CHARITIES DIGEST 2017

Selected Charities & Voluntary Organisations

123rd edition

Wilmington plc

Published by
Wilmington Business Intelligence
6-14 Underwood Street, London, N1 7JQ
Tel: 020 7490 0049
DX: 122030 Finsbury 3
E-mail: claudia.rios@wilmingtonplc.com
Website: www.charitychoice.co.uk

CONTENTS

Publisher
Tanya Noronha

Product Manager
Claudia Rios

Production Manager
Susan Sixtensson

Marketing Manager
Gabrielle Williams

Database Manager
Stephen Grainge

Customer Services
Emily Martin

Publishing Services
Jacqueline Hobbs
Stacey Perryment

Ad Sales Enquiries:
Danniella Gomes
Tel: 020 7324 2372

Editorial and Advertising:
Tel: 020 7490 0049 *DX:* 122030 Finsbury 3

Orders:
Marketing Department, Wilmington Business Intelligence
Tel: 020 7490 0049

ISBN 978-1-85783-239-6

Printed in the UK by Latimer Trend & Company Limited, Plymouth
Typesetting by Alpha Index, Brighton

PPA Wilmington is a member of the Professional Publishers Association

ABOUT CHARITIES DIGEST

Charities Digest was first published in 1882 for the information and guidance of those concerned with charitable organisations, with the intention that its reference section should be updated and reprinted annually. Information included in the Digest is submitted to us by charities and is researched and updated each year.

Charities Digest is published by Wilmington Business Intelligence.

Registered Charities

There are over 160,000 registered charities in the UK. Charities Digest concentrates on national and regional charities. These charities appear in the alphabetical section, which forms the larger part of this book. Key local organisations are also listed. Most of them are registered charities, but we also include some charities which are excepted or exempt from registration under the Charities Act. Some Scottish and Northern Irish charities are also listed. A small number of organisations whose purposes are not exclusively charitable but whose addresses may be of assistance to users of the Digest also feature in the directory. We also include Object Codes to indicate charities prepared to offer grants and other financial services.

How the book works

Charities are listed in alphabetical order.

The basic information for each charity follows a standard format, which includes the name of the organisation; the date of foundation; the charity registration number or other information about charitable status; and their address and telephone number. Some charities also provide contact names, while other listings include bank details for donation purposes. Many entries will also feature additional text about their causes, aims, and history. The back of the book features an index which lists selected charities according to their main charitable objectives.

Wilmington Business Intelligence makes every effort to ensure that all organisations included are bona fide, but inclusion in or omission from Charities Digest does not indicate approval or otherwise by Wilmington Business Intelligence.

New entries are welcomed for consideration. For more information, please contact claudia.rios@wilmingtonplc.com.

Other voluntary organisations

Charities Digest also contains updated directory listings of other relevant organisations that help people in need, including: Citizens Advice Bureaux, Community Foundations, Voluntary Organisations for Blind & Partially Sighted People, and Hospice Services. These listings are located in the second half of this publication and are arranged by region.

Acknowledgements

We are indebted to the Charity Commission, the Office of the Scottish Charity Regulator, the Charity Commission for Northern Ireland, Action on Hearing Loss (previously known as RNID), Action with Communities in Rural England (ACRE), the Almshouse Association, the UK Community Foundations Network, DIAL UK (Scope), Disability Rights UK, the Equality & Human Rights Commission (EHRC), Hospice UK, the Law Centres Federation, the National Association for Voluntary & Community Action (NAVCA), the National Association of Citizens Advice Bureaux, Northern Ireland Council for Voluntary Action (NICVA), the Royal National Institute for the Blind (RNIB), Volunteering England and Wales Council for Voluntary Action (WCVA).

Photo: Gavin Bernard / Barcroft Media
With your help
we can secure her future.

News from The Passage

The Passage is about long term, lasting solutions and seeks to address the root causes that led to a person becoming homeless in the first place so that their cycle of homelessness can be broken for good. Recent achievements include:

92% of all new rough sleepers in South Westminster were either supported to return to their home area or linked into support services and accommodation off the streets within 2 contacts by The Passage Street Outreach team during 2011/12.

The Passage helped 117 entrenched rough sleepers off the streets of South Westminster during the same period.

For the 3rd year running every client moving on from The Passage's supported accommodation scheme and into their own tenancy has sustained that tenancy.

Over the last 10 years The Passage has helped nearly 600 homeless people into full time employment.

The Passage has ninety staff and a volunteer to staff ratio of over 3:1. It costs nearly £4 million per year to run The Passage, and half of that income is dependent on voluntary donations. For every £1 donated in voluntary income, over 90% goes straight to our frontline services.

בס״ד

FINDING CHARITY INFORMATION ONLINE

Supporting Charities Online at www.charitychoice.co.uk

Charity Choice has been helping people to find charities for over 25 years. Our award-winning website includes a free online directory which gives information on over 160,000 charities from England, Wales, Scotland and Northern Ireland. It is the most popular charity directory in the UK, enabling people to easily find charities by cause, location, or name.

The site also allows charity supporters to search for fundraising events, make donations, find out about leaving a gift in their will, offer to volunteer, set up fundraising pages, or donate goods to charity. Charity Choice's aim is to support people who are deciding which charity to help, and offer them guidance with a range of free information and giving options.

Free Charity Financial Reports

In an effort to give people more information about how charities really spend their money, Charity Choice has now released free financial reports for each of the top 10,000 UK charities. The reports aim to clear up common myths about how charity donations are spent, and help people to make more informed decisions on which charities to support with their time and money.

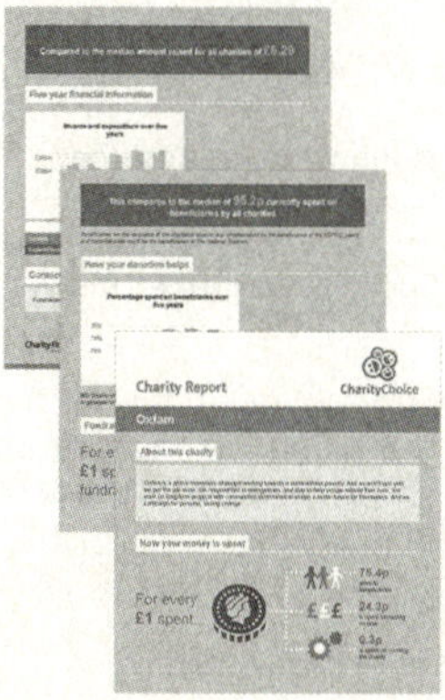

The reports feature

- How much the charity spends on beneficiaries, fundraising and admin per £1 spent
- How much income is raised for every £1 spent on fundraising
- Five year financial information on income and expenditure

To download a free charity report simply go to **www.charitychoice.co.uk**, click on the "Find a charity" tab to begin your search then click on the "Free Report" button!

CHARITIES IN THE UK

Definitions

To qualify as a charity an organisation must exist for charitable purposes. The Charities Act 2006 lists purposes that can be defined as charitable, which include the relief of poverty, the advancement of education, the advancement of religion, or for other purposes beneficial to the community, such as community development or urban regeneration.

A full list can be viewed in the text of the Act itself or online at www.legislation.gov.uk.

The definitions themselves are at some times vague and have been the subject matter of extensive judicial interpretation, so legal advice is essential in the formation of any trust or organisation which intends to register as a charity.

The law governing registration applies to England and Wales only. Charities in Scotland are regulated by the Office of the Scottish Charity Regulator (OSCR) and Northern Irish charities are in the process of being registered by the new Charity Commission for Northern IReland.

ENGLAND AND WALES

Registration and exemptions

Section 3 of the Charities Act 2006 requires all charities to register with the Charity Commission, with specified exceptions. Charities excepted or exempt from registration are:

(a) any charity comprised in the second schedule to the 2006 Act referred to as an "exempt charity"
(b) any charity excepted by order or regulations
(c) any charity whose income from all sources does not exceed £5,000 in any year.

No charity is required to be registered in respect of any registered place of worship.

Charities exempt from the Commissioners' regulatory powers, although they may request the Commissions' advice or guidance, include certain universities and colleges, the British Museum, the Church Commissioners and certain institutions administered by them, and registered societies within the Industrial and Provident Societies Act 1965 or the Friendly Societies Act 1974.

Setting up a charity: preliminary steps

In every case, before seeking registration and obtaining legal advice to that end, any founders of a would-be charity should consider the following guidance offered by the Charity Commission before consulting an expert adviser:

- Is a new charity the best way forward?
- Are there existing charities with the same purposes and activities as yours?
- Do you understand how a charity must operate?

After forming clear, positive ideas of the answers to these questions, founders should move forward.

Setting up a charity: secondary steps

Assuming it is decided to seek registration, the founders should consult the National Council for Voluntary Organisations (NCVO). The NCVO is based at Regent's Wharf, 8 All Saints Street, London N1 9RL, Tel: 020 7713 6161. Local voluntary councils can be found on the National Association for Voluntary and Community Action (NAVCA) website, www.navca.org.uk, while in Wales if would be best to use the Wales Council for Voluntary Action (WCVA), www.wcva.org.uk. It would be useful to consult the Charity Commission's official guidance, 'Registering as a Charity' (CC21a) which sets out the legal requirements and procedure for registration.

It may also be necessary consult a qualified lawyer who has knowledge and experience of the workings of charity law and charities, or to engage a solicitor. Suitable legal advice can be found from Citizens Advice (www.citizensadvice.org.uk), or the Charity Law Association (CLA), who are online at www.charitylawassociation.org.uk).

Setting up a charity: governance

The would-be founders would also need to draft a governing document for the charity in the form of a Constitution, deed, set of rules, or memorandum and articles of association.

In most cases this should be done by the founders' legal adviser.

Founders would also have to appoint trustees, who would form the charity's board. They would be recruited as per the process for standard job recruitment, although trustees are generally unpaid.

Potential charities are also required to prove that their existence would benefit the public. This means that they have to fit in to the Charities Act 2006 as having a charitable purpose. More guidance on this matter is available from the Charity Commission.

Before registering with the Commission, charities will also be required to choose a name, which will appear on the Register of Charities. It is advised that names are made as specific and unique as possible.

Setting up a charity: registration

Once these measures are all in place, founders can, if necessary, register with the Charity Commission. This can now be done online. Find information at https://www.gov.uk/setting-up-charity

Charities with an income of under £5,000 per year are not required to register, and should instead apply for tax relief from Her Majesty's Revenue & Customs (HMRC).

Fiscal benefits

Charities, whether registered or not, may be entitled to certain fiscal benefits such as relief from income tax, corporation tax, capital gains tax and local council tax. Applications and enquiries regarding relief from income tax or capital gains tax should be addressed to HMRC at: St John's House, Merton Road, Bootle, Merseyside L69 9BB. Tel: 0300 123 1073.

Enquiries about all aspects of VAT as applied to charities should be addressed to the Collector of the local Customs and Excise VAT Office.

Fundraising from the public and from major sources of funds for voluntary organisations (e.g. charitable trusts and business firms) will be much easier if the organisation is a registered charity. In particular, many charitable trusts are prevented by their constitutions from making grants to other than registered charities.

THE CHARITY COMMISSION FOR ENGLAND & WALES

The Charity Commissioners have been in existence since 1853, and offer a large number of services via their website, www.gov.uk/government/organisations/charity-commission.

The Commission registers and regulates charities in England and Wales. It offers them advice and provide a wide range of services and guidance to help them run as effectively as possible. It also keeps the online Register of Charities, which provides information about each of the thousands of registered charities in England and Wales.

The Commission's particular functions include the maintenance of a central register of charities, the institution of inquiries, the protection of the endowments of charities, control of the taking of legal proceedings, the making of schemes and orders to modernise the purposes and administrative machinery of charities, and the giving of advice to trustees. The Commission acts as both a regulator and an enabler and stresses its support role in relation to charity trustees and encourages them to contact the Commission at an early stage if in doubt or difficulty. One of its stated objectives is to increase public trust and confidence in charities and it encourages charities to enhance their accountability and transparency in a range of ways. It does not provide funding and may not act in the administration of a charity.

The Charities Act 2006

The Charities Act 2006 was passed on the 8th November 2006 and its various provisions came into force from 2007 onwards.

The new income level for registration is £5,000, and all charities with a lower income are exempt. Previously, small charities with an income of £1,000 or less were required to register if they had a permanent endowment or the use or occupation of land. The Act underlined that all charities must exist for the public benefit, and the Commission has a new objective to promote understanding and awareness of the public benefit requirement.

The Act also ensured that both exempt and excepted charities are monitored for their compliance to charity law. Previously excepted charities such as some religious charities, armed forces charities and Boy Scout and Girl Guides, may also now have to register with the Commission if they have an annual income of £100,000 or more. Those with a lower income do not have to register but still come under the jurisdiction of the Commission.

The new Act liberalised and extended the powers for charities to make changes to their purposes, and allowed smaller charities to take certain actions without permission from the Commission. It also proposed the creation of a Register of Mergers to be held by the Commission to help ensure that legacies and donations left to charities which subsequently merged are transferred to the new charity. A new structure for charities was created by the Act, the Charitable Incorporated Organisation (CIO). This allows charities which want a corporate structure to have the benefits of incorporation without the burden of dual regulation with Companies House and the Commission.

The Act also created a new Charity Tribunal which allowed charities to appeal against decisions made by the Commission. The Charity Tribunal has since merged with HM Courts Service.

SCOTLAND

Only a body granted charitable status by the Office of the Scottish Charity Regulator (OSCR) or one recognised by the Charity Commission of England and Wales may represent itself as a charity in Scotland. OSCR is the body responsible for supervising and regulating charities in Scotland and they publish an index of recognised charities on their website, www.oscr.org.uk.

Under existing legislation, charities with an income of over £25,000 must complete as Annual Return form and a Supplementary Monitoring Return form. Charities must also complete and file an Annual Report to OSCR within 9 months of the end of their financial year. Charities that fail to comply with this measure are considered for removal from the Register. OSCR also perform a continuous review of their Register as per the Charities and Trustee Investment (Scotland) Act 2005, which allows them to confirm charities' details from time to time.

While OSCR doesn't publish listings of a charity's trustees as the Charity Commission does, trustees are responsible for keeping charity details up-to-date.

To make general enquiries, a complaint, or to set up a new charity, please contact OSCR at: 2nd Floor, Quadrant House, 9 Riverside Drive, Dundee DD1 4NY, Tel: 01382 220446, info@oscr.org.uk.

NORTHERN IRELAND

The Charities Act (NI) 2008 announced the creation of the Charity Commission for Northern Ireland (CCNI). It was launched as Northern Ireland's independent regulator in 2010. The Charity Commission for Northern Ireland has published a list of all Northern Irish charities falling within its power on its website, www.charitycommissionni.org.uk.

The CCNI has replaced the The Department for Social Development (DSD), which was previously the the main charity authority in Northern Ireland.

The CCNI offers a range of services through its website for charity registration as well as information on registered charities for the public.

The CCNI is based at: 257 Lough Road, Lurgan, Craigavon BT66 6NQ. Tel: 028 3832 0220, Monday to Friday 9 - 5pm. Textphone: 028 3834 7639.

GUIDE TO CODES USED IN THE MAIN ENTRIES

	Objects
1A	Grants made to individuals
1B	Grantmaking organisation
2	Member organisation
3	Services Provider
A	Grants of money of varying amounts
B	Pensions, benefits or scholarships
C	Sheltered accommodation & hostels
D	Housing
E	Day Centres
F	Advice, counselling, information
G	Education, training
H	Publications and/or free literature
I	Crime prevention
J	Co-ordination, liaison
K	Workshops & other employment
L	Casework, welfare
M	Care equipment, practical services
N	Medical treatment, nursing
O	Rehabilitation, therapy
P	Social activities & relationships
Q	Adoption, fostering
R	Missionary & outreach work at home or abroad
S	Cultural pursuits
T	Reconciliation
U	Overseas aid or service
V	Holidays
W	Medical research
X	Protection against domestic violence
Y	Relief of poverty
Z	Social welfare and casework
W1	Animals and/or birds
W2	Conservation & environment
W3	Children, young people
W4	Older people
W5	Disabled people
W6	Blind people
W7	Deaf people
W8	Women
W9	Armed services & ex-services
W10	Ethnic minorities
W11	Ex professional or trade workers
W12	Museums, memorials
W13	Merchant Navy & Fishing Fleet
W14	Residential care
W15	Families
W16	Homeless people

	Charity Registration
CR	Registered under the Charities Act 2006
Exempt	Excepted or exempt from registration
FS	Exempt under Friendly Societies Act/Provident Societies Act
SC	Scottish Charity
XN	Northern Irish Charity

Numeric

4CHILDREN
CR288285
5th Floor, City Reach, 5 Greenwich View Place, London E14 9NN
Tel: 020 7512 2100
Email: . . . . info@4Children.org.uk
Object: W3

21ST CENTURY LEARNING INITIATIVE (UK), THE
Founded: 1991 CR1003067
3 Grosvenor Place, Bath, Bath & North East Somerset BA1 6AX
Tel: 01225 333376
Objects: W3,G,H

42ND STREET - WORKING WITH YOUNG PEOPLE UNDER STRESS
Founded: 1990 CR702687
2nd Floor, Swan Buildings, 20 Swan Street, Manchester, Greater Manchester M4 5JW
Tel: . . . . 0161 832 0169; 0161 832 0170 Helpline
Email: . . . . theteam@42ndstreet.org.uk
Objects: F,W6,W3,W7,W5,G,W10,O,3,P,W8

1930 FUND FOR DISTRICT NURSES
Founded: 1930 CR208312
Charity Business (CC), 6 Trull Farm Buildings, Tetbury, Gloucestershire GL8 8SQ
Tel: 01285 841900
Email: . . . . info@thetrustpartnership.com

1989 WILAN CHARITABLE TRUST, THE
Founded: 1990 CR802749
C/O The Community Foundation Serving Tyne & Wear & Northumberland, Cale Cross, 156 Pilgrim Street, Newcastle upon Tyne, Tyne & Wear NE1 6SU
Objects: W6,W3,E,W7,W5,G,W10,1B,W4,P,W8

A

ABANDONED ANIMALS ASSOCIATION
CR518901
8 Nant-y-Gammar Road, Craig-y-Don, Llandudno, Conwy LL30 1YE
Email: . . . . phil.waldock@btinternet.com

ABBEYFIELD (BRISTOL) SOCIETY
CR257532
29 Alma Vale Road, Clifton, Bristol BS8 2HL
Tel: 0117 973 6997
Email: . . . . e-mail@abbeyfield-bristol.co.uk

ABBEYFIELD - MAKING TIME FOR OLDER PEOPLE
Founded: 1956 CR200719
St Peter's House, 2 Bricket Road, St Albans, Hertfordshire AL1 3JW
Tel: 01727 734095
Email: . . . . fundraisingteam@abbeyfield.com
Web: . . . . www.abbeyfield.com
Since 1956 Abbeyfield has been alleviating the crippling loneliness felt by older people and making their lives easier and more fulfilling. Our safe, happy homes are where people can really live, not just be cared for. Donations and gifts in Wills are vital so we can build new

homes - including innovative dementia care centres - to make later life a truly happy life.

See advert on page 1

ABBEYFIELD WALES SOCIETY LIMITED

CR200719
1 Derwen Villas, Wrexham Road, Mold, Flintshire CH7 1HZ
Tel: 01352 751992
Email: . . . . abbeyfieldcymru@yahoo.co.uk

ABF THE SOLDIERS' CHARITY

Founded: 1944 CR1146420; SC039189
Mountbarrow House, 6-20 Elizabeth Street, London SW1W 9RB
Tel: 0207 901 8900
Email: . . . . enquiries@armybenfund.org
Objects: W9,A

ABILITYNET ADVICE AND INFORMATION - UK'S LEADING AUTHORITY ON DISABILITY AND COMPUTING

Founded: 1992 CR1067673
PO Box 94, Warwick, Warwickshire CV34 5WS
Tel: 01926 312847
Email: . . . . enquiries@abilitynet.org.uk
Objects: F,W6,W3,W7,W5,W4,3

THE ACADEMY OF THE SCIENCE OF ACTING AND DIRECTING

Founded: 1992 CR1014419
9-15 Elthorne Road, Archway, London N19 4AJ
Tel. 020 7272 0027
Objects: W3,G,3

ACCORD HOSPICE, PAISLEY

SC013682
Morton Avenue, Paisley, Renfrewshire PA2 7BW
Tel: 0141 581 2000
Email: . . . . office@accord.org.uk
Objects: N,3

ACORN CHRISTIAN HEALING FOUNDATION

Founded: 1983 CR1080011
Whitehill Chase, High Street, Bordon, Hampshire GU35 0AP
Tel: 01420 478121
Email: . . . . info@acornchristian.org
Objects: Q,W3,G,W4,T

ACORNS CHILDREN'S HOSPICE, WEST MIDLANDS

Founded: 1986 CR700859
Acorns House, 4B Truemans Heath Lane, Birmingham, West Midlands B47 5QB
Tel: 0121 248 4800
Email: . . . . legacies@acorns.org.uk
Objects: F,W3,G,N,3

ACRE (ACTION WITH COMMUNITIES IN RURAL ENGLAND)

Founded: 1987 CR1061568
Somerford Court, Somerford Road, Cirencester, Gloucestershire GL7 1TW
Tel: 01285 653477
Email: . . . . acre@acre.org.uk
Objects: F,W3,J,G,D,2,W4,H,W8

ACRE GOSPEL MISSION

XN47625A
33 Ravensdene Park, Belfast BT6 0DA
Tel: 028 9064 2638
Email: . . . . info@acremission.co.uk
Object: R

ACT AGAINST BULLYING

CR1100132
PO Box 57962, London W4 2TG
Tel: 020 8995 9500
Email: . . . . info@actagainstbullying.org

ACTION AGAINST MEDICAL ACCIDENTS

Founded: 1982 CR299123
44 High Street, Croydon, London CRO 1YB
Tel: 0845 123 2352 Mon-Fri 10am-5pm; 020 8688 9555 admin line
Email: . . . . advice@avma.org.uk
Objects: F,W3,W5,G,W4,H,3

ACTION DEAFNESS

CR226864
Centre for Deaf People, 135 Welford Road, Leicester, Leicestershire LE2 6BE
Tel: . . 0116 257 4800 Voice; 0116 257 4850 Text
Email: . . . . enquiries@actiondeafness.org.uk
Objects: F,M,W3,J,S,E,W7,G,W10,W11,2,R,W4, H,O,3,P,W8,K

ACTION FOR BLIND PEOPLE - PART OF RNIB GROUP

Founded: 1857 CR205913
105 Judd Street, London WC1H 9NE
Tel: 0303 123 9999
Email: . . . . supportercare@afbp.org.uk
Objects: F,W6,W5,G,1A,A,V,D,B,H,3,C,K

ACTION FOR CHILDREN

Founded: 1869 CR1097940; SC038092
CEO: Sir Tony Hawkhead
3 The Boulevard (CD), Ascot Road, Watford, Hertfordshire WD18 8AG
Tel: 01923 361500; 0300 123 2112
Email: . . . . . . legacies@actionforchildren.org .uk
Web: . . . . www.actionforchildren.org.uk
Objects: Q,W3,E,3,P,Z

For over 145 years, Action for Children has worked in local communities to protect and support the young and vulnerable, as they grow up.
When it comes to children, Action for Children is on the ground making their lives better – now, tomorrow, every day. We run around 650 services, from children's centres to intensive family support, from fostering and adoption to short breaks for disabled children. In the past year we have helped more children and their families across the UK than any other charity.
We hope you agree that we must continue to be there for future generations of vulnerable children.By remembering Action for Children with a gift in your will, you can help us carry on the amazing work. So once you have provided for your own family, please consider helping us carry on supporting the children who need us most.
We never give up.

See advert on previous page

ACTION FOR KIDS CHARITABLE TRUST

Founded: 1991 CR1068841
Ability House, 15a Tottenham Lane, Hornsey, London N8 9DJ
Tel: 020 8347 8111
Email: . . . . info@actionforkids.org

ACTION FOR SICK CHILDREN (NATIONAL ASSOCIATION FOR THE WELFARE OF CHILDREN IN HOSPITAL)
CR296295
3 Abbey Business Centre, Keats Lane, Earl Shilton, Leicestershire LE9 7DQ
Tel: 01455 845600
Email: . . . . . enquiries@actionforsickchildren.org
Objects: F,W3,J,G,2,H

ACTION MEDICAL RESEARCH
Founded: 1952 CR208701; SC039284
Vincent House, North Parade, Horsham, West Sussex RH12 2DP
Tel: 01403 327413
Email: . . . . info@action.org.uk
Objects: W3,W5,1A,A,1B,N,W4,H,W8

ACTION ON ADDICTION
Founded: 2007 CR1117988
Clouds House, East Knoyle, Salisbury, Wiltshire SP3 6BE
Tel: 01747 832028
Email: . . . . action@aona.co.uk
Objects: F,W6,W3,G,W10,N,O,3

ACTION ON POVERTY
CR290836
Nicholas House, Heath Park, Main Road, Cropthorne, Pershore, Worcestershire WR10 3NE
Tel: 01386 861294
Email: . . . . info@aptuk.org.uk
Objects: W5,U,Y,W8

ACTIONAID
Founded: 1972 CR274467
Hamlyn House, Macdonald Road, Archway, London N19 5PG
Tel: 020 7561 7561
Email: . . . . mail@actionaid.org.uk
Object: U

ADDACTION
Founded: 1967 CR1001957
67-69 Cowcross Street, Smithfield, London EC1M 6PU
Tel: 020 7251 5860
Email: . . . . info@addaction.org.uk
Objects: F,W3,J,G,W10,W15,W16,N,R,W4,H,O,3, P,Z,W8,K

ADDICTION RECOVERY AGENCY
Founded: 1987 CR1002224
61 Queen Charlotte Street, Bristol BS1 4HQ
Tel: 0117 930 0282
Email: . . . . info@addictionrecovery.org.uk
Objects: F,E,D,O,3,C

ADDITIONAL CURATES SOCIETY
Founded: 1837 CR209448
Gordon Browning House, 8 Spitfire Road, Birmingham, West Midlands B24 9PB
Tel: 0121 382 5533
Email: . . . . info@additionalcurates.co.uk
Objects: A,1B,R,H

ADFAM NATIONAL
Founded: 1986 CR1067428
25 Corsham Street, London N1 6DR
Tel: 020 7553 7640
Email: . . . . admin@adfam.org.uk
Objects: F,W9,W6,W3,W7,W5,G,W10,W11,W4,H, 3,W8

ADJUTANT GENERAL'S CORPS REGIMENTAL ASSOCIATION
Founded: 1992 CR1035939
Regimental Headquarters, Gould House, Worthy Down, Winchester, Hampshire SO21 2RG
Tel: 01962 887254; 01962 887435
Email: . . . . secretary@agcorps.org
Objects: W9,1A,A,V,2,P

ADOPTION FOCUS
CR1129095
Kemp House, 152 City Road, London EC1V 2NX
Tel: 0845 519 0539
Email: . . . . info@adoption-focus.org.uk

ADOPTION UK - SUPPORTING ADOPTIVE FAMILIES BEFORE, DURING AND AFTER ADOPTION
CR326654
Units 11 and 12, Vantage Business Park, Bloxham Road, Banbury, Oxfordshire OX16 9UX
Tel: . . . 0844 848 7900 (Helpline); 01295 752240
Email: . . . . enquiries@adoptionuk.org.uk
Objects: Q,2

ADREF LTD
Founded: 1990 CR703130
54-55 Bute Street, Aberdare, Rhondda Cynon Taff CF44 7LD
Tel: 01685 878755

ADS (ADDICTION DEPENDENCY SOLUTIONS)
Founded: 1973 CR702559
135 – 141 Oldham Street, Manchester, Greater Manchester M4 1LN
Tel: 0161 831 2400
Email: . . . . headoffice@adsolutions.org.uk
Objects: F,W3,E,G,W10,W4,O,3,C,W8

ADVENTURE SERVICE CHALLENGE SCHEME ASC SCHEME
CR292690
East Lynn, Lansdown Lane, Weston, Bath, Bath & North East Somerset BA1 4NB
Tel: 01225 329838
Email: . . . . asc@asc-scheme.org.uk
Objects: W3,G,2,P

ADVISORY CENTRE FOR EDUCATION (ACE) LTD - ADVICE FOR PARENTS, A VOICE FOR PARENTS
Founded: 1960 CR313142
1c, Aberdeen Studios, 22 Highbury Grove, London N5 2DQ
Tel: . . . 0808 800 5793 General Advice; 020 7704 9822 Exclusions; 020 7704 3370 Admin
Email: . . . . enquiries@ace-ed.org.uk
Objects: F,W3,G,2,3

ADVISORY COMMITTEE ON PROTECTION OF THE SEA (ACOPS)
Founded: 1952 CR290776
11 Dartmouth Street, London SW1H 9BN
Tel: 020 7799 3033
Email: . . . . acopsadmin@googlemail.com
Objects: W2,G,H

AECC CHIROPRACTIC COLLEGE
CR306289
13-15 Parkwood Road, Bournemouth BH5 2DF
Tel: 01202 436200
Email: . . . . sachabillett@aecc.ac.uk

AFASIC - HELPING CHILDREN AND YOUNG PEOPLE WITH SPEECH, LANGUAGE & COMMUNICATION IMPAIRMENTS

CR1045617

1st Floor, 20 Bowling Green Lane, London EC1R 0BD

Tel: .... 020 7490 9410; 0845 355 5577 Helpline

Email: .... info@afasic.org.uk

Objects: F,M,W3,J,G,H,P,K

AFGHANAID

CR1045348

Development House, 56-64 Leonard Street, London EC2A 4LT

Tel: 020 7065 0825

Email: .... info@afghanaid.org.uk

Objects: W3,U,W8

AFRICAN CHILDREN'S EDUCATIONAL TRUST (A-CET)

CR1066869

PO Box 8390, Leicester, Leicestershire LE5 4YD

Tel: 0800 652 9475

Email: .... dgs@a-cet.org

Objects: W3,G,U

AFRICAN PASTORS' FELLOWSHIP

CR282756

2 Binley Avenue (CC), Binley, Coventry, West Midlands CV3 2EE

Tel: 024 7644 8068

Email: .... africanpastors@aol.com

AFTAID - AID FOR THE AGED IN DISTRESS

CR299276

9 Bonhill Street, London EC2A 4PE

Tel: 0870 803 1950

Email: .... info@aftaid.org.uk

Object: W4

AFTER ADOPTION

Founded: 1990 CR1000888

Unit 5 Citygate, 5 Blantyre Street, Manchester, Greater Manchester M15 4JJ

Tel: 0161 839 4932

Email: .... information@afteradoption.org.uk

Objects: Q,F,W3,H,3,W8

AGE CONCERN PLYMOUTH

CR281820

Elspeth Sitters House, Hoegate Street, Plymouth, Devon PL1 2JB

Tel: 01752 665424

Objects: F,M,E,W4,H,P

AGE SCOTLAND

Founded: 1943SC010100

Causewayside House, 160 Causewayside, Edinburgh EH9 1PR

Tel: 0333 323 2400

Email: .... enquiries@agescotland.org.uk

Objects: F,1B,D,2,W4,H

AGE UK

Founded: 1940 CR1128267

Tavis House, 1-6 Tavistock Square, London WC1H 9NA

Tel: 020 3033 1421

Email: .... legacies@ageuk.org.uk

AGE UK CALDERDALE & KIRKLEES

CR1102020

4-6 Woolshops, Halifax, West Yorkshire HX 1 1RJ

Tel: ... 01422 252 040 (Shopmobility) 01422 399 830

Email: ... jbarcoe@ageconcerncalderdale.org.uk

Objects: F,M,J,A,2,W4,B,H,3,P

AGE UK CHESHIRE

CR1091608

314 Chester Road, Hartford, Cheshire CW8 2AB

Tel: 01606 881660; 01606 881 663

Email: .... admin@ageukcheshire.org.uk

AGE UK CORNWALL & THE ISLES OF SCILLY

Founded: 1990 CR900542

Boscawen House, Chapel Hill, Truro, Cornwall TR1 3BN

Tel: 01872 266388

Email: .... email@ageukcornwall.org.uk

Objects: F,J,E,W5,W4,H

AGE UK DONCASTER

CR1077339

109 Thorne Road, Doncaster, South Yorkshire DN2 5BE

Tel: 01302 812345

Email: .... admin@ageukdoncaster.org.uk

AGE UK EALING

Founded: 1990 CR1100474

135 Uxbridge Road, London W13 9AU

Tel: 020 8567 8017

Email: .... reception@ageukealing.org.uk

Objects: F,J,W4,O,3

AGE UK EAST SUSSEX

CR265532

County Office, 54 Cliffe High Street, Lewes, East Sussex BN7 2AN

Tel: 01273 476704

Email: .... information@ageukeastsussex.org.uk

AGE UK EAST SUSSEX - HASTINGS OFFICE

CR265532

50 Robertson Street, Hastings, East Sussex TN34 1HL

Tel: 01424 426162

Email: ...... hastingsinfo@aceastsussex.org.uk

Objects: F,E,2,W4,B,Y,3,P,Z

AGE UK GATESHEAD

Founded: 1990 CR702561

341-343 High Street, Gateshead, Tyne & Wear NE8 1EQ

Tel: 0191 477 3559

Email: .... admin@ageconcerngateshead.org.uk

Objects: F,J,E,W5,W4,3,P

AGE UK HILLINGDON

Founded: 1990 CR1051711

Globe House, Bentinck Road, West Drayton, Middlesex UB7 7RQ

Tel: 01895 431331

Objects: F,P

AGE UK LANCASHIRE FORMERLY KNOWN AS AGE CONCERN LANCASHIRE

CR1142294

Head Office, 61-63 St Thomas's Road, Chorley, Lancashire PR7 1JE

Tel: 01257 233200
Email: . . . . admin@ageuklancs.org.uk
Objects: F,M,S,E,W4,O,3,P

AGE UK LEICESTER & RUTLAND

CR512991
Clarence House, 46 Humberstone Gate, Leicester, Leicestershire LE1 3PJ
Tel: 0116 222 0555
Email: . . . . enquiries@ageukleics.org.uk

AGE UK LINCOLN

CR1078539
23 Sixfield Close, Lincoln, Lincolnshire LN6 0EJ
Tel: 01522 696000
Email: . . . . barry.earnshaw@ageuklincoln.org.uk
Objects: F,M,J,S,E,G,2,W4,B,3,P

AGE UK LONDON

Founded: 1966 CR1092198
1st Floor (CC), 21 St Georges Road, London SE1 6ES
Tel: 020 7820 6770
Email: . . . aalao@ageuklondon.org.uk; apurser@ageuklondon.org.uk
Objects: F,J,G,2,H

AGE UK MANCHESTER

CR1083242
Canada House (CD), 3 Chepstow Street, Manchester, Greater Manchester M1 5FW
Tel: 0161 817 2351
Email: . . . . . enquiries@ageukmanchester.org.uk
Objects: F,E,W4,B,3,P

AGE UK NEWHAM

Founded: 1990 CR802908
82 Russia Lane, Bethnal Green, London E2
Tel: 0208 981 7124
Email: . . . . info@ageukeastlondon.org.uk
Objects: F,W10,1A,W4,H,3,P

AGE UK NORTH STAFFORDSHIRE

Founded: 1991 CR1087774
83-85 Trinity Street, Hanley, Stoke-on-Trent, Staffordshire ST1 5NA
Tel: 01782 286209
Email: . . . . info@ageuknorthstaffs.org.uk
Objects: F,J,W10,V,D,2,W4,B,H,O,3,P

AGE UK NORTH YORKSHIRE

North Yorkshire
age UK

Founded: 2000 CR1124567
CEO: Ms Alexandra Bird
Harrogate Community House, 46-50 East Parade, Harrogate, North Yorkshire HG1 5RR
Tel: 01423 530628
Email: harrogate@ageuknorthyorkshire.org.uk
Web: . . . . . www.ageuk.org.uk/northyorkshire/
Object: W4
Age UK N. Yorkshire provides services and support for older people in the Harrogate, Hambleton, Richmondshire and South Craven districts within

North Yorkshire. We aim to help promote and improve the well-being of older people and reduce isolation and loneliness,and making later life enjoyable.

See advert on previous page

AGE UK NORWICH
CR1094623
Boardman House, Redwell Street, Norwich, Norfolk NR2 4SL
Tel: 01603 496333
Email: . . . . enquiries@ageuknorwich.org.uk
Objects: F,M,E,W4,B,3,P

AGE UK SHEFFIELD
CR1108413
44 Castle Square, Sheffield, South Yorkshire S1 2GF
Tel: 0114 250 2850
Email: . . . enquiries@ageconcernsheffield.org.uk
Objects: F,M,E,W4,P

AGE UK SOLIHULL
CR1055887
The Core, Central Library Building, Homer Road, Solihull, West Midlands B91 3RG
Tel: 0121 704 7840
Email: . . . . info@ageuksolihull.org.uk

AGE UK SUFFOLK
CR1085900
Head Office, 14 Hillview Business Park, Old Ipswich Road, Claydon, Suffolk IP6 0AJ
Tel: 01473 359911
Email: . . . . office@ageuksuffolk.org

AGE UK TEESSIDE
CR702714
190 Borough Road, Middlesbrough, North Yorkshire TS1 2EH
Tel: 01642 805500
Email: . . . . admin@ageukteesside.org.uk
Objects: F,E,G,W10,2,W4,3,P

AGE UK WILTSHIRE
Founded: 1990 CR800912
13 Market Place, Devizes, Wiltshire SN10 1HT
Tel: 01380 727767
Email: . . . . info@ageukwiltshire.org.uk
Objects: F,M,J,E,G,1A,A,1B,2,W4,B,H,O,3,P

AGGIE WESTON'S ROYAL SAILORS REST (AGGIE'S)
Founded: 1876 CR238748
Castaway House, 311 Twyford Avenue, Portsmouth, Hampshire PO2 8RN
Tel: 023 9265 0505
Email: . . . . office@aggies.org.uk
Objects: W9,W3,R,3,P

AHIMSA
Founded: 1990 CR328598
6 Victoria Place, Millbay Road, Plymouth, Devon PL1 3LP
Tel: 01752 213535
Email: . . . . enquiries@ahimsa.org.uk
Objects: F,W3,G,O,3,W8

THE ROYAL SURGICAL AID SOCIETY
Founded: 1862 CR216613
47 Great Russell Street, London WC1B 3PA
Tel: 020 7637 4577
Email: . . . . info@thersas.org.uk
Objects: G,W4,3,C

AID TO THE CHURCH IN NEED
Founded: 1947 CR1097984
1 Times Square, Sutton, Surrey SM1 1LF
Tel: 020 8642 8668
Email: . . . . acn@acnuk.org
Object: R

AIM INTERNATIONAL
Founded: 1895 CR1096364
Halifax Place, Nottingham, Nottinghamshire NG1 1QN
Tel: 0115 983 8120
Email: . . . . admin.eu@aimint.org
Objects: R,3

AIR LEAGUE EDUCATIONAL TRUST - FOR BRITAIN'S YOUTH
CR1129969
Broadway House, Tothill Street, London SW1H 9NS
Tel: 020 7222 8463
Email: . . . . flying@airleague.co.uk
Objects: W3,G,1A,3

AIR TRAINING CORPS (GENERAL PURPOSES FUND)
CR256391
Headquarters Air Cadets (TG2), RAF College Cranwell, Sleaford, Lincolnshire NG34 8HB
Tel: 01400 267619
Email: . . . . tg2@atc.raf.mod.uk

AIRBORNE FORCES SECURITY FUND
Founded: 1942 CR206552
c/o RHQ The Parachute Regiment, Flagstaff House, Napier Road, Colchester, Essex CO2 7SW
Tel: . . . . 01206 541748 ; 01206 782342
Email: . . . . abfsyfund@btopenworld.com
Objects: F,J,1A,A,V

AJEX CHARITABLE FOUNDATION
CR1082148
Shield House, Harmony Way, London NW4 2BZ
Tel: 020 8202 2323
Objects: F,A,D

AL-MAHDI (AS) INSTITUTE
CR1080962
532 Moseley Road, Birmingham, West Midlands B12 9AE
Tel: 0870 774 4304
Email: . . . . almahdi@iname.com
Objects: G,3,P

ALABARE CHRISTIAN CARE AND SUPPORT
Founded: 1991 CR1006504
Riverside House, 2 Watt Road, Churchfields, Salisbury, Wiltshire SP2 7UD
Tel: 01722 322882
Email: . . . . enquiries@alabare.co.uk
Objects: F,W9,W3,W5,G,D,W4,3,C,W8,K

ALBRIGHTON TRUST
Founded: 1990 CR1000402
Blue House Lane, Albrighton, Wolverhampton, West Midlands WV7 3FL
Tel: 01902 372441
Email: . . . . moat@albrightontrust.org.uk
Objects: W6,W3,W2,E,W7,W5,G,W4

ALCOHOL FOCUS SCOTLAND
SC009538
166 Buchanan Street, Glasgow G1 2LW
Tel: 0141 572 6700
Email: . enquiries@alcohol-focus-scotland.org.uk
Objects: F,W3,J,G,W4,H,O,W8,K

ALCOHOL RESEARCH UK
Founded: 1982 CR1140287
83 Victoria Street, London SW1H 0HW
Tel: 020 3585 4155
Email: . . . . andrea.tilouche@aerc.org.uk
Objects: 1A,A,1B,B

ALCOHOLICS ANONYMOUS
Founded: 1947 CR226745; SC038023
PO Box 1, 10 Toft Green, York, North Yorkshire YO1 7NJ
Tel: . . . . 01904 644026; 0845 769 7555 (National Helpline)
Objects: H,O,P

ALDER HEY CHILDREN'S CHARITY
CR1160661
Alder Hey Children's Hospital, Eaton Road, Liverpool, Merseyside L12 2AP
Tel: 0151 252 5716
Email: . . . . info@alderheycharity.org
Objects: W3,N

ALDERMAN TOM F SPENCE CHARITY, THE
Founded: 1991 CR1002235
c/o Rippon City Council, Town Hall, Ripon, North Yorkshire HG4 1PA
Tel: 01765 604097
Objects: W3,W2,3

ALL NATIONS CHRISTIAN COLLEGE
CR311028
Easneye, Ware, Hertfordshire SG12 8LX
Tel: 01920 443500
Email: . . . . info@allnations.ac.uk
Objects: G,R,3

ALL SAINTS EDUCATIONAL TRUST
Founded: 1979 CR312934
Suite 8c, First Floor, Royal London House, 22-25 Finsbury Square, London EC2A 1DX
Tel: 020 7920 6465
Email: . . . . aset@aset.org.uk
Objects: G,1A,1B

ALMOND TRUST, THE
Founded: 1990 CR328583
19 West Square, London SE11 4SN
Objects: 1A,A,1B,R

ALMSHOUSE ASSOCIATION
Founded: 1956 CR245668
Billingbear Lodge, Maidenhead Road, Wokingham RG40 5RU
Tel: 01344 452922
Email: . . . . naa@almshouses.org
Objects: F,J,A,1B,D,2,W4,H

ALONE IN LONDON
Founded: 1972 CR1107432
188 King's Cross Road, London WC1X 9DE
Tel: . . . . . 020 7278 4486 Admin; 020 7278 4224 Advice
Email: . . . . enquiries@als.org.uk
Objects: F,W3,D,T,3,C

ALTERNATIVE FUTURES LTD
Founded: 1992 CR1008587
Lion Court, Kings Drive, Kings Business Park, Prescot, Merseyside L34 1BN
Tel: 0845 0176 744
Email: . . . . mail@alternativefutures.co.uk

ALZHEIMER'S RESEARCH UK
CR1077089; SC042474
3 Riverside, Granta Park, Cambridge, Cambridgeshire CB21 6AD
Tel: 0300 111 5555
Email: . . . . enquiries@alzheimersresearchuk.org
Objects: W6,W7,W5,W10,W11,1B,W4,W8

ALZHEIMER SCOTLAND
SC022315
22 Drumsheugh Gardens, Edinburgh EH3 7RN
Tel: 0131 243 1453
Email: . . . . cthomas@alzscot.org

AMELIA METHODIST TRUST FARM
Founded: 1991 CR1001546
Five Mile Lane, Barry, Vale of Glamorgan CF62 3AS
Tel: 01446 781427
Email: . . . . general@ameliatrust.org.uk
Objects: W3,W2,G,V,O,3,P,K

AMNESTY INTERNATIONAL (UK SECTION) CHARITABLE TRUST
Founded: 1986 CR1051681
The Human Rights Action Centre, 17-25 New Inn Yard, London EC2A 3EA
Tel: . 020 7033 1500; 020 7033 1664 (textphone)
Email: . . . . legacy@amnesty.org.uk
Objects: G,U

ANCHOR TRUST
CR1052183
2nd Floor, 25 Bedford Street, London WC2E 9ES
Tel: 020 7759 9100
Email: . . . . enquiries@anchor.org.uk
Objects: F,M,E,W5,1A,D,W4,3,C

ANCIENT MONUMENTS SOCIETY
Founded: 1924 CR209605
St Ann's Vestry Hall, 2 Church Entry, London EC4V 5HB
Tel: 020 7236 3934
Email: . office@ancientmonumentssociety.org.uk
Objects: F,W2,G,2,H

ANGLICAN SOCIETY FOR THE WELFARE OF ANIMALS
CR1087270
PO Box 7193, Hook, Hampshire RG27 8GT
Tel: 01252 843093
Email: . . . . angsocwelanimals@aol.com
Objects: F,W1,R,H

ANGLO-CATHOLIC ORDINATION CANDIDATES FUND
Founded: 1926 CR220121
57 Kenworthy Road, Braintree, Essex CM7 1JJ
Objects: G,1A,A,1B,2,R

ANGLO-RUSSIAN OPERA AND BALLET TRUST / THE MARIINSKY THEATRE TRUST
Founded: 1992 CR1010450
Mare Street Studios – Unit 305, 203-213 Mare Street, London E8 3QE

Tel: 020 8510 9262
Email: . . . . mail@mariinskyfriends.co.uk
Objects: S,G,A,2

ANIMAL CARE (LM&D)
CR508819
Blea Tarn Road, Scotforth, Lancaster, Lancashire LA2 0RD
Tel: 01524 65495 (11AM-3PM)
Email: . . . . . . admin@animalcare-lancaster.co.uk

ANIMAL CARE TRUST
CR281571
The Royal Veterinary College Animal Care Trust, Room CC1A, Hawkshead Lane, North Mymms, Hatfield, Hertfordshire AL9 7TA
Tel: 01707 666039
Email: . . . . legacy@rvc.ac.uk
Objects: W1,G

ANIMAL CONCERN ADVICE LINE (ACAL)
Founded: 2000SC030982
c/o Animal Concern, PO Box 5178, Dumbarton, West Dunbartonshire G82 5YJ
Tel: 01389 841111
Email: . . . . acal@jfrobins.force9.co.uk
Objects: F,W1,W2

ANIMAL RESCUE CUMBRIA (THE WAINWRIGHT SHELTER) CIO
CR1153737
"Kapellan", Grayrigg, Kendal, Cumbria LA8 9BS
Tel: . . . . 01539 824293 or 01539 724707
Email: . . . . . admin@animalrescuecumbria.co.uk
Web: . . . . www.animalrescuecumbria.co.uk
Object: W1
Animal Rescue Cumbria, called The Wainwright Shelter after our benefactor, well-known walker and writer Alfred Wainwright who, until his death in 1991, generously donated royalties from his books to ensure on-going support for the cats and dogs in our care. From humble beginnings in 1972 our staff and volunteers provide dedicated year round care.

ANIMAL WELFARE FOUNDATION
CR287118
7 Mansfield Street (CC), London W1G 9NQ

Tel: 020 7908 6375
Email: . . . . bva-awf@bva.co.uk
Objects: W1,1A,A,1B,H

ANIMALS IN DISTRESS SANCTUARY

Founded: 1967 CR515886
55 Silver Street (CC), Irlam, Manchester, Greater Manchester M44 6HT
Tel: 0161 775 2221
Email: . . . . . fieldofdreams@btconnect.com
Web: . . . . . www.animals-in-distress.co.uk
Objects: F,W1
AID was founded to alleviate the suffering of sick and injured animals. This includes a 24hr rescue service, veterinary treatment, neutering, micro-chipping then rehoming.
Unfortunately this all costs Please help - thank you.

ANIMALS IN NEED (NORTHAMPTONSHIRE)
CR1068222
Pine Tree Farm, London Road, Little Irchester, Wellingborough, Northamptonshire NN8 2EH
Tel: 01933 278080
Email: . . . . admin@animals-in-need.org
Object: W1

ANITA GOULDEN TRUST, THE
Founded: 1991 CR1004116
144 Bronsart Road, London SW6 6AB
Tel: 020 7385 1483
Email: . . . . annabuchan@aol.com
Objects: W3,W5,N,U

ANTHONY NOLAN
Founded: 1990 CR803716; SC038827
The Royal Free Hospital, Pond Street, Hampstead, London NW3 2QG
Tel: 020 7284 1234
Email: . . . . support@anthonynolan.org
Objects: W3,W5,N,3,W8

APEX CHARITABLE TRUST LTD
Founded: 1965 CR284736
St Alphage House, Wingate Annexe, 2 Fore Street, London EC2Y 5DA
Tel: 020 7638 5931
Email: . . . . jobcheck@apextrust.com
Objects: F,J,G,H,3,K

APLASTIC ANAEMIA TRUST
Founded: 1985 CR1107539
St Georges Hospital Medical School, Cranmer Terrace, London SW17 0RE
Tel: 0870 487 7778
Email: . . . . info@theaat.org.uk

APOSTLESHIP OF THE SEA
CR1069833
39 Eccleston Square, London SW1V 1BX
Tel: 02079011931
Email: . . . . info@apostleshipofthesea.org.uk
Objects: 1B,2,R,P

APULDRAM CENTRE, THE
Founded: 1990 CR801169
Common Farm, Apuldram Lane, Chichester, West Sussex PO20 7PE

Tel: 01243 783 370
Email: . . . . info@apuldram.org
info@apuldram.org

AQUARIUS
Founded: 1992 CR1014305
Sixth Floor, The White House, 111 New Street, Birmingham, West Midlands B2 4EU
Tel: 0121 622 8181
Objects: F,G,H,O,3,C,P

ARCH NORTH STAFFS LIMITED
Founded: 1989 CR701376
Canalside, Pelham Street, Hanley, Stoke-on-Trent, Staffordshire ST1 3LL
Tel: 01782 204479
Email: . . . . info@archnorthstaffs.org.uk
Objects: F,W3,G,D,3,C,P,W8

ARCHITECTS BENEVOLENT SOCIETY
Founded: 1850 CR265139
43 Portland Place, London W1B 1QH
Tel: 020 7580 2823
Email: . . . . help@absnet.org.uk
Objects: F,W5,W11,1A,A,V,D,W4,C

THE ARCHITECTURAL HERITAGE FUND
Founded: 1976 CR266780; SC043840
3 Spital Yard, Spitalfields, London E1 6AQ
Tel: 020 7925 0199
Email: . . . . ahf@ahfund.org.uk
Objects: W2,S,A,1B,3

ARDIS
Founded: 1986 CR297811
14 Gundreda Road, Lewes, East Sussex BN7 1PX
Tel: 01273 472049
Objects: E,1B,2,W4,C

ARMED FORCES' CHRISTIAN UNION
Founded: 1851 CR249636
Havelock House, Barrack Road, Aldershot, Hampshire GU11 3NP
Tel: 01252 311221
Email: . . . . office@afcu.org.uk
Objects: W9,2,R

ARMS AROUND THE CHILD
CR1123038
Communications House, 26 York Street, London W1U 6PZ
Tel: 0845 094 9491
Email: . . . . ukinfo@keepachildalive.org

ARROWE PARK HOSPITAL POSTGRADUATE EDUCATION CENTRE TRUST
Founded: 1990 CR703069
Arrowe Park Road, Upton, Wirral, Merseyside CH49 5PE
Tel: 0151 604 7196
Objects: G,N,3

ART FUND, THE
Founded: 1903 CR209174
Millais House, 7 Cromwell Place, South Kensington, London SW7 2JN
Tel: 020 7225 4800
Email: . . . . info@artfund.org
Objects: S,A,1B,2,W12,3

ART IN HEALTHCARE
Founded: 2005SC036222
The Drill Hall, 32-36 Dalmeny Street, Edinburgh EH6 8RG
Tel: 0131 555 7638
Email: . . . . admin@artinhealthcare.org.uk
Objects: W3,W2,S,W7,W5,W10,W4,O,3,W8

ARTHRITIC ASSOCIATION - TREATING ARTHRITIS NATURALLY
CR292569
8th Floor (CC), 64 Victoria Street, London SW1E 6QP
Tel: 01323 416550; 020 7491 0233
Email: . . . . info@arthritisaction.org.uk
Objects: F,1A,2,W4,H

ARTHRITIS CARE
CR206563; SC038693
Floor 4, Linen Court, 10 East Road, London N1 6AD
Tel: 020 7380 6500
Email: . . . . info@arthritiscare.org.uk
Objects: F,W3,W5,G,2,H,3,P

ARTHRITIS RESEARCH UK
Founded: 1936 CR207711; SC041156
Copeman House, St. Mary's Court, St Mary's Gate, Chesterfield, Derbyshire S41 7TD
Tel: 0300 790 0400
Email: . . . . legacies@arthritisresearchuk.org
Objects: F,1A,1B,H

ARTISTS' GENERAL BENEVOLENT INSTITUTION
Founded: 1814 CR212667
Burlington House, Piccadilly, London W1J 0BB
Tel: 020 7734 1193
Email: . . . . agbi1@btconnect.com
Object: 1A

ARTISTS' ORPHAN FUND
CR219356
Burlington House, Piccadilly, London W1J 0BB
Tel: 020 7734 1193
Email: . . . . agbi1@btconnect.com
Objects: 1A,Y

ARTLINK WEST YORKSHIRE
Founded: 1990 CR702492
Community Arts Centre, 191 Belle Vue Road, Leeds, West Yorkshire LS3 1HG
Tel: 0113 243 1005
Objects: F,W3,S,W5,G,W10,W4,3,K

ASH - ACTION ON SMOKING & HEALTH
Founded: 1971 CR262067
First Floor, 144-145 Shoreditch High Street, London E1 6JE
Tel: 020 7739 5902
Email: . . . . enquiries@ash.org.uk
Objects: F,W3,W4,H

ASIAN PEOPLE'S DISABILITY ALLIANCE
Founded: 1990 CR803283
Daycare and Development Centre, Alric Avenue, Harlesden, London NW10 8RA
Tel: 020 8961 6773
Email: . . . . apdmcha@aol.com
Objects: F,W6,S,E,W7,W5,G,W10,W4,3,P

ASPIRE - SUPPORTING PEOPLE WITH SPINAL INJURY

Founded: 1983 CR1075317
ASPIRE National Training Centre (CC), Wood Lane, Stanmore, Middlesex HA7 4AP
Tel: . . . . 020 8954 5759; 020 8420 6506 Minicom
Email: . . . . info@aspire.org.uk
Objects: W5,1A,D

ASSESSMENT AND QUALIFICATIONS ALLIANCE

Founded: 1992 CR1073334
Stag Hill House, Guildford, Surrey GU2 7XJ
Tel: 0800 197 7162
Objects: G,3

ASSISI ANIMAL CHARITIES FOUNDATION

CR1102985
Assisi, Home Close Farm, Shilton Road, Burford, Oxfordshire OX18 4PF
Tel: 0870 609 2810
Email: . . . . enquiries@assisi.org.uk
Objects: W1,2

ASSOCIATION FOR LANGUAGE LEARNING, THE

Founded: 1991 CR1001826
14 Salisbury Road, Leicester, Leicestershire LE1 7QR
Tel: 0116 229 7600
Email: . . . . info@all-languages.org.uk
Objects: G,2,H

ASSOCIATION FOR REAL CHANGE

Founded: 1976 CR285575
ARC House, Marsden Street, Chesterfield, Derbyshire S40 1JY
Tel: 01246 555043
Email: . . . . contact.us@arcuk.org.uk
Objects: F,W3,J,E,W5,G,2,W4,H,3,C

ASSOCIATION FOR RESEARCH INTO STAMMERING IN CHILDHOOD

CR801171
Michael Palin Centre For Stammering Children, 13-15 Pine Street, Pine Street, London EC1R 0JH
Tel: 020 3316 8100
Email: . . . . info@stammeringcentre.org
Objects: F,W3,G,3

ASSOCIATION OF CHARITY OFFICERS

Founded: 1946 CR1118605
Central House, 14 Upper Woburn Place, London WC1H 0NN
Tel: 020 7255 4480
Email: . . . . info@aco.uk.net
Objects: F,W9,W6,W3,J,W7,W5,W10,W11,2,W4, W8

ASSOCIATION OF DISABLED PROFESSIONALS

Founded: 1971 CR1121706
BCM ADP, London WC1N 3XX
Tel: 01204 431638
Email: . . . . info@adp.org.uk
Objects: F,W5

ASSOCIATION OF INTERCHURCH FAMILIES

Founded: 1968 CR283811
27 Tavistock Square, London WC1H 9HH
Tel: 020 3384 2947
Email: . . . . info@interchurchfamilies.org.uk
Objects: F,W3,J,G,2,H,3

ASSOCIATION OF PRESERVATION TRUSTS

CR1027919
9th Floor, Alhambra House, 27-31 Charing Cross Road, London WC2H 0AU
Tel: 020 7930 1629
Email: . . . . apt@ahfund.org.uk

ASSOCIATION OF PROFESSIONAL FORESTERS EDUCATION AND PROVIDENT FUND

CR1061322
Woodland Place, West Street, Belford, Northumberland NE70 7QA
Tel: 01668 213937
Email: . . . . jane@apfs.demon.co.uk

ASSOCIATION OF ROYAL NAVY OFFICERS

Founded: 1925 CR313113
70 Porchester Terrace, Bayswater, London W2 3TP
Tel: 020 7402 5231
Email: . . . . asec@arno.org.uk
Objects: F,W9,G,1A,A,2,B,3

ASSOCIATION OF TAXATION TECHNICIANS

Founded: 1990 CR803480
12 Upper Belgrave Street, London SW1X 8BB
Tel: 020 7235 2544
Email: . . . . info@att.org.uk
Objects: G,2

ASTHMA UK

Founded: 1990 CR802364; SC039322
Chief Executive: Kay Boycott
Legacies Team (CD16), 18 Mansell Street, London E1 8AA
Tel: . . . . 020 7786 4990; 0300 222 5800 (Helpline)
Email: . . . . info@asthma.org.uk
Web: . . . www.asthma.org.uk/get-involved/leave-a-gift/
Objects: F,W3,J,G,1A,1B,2,H,3,W

Every 10 seconds, someone in the UK suffers a terrifying and potentially life threatening asthma attack and three of those people will die each day. Two thirds of these deaths are preventable. 250,000 people have asthma so severe current treatments don't work. We work to stop asthma attacks and, ultimately, cure asthma by funding world leading research and scientists, campaigning for improved care and supporting people with asthma to reduce their risk of an asthma attack. We are entirely funded by voluntary donations.

Gifts in Wills fund one in every three research projects and are vital in helping to reduce the time it takes to achieve our mission. Together we can do more than treat asthma we can cure asthma too.

ASYLUM AID
Founded: 1990 CR328729
Club Union House, 253-254 Upper Street, London N1 1RY
Tel: 020 7354 9631
Email: . . . . info@asylumaid.org.uk
Objects: F,W3,W5,W10,2,W4,3,W8

ASYLUM WELCOME
CR1092265
Unit 7 Newtec Place, Magdalen Road, Oxford, Oxfordshire OX4 1RE
Tel: 01865 722082
Email: . . . . asylum-welcome@supanet.com
Objects: F,W3,S,G,W10,V,2,3,W8

AT HOME IN THE COMMUNITY LTD
Founded: 1990 CR803280
391 West Road, Newcastle upon Tyne, Tyne & Wear NE15 7PY
Tel: 0191 228 8300
Email: . . . . info@athome.uk.net
Objects: W5,3

ATAXIA UK
Founded: 1964 CR1102391
12 Broadbent Close, London N6 5JW
Tel: . . . 0845 644 0606 (Helpline); 020 7582 1444
Email: . . . . enquiries@ataxia.org.uk
Objects: F,W3,W5,1A,A,1B,W4,H,3,P

THE ATHLONE TRUST
CR277065
36 Nassau Road Barnes, London SW13 9QE
Tel: 07496 653542
Fax: 020 8251 9563
Email: . . . . athlonetrust@outlook.com
Web: . . . . www.athlonetrust.com
See advert on this page

ATHOLL CENTRE (ATHOLL BAPTIST CENTRE LTD)
SC015113
Atholl Road, Pitlochry, Perth & Kinross PH16 5BX
Tel: 01796 473044
Email: . . . . admin@athollcentre.org.uk
Objects: W3,W5,V,R,W4

ATLANTIC FOUNDATION, THE
Founded: 1990 CR328499
Atlantic House, Cardiff Gate Business Park, Greenwood Wharf, Cardiff CF23 8RD
Tel: 029 2054 5680

ATS & WRAC ASSOCIATION BENEVOLENT FUND
Founded: 1964 CR206184
AGC Centre, Worthy Down, Winchester, Hampshire SO21 2RG
Tel: 01962 887612
Email: benfund.wracassociation@googlemail.com
Objects: F,W9,1A,A,B,W8

ATTEND
Founded: 1949 CR1113067
11-13 Cavendish Square, London W1G 0AN
Tel: 0845 450 0285
Email: . . . . info@attend.org.uk
Objects: F,W3,J,W5,G,W10,A,1B,2,W4,W8,K

AUTISM ANGLIA
CR1063717
Century House, Riverside Office Centre, North Station Road, Colchester, Essex CO1 1RE
Tel: 01206 577678
Email: .... info@autism-anglia.org.uk
Objects: F,W5,G

AUTISM INITIATIVES UK
Founded: 1990 CR702632
7 Chesterfield Road, Crosby, Merseyside L23 9XL
Tel: 0151 330 9500
Email: .... sfr@autisminitiatives.org
Objects: F,W3,E,W5,G,D,W4,H,P,K

AUTISM LONDON
Founded: 1992 CR1009720
One Hermitage Court, Hermitage Lane, Maidstone, Kent ME16 9NT
Tel: 01622 722400
Email: .... info@autismlondon.org.uk
Objects: F,W5,2,3,C

AVERT
Founded: 1986 CR1074849
First Floor South, 6-7 Lovers Walk, Brighton, Brighton & Hove BN1 6AH
Tel: 01273 947749
Email: .... info@avert.org
Objects: F,W3,G,1B,U,3

AVIATION ENVIRONMENT TRUST
Founded: 1978 CR276987
Broken Wharf House, 2 Broken Wharf, London EC4V 3DT
Tel: 020 7248 2223
Email: .... info@aet.org.uk
Objects: F,J,W2,G,H,3

AVOCET TRUST
Founded: 1991 CR1004537
Head Office, Clarence House, 60-62 Clarence Street, Hull, Kingston upon Hull HU9 1DN
Tel: 01482 329226
Email: .... info@avocettrust.co.uk

AXIS WEB
Founded: 1991 CR1002841
Round Foundry Media Centre, Foundry Street, Leeds, West Yorkshire LS11 5QP
Tel: 0870 443 0701
Email: .... hello@axisweb.org
Objects: F,W6,W3,J,W2,S,W7,W5,G,W10,W12, W4,H,3,W8,K

AYRSHIRE CANCER SUPPORT
SC016098
16 Portland Road, Kilmarnock, East Ayrshire KA1 2BS
Tel: 01563 538008
Email: .... admin@ayrshirecs.org

B

BABY LIFELINE LTD
Founded: 1991 CR1006457
The Granary, Fernhill Court, Balsall Street East, Balsall Common, Coventry, West Midlands CV7 7FR
Tel: 01676534671
Email: .... info@babylifeline.org.uk
Objects: W3,G,A,W8

BACKCARE (REGISTERED AS THE NATIONAL BACK PAIN ASSOCIATION)
Founded: 1968 CR256751
16 Elmtree Road, Teddington, Middlesex TW11 8ST
Tel: 020 8977 5474
Email: .... info@backcare.org.uk
Objects: F,W3,J,W5,G,A,1B,2,W4,H,O,3,P,W8

BAKERS' BENEVOLENT SOCIETY
Founded: 1832 CR211307
The Mill House, 23 Bakers Lane, Epping, Essex CM16 5DQ
Tel: 01992 575951
Objects: W5,1A,A,D,W4,B,3

BAKEWELL & EYAM COMMUNITY TRANSPORT
Founded: 1996 CR1049389
South Lodge Newholme Hospital, 3 Baslow Road, Bakewell, Derbyshire DE45 1AD
Tel: 01629 814889
Objects: W6,M,W3,W7,W5,2,W4,3,W8

BANK WORKERS CHARITY
Founded: 1883 CR313080
Pinners Hall, 105-108 Old Broad Street, London EC2N 1EX
Tel: 020 7216 8981
Email: .... help@bbfund.org.uk
Objects: W3,W5,1A,A,2,W4

BAPTIST MINISTERS' PENSION FUND
PO Box 44, Baptist House, 129 Broadway, Didcot, Oxfordshire OX11 8RT
Tel: 01235 517700
Email: .... pensions@baptist.org.uk
Objects: B,3

BAPTIST UNION OF GREAT BRITAIN
CR1125912
PO Box 44, 129 Broadway, Didcot, Oxfordshire OX11 8RT
Tel: 01235 517700
Objects: F,G,R,H,P

THE BARCLAY FOUNDATION
Founded: 1990 CR803696
3rd Floor, 20 St James's Street, London SW1A 1ES
Tel: 020 7915 0915
Objects: W3,1B

BARNARDO'S

Believe in children

Barnardo's

Founded: 1866 CR216250; SC037605
Tanners Lane, Barkingside, Ilford, Essex
IG6 1QG
Tel: 020 8498 7880
Email: ..... giftsinwills@barnardos.org.uk
Web: .. www.barnardos.org.uk/giftsinwills

Objects: Q,F,M,W3,E,G,D,H,3,C,P,K

Barnardo's transforms the lives of vulnerable and disadvantaged children through the work of our services, and through our campaigning and research expertise. As one of the UK's leading children's charities we work directly with over 240,000 children, young people and their families each year, and run more than 960 services across the UK.

Barnardo's aim is always the same; to bring out the best in any child, no matter who they are, what they have done, or what they have been through.

Our work includes support for young people leaving care, counselling for children who've been mistreated, vocational training for young people not in mainstream education or employment and specialist help for disabled children and their families.

We believe that every child deserves the best start in life and the chance to fulfil their potential. We depend heavily on the generosity and support of the public to help us continue and expand our vital work. By leaving a gift in your Will to Barnardo's - however large or small - you can help ensure that the most vulnerable children have someone to turn to, long into the future.

BARNSTONDALE CENTRE

Founded: 1990 CR1087502
Storeton Lane, Barnston, Wirral, Merseyside
CH61 1BX
Tel: 0151 648 1412
Email: .... info@barnstondale.org

Objects: W6,W3,W7,W5,G,V,3,P

BAROW HILLS SCHOOL WITLEY

Founded: 1990 CR1000190
Roke Lane, Witley, Godalming, Surrey GU8 5NY
Tel: 01428 683639
Email: .... info@barrowhills.org

BARRISTERS' BENEVOLENT ASSOCIATION

BBA

Founded: 1873 CR1106768
Secretary: Mrs Susan Eldridge
14 Gray's Inn Square, London WC1R 5JP
Tel: 020 7242 4761
Fax: 020 7831 5366
Email: .... susan@the-bba.com
Web: .... www.the-bba.com

Objects: F,M,W15,1A

The object of the Association is to help needy and deserving members of the English Bar who are, or have been, in practice in England or Wales, their husbands or wives, widows or widowers, children and, in exceptional circumstances, dependants. Application to Secretary.

See advert on next page

BARRY GREEN MEMORIAL FUND

CR1000492
Claro Chambers, Bridge Street, Boroughbridge, York, North Yorkshire YO51 9LD
Email: .... info@fitz-law.co.uk

Objects: W1,A,1B

BASE - BRITISH ASSOCIATION FOR SERVICE TO THE ELDERLY

Founded: 1968 CR269853
119 Hassell Street, Newcastle-under-Lyme, Staffordshire ST5 1AX
Tel: 01782 661033
Email: .... basenul@intonet.co.uk

Objects: G,2,W4,H,3

BASINGSTOKE DIAL-A-RIDE

Founded: 1990 CR900594
Whiteditch Playing Field, Sherbourne Road, Basingstoke, Hampshire RG21 5UT
Tel: 01256 816069

Objects: M,W4,3

BASPCAN (BRITISH ASSOCIATION FOR THE STUDY AND PREVENTION OF CHILD ABUSE AND NEGLECT)

Founded: 1979 CR279119
17 Priory Street, York, North Yorkshire YO1 6ET
Tel: 01904 613605
Email: .... baspcan@baspcan.org.uk

Objects: W3,J,G,2,H,P

BASSETLAW HOSPICE OF THE GOOD SHEPHERD, RETFORD

CR701876
Cedar House, North Road, Retford, Nottinghamshire DN22 7XF
Tel: 01777 869239
Email: .... give@hospiceappeal.org.uk

Objects: E,N,3

BAT CONSERVATION TRUST

Founded: 1990 CR1012361
5th floor, Quadrant House, 250 Kennington Lane, London SE11 5RD

Tel: 020 7627 2629; 0845 130 0228
Email: . . . . enquiries@bats.org.uk
Objects: F,W1,W3,W2,G,2,H

BATH INSTITUTE FOR RHEUMATIC DISEASES
CR1040650
1 Trimbridge, Bath, Bath & North East Somerset BA1 1HD
Tel: 01225 448444
Email: . . . . fundraising@birdbath.org.uk
Objects: W3,W5,G,1B,N,W4,3,W8

BATTERSEA DOGS & CATS HOME
Founded: 1860 CR206394
4 Battersea Park Road (LCD2012), London SW8 4AA
Tel: 020 7627 9247
Email: . . . . fundraising@battersea.org.uk; info@battersea.org.uk
Objects: Q,F,W1,G,O

BAYC (BIRMINGHAM ASSOCIATION OF YOUTH CLUBS)
Founded: 1898 CR1090789
Hilda Simister House, 581 Pershore Road, Selly Park, Birmingham, West Midlands B29 7EL
Tel: 0845 241 0923
Email: . . . . info@bayc.org
Objects: F,W3,J,S,G,2,H,3,P

BCPC
Founded: 1992 CR1075620
1 Trim Bridge, London Road, Bath, Bath & North East Somerset BA1 1HD
Tel: 01225 429720
Email: . . . . admin@bcpc.org.uk
Objects: F,G,2,3

BEACON CENTRE FOR THE BLIND
Founded: 1875 CR216092
Wolverhampton Road East, Wolverhampton, West Midlands WV4 6AZ
Tel: 01902 880111
Email: . . . . enquiries@beacon4blind.co.uk
Objects: F,W6,M,W3,E,W5,G,V,W4,O,3,C,P,K

BEAUMOND HOUSE COMMUNITY HOSPICE
CR1025442
32 London Road, Newark, Nottinghamshire NG24 1TW
Tel: 01636 610556
Object: 3

BEDFORD DAYCARE HOSPICE
Founded: 1991 CR1001614
3 Linden Road, Bedford, Bedfordshire MK40 2DD
Tel: 01234 352015
Email: . . . . . . info@bedforddaycarehospice.co.uk
Objects: F,W9,W6,M,J,E,W7,W5,W10,W11,N,W4,H,O,3,P,W8

BEDFORDSHIRE AND HERTFORDSHIRE HISTORIC CHURCHES TRUST

***Founded:* 1991 CR1005697**
Church Cottage, Southill Park, Southill, Biggleswade, Bedfordshire SG18 9LL
Tel: 01442 864867
Email: .... wmarsterson@yahoo.co.uk
Web: .... www.bedshertshct.org.uk
Aims:
• To assist with the care of places of worship of all denominations in the two counties;
• To grant funds for their restoration, maintenance, preservation, repair and reconstruction.

Objectives:
• To generate income from members to fund the Trust's activities;
• To raise substantial income through the annual Bike 'n Hike event, and also via legacies;
• To co-operate with other bodies making funds available for the purposes above;
• To foster the appreciation of the history and architecture of these places of worship.

BEIS AHARON

Founded: 1992 CR1010420
86 Darenth Road, London N16 6ED

BELL MEMORIAL HOME (INC)

Founded: 1890 CR206244
Methold House, North Street, Worthing, West Sussex BN11 1DU
Tel: 01903 528600
Objects: W5,G,W4,3

BEN - THE AUTOMOTIVE INDUSTRY CHARITY

Founded: 1905 CR297877; SC039842
Lynwood, Sunninghill, Ascot, Windsor & Maidenhead SL5 0AJ
Tel: 01344 620191
Email: .... info@ben.org.uk
Objects: F,E,W11,1A,A,D,N,B,3,C

BENSLOW MUSIC TRUST AND INSTRUMENT LOAN SCHEME

Founded: 1960 CR313755, 313663
Little Benslow Hills, Benslow Lane, Hitchin, Hertfordshire SG4 9RB
Tel: 01462 420748
Email: .... loanscheme@benslow.org
Objects: W3,S,G,2,3

BERKSHIRE, BUCKINGHAMSHIRE & OXFORDSHIRE WILDLIFE TRUST

Founded: 1960 CR204330
The Lodge, 1 Armstrong Road, Littlemore, Oxford, Oxfordshire OX4 4XT
Tel: 01865 775476
Email: .... info@bbowt.org.uk
Objects: W2,2

THE BERKSHIRE MS THERAPY CENTRE

Founded: 1982 CR800419
Bradbury House, 23a August End, Brock Gardens, Reading RG30 2JP
Tel: 0118 901 6000
Email: .... ms@bmstc.org
Objects: F,E,W5,G,N,H,O,3

BETHESDA HOSPICE, STORNOWAY

Founded: 1987 CR44253; SC015783
Springfield Road, Stornoway, Western Isles HS1 2PS
Tel: 01851 706222
Fax: 01851 706285
Email: .... bethesdahospice@hotmail.com
Web: .... bethesdahospice.co.uk
Objects: W5,N,W4,W14

BFMS (THE BRITISH FALSE MEMORY SOCIETY)

CR1040683
Newtown, Bradford-on-Avon, Wiltshire BA15 1NF
Tel: 01225 868682
Objects: F,W6,W3,W7,W5,W10,2,W4,T,W8

BIBIC - CHANGING CHILDREN'S LIVES

CR1057635; SC043909
Old Kelways, Somerton Road, Langport, Somerset TA10 9SJ
Tel: 01458 253344
Email: .... giftsinwills@bibic.org.uk
Objects: W3,G,W15,O,3

THE BIBLE NETWORK

CR299943
Hornchurch, Essex RM11 2EG
Email: .... johnsavageuk@aol.com
The Bible Network trains Christians worldwide to share God's Word, to lead people to Jesus Christ, and to connect them to a local church.

The process continues as new Bible-believing Christians go on to tell others about the Saviour who loves them and gave His life for them.

BIBLE SOCIETY

Founded: 1804 CR232759
Stonehill Green, Westlea, Swindon, Wiltshire SN5 7DG
Tel: 01793 418100
Email: .... contactus@biblesociety.org.uk
Objects: W9,W6,W3,W7,W5,G,W10,1B,R,W4,U,H,3,W8

BILD (BRITISH INSTITUTE OF LEARNING DISABILITIES)

CR1019663
Campion House, Green Street, Kidderminster, Worcestershire DY10 1JL
Tel: 01562 723010
Email: .... enquiries@bild.org.uk
Objects: F,W5,G,2,H

BIPOLAR UK

Founded: 1983 CR293340
11 Belgrave Road, London SW1V 1RB
Tel: 020 7931 6480
Email: .... mdf@mdf.org.uk
Objects: F,W3,W5,G,2,H,3,P

BIRCHINGTON CONVALESCENT BENEFIT FUND
CR249574
Dean Wace House, 16 Rosslyn Road, Watford, Hertfordshire WD18 0NY
Tel: 01923 235111
Email: .... finance@churchsociety.org
Objects: W3,1A,A,1B,V

BIRDLIFE INTERNATIONAL
CR1042125
Wellbrook Court, Girton Road, Cambridge, Cambridgeshire CB3 0NA
Tel: 01223 277318
Email: .... birdlife@birdlife.org

BIRKENHEAD YOUNG MEN'S CHRISTIAN ASSOCIATION
Founded: 1990 CR1000601
Birkenhead YMCA, Hope Prospect, 56 Whetstone Lane, Birkenhead, Merseyside CH41 2TJ
Tel: 0151 650 1015
Email: .... reception@birkenheadymca.co.uk
Objects: W3,G,D,2,3,C,W8

BIRMINGHAM CHILDREN'S HOSPITAL CHARITY

Birmingham Children's Hospital Charity
Registered Charity Number: 1160875

Founded: 1862 CR1160875
Fundraising Team, Birmingham Children's Hospital, Steelhouse Lane, Birmingham, West Midlands B4 6NH
Tel: 0121 333 8506
Fax: 0121 233 1923
Email: .... fundraising@bch.org.uk
Web: .... www.bch.org.uk/gifts
Objects: W3,N
Birmingham Children's Hospital is a world-class centre helping to save an unprecedented number of children with life-threatening conditions. We invest in research for the best medical discoveries, the best spaces and the best experiences for our patients while they're in our care.

BIRMINGHAM CHRISTIAN COLLEGE
Founded: 1953 CR1002205
Hamilton Drive, Selly Oak, Birmingham, West Midlands B29 6AJ
Tel: 0121 472 0726
Email: .... info@bhxc.ac.uk
Objects: G,R,3

BIRMINGHAM CONTEMPORARY MUSIC GROUP
Founded: 1991 CR1001474
CBSO Centre, Berkley Street, Birmingham, West Midlands B1 2LF
Tel: 0121 616 2616
Email: .... info@bcmg.org.uk
Objects: S,G,3

BIRMINGHAM DOGS' HOME, THE
CR222436
Catherine-De-Barnes Lane (CC), Catherine-De-Barnes, Solihull, West Midlands B92 0DJ
Tel: 0121 643 5211
Email: ...... info@birminghamdogshome.org.uk
Object: W1

BIRMINGHAM MIND
Founded: 1991 CR1003906
17 Graham Street, Birmingham, West Midlands B1 3JR
Tel: 0121 608 8001
Email: .... info@birminghammind.org
Objects: F,E,3,C

BIRMINGHAM REPERTORY THEATRE LTD
Founded: 1991 CR223660
Birmingham Repertory Theatre, Centenary Square, Broad Street, Birmingham, West Midlands B1 2EP
Tel: 0121 245 2000
Email: .. yvonne.stevens@birmingham-rep.co.uk
Objects: S,G

BISHOP HO MING WAH ASSOCIATION
Founded: 1984 CR290398
Bishop Ho Ming Wah Community Centre, Lower Crypt, St.Martin-in-the-Fields Church, Trafalgar Square, London WC2N 4JJ
Tel: 020 7766 1141; 020 7839 1874
Email: .... enquiry@bhmwa.com
Objects: F,W3,J,S,E,G,W10,W4,3,P,W8

BLACK CULTURAL ARCHIVES
CR1051087
1 Othello Close, Kennington, London SE11 4RE
Tel: 020 7582 8516
Email: .... info@bcaheritage.org.uk
Objects: S,G,H,3

BLACK WOMEN'S HEALTH & FAMILY SUPPORT
Founded: 1991 CR1083654
1st Floor, 82 Russia Lane, London E2 9LU
Tel: 020 8980 3503
Email: .... bwhafs@btconnect.com

BLACKBURN CHILD CARE SOCIETY
CR222533
Registered Office, Whalley Road, Wilpshire, Blackburn, Lancashire BB1 9LL
Tel: 01254 244700
Email: .... enquiries@bccs-uk.org
Objects: Q,F,W3,3

BLANDFORD MUSEUM OF FASHION
CR1052471
Lime Tree House, The Plocks, Church Lane, Blandford Forum, Dorset DT11 7AA
Tel: 01258 453006
Objects: W3,S,G,W4,3

BLEAKHOLT ANIMAL SANCTUARY
CR1110503
30 Stuart Road, Stretford, Greater Manchester M32 0DQ
Tel: 0161 865 0457
Email: .... info@bleakholt.org
Object: W1

BLESMA, THE LIMBLESS VETERANS
Founded: 1932 CR1084189; SC010315
Frankland Moore House (CC), 185-187 High Road, Chadwell Heath, Essex RM6 6NA

Tel: 020 8548 3517
Email: . . . . fundraising@blesma.org
Web: . . . . www.blesma.org

Objects: F,W9,M,W5,1A,A,1B,V,2,B,H,O,3,C,P

Blesma, The Limbless Veterans helps all serving and ex-Service men and women who have lost limbs, or lost the use of limbs or eyes, to rebuild their lives by providing rehabilitation activities and welfare support. Our programmes allow Members and their families to face the challenges ahead with renewed confidence and self-belief. We work tirelessly for our Members when the conflicts that have affected their lives are no longer a focal point in the nation's media. Blesma is for life.

See advert on previous page

BLIND VETERANS UK

Founded: 1915 CR216227; SC039411
12-14 Harcourt Street, London W1H 4HD
Tel: 020 7616 7953
Email: . . . . james.allport@st-dunstans.co.uk

Objects: F,W9,W6,M,E,W5,G,1A,A,D,N,W4,B,H,O,3,C,P,K

BLINDAID

BlindAid

Founded: 1834 CR262119
Lantern House, 102 Bermondsey Street, London SE1 3UB
Tel: 020 7403 6184
Fax: 020 7234 0708
Email: . . . . enquiries@blindaid.org.uk
Web: . . . . www.blindaid.org.uk

Objects: F,W6,1A,A,1B,3,P

BlindAid has over 180 years of experience. Working in the 12 Inner London Boroughs, we provide vital home visits to over 600 isolated blind and visually impaired people offering friendship, company and conversation.

BLISS

Founded: 1979 CR1002973; SC040006
2nd Floor, Chapter House, 18-20 Crucifix Lane, London SE1 3JW
Tel: . . . 020 7378 1122; 0500 618140 Freephone Family Support Helpline
Email: . . . . ask@bliss.org.uk

Objects: F,W3,G,1A,N,H

BLOND MCINDOE RESEARCH FOUNDATION

Founded: 1960 CR1106240
Queen Victoria Hospital, East Grinstead, West Sussex RH19 3DZ
Tel: 01342 313088
Email: . . . . enquiries@blondmcindoe.com

Object: 3

BLOOD PRESSURE ASSOCIATION

CR1058944; SC040230
60 Cranmer Terrace (CC), London SW17 0QS
Tel: 020 8772 4994
Email: . . . . kyn@bloodpressureuk.org

Objects: F,2,H

BLOODWISE

Bloodwise
Beating blood cancer since 1960

Founded: 1960 CR216032; SC037529
Chief Executive: Ms Cathy Gilman
39-40 Eagle Street, London WC1R 4TH
Tel: 020 7504 2200
Email: . . . . info@bloodwise.org.uk

Objects: F,W3,J,A,1B,N,2,W4,H,3

Life is a gift. Give it through a legacy.

Every year 38,000 people are diagnosed with blood cancer – one person every 14 minutes. By leaving a gift in your Will to Bloodwise, the new name for Leukaemia & Lymphoma Research, you'll fund ground-breaking research and vital patient support to change the lives of every single person affected by blood cancer. We can see a future without blood cancer. Help us make it happen.

Find out more at bloodwise.org.uk/legacies or call 020 7504 2200

BLUE CROSS

Founded: 1897 CR224392; SC040154
Registered Office, Shilton Road, Burford, Oxfordshire OX18 4PF
Tel: 0300 777 1897
Email: . . . . info@bluecross.org.uk

Objects: W1,E,G,H,3

BLUEBELL RAILWAY TRUST

CR292497
The Bluebell Railway, Sheffield Park Station, Uckfield, East Sussex TN22 3QL
Tel: 01825 720800
Email: . . . . roger.kelly@bluebell-railway.co.uk

Objects: W2,S,G,1A,A,1B,W12

BLYTHSWOOD CARE

SC021848
Highland Deephaven Industrial Estate, Evanton, Highland IV16 9XJ
Tel: 01349 830777
Email: . . . . info@blythswood.org

Objects: W3,W10,R,U,H,K

BMA CHARITIES

Founded: 1925 CR219102
Director: Ms Marian Flint
Chairman: Dr A Mowat
BMA House, Tavistock Square, London WC1H 9JP
Tel: 020 7383 6142
Email: . . . . info.bmacharities@bma.org.uk
Web: . . www.bma.org.uk/about-us/bma-charities

Objects: F,W11,1A,A

Helps doctors and their dependants and medical students in times of financial crisis.

BMS WORLD MISSION

Founded: 1792 CR233782
PO Box 49, 129 Broadway, Didcot, Oxfordshire OX11 8XA
Tel: 01235 517700
Email: . . . . mail@bmsworldmission.org

Objects: W3,W7,G,W10,W15,A,1B,W16,2,R,W4,U,B,H,Y,P,W8,L

BNTL 'FREEWAY' (THE BRITISH NATIONAL TEMPERANCE LEAGUE)
CR224555
30 Keswick Road, Worksop, Nottinghamshire S81 7PT
Tel: 01909 477882
Email: . . . . bntl@btconnect.com
Objects: W3,G,3

BOB CHAMPION CANCER TRUST
CR1024664
6 Old Garden House, The Lanterns, Bridge Lane, London SW11 3AD
Tel: 020 7924 3553
Email: . . . . ask@bobchampion.org.uk

BOBATH CENTRE FOR CHILDREN WITH CEREBRAL PALSY
Founded: 1957 CR229663
250 East End Road, London N2 8AU
Tel: 020 8444 3355
Email: . . . . fundraising@bobathlondon.co.uk
Objects: W3,W5,G,O,3

BOBATH CHILDREN'S THERAPY CENTRE WALES
CR1010183
19 Park Road, Whitchurch, Cardiff CF14 7BP
Tel: 029 2052 2600
Email: . . . . info@bobathwales.org; fundraising@bobathwales.org
Objects: W3,W5

BODY POSITIVE NORTH EAST LIMITED
Founded: 1990 CR1000714
12 Princess Square, Newcastle upon Tyne, Tyne & Wear NE1 8ER
Tel: 0191 232 2855
Email: . . . . bpne@btinternet.com
Objects: F,W6,M,W3,J,E,W7,W5,G,W10,W4,H,3,P,W8

BODY POSITIVE NORTH WEST LIMITED
Founded: 1991 CR1002475
39 Russell Road, Whalley Range, Manchester, Greater Manchester M16 8DH
Tel: . . . 0161 882 2200; 0161 882 2202 (Helpline)
Email: . . . . info@bpnw.org.uk
Objects: F,E,G,D,O,3

BOLENOWE ANIMAL SANCTUARY
CR296673
Bonaventure Farm, Ruan Minor, Helston, Cornwall TR12 7LW
Tel: 01326 291 272
Email: . . . . info@bolenowe.co.uk

BOLTON COMMUNITY & VOLUNTARY SERVICE
Founded: 1991 CR1003123
Bridge House, Pool Street South, Bolton, Greater Manchester BL1 2BA
Tel: 01204 546010
Email: . . . . shafiqa@boltoncvs.org.uk
Objects: F,2,H

BOLTON YMCA
Founded: 1991 CR1001884
125 Deansgate, Bolton, Greater Manchester BL1 1HA
Tel: 01204 522855
Objects: W3,E,A,2,3,P

THE BOOK TRADE CHARITY (BTBS)
CR1128129
The Foyle Centre, The Retreat, Kings Langley, Hertfordshire WD4 8LT
Tel: 01923 263128
Email: . . . . david@btbs.org
Objects: F,W6,W7,W5,W11,1A,V,D,W4,C,W8

BOOTSTRAP COMPANY (BLACKBURN) LIMITED
Founded: 1990 CR702427
35 Railway Road, Blackburn, Lancashire BB1 1EZ
Tel: 01254 680367
Objects: G,3

BORDER COLLIE TRUST GB
CR1053585
Heathway, Colton, Rugeley, Staffordshire WS15 3LY
Tel: 0871 560 2282
Email: . . . . info@bordercollietrustgb.org.uk

BOSCO SOCIETY
Founded: 1991 CR1129588
59/61 Merton Road, Bootle, Liverpool, Merseyside L20 7AP
Tel: 0151 944 1818
Objects: G,2,O,C

BOTANIC GARDENS CONSERVATION INTERNATIONAL - BGCI
Founded: 1987 CR1098834
Descanso House, 199 Kew Road, Richmond, Surrey TW9 3BW
Tel: 020 8332 5953
Email: . . . . info@bgci.org
Objects: W2,G,U

BOWEL & CANCER RESEARCH
CR1119105
National Centre for Bowel Research and Surgical Innovation, Barts & The London School of Medicine and Dentistry, 1st Floor, Abernethy Building, 2 Newark Street, London E1 2AT
Tel: 020 7882 8749
Email: . . . . mail@bowelcancerresearch.org
Objects: W3,W5,W10,W4,W8

BOWEL CANCER UK
CR1071038; SC040914
Willcox House, 140-148 Borough High Street, London SE1 1LB
Tel: . . . . . 020 7381 9711; 0800 840 3540 Bowel Cancer Advisory Service
Email: . . . . legacy@bowelcanceruk.org.uk
Objects: F,N

THE BOYS' BRIGADE (NATIONAL OFFICE)

Founded: 1883 CR305969; SC038016
Headquarters, Felden Lodge, Hemel Hempstead, Hertfordshire HP3 0BL
Tel: 01442 231681
Fax: 01442 235391
Email: . . . . enquiries@boys-brigade.org.uk
Web: . . . . www.boys-brigade.org.uk
Objects: W3,J,S,G,2,R,H,3

The BB seeks to care for and challenge young people for life through a programme of informal education underpinned by the Christian faith. Currently there are 60,000 members sharing activities in 1400 churches throughout the British Isles. You can help by giving of your time to your local Company, offering financial support or remembering us in your will.

BRACE - ALZHEIMER'S RESEARCH

Founded: 1987 CR297965
The BRACE Charity Office, Elgar House, Southmead Hospital, Bristol BS10 5NB
Tel: 0117 414 4831
Email: . . . . admin@alzheimers-brace.org
Object: W4

BRADFIELD FOUNDATION, THE

Founded: 1990 CR900457
Bradfield College, Bradfield, Reading RG7 6AU
Tel: 0118 964 4840
Email: . . . . . foundation@bradfieldcollege.org.uk
Objects: W3,S,G,A,D,B

BRADFORD COMMUNITY FOR VOLUNTARY SERVICE

Founded: 1991 CR1090036
19-25 Sunbridge Road, Bradford, West Yorkshire BD1 2AY
Tel: 01274 722772
Email: . . . . cvs@bradfordcvs.org.uk
Objects: F,J,2,H,3

BRAIN AND SPINE FOUNDATION

Founded: 1992 CR1098528
Office LG1, Lincoln House, Kennington Park, 1-3 Brixton Road, London SW9 6DE
Tel: . . . 020 7793 5900; Brain and Spine Helpline 0808 808 1000 (freephone)
Email: . . . . info@brainandspine.org.uk
Objects: F,W3,W5,G,W10,W4,H,3,W8

BRAIN INJURY REHABILITATION TRUST

CR800797
3 Westgate Court, Silkwood Park, Wakefield, West Yorkshire WF5 9TJ
Tel: 01924 266344
Email: . . . . director@birt.co.uk
Objects: W5,O,3,C

BRAIN RESEARCH TRUST

Founded: 1971 CR1137560
Dutch House, 307-308 High Holborn, London WC1V 7LL
Tel: 020 7404 9982
Email: . . . . info@brt.org.uk
Object: W

THE BRAIN TUMOUR CHARITY

CR1150054; SC045081
Hartshead House, 61-65 Victoria Road, Farnborough, Hampshire GU14 7PA
Tel: 0845 4500 386
Email: . . . . . . fundraising@braintumouruk.org.uk
Objects: F,J,W5,G,N,H,P

BRAINWAVE

CR1073238
Marsh Lane, Huntworth Gate, Bridgwater, Somerset TA6 6LQ
Tel: 01278 429089
Email: . . . . alexishawkes@brainwave.org.uk
Objects: W3,W5,O,3

BRAMBLEY HEDGE CHILDRENS CENTRE CHARITY LIMITED

Founded: 1979 CR278497
Brambley Hedge Childrens Centre, Tower Street, Dover, Kent CT17 0AW
Tel: 01304 211811
Objects: W3,E,3

BREAK: HIGH QUALITY SUPPORT FOR VULNERABLE CHILDREN AND FAMILIES

Founded: 1968 CR286650
Davison House, 1 Montague Road, Sheringham, Norfolk NR26 8WN
Tel: 01263 822161
Email: . . . . office@break-charity.org
Objects: W3,E,W5,V,W4,3

BREAST CANCER CARE

CR1017658; SC038104
5-13 Great Suffolk Street, London SE1 0NS
Tel: 0845 092 0800
Email: . . . . info@breastcancercare.org.uk
Objects: F,M,G,H,3

BREAST CANCER NOW

CR1160558; SC045584
Fifth Floor, Ibex House, 42-47 Minories, London EC3N 1DY
Tel: 0333 20 70 300
Email: . . . . legacies@breakthrough.org.uk
Objects: W5,W10,W15,1B,W4,W8,W

BREAST CANCER NOW

CR1160558; SC045584
Fifth Floor, Ibex House, 42-47 Minories, London EC3N 1DY
Tel: 0333 20 70 300
Email: . . . . info@bcc-uk.org
Objects: W5,W10,W15,1B,W4,W8,W

BRENDONCARE FOUNDATION

CR326508
The Old Malthouse, Victoria Road, Winchester, Hampshire SO23 7DU
Tel: 01962 852133
Email: . . . . enquiries@brendoncare.org.uk

BRENT WOMEN'S ADVISORY CENTRE

CR1099581
2 Burton Road, Brent, London NW6 7LN
Tel: 020 7328 7805

BRISTOL ASSOCIATION FOR NEIGHBOURHOOD DAYCARE LTD (BAND LTD)

Founded: 1978 CR1017307
The Proving House, Sevier Street, St. Werburghs, Bristol BS2 9LB
Tel: 0117 954 2128
Email: . . . . admin@bandltd.org.uk
Objects: F,W3,G,W15,2,3

BRISTOL OLD VIC THEATRE SCHOOL LTD

Founded: 1990 CR900280
2 Downside Road, Bristol BS8 2XF
Tel: 0117 973 3535
Email: . . . . enquiries@oldvic.drama.ac.uk
Objects: G,3

BRITAIN NEPAL MEDICAL TRUST

Founded: 1968 CR255249
Export House (CD 2014), 130 Vale Road, Tonbridge, Kent TN9 1SP
Tel: 01732 360284
Email: . . . . . info@britainnepalmedicaltrust.org.uk

BRITISH AMERICAN SECURITY INFORMATION COUNCIL (BASIC)

Founded: 1990 CR1001081
3 Whitehall Court, London SW1A 2EL
Tel: 020 7766 3461
Email: . . . . basicuk@basicint.org
Objects: G,3

BRITISH AND FOREIGN SCHOOL SOCIETY

Founded: 1808 CR314286
Maybrook House, Godstone Road, Caterham, Surrey CR3 6RE
Tel: 01883 331177
Email: . . . . enquiries@bfss.org.uk
Objects: W3,G,1A,A,1B,2

BRITISH ASSOCIATION FOR ADOPTION & FOSTERING

Founded: 1980 CR275689
Saffron House, 6-10 Kirby Street, London EC1N 8TS
Tel: 020 7421 2600
Email: . . . . mail@baaf.org.uk
Objects: Q,F,W3,J,G,W10,2,H,3

BRITISH ASSOCIATION FOR COUNSELLING AND PSYCHOTHERAPY

Founded: 1977 CR298361
BACP House, 35-37 Albert Street, Rugby, Warwickshire CV21 2SG
Tel: 0870 443 5252
Email: . . . . bacp@bacp.co.uk
Objects: F,W9,W6,W3,J,W7,W5,G,W10,2,W4,H,3,W8

BRITISH ASSOCIATION FOR IMMEDIATE CARE - BASICS

Founded: 1977 CR276054
Turret House, Turret Lane, Ipswich, Suffolk IP4 1DL
Tel: 01473 218407
Email: . . . . admin@basics.org.uk
Objects: J,G,N,2,H,3

BRITISH ASSOCIATION OF PLASTIC RECONSTRUCTIVE AND AESTHETIC SURGERY (BAPRAS)

Founded: 1946 CR1005353
The Royal College of Surgeons, 35-43 Lincolns Inn Fields, London WC2A 3PN
Tel: 020 7831 5161
Email: . . . . secretariat@bapras.org.uk
Objects: W9,W3,W5,G,1A,A,2,W4

BRITISH COUNCIL FOR PREVENTION OF BLINDNESS

CR270941
4 Bloomsbury Square, London WC1A 2RP
Tel: 020 7404 7114
Email: . . . . info@bcpb.org
Objects: W6,1B,U

BRITISH DEAF ASSOCIATION

Founded: 1890 CR1031687; SC042409
3rd Floor, 356 Holloway Road, London N7 6PA
Tel: . 020 7588 3520 Voice; 020 7588 2529 Text; 0800 652 2965 Helpline Text; 0870 770 3300 Voice
Email: . . . . bda@bda.org.uk
Objects: F,J,S,W7,G,V,2,U,H,3,P

BRITISH DEAF SPORTS COUNCIL LTD

Founded: 1930 CR1014541
7 Maes Talcen, Brackla, Bridgend CF31 2LG
Tel: . . . . . 01943 850214; 01943 850081 Minicom
Objects: W7,2,3,P

BRITISH DENTAL ASSOCIATION BENEVOLENT FUND

CR208146
64 Wimpole Street, London W1G 8YS
Tel: 020 7486 4995
Objects: W11,1A,A

BRITISH DENTAL HEALTH FOUNDATION

CR263198
Smile House, 2 East Union Street, Rugby, Warwickshire CV22 6AJ
Tel: 0870 770 4000
Email: . . . . mail@dentalhealth.org
Objects: F,W2,W7,W5,W10,2,W4,H,3,W8

BRITISH DISABLED WATER SKI ASSOCIATION, THE

Founded: 1979 CR1063678
The Tony Edge National Centre, Heron Lake, Hythe End, Staines, Middlesex TW19 6HW
Tel: 01784 483664
Objects: W6,W7,W5,G,3,P

BRITISH DYSLEXIA ASSOCIATION

Founded: 1972 CR289243
Unit 8, Bracknell Beeches, Old Bracknell Lane, Bracknell, Bracknell Forest RG12 7BW
Tel: . . . . 0845 251 9003 (Office); 0845 251 9002 (Helpline)
Email: . . . . admin@bdadyslexia.org.uk
Objects: F,J,W5,G,2,H,3

BRITISH FRIENDS OF NEVE SHALOM/ WAHAT AL-SALAM (OASIS OF PEACE UK)

CR290062
Premier House, 112 Station Road, Edgware, Middlesex HA8 7BJ
Tel: 020 8952 4717
Email: . . . . british.friends@nswas.org

BRITISH HEART FOUNDATION

Founded: *1961 CR225971; SC039426*
Greater London House, 180 Hampstead Road, London NW1 7AW
Tel: 020 7554 0330; 020 7554 0000
Fax: 020 7554 0100
Email: .... legacies@bhf.org.uk
Web: .... http://www.bhf.org.uk

Coronary heart disease is still the UK's single biggest killer, claiming more than 73,000 lives every year. We believe that one day we can help to create a world where people no longer die prematurely from heart disease. The British Heart Foundation is dedicated to keeping vulnerable hearts beating through our pioneering research, vital prevention work and quality care and support. We also run numerous campaigns to deliver essential information to help people understand and care for their own heart health. As the nation's heart charity, we rely on your support and your donations of time and money to continue our life saving work. Only by working together can we fight for every heartbeat.

BRITISH HEDGEHOG PRESERVATION SOCIETY

CR1164542
Hedgehog House (CC), Clee Hill, Dhustone, Ludlow, Shropshire SY8 3PL
Tel: 01584 890801
Email: .... info@britishhedgehogs.org.uk

THE BRITISH HOME - CARING FOR SEVERELY DISABLED PEOPLE

Founded: 1861 CR206222
Crown Lane, Streatham, London SW16 3JB
Tel: 020 8670 8261
Email: .... info@britishhome.org.uk
Objects: M,N,B,C

THE BRITISH HORSE SOCIETY

Founded: 1947 CR210504; SC038516
Abbey Park (CC), Stareton, Kenilworth, Warwickshire CV8 2XZ
Tel: 02476 840 500
Email: .... enquiry@bhs.org.uk
Objects: W1,W2,G,2

BRITISH-ITALIAN SOCIETY

Founded: 1941 CR253386
Hurlingham Studios (Unit 4), Ranelagh Gardens, London SW6 3PA
Tel: .... 020 8150 9167 (Membership); 020 7371 7141 (Events)
Email: jj@british-italian.org (Membership); reiko@british-italian.org (Events)
Objects: S,A,P

BRITISH KIDNEY PATIENT ASSOCIATION (BKPA)

Founded: 1975 CR270288
Ms Suzan Yianni
3 The Windmills, St Mary's Close, Turk Street, Alton, Hampshire GU34 1EF
Tel: 01420 541424
Web: .... www.britishkidney-pa.co.uk
Objects: W3,W5,A

The British Kidney Patient Association is a well established charity working to improve the quality of life for all kidney patients living with the mental and physical demands of kidney disease. The funds we raise are used to help provide valuable advice, information and much needed financial aid to patients and their families during difficult times, as well as supporting the development of quality facilities within kidney units around the UK.

BRITISH OCCUPATIONAL HEALTH RESEARCH FOUNDATION

Founded: 1991 CR1077273
6 St Andrew's Place, London NW1 4LB
Tel: 020 7317 5898
Email: .... admin@bohrf.org.uk
Objects: A,1B,2

BRITISH ORNITHOLOGISTS' UNION

Founded: 1858 CR249877
Dept of Zoology, South Parks Road, Oxford, Oxfordshire OX1 3PS
Tel: 01865 281842
Email: .... bou@bou.org.uk
Objects: 1A,A,2,H

BRITISH PLUMBING EMPLOYERS COUNCIL (TRAINING) LIMITED

Founded: 1992 CR1012890
2 Mallard Way, Pride Park, Derby, Derbyshire DE24 8GX
Tel: 0845 644 6558
Email: .... info@bpec.org.uk
Objects: G,H,3

BRITISH POLIO FELLOWSHIP

Founded: 1939 CR1108335; SC038863
Eagle Office Centre, The Runway, South Ruislip, Middlesex HA4 6SE
Tel: 0800 018 0586
Email: .... info@britishpolio.org.uk
Objects: F,M,W5,1A,A,V,2,H,P

BRITISH RECORD INDUSTRY TRUST

Founded: 1990 CR1000413
Riverside Building, County Hall, Westminster Bridge Road, London SE1 7JA
Tel: 020 7803 1300
Email: .... brittrust@bpi.co.uk
Objects: W3,G,1B

BRITISH RED CROSS

CR220949; SC037738
44 Moorfields, London EC2Y 9AL
Tel: 0844 412 2848
Email: .... legacy@redcross.org.uk

BRITISH SKIN FOUNDATION
CR313865
4 Fitzroy Square, London W1T 5HQ
Tel: 020 7391 6341
Email: . . . . . admin@britishskinfoundation.org.uk
Objects: W9,W6,W3,W7,W5,W10,W11,W15,1A, W16,W4,W8,W

BRITISH SOCIETY FOR HAEMATOLOGY, THE
Founded: 1960 CR1005735
100 White Lion Street, London N1 9PF
Tel: 020 7713 0990
Email: . . . . info@b-s-h.org.uk
Objects: G,1A

BRITISH SPORTS TRUST - TRADING AS SPORTS LEADERS UK
CR1095326
23-25 Linford Forum, Rockingham Drive, Linford Wood, Milton Keynes MK14 6LY
Tel: 01908 689180
Email: . commercialdevelopment@sportsleaders.org

BRITISH STAMMERING ASSOCIATION
Founded: 1978 CR1089967
15 Old Ford Road, Bethnal Green, London E2 9PJ
Tel: . . . . 020 8983 1003; 0845 603 2001 Helpline
Email: . . . . mail@stammering.org
Objects: F,W3,J,W5,G,2,H,O

BRITISH TRUST FOR ORNITHOLOGY - BTO
Founded: 1933 CR216652; SC039193
The Nunnery, Thetford, Norfolk IP24 2PU
Tel: 01842 750050
Email: . . . . info@bto.org
Objects: W1,W2,1A,2,3

BRITISH WIRELESS FOR THE BLIND FUND (BWBF)
CR1078287
10 Albion Place, Maidstone, Kent ME14 5DZ
Tel: 01622 754757
Email: . . . . info@blind.org.uk
Object: W6

BRITTLE BONE SOCIETY
Founded: 1972 CR272100
30 Guthrie Street, Dundee DD1 5BS
Tel: 01382 204446
Email: . . . . bbs@brittlebone.org
Objects: F,M,W3,W5,A,2,H,P

BROADENING CHOICES FOR OLDER PEOPLE
CR1074954
Imperial Court, 40b 1st Floor, Kings Norton Business Centre, Pershore Road South, Kings Norton, Birmingham, West Midlands B30 3ES
Tel: 0121 459 7670
Email: . . . . info@bcop.org.uk
Objects: D,W4

BROMLEY & SHEPPARD'S COLLEGES
Founded: 1666 CR210337
c/o Chaplain's House, Bromley College, London Road, Bromley, Kent BR1 1PE
Tel: 020 8460 4712
Objects: D,W4,C

BROMLEY AUTISTIC TRUST
CR1002032
Burgess Autistic Trust, 164a Lee High Road, Lewisham, London SE13 5PL
Tel: 020 8464 2897
Email: . . . . info@bromleyautistictrust.co.uk
Objects: W3,E,W5,D,W4,3,P

BROOK
Founded: 1964 CR239966
421 Highgate Studios, 53-79 Highgate Road, London NW5 1TL
Tel: . 020 7284 6040; 0800 0185 023 (Freephone helpline for under 25's)
Email: . . . . admin@brookcentres.org.uk
Objects: F,W3,G,N,H,3

BT BENEVOLENT FUND
Founded: 1853 CR212565
Room 323 (CD), Reading Central TE, 41 Minster Street, Reading RG1 2JB
Tel: 0208 726 2145
Email: . . . . benevolent@bt.com
Objects: W11,1A,A,2

BUCKINGHAMSHIRE MIND
CR1103063
Ashton House, 14 Granville Street, Aylesbury, Buckinghamshire HP20 2JR
Tel: 01494 463364
Email: . . . . carolyn.smyth@bucksmind.org.uk
Objects: F,J,E,W5,G,D,2,W4,H,3,P

BUCKS COUNTY AGRICULTURAL ASSOCIATION
Founded: 1990 CR1000652
No. 5 Lilies, High Street, Weedon, Buckinghamshire HP22 4NS
Tel: 01296 680400
Email: . . . . alison@buckscountyshow.co.uk

BULLYING UK
CR1077722
10c Mornington Terrace, Harrogate, North Yorkshire HG1 5DH
Tel: . . . . . 020 7284 5500 Admin; 0808 800 2222 HelpLine / 0800 783 6783 Textphone
Email: . . . . help@bullying.co.uk
Objects: F,W3,G,H

THE BURMA STAR ASSOCIATION
Founded: 1951 CR1043040
34 Grosvenor Gardens, London SW1W 0DH
Tel: 020 7823 4273
Email: . . . . mrnbsa@btconnect.com
Objects: F,W9,1A,A,2,W4

BURTON CONSTABLE FOUNDATION, THE
Founded: 1992 CR1010121
Burton Constable Hall, Burton Constable, Skirlaugh, East Riding of Yorkshire HU11 4LN
Tel: 01964 562400
Email: . . . . enquiries@burtonconstable.com
Objects: W3,W2,S,G,W12,W4,3

BUSINESS IN THE COMMUNITY
CR297716
137 Shepherdess Walk, London N1 7RQ
Tel: 0870 600 2482
Email: . . . . info@bitc.org.uk
Objects: W3,J,G,W10,2,H,W8

BUSINESSDYNAMICS TRUST
Founded: 1991 CR1004426
Enterprise House, 59-65 Upper Ground, London SE1 9PQ
Tel: 020 7620 0735
Objects: W6,W3,W7,G,3

BUTTERFLY CONSERVATION
CR254937
Manor Yard, East Lulworth, Wareham, Dorset BH20 5QP
Tel: 01929 400209
Email: .... info@butterfly-conservation.org
Objects: W2,2,H

BUTTLE UK
CR313007
Audley House, 13 Palace Street, London SW1E 5HX
Tel: 020 7828 7311
Email: .... info@buttleuk.org
Objects: W3,G,Y

C

CAIRN TERRIER RELIEF FUND
CR803599
288 Lichfield Road (CC), Barton-Under-Needwood, Burton-on-Trent, Staffordshire DE13 8ED
Tel: 01283 712498
Email: .... chrismroberts1@gmail.com

CALDECOTT FOUNDATION
Founded: 1911 CR307889
Caldcott House, Smeeth, Ashford, Kent TN25 6SP
Tel: 01303 815678
Objects: W3,G,O

CALIBRE AUDIO LIBRARY
Founded: 1974 CR286614
New Road, Weston Turville, Aylesbury, Buckinghamshire HP22 5XQ
Tel: 01296 432339
Email: .... enquiries@calibre.org.uk
Objects: W6,W3,S,W5,G,2,W4,H,O,3

THE CALVERT TRUST
CR1042423
Kielder Water & Forest Park, Hexham, Northumberland NE48 1BS
Tel: 01434 250232
Email: .... enquiries@calvert-kielder.com

CALVERT TRUST EXMOOR
Founded: 1991 CR1005776
Wistlandpound, Kentisbury, Barnstaple, Devon EX31 4SJ
Tel: 01598 763221
Email: .... exmoor@calvert-trust.org.uk
Objects: W6,W3,W7,W5,V,3,P

CAM SIGHT (THE CAMBRIDGESHIRE SOCIETY FOR THE BLIND & PARTIALLY SIGHTED)
Founded: 1912 CR201640
167 Green End Road, Cambridge, Cambridgeshire CB4 1RW
Tel: 01223 420033
Email: .... info@camsight.org.uk
Objects: F,W6,M,W3,J,S,W5,G,W10,W4,O,3,P,K

THE CAMBRIDGE FOUNDATION
XN81946
1 Quayside, Bridge Street, Cambridge, Cambridgeshire CB5 8AB
Tel: 01223 332288
Email: .... enquiries@foundation.cam.ac.uk
Object: G

CAMBRIDGE HOUSE AND TALBOT
Founded: 1897 CR265103
131-139 Camberwell Road, London SE5 OHF
Tel: 020 7703 5025
Objects: F,W3,S,W5,G,W10,H,3,P,W8

CAMDEN COMMUNITY NURSERIES LIMITED
Founded: 1991 CR1002534
16 Acol Road, London NW6 3AG
Tel: 020 7624 2937
Email: . admin@camdencommunitynurseries.org.uk

THE CAMERON FUND
CR261993
Tavistock House North, Tavistock Square, London WC1H 9HR
Tel: 020 7388 0796
Email: .... secretary@cameronfund.org.uk
Objects: W11,1A,A

CAMPAIGN FOR NATIONAL PARKS
CR295336
5-11 Lavington Street, London SE1 0NZ
Tel: 020 7981 0890
Email: .... info@cnp.org.uk
Objects: F,J,W2,2

CAMPAIGN FOR THE PROTECTION OF RURAL WALES
Founded: 1928 CR239899
Ty Gwyn, 31 High Street, Welshpool, Powys SY21 7YD
Tel: 01938 552525; 01938 556212
Email: .... info@cprwmail.org.uk
Objects: W2,2

CAMPAIGN TO PROTECT RURAL ENGLAND - CPRE
Founded: 1926 CR1089685
5-11 Lavington Street, London SE1 0NZ
Tel: 020 7981 2855
Email: .... info@cpre.org.uk
Objects: F,W1,J,W2,S,2,H

CAMPDEN CHARITIES
CR1104616
27A Pembridge Villas, London W11 3EP
Tel: 020 7243 0551
Objects: F,M,W3,J,E,W5,G,W10,1A,A,1B,V,D,2, W4,B,O,C,P,W8,K

CAMPHILL HOUSES, STOURBRIDGE
CR232402
19 South Road, Stourbridge, West Midlands DY8 3YA
Tel: 01384 441505
Objects: F,W5,D,3

CAMPHILL SCHOOL ABERDEEN
Founded: 1940SC015588
Central Office, Murtle House, Bieldside, Aberdeen AB15 9EP

Tel: 01224 867935
Email: . . . . office@crss.org.uk
Objects: M,W3,W5,G,N,O,3,P

CAMPHILL VILLAGE TRUST
Founded: 1954 CR232402
Camphill Family Appeals Office, Botton Village, Danby, Whitby, North Yorkshire YO21 2NJ
Tel: 01287 661294
Email: . . . . family@camphill.org.uk
Objects: W2,S,W5,D,W4,W14,3,K

CAN - DRUGS, ALCOHOL & HOMELESSNESS
CR1025395
Denmark House, 8 Billing Road, Northampton, Northamptonshire NN1 5AW
Tel: 01604 824777
Email: . . . . administration@can.org.uk
Objects: F,W3,G,W15,D,W8

CANBURY SCHOOL LIMITED
Founded: 1990 CR803766
Kingston Hill, Kingston upon Thames, Surrey KT2 7LN
Tel: 020 8549 8622
Email: . . . . Enquiries@canburyschool.co.uk
Objects: W3,G,3

CANCER FOCUS NORTHERN IRELAND
101307
40-44 Eglantine Avenue, Belfast BT9 6DX
Tel: . 028 9066 3281; 0800 783 3339 (Freephone Information Helpline)
Email: . . . . hello@cancerfocusni.org

CANCER LARYNGECTOMEE TRUST (INCORPORATING NATIONAL ASSOCIATION OF NECK BREATHERS)
CR326653
PO Box 618, Halifax, West Yorkshire HX3 8WX
Tel: 01422 205522
Email: . . . . info@cancerlt.org
Objects: F,W5,1A,A,2,H,3

CANCER RESEARCH UK
CR1089464; SC041666
Angel Building, 407 St John Street, London EC1V 4AD
Tel: 0300 123 1861
Email: . . . . fws.administration@cancer.org.uk

CANCER RESEARCH WALES
CR248767
Velindre Hospital, Whitechurch, Cardiff CF14 2TL
Tel: 029 2031 6976
Email: . . . . crw@wales.nhs.uk

CANCER SUPPORT SCOTLAND
SC012867
75 Shelley Court, Gartnavel Complex, Glasgow G12 0ZE
Tel: 0141 337 8199
Email: . . . . info@cancersupportscotland.org
Objects: F,W3,W4,O,3,W8

CANCERWISE
Founded: 1982 CR290574
Tavern House, 4 City Business Centre, Basin Road, Chichester, West Sussex PO19 8DU
Tel: 01243 778516
Email: . . . . enquiries@cancerwise.org.uk
Objects: F,J,G,H,O,3

CANINE CONCERN SCOTLAND TRUST (INCORPORATING THERAPET)
SC014924
81-85 Portland Street (CC), Edinburgh EH6 4AY
Tel: 0131 553 0034
Email: . . . . . info@canineconcernscotland.org.uk
Objects: W1,W3,G,W4,O,3

CANINE PARTNERS
Founded: 1990 CR803680; SC039050
PO Box 3460, Glasgow G62 9AT
Tel: 0845 481 1915
Email: . . . . info@caninepartners.org.uk
Objects: W5,3

CANTERBURY DAY NURSERY, HOLIDAY PLAYSCHEME AND AFTER SCHOOL CLUB
Founded: 1991 CR1001989
Havelock Street, Canterbury, Kent CT1 1NP
Tel: 01227 454557
Email: . . . . anterburydaynursery@btconnect.com
Object: G

CANTERBURY DISTRICT C.A.B
Founded: 1990 CR803115
3 Westgate Hall Road, Canterbury, Kent CT1 2BT
Tel: 01227 452762
Objects: F,W9,W6,W7,W5,W10,W11,2,W4,3,W8

CANTERBURY OAST TRUST & SOUTH OF ENGLAND RARE BREEDS CENTRE
Founded: 1985 CR291662
Highlands Farm, Woodchurch, Ashford, Kent TN26 3RJ
Tel: 01233 861493
Email: . . . . enquiries@canterburyoasttrust.org.uk
Objects: W2,W5,G,D,3

CAPABILITY SCOTLAND
Founded: 1946SC011330
5-11 Ellersly Road, Edinburgh EH12 6HY
Tel: 0131 337 9876
Email: . . . . capability@capability-scotland.org.uk
Objects: F,W6,M,W3,J,S,E,W7,W5,G,1A,V,W4,H,O,3,P,K

CAPITB TRUST
Founded: 1990 CR1000290
PO Box 91, Brighouse, West Yorkshire HD6 2WB
Tel: 0113 227 3345
Objects: G,3

CARDIAC RESEARCH AND DEVELOPMENT FUND
Founded: 1990 CR328613
PricewaterhouseCoopers, One Kingsway, Cardiff CF10 3PW
Email: . . . . simon.r.strong@uk.pwc.com

CARDIFF ACTION FOR SINGLE HOMELESS - YMGYRCH CAERDYDD DROS Y DIGARTEF SENGL
Founded: 1990 CR703074
Huggard Centre, Tresillian Terrace, Cardiff CF10 5JZ
Tel: 029 2034 9980
Email: . . . . adrianburke@c-a-s-h.org.uk
Objects: F,J,E,G,D,3,C

CARDIFF CHINESE CHRISTIAN CHURCH
Founded: 1991 CR1004056
65 Llandaff Road, Canton, Cardiff CF11 9NG

Tel: 029 2038 8724
Email: . . . . samwong@cardiffcccc.org

CARE
Founded: 1966 CR250058
9 Weir Road, Kibworth, Leicester, Leicestershire LE8 0LQ
Tel: 01732 782711
Email: . . . . info@care.ltd.co.uk

CARE FOR THE WILD INTERNATIONAL
Founded: 1984 CR288802
72 Brighton Road, Horsham, West Sussex RH13 5BQ
Tel: 01403 249832
Email: . . . . info@careforthewild.com
Objects: Q,W1,W2,1B

CARE INTERNATIONAL UK
CR292506
9th Floor, 89 Albert Embankment, London SE1 7TP
Tel: 020 7091 6000
Email: . . . . donorservices@careinternational.org
Objects: W3,U

CARERS RELIEF SERVICE
Founded: 1983 CR1051841
Lingley House, Rooms 2 & 3, Commissioners Road, Strood, Rochester, Kent ME2 4EE
Tel: 01634 715995
Objects: M,W5,3,P

CARERS UK
Founded: 1988 CR246329
20 Great Dover Street, London SE1 4LX
Tel: 020 7378 4999
Email: . . . . fundraising@carersuk.org
Objects: F,W3,J,G,2,W4,H,3

CARITAS SOCIAL ACTION
Founded: 1929 CR1101431
39 Eccleston Square, Hendon, London SW1V 1BX
Tel: 020 7901 4875
Objects: Q,F,W3,J,E,2,C,P

CASUALTIES UNION
CR234672
PO Box 1942, London E17 6YU
Tel: 0870 078 0590
Email: . . . . hq.cu@casualtiesunion.org.uk
Objects: G,N,3

CAT ACTION TRUST
CR1063947; SC041997
The Kings Mill Partnership, Chartered Accountants, 75 Park Lane, Croydon, Surrey CR9 1XS
Tel: 01406 701 001
Email: . . . . info@catactiontrust.org.uk
Object: W1

CAT & KITTEN CARE
CR1100897
6 Northbank Road (CC), Waltham Forest, London E17 4JZ
Tel: 020 8531 3469
Email: . . . . catandkittencare@btinternet.com

CAT SURVIVAL TRUST

CR272187

The Centre, 46-52 Codicote Road, Welwyn, Hertfordshire AL6 9TU

Tel: 01438 716873
Fax: 01438 717535
Email: cattrust@aol.com
Web: www.catsurvivaltrust.org

Objects: W1,W2,G

Formed in 1976 for the captive breeding and preservation in the wild of the 37 endangered species of wild cat and their habitat. Also research the effect of climate change on all life including humans! Purchased 10,000 acres of virgin forest in north east Argentina.

CAT WELFARE TRUST

Founded: 1988 CR800719

Hon. Secretary: Mrs Rosemary Fisher

GCCF, 5 Kings Castle Business Park, The Drove, Bridgwater, Somerset TA6 4AG

Tel: 01278 427575
Fax: 01278 446627
Email: info@gccfcats.org
Web: www.catwelfaretrust.org

The Cat Welfare Trust helps fund research projects into feline disease. The current project, a collaboration between three major Universities, is researching into the genes that play a pivotal role in the control of infectious diseases in cats. All donations are spent on the work of the Trust, not administration or salaries.

See advert on previous page

CATASTROPHES CAT RESCUE

Catastrophes CAT RESCUE

CR1017304

Half Moon Cottage, Bakers Lane, Dallington, Heathfield, East Sussex TN21 9JS

Tel: 01435 830212
Fax: 01825 768012
Email: lizzie@catastrophescats.org
Web: www.catastrophescats.org

Object: W1

Catastrophes Cat Rescue in East Sussex provides a safe haven for unwanted cats in the UK. Many of the cats we rescue have been abandoned or need a new home because of a change in their owners' circumstances. Some have been ill treated. They are all in need of love and care. Catastrophes' aim is to help any cat in need, regardless of age, temperament or behavioural problems. Consequently we often receive calls for help with elderly or feral cats, or animals that are difficult to rehome. We do not believe in putting animals to sleep unnecessarily and we actively encourage spaying and neutering as a vital part of responsible pet ownership. Please remember us in your will. Your donation or legacy will help us continue to provide a vital lifeline and a bright future for cats in desperate need.

See advert on this page

Registered charity number 1049274

CATHARINE HOUSE TRUST
Founded: 1988 CR801656
Ridge Cottage, New Cut, Westfield, East Sussex TN35 4RL
Objects: W9,W6,M,W3,W7,W5,W10,W11,1A,A,1B,N,2,W4,O,W8

CATHOLIC AGENCY FOR OVERSEAS DEVELOPMENT (CAFOD)
Founded: 1962 CR1160384
Romero House, 55 Westminster Bridge Road, London SE1 7JB
Tel: 020 7095 5367
Email: . . . . hqcafod@cafod.org.uk
Objects: G,A,U,H

CATHOLIC CHILDREN'S SOCIETY (SALFORD DIOCESE)
CR239172
390 Parrs Wood Road, Didsbury, Manchester, Greater Manchester M20 5NA
Tel: 0161 445 7741
Objects: Q,F,W3,W5,3,C

CATHOLIC DEAF ASSOCIATION UK
CR262362
Hollywood House, Sudell Street, Collyhurst, Manchester, Greater Manchester M4 4JF
Tel: . . . . 0161 834 8828; 0161 835 1767 Minicom
Email: . . . . catholicdeaf1971@gmail.com
Objects: F,S,W7,2,R,P

CATS PROTECTION (CP)
Founded: 1927 CR203644; SC037711
National Cat Centre, Chelwood Gate, Haywards Heath, West Sussex RH17 7TT
Tel: 01825 741271
Email: . . . . giftsinwills@cats.org.uk
Objects: F,W1,H

THE CAUDWELL CHARITY
CR1079770
Minton Hollins Building, Shelton Old Road, Stoke-on-Trent, Staffordshire ST4 7RY
Tel: 01782 600437; 08453 001348
Email: . communityaffairs@caudwellchildren.com

CAVELL NURSES TRUST - THE EDITH CAVELL FUND FOR NURSES
CR210571; SC041453
Grosvenor House, Prospect Hill, Redditch, Worcestershire B97 4DL
Tel: 01527 595999
Email: . . . . admin@cavellnursestrust.org
Objects: F,1A,A,B

CBM
Founded: 1996 CR1058162; SC041101
Vision House, 7/8 Oakington Business Park, Oakington, Cambridge, Cambridgeshire CB24 3DQ
Tel: 01223 484700
Email: . . . . info@cbmuk.org.uk
Objects: W6,W3,W7,W5,G,N,U,O,3

CCHF ALL ABOUT KIDS
Founded: 1884 CR206958
42-43 Lower Marsh, London SE1 7RG
Tel: 020 7928 6522
Email: . . . . cchf@dircon.co.uk
Objects: W3,V,3

CCS ADOPTION (CLIFTON CHILDREN'S SOCIETY)
CR286814
162 Pennywell Rd, Easton, Bristol BS5 0TX
Email: . . . . info@ccsadoption.org
Objects: Q,F,W3,3

CELIA HAMMOND ANIMAL TRUST
Founded: 1986 CR293787
High Street, Wadhurst, East Sussex TN5 6AG
Tel: . . . . 01892 783820 / 01892 783367
Email: . . . . headoffice@celiahammond.org
Objects: F,W1,3

CENTRAL AFRICA'S RIGHTS & AIDS (CARA) SOCIETY
CR1135610
Unit 4, 2nd Floor, The Printhouse, 18-22 Ashwin Street, Dalston, London E8 3DL
Tel: 020 7254 6415
Email: . . . . info@cara-online.org

CENTRAL BRITISH FUND FOR WORLD JEWISH RELIEF
Founded: 1990 CR290767
c/o World Jewish Relief, Oscar Joseph House, 54 Crewys Road, London NW2 2AD
Tel: 020 8736 1250
Email: . . . . info@wjr.org.uk

CENTRAL MANCHESTER UNIVERSITY HOSPITALS NHS FOUNDATION TRUST CHARITY

Central Manchester University Hospitals NHS Foundation Trust **Charity**
supporting excellence in treatment, research and care

CR1049274
Citylab 1, Maurice Watkins Building, Oxford Road, Manchester, Greater Manchester M13 9NQ
Tel: 0161 276 4522
Fax: 0161 276 4241
Email: . . . . charity.office@cmft.nhs.uk
Web: . . . . www.cmftcharity.org.uk
Objects: W3,N,W4

See advert on previous page

CENTRAL YOUNG MEN'S CHRISTIAN ASSOCIATION LIMITED, THE
Founded: 1844 CR213121
112 Great Russell Street, London WC1B 3NQ
Tel: 020 7343 1844
Email: . . . . info@ymca.co.uk
Objects: W3,G,H,P

CENTRE 33
CR1074974
33 Clarendon Street, Cambridge, Cambridgeshire CB1 1JX
Tel: . . . . . 01223 316488 Helpline; 01223 314763 Office/Admin
Email: . . . . office@centre33.org.uk
Objects: F,W3,H,3

NATIONAL CENTRE FOR CIRCUS ARTS
Founded: 1991 CR1001839
Coronet Street, Hackney, London N1 6HD

Tel: 020 7613 4141
Email: . . . . charity@nationalcircus.org.uk
Objects: W3,S,G,3

CENTRE FOR LOCAL ECONOMIC STRATEGIES

Founded: 1990 CR1089503
Express Networks, 1 George Leigh Street, Manchester, Greater Manchester M4 5DL
Tel: 0161 236 7036
Email: . . . . info@cles.org.uk
Objects: W3,W7,W5,G,W10,2,W4,H,3,W8

CENTREPOINT

Founded: 1969 CR292411
Central House, 25 Camperdown Street, London E1 8DZ
Tel: 0845 466 3400; 020 7426 6809
Email: . . . . yoursupport@centrepoint.org
Objects: F,W3,J,G,D,H,3,C,P

CEREBRA, THE FOUNDATION FOR BRAIN INJURED INFANTS AND YOUNG PEOPLE

Founded: 1991 CR1089812
Second Floor Offices, The Lyric Building, King Street, Carmarthen, Carmarthenshire SA31 1BD
Tel: 01267 244200
Email: . . . . info@cerebra.org.uk
Objects: F,W3,1B,H

CEREBRAL PALSY MIDLANDS

Founded: 1947 CR529464
17 Victoria Road, Harborne, Birmingham, West Midlands B17 0AQ
Tel: 0121 427 3182
Email: . . . . info@cpmids.free-online.co.uk
Objects: F,W6,M,W3,J,S,E,W7,W5,G,W10,1A,A,V,D,H,O,3,C,P,K

CFBT EDUCATION TRUST

Founded: 1968 CR270901
60 Queens Road, Reading RG1 4BS
Tel: 0118 902 1000
Email: . . . . enquiries@cfbt.com
Objects: G,H,3

CFBT SCHOOLS TRUST

Founded: 2010 CR270901
Highbridge House, 16-18 Duke Street, Reading RG1 4RU
Tel: 0118 902 1000
Email: . . . . enquiries@cfbt.com
Objects: G,3

CGD SOCIETY

Founded: 1991 CR1143049
CGD Office, Manor Farm, Wimborne St Giles, Dorset BH21 5NL
Tel: 01725 517977
Email: . . . . events@cgdsociety.org
Objects: F,W3,A,1B,N,2,W4,H,3

CHAI CANCER CARE

CR1078956
Chief Executive: Ms Lisa Steele
142-146 Great North Way, London NW4 1EH
Tel: 020 8202 2211
Fax: 020 8202 2111
Email: . . . . info@chaicancercare.org
Web: . . . . www.chaicancercare.org
Chai Cancer Care is the Jewish Community's Cancer Support Organisation, enabling patients, their families and friends to cope with the impact of a cancer diagnosis.

Chai offers an extensive range of services including counselling, therapies, complementary therapies, advisory services and group activities.

CHANGING FACES - SUPPORTING PEOPLE WITH DISFIGUREMENTS

Founded: 1992 CR1011222
Changing Faces Centre, 33-37 University Street, London WC1E 6JN
Tel: 0845 450 0275
Email: . . . . info@changingfaces.org.uk
Objects: F,W3,W5,G,H,O,3,W8

CHARITIES AID FOUNDATION

Founded: 1924 CR268369
25 Kings Hill Avenue, Kings Hill, West Malling, Kent ME19 4TA
Tel: 03000 123 504
Email: . . . . legacies@cafonline.org
Objects: F,G,A,1B,U,H

THE CHARITY FOR CIVIL SERVANTS (FORMERLY THE CIVIL SERVICE BENEVOLENT FUND)

CR1136870
Fund House, 5 Anne Boleyn's Walk, Cheam, Sutton SM3 8DY
Tel: . . 020 8240 2400 (Administration); 0800 056 2424 (Freephone Helpline)
Email: . . . . info@foryoubyyou.org.uk

CHARITY FOR ST JOSEPH'S MISSIONARY SOCIETY (GENERALATE)

CR1148980
PO Box 3608, Maidenhead, Windsor & Maidenhead SL6 7UX
Tel: 01628 673178
Email: . . . . office@millhillmissionaries.com
Object: R

CHARITY SEARCH - FREE ADVICE FOR OLDER PEOPLE

Founded: 1987 CR296999
25 Portview Road, Avonmouth, Bristol BS11 9LD
Tel: 0117 982 4060
Email: . . . . info@charitysearch.org.uk
Objects: F,W4,3

THE CHARITY SERVICE LTD

Founded: 1992 CR1011293
6 Great Jackson Street, Manchester, Greater Manchester M15 4AX
Tel: 0161 839 3291
Email: . . . . . michael.colin@charityservice.org.uk
Objects: A,1B,3

CHARTERED ACCOUNTANTS' BENEVOLENT ASSOCIATION

Founded: 1886 CR1116973
8 Mitchell Court, Castle Mound Way, Rugby, Warwickshire CV23 0UY
Tel: . . . . 01788 556366 - Helpline 0800 107 6163
Email: . . . . enquiries@caba.org.uk
Objects: F,1A,A,2,3

CHARTERED INSTITUTE OF ARBITRATORS

Founded: 1990 CR803725
International Arbitration and Mediation Centre, 12 Bloomsbury Square, London WC1A 2LP
Tel: 020 7421 7444
Email: . . . . info@arbitrators.org
Object: 2

CHARTERED INSTITUTE OF BUILDING BENEVOLENT FUND LTD

Founded: 1992 CR1013292
Englemere, King's Ride, Ascot, Windsor & Maidenhead SL5 7TB
Tel: 01344 630700
Email: . . . . fjmacdonald@ciob.org.uk
Objects: F,A

CHARTERED INSTITUTE OF JOURNALISTS

Founded: 1894 CR208176
2 Dock Offices, Surrey Quays Road, London SE16 2XU
Tel: 020 7252 1187
Email: . . . . memberservices@cioj.co.uk
Objects: A,B

CHARTERED INSTITUTE OF LIBRARY AND INFORMATION PROFESSIONALS (CILIP)

Founded: 1898 CR313014
7 Ridgmount Street, London WC1E 7AE
Tel: 020 7255 0500
Email: . . . . info@cilip.org.uk
Objects: G,2

CHARTERED INSTITUTE OF LOGISTICS AND TRANSPORT (UK), THE

Founded: 1991 CR1004963
Logistics and Transport Centre, Earlstrees Court, Earlstrees Road, Corby, Northamptonshire NN17 4AX
Tel: 01536 740100
Email: . . . . membership@ciltuk.org.uk
Objects: G,W11,1B,2,B,H,3

CHARTERED INSTITUTE OF MANAGEMENT ACCOUNTANTS BENEVOLENT FUND

Founded: 1969 CR261114
26 Chapter Street, London SW1P 4NP
Tel: . 020 7663 5441 CIMA Main Lines; 020 8849 2221 Direct Line
Email: . . . . benevolent.fund@cimaglobal.com
Objects: F,M,J,1A,A,2

CHARTERED INSTITUTION OF CIVIL ENGINEERING SURVEYORS

Founded: 1972 CR1131469
Dominion House, Sibson Road, Sale, Greater Manchester M33 7PP
Tel: 0161 972 3100
Email: . . . . admin@cices.org
Objects: G,2,H

CHARTERED SOCIETY OF PHYSIOTHERAPY'S MEMBERS' BENEVOLENT FUND

CHARTERED SOCIETY OF PHYSIOTHERAPY

Founded: 1894 CR279882
14 Bedford Row, London WC1R 4ED
Tel: 020 7306 6666
Fax: 020 7306 6623
Email: . . . . enquiries@csp.org.uk
Web: . . . . http://www.csp.org.uk
Objects: F,J,G,1A,A,2,H,O

The Chartered Society of Physiotherapy (CSP) is the professional, educational and trade union body for the UK's 54,000 chartered physiotherapists, physiotherapy students and support workers. The CSP's Members' Benevolent Fund (MBF) makes financial awards to members, support workers and students (including retired members) who need help. Whether as a result of illness or injury, job loss or bereavement, the MBF exists to support CSP members.

SHOOTING STAR CHASE

CR1042495
Bridge House, Addlestone Road, Guildford, Surrey KT15 2UE
Tel: 01932 823100
Email: . . . . hello@shootingstarchase.org.uk

THE CHASELEY TRUST - CARING FOR PEOPLE WITH SEVERE DISABILITIES

CR1090579
Chaseley Bungalows, South Cliff, 9 The Sidings, Eastbourne, East Sussex BN20 7JH
Tel: 01323 744200
Email: . . . . info@chaseleytrust.org
Objects: W9,W5,N,O,3

CHATHAM HISTORIC DOCKYARD TRUST

Founded: 1984 CR292101
The Historic Dockyard, Chatham, Kent ME4 4TZ
Tel: 01634 823800
Email: . . . . info@chdt.org.uk
Objects: W2,G,W12,3,K

CHELMSFORD MENCAP

CR245421
PO Box 10476, Chelmsford, Essex CM1 9NE
Email: . . . . info@chelmsfordmencap.org.uk
Objects: W6,W3,W7,W5,G,W15,W4,Y,3,P,Z

CHEMICAL ENGINEERS BENEVOLENT FUND

Founded: 1934 CR221601
165-189 Railway Terrace, Rugby, Warwickshire CV21 3HQ
Tel: 01788 578214
Email: . . . . jdownham@icheme.org
Objects: W11,1A,A

CHERNOBYL CHILDREN LIFE LINE

Founded: 1992 CR1014274; SC060136
6 Hartley Park Farm, Selborne Road, Alton, Hampshire GU34 3HD
Tel: 01420 511700
Email: . . . . vicmizzi@nildram.co.uk
Objects: W3,V,U,3

CHESHIRE REGIMENT ASSOCIATION

Founded: 1933 CR1036982
The Castle, Chester, Cheshire CH1 2DN
Tel: 01244 327617
Email: . . cheshire.regt.association@hotmail.com
Objects: F,W9,J,1A,A,2,H,P

CHESTER ZOO (NORTH OF ENGLAND ZOOLOGICAL SOCIETY)

CR306077
Zoological Gardens, Upton-by-Chester, Cheshire CH2 1LH
Tel: 01244 380280
Email: . . . . info@chesterzoo.co.uk
Objects: W1,W2

CHESTNUT TREE HOUSE CHILDREN'S HOSPICE

CR256789
Dover Lane, Poling, Arundel, West Sussex BN18 9PX
Tel: . 01903 871800/01903 871 820 (fundraising)
Email: ... enquiries@chestnut-tree-house.org.uk
Web: .... www.chestnut-tree-house.org.uk

CHILD ACCIDENT PREVENTION TRUST

CR1053549
PO Box 3588, Cloister Court, Barnet, Hertfordshire EN5 9QU
Tel: 020 7608 3828
Email: .... safe@capt.org.uk
Objects: F,W3,J,G,H,3

CHILD BEREAVEMENT CHARITY

Founded: 1994 CR1040419
Aston House, High Street, West Wycombe, High Wycombe, Buckinghamshire HP14 3AG
Tel: 01494 446648
Email: ..... enquiries@childbereavement.org.uk
Objects: F,W3,G,W10,H,3,W8

CHILD BRAIN INJURY TRUST

Founded: 1988 CR1113326
Unit 1, The Great Barn, Baynards Green Farm, Baynards Green, Near Bicester, Oxford, Oxfordshire OX2 6HE
Tel: 01869 341075
Email: .... info@cbituk.org
Objects: F,W3,J,2,H,O,3

CHILD GROWTH FOUNDATION

Founded: 1977 CR274325
2 Mayfield Avenue, Chiswick, London W4 1PW
Tel: 020 8995 0257; 020 8994 7625
Email: .... cgflondon@aol.com
Objects: F,M,W3,G,1A,1B,H,3

CHILD HEALTH RESEARCH APPEAL TRUST

Founded: 1976 CR271834
Institute of Child Health, University College London, 30 Guilford Street, London WC1N 1EH
Tel: 020 7905 2681
Email: .... d.rob@ich.ucl.ac.uk
Object: W3

CHILDCARE - BRENTWOOD CATHOLIC CHILDREN'S SOCIETY

CR1000661
Childcare House, Little Wheatley Chase, Rayleigh, Essex SS6 9EH
Tel: 01268 784544
Email: .... headoffice@childcare.org
Objects: F,W3,J,G,V,O,3,P

CHILDHOOD FIRST

Founded: 1973 CR286909
210 Borough High Street, London SE1 1JX
Tel: 020 7928 7388
Email: .... enquiries@childhoodfirst.org.uk
Objects: Q,F,W3,J,G,O,3

CHILDHOPE UK

CR328434
Development House (CC), 56-64 Leonard Street, London EC2A 4LT
Tel: 020 7065 0950
Email: .... info@childhope.org.uk

CHILDLINE

Founded: 1986 CR216401
Weston House, 42 Curtain Road, London EC2A 3NH
Tel: .... 020 7650 3200; 0800 1111 Helpline
Email: .... reception@childline.org.uk
Objects: F,W3,3

CHILDREN 1ST - ROYAL SCOTTISH SOCIETY FOR PREVENTION OF CRUELTY TO CHILDREN

SC016092
83 Whitehouse Loan, Edinburgh EH9 1AT
Tel: ... 0131 446 2300; 0845 108 0111 (Donation Line)
Email: .... fundraising@children1st.org.uk
Objects: F,W3,H,O,3,W8

CHILDREN ENGLAND

Founded: 1942 CR1044239
Unit 25, 1st Floor, Angel Gate, City Road, London EC1V 2PT
Tel: 020 7833 3319
Email: .... office@ncvcco.org
Objects: F,W3,J,G,2,H

CHILDREN IN CRISIS

Founded: 1993 CR1020488
206-208 Stewarts Road, London SW8 4UB
Tel: 020 7627 1040
Email: .... info@childrenincrisis.org
Objects: W3,U

CHILDREN IN DISTRESS UK

Founded: 1989 CR1001327; SC039383
Suite 30, Ladywell Business Centre, 94 Duke Street, Glasgow G4 0UW
Tel: 0141 559 5690
Email: .... admin2@childrenindistress.org.uk
Objects: W3,W5,G,N,U,Y

CHILDREN NORTH EAST

CR222041
89 Denhill Park, Newcastle upon Tyne, Tyne & Wear NE15 6QE

Tel: 0191 256 2444
Email: . . . . enquiries@children-ne.org
Object: W3

CHILDREN'S CANCER AND LEUKAEMIA GROUP (CCLG)

Children's Cancer and Leukaemia Group

Founded:* 1977 *CR286669
University of Leicester, Clinical Sciences Building, Leicester Royal Infirmary, Leicester, Leicestershire LE2 7LX
Tel: 0116 252 5858
Email: . . . . info@cclg.org.uk
Web: . . . . www.cclg.org.uk
Objects: W3,N,2,H,3,W

More than 30 children are diagnosed with cancer and leukaemia each week in the UK. CCLG funds, promotes and supports research into childhood cancer and leukaemia.
We are a leading provider of awarding-winning information for patients and families.
Through a network of specialist centres, CCLG members provide the best possible treatment for all children with cancer and leukaemia.
Over the last 40 years, the survival rate for childhood cancer has dramatically improved, but sadly around 2 in 10 children will not survive their disease, and for some cancers the prognosis is much worse.
Please help us save more young lives

CHILDREN'S FAMILY TRUST

Founded: 1945 CR208607
Hanbury Court, Harris Business Park, Hanbury Road
Stoke Prior, Bromsgrove, Worcestershire B60 4DJ
Tel: 01905 798229
Email: . . . . carolyn@thecft.org.uk
Objects: Q,W3,3

CHILDREN'S FOUNDATION: YELLOW BRICK ROAD APPEAL

Founded: 1990 CR1000013
PO Box 2YB, Queen Victoria Road, Newcastle upon Tyne, Tyne & Wear NE99 2YB
Tel: 0191 282 0000
Email: . . . . childrens.foundation@nuth.nhs.uk
Objects: W3,A,1B,2

CHILDREN'S HEART FEDERATION

CR1120557
Office SB3, Dragon Enterprise Centre, Cullen Mill, Braintree Road, Witham, Essex CM8 2DD
Tel: 01376 780 044
Email: . . . . info@chfed.org.uk
Objects: F,M,W3,W5,1A,A,V,H,3

CHILDREN'S HEART SURGERY FUND

CR1148359
Room 003, B Floor, Brotherton Wing, Leeds General Infirmary, Leeds, West Yorkshire LS1 3EX
Tel: 0113 392 5742
Email: . . . . info@chsf.org.uk

CHILDREN'S HOSPICE SOUTH WEST

Founded:* 1991 *CR1003314
Head Office, Little Bridge House, Redlands Road, Fremington, Barnstaple, Devon EX31 2PZ
Tel: 01271 325270
Fax: 01271 328640
Email: . . . . rob.emery@chsw.org.uk
Web: . . . . www.chsw.org.uk
Objects: W3,N,3

Children's Hospice South West provides the only hospice care in the South West for children with life-limiting conditions. Our three hospices, Little Bridge House in North Devon, Charlton Farm in North Somerset, and Little Harbour in Cornwall provide respite, emergency care and support for in excess of 400 families. Of these some come to us for planned respite and a rare opportunity for a break, others will also be supported through our bereavement team after the loss of their child.
Children's Hospice South West is the only organisation in the region offering this vital service in a home from home environment and is almost entirely funded by the generosity of people in the South West.

THE CHILDREN'S SOCIETY

Founded: 1881 CR221124
Edward Rudolf House, Margery Street, London WC1X 0JL
Tel: 020 7841 4400
Email: . . . . legacies@childrenssociety.org.uk
Objects: Q,F,W3,J,E,H,3

THE CHILDREN'S TRUST

Founded: 1983 CR288018
Tadworth Court, Tadworth, Surrey KT20 5RU
Tel: 01737 365081
Email: . . . . . . enquiries@thechildrenstrust.org.uk
Objects: F,M,W3,J,W5,G,N,R,H,O,3,P

CHOLMONDELEYS, THE

Founded: 1991 CR1001606
LF1.1 Lafone House, The Leathermarket, 11-13 Leathermarket Street, London SE1 3HN
Tel: 020 7378 8800
Objects: S,G,3

CHRIST'S HOSPITAL

Founded: 1552 CR306975
The Counting House, Christ's Hospital, Horsham, West Sussex RH13 OYP
Tel: 01403 211293
Email: . . . . enquiries@christs-hospital.org.uk
Objects: W3,G,3

CHRISTIAN AID

CR1105851
PO Box 100, London SE1 7RT
Tel: 020 7620 4444
Email: . . . . info@christian-aid.org
Objects: W6,M,W3,W2,W7,W5,G,W10,A,1B,W4, U,H,T,O,W8

THE CHRISTIAN BUILDING TRUST

CR1084616
PO Box 27, Llangefni, Anglesey LL77 7BZ
Tel: 01248 724806
Email: . . . . david@davidjebb.co.uk
Objects: N,R,U

CHRISTIAN CHILD CARE FORUM

CR1049477

10 Crescent Road, South Woodford, London E18 2JB

Tel: 020 8504 2702

Email: . . . . . . info@christianchildcareforum.co.uk

Objects: F,W3,J,2

CHRISTIAN COMMUNITY MINISTRIES

CR1020071

97 Runcorn Road, Barnton, Northwich, Cheshire CE8 4EX

Tel: 01606 782244

Email: . . . . office@ccm-international.org

Objects: W3,W15,W16,R,U,Y

THE CHRISTIAN COMMUNITY - MOVEMENT FOR RELIGIOUS RENEWAL

CR210029

Malin House, St Mary Street, Ilkeston, Derbyshire DE7 8AF

Tel: 0115 932 8341

Email: . . . . lcmadsen@talktalk.net

Objects: W3,W4

CHRISTIAN EDUCATION MOVEMENT

Founded: 1882 CR1086990

1020 Bristol Road, Selly Oak, Birmingham, West Midlands B29 6LB

Tel: 0121 472 4242

Email: . . . . . enquiries@christianeducation.org.uk

Objects: W3,G,1B,W4,H,P

CHRISTIAN FAMILY CONCERN

Founded: 1893 CR279962

Wallis House, 42 South Park Hill Road, Croydon, Surrey CR2 7YB

Tel: 020 8688 0251

Email: . . . . . . info@christianfamilyconcern.org.uk

Objects: W3,D,R,3,C,P,W8

CHRISTIAN MEDICAL FELLOWSHIP

CR1131658

6 Marshalsea Road, London SE1 1HL

Tel: 020 7234 9660

Email: . . . . info@cmf.org.uk

Objects: F,1A,R,H,3

CHRISTIAN WITNESS TO ISRAEL

CR271323

166 Main Road, Sundridge, Sevenoaks, Kent TN14 6EL

Tel: 01959 565955

Email: . . . . cwi@cwi.org.uk

Objects: G,W10,R,H,3

CHRISTINA NOBLE CHILDREN'S FOUNDATION

Founded: 1992 CR1007484

11-15 Lillie Road, West Brompton, London SW6 1TX

Tel: 020 7381 8550

Fax: 020 7385 9228

Email: . . . . uk@cncf.org

Web: . . . . www.cncf.org

Objects: W6,M,W3,S,E,W7,W5,G,W10,D,N,U,O,3,C,W8

Primary objective to care for disadvantaged and street children in Vietnam and Mongolia.

CHRISTOPHER PLACE

Founded: 1991 CR1002463

1-5 Christopher Place, Chalton Street, London NW1 1JF

Tel: 020 7383 3834

Email: . . . . info@speech-lang.org.uk

Objects: W3,G,O,3,K

CHRYSALIS AIDS FOUNDATION CHARITABLE TRUST

Founded: 1991 CR1001550

c/o Professor Pinching, Peninsula Medical School, Royal Cornwall Hospital, Truro, Cornwall TR1 3HD

Tel: 01872 256402

Object: 1B

CHURCH ACTION ON POVERTY

Founded: 1990 CR1079986

Central Buildings, Oldham Street, Manchester, Greater Manchester M1 1JQ

Tel: 0161 236 9321

Email: . . . . info@church-poverty.org.uk

Objects: G,2,H

CHURCH ARMY

Founded: 1882 CR226226

Marlowe House, 109 Station Road, Sidcup, Kent DA15 7AD

Tel: 020 8309 3519

Email: . . . . info@churcharmy.org.uk

Objects: W9,W3,E,G,R,W4,3,C,P,W8

CHURCH HOUSING TRUST

Founded: 1984 CR802801

Director: Miriam Morris

PO Box 50296, Premier House, 12-13 Hatton Garden EC1N 8AN

Tel: 020 7269 1630

Email: . . . . info@churchhousingtrust.org.uk

Objects: W16,D,C

CHURCH IN WALES, REPRESENTATIVE BODY OF THE

CR1142813

39 Cathedral Road, Cardiff CF11 9XF

Tel: 029 2034 8200

Email: . . . . . . information@churchinwales.org.uk

Object: R

CHURCH LADS' & CHURCH GIRLS' BRIGADE

CR276821

2 Barnsley Road, Wath upon Dearne, Rotherham, South Yorkshire S63 6PY

Tel: 01709 876535

Email: . . . . brigadesecretary@clcgb.org.uk

Objects: W3,G,2

THE CHURCH OF ENGLAND PENSIONS BOARD – RETIREMENT HOUSING FOR CLERGY PENSIONERS

Founded: 1926 CR236627

29 Great Smith Street (CC), Westminster, London SW1P 3PS

Tel: 020 7898 1808

Email: . . . . . cepbappeals@churchofengland.org

Objects: 1A,D,N,W4,B,3,C

CHURCH OF ENGLAND SOLDIERS', SAILORS' & AIRMEN'S CLUBS
Founded: 1891 CR226684
1 Shakespeare Terrace, 126 High Street, Portsmouth, Hampshire PO1 2RH
Tel: 023 9282 9319
Objects: W9,W4,3,C,P

CHURCH OF SCOTLAND GUILD
SC011353
121 George Street, Edinburgh EH2 4YN
Tel: 0131 240 2217
Email: . . . . guild@cofscotland.org.uk
Objects: G,A,1B,2,R,H,T,W8

CHURCH OF SCOTLAND HOUSING & LOAN FUND FOR RETIRED MINISTERS & WIDOWS AND WIDOWERS OF MINISTERS
SC011353
121 George Street, Edinburgh, Midlothian EH2 4YN
Tel: 0131 225 5722
Email: . lmacmillan@churchofscotland.org.uk
Web: . . . . . . www.churchofscotland.org.uk
Objects: W11,W4,Y
The Fund endeavours, wherever possible, to assist Ministers and Widow(er)s of Ministers with their retirement housing, by way of a house to rent or a house purchase loan. The Trustees may grant the tenancy, on advantageous terms, of a house. Alternatively the Trustees may grant a loan up to 70% of a house purchase price at favourable rates of interest. House prices are capped for both rentals and loans. The Trustees are also prepared to consider assisting those who are already housed, but are seeking to move to more suitable accommodation. Further information may be obtained from The Secretary; Miss L.J.Macmillan, MA, at the above address.

CHURCH PASTORAL AID SOCIETY
Founded: 1836 CR1007820
Athena Drive, Tachbrook Park, Warwick, Warwickshire CV34 6NG
Tel: 01926 458458
Email: . . . . mail@cpas.org.uk
Objects: W3,R,3,W8

CHURCH SCHOOLMASTERS' & SCHOOLMISTRESSES' BENEVOLENT INSTITUTION
Founded: 1857 CR207236
Glen Arun, 9 Athelstan Way, Horsham, West Sussex RH13 6HA
Tel: 01403 253881
Objects: 1A,A,N

CHURCHES CHILD PROTECTION ADVISORY SERVICE - (PCCA)
Founded: 1991 CR1004490
PO Box 133, Swanley, Kent BR8 7UQ
Tel: . . . . 0845 120 4550; 0845 120 4552 Helpline
Email: . . . . info@ccpas.co.uk
Objects: Q,F,W6,W3,W7,W5,G,W10,W4,H,3,W8

CHURCHES COMMUNITY WORK ALLIANCE
CR1004053
218 York Street, Belfast BT15 1GY
Tel: 02890740077
Email: . . . . info@ccwa.org.uk
Objects: F,J,G,2,H,3

CHURCHES TOGETHER IN ENGLAND
Founded: 1991 CR1110782
27 Tavistock Square, London WC1H 9HH
Tel: 020 7529 8131
Objects: 1B,2,T

CHURCH'S MINISTRY AMONG JEWISH PEOPLE (CMJ)
Founded: 1809 CR228519
Eagle Lodge, Hexgreave Hall Business Park, Farnsfield, Nottinghamshire NG22 8LS
Tel: 01623 883960
Email: . . . . enquiries@cmj.org.uk
Objects: R,T

CINEMA & TELEVISION BENEVOLENT FUND (CTBF)
Founded: 1924 CR1099660
Providing Care Behind The Scenes, 22 Golden Square, London W1F 9AD
Tel: 020 7437 6567
Email: . . . . charity@ctbf.co.uk
Objects: W11,1A,3

CIRCULATION FOUNDATION
Founded: 1992 CR1102769
35-43 Lincoln's Inn Fields, London WC2A 3PE
Tel: 020 7869 6937
Email: . . . . info@circulationfoundation.org.uk
Objects: F,W10,A,1B,N,W4,H,3,W8,W

CIRDAN SAILING TRUST
CR1091598
Fullbridge Wharf, 3 Chandlers Quay, Maldon, Essex CM9 4LF
Email: . . . . info@cirdantrust.org
Objects: W3,W5,G,W10,2,3,P

CISV INTERNATIONAL LTD (THE INTERNATIONAL ASSOCIATION OF CHILDRENS INTERNATIONAL SUMMER VILLAGES)
Founded: 1950 CR1073308
MEA House, Ellison Place, Newcastle upon Tyne, Tyne & Wear NE1 8XS
Tel: 0191 232 4998
Email: . . . . international@cisv.org
Objects: W3,G

CITIZEN'S INCOME TRUST
Founded: 1984 CR328198
Citizens Income Study Centre at London School of Economics, Sheffield Street, London WC2A 2EX
Tel: 020 7955 7453
Email: . . . . citizens-income@lse.ac.uk
Objects: F,J,G,W10,2,W4,H,3,W8

CITIZENS ADVICE
CR279057
3rd Floor North, 200 Aldergate Street, London EC14 4HD
Email: . . . . legacies@citizensadvice.org.uk
Objects: F,W9,W6,W3,W7,W5,W10,W11,2,W4,3,W8

CITY LITERARY INSTITUTE
Founded: 1990 CR803007
1-10 Keeley Street, London WC2B 4BA

Tel: 020 7242 9872
Email: .... denise.gill@citylit.ac.uk
Objects: G,3

CITY OF BIRMINGHAM SYMPHONY ORCHESTRA
CR506276
CBSO Centre, Berkley Street, Birmingham, West Midlands B1 2LF
Tel: 0121 616 6500
Email: .... information@cbso.co.uk

CITY OF EXETER Y M C A
Founded: 1990 CR803226
39-41 St Davids Hill, Exeter, Devon EX4 4DA
Tel: 01392 410530
Objects: W3,D,3,C

CITY SOLICITORS EDUCATIONAL TRUST, THE
Founded: 2007 CR1121091
4 College Hill, London EC4R 2RB
Tel: 020 7329 2173
Email: .... mail@citysolicitors.org.uk
Objects: G,1B

THE CIVIL SERVICE RETIREMENT FELLOWSHIP
Founded: 1968 CR255465; SC039049
Suite 2, 80A Blackheath Road, London SE10 8DA
Tel: 020 8691 7411
Email: .... info@csrf.org.uk
Objects: F,V,W4,H,P

CLAIRE HOUSE CHILDREN'S HOSPICE
Founded: 1991 CR1004058
Fundraising Centre, Clatterbridge Road, Bebington, Merseyside CH63 4JD
Tel: 0151 343 0883
Email: .... appeals@claire-house.org.uk
Objects: F,W3,N,3

CLAN CANCER SUPPORT
SC022606
CLAN House, 120 Westburn Road, Aberdeen AB25 2QA
Tel: .. 01224 647000; 0800 783 7922 (freephone)
Email: .... enquiries@clanhouse.org
Objects: F,W3,W4,3

CLARENDON TRUST LTD
CR1069942
21-23 Clarendon Villas, Hove, Brighton & Hove BN3 3RE
Tel: 01273 747687
Email: .... office@cck.org.uk
Objects: G,1A,2,R,U

CLARITY - EMPLOYMENT FOR BLIND PEOPLE
Founded: 1854 CR210794
Unit 7 Highams Park Industrial Estate, Jubilee Avenue, Highams Park, London E4 9JD
Tel: 020 3078 8950
Objects: W6,W5,G,B,3,C,K

CLEFT LIP & PALATE ASSOCIATION (CLAPA)
CR1108160
1st Floor, Green Man Tower, 332B Goswell Road, London EC1V 7LQ
Tel: 020 7833 4883
Email: .... info@clapa.com
Objects: F,M,W3,W5,N,W4,H,3,P

THE CLERK MAXWELL CANCER RESEARCH FUND
SC028098
14 India Street, Edinburgh EH3 6EZ
Tel: 0131 343 1036
Email: .... admin@maxwellcancerfund.org

CLIC SARGENT
CR1107328; SC039857
Room CC16 (CD13), 77-85 Fulham Palace Road, London W6 8JA
Tel: 0845 125 2625
Email: .... info@clicsargent.org.uk
Objects: F,W3,N,H

CLIC SARGENT (SCOTLAND)
CR1107328; SC039857
Room 14, 5th Floor (SCC), Mercantile Chambers, 53 Bothwell Street, Glasgow G2 6TS
Tel: 0141 572 5700
Email: .... giftsinwills@clicsargent.org.uk
Objects: F,W3,1A,A,V,H

CLIFF COLLEGE
Founded: 1883 CR529386
Calver, Hope, Derbyshire S32 3XG
Tel: 01246 584200
Email: .... admin@cliffcollege.ac.uk
Objects: G,3

CLIMB - CHILDREN LIVING WITH INHERITED METABOLIC DISEASE
CR1089588
Climb Building (CDPR2010), 176 Nantwich Road, Crewe, Cheshire CW2 6BG
Tel: 0845 241 2172
Email: .... info.svcs@climb.org.uk
Objects: F,W3,G,1A,A,2,H

CLOWNE AND DISTRICT COMMUNITY TRANSPORT
Founded: 1990 CR1055035
Unit 10, 10 Creswell Road, Clowne, Chesterfield, Derbyshire S43 4PW
Tel: 01246 573040
Objects: M,W3,W5,W4,3,W8

CLUBS FOR YOUNG PEOPLE (CYP)
Founded: 1925 CR306065
Headquarters, 371 Kennington Lane, London SE11 5QY
Tel: 020 7793 0787
Email: ...... office@clubsforyoungpeople.org.uk
Objects: M,W3,J,S,G,2,H,3,P

COAL TRADE BENEVOLENT ASSOCIATION
Founded: 1888 CR212688
6 Bridge Wharf, 156 Caledonian Road, London N1 9UU
Tel: 020 7278 3239
Email: .... coalbenev@aol.com
Objects: F,W9,W6,M,W3,W7,W5,G,W10,W11,1A, V,N,W4,B,O,W8

CODA INTERNATIONAL TRAINING
Founded: 1990 CR1000717
ADKC Centre, Whitstable House, Silchester Road, London W10 6SB
Tel: 02089608888
Email: ..... enquiries@coda-international.org.uk
Objects: W3,J,W2,W5,G,W10,1B,W4,U,W8

COED CYMRU
CR702443
The Old Sawmill, Tregynon, Newtown, Powys SY16 3PL
Tel: 01686 650777
Email: . . . . coedcymru@coedcymru.org.uk
Objects: F,J,W2,G,A,3,K

COELIAC UK
Founded: 1968 CR1048167
Suites A-D, Octagon Court, High Wycombe, Buckinghamshire HP11 2HS
Tel: 01494 437278
Email: . . . . info@coeliac.co.uk
Objects: F,W9,W6,W3,J,W7,W5,W10,W11,1B,2, W4,H,W8

COIF CHARITY FUNDS
Founded: 1962 CR218873, 803610, 1046
80 Cheapside, London EC2V 6DZ
Tel: 020 7489 6000
Object: 3

COLCHESTER COMMUNITY VOLUNTARY SERVICES
CR1092567
Winsley's House, High Street, Colchester, Essex CO1 1UG
Tel: 01206 505250
Email: . . . . information@ccvs.org
Objects: W6,W3,J,W7,W5,W10,W15,W16,W4,3, W8

COLLEGE FOR HIGHER RABBINICAL STUDIES TCHABE KOLLEL
Founded: 1990 CR803466
4-6 Windus Mews, Windus Road, London N16 6UP
Tel: 020 8880 8910

THE COLLEGE OF ST. BARNABAS
Founded: 1895 CR205220
Blackberry Lane, Lingfield, Surrey RH7 6NJ
Tel: 01342 870260
Email: . . . . . . warden@collegeofstbarnabas.com
Objects: W9,W6,W7,W5,N,W4,3,C,W8

COMBAT STRESS
Founded: 1919 CR206002; SC038828
Tyrwhitt House, Oaklawn Road, Leatherhead, Surrey KT22 0BX
Tel: 01372 587000
Email: . . . . fundraising@combatstress.org.uk
Objects: F,W9,N,O

COMMUNITY ACTION HALFWAY HOME LTD
Founded: 1991 CR1005379
23 Filey Street, Sheffield, South Yorkshire S10 2FG
Tel: 0114 279 6777
Objects: D,R,3,C,P

COMMUNITY FIRST IN HEREFORDSHIRE & WORCESTERSHIRE
Founded: 1990 CR703072
Community Centre, 52 Prospect Close, Malvern, Worcestershire WR14 2FD
Tel: 01684 312730
Email: . . . . info@comfirst.org.uk
Objects: F,J,W5,G,W10,A,1B,2,W4,H,3,W8

COMMUNITY HOUSING AND THERAPY
Founded: 1994 CR1040713
Bishop Creighton House, 378 Lillie Road, London SW6 7PH
Tel: 020 7381 5888
Email: . . . . chtcharity@yahoo.co.uk
Objects: F,C

COMMUNITY MATTERS (NATIONAL FEDERATION OF COMMUNITY ORGANISATIONS)
Founded: 1991 CR1002383
12 - 20 Baron Street, London N1 9LL
Tel: 020 7837 7887
Email: . . communitymatters@communitymatters.org.uk
Objects: F,W3,J,G,W10,2,W4,H,3

COMMUNITY NETWORK
CR1000011
Ground Floor, 12-20 Baron Street, London N1 9LL
Tel: 020 7923 5250
Email: . . . . info@community-network.org
Objects: W5,W10,W4,3,P

COMMUNITY SECURITY TRUST (CST)
CR1042391
Freepost 12303, London NW1 0YY
Tel: 020 8457 9999
Email: . . . . enquiries@thecst.org.uk

COMMUNITY TRANSPORT ASSOCIATION UK
Founded: 1991 CR1002222
Aeroworks, 5 Adair Street, Hyde, Greater Manchester M1 2NQ
Tel: 0161 351 1475
Email: . . . . info@ctauk.org
Objects: F,W6,W3,W7,W5,G,W10,2,W4,H,3,W8

COMPASSION IN WORLD FARMING
CR1095050
River Court, Mill Lane, Godalming, Surrey GU7 1EZ
Tel: 01483 521953
Email: . . . . legacy@ciwf.org.uk
Objects: W1,W2

COMPTON HOSPICE
CR512387
4 Compton Road West, Wolverhampton, West Midlands WV3 9DH
Tel: 0845 225 5497
Email: . . . . fundraising@compton-hospice.org.uk
Objects: W3,N,W4,3,W8

COMPUTER AID INTERNATIONAL
CR1069256
Brunswick Industrial Park, Brunswick Way, London N11 1JL
Tel: 020 8361 5540
Email: . . . . info@computeraid.org
Objects: G,U

CONNECTION AT ST MARTIN'S, THE
Founded: 1990 CR1078201
12 Adelaide Street, London WC2N 4HW
Tel: 020 7766 5555
Email: . . . . info@cstm.org.uk
Objects: F,M,W3,E,G,W4,3,P,K

CONSTRUCTION YOUTH TRUST
CR1094323
The Building Centre, 26 Store Street, London WC1E 7BT
Tel: 020 7467 9540
Email: .... hello@constructionyouth.org.uk
Objects: W3,G,1A,1B,3

CONTACT A FAMILY
Founded: 1979 CR284912; SC039169
209-211 City Road, London EC1V 1JN
Tel: ..... 020 7608 8700 Admin; 0808 808 3556 Textphone; 0808 808 3555 Mon - Fri, 10-4pm; Mon 5:30-7:30pm
Email: .... fundraising@cafamily.org.uk
Objects: F,W3,W10,H,3

CONTACT THE ELDERLY
Founded: 1965 CR1146149; SC039377
2 Grosvenor Gardens, London SW1W 0DH
Tel: 020 7240 0630
Email: .... info@contact-the-elderly.org.uk
Objects: W4,3,P

CORAM FAMILY
CR312278
Coram Community Campus, 49 Mecklenburgh Square, London WC1N 2QA
Tel: 020 7520 0329
Email: .... reception@coram.org.uk
Objects: Q,F,W3,G,3,C,P

CORDA - PREVENTING HEART DISEASE AND STROKE
Founded: 1976 CR271070
Chelsea Square, London SW3 6NP
Tel: 020 7349 8686
Email: .... corda@rbht.nhs.uk
Objects: A,1B

CORNERSTONE TRUST
Founded: 1991 CR1003948
132 Thicketford Road, Bolton, Greater Manchester BL2 2LU
Tel: 01204 392 043
Email: .... tracy@thecornerstonetrust.org.uk
Objects: F,W5

CORNWALL AIR AMBULANCE TRUST
CR1133295
Victoria Square, Roche, St Austell, Cornwall PL26 8LQ
Tel: 01726 890444
Email: . enquiries@cornwallairambulancetrust.org

CORNWALL BLIND (AND PARTIALLY SIGHTED) ASSOCIATION
Founded: 1856 CR1108761
The Sight Centre, Newham Road, Truro, Cornwall TR1 2DP
Tel: 01872 261110
Email: .... info@cornwallblind.org.uk
Objects: F,W6,M,W3,S,G,1A,A,1B,V,2,W4,H,O,3,P

CORONA WORLDWIDE
Founded: 1950 CR204802
Southbank House, Black Prince Road, London SE1 7SJ
Tel: 020 7793 4020
Email: .... corona@coronaworldwide.org
Objects: F,J,G,2,U,H,3,P,W8

CORONARY PREVENTION GROUP
Founded: 1979 CR277243
2 Taviton Street, London WC1H 0BT
Tel: 020 7927 2125
Email: .... cpg@lshtm.ac.uk
Objects: J,W4,H

CORPORATION OF THE SONS OF THE CLERGY
Founded: 1655 CR207736
1 Dean Trench Street, Westminster, London SW1P 3HB
Tel: 020 7799 3696
Email: .... enquiries@sonsoftheclergy.org.uk
Objects: W11,Y

CORRYMEELA COMMUNITY
Founded: 1965XN48052A
8 Upper Crescent, Belfast BT7 1NT
Tel: 028 9050 8080
Email: .... belfast@corrymeela.org
Objects: F,W3,J,E,W5,G,2,R,W4,H,T,P,W8

COTSWOLD ARCHAEOLOGY LIMITED
Founded: 1991 CR1001653
Building 11, Kemble Enterprise Park, Cirencester, Gloucestershire GL7 6BQ
Tel: 01285 771022
Email: .. enquiries@cotswoldarchaeology.org.uk
Objects: S,G,H,3

COUNCIL FOR BRITISH ARCHAEOLOGY
CR287815; SC041971
Beatrice de Cardi House, 66 Bootham, York, North Yorkshire YO30 7BZ
Tel: 01904 671417
Email: .... admin@archaeologyUK.org
Objects: W3,W2,G,1B,2,H

COUNCIL FOR WORLD MISSION
Founded: 1977 CR1097842
32-34 Great Peter Street, London SW1P 2DB
Tel: 020 7222 4214
Email: .... council@cwmission.org
Objects: 2,R

COUNCIL OF ETHNIC MINORITY VOLUNTARY SECTOR ORGANISATIONS
CR1077004
Boardman House, 64 Broadway, Stratford, London E15 1NG
Tel: 020 8432 0000
Email: .... enquiries@cemvo.org.uk
Objects: G,W10,1B,W4,H,W8

COUNSEL AND CARE
Founded: 1954 CR203429
Twyman House, 16 Bonny Street, London NW1 9PG
Tel: . 020 7241 8555; 0845 300 7585 Advice Line (Mon-Fri 10-4, Wed 10-1)
Email: .... advice@counselandcare.org.uk
Objects: F,1A,2,W4,B,H,3,P

COUNTRY HOUSES FOUNDATION
Founded: 2005 CR1111049
Sheephouse Farm, Uley Road, Dursley, Gloucestershire GL11 5AD
Tel: 0845 402 4102
Email: ... info@countryhousesfoundation.org.uk
Objects: W2,1A,1B

COUNTRY TRUST
Founded: 1978 CR1122103
The Technology Centre, Framlingham, Suffolk IP13 9EZ
Tel: 01728 720176
Email: . . . . info@countrytrust.org.uk
Objects: W3,W2,G

COUNTRYSIDE RESTORATION TRUST
CR1142122
Bird's Farm, Haslingfield Road, Barton, Cambridgeshire CB23 7AG
Tel: 01223 262999
Email: . . . . info@countrysiderestorationtrust.com

COVENANT MINISTRIES INTERNATIONAL
Founded: 1990 CR328513
Nettle Hill, Brinklow Road, Ansty, Coventry, West Midlands CV7 9JL
Tel: 024 7660 2777
Objects: G,R,U,H

COVENTRY CYRENIANS LTD
CR502421
McRaye House, 98-101 Far Gosford Street, Coventry, West Midlands CV1 5EA
Tel: 024 7622 8099
Email: . . . . info@coventrycyrenians.org
Objects: F,W3,W10,D,R,3,C,W8

CREATION RESOURCES TRUST
CR1016666
PO Box 3237, Yeovil, Somerset BA22 7WD
Tel: 01935 850569
Email: . . . . info@crt.org.uk
Objects: W3,G,H

CRESCENT ARTS CENTRE
XI8909
2-4 University Road, Belfast BT7 1NH
Tel: 028 9024 2338
Email: . . . . info@crescentarts.org
Objects: S,G,P

CRESWELL GROUNDWORK TRUST
Founded: 1991 CR1004253
146 Creswell Road, Clowne, Chesterfield, Derbyshire S43 4NA
Tel: 01246 570977
Email: . . . . info@groundwork-creswell.org.uk

CREWE/NANTWICH BOROUGH AND CONGLETON BOROUGH DIAL-A-RIDE ASSOCIATION
Founded: 1990 CR702629
Units 12 & 15, Brierley Business Centre, Mirion Street, Crewe, Cheshire CW1 2AZ
Tel: 01270 251662

CRIMESTOPPERS TRUST
CR1108687
Leo House, Railway Approach, Wallington, Surrey SM6 6BG
Tel: 020 8835 3700
Email: . . . . cst@crimestoppers-uk.org
Objects: W3,G,H,3

CRIPPLEGATE FOUNDATION
Founded: 1891 CR207499
76 Central Street, London EC1V 8AG
Tel: 020 7549 8181
Objects: F,M,W3,W5,G,1A,A,1B,V,W4,O,P

CROFT CARE TRUST
Founded: 1990 CR703194
The Croft, Hawcoat Lane, Barrow-in-Furness, Cumbria LA14 4HE
Tel: 01229 820090
Objects: W5,3

CROHN'S AND COLITIS UK
Founded: 1979 CR1117148; SC038632
45 Grosvenor Road, St Albans, Hertfordshire AL1 3AW
Tel: 01727 830038 (Admin & Membership); 0845 130 2233 (Information & Support)
Email: . . . . enquiry@crohnsandcolitis.org.uk
Objects: F,W3,W5,1A,2,W4,H,3,P,W

CROHN'S IN CHILDHOOD RESEARCH ASSOCIATION
Founded: 1978 CR278212; SC040700
Parkgate House, 356 West Barnes Lane, Motspur Park, Surrey KT3 6NB
Tel: 020 8949 6209
Email: . . . . support@cicra.org
Objects: F,W3,J,G,1A,A,1B,2,H,3

CROSSROADS GREENWICH & LEWISHAM LTD
Founded: 1997 CR1062951
2a Wildfell Road, London SE6 4HU
Tel: 020 8690 8554
Objects: M,W3,W5,W10,W4,3

CROSSWAYS COMMUNITY
Founded: 1991 CR1007156
8 Culverden Park Road, Tunbridge Wells, Kent TN4 9QX
Tel: 01892 529321
Email: . . . . info@crosswayscommunity.org.uk
Objects: W5,O,3,C

CROSSWAYS TRUST LIMITED
Founded: 1949 CR230160
Columbia House, Columbia Drive, Worthing, West Sussex BN13 3HD
Tel: 01903 276030
Objects: W9,E,W5,W11,N,2,W4,H,3,C,P

CRUSAID
Founded: 1986 CR1011718
1-5 Curtain Road, London EC2A 3JX
Tel: 020 7539 3880
Email: . . . . office@crusaid.org.uk
Objects: W5,1A,A,1B

CRUSE BEREAVEMENT CARE
Founded: 1959 CR208078
PO Box 800, Richmond, Surrey TW9 1RG
Tel: . . . . 020 8939 9530; 0844 477 9400 Helpline
Email: . . . . info@cruse.org.uk
Objects: F,W3,G,W4,H,3,P

CSHS
Founded: 1990 CR328742
1st Floor, Elgar House, Shrub Hill Road, Worcester, Worcestershire WR4 9EE
Tel: 01905 21155
Email: . . . . cshs@cornwall.co.uk
Objects: J,G,W10,D,W4,H,3,K

CSV (COMMUNITY SERVICE VOLUNTEERS)
CR291222
237 Pentonville Road, London N1 9NJ

Tel: 020 7278 6601
Email: . . . . information@csv.org.uk
Objects: W3,W2,W5,G,W10,W4,3,W8

THE CTBI - THE SALESPEOPLES CHARITY

Founded: 1849 CR216538
2 Fletcher Road, Ottershaw, Chertsey, Surrey KT16 0JY
Tel: 01932 429636
Email: . . . . sec.ctbi@ntlworld.com
Objects: W11,1A,A

CUMBERLAND AND WESTMORLAND CONVALESCENT INSTITUTION

Founded: 1862 CR223946
Nursing and Residential Care, Silloth, Wigton, Cumbria CA7 4JH
Tel: 01697 331493
Objects: W5,N,W4,3

CUMBRIA MINERS WELFARE TRUST FUND

Founded: 1977 CR506515
c/o Coal Industry Social Welfare Organisation, 6 Bewick Road, Gateshead, Tyne & Wear NE8 4DP
Tel: 0191 477 7242
Objects: W3,W5,G,1A,A,1B,2,W4,P

THE CURE PARKINSON'S TRUST

CR1111816; SCO44368
120 Baker Street, London W1U 6TU
Tel: 0207 487 3892
Email: . . . . cptinfo@cureparkinsons.org.uk

CWMNI THEATR ARAD GOCH

Founded: 1990 CR702506
Stryd Y Baddon, Aberystwyth, Ceredigion SY23 2NN
Tel: 01970 617998
Objects: W3,G,3

CYNTHIA SPENCER HOSPICE

CR1002926
Manfield Health Campus, Kettering Road, Northampton, Northamptonshire NN3 6NP
Tel: 01604 678086
Email: . . . . . . cshfundraising@nhft.nhs.uk
Web: . . . . www.cynthiaspencer.org.uk
Objects: N,3
Providing specialist palliative care for people with life-limiting and terminal illnesses and their families across Northamptonshire, either at the Hospice itself or in the Community through our Hospice at Home Team.

CYSTIC FIBROSIS TRUST

Founded: 1964 CR1079049; SC040196
1 Aldgate, London EC3N 1RE
Tel: 020 8464 7211
Email: . . . . legacies@cysticfibrosis.org.uk
Objects: F,H

D

DAIN FUND, THE

Founded: 1940 CR313108
Chairman: Dr Bill Strange
Director: Ms Marian Flint
BMA Charities, BMA House, Tavistock Square, London WC1H 9JP
Tel: 020 7383 6142
Email: . . . . info.bmacharities@bma.org.uk
Web: . . . . https://www.bma.org.uk
Objects: G,W11,1A
Helps with the education costs and support of doctors' children in times of financial crisis.

DAME HANNAH ROGERS TRUST - TRANSFORMING DISABLED YOUNG PEOPLES' LIVES

CR306948
Woodland Road, Ivybridge, Devon PL21 9HQ
Tel: 01626 325800
Email: . Imogen.Middleton@discoverhannahs.org
Objects: W3,W5,G

THE DAME VERA LYNN TRUST FOR CHILDREN WITH CEREBRAL PALSY

CR1089657
Trust Office, Ingfield Manor, Five Oaks, Billinghurst, West Sussex RH14 9AX
Tel: 01403 780444; 01403 783111
Objects: W3,G,3

DANCE EAST

CR1066825
Jerwood DanceHouse, Foundry Lane, Ipswich, Suffolk IP4 1DW
Tel: 01473 639230
Email: . . . . info@danceeast.co.uk
Objects: F,W3,J,W2,S,W5,G,W10,W4,H,3,P

DANENBERG OBERLIN-IN-LONDON PROGRAM

Founded: 1991 CR297071
F.S.U. Study Centre, Room 29, 99-103 Great Russell Street, London WC1B 3LA
Tel: 020 7419 1178
Objects: W3,G

DANIELL'S (MISS) SOLDIERS' HOMES

Founded: 1863 CR233658
Havelock House, Barrack Road, Aldershot, Hampshire GU11 3NP
Tel: 01252 310033
Email: . . . . mdsh@sasra.org.uk
Objects: W9,R,3,P

DAPHNE JACKSON TRUST, THE

Founded: 1992 CR1125867
Department of Physics, University of Surrey, Guildford, Surrey GU2 7XH
Tel: 01483 689166
Email: . . . . djmft@surrey.ac.uk
Objects: G,W11,1A,B,W8

DARK HORSE VENTURE

Founded: 1989 CR328662
St Mary's Millennium Centre, Meadow Lane, Liverpool, Merseyside L12 5EA
Tel: 0151 256 8866
Email: . . . . barbaradhv@yahoo.co.uk
Objects: S,W5,2,W4,P

David Livingstone, the greatest Scottish missionary spent his life in Africa and India where he fought slavery and for women and girls to be respected, he opened up great areas of these countries so that others could follow and continue the work which he started.

Our education programme is proving that there is only one way out of poverty and many of our children are gaining degrees in various subjects whilst our vocational training is enabling adults as well as children to produce worthwhile items for sale. This is helping poverty stricken villagers to gain respect and confidence.

Graduates 2016
in well paid employment

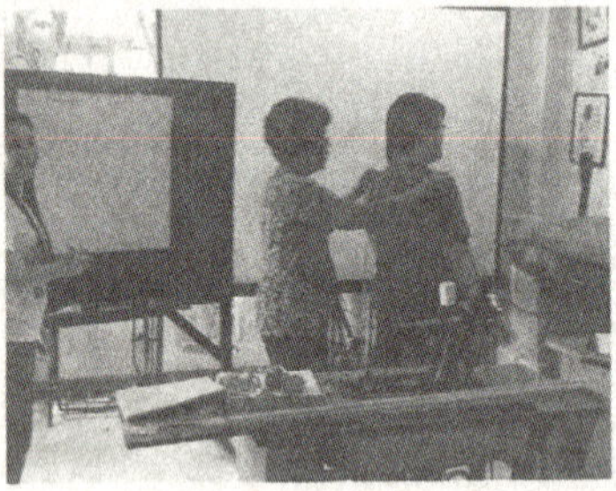

Sewing Classes for women
Learning to earn

Children's camps are attended by children and adults who are shown how to cook nourishing meals and help in our feeding programmes and relief work.

We are inundated with requests for help from other villages and all our graduates are offering financial aid and sharing the burden of those in abject poverty but it is not enough. Funds are needed to continue our self help programme. This is exciting work please help us to respond to these opportunities, join the world-wide David Livingstone Family reaching out to the oppressed we need to open three more children's centres at a cost of £75,000 each. These centres will meet not only the children's needs but also the widows and sick elderly family members.

NO SALARIES OR ALLOWANCES ARE PAID TO ANY OF OUR DIRECTORS OR OFFICERS ALL ARE VOLUNTEERS

DARTFORD, GRAVESHAM & SWANLEY MIND
Founded: 1969 CR1103790
The Almhouses, 16 West Hill, Dartford, Kent DA1 2EP
Tel: 01322 291380
Email: .... admin@northkentmind.co.uk
Objects: F,E,G,D,H,3,C,P,K

DAVE LEE'S HAPPY HOLIDAYS
Founded: 1995 CR1045416
Jester, 15 Curtis Wood Park Road, Herne, Herne Bay, Kent CT6 7TY
Tel: 01227 371022
Email: .... dlegge7288@aol.com
Objects: W3,W5,V,3

DAVID LEWIS CENTRE FOR EPILEPSY
Founded: 1990 CR1000392
The David Lewis Centre, Mill Lane, Warford, Alderley Edge, Cheshire SK9 7UD
Tel: 01565 640000
Email: .... enquiries@davidlewis.org.uk
Objects: W3,W5,G,N,2,W4,O,3,C,K

DAVID LIVINGSTONE INTERNATIONAL LTD
SC010894
47 Brynsworthy Park, Roundswell, Barnstaple, Devon EX31 3RB
Tel: 01271 321210
Fax: 01271 321210
Email: .... upservant2008@talktalk.net
Web: .... www.davidlivingstone-int-ltd.com
Objects: W3,G,N,R,U,Y,W8

DLI the charity with a difference it enjoys free office accommodation, heating and telephone, no salaries or allowances are paid to the directors or officers in the UK or abroad. It operates through ministers and national workers and seeks to respond to crisis situations in emergencies. DLI supports nearly 2,000 orphans and children in homes and schools in **Thailand, The Philippines, India** and various parts of **Africa**. It carries out an active medical programme treating **cleft palate** children with follow up dentistry, speech therapy and catch up education. Care for patients with TB, cancer and the frail elderly is part of seeking to meet part of the family needs. **Clean water is a vital part** of the provision and every year new **bore holes and water pumps** are installed in slum villages where weekly feeding programmes for malnourished children and training of mothers to prepare food in hygienic conditions are provided. **Education is the only way out of poverty** and children are encouraged to obtain the highest qualifications academically or vocationally in 2016 seventeen of our students received university degrees, please help us, join our winning team and increase our successes.
Your donation and legacies are urgently needed today.
See advert on previous page

DAY ONE CHRISTIAN MINISTRIES INCORPORATING LORD'S DAY OBSERVANCE SOCIETY
Founded: 1831 CR233465
Ryelands Road, Leominster, Herefordshire HR6 8NZ
Tel: 01568 613740
Email: .... info@lordsday.co.uk
Objects: R,H,3

DE HAVILLAND AIRCRAFT HERITAGE CENTRE - INCORPORATING THE MOSQUITO AIRCRAFT MUSEUM
CR286794
PO Box 107, London Colney, Hertfordshire AL2 1EX
Tel: ... 01727 822051 (Info only); 01727 862400
Email: .... w4060.dhamt@fsmail.net
Objects: W9,S,G,W12

DE SOUSA DEIRO (MARGARET) FUND
Founded: 1927 CR210615
PO Box 135, Buntingford, Hertfordshire SG11 2XJ
Tel: 01763 274781
Objects: M,1A,N,O,W8

DEAF DIRECT
CR1105044
Community Manager: Mr Gordon Hay
Vesta Tilley House, Lowesmoor, Worcester, Worcestershire WR1 2RS
Tel: .... 01905 746301; 01905 746300 (Text)
Fax: 01905 746302
Email: .... info@deafdirect.org.uk
Web: .... www.deafdirect.org.uk
Objects: F,J,W7,G,3
Working to promote independence and equality of opportunity for deaf and hard of hearing people of all ages, living in Herefordshire, Oxfordshire and Worcestershire. Deaf Direct provides communication services, training, support and advice.

DEAF EDUCATION THROUGH LISTENING AND TALKING - DELTA
Founded: 1988 CR1115603
The Con Powell Centre, Alfa House, Molesey Road, Walton-on-Thames, Surrey KT12 3PD
Tel: 0845 108 1437
Email: .... enquiries@deafeducation.org.uk
Objects: F,W3,W7,G,V,2,H

DEAFCONNECT NORTHANTS AND RUTLAND
CR208164
Spencer Dallington Community Centre, Tintern Avenue, Northampton, Northamptonshire NN5 7BZ
Tel: ... 01604 880777; 01604 799020 Textphone
Email: .... general@deafconnect.org.uk

DEAFPLUS
Founded: 1970 CR1073468
First Floor Trinity Centre, Key Close, Whitechapel, London E1 4HG
Tel: .. 020 7790 6147; 020 7790 5999 Textphone
Email: .... janet.plunkett@deafplus.org
Objects: F,M,J,W7,G,W4,3,P

DEBRA
Founded: 1978 CR1084958; SC039654
DEBRA House, 13 Wellington Business Park, Dukes Ride, Crowthorne, Wokingham RG45 6LS
Tel: 01344 771961
Email: .... debra@debra.org.uk
Objects: F,M,W5,1A,A,1B,V,N,2,H,3

DEBTORS' RELIEF FUNDS CHARITY
Founded: 1772 CR234144
14 Hall Farm Gardens, East Winch, King's Lynn, Norfolk PE32 1NS
Objects: F,A,1B,O

DELPHSIDE LTD
Founded: 1991 CR1006024
11 Standstone Drive, Prescot, Merseyside
L35 7LS
Tel: 0151 431 0330

DEMAND - DESIGN AND MANUFACTURE FOR DISABILITY
Founded: 1992 CR1008128
The Old Chapel, Mallard Road, Abbots Langley, Hertfordshire WD5 0GQ
Tel: 01923 681800
Email: . . . . info@demand.org.uk

DEMENTIA SERVICES DEVELOPMENT TRUST
Founded: 1989SC016905
Iris Murdoch Building, University of Stirling, Stirling
FK9 4LA
Tel: 01786 467740
Email: . . dementia@stir.ac.uk/ dsdtrust_stirling@yahoo.com
Objects: F,G,H,K

DEPAUL UK
Founded: 1989 CR802384
291-299 Borough High Street, London SE1 1JG
Tel: 020 7939 1273
Email: . . . . depaul@depauluk.org
Objects: W3,W16

DEPRESSION ALLIANCE
CR1096741
63-71 Collier Street, London N1 9BE
Tel: 020 7833 2500
Email: . . . . . information@depressionalliance.org
Objects: F,G,2,H

DEPRESSION UK
Founded: 1979 CR294482
Self Help Nottingham, Ormiston House, 32-36 Pelham Street, Nottingham, Nottinghamshire
NG1 2EG
Tel: 0870 774 4320
Email: . . . . info@depressionuk.org
Objects: F,2,H,O,W

DERBY COUNCIL FOR VOLUNTARY SERVICE
CR1043482
4 Charnwood Street, Derby, Derbyshire DE1 2GT
Tel: . . . 01332 346266; 01332 341576 (Minicom)
Email: . . . . cvs@cvsderby.co.uk

DEREK PRINCE MINISTRIES - CHINA
Founded: 1992 CR1010850
Kingsfield, Hadrian Way, Baldock, Hertfordshire
SG7 6AN
Tel: 01462 492110
Email: . . . . enquires@dpmuk.org

DERIAN HOUSE CHILDREN'S HOSPICE FOR THE NORTH WEST
Founded: 1991 CR1005165
Derian House, Chancery Road, Astley Village, Chorley, Lancashire PR7 1DH
Tel: 01257 271271
Email: . . . . derian.house@virgin.net
Objects: W3,3

DESIGN AND TECHNOLOGY ASSOCIATION
Founded: 1992 CR1062270
16 Wellesbourne House, Walton Road, Wellesbourne, Warwickshire CV35 9JB
Tel: 01789 470007
Email: . . . . data@data.org.uk
Objects: G,2,H

DEVON AIR AMBULANCE TRUST
Founded: 1991 CR1077998
5 Sandpiper Court, Harrington Lane, Exeter, Devon EX4 8NS
Tel: 01392 466666
Email: . . . . info@daat.org
Objects: N,3

DIABETES TRUST RESEARCH AND CARE FUND
CR1058284
c/o InDependent Diabetes Trust, PO Box 294, Northampton, Northamptonshire NN1 4XS
Tel: 01604 622837
Fax: 01604 622838
Email: . . . . enquiries@iddtinternational.org
Web: . . . . www.iddtinternational.org

DIABETES UK
Founded: 1934 CR215199; SC039136
Macleod House, 10 Parkway, London NW1 7AA
Tel: 0345 123 2399
Email: . . . . legacies@diabetes.org.uk
Objects: F,W3,J,G,W10,A,V,2,H,3

THE DIAGEO FOUNDATION
Founded: 1992 CR1014681
8 Henrietta Place, London W1G 0NB
Tel: 020 7927 5200

DIAGRAMA FOUNDATION
Founded: 1887 CR1128532
49 Russell Hill Road, Purley, Surrey CR8 2LD
Tel: 020 8668 2181
Email: . . . . info@cabrini.org.uk
Objects: Q,F,W3,E,V,O,3,P

THE DICK VET ANIMAL HEALTH AND WELFARE FUND
SC004307
The University of Edinburgh, Easter Bush Veterinary Centre, Roslin, Midlothian EH25 9RG
Tel: 0131 650 6261
Email: . . . . edinburghcampaign@ed.ac.uk

DIOCESE OF CYPRUS AND THE GULF ENDOWMENT FUND
Founded: 1990 CR1000307
19 Little Breach, Chichester, West Sussex
PO19 5TX
Tel: 01243 787507

DIRECTORY OF SOCIAL CHANGE
Founded: 1975 CR800517
24 Stephenson Way, London NW1 2DP
Tel: 0845 077 7707
Email: . . . . enquiries@dsc.org.uk
Objects: G,H,3

DISABILITY ADVICE BRADFORD
CR700084
103 Dockfield Road, Shipley, West Yorkshire
BD17 7AR
Tel: 01274 594173
Email: . . . . enquiry@disabilityadvice.org.uk

We promise we'll never put down a healthy dog.
Please promise to help us with a gift in your Will.
Every year, Dogs Trust cares for around 17,000 dogs in our 20 rehoming centres across the UK. We never put down a healthy dog. By leaving a gift in your Will, your love of dogs can live on and help us make the world a better place for them.
Call: 020 7837 0006
Email: infopack@dogstrust.org.uk
Please quote "113378"
DogsTrust
www.dogstrust.org.uk
Reg Charity Nos: 227523 & SC037843

DISABILITY ESSEX (ESSEX DISABLED PEOPLES ASSOCIATION LTD)

Founded: 1949 CR1102596
The Centre for Disability Studies, Adult Community College Rocheway, Rochford, Essex SS4 1DQ
Tel: 08444 121771
Email: . . . . info@disabilityessex.org
Objects: F,W6,W7,W5,G,V,2,W4,3,P

DISABILITY RIGHTS UK

Founded: 1977 CR1138585
CAN Mezzanine, 49-51 East Road, London N1 6AH
Tel: . . . . 020 7250 3222; 020 7250 4119 Minicom
Email: . . . . enquiries@disabilityrightsuk.org
Objects: F,J,W5,G,V,D,H

DISABLED LIVING

CR224742
Redbank House, 4 St Chad's Street, Cheetham, Manchester, Greater Manchester M8 8QA
Tel: 0161 214 5959
Email: . . . . information@disabledliving.co.uk
Objects: F,W6,M,W3,E,W7,W5,G,V,O,3,P

DISABLED LIVING FOUNDATION

Founded: 1971 CR290069
DMS, 380-384 Harrow Road, London W9 2HU
Tel: . . . . 020 7289 6111; 0845 130 9177 Helpline
Email: . . . . info@dlf.org.uk
Objects: F,W9,W6,M,W3,W7,W5,G,W10,W11, W4,H,3,W8

DISABLED MOTORING UK

CR1111826
National Headquarters, Ashwellthorpe, Norwich, Norfolk NR16 1EX
Tel: 01508 489449
Email: . . . . enquiries@mobilise.info
Objects: F,J,W5,2,H,3,P

DOG AID SOCIETY OF SCOTLAND

Founded: 1956SC001918
60 Blackford Avenue, Edinburgh EH9 3ER
Tel: 0131 668 3633
Email: . . . . enquiries@dogaidsociety.com
Object: W1

DOG CARE ASSOCIATION (AND CATS)

CR518996
Ponderosa Kennels, Allerton Bywater, Castleford, West Yorkshire WF10 2EW
Tel: 01977 552303
Email: . . . . . . michael@pondarosakennel.org.uk
Object: W1

DOGS FOR GOOD

Founded: 1986 CR1092960
The Frances Hay Centre, Blacklocks Hill, Banbury, Oxfordshire OX17 2BS
Tel: 01295 252600
Email: . . . . info@dogsforgood.org
Objects: M,W3,W5,3

DOGS TRUST

Founded: 1891 CR227523; SC037843
Veterinary Director: Ms Paula Boyden
Chief Executive: Mr Adrian Burder
Finance Director: Mr Jim Monteith
Clarissa Baldwin House, 17 Wakley Street, London EC1V 7RQ
Tel: 020 7837 0006
Fax: 020 7833 2701
Email: . . . . infopack@dogstrust.org.uk
Web: . . . . www.dogstrust.org.uk
Objects: Q,F,W1,J,G,2,H

Dogs Trust is the UK's largest dog welfare charity, and last year cared for nearly 17,000 stray and abandoned dogs at our nationwide network of rehoming centres. We never put down a healthy dog, and work hard to match the right dog with the right owner, no matter how long this may take. We believe that all dogs should live in permanent, loving homes with responsible owners, and that a dog really is for life. We are working towards the day when no healthy dog is put down for want of a loving home.

Dogs Trust also offers peace of mind to dog owners with its special free service, the Canine Care Card. If you ever wonder "What would happen to my dog if I were to die suddenly?" Dogs Trust provides the answer. By carrying a Canine Care Card, we undertake to look after and find a new, loving home for your dog in the event of your death. That way, you can rest assured that your dog's future can be a safe and happy one after your lifetime.

Dogs Trust relies entirely on legacies and donations to fund its work. Every gift received helps more dogs in need.

See advert on page 45

DONCASTER PARTNERSHIP FOR CARERS LIMITED (DPFC)

Founded: 1991 CR1075455
St Wilfrid's, 74 Church Lane, Bessacarr, Doncaster, South Yorkshire DN4 6QD
Tel: 01302 531333
Email: . . . . dpfc@doncastercarers.org.uk
Objects: F,W6,W3,W7,W5,G,W10,W4,3

THE DONKEY SANCTUARY

THE DONKEY SANCTUARY

Founded: 1969 CR264818
Chief Executive: Mr Mike Baker
Slade House Farm (Dept CD), Sidmouth, Devon EX10 0NU
Tel: 01395 578222
Fax: 01395 579266
Email: . enquiries@thedonkeysanctuary.org.uk
Web: . . . . . . www.thedonkeysanctuary.org.uk

We prevent the suffering of donkeys through the provision of high quality professional advice, training and support on donkey care and welfare. Welfare advisers in the UK and Ireland provide advice and practical support to donkey owners and follow up complaints of mistreatment or neglect of donkeys and our veterinary team shares their knowledge with practitioners around the world.

See advert on previous page

THE DONKEY SANCTUARY INTERNATIONAL

THE DONKEY SANCTUARY

Founded: 1969 CR264818
Chief Executive: Mr Mike Baker
Slade House Farm (Dept CDO), Sidmouth, Devon EX10 0NU
Tel: 01395 578222
Fax: 01395 579266
Email: . enquiries@thedonkeysanctuary.org.uk
Web: . . . . . . www.thedonkeysanctuary.org.uk

Our mission is to transform the quality of life for donkeys, mules and people worldwide through greater understanding, collaboration and support, and by promoting lasting, mutually life-enhancing relationships. A world where donkeys and mules live free from suffering and their contribution to humanity is fully valued.

See advert on previous page

DORCAS MINISTRIES

Founded: 1996 CR1055427
62 Lebrun Square, Greenwich, London SE3 9NS
Tel: 020 8856 7876
Objects: F,W9,W3,D,R,U,O,3,C,P,W8

DORIS FIELD CHARITABLE TRUST

Founded: 1990 CR328687
Buxton Court, 3 West Way, Oxford, Oxfordshire OX2 0SZ
Tel: 01865 262600
Objects: 1A,A,1B

DOROTHY KERIN TRUST, THE

Founded: 1948 CR1095940
Burrswood, Groombridge, Tunbridge Wells, Kent TN3 9PY
Tel: 01892 863637
Email: . . . . admin@burrswood.org.uk
Objects: F,W3,W5,1A,N,R,W4,O,3,W8

DORSET RESIDENTIAL HOMES

Founded: 1991 CR1003779
Connaught House, 22 Cornwall Road, Dorchester, Dorset DT1 1RU
Tel: 01305 267483
Email: . . . . doresd@aol.com
Objects: W5,O,3,C

DORUS TRUST

Founded: 1990 CR328724
Kings Hill, West Malling, Kent ME19 4TA
Tel: 01732 520081
Objects: F,W6,W3,W2,W7,W5,A,1B,W4,O

DOWN'S SYNDROME ASSOCIATION

CR1061474
Langdon Down Centre, 2a Langdon Park, Teddington, Middlesex TW11 9PS
Tel: 0333 121 2300
Email: . . . . alexa.dizon@downs-syndrome.org.uk
Objects: F,W3,J,G,2,W4,H,P

DOWN'S SYNDROME SCOTLAND

SC011012
158-160 Balgreen Road, Edinburgh EH11 3AU
Tel: 0131 313 4225
Email: . . . . info@dsscotland.org.uk
Objects: F,W5,2

DOWNLANDS EDUCATIONAL TRUST

Founded: 1975 CR270943
15 Trent Close, Sompting, Lancing, West Sussex BN15 0EJ
Tel: 01903 523206
Email: . . . . sec@downlandsedtrust.org
Objects: W3,A,1B

DR GRAHAM'S HOMES, KALIMPONG, INDIA, UK COMMITTEE

SC016341
101 Caiyside (CC), Edinburgh EH10 7HR
Tel: 0845 094 8839
Email: . . . sponsorship@drgrahamshomes.co.uk
Objects: W3,G,1B,2,R

DREAMFLIGHT - HOLIDAYS FOR DISABLED CHILDREN

Founded: 1990 CR1117303
15 Chiltern Court, Asheridge Road, Chesham, Buckinghamshire HP5 2PX
Tel: 01494 722733
Email: . . . . office@dreamflight.org
Objects: W3,W5,V

DRIVE

Founded: 1990 CR703002
Unit 8, Cefn Coed, Parc Nantgarw, Nantgarw, Cardiff CF15 7QQ
Tel: 01443 845260
Objects: W5,D,3,P

DRUGSCOPE

Founded: 1968 CR255030
2nd Floor, Prince Consort House, 109-111 Farringdon Road, London EC1R 3BW
Tel: 020 7520 7550
Email: . . . . info@drugscope.org.uk
Objects: F,J,H

DUDLEY MIND

Founded: 1976 CR1002257
221 Hagley Road, Oldswinford, Stourbridge, West Midlands DY8 2JP
Tel: 01384 442938
Email: . . . . . margaret.allen@dudley-mind.org.uk
Objects: E,D,2,O,3,C,P

THE DUKE OF EDINBURGH'S AWARD

Founded: 1956 CR1072490
Gulliver House, Madeira Walk, Windsor, Windsor & Maidenhead SL4 1EU
Tel: 01753 727400
Email: . . . . info@DofE.org
Objects: W6,W3,W2,S,W7,W5,G,W10,H,3,P,W8

DUNDEE INTERNATIONAL WOMEN'S CENTRE

SC014949
Unit 9, Manhattan Business Park, Dundonald Street, Dundee DD3 7PY
Tel: 01382 462058
Email: . . . . enquiries@diwc.co.uk
Objects: W3,G,W10,W4,3,P,W8

DURHAM LESOTHO DIOCESAN LINK, THE

Founded: 1990 CR702809
26 Allergate, Durham, Co. Durham DH1 4ET

Tel: 0191 384 8385
Email: .... tpjeff@sagainternet.co.uk
Objects: W3,G,A,R,3,P,W8

DWARF SPORT ASSOCIATION UK
Founded: 1993 CR1041961
PO Box 4269, Dronfield, Derbyshire S18 9BG
Tel: 01246 296485
Objects: W5,W15

DYSLEXIA ACTION
Founded: 1972 CR268502; SC039177
Parkhouse, Wick Road, Egham, Surrey TW20 0HH
Tel: 01784 222300
Email: .... info@dyslexiaaction.org.uk
Objects: F,W3,G,W4,H,3

DYSPRAXIA FOUNDATION
Founded: 1987 CR1058352
8 West Alley, Hitchin, Hertfordshire SG5 1EG
Tel: 01462 455016; 01462 454986 Helpline (Mon-Fri 10am-1pm)
Email: ... dyspraxia@dyspraxiafoundation.org.uk
Objects: F,W3,J,H

E

EARL MOUNTBATTEN HOSPICE, NEWPORT, ISLE OF WIGHT
CR1039086
Fundraising, Halberry Lane, Newport, Isle of Wight PO30 2ER
Tel: 01983 528989
Email: .... info@emhfunding.com

EARLS COURT COMMUNITY PROJECT (YWAM)
Founded: 1991 CR1002189
24 Collingham Road, London SW5 0LX
Tel: 020 7370 4424
Objects: F,E,G,R,O,3,P

EARTHWATCH INSTITUTE (EUROPE)
CR1094467
267 Banbury Road, Oxford, Oxfordshire OX2 7HT
Tel: 01865 318875
Email: .... info@earthwatch.org.uk
Objects: W1,W2,1B,2,H

EASINGTON DISTRICT COUNCIL OF VOLUNTARY SERVICE
CR1117642
Community House, Yoden Road, Peterlee, Co. Durham SR8 5DP
Tel: 0191 569 3511
Email: .... info@eastdurhamtrust.org.uk
Objects: F,G,A,1B,H,3

EAST ANGLIAN AIR AMBULANCE
CR1083876
Hangar E, Gambling Close, Norwich Airport, Norwich, Norfolk NR6 6EG
Tel: 0845 066 9999
Email: .... info@eaaa.org.uk

EAST BELFAST MISSION
XN68566
239 Newtownards Road, Belfast BT4 1AF
Tel: 028 9045 8560
Objects: W3,R,W4,3

EAST CHESHIRE HOUSING CONSORTIUM LTD
Founded: 1991 CR1001923
26A Jordangate, Macclesfield, Cheshire SK10 1EW
Tel: 01625 500166

EAST LONDON COMMUNITY FOUNDATION
Founded: 1990 CR1133535
Unit G12, Office 7, Chadwell Heath Ind.Park, Chadwell Heath, Essex RM8 1SL
Tel: 0300 303 1203
Email: .... enquiries@elcf.org.uk
Objects: W6,W3,W7,W5,W10,W15,A,1B,W16,W4

EAST MIDDLESBROUGH COMMUNITY VENTURE
Founded: 1990 CR702916
The Greenway Centre, Thorntree, Middlesbrough, North Yorkshire TS3 9PA
Tel: 01642 230314

EATON FUND FOR ARTISTS, NURSES AND GENTLEWOMEN
CR236060
PO Box 172, Lewes, East Sussex BN7 9FF
Tel: 01273 480606
Email: .... admin@eatonfund.org.uk
Objects: A,W4,W8

ECL DOOR OF HOPE
CR1083260
PO Box 60, Battle, East Sussex TN33 0WW
Tel: 01424 870836
Email: .... doorhope@aol.com
Objects: W3,G,W10,3

ECUMENICAL SOCIETY OF THE BLESSED VIRGIN MARY
CR282748
11 Belmont Road, Wallington, Surrey SM6 8TE
Tel: 020 8647 5992

EDINBURGH CAT PROTECTION LEAGUE
SC014916
3 Casselbank Street, Edinburgh EH6 5HA
Tel: 0131 554 5521

EDUCATION ACTION INTERNATIONAL (REFUGEE EDUCATION & TRAINING ADVISORY SERVICE)
Founded: 1920 CR1003323
3 Dufferin Street, London EC1Y 8NA
Tel: .... 020 7426 5800 RETAS; 020 7426 5820 International
Email: ..... international@education-action.org; retas@educational-action.org
Objects: F,G,W10,2,U,3,W8

EDWARD LLOYD TRUST, THE
Founded: 1991 CR1005124
Harcourt House, 19 Cavendish Square, London W16 0AJ
Tel: 020 7636 1616
Object: 3

THE EHLERS-DANLOS SUPPORT UK
CR1157027
PO Box 748, Borehamwood, Hertfordshire WD6 9HU
Tel: 020 8736 5604
Email: .... info@ehlers-danlos.org
Objects: W5,H,3

ELDERLY ACCOMMODATION COUNSEL
Founded: 1985 CR292552
3rd Floor, 89 Albert Embankment, London SE1 7TP
Tel: 0800 377 7070
Email: . . . . enquiries@eac.org.uk
Objects: F,W9,W6,W7,W5,W10,W11,W15,V,D, W4,B,3,C,Z,W8

ELFRIDA SOCIETY, THE
CR282716
34 Islington Park Street, London N1 1PX
Tel: 020 7359 7443
Email: . . . . elfrida@elfrida.com

ELISABETH SVENDSEN TRUST FOR CHILDREN AND DONKEYS, THE
Founded: 1989 CR801070
Slade House Farm (Dept ESJ), Sidmouth, Devon EX10 0NU
Tel: 01395 573133
Email: . . . . . info@elisabethsvendsentrust.org.uk
Objects: Q,W6,W3,W7,W5,G,O,3,P

ELIZABETH FOUNDATION FOR DEAF CHILDREN
Founded: 1981 CR293835
Southwick Hill Road, Cosham, Portsmouth, Hampshire PO6 3LL
Tel: 023 9237 2735
Email: . . . . info@elizabeth-foundation.org
Objects: F,W3,W7,G,3

ELLENORLIONS HOSPICES, NORTHFLEET
CR1121561
Coldharbour Road, Northfleet, Gravesend, Kent DA11 7HQ
Tel: 01474 320007
Objects: N,3

ELLYS EXTRA CARE LIMITED
Founded: 1990 CR703127
1 Ellys Road, Radford, Coventry, West Midlands CV1 4EW
Tel: 024 7625 6859

ELSE AND LEONARD CROSS CHARITABLE TRUST, THE
Founded: 1992 CR1008038
The Wall House, 2 Lichfield Road, Richmond, Surrey TW9 3JR
Tel: 020 8948 4950

EMERGE POVERTY FREE
CR1045672; SC038093
5 Skylines Village, Limeharbour, London E14 9TS
Tel: 020 7839 3854
Email: . . . . jeremy@emergepovertyfree.org

EMERGENCY EXIT ARTS
Founded: 1991 CR1004137
PO Box 570, Greenwich, London SE10 0EE
Tel: 020 8853 4809
Email: . . . . info@eea.org.uk
Objects: W3,W2,S,G,W10,W4,3

EMFEC
Founded: 1991 CR1004087
Robins Wood House, Robins Wood Road, Aspley, Nottingham, Nottinghamshire NG8 3NH
Tel: 0115 854 1616
Email: . . . . enquiries@emfec.co.uk
Objects: G,2,H,3

EMMANUEL CHRISTIAN SCHOOL ASSOCIATION
Founded: 1990 CR900505
Sandford Road, Littlemore, Oxford, Oxfordshire OX4 4PU
Tel: 01865 395236
Objects: W3,G,3

EMMANUEL INTERNATIONAL UK
Founded: 1978 CR289036
Forum House, Stirling Road, Chichester, West Sussex PO20 3UF
Tel: 01243 931094
Email: . . . . info@eiuk.org.uk
Web: . . . . www.eiuk.org.uk
Objects: W3,W2,W11,W15,2,R,W4,U,W8
Emmanuel International works in Developing Countries world-wide through practical, caring action and culturally sensitive mission - to meet the needs of people practically, spiritually and emotionally.
See advert on previous page

EMMAUS UK
Founded: 1992 CR1064470
76-78 Newmarket Road, Cambridge, Cambridgeshire CB5 8DZ
Tel: 01223 576103
Email: . . . . contact@emmaus.org.uk
Objects: W2,G,D,O,3,C,P,K

BRITISH EMUNAH FUND
CR215398
Shield House, Harmony Way, London NW4 2BZ
Tel: 020 8203 6066
Email: . . . . info@emunah.org.uk
Objects: F,W3,E,G,W4,O,P,W8

ENABLE CARE & HOME SUPPORT LIMITED
Founded: 1990 CR1001704
Ellen House, Heath Road, Holmewood, Chesterfield, Derbyshire S42 5RB
Tel: 01246 599999
Objects: E,W5,D,N,W4,3,P

ENABLE SCOTLAND
Founded: 1954SC009024
Inspire House, 3 Renshaw Place, Eurocentral, North Lanarkshire ML1 4UF
Tel: 01698 737000
Email: . . . . enable@enable.org.uk
Objects: F,W3,E,W5,G,V,2,H,3,C,P,K

THE ENCEPHALITIS SOCIETY
Founded: 1995 CR1087843
7B Saville Street, Malton, North Yorkshire YO17 7LL
Tel: . . . . . . 01653 699599; 01653 692583 Admin
Email: . . . . mail@encephalitis.info
Objects: F,W6,W3,W7,W5,G,W10,1B,2,W4,H

ENDOMETRIOSIS UK
Founded: 1982 CR1035810
50 Westminster Palace Gardens, 1-7 Artillery Row, London SW1P 1RR
Tel: 020 7222 2781
Email: . . . . info@endometriosis-uk.org
Objects: F,2,H,W8

ENFIELD COMMUNITY TRANSPORT
Founded: 1991 CR1086730
Morson Road Depot, 9 Morson Road, Enfield, Middlesex EN3 4NQ
Tel: 020 8363 2255

ENFIELD VOLUNTARY ACTION
Founded: 1991 CR1077857
Community House, 311 Fore Street, London N9 0PZ
Tel: 020 8373 6299

ENGLISH AND MEDIA CENTRE, THE
Founded: 1990 CR803031
18 Compton Terrace, London N1 2UN
Tel: 020 7359 8080
Email: . . . . info@englishandmedia.co.uk

ENGLISH FOLK DANCE AND SONG SOCIETY
CR305999
Cecil Sharp House, 2 Regents Park Road, London NW1 7AY
Tel: 020 7485 2206
Email: . . . . info@efdss.org
Objects: S,G,2,W12

THE ENGLISH HERITAGE FOUNDATION
CR1140351
1 Waterhouse Square, 138-142 Holborn, London EC1N 2ST
Tel: 020 7973 3797
Email: . . . . . foundation@english-heritage.org.uk
Objects: W2,S,2

ENGLISH SCHOOLS FOOTBALL ASSOCIATION
CR306003
4 Parker Court, Staffordshire Technology Park, Stafford, Staffordshire ST18 0WP
Tel: 01785 785970
Email: . . . . office@esfa.co.uk

ENHAM TRUST
Founded: 1917 CR211235
Enham Alamein, Andover, Hampshire SP11 6JS
Tel: 01264 345800
Email: . . . . info@enham.co.uk
Objects: F,W6,M,J,E,W7,W5,G,D,O,C,K

THE ENVIRONMENT COUNCIL
Founded: 1969 CR294075
212 High Holborn, London WC1V 7BF
Tel: 020 7836 2626
Email: . . . . info@envcouncil.org.uk
Objects: F,J,W2,G,2,H,3

ENVIRONMENTAL INVESTIGATION AGENCY
CR1145359
62-63 Upper Street, London N1 0NY

Tel: 020 7354 7960
Email: . . . . legacy@eia-international.org
Objects: W1,W2

ENVIRONMENTAL PROTECTION UK
Founded: 1959 CR221026
44 Grand Parade, Brighton, Brighton & Hove BN2 9QA
Tel: 01273 878770
Email: . . . . admin@nsca.org.uk
Objects: J,W2,G,2,H,3

EPIGONI TRUST
Founded: 1990 CR328700
Charities Aid Foundation, The Trust Department, Kings Hill, West Malling, Kent ME19 4TA
Tel: 01732 520028
Objects: F,W6,W3,W2,W7,W5,A,1B,N,O

EPILEPSY ACTION
Founded: 1950 CR234343
New Anstey House, Gate Way Drive, Yeadon, Leeds, West Yorkshire LS19 7XY
Tel: . . . . 0113 210 8800; 0808 800 5050 Epilepsy Helpline
Email: . . . . helpline@epilepsy.org.uk
Objects: F,M,W3,J,W5,G,W10,N,2,W4,H,P,W8,K

EPILEPSY CONNECTIONS
Founded: 2000SC030677
100 Wellington Street, Glasgow G2 6DH
Tel: 0141 248 4125
Email: . . . . info@epilepsyconnections.org.uk
Objects: W5,G,W10,Z

EPILEPSY RESEARCH UK
Founded: 2003 CR1100394
Chairman: Dr Graeme Sills
PO Box 3004, London W4 4XT
Tel: 0208 747 5024
Fax: 0870 838 1069
Email: . . . . info@eruk.org.uk
Web: . . . . www.epilepsyresearch.org.uk
Objects: W3,W5,A,1B,N,W4,W8
See advert on previous page

EPILEPSY SCOTLAND
Founded: 1954SC000067
48 Govan Road, Glasgow G51 1JL
Tel: . . . . 0808 800 2200 Freephone
Email: . . . . . . enquiries@epilepsyscotland.org.uk
Objects: F,W3,W5,G,2,W4,H,3,P,W8

EQUALITY NOW
CR1107613
1 Birdcage Walk, London SW1H 9JJ
Tel: 0207 304 6902
Email: . . . . ukinfo@equalitynow.org
Objects: Y,W8

EQUITY CHARITABLE TRUST
Founded: 1989 CR328103
Plouviez House, 19-20 Hatton Place, London EC1N 8RU
Tel: 020 7831 1926
Fax: 020 7242 7995
Email: . . . . info@equitycharitabletrust.org.uk
Web: . . . . http://www.equitycharitabletrust.org.uk
Objects: F,W11,1A,A

The Equity Charitable Trust provides Educational Bursaries to enable professional actors with a minimum of ten years professional adult experience to retrain, re-qualify and develop a new skill set. Depending on your circumstances, grants can cover some or even all of the fees. We also provide benefit and debt advice to professional performers who are experiencing financial hardship and may qualify for a one-off financial grant. For information and to download an application form for either a Welfare or Education Grant, please call us or visit our website www.equitycharitabletrust.org.uk

ERIC (EDUCATION AND RESOURCES FOR IMPROVING CHILDHOOD CONTINENCE)
Founded: 1991 CR1002424
34 Old School House, Britannia Road, Kingswood, Bristol BS18 8DB
Tel: 0845 370 8008
Email: . . . . info@eric.org.uk
Objects: F,W3,H,3

ERSKINE - CARING FOR VETERANS
SC006609
Erskine, Bishopton, Renfrewshire PA7 5PU
Tel: 0141 812 1100
Email: . . . . enquiries@erskine.org.uk

THE ESTHER BENJAMINS TRUST
Founded: 1999 CR1078187
32-36 Loman Street, London SE1 0EH
Tel: 020 7600 5654
Email: . . . . info@ebtrust.org.uk
Objects: W3,S,E,W7,W5,G,U,O,Y,P,W8

EUROPEAN CHILDREN'S TRUST
Founded: 1990 CR803070
4 Bath Place, Rivington Street, London EC2A 3DR
Tel: 020 7749 2468
Email: . . . . gen@everychild.org.uk
Objects: Q,W3,J,G,U

EUROPEAN SIDHALAND ASSOCIATION
Founded: 1991 CR1002335
The Dome Woodley, Park Road, Ashurst, Skelmersdale, Lancashire WN8 6UQ
Tel: 01695 728847
Objects: W3,G,1A,A,2,W4,U,O,3

EUROVISION MISSION TO EUROPE
Founded: 1992 CR1126438
41 Healds Road, Dewsbury, West Yorkshire WF13 4HU
Tel: 01924 453693
Email: . . . . uk@propheticvision.org.uk
Objects: R,U,3

EVANGELICAL FELLOWSHIP IN THE ANGLICAN COMMUNION
CR212314
Trinity College, Stoke Hill, Bristol BS9 1JP
Tel: 0117 968 2803
Objects: W3,J,S,G,W10,R,W8

EVANGELICAL LIBRARY, THE
Founded: 1928 CR1040175
5/6 Gateway Mews, Ringway, Bounds Green Road, London N11 2UT
Tel: 020 8362 0868
Email: . . . . elenquire@gmail.com
Objects: F,G,3

EVELYN NORRIS TRUST
Founded: 1969 CR260078
Plouviez House, 19-20 Hatton Place, London EC1N 8RU
Tel: 020 7831 1926
Email: . . . . info@equitycharitabletrust.org.uk
Objects: W11,V

EVERGREEN TRUST
Founded: 1991 CR1004289
Brixton Warehouse Shop, 126-128 Brixton Hill, London SW2 1RP
Tel: 020 8674 3065

EWELL CHRISTIAN FELLOWSHIP TRUST
Founded: 1991 CR1002721
Generation Resource Centre, Ruxley Lane, Epsom, Surrey KT19 0JG
Tel: 020 8786 8221
Email: .... info@generation.co.uk
Objects: F,W3,W5,G,R,W4,3,P

EX CATHEDRA LTD
Founded: 1969 CR1004086
611b The Big Peg, 120 Vyse Street, Birmingham, West Midlands B18 6NF
Tel: 0121 200 1511
Email: .... info@excathedra.org
Objects: W3,S,W5,G,R,3,P

EX-SERVICES HOUSING SOCIETY
CR1004070
Kingsley Place, 46 Mote Road, Maidstone, Kent ME15 6ES
Tel: 01622 768400
Email: .... tony@primesafety.com
Objects: F,D

EX-SERVICES MENTAL WELFARE SOCIETY
See Combat Stress

EXCEED WORLDWIDE
CR1032476
UK Support Team, Unit 4, Rosevale Industrial Estate, 171 Moira Road, Lisburn, Co. Antrim BT28 1RW
Email: .... office@exceed-worldwide.org

EYELESS TRUST, THE
Founded: 1993 CR1028896
Quemerford Cottage, 50 Malthouse Square, Lakes Lane, Beaconsfield, Buckinghamshire HP9 2LE
Tel: 01494 672006
Objects: M,J,S,A,V,R

F

F.O.R.C.E. CANCER CHARITY
CR296884
Corner House, Barrack Road, Exeter, Devon EX2 5DW
Tel: 01392 402875
Email: .... forcefr@forcecancercharity.co.uk
Objects: F,C

FACT, THE FOUNDATION FOR ART & CREATIVE TECHNOLOGY
Founded: 1990 CR702781
88 Wood Street, Liverpool, Merseyside L1 4DQ
Tel: 0151 707 4444
Email: .... fact@fact.co.uk
Objects: W3,J,S,G,W4,H

FACTORY COMMUNITY PROJECT AND YOUTH CENTRE
Founded: 1991 CR291360
The Walnut Tree, Bronte House, Mayville Est, London N16 8LG
Tel: 020 7241 1520
Objects: W3,G,W10,W4,3,W8

FACULTY OF PHARMACEUTICAL MEDICINE OF THE ROYAL COLLEGES OF PHYSICIANS OF THE UNITED KINGDOM
Founded: 1992 CR1130573
Faculty of Pharmaceutical Medicine, 1 St Andrew's Place, Regent's Park, London NW1 4LB
Tel: 020 7224 0343

FAIRBRIDGE
Founded: 1909 CR206807
207 Waterloo Road, London SE1 8XD
Tel: 020 7928 1704
Email: .... info@fairbrige.org.uk
Objects: F,W3,G,P

FALKIRK AND DISTRICT WOMEN'S AID
SC000058
4 Wellside Place, Falkirk FK1 5RL
Tel: 01324 635661
Email: .... info@fdwa.org.uk
Objects: F,W3,3,P,Z,W8

FAMILIES NEED FATHERS
Founded: 1974 CR276899
134 Curtain Road, London EC2A 3AR
Tel: 0300 030 0110
Email: .... fnf@fnf.org.uk

FAMILY ACTION
Founded: 1869 CR264713
501-505 Kingsland Road, Dalston, London E8 4AU
Tel: 020 7254 6251
Email: .... fwa.headoffice@fwa.org.uk
Objects: F,M,W3,E,G,1A,A,V,D,O,3

FAMILY FOUNDATIONS TRUST LTD
CR284006
Dalesdown, Honeybridge Lane, Dial Post, Horsham, West Sussex RH13 8NX
Tel: 01403 710712
Email: .... admin@dalesdown.org.uk
Objects: W3,G,V,R

FAMILY HOLIDAY ASSOCIATION
Founded: 1975 CR800262
16 Mortimer Street, London W1T 3JL
Tel: 020 3117 0650
Email: .... info@fhaonline.org.uk
Objects: W3,A,1B,V,P,W8

FATHER MAREK SUJKOWSKI, CHILDREN'S AID TO UKRAINE, ROMANIA AND POLAND
Founded: 1994 CR1031451
48 Achilles Road, London NW6 1EA
Tel: 020 7794 7891 (10am-10pm)
Objects: W6,W3,W5,N,U

FAUNA & FLORA INTERNATIONAL (CONSERVATION OF SPECIES AND HABITATS WORLDWIDE)
Founded: 1903 CR1011102
Great Eastern House, Tenison Road, Cambridge, Cambridgeshire CB1 2TT

Tel: 01223 571000
Email: .... info@fauna-flora.org
Objects: W1,W2

FEGANS CHILD & FAMILY CARE
Founded: 1870 CR209930
160 St James' Road, Tunbridge Wells, Kent TN1 2HE
Tel: 01892 538288
Objects: F,W3,E,R,3

FELINE CAT RESCUE
CR803055
Hurst Way, Luton, Bedfordshire LU3
Tel: 01582 732347

THE FELLOWSHIP HOUSES TRUST
Founded: 1937 CR205786
Rosemary House, Portsmouth Road, Esher, Surrey KT10 9AA
Tel: 01372 461440
Email: .... housing@rsmha.org.uk
Objects: D,W4,3,C

FELLOWSHIP OF ST. NICHOLAS
Founded: 1939 CR208446
66 London Road, St Leonards-on-Sea, East Sussex TN37 6AS
Tel: 01424 423683
Email: .... fsn@stleonards3.fsnet.co.uk
Objects: F,W3,E,G,V,3

FELTHAM COMMUNITY SCHOOL ASSOCIATION
Founded: 1991 CR1001996
Feltham Community College, Browells Lane, Feltham, Middlesex TW13 7EF
Tel: 020 8831 3000
Objects: W3,W5,2

FERN STREET SETTLEMENT
Founded: 1907 CR250500
Fern Street, Bow, London E3 3PS
Tel: 020 7987 1949
Email: .... pat.burton@classmail.co.uk
Objects: F,W3,E,G,V,W4,3,P

FERNE ANIMAL SANCTUARY, CHARD
CR245671
Wambrook, Chard, Somerset TA20 3DH
Tel: 01460 65214
Email: .... info@ferneanimalsanctuary.org

FIELD - (FOUNDATION FOR INTERNATIONAL ENVIRONMENTAL LAW AND DEVELOPMENT)
Founded: 1990 CR802934
3 Endsleigh Street, London WC1H 0DD
Tel: 020 7388 2117
Email: .... field@field.org.uk
Objects: F,J,W2,G,W10,H,3,K

FIELD LANE
Founded: 1841 CR207493
2nd Floor, The Victoria Charity Centre, 11 Belgrave Road, London SW1V 1RB
Tel: 020 7748 0303
Email: .... info@fieldlane.org.uk
Objects: W3,E,D,N,W4,3,C

FIELD STUDIES COUNCIL (FSC)
CR313364
Head Office, Preston Montford, Montford Bridge, Shrewsbury, Shropshire SY4 1HW
Tel: 01743 852100
Email: .. fsc.headoffice@field-studies-council.org
Objects: G,2,3

FIELDS IN TRUST
Founded: 1925 CR306070
2nd Floor, 15 Crinan Street, London N1 9SQ
Tel: 0207 427 2110
Email: .... info@fieldsintrust.org
Objects: F,W3,J,W2,S,G,2,H,3,P

FIFE SOCIETY FOR THE BLIND
SC001354
Fife Sensory Impairment Centre, Wilson Avenue, Kirkcaldy, Fife KY2 5EF
Tel: 01592 644979
Email: .... info@fsbinsight.co.uk
Objects: W6,O,3,P

FIGHT FOR SIGHT
Founded: 1965 CR1111438
1st floor, 18 Mansell Street, London E1 8AA
Tel: 020 7264 3900
Email: .... info@fightforsight.org.uk
Objects: F,W6,M,W3,N,H

FINCHALE TRAINING COLLEGE FOR DISABLED PEOPLE
Founded: 1943 CR1001027
Finchale Training College, Durham, Co. Durham DH1 5RX
Tel: 0191 386 2634
Email: .... enquiries@finchalecollege.co.uk
Objects: F,W9,W5,G,W10,W11,W4,O,3,W8

FINCHLEY CHARITIES
CR206621
41a Wilmot Close, London N2 8HP
Tel: 020 8346 9464
Email: .... info@thefinchleycharities.org

THE FIRCROFT TRUST
Founded: 1967 CR802456
Fircroft, 96 Ditton Road, Surbiton, Surrey KT6 6RH
Tel: 020 8399 1772
Email: .... office@thefircrofttrust.org
Objects: F,E,W5,3,C

FIREPOWER - THE ROYAL ARTILLERY MUSEUM
Founded: 1778 CR803006
Royal Arsenal, Woolwich, London SE18 6ST
Tel: 020 8312 7102
Email: .... info@firepower.org.uk
Objects: S,G,W12

FISHERMEN'S MISSION - ROYAL NATIONAL MISSION TO DEEP SEA FISHERMEN
Founded: 1881 CR232822; SC039088
Mather House (CC), 4400 Parkway, Solent Business Park, Whiteley, Fareham, Hampshire PO15 7FJ
Tel: 01489 566926
Email: .... enquiries@rnmdsf.org.uk
Objects: F,M,W5,1A,R,W4,H,O,3,C

FISHMONGERS' AND POULTERERS' INSTITUTION
Founded: 1835 CR209013
Butchers' Hall, 87 Bartholomew Close, London EC1A 7EB

Tel: 020 7606 4106
Email: .... fpi@butchershall.com
Objects: W11,1A,A,B

FISHMONGERS' COMPANY'S CHARITABLE TRUST
Founded: 1972 CR263690
Fishmongers' Hall, London EC4R 9EL
Tel: 020 7626 3531
Objects: F,W9,M,W2,W5,G,A,1B,W16,N,R,B,O,Y,Z,W

FITZROY
Founded: 1962 CR1011290
FitzRoy House, 8 Hylton Road, Petersfield, Hampshire GU32 3JY
Tel: 01730 711111
Email: .... fundraising@fitzroy.org
Objects: F,M,E,W5,G,N,O,3,C,P

FLEDGELING CHARITY FUNDS, THE
Founded: 1992 CR1014756, 1014758
Finsbury Dials, 20 Finsbury Street, London EC2Y 9AQ
Tel: 020 7742 6000
Object: 3

FLEET AIR ARM MUSEUM
CR1143023
Box No D6, RNAS Yeovilton, Ilchester, Somerset BA22 8HT
Tel: 01935 840565
Email: .... info@fleetairarm.com

FLORENCE NIGHTINGALE HOSPICE - FLORENCE NIGHTINGALE HOSPICE CHARITY
Founded: 1989 CR802733
Unit 4, Aylesbury Business Centre, Chamberlain Road, Aylesbury, Buckinghamshire HP19 8DY
Tel: 01296 429975
Email: .... enquiries@fnhospice.org.uk

FLUENCY TRUST, THE
Founded: 1995 CR1044910
31 Harrow Close, Swindon, Wiltshire SN3 4QD
Tel: 01793 823986
Objects: F,W3,O,P

FOCUS
Founded: 1988 CR1068467
73 Churchgate, Leicester, Leicestershire LE1 3AN
Tel: 0116 251 0369
Email: .... admin@focus-charity.co.uk
Objects: W3,W5,G,3,P

FOCUS ON ISRAEL
CR803140
PO Box 3197, Leytonstone, London E11 1XT
Tel: 020 8556 3229
Email: .... mervyn.tilley@ntlworld.com

FOLKESTONE & DISTRICT MIND RESOURCE CENTRE
Founded: 1989 CR1089472
Folkestone MIND Resource Centre, 3 Mill Bay, Folkestone, Kent CT20 1JS
Tel: 01303 250090
Objects: F,E,W5,2,H,3,P

FOOTWEAR BENEVOLENT SOCIETY, THE (FOOTWEAR FRIENDS)
Founded: 1836 CR222117
5th Floor, 15-16 Margaret Street, London W1W 8RW
Tel: 020 7323 2362
Email: .... info@footwearfriends.org.uk
Objects: W11,1A,A

FORCES PENSION SOCIETY WIDOWS' FUND
Founded: 1972 CR264524
68 South Lambeth Road, Vauxhall, London SW8 1RL
Tel: 020 7820 9988
Objects: F,A,1B

FOREST OF CARDIFF
Founded: 1991 CR1002867
The Walled Garden, Old Coedarhydyglyn, St Nicholas, Cardiff CF5 6SG
Tel: 029 2059 9300
Objects: W2,G,3

FOREST YMCA
Founded: 1970 CR803442
642 Forest Road, Walthamstow, London E17 3EF
Tel: 020 8509 4600
Email: .... info@forestymca.org.uk
Objects: W3,W16,D,3,C,P

FOREVER HOUNDS TRUST
CR1131399
PO Box 4243, Radstock, Bath, Bath & North East Somerset BA3 3ZL
Tel: 07000 785092
Email: .... legacy@grwe.com

FORFARSHIRE SOCIETY FOR THE BLIND
Founded: 1869SC008915
76 High Street, Arbroath, Angus DD11 1AW
Tel: 01241 871215
Objects: F,W6,M,1A,A,3

FORTUNE CENTRE OF RIDING THERAPY
Founded: 1976 CR1045352
Avon Tyrrell, Bransgore, Christchurch, Dorset BH23 8EE
Tel: 01425 673297
Email: .... info@fortunecentre.org.uk
Objects: W3,G,O

THE FOSTERING NETWORK
Founded: 1974 CR280852
87 Blackfriars Road, London SE1 8HA
Tel: 020 7620 6400
Email: .... info@fostering.net
Objects: Q,F,W3,G,2,H,3

THE FOUNDATION FOR LIVER RESEARCH
Founded: 1973 CR1134579
111 Coldharbour Lane, London SE5 9NT
Tel: 020 7255 9830
Fax: 020 7380 0405
Email: .... n.day@researchinliver.org.uk
Web: .... www.liver-research.org.uk

The Foundation for Liver Research was established in 1973 to support research into disorders of the liver. Current research programmes are looking at the hepatitis viruses; severe infection in acute and chronic liver disease; development, diagnosis and treatment of liver cell cancer and the study of factors promoting liver recovery and regeneration. It is the Trustees intention to make the Institute of Hepatology a Centre of Excellence

in this country and to link it with other centres specialising in liver disease throughout the world. The Foundation depends entirely on voluntary donations and legacies.
For more details and discussion of collaborative/sponsorship opportunities, please contact: Professor Roger Williams, CBE, Director, at the address above or on r.williams@researchinliver.org.uk

FOUNDATION FOR THEOSOPHICAL STUDIES

Founded: 1992 CR1014648
Keymer Haslam and Co, 4/6 Church Road, Burgess Hill, West Sussex RH15 9AE
Tel: 01444 247871
Email: . . . inquiries@theosophical-society.org.uk

FOUNDATION FOR YOUNG MUSICIANS, THE

Founded: 1990 CR1000825
CYM, 61 Westminster Bridge Road, London SE1 7HT
Tel: 020 7928 3844
Email: . . . . info@fymlondon.co.uk
Objects: W3,S,G

FOUNDATION HOUSING

Founded: 1984 CR515517
Tennant Hall, Blenheim Grove, Leeds, West Yorkshire LS2 9ET
Tel: 0113 368 8800
Objects: F,W3,G,D,3,C,W8

FPA - FORMERLY THE FAMILY PLANNING ASSOCIATION

Founded: 1930 CR250187
23-28 Penn Street, London N1 5DL
Tel: 020 7608 5240
Email: . . . . membership@fpa.org.uk
Objects: F,G,2,H

FRAME (FUND FOR THE REPLACEMENT OF ANIMALS IN MEDICAL EXPERIMENTS)

Founded: 1969 CR259464
Russell & Burch House, 96-98 North Sherwood Street, Nottingham, Nottinghamshire NG1 4EE
Tel: 0115 958 4740
Email: . . . . frame@frame.org.uk
Object: W1

FRANCIS HOUSE CHILDREN'S HOSPICE (RAINBOW FAMILY TRUST), MANCHESTER

Founded: 1990 CR328659
390 Parrswood Road, East Didsbury, Manchester, Greater Manchester M20 5NA
Tel: 0161 434 4118
Email: . . . . sr.austin@francishouse.org.uk
Objects: W3,N,3

FRANCISCAN MISSIONARIES OF MARY

CR249515
5 Vaughan Avenue, London W6 0XS
Tel: 020 8748 4077
Email: . . . . provsecuk@aol.com

FREDERICK ANDREW CONVALESCENT TRUST

FACT

Founded: 1970 CR211029
Clerk to the Trustees: Mrs Karen Armitage
PO Box 1291, Lincoln, Lincolnshire LN55RA
Tel: 01522 705536
Fax: 01522 518911
Email: . . . . info@factonline.co.uk
Web: . . . . www.factonline.co.uk
Objects: 1A,A,1B,W8

Grants made to women towards the cost of medically recommended convalescence, HCPC registered therapy or help in the home after illness or injury. Further information and application forms from the above address.

See advert on previous page

FREE CHURCHES GROUP, THE

CR236878
27 Tavistock Square, London WC1H 9HH
Tel: 020 7529 8130
Email: . . . . freechurch@cte.org.uk
Objects: J,G,2,H

FREEDOM CENTRE - WORKING WITH PEOPLE WITH PHYSICAL DISABILITIES

CR1007683
c/o Freedom Centre, Blain Pritchard & Co, 29 High Street, Blue Town, Sheerness, Kent ME12 1RN
Tel: 01795 666233
Objects: W6,S,E,W7,W5,G,W10,W11,2,H,3,P,W8

FREEDOM FROM TORTURE (FORMERLY MEDICAL FOUNDATION FOR THE CARE OF VICTIMS OF TORTURE)

Founded: 1990 CR1000340
111 Isledon Road, London N7 7JW
Tel: 020 7697 7777
Email: . . . . info@freedomfromtorture.org
Objects: F,W3,G,N,U,O,3

FREEMASONS' GRAND CHARITY

CR281942
60 Great Queen Street, London WC2B 5AZ
Tel: 020 7395 9261
Email: . . . . info@the-grand-charity.org
Objects: W6,W3,W7,W5,1A,A,1B,2,W4,U

FRIENDS OF AFRICA FOUNDATION, THE

CR1079522
Oakhurst Court Nursing Home, Tilburstow Hill Road, South Godstone, Godstone, Surrey RH9 8JY
Tel: 01342 893555
Email: . . . . ukoffice@friendsofafrica.net
Objects: W3,1B,U,3

FRIENDS OF AMWELL VIEW SCHOOL, THE

Founded: 1990 CR803181
Amwell View School, Stanstead Abbotts, Ware, Hertfordshire SG12 8EH
Tel: 01920 870027
Objects: W3,G,1B,2

FRIENDS OF CANTERBURY CATHEDRAL

CR256575
8 The Precincts, Canterbury, Kent CT1 2EE
Tel: 01227 865292
Email: . . . . friends@canterbury-cathedral.org
Objects: S,A,V,2,W12,H,P

FRIENDS OF FRIENDLESS CHURCHES

Founded: 1957 CR1113097
St Ann's Vestry Hall, 2 Church Entry, London EC4V 5HB
Tel: 020 7236 3934
Email: office@friendsoffriendlesschurches.org.uk
Objects: W2,2,3

FRIENDS OF HARROGATE HOSPITAL AND COMMUNITY CHARITY

Friends of Harrogate Hospital & Community Charity

Founded: 1966 CR1050008
c/o General Office, Harrogate District Hospital, Lancaster Park Road, Harrogate, North Yorkshire HG2 7SX
Tel: 01423 501513
Web: . www.hdft.nhs.uk/hhcc/friends-of-hhcc/
Objects: N,O

The Friends exists to enhance the patient experience both in hospital and in the community. Money raised is used to purchase equipment that is currently unaffordable. Purchases have ranged from an MRI scanner to smaller items for use in the community and in the hospital.
Any legacy received will make a huge difference to our work.

FRIENDS OF MICHAEL SOBELL HOUSE

CR1079638
Mount Vernon Hospital, Rickmansworth Road, Northwood, Middlesex HA6 2RN
Tel: 01923 844906
Email: . . . . . . ccohen@michaelsobellhouse.co.uk
Objects: E,G,N,W4

FRIENDS OF THE CLERGY CORPORATION

CR264724
1 Dean Trench Street, London SW1P 3HB
Tel: 020 7799 3696
Email: . . . . enquiries@clergycharities.org.uk
Objects: W11,1A,Y

FRIENDS OF THE EARTH SCOTLAND

SC003442
Thorn House, 5 Rose Street, Edinburgh EH2 2PR
Tel: 0131 243 2700
Email: . . . . info@foe-scotland.org.uk
Objects: W2,2

FRIENDS OF THE ELDERLY

Founded: 1905 CR226064
40-42 Ebury Street, London SW1W 0LZ
Tel: 020 7730 8263
Email: . . . . enquiries@fote.org.uk
Objects: F,M,J,E,1A,A,N,W4,3,C

FRIENDS OF THE HOLY FATHER
CR280489
Culver Farn, Old Compton Lane, Farnham, Surrey GU9 8GJ
Tel: 01252 724924

FRIENDS OF THE ISRAEL CANCER ASSOCIATION
CR260710
c/o Berwin Leighton Paisner LLP, Adelaide House, London Bridge, London EC4R 9HA
Tel: 020 3400 1000
Email: . . . . jonathan.morris@blplaw.com
Objects: F,N

FRIENDS OF THE LAKE DISTRICT
Founded: 1934 CR1100759
Murley Moss Business Park, Oxenholme Road, Kendal, Cumbria LA9 7SS
Tel: 01539 720788
Email: . . . . info@fld.org.uk
Objects: F,J,W2,S,A,1B,2,H

FRIENDS OF THE PEAK DISTRICT
CR1094975
The Stables, 22a Endcliffe Crescent, Sheffield, South Yorkshire S10 3EF
Tel: 0114 266 5822
Email: . . . . info@friendsofthepeak.org.uk

FRIENDS OF THE UNITED INSTITUTIONS OF ARAD
Founded: 1992 CR1012222
5 Windus Road, London N16 6UT
Tel: 020 8880 8910

FRIENDS OF WESTMINSTER CATHEDRAL
CR272899
Clergy House, 42 Francis Street, London SW1P 1QW
Tel: 020 7798 9059
Email: . . . . friends@westminstercathedral.org.uk

FRIENDS' SCHOOL, SAFFRON WALDEN
Founded: 1990 CR1000981
Friends School, Mount Pleasant Road, Saffron Walden, Essex CB11 3EB
Tel: 01799 525351
Objects: W3,G,1A,B,3

FRONTIERS
Founded: 1992 CR1012566
PO Box 600, Hemel Hempstead, Hertfordshire HP3 9UG
Email: . . . . info@frontiers.org.uk
Objects: R,U,3

FULBRIGHT FOUNDATION, THE
Founded: 1990 CR328571
Fulbright House, 62 Doughty Street, London WC1N 2JZ
Tel: 020 7404 6880
Email: . . . . education@fulbright.co.uk
Objects: G,U

FULL EMPLOYMENT UK TRUST
Founded: 1990 CR328739
35 The Avenue, Richmond, Surrey TW9 2AL
Tel: 020 7348 5070

FUND FOR REFUGEES IN SLOVENIA, THE

Founded: 1992 CR1013193
19 Elmtree Green, Great Missenden, Buckinghamshire HP16 9AF
Tel: 0870 410 0088
Objects: W3,W5,G,1A,N,W4,U,T,3

G

THE G J & S LIVANOS CHARITABLE TRUST

Founded: 1991 CR1002279
Jeffrey Green Russell, Apollo House, 56 New Bond Street, London W1S 1RG
Tel: 020 7339 7000

GADS HILL SCHOOL

CR803153
Higham, Rochester, Kent ME3 7PA
Tel: 01474 822366
Objects: W3,W2,S,G,B

GALLOWAY'S SOCIETY FOR THE BLIND

Founded: 1867 CR526088
Howick House, Howick Park Avenue, Penwortham, Preston, Lancashire PR1 0LS
Tel: 01772 744148
Email: .... peter.taylor@galloways.org.uk
Objects: F,W6,M,G,A,V,2,O,3,C,P

GALTON INSTITUTE

Founded: 1907 CR209258
19 Northfields Prospect, Northfields, London SW18 1PE
Tel: 020 8874 7257
Email: .... betty.nixon@talk21.com
Objects: G,2,P

THE GAMBIA HORSE AND DONKEY TRUST

Founded: 2002 CR1096814
Ms Heather Armstrong
Brewery Arms Cottage (CD), Stane Street, Ockley, Surrey RH5 5TH
Tel: 01306 627568
Email: . ghdt@gambiahorseanddonkey.org.uk
Web: ... www.gambiahorseanddonkey.org.uk
We aim to reduce rural poverty by increasing the productivity of the working equines through the provision of training in management and welfare. We train harness makers, paravets, farmers groups and we teach in schools. We would like to provide the Gambian people with the knowledge and skills to deal with and even prevent the problems that we see.

We believe that learning should be fun and we encourage young boys who traditionally care for the donkeys to have fun and build a rapport with their donkeys through games and sport.
We provide basic veterinary treatment and have mobile clinics and hospital facilities at our centre and we run a bit exchange programme.

We believe that poverty is the cause of many of the animal welfare problems that we see so we are involved in community development projects which will increase the economic growth of the area.“

See advert on previous page

GAME & WILDLIFE CONSERVATION TRUST

CR279968
Burgate Manor, Fordingbridge, Hampshire SP6 1EF
Tel: 01425 652381
Email: .... admin@gwct.org.uk
Objects: W1,W2

THE GAME AND WILDLIFE CONSERVATION TRUST

Founded: 1992 CR1010814
Loddington House, Main Street, Loddington, Leicestershire LE7 9XE
Tel: 01572 717220
Email: .... aleake@gct.org.uk
Objects: F,W1,W2,2

THE GARDEN TOMB (JERUSALEM) ASSOCIATION

Founded: 1894 CR1004062
Maybury Copse, The Ridge, Woking, Surrey GU22 7EQ
Tel: 01483 763298
Email: .... mail@gardentomb.com
Objects: R,3

GARDENING FOR DISABLED TRUST

CR255066
The Freight, Cranbrook, Kent TN17 3PG
Tel: 01580 712196
Email: ... info@gardeningfordisabledtrust.org.uk
Objects: F,W5,A,H

GARDNER'S TRUST FOR THE BLIND

CR207233
117 Charterhouse Street, London EC1M 6PN
Tel: 020 7253 3757

GARNETHILL CENTRE LTD

SC002096
28 Rose Street, Glasgow G3 6RE
Tel: 0141 333 0730
Email: .... admin@garnethillcentre.org.uk

GATESHEAD CROSSROADS - CARING FOR CARERS

Founded: 1991 CR1059917
The Old School, Smailes Lane, Highfield, Rowlands Gill, Tyne & Wear NE39 2DB
Tel: ... 01207 549780; 0191 478 6284 (Minicom)
Email: .. enquiries@gatesheadcrossroads.org.uk
Objects: F,W6,M,W3,J,S,E,W7,W5,G,W10,R,W4, B,H,3,P,W8,K

GEFFRYE MUSEUM, LONDON

Founded: 1990 CR803052
Geffrye Museum, Kingsland Road, London E2 8EA
Tel: 020 7739 9893
Object: S

THE GENETIC ALLIANCE UK LTD

Founded: 1990 CR1114195
4D Leroy House, 436 Essex Road, London N1 3QP
Tel: 020 7704 3141
Email: .... mail@gig.org.uk
Objects: F,J,W5,N,2,O

GEOLOGICAL SOCIETY

CR210161
Burlington House, Piccadilly, London W1J 0BG

Tel: 020 7434 9944
Email: . . . . enquiries@geolsoc.org.uk
Object: 2

GERMAN WELFARE COUNCIL
CR288538
35 Craven Terrace, London W2 3EL
Tel: 020 7262 2463
Email: . . . . info@gwc-london.org.uk

GIDEONS INTERNATIONAL
Founded: 1949 CR221605
Western House, 24 George Street, Lutterworth, Leicestershire LE17 4EE
Tel: 01455 554241
Email: . . . . hq@gideons.org.uk
Object: R

GILEAD FOUNDATION
Founded: 1991 CR1002909
Risdon Farm, Jacobstowe, Inwardleigh, Okehampton, Devon EX20 3AJ
Tel: 01837 851240
Email: . . . . pr@gilead.org.uk
Objects: F,W3,G,W10,W11,1A,R,W4,T,O,P,W8,K

GINGERBREAD
CR230750
520 Highgate Studios, 53-79 Highgate Road, London NW5 1TL
Tel: . 020 7428 5400; 020 7428 5416 Press Office
Email: . . . . info@oneparentfamilies.org.uk
Objects: F,W3,W15,2,H,3,P,Z,W8

GIRLGUIDING
Founded: 1910 CR306016
17-19 Buckingham Palace Road, London SW1W 0PT
Tel: 020 7834 6242
Email: . . . . supporters@girlguiding.org.uk
Objects: W3,G,2,H,P,W8

GIRLS' BRIGADE NORTHERN IRELAND
XN48488
16 May Street, Belfast BT1 4NL
Tel: 028 9023 1157
Email: . . . . info@gbni.co.uk
Objects: F,W3,G,2,R,P

GLASGOW CHILDREN'S HOLIDAY SCHEME
Founded: 1955SC022654
Fifth Floor, 30 George Square, Glasgow G2 1EG
Tel: 0141 248 7255
Email: . admin@glasgowchildrensholidayscheme.org.uk
Objects: W3,V,P

GLASGOW EDUCATIONAL & MARSHALL TRUST
SC012582
21 Beaton Road, Glasgow G41 4NW
Tel: 0141 433 4449
Email: . . . . sloanea@hutchesons.org
Objects: W3,W11,A

GLOBAL CAST TRUST
Founded: 2000 CR1083094
21 Winsor Court, Rutherford Close, Borehamwood, Hertfordshire WD6 5RZ
Tel: 020 8207 5326

GLOBAL PARTNERS UK
CR1009755
Kingsgate House, High Street, Redhill, Surrey RH1 1SG
Tel: 01737 779040

GLOBE CENTRE, THE
Founded: 1991 CR1001582
159 Mile End Road, London E1 4AQ
Tel: 020 7791 2855
Email: . . . . info@theglobecentre.co.uk
Objects: F,E,W5,W10,O,3,P,K

GLOUCESTERSHIRE ANIMAL WELFARE ASSOCIATION AND CHELTENHAM ANIMAL SHELTER
CR1081019
Gardners Lane, Cheltenham, Gloucestershire GL51 9JW
Tel: 01242 523521
Email: . . . . fundraising@gawa.org.uk

GOAL UK
CR1107403
7 Hanson Street, London W1W 6TE
Tel: 020 7631 3196
Email: . . . . info@goal.ie

GOATS, BUTTERCUPS SANCTUARY
CR1099627
Wierton Hall, East Hall Hill, Boughton Monchelsea, Maidstone, Kent ME17 4JU
Tel: 01622 746410
Email: . . . . enquiries@buttercups.org.uk

GODINTON HOUSE PRESERVATION TRUST, THE
Founded: 1991 CR1002278
Estate Office, Godinton House, Godinton Lane, Ashford, Kent TN23 3BP
Tel: 01233 632652
Email: . . . . ghpt@godinton.fsnet.co.uk
Objects: S,G,3

GODOLPHIN SCHOOL, THE
Founded: 1726 CR309488
The Godolphin School, Milford Hill, Salisbury, Wiltshire SP1 2RA
Tel: 01722 430511
Email: . . . . . admissions@godolphin.wilts.sch.uk
Objects: W3,G,1A

GOFAL
Founded: 1990 CR1000889
2nd Floor, Derwen House, 2 Court Road, Bridgend CFR31 1BN
Tel: 01656 647722
Email: . . . . centraloffice@gofalcymru.org.uk
Objects: F,G,D,N,O,3,C

GOLF FOUNDATION - DEVELOPING JUNIOR GOLF
CR285917
Foundation House, The Spinney, Hoddesdon Road, Stanstead Abbotts, Ware, Hertfordshire SG12 8GF
Tel: 01920 876200
Email: . . . . admin@golf-foundation.org
Objects: W3,G,A,1B,H,3

THE GORILLA ORGANIZATION (FORMERLY THE DIAN FOSSEY GORILLA FUND)
CR1117131
110 Gloucester Avenue, London NW1 8HX

Tel: 020 7916 4974
Email: . . . . legacy@gorillas.org
Web: . . . . www.gorillas.org

Objects: W1,W2

The Gorilla Organization was established by the acclaimed conservationist Dr Dian Fossey in 1978 after poachers killed her favourite gorilla. Mountain Gorilla numbers had fallen to a perilous 260 and trade in infant gorillas was rife. Today there are still fewer than 900 mountain gorillas in existence – and they could disappear in this generation. Habitat loss, poaching, war and human disease are the main threats to gorilla survival. The Gorilla Organization is tackling these threats by working alongside local communities through community-based conservation, anti-poaching patrols and conservation education. Your support is vital to ensure that mountain gorillas survive into the next century and beyond.

GRACE & COMPASSION BENEDICTINES

Founded: 1954 CR1056064
38/39 Preston Park Avenue, Brighton, Brighton & Hove BN1 6HG
Tel: 01273 502129
Fax: 01273 552540
Email: . . . . osb@graceandcompassion.co.uk
Web: www.graceandcompassionbenedictines.org.uk

Founded in 1954 for the care of the old, sick and frail, we run care homes and retirement accommodation in the south of England. We also provide wide ranging services overseas, in India, Sri Lanka, Kenya and Uganda, where we work with the poor and sick of all ages, in care homes, hospital, village clinics, school of nursing, vocational training, farming, nursery and primary schools. There is so much to be done. Please support our work with a donation or a legacy.

GRACE WYNDHAM GOLDIE (BBC) TRUST FUND

Founded: 1950 CR212146
Administrator: Ms Cheryl Miles
BBC Pension and Benefits Centre, Ty Oldfield, BBC Broadcasting House, Llandaff, Cardiff CF5 2YQ
Tel: 029 2032 3772
Fax: 029 2032 2408
Web: www.bbc.co.uk/charityappeals/grant/gwg.shtml

Objects: G,1A,A

The Fund makes modest grants for education and specific short term unexpected needs to persons who have been engaged in broadcasting or any associated activity and to their children and dependants.

GRAFF FOUNDATION

Founded: 1992 CR1012859
c/o Kerman & Co Solicitors, 7 Savoy Court, London WC2R 0ER
Tel: 020 7539 7272

GRAHAM KIRKHAM FOUNDATION, THE

Founded: 1991 CR1002390
Bentley Moore Lane, Adwick Le Street, Doncaster, South Yorkshire DN6 7BD
Tel: 01302 330365

GRAND LODGE OF MARK MASTER MASONS FUND OF BENEVOLENCE

Founded: 1868 CR207610
Mark Masons Hall, 86 St James's Street, London SW1A 1PL
Tel: 020 7839 5274

Objects: 1A,A,1B,2

GRAND LODGE OF SCOTLAND

SC001996
Freemasons' Hall, 96 George Street, Edinburgh EH2 3DH
Tel: 0131 225 5577
Email: . . . . . . glhomes@grandlodgescotland.org

GRANGEWOOD EDUCATIONAL ASSOCIATION

Founded: 1990 CR803492
Grangewood School, Chester Road, Forest Gate, London E7 8QT
Tel: 020 8472 3552

Objects: G,3

GREAT NORTH AIR AMBULANCE SERVICE

Founded: 1991 CR1092204
Northumberland Wing, The Imperial Centre, Grange Road, Darlington, Co. Durham DL1 5NQ
Tel: 01325 487263
Email: . . . . . info@greatnorthairambulance.co.uk

Objects: N,3

GREAT ORMOND STREET HOSPITAL CHILDREN'S CHARITY

CR1160024
Great Ormond Street, London WC1N 3JH
Tel: 020 3841 3105
Email: . . . . legacy@gosh.org

Objects: W3,N

GREAT WESTERN AIR AMBULANCE CHARITY

CR1121300
County Gates, 3rd Floor, Ashton Road, Bristol BS3 2JH
Tel: 0303 4444 999
Email: . . . . info@greatwesternairambulance.com

Object: N

GREATER LONDON FUND FOR THE BLIND

Founded: 1921 CR1074958
Sir John Mills House, 11-12 Whitehorse Mews, 37 Westminster Bridge Road, London SE1 7QD
Tel: 020 7620 2066
Email: . . . . info@glfb.org.uk

Objects: W6,1B

GREATER NOTTINGHAM GROUNDWORK TRUST

Founded: 1991 CR1003426
Denman Street East, Nottingham, Nottinghamshire NG7 3GX
Tel: 0115 978 8212
Email: . . . . gn@groundwork.org.uk

Objects: F,W6,W3,J,W2,S,W7,W5,G,W10,A,1B,W4,H,3,P,W8,K

GREEK AND GREEK CYPRIOT COMMUNITY OF ENFIELD

CR1084004
Community House, 311 Fore Street, London N9 0PZ

Tel: 020 8373 6299; 020 8373 6251
Email: .... enquires@ggcce.org.uk
Objects: F,W6,M,W3,J,S,E,W7,W5,G,W10,W15, V,W16,D,W4,B,H,O,Y,C,P,Z,W8,I

GREEN SHOOTS FOUNDATION

CR1138412
57/59 Gloucester Place, London W1U 8JH
Tel: 020 7935 8128
Email: .... jm@greenshootsfoundation.org

GREENDOWN TRUST LIMITED

Founded: 1990 CR328465
Dyneley House, 10 Alerton Hill, Chapel Allerton, Leeds, West Yorkshire LS7 3QB
Tel: 0113 268 1812
Objects: W4,3,C

GREENFIELDS CENTRE LIMITED

Founded: 1990 CR702308
Greenfields, 139 Russell Road, Forest Fields, Nottingham, Nottinghamshire NG7 6GX
Tel: 0115 841 8440
Objects: W3,3,W8

GREENPEACE ENVIRONMENTAL TRUST

GREENPEACE

CR284934
Canonbury Villas (CC), London N1 2PN
Tel: 020 7865 8116
Email: .... info.uk@greenpeace.org
Web: .... www.greenpeace.org.uk/legacy
Objects: W2,G,1A,A,1B,2,H

The Trust complements the activities of Greenpeace by engaging in educational activities and funding scientific research and investigative projects into world ecology. Some of the research activities funded by the Trust were increasing the efficiency of solar cells, the regional effects of the Chernobyl disaster on health and the environment, the effects of toxic pollution on marine mammals such as whales, seals and dolphins and the link between health and contamination of the environment and the food chain. The Trust also produces educational leaflets for students. For further information about the activities of the Trust, or for a legacy leaflet, please write to the above address.

GREENSLEEVES HOMES TRUST

Founded: 1996 CR1060478
Unit 2, Regent Terrace, Rita Road, London SW8 1AW
Tel: 020 7793 1122
Email: .... headoffice@greensleeves.org.uk
Objects: M,N,W4,3

GREENWICH CRE

Founded: 1968 CR803231
1st Floor, 1-4 Beresford Square, Woolwich, London SE18 6BB
Tel: 020 8855 7191
Email: .... gcre@supranet.com
Objects: F,W10,2,W4,3

GREENWICH HOSPITAL

3 Creed Court, 5 Ludgate Hill, London EC4M 7AA
Tel: 020 7396 0150
Email: .... enquiries@grenhosp.org.uk
Objects: W9,W3,G,1A,A,1B,W4,B,C

GRENFELL ASSOCIATION OF GREAT BRITAIN AND IRELAND (GAGBI)

Founded: 1928 CR210040
Ormonde, D'urton Lane, Broughton, Preston, Lancashire PR3 5LE
Tel: 01772 862212
Objects: N,O,C

GREYHOUND RESCUE

CR702522
Crimea Cottage, Sutterton Drove, Amber Hill, Boston, Lincolnshire PE20 3RP
Tel: 01205 290145

GREYHOUND RESCUE WALES

CR1059733
Lawnswood, Sandy Lane, Parkmill, Swansea SA3 2EW
Tel: 0300 0123 999
Email: ...... info@greyhoundrescuewales.co.uk

GREYHOUNDS IN NEED

CR1069438
5 Greenways, Egham, Surrey TW20 9PA
Tel: 01784 436845
Email: .... info@greyhoundsinneed.co.uk

GRIMSBY AND CLEETHORPES AREA DOORSTEP

Founded: 1990 CR702881
115 Pasture Street, Grimsby, North East Lincolnshire DN32 9EE
Tel: 01472 321444
Objects: F,W3,E,G,D,3,C

GROCERYAID

Founded: 1964 CR1095897; SC039255
2 Lakeside Business Park, Swan Lane, Sandhurst, Slough GU47 9DN
Tel: 01252 875925
Email: .... info@groceryaid.org.uk
Objects: F,W11,1A,A,W4,B,3

GROUND LEVEL MINISTRY TEAM

Founded: 1991 CR1001599
24 Newland, Lincoln, Lincolnshire LN1 1XD
Tel: 01522 533535
Email: .... admin@groundlevel.org.uk
Objects: J,G,1A,A,1B,R,O

GROUNDWORK BLACK COUNTRY

Founded: 1989 CR702917
The Groundwork Environment Centre, Dolton Way, Tipton, West Midlands DY4 9AL
Tel: 0121 530 5500
Email: .... bc@groundwork.org.uk
Objects: W3,W2,G,W10,3,P,K

GROUNDWORK LEICESTER & LEICESTERSHIRE LTD

Founded: 1990 CR703009
Parkfield, Western Park, Hinkley Road, Leicester, Leicestershire LE3 6HX
Tel: 0116 222 0222
Email: .... info@gwll.org.uk
Objects: F,W1,W3,J,W2,G,1B,H,3,K

GROUNDWORK NORTH WALES

CR1004132
3-4 Plas Power Road, Tanyfron, Wrexham LL11 5SZ
Tel: 01978 757524
Email: .... wx@groundwork.org.uk

GROUNDWORK NORTHERN IRELAND
63-75 Duncairn Gardens, Belfast BT15 2GB
Tel: 028 9074 9494
Email: .... info@groundworkni.co.uk

GROUNDWORK UK
Founded: 1985 CR291558
Lockside, 5 Scotland Street, Birmingham, West Midlands B1 2RR
Tel: 0121 236 8565
Email: .... info@groundwork.org.uk
Objects: W3,J,W2,G,3

GROVE HOUSE
Founded: 1991 CR1003462
St Albans and Dacorum Day Hospice, 4 Broadfields, Harpenden, Hertfordshire AL5 2HJ
Tel: 01582 621303
Objects: F,M,E,G,N,W4,O,3,P,W8

GRUBB INSTITUTE
Founded: 1969 CR890637
The Grubb Institute, Cloudesley Street, London N1 0HU
Tel: 020 7278 8061
Email: .... info@grubb.org.uk
Objects: F,W3,G,3

THE GUIDE DOGS FOR THE BLIND ASSOCIATION
Founded: 1934 CR209617; SC038979
Hillfields (C1), Reading Road, Burghfield Common, Reading RG7 3YG
Tel: 0800 953 0113
Fax: 0118 983 6326
Email: .... giftsinwills@guidedogs.org.uk
Web: ... http://www.guidedogs.org.uk/giftsinwills
Objects: W1,W6

Did you know it costs Guide Dogs around £50,000 to support a guide dog from birth to retirement?
That's why we rely on the generosity of people who leave us a gift in their Will. It all adds up to make a big difference for people who are blind and partially sighted.

GUIDEPOSTS TRUST
CR272619
Two Rivers Industrial Estate, Station Lane, Witney, Oxfordshire OX28 4BH
Tel: 01993 772886
Email: .... gpt@guidepoststrust.org.uk
Objects: M,E,W5,N,W4,3,P,K

GUILD OF AID FOR GENTLEPEOPLE
Founded: 1904FS 31BEN
10 St Christopher's Place, London W1U 1HZ
Tel: 020 7935 0641
Email: .... thead@pcac.org.uk
Objects: J,1A,A,W4

GUILD OF BENEVOLENCE OF THE INSTITUTE OF MARINE ENGINEERING, SCIENCE & TECHNOLOGY
Founded: 1934 CR208727
1 Birdcage Walk, London SW1H 9JJ
Tel: 020 7382 2600
Email: .... guild@imarest.org
Objects: W9,W11,1A,A,3

GUILDHALL STRING ENSEMBLE CONCERTS TRUST, THE
Founded: 1990 CR1001256
13 West End, Whittlesford, Cambridge, Cambridgeshire CB2 4LX
Tel: 01223 839744
Object: S

GUILDHE LIMITED
Founded: 1992 CR1012218
Woburn House, 20 Tavistock Square, London WC1H 9HB
Tel: 020 7387 7711
Email: .... info@guildhe.ac.uk
Objects: G,2

GUILLAIN-BARRE SYNDROME SUPPORT GROUP
Founded: 1985 CR327314
Lincs County Council Offices, Eastgate, Sleaford, Lincolnshire NG34 7EB
Tel: 01529 304615
Email: .... admin@gbs.org.uk
Objects: F,W5,G,H

GURNEY FUND FOR POLICE ORPHANS
Founded: 1890 CR261319
9 Bath Road, Worthing, West Sussex BN11 3NU
Tel: 01903 237256
Objects: W3,G,1A,A

THE GYDE CHARITY
Founded: 1909 CR311529
14 Green Close, Uley, Dursley, Gloucestershire GL11 5TH
Tel: 01453 860378
Email: .... info@thegydecharity.org
Objects: W3,A,1B

H

A H WHITELEY AND B C WHITELEY CHARITY
Founded: 1991 CR1002220
Regent Chambers, 2A Regent Street, Mansfield, Nottinghamshire NG18 1SW
Tel: 01623 655111

HABERDASHERS' ASKE'S HATCHAM COLLEGE
Founded: 1991 CR1001489
Pepys Road, New Cross, London SE14 5SF
Tel: 020 7652 9500

HABITAT FOR HUMANITY GREAT BRITAIN
CR1043641
10 The Grove, Slough SL1 1QP
Tel: 01753 313 539
Email: .... enquiries@habitatforhumanity.org
Objects: W3,G,W10,W16,D,U,Y,3,W8

HABITAT FOR HUMANITY NORTHERN IRELAND
Unit 29, Enterprise Park, 638 Springfield Road, Belfast BT12 7DY

Tel: 028 9024 3686
Email: ....

info@habitatni.co.uk

HACT – THE HOUSING ACTION CHARITY
Founded: 1960 CR1096829
78 Quaker Street, London E1 6SW
Tel: 020 7247 7800
Email: .... hact@hact.org.uk
Objects: F,W5,W10,A,1B,D,W4,H,C,W8

HAEMOPHILIA SOCIETY
Founded: 1950 CR288260
Willcox House, 140-148 Borough High street, London SE1 1LB
Email: .... info@haemophilia.org.uk
Objects: F,W3,J,W5,1A,A,1B,2,W4,H,3,W8

HAIL WESTON VILLAGE HALL
CR1097874
Manor Farm House, Ford End, Hail Weston, St Neots, Cambridgeshire PE19 5JR
Tel: 01480 211693

THE HAIRDRESSERS CHARITY - PREVIOUSLY KNOWN AS THE HAIR AND BEAUTY BENEVOLENT (HABB)
Founded: 1853 CR1166298
1st Floor, 9 Cheam Road, Ewell, Surrey KT17 1SP
Tel: 01737 212494
Email: .... info@thehairdresserscharity.org
Web: .... www.thehairdresserscharity.org/
Objects: 1A,2

We provide direct assistance to hairdressers or persons connected with the hairdressing and beauty industries, in times of hardship due to ill-health, disability or old age. One-off help or small pensions can be granted, dependant upon need. The past few years have seen a marked increase in the number of calls on our limited funds. Many fundraising events are organised each year, but as a small charity, we actively seek donations, Deeds of Covenant and legacies, which are very gratefully received.

HALLAM COMMUNITY PHYSIOTHERAPY PROJECT, THE
Founded: 1990 CR702486
24 Stumperlowe View, Sheffield, South Yorkshire S10 3QU
Tel: 0114 230 5044

HALLIWICK ASSOCIATION OF SWIMMING THERAPY
Founded: 1952 CR250008
c/o ADKC Centre, Whitstable House, Silchester Road, London W10 6SB
Tel: 01727 825 524
Email: ...... patrick.hastings@btopenworld.com
Objects: W6,M,J,W7,W5,G,H,O,3,P

HALT (HELP, ADVICE, & THE LAW TEAM) DOMESTIC VIOLENCE
CR1087583
PO Box 332, Leeds, West Yorkshire LS1 3RD
Tel: .... 0113 244 2578 Admin
Email: .... info@halt.org.uk

HAMELIN TRUST
Founded: 1991 CR1004432
19 Radford Crescent, Billericay, Essex CM12 0DP
Tel: 01277 653889
Email: .... legacy@hamelintrust.org.uk
Objects: M,W3,E,W5,V,2,3,C,P,K

HAMILTON TRUST
Founded: 1991 CR1004205
1a Howard Street, Oxford, Oxfordshire OX4 3AY
Tel: 01865 253980
Email: .... info@hamilton-trust.org.uk
Objects: W3,G

HAMLET CENTRE TRUST, THE
Founded: 1972 CR1000653
The Hamlet Centre (CD), Ella Road, Norwich, Norfolk NR1 4BP
Tel: 01603 616094
Email: .... admin@hamletcentre.org.uk
Objects: W3,S,E,W5,G,3,P

HAMPSHIRE & ISLE OF WIGHT MILITARY AID FUND (1903)
Founded: 1903 CR202363
Serles House, Southgate Street, Winchester, Hampshire SO23 9EG
Tel: 01962 852933
Email: .... hantsandiowmaf@dsl.pipex.com
Objects: W9,1A,A,3

HAMPSTEAD HEATH
Founded: 1990 CR803392
Corporation of London, PO Box 270, Guildhall, London EC2P 2EJ
Tel: 020 7332 1334

HANDICAP INTERNATIONAL UK
CR1082565
27 Broadwall, London SE1 9PL
Tel: 0870 774 3737
Email: .... hi-uk@hi-uk.org

HANDICAPPED AID TRUST
Founded: 1981 CR284791
Windmill House,
Church Road, Lytham St Anne's, Lancashire FY8 5LH
Tel: 01253 796441
Email: .... hazel.preston@pmms-group.com
Objects: W5,1A,A,1B,V

HANDS ROCHESTER VOLUNTEER CENTRE
CR284288
5a New Road Avenue, Chatham, Kent ME4 6BB
Tel: 01634 830371
Email: .... rochestervb@pcihosting.co.uk

HANDSWORTH COMMUNITY CARE CENTRE
Founded: 1991 CR1002669
63 Heathfield Road, Handsworth, Birmingham, West Midlands B19 1HE
Tel: 0121 554 4755

HAPPY DAYS CHILDREN'S CHARITY
Founded: 1992 CR1010943
3rd Floor, Clody House, 90-100 Collingdon Street, Luton, Bedfordshire LU1 1RX
Tel: 01582 755999
Email: .... enquiries@happydayscharity.org
Objects: W3,S,W5,G,1A,A,1B,V,3,P

HARBOUR, THE (FORMERLY RED ADMIRAL PROJECT - BRISTOL)
Founded: 1992 CR1008360
30 Frogmore Street, Bristol BS1 5NA
Tel: 0117 925 9348
Email: .... info@the-harbour.co.uk
Objects: F,W5,W4,3,W8

HARINGEY IRISH CULTURAL AND COMMUNITY CENTRE
Founded: 1987 CR1003015
Haringey Irish Centre, Pretoria Road, Tottenham, London N17 8DX
Tel: 020 8885 3490
Objects: F,E,W10,W4,P

HARNHILL CENTRE OF CHRISTIAN HEALING
CR292173
Harnhill Manor, Harnhill, Cirencester, Gloucestershire GL7 5PX
Tel: 01285 850283
Email: .... office@harnhillcentre.org.uk
Objects: F,W5,R,W4,3,W8

HARRIS HOSPISCARE WITH ST CHRISTOPHER'S
Founded: 1984 CR1003903
Caritas House, Tregony Road, Orpington, Kent BR6 9XA
Tel: 01689 825755
Email: .... info@harrishospiscare.org.uk

HARROW SCHOOL OF GYMNASTICS
Founded: 1991 CR1002258
186 Christchurch Avenue, Harrow, Middlesex HA3 5BD
Tel: 020 8427 5611
Objects: W3,G,3

HASTINGS VOLUNTARY ACTION
Founded: 1990 CR802632
31A Priory Street, Hastings, East Sussex TN34 1EA
Tel: 01424 444010
Email: .. infoworker@hastingsvoluntaryaction.org

HATCH CAMPHILL COMMUNITY
CR307104
The Office, The Hatch Camphill Community, Chestnut, Castle Street, Thornbury, South Gloucestershire BS35 1HG
Tel: 01454 413010
Email: .... hatchcamphill@aol.com
Objects: E,W5,D,3,C,P

HAVERING CITIZENS ADVICE BUREAU
Founded: 1991 CR1002593
719 Victoria Road, Romford, Essex RM1 2JT
Tel: 01708 735325
Email: .... advice@haveringcab.org.uk
Objects: F,3

HAWK CONSERVANCY TRUST
CR1092349
Visitor Centre, Sarson Lane, Weyhill, Andover, Hampshire SP11 8DY
Tel: 01264 773850
Email: .... info@hawkconservancy.org
Objects: W1,W2,G,O,3

HAYWARD HOUSE CANCER CARE TRUST
Founded: 1992 CR1014356
Hayward House, Nottingham University Hospitals, City Campus, Hucknall Road, Nottingham, Nottinghamshire NG5 1PB
Tel: 0115 962 7996
Objects: M,N

HCPT - THE PILGRIMAGE TRUST
Founded: 1956 CR281074
Oakfield Park, 32 Bilton Road, Rugby, Warwickshire CV22 7HQ
Tel: 01788 564646
Email: .... hq@hcpt.org.uk
Objects: W6,W3,W7,W5,V

HEADWAY THAMES VALLEY LIMITED
Founded: 1990 CR900591
Townlands Hospital, York Road, Henley-on-Thames, Oxfordshire RG9 2EB
Tel: 01491 411469; 01491 636108
Email: .... hwthamesvalley@aol.com
Objects: F,J,E,W5,V,2,R,H,O,3,P

HEADWAY - THE BRAIN INJURY ASSOCIATION
Founded: 1979 CR1025852
190 Bagnall Road, Old Basford, Nottingham, Nottinghamshire NG3 8SF
Tel: .... 0115 924 0800; 0808 800 2244 Helpline
Email: .... enquiries@headway.org.uk
Objects: F,J,E,W5,G,2,H,O,3,P

HEALTH POVERTY ACTION
Founded: 1984 CR290535
Ground Floor, 31-33 Bondway, London SW8 1SJ
Tel: 020 7840 3777
Email: .... general@healthunlimited.org
Objects: W3,G,W10,N,R,U

HEALTHCARE FINANCIAL MANAGEMENT ASSOCIATION
Founded: 1952 CR1114463; SC041994
Suite 32, Albert House, 111-7 Victoria Street, Bristol BS1 6AX
Tel: 0117 929 4789
Email: .... info@hfma.org.uk
Objects: G,2,H

HEALTHLINK WORLDWIDE
Founded: 1977 CR274260
Development House, 56-64 Leonard Street, London EC2A 4LT
Tel: 020 7549 0240
Email: .... info@healthlink.org.uk
Objects: F,W3,W5,G,U,H,W8,K

HEALTHPROM
Founded: 1984 CR1100459
Star House, 104-108 Grafton Road, London NW5 4BD
Tel: 020 7284 1620
Email: .... healthprom@healthprom.org
Objects: F,W3,J,G,2,W4,U,3,W8

HEARING DOGS FOR DEAF PEOPLE (HEAD OFFICE)
Founded: 1985 CR293358; SC040486
The Grange, Wycombe Road, Saunderton, Princes Risborough, Buckinghamshire HP27 9NS
Tel: 01844 348100
Email: .... info@hearing-dogs.co.uk
Objects: W1,W3,W7

HEARING LINK
Founded: 1972 CR264809; SC037688
27-28 The Waterfront, Eastbourne, East Sussex BN23 5UZ
Tel: 01323 638230 Voice; 01323 739998 Minicom
Email: .... info@linkdp.org
Objects: F,M,J,W7,W5,G,W4,H,O,3,P

HEART OF ENGLAND CARE

Founded: 1991 CR1002167
Bridge House Annex, Paper Mill End, 509 Aldridge Road, Great Barr, Birmingham, West Midlands B44 8NA
Tel: 0121 331 4722
Email: .... enquiries@heartofenglandcare.org.uk
Objects: N,W4,O,3,P

HEARTSWELL SOUTH WEST

CR1092779
HeartSWell Lodge, 7 Blunts Lane, Derriford, Plymouth, Devon PL6 8BE
Tel: 01752 315929
Email: .... info@heartswell.org.uk
Objects: F,M,W15,N,W4,W8

HELP FOR HEROES

CR1120920
14 Parker's Close, Downton Business Centre, Downton, Salisbury, Wiltshire SP5 3RB
Tel: 01725 513212
Email: .... info@helpforheroes.org.uk
Objects: W9,1B,O

HELP MUSICIANS UK

Founded: 1921 CR228089
7-11 Britannia Street, London WC1X 9JS
Tel: 020 7239 9100
Email: .... info@helpmusicians.org.uk

HELP THE HOMELESS

Founded: 1975 CR271988
6th Floor, 248 Tottenham Court Road, London W1T 7QZ
Tel: 020 7323 7411
Email: .... hth@help-the-homeless.org.uk
Objects: A,1B,D,C

HELPING THE POOR AND NEEDY

CR1121950
1 Matthews Lane, Manchester, Greater Manchester M12 4QW
Tel: 0161 225 2307
Email: .... enquiries@hpan.org.uk

THE HENRY MOORE FOUNDATION

Founded: 1977 CR271370
Dane Tree House, Perry Green, Much Hadham, Hertfordshire SG10 6EE
Tel: 01279 843333
Email: .... admin@henry-moore-fdn.co.uk
Objects: G,A,1B,H

HENSHAWS SOCIETY FOR BLIND PEOPLE

Founded: 1837 CR221888
Fundraising (CC), Atherton House, 88-92 Talbot Road, Old Trafford, Manchester, Greater Manchester M16 0GS
Tel: 01423 814385
Email: .... info@henshaws.org.uk
Objects: F,W6,M,G,A,V,D,N,O,3,C,K

HEREFORDSHIRE ASSOCIATION FOR THE BLIND

CR220171
36 Widemarsh Street, Hereford, Herefordshire HR4 9EP
Tel: 01432 352297

HEREFORDSHIRE LIFESTYLES

Founded: 1991 CR1003132
41a Millbrook Street, Hereford, Herefordshire HR4 9LF
Tel: 01432 277968
Email: ...... mainoffice@lifestyles.demon.co.uk
Objects: M,W5,2,3,P

HEREWARD COLLEGE FOR THE PHYSICALLY AND SENSORY DISABLED, COVENTRY

Bramston Cresent, Tile Hill Lane, Coventry, West Midlands CV4 9SW
Tel: 024 7646 1231
Email: .... enquiries@hereward.ac.uk

HERITAGE LINCOLNSHIRE

Founded: 1991 CR1001463
The Old School, Cameron Street, Heckington, Sleaford, Lincolnshire NG34 9RW
Tel: 01529 461499
Email: .... info@lincsheritage.org

HERPES VIRUSES ASSOCIATION

Founded: 1985 CR291657
41 North Road, Islington, London N7 9DP
Tel: .. 020 7607 9661 & Minicom; 0845 123 2305 Helpline
Objects: F,W9,W6,W3,W7,W5,W10,W11,N,2,W4, H,W8

HERTFORDSHIRE CONVALESCENT TRUST

Founded: 1876 CR212423
140 North Road, Hertford, Hertfordshire SG14 2BZ
Tel: 01992 505886
Objects: F,W9,W6,W3,W7,W5,W10,W11,1A,A,V, W4,W8

HESTIA HOUSING AND SUPPORT

CR294555
Maya House, 134-138 Borough High Street, London SE1 1LB
Email: .... info@hestia.org

HFT

Founded: 1962 CR313069
5/6 Brook Office Park, Folly Brook Road, Emersons Green, Bristol BS16 7FL
Tel: 0117 906 1700
Email: .... info@hft.org.uk
Objects: F,M,J,E,W5,G,V,D,2,H,O,3,C,P,K

HIGH BLOOD PRESSURE FOUNDATION

Founded: 1990SC022286
Dept. of Medical Sciences, Western General Hospital, Edinburgh EH4 2XU
Tel: 0131 332 9211
Email: .... hbpf@hbpf.org.uk
Objects: F,G,N,3

HIGHSCOPE GB

Founded: 1991
Anerley Business Centre, Anerley Road, London SE20 8BD
Tel: 0870 777 7680; 0870 777 7681
Email: .... highscope@btconnect.com
Objects: W3,G,3

HOME-START BANBURY & CHIPPING NORTON

CR114860
Britannia Road Childrens Centre, Grove Street, Banbury, Oxfordshire OX16 5DN
Tel: 01295 266358
Email: .... info@home-startbanbury.org.uk
Objects: W3,3,W8

REALL (FORMERLY HOMELESS INTERNATIONAL)

CR1017255; SC041976
Queen's House, 16 Queen's Road, Coventry, West Midlands CV1 3EG
Tel: 024 7663 2802
Email: .... info@reall.xyz
Objects: D,2,U

HOMELESS OUTREACH PROJECT

SC029897
1a Grindlay Street Court, Edinburgh EH3 9AR
Tel: 0131 554 3961
Email: .... mail@hopuk.org
Objects: F,D,W8

HONOURABLE SOCIETY OF GRAY'S INN TRUST FUND

Founded: 1992 CR1014798
8 South Square, Gray's Inn, London WC1R 5EU
Tel: 020 7458 7800
Objects: G,2,3

HOPE AND HOMES FOR CHILDREN

CR1089490
East Clyffe, Salisbury, Wiltshire SP3 4LZ
Tel: 01722 790111
Email: .... info@hopeandhomes.org
Object: W3

HOPE FOR CHILDREN

CR1041258
22 Ben Sayers Park, North Berwick, East Lothian EH39 5PT
Tel: 0844 779 9774
Email: .... mw@hope4c.org

HOPE HOUSE CHILDREN'S HOSPICES

Founded: 1991 CR1003859
Nant Lane, Morda, Oswestry, Shropshire SY10 9BX
Tel: 01691 671671
Email: .... appeals@hopehouse.org.uk
Objects: F,W3,J,W5,N,3

HOPE ROMANIA

CR1011626
Birch Lodge, 52 Cossington Road, Canterbury, Kent CT1 3HU
Tel: 01227 462200
Email: .... pbaxter@hoperomania.co.uk

HOPE UK (DRUG EDUCATION) (FORMERLY THE BAND OF HOPE)

Founded: 1855 CR1044475
25(f) Copperfield Street, London SE1 0EN
Tel: 020 7928 0848
Email: .... a.wilson@hopeuk.org
Objects: W3,G,H,3

THE HORDER CENTRE

Founded: 1954 CR1046624
St John's Road, Crowborough, East Sussex TN6 1XP
Tel: 01892 665577
Email: .... info@hordercentre.co.uk
Objects: M,W5,G,N,W4,O,3

HORNIMAN MUSEUM AND GARDENS

CR802725
100 London Road, Forest Hill, London SE23 3PQ
Tel: 020 8699 1872
Email: .... fundraising@horniman.ac.uk
Objects: S,3

HORSES AND PONIES PROTECTION ASSOCIATION

CR1085211
Taylor Building, Shores Hey Farm, Halifax Road, Briercliffe, Burnley, Lancashire BB10 3QU
Tel: 01282 455992
Email: .... enquiries@happa.org.uk

HORSEWORLD TRUST (FRIENDS OF BRISTOL HORSES SOCIETY)

CR1121920
Delmar Hall, Keynes Farm, Staunton Lane, Whitchurch, Bristol BS14 0QL
Tel: 01275 893021
Email: .... info@horseworld.org.uk

HOSPICE AT HOME WEST CUMBRIA

CR1086837
Workington Community Hospital, Park Lane, Workington, Cumbria CA14 2RW
Tel: ... 01900 705200; 01900 873173 (Finance & Fundraising)
Email: . info@hospiceathomewestcumbria.org.uk
Objects: F,E,N,3

HOSPICE OF ST. FRANCIS (BERKHAMSTED) LTD

Founded: 1979 CR280825
Spring Garden Lane, Off Shooters Way, Northchurch, Berkhamsted, Hertfordshire HP4 3GW
Tel: 01442 869550
Email: .... admin@stfrancis.org.uk
Objects: F,E,W5,G,N,W4,O,3

HOSPICE OF THE GOOD SHEPHERD (CHESHIRE)

CR515516
49 Woodland Road, Ellesmere Port, Cheshire CH65 6PW
Email: .... info@hospicegs.com

HOSPICE UK

Founded: 1984 CR1014851; SC041112
Individual Giving & Legacy Executive: Ms Clare Young
Hospice House, 34-44 Britannia Street, London WC1X 9JG
Tel: 020 7520 8200
Fax: 020 7278 1021
Email: .... fundraising@hospiceuk.org
Web: .... www.hospiceuk.org
Objects: W3,N,W4

Everyone, no matter who they, where they are or why they're ill, should receive the best care at the end of their life.

Hospice UK is the national charity for hospice care. Hospice care transforms lives. It is with you through life, through death and through grief.

At Hospice UK we champion and support the work of more than 200 member hospices, which provide hospice care across the UK, so that they can deliver the highest quality of care to people with terminal or life limiting conditions, and support their families.

Hospice care is provided free to patients, and with limited government funding, hospices across the country depend on the support of their local communities to help them continue their services. A gift in your will, however large or small, will make sure that we can continue supporting hospice care throughout the UK, so it is there for everyone who needs it, now and for generations to come.

HOSPITAL SATURDAY FUND CHARITABLE TRUST
Founded: 1873 CR1123381
24 Upper Ground, London SE1 9PD
Tel: 020 7202 1365
Email: . . . . charity@hsf.co.uk
Objects: 1A,A,1B,N,O

HOSPITALITY ACTION
Founded: 1837 CR208855
62 Britton Street, London EC1M 5UY
Tel: 0870 351 0160
Email: . . . . info@hospitalityaction.org.uk
Objects: F,G,W11,1A,Y,3,P

HOUSING 21
Founded: 1964 CR1015049
The Triangle, Baring Road, Beaconsfield, Buckinghamshire HP9 2NA
Tel: 01494 685200
Objects: M,D,W4,3,C

HOUSING FOR WOMEN
Founded: 1933 CR211351
6th Floor, Blue Star House, 234-244 Stockwell Road, London SW9 9SP
Tel: 020 7501 6120
Email: . . . . info@h4w.co.uk
Objects: D,3,C,W8

HOUSING JUSTICE
Founded: 1956 CR294666
22-25 Finsbury Square, London EC2A 1DX
Tel: 020 7920 6600
Email: . . . . info@housingjustice.org.uk
Objects: F,W9,G,W10,D,2,W4,H,W8

HOUSING RIGHTS SERVICE
XN48275
4th Floor, Middleton Buildings, 10-12 High Street, Belfast BT1 2BA
Tel: 028 9024 5640
Email: . . . . hrs@housingrights.org.uk

HUGGENS' COLLEGE
Founded: 1844 CR210336
20 Sallows Shaw, Sole Street, Cobham, Gravesend, Kent DA13 9BS
Tel: 01474 814587
Email: . . . . secretary@huggenscollege.org
Objects: W4,3,C

HUGO LONDON
Founded: 1992 CR1008230
20 Church Lane, Cheddington, Leighton Buzzard, Bedfordshire LU7 0RU
Tel: 020 7935 8085

HUMAN APPEAL INTERNATIONAL
Founded: 1991 CR1005733
Victoria Court, 376 Wilslow Road, Manchester, Greater Manchester M14 6AX
Tel: 0161 225 0225

HUMAN VALUES FOUNDATION (HVF)
Founded: 1995 CR1048755
The Coach House (CD), Salisbury Road, Horsham, West Sussex RH13 0AJ
Tel: 01403 259711
Email: . . . . yes2values@hvf.org.uk
Objects: F,W3,J,G,H,T,O,3,P

THE HUMANE RESEARCH TRUST
Founded: 1974 CR267779
Brook House, 29 Bramhall Lane South, Bramhall, Stockport, Greater Manchester SK7 2DN
Tel: 0161 439 8041
Email: . . . . info@humaneresearch.org.uk
Objects: W1,W3,G,1A,W4,W8,W

HUMANE SLAUGHTER ASSOCIATION
Founded: 1911 CR1159690
The Old School, Brewhouse Hill, Wheathampstead, Hertfordshire AL4 8AN
Tel: 01582 831919
Email: . . . . info@hsa.org.uk
Objects: F,W1,G,1A,A,1B,2,H

HUNTINGDONSHIRE COMMUNITY CHURCH
Founded: 1990 CR803355
83A High Street, Huntingdon, Cambridgeshire PE29 3DP
Tel: 01480 411665
Objects: W3,W5,R,W4,3

HUNTINGDONSHIRE SOCIETY FOR THE BLIND
Founded: 1927 CR202573
8 St Mary's Street, Huntingdon, Cambridgeshire PE29 3PE
Tel: 01480 453438
Email: . . . . huntsblind@btconnect.com
Objects: F,W6,M,J,V,2,O,3,P

HYDE PARK APPEAL
Founded: 1991 CR1005326
35 Sloane Gardens, London SW1W 8EB
Tel: 07767 498096
Email: . . . . info@hydeparkappeal.org
Objects: W5,W4,3

HYELM
Founded: 1926 CR215575
79 Fitzjohn's Avenue, Hampstead, London NW3 6PA
Tel: 020 7435 8793
Objects: W3,C

HYPERACTIVE CHILDREN'S SUPPORT GROUP - FOR HYPERACTIVE/ALLERGIC/ ADHD CHILDREN
CR277643
71 Whyke Lane, Chichester, West Sussex PO19 7PD
Tel: 01243 539966
Email: . . . . hyperactive@hacsg.org.uk
Objects: F,W3,2,3

I

I CAN - HELPS CHILDREN COMMUNICATE
Founded: 1888 CR210031
8 Wakley Street, London EC1V 7QE

Tel: 0845 225 4071
Email: . . . . ican@ican.org.uk
Objects: W3,G,H,3

IBERO-AMERICAN BENEVOLENT SOCIETY

Founded: 1889FS27BEN
108 Cannon Street, London EC4N 6EU
Tel: 020 7623 3060
Objects: 1A,A

ICHTHUS COMMUNITY PROJECTS LIMITED

Founded: 1990 CR1000655
7 Greenwich Quay, Clarence Road, Greenwich, London SE8 3EY
Tel: 020 8694 7171
Objects: F,W3,G,U,3

ICSA BENEVOLENT FUND

Founded: 1897 CR1152784
ICSA, Saffron House, 6-10 Kirby Street, London EC1N 8TS
Tel: 020 7612 7048
Email: . . . . icsacharities@icsaglobal.com
Objects: W3,W11,1A,A,2,W4

IMPACT FOUNDATION

Founded: 1985 CR290992
151 Western Road, Haywards Heath, West Sussex RH16 3LH
Tel: 01444 457080
Email: . . . . impact@impact.org.uk
Objects: W6,W3,W7,W5,G,1B,N,U,3

IN-VOLVE

Founded: 1987 CR803244
Abbey House, 361 Barking Road, Plaistow, London E13 8EE
Tel: 020 7474 2222
Email: . . . . headoffice@in-volve.org.uk
Objects: F,W3,E,G,W10,O,3,W8

INCLUDE

Founded: 1990 CR803333
c/o The Centre for British Teachers, 60 Queens Road, Reading RG1 4BS
Tel: 0118 902 1000; 0118 902 1404
Objects: W3,J,G,3

INCORPORATED BENEVOLENT FUND OF THE INSTITUTION OF GAS ENGINEERS AND MANAGERS

Founded: 1863 CR214010
Charnwood Wing, Holywell Park, Ashby Road, Loughborough, Leicestershire LE11 3GH
Tel: 01509 282728
Email: . . . . general@igem.org.uk
Objects: M,1A,A,V,N,2,C

INDEPENDENT AGE

Founded: 1863 CR210729
18 Avonmore Road (CC), London W14 8RR
Tel: 020 7605 4200
Email: . . . . legacies@independentage.org
Objects: F,M,A,V,W4,H,P

INDEPENDENT DIABETES TRUST

Founded: 1984 CR1058284
PO Box 294, Northampton, Northamptonshire NN1 4XS
Tel: 01604 622837
Fax: 01604 622838
Email: . . . . enquiries@iddtinternational.org
Web: . . . . www.iddtinternational.org
Objects: F,W3,N,W4,W
The InDependent Diabetes Trust offers FREE support and information to people with diabetes, their families and health professionals on the issues that are important to them.
See advert on previous page

INDEPENDENT HEALTHCARE FORUM

CR296103
Centre Point, 103 New Oxford Street, London WC1A 1DU
Tel: 020 7379 7721
Email: . . . . info@ihf.org.uk
Objects: F,W9,W6,W3,J,W7,W5,G,W11,N,2,W4,H,O,3,W8

INDIVIDUAL CARE SERVICES

Founded: 1992 CR1008195
Kingfisher Court, The Oaks, Clews Road, Redditch, Worcestershire B98 7ST
Tel: 01527 546000

INSTITUTE FOR EUROPEAN ENVIRONMENTAL POLICY, LONDON

Founded: 1990 CR802956
15 Queen Anne's Gate, London SW1H 9BU
Tel: 020 7799 2244
Email: . . . . central@ieep.eu
Objects: F,W2,H,3

INSTITUTE FOR OPTIMUM NUTRITION

CR1013084
Avalon House, 72 Lower Mortlake Road, Richmond, Surrey TW9 2JY
Tel: 020 8614 7804
Email: . . . . reception@ion.ac.uk
Objects: F,W3,G,2,W4,H,O,3,W8

INSTITUTE OF AGRICULTURAL MANAGEMENT, THE

Founded: 1990 CR802635
Farm Management Unit, University of Reading, PO Box 236, Reading RG6 6AT
Tel: 01275 843825
Email: . . . . iagrm@reading.ac.uk
Objects: W2,G,2,B,H

THE INSTITUTE OF CANCER RESEARCH

Exempt
Dept CD 2009, 123 Old Brompton Road, London SW7 3RP
Tel: 0800 731 9468
Email: . . . . legacy@icr.ac.uk
Object: N

INSTITUTE OF CREDIT MANAGEMENT

Founded: 1939 CR1012200
The Water Mill, Station Road, South Luffenham, Oakham, Leicestershire LE15 8NB

Tel: 01780 722900
Email: .... info@icm.org.uk
Objects: F,J,G,2,H

INSTITUTE OF DIRECT MARKETING, THE
Founded: 1991 CR1001865
1 Park Road, Teddington, Middlesex TW11 0AR
Tel: 020 8977 5705
Objects: G,H

INSTITUTE OF HEALTHCARE MANAGEMENT BENEVOLENT FUND
Founded: 1913 CR208225
18-21 Morley Street, London SE1 7QZ
Tel: 01474 853014; 020 7460 7654
Email: .... ihmfund@stoneham.org
Objects: F,G,W11,1A,A,2

INSTITUTE OF NEUROLOGY
The National Hospital, Queen Square, London WC1N 3BG
Tel: .... 020 7837 3611 ext. 4137
Objects: W5,N,W4,O,3

INSTITUTION OF CIVIL ENGINEERS' BENEVOLENT FUND
Founded: 1864 CR1126595
30 Mill Hill Close, Haywards Heath, West Sussex RH16 1NY
Tel: 01444 417979
Email: .... benfund@ice.org.uk
Objects: F,J,1A,A,D

INSTITUTION OF ENGINEERING AND TECHNOLOGY
Founded: 1871 CR211014; SC038698
Michael Faraday House, Six Hills Way, Stevenage, Hertfordshire SG1 2AY
Tel: 01438 313311
Email: .... postmaster@theiet.org
Objects: J,G,1A,A,2,H,W8

INSTITUTION OF STRUCTURAL ENGINEERS BENEVOLENT FUND
CR1049171
11 Upper Belgrave Street, London SW1X 8BH
Tel: 020 7235 4535
Email: .... benfund@istructe.org
Objects: W11,1A,A,2

INSURANCE CHARITIES, THE
CR206860
20 Aldermanbury, London EC2V 7HY
Tel: 020 7606 3763
Email: .... info@theinsurancecharities.org.uk
Objects: F,1A,A,V,3

INTEGRATION TRUST LIMITED, THE
Founded: 1991 CR1003124
Howcans, Front Street, Esh, Durham, Co. Durham DH7 9QS
Tel: 0191 373 3804

INTER-ACTION TRUST
Founded: 1968 CR257281
HMS President (1918), Near Blackfriars Bridge, Victoria Embankment, London EC4Y 0HJ
Tel: 020 7515 4449
Email: .... inter.action@btconnect.com
Objects: F,W3,W2,S,W5,G,W10,W4,H,3,P,W8,K

INTERCHANGE STUDIOS
Founded: 1975 CR267043
Hampstead Town, Hall Centre, 213 Haverstock Hill, London NW3 4QP
Tel: 020 7692 5808
Email: .... bookings@interchange.org.uk

INTERCONTINENTAL CHURCH SOCIETY (FORMERLY KNOWN AS COLONIAL AND CONTINENTAL CHURCH SOCIETY)
Founded: 1823 CR1072584
Unit 11 Ensign Business Centre, Westwood Way, Westwood Business Park, Coventry, West Midlands CV4 8JA
Tel: 024 7646 3940
Email: .... enquiries@ics-uk.org
Objects: 2,R,3

INTERCOUNTRY ADOPTION CENTRE
CR1067313
64-66 High Street, Barnet, Hertfordshire EN5 5SJ
Tel: 020 8449 2562
Email: .... info@icacentre.org.uk
Objects: Q,F,H

INTERNATIONAL ANIMAL RESCUE

International
Animal Rescue
internationalanimalrescue.org

CR1118277
Lime House, Regency Close, Uckfield, East Sussex TN22 1DS
Tel: 01825 767688
Fax: 01825 768012
Email: info@internationalanimalrescue.org
Web: . www.internationalanimalrescue.org
Objects: W1,W2

At International Animal Rescue (IAR) we do exactly what our name says: we save animals from suffering around the world.
In Borneo, our Orangutan Conservation Project rescues orphaned and displaced orangutans. We rehabilitate them at our Orangutan Rescue Centre, with the aim of releasing as many as possible back into protected areas of wild rainforest. We are working on holistic solutions to protect habitat from destruction and improving the welfare of the inhabitants.
Our clinics in India sterilise and vaccinate stray dogs and cats to regulate their numbers and protect them from diseases. The vets also treat snakes, monkeys and other wildlife, as well as sacred cows that roam the streets and beaches. When a disaster strikes like the Asian tsunami, our rescue teams rush to the aid of its victims.
IAR's sanctuaries in India are home to hundreds of dancing bears that we have rescued from the streets. The bears are nursed back to health and live free from fear and pain in a safe, semi-natural forest environment. At the end of 2009 IAR and our partners made animal welfare history by rescuing the last dancing bear in India and ending this cruel practice forever.
At our bird hospital in Malta we rescue and rehabilitate migrating birds that have been shot by hunters. We also campaign for better legislation to protect wild and domestic animals across the EU.
We cannot continue this work without your help. Please consider becoming a regular supporter to help us save an animal's life today, or pledge a lasting legacy that will provide sanctuary for suffering animals in future.
See advert on next page

INTERNATIONAL ASSOCIATION FOR RELIGIOUS FREEDOM (IARF)
CR1026699
Upper Chapel, Norfolk Street, Sheffield, South Yorkshire S1 2JD
Tel: 0114 276 7114
Email: .... hq@iarf.net
Objects: J,G,2

INTERNATIONAL CEREBRAL PALSY SOCIETY
CR273102
78 Romulus Court, 1 Justin Close, Brentford, Middlesex TW8 8QJ
Tel: 020 8568 0709
Email: .... anita.loring@mac.com

INTERNATIONAL CHINA CONCERN
Founded: 1990 CR1068349
PO BOX 20, Morpeth, Northumberland NE61 3YP
Tel: 01670 505622; 07799 413095
Email: .... uk@intlchinaconcern.org
Objects: W3,W5,G,U,O,3

INTERNATIONAL CHRISTIAN COLLEGE
SC028032
70 Cathedral Street, Glasgow G4 0RD
Tel: 0141 552 4040
Email: .... college@icc.ac.uk

INTERNATIONAL CONNECTIONS TRUST
Founded: 1992 CR1113099
93 Acre Lane, Brixton, London SW2 5TU
Tel: 020 7924 9700
Email: .... connuk@gol.com
Objects: 1A,1B,R,U,3

INTERNATIONAL FOOD INFORMATION SERVICE
Founded: 1968 CR1068176
Lane End House, Shinfield Road, Shinfield, Reading RG2 9BB
Tel: 0118 988 3895
Email: .... ifis@ifis.org
Objects: G,H,3

INTERNATIONAL FUND FOR CAT WELFARE FELINE ADVISORY BUREAU
Founded: 1958 CR1117342
Taeselbury, High Street, Tisbury, Wiltshire SP3 6LD
Tel: 01747 871872
Email: .... info@icatcare.org
Objects: F,W1,G,2,B,H

INTERNATIONAL GLAUCOMA ASSOCIATION
Founded: 1974 CR274681; SC041550
Woodcote House, 15 Highpoint Business Village, Henwood, Ashford, Kent TN24 8DH
Tel: 01233 648170
Email: .... info@iga.org.uk
Objects: W6,G,W4,H

INTERNATIONAL NEPAL FELLOWSHIP
CR1047178
The Cottage, 22 Weoley Park Road, Selly Oak, Birmingham, West Midlands B29 6QU
Tel: 0121 472 2425
Email: .... ukoffice@inf.org.uk
Objects: G,N,R

INTERNATIONAL ORGAN FESTIVAL SOCIETY LTD, THE
Founded: 1991 CR1006151
Spinney Corner, Green Lane, Apsley Guise, Milton Keynes MK17 8EN
Object: S

INTERNATIONAL RECORDS MANAGEMENT TRUST, THE
Founded: 1991 CR1068975
4th Floor, 7 Hatton Garden, London EC1N 8AD
Tel: 020 7831 4101
Email: .... info@irmt.org
Objects: S,G,U,H,3,K

INTERNATIONAL SOCIAL SERVICE OF THE UNITED KINGDOM
Founded: 1955 CR1085541
3rd Floor, Cranmer House, 39 Brixton Road, London SW9 6DD
Tel: 020 7735 8941
Email: .... issuk@charity.vfree.com
Objects: Q,F,W3,J,W4,U,3

INTERNATIONAL STUDENTS HOUSE TRUST
CR294448
1 Park Crescent, Regents Park, London W1B 1SH
Tel: 020 7631 8300
Email: .... info@ish.org.uk

INTERNATIONAL WATER ASSOCIATION
CR289269
Alliance House, 12 Caxton Street, London SW1H 0QS
Tel: 020 7654 5500
Email: .... water@iwahq.org.uk
Objects: J,2

INTERNATIONAL WHEELCHAIR & AMPUTEE SPORTS FEDERATION (IWAS)
Founded: 1992 CR1011552
IWAS Secretariat, Olympic Village, Guttmann Road, Aylesbury, Buckinghamshire HP21 9PP
Tel: 01296 436179
Email: .... info@iwasf.com
Objects: W3,J,W5,G,2,U,K

INTRAC (INTERNATIONAL NGO TRAINING & RESEARCH CENTRE)
CR1016676
Oxbridge Court, Osney Mead, Oxford, Oxfordshire OX2 0ES
Tel: 01865 201851
Email: .... info@intrac.org
Objects: U,H

IPA TRUST, THE
Founded: 1991 CR1071752
International Psychoanalytical Assn, Registered Office, Bromhills, Woodside Lane, London N12 8UD
Tel: 020 7380 7896

IRIE! DANCE THEATRE
Founded: 1985 CR1003947
The Moonshot Centre, Fordham Park, Angus Street, New Cross, London SE14 6LY
Tel: 020 8691 6099
Email: .... info@iriedancetheatre.org
Objects: W3,S,G,W10,W4,3,W8,K

IRONBRIDGE (TELFORD) HERITAGE FOUNDATION LIMITED, THE
Founded: 1990 CR1001039
14 The Square, Broad Street, Edgbaston, Birmingham, West Midlands B15 1AS
Tel: 0121 603 9000

ISIS
Founded: 1989 CR1059698
183-185 Rushey Green, Catford, London SE6 4BD
Tel: 020 8695 1955
Objects: F,J,S,E,W5,G,W10,O,3,P,K

ISLE OF ANGLESEY CHARITABLE TRUST, THE
Founded: 1990 CR1000818
Isle of Anglesey Charitable Trust, County Offices, Llangefni, Anglesey LL77 7TW
Objects: A,1B

ISLE OF WIGHT DONKEY SANCTUARY
Founded: 1990 CR1001061
Lower Winstone Farm (Dept. CD), Wroxall, Isle of Wight PO38 3AA
Tel: 01983 852693
Email: . . . . info@iwdonkey-sanctuary.com
Objects: W1,G,3

ISLINGTON MIND
CR294535
Unit 4, Archway Business Centre, Wedmore Street, London N19 4RU
Tel: 020 3301 9850
Email: . . . . admin@islingtonmind.org.uk

J

JAMES CLERK MAXWELL FOUNDATION (INTERNATIONAL STUDY CENTRE AND MUSEUM)
SC015003
14 India Street, Edinburgh EH3 6EZ
Tel: 0131 343 1036
Email: . . . . . admin@clerkmaxwellfoundation.org

JAMI MOSQUE AND ISLAMIC CENTRE (BIRMINGHAM) TRUSTEES LIMITED
Founded: 1975 CR1000355
Jami Masjid and Islamic Centre, 521 Coventry Road, Small Heath, Birmingham, West Midlands B10 0LL
Tel: 0121 772 6408
Objects: F,W6,W3,J,S,W7,W5,G,W10,2,R,W4,H,T,O,3,P,W8,K

JAPAN ANIMAL WELFARE SOCIETY
Founded: 1966 CR244534
Lyell House, 51 Greencoat Place, London SW1P 1DS
Tel: 020 7630 5563
Email: . . . . jawsuk@jawsuk.org.uk
Objects: W1,1A,2

JDRF
CR295716; SC040123
19 Angel Gate, City Road, London EC1V 2PT
Tel: 020 7713 2030
Email: . . . . info@jdrf.org.uk
Objects: W3,W

JEAN SAINSBURY ANIMAL WELFARE TRUST
Founded: 1982 CR326358
PO Box 50793, London NW6 9DE
Objects: W1,1B,2

JEELY PIECE CLUB RESOURCE CENTRE (INCORPORATING PLAY IT SAFE)
SC035027
The Tower, 55 Machrie Drive, Castlemilk, Glasgow G45 0AL
Tel: 0141 634 7305
Email: . . . michelleclelland@jeelypiececlub.org.uk

JERRY GREEN DOG RESCUE
CR1155042
Broughton, Brigg, Lincolnshire DN20 0BJ
Tel: 01652 657820
Email: . . . . . . fundraising@jerrygreendogs.org.uk
Objects: Q,F,W1,2,3

JERUSALEM AND THE MIDDLE EAST CHURCH ASSOCIATION
Founded: 1888 CR248799
1 Hart House, The Hart, Farnham, Surrey GU9 7HJ
Tel: 01252 726994
Email: . . . . secretary@jmeca.eclipse.co.uk
Objects: W6,W3,W7,W5,G,W10,W15,1A,A,1B,N,R,W4,U,Y,W8

JESMOND SWIMMING PROJECT
Founded: 1992 CR1010563
Jesmond Swimming Pool, St Georges Terrace, Jesmond, Newcastle upon Tyne, Tyne & Wear NE2 2DL
Tel: 0191 281 2482
Objects: W3,S,W7,W5,G,W10,W4,O,P,W8

JESSE MARY CHAMBERS ALMSHOUSES
Founded: 1924 CR1001479
21 Rodney Road, Cheltenham, Gloucestershire GL50 1HX
Tel: 01242 522180
Objects: W4,3,C

JESUIT MISSIONS
CR230165
11 Edge Hill, London SW19 4LR
Tel: 020 8946 0466
Email: . . . . director@jesuitmissions.org.uk
Objects: R,U,3

JEWISH AID COMMITTEE
CR801096
Carradine House, 237 Regents Park Road, London N3 3LF
Tel: 020 8343 4156
Email: . . . . admin@one-to-one.org
Objects: M,E,W5,G,W10,1A,A,1B,N,W4,U,O,P,W8

JEWISH CARE
CR802559
Merit House, 508 Edgware Road, The Hyde, Colindale, London NW9 5AB
Tel: 020 8922 2000
Email: . . . . info@jcare.org
Objects: F,W6,M,J,S,E,W5,N,W4,H,O,3,C,P,K

JEWISH CARE SCOTLAND
SC005267
The Walton Community Care Centre, May Terrace, Giffnock, Glasgow G46 6LD

Tel: 0141 620 1800
Email: .... admin@jcarescot.org.uk

JEWISH MARRIAGE COUNCIL

Founded: 1946 CR1078723
23 Ravenshurst Avenue, London NW4 4EE
Tel: 020 8203 6311
Email: .... info@jmc-uk.org
Objects: F,G,W10,3,P

JEWISH MUSIC INSTITUTE

Founded: 1989 CR328228
PO Box 232, Harrow, Middlesex HA1 2NN
Tel: 020 8909 2445
Email: .... jewishmusic@jmi.org.uk
Objects: F,W6,W3,J,S,W7,W5,G,W10,1A,W4,H,T, W8,K

JEWS FOR JESUS TRUST

Founded: 1991 CR1110425
106-110 Kentish Town Road, London NW1 9PX
Tel: 020 7431 9636
Email: ...... pbquestions@jews-for-jesus.org.uk
Object: R

JNF CHARITABLE TRUST (JEWISH NATIONAL FUND FOR ISRAEL, KKL EXECUTOR & TRUSTEE CO. LTD)

Founded: 1901 CR225910
JNF House, Spring Villa Park, Edgware, Middlesex HA8 7ED
Tel: 020 8732 6100
Email: .... info@jnf.co.uk
Objects: W2,S,G,U,H

THE JOE HOMAN CHARITY

Founded: 1991 CR1006060
PO Box 54, Peterborough, Cambridgeshire PE4 6JP
Tel: 01733 574886
Objects: W3,U

JOHN INNES CENTRE

CR223852
Norwich Research Park, Colney, Norwich, Norfolk NR4 7UH
Tel: 01603 450000
Email: .... sce.mail@bbsrc.ac.uk
Objects: G,3

JOHN MUIR TRUST

SC002061
Tower House, Station Road, Pitlochry, Perth & Kinross PH16 5AN
Tel: 0131 554 0114
Email: .... adam.pinder@jmt.org
Objects: W2,G

JOINT COMMITTEE OF THE ORDER OF ST. JOHN & THE BRITISH RED CROSS SOCIETY

Founded: 1920 CR225753
5th Floor, 22-26 Albert Embankment, London SE1 7TJ
Tel: 020 7735 9800
Email: balwinder@jointcommittee.freeserve.co.uk
Objects: W9,A,1B

JOINT EDUCATIONAL TRUST

CR313218
6-8 Fenchurch Buildings, London EC3M 5HT
Tel: 020 3217 1100
Email: .... admin@jetcharity.org
Objects: W3,G,1A,A

JOLT

Founded: 1983 CR1088591
34 Whitehall Road, Harrow-on-the-Hill, Harrow, Middlesex HA1 3AJ
Tel: 020 8426 6686
Objects: W3,V,3

JOURNALISTS' CHARITY

Founded: 1864 CR208215
Dickens House, 35 Wathen Road, Dorking, Surrey RH4 1JY
Tel: 01306 887511
Email: ...... enquiries@journalistscharity.org.uk
Objects: W11,1A,A,2,C

JUBILEE ACTION

Founded: 1992 CR1013587
Carroll House, 11 Quarry Street, Guildford, Surrey GU1 3UY
Tel: 01483 230250
Email: .... info@jubileeaction.co.uk
Objects: W3,E,W10,A,1B,D,U,O,P,W8

JUBILEE DEBT CAMPAIGN

Founded: 1996 CR1055675
The Grayston Centre, 28 Charles Square, London N1 6HT
Tel: 020 7324 4722
Email: .... info@jubileedebtcampaign.org.uk
Objects: W3,J,W2,G,2,W4,H,W8

JUSTICE

CR1058580
59 Carter Lane, London EC4V 5AQ
Tel: 020 7329 5100
Email: .... admin@justice.org.uk
Objects: F,W6,W3,W7,W5,G,W10,2,W4,H,W8

K

KATHARINE HOUSE HOSPICE (STAFFORD)

CR1011712
Weston Road, Stafford, Staffordshire ST16 3SB
Tel: 01785 254645
Email: .... info@khhospice.org.uk
Objects: E,N,3

KELLY HOLDSWORTH ARTILLERY TRUST

Founded: 1914 CR208359
Artillery House, Artillery Centre, Larkhill, Salisbury, Wiltshire SP4 8QT
Tel: 01980 845698
Email: . artycen-rhqra-racf-race-gensec@mod.uk
Objects: F,W9,J,G,1A,A,B,P

KENT ASSOCIATION FOR THE BLIND

CR1062354
72 College Road, Maidstone, Kent ME15 6SJ
Tel: 01622 691357
Email: ..... amanda.croft-pearman@kab.org.uk

KENT COMMUNITY HOUSING TRUST

Founded: 1991 CR1002727
Bridgewood House, Rochester Airport Industrial Estate, 8 Laker Road, Rochester, Kent ME1 3QX
Tel: 01634 869880
Email: .... debbie.pert@kcht.org.uk
Objects: F,M,W3,E,W5,G,A,D,W4,O,3,C,P,K

KENT COUNTY AGRICULTURAL SOCIETY
CR1001191
County Showground, Detling, Maidstone, Kent ME14 3JF
Tel: 01622 630975
Email: . . . . info@kentshowground.co.uk
Objects: W1,W2,1A,1B,B

THE KENT, SURREY & SUSSEX AIR AMBULANCE
Founded: 1993 CR1021367
Head Office: Wheelbarrow Park Estate, Pattenden Lane, Marden, Kent TN12 9QJ
Tel: 01622 833833
Email: . . . . info@kssairambulance.org.uk
Objects: N,3

KENT WILDLIFE TRUST
Founded: 1958 CR239992
Tyland Barn, Sandling, Maidstone, Kent ME14 3BD
Tel: 01622 662012
Email: . . . . info@kentwildlife.org.uk
Objects: W1,W2,G,2,P

KENTISBEARE COMMUNITY HALL FUND
Founded: 1990 CR1052482
Quenton House, Cullompton, Devon EX15 1PB
Tel: 01884 798342

KENWARD TRUST
CR265394
Kenward House, Kenward Road, Yalding, Maidstone, Kent ME18 6AH
Tel: 01622 814187
Email: . . . . enquiry@kenwardtrust.org.uk

KEYCHANGE CHARITY
Founded: 1920 CR1061344
5 St George's Mews, 43 Westminster Bridge Road, London SE1 7JB
Tel: 020 7633 0533
Email: . . . . info@keychange.org.uk
Objects: W15,D,W4,H,C,W8

KEYRING-LIVING SUPPORT NETWORKS
Founded: 1990 CR1054234
1st Floor Impact Centre, 12-18 Hoxton Street, London N1 6NG
Tel: 020 7749 9411
Objects: W5,D,3

KIDASHA
CR1106156
55 East Road, London N1 6AH
Tel: 020 7017 8989
Email: . . . . enquiries@kidasha.org
Objects: W3,G,N,3

KIDNEY RESEARCH UK (FORMERLY THE NATIONAL KIDNEY RESEARCH FUND)
CR252892; SC039245
Nene Hall, Lynch Wood Park, Peterborough, Cambridgeshire PE2 6FZ
Tel: . . 01733 704656; 0845 300 1499 Helpline for Patients and Carers
Email: . . . . enquiries@nkrf.org.uk

KIDNEY WALES FOUNDATION
CR700396
2 Radnor Court, 256 Cowbridge Road East, Cardiff CF5 1GZ
Tel: 029 2034 3940
Email: . . . . chris@kidneywales.com

KIDS
Founded: 1970 CR275936
7-9 Elliott's Place (CC), London N1 8HX
Tel: 020 7359 3635
Email: . . . . enquiries@kids.org.uk
Objects: F,M,W3,J,W5,G,3,P

KIDS KIDNEY RESEARCH
CR266630
10 Beechwood, Southwater, Horsham, West Sussex RH13 9JU
Tel: 01403 732291
Email: . . . . paul@kidskidneyresearch.org
Web: . . . . www.kidskidneyresearch.org
Object: W3

Each year a significant number of babies are born with serious abnormalities of their kidneys, which may result in total failure of kidney function, needing dialysis treatment and/or a kidney transplant. Treatments on offer allow varying extension of life. However there is no cure.

Please help us to find ways of eradicating disease of the kidney and bladder. We support the vital research at the Institute of Child Health, which works in conjunction with Great Ormond Street Hospital renal unit. We also fund renal projects nationwide under the guidance of the British Association for Paediatric Nephrology. We are a member of the Association of Medical Research Charities.

KING EDWARD'S SCHOOL WITLEY
Founded: 1553 CR273208
Witley, Godalming, Surrey GU8 5SG
Tel: 01428 686735
Email: . . . . admissions@kesw.surrey.sch.uk
Objects: W3,G,3

KING EDWARD VII'S HOSPITAL SISTER AGNES
Founded: 1899 CR208944
Beaumont Street, London W1G 6AA
Tel: 020 7467 3920
Email: . . . . fundraising@kingedwardvii.com
Objects: W9,W6,W7,W5,1A,A,N,W4,3,W8

KING'S FUND (KING EDWARD'S HOSPITAL FUND FOR LONDON)
Founded: 1897 CR207401
11-13 Cavendish Square, London W1G 0AN
Tel: 020 7307 2400
Objects: F,G,A,1B,2,H

KINGS CROSS-BRUNSWICK NEIGHBOURHOOD
CR1083901
Marchmont Community Centre, 62 Marchmont Street, London WC1N 1AB
Tel: 020 7278 5635
Email: . . . . kcbna@aol.com
Objects: F,W3,W10,W4,3

KINGSTON CHURCHES ACTION ON HOMELESSNESS
CR1075890
36a Fife Road, Kingston upon Thames, Surrey KT1 1SU
Tel: 020 8255 7400; 020 8255 2439
Email: . . . . kcah@dial.pipex.com
Objects: F,D,3

KINLOCH BEQUEST
Founded: 1818 CR210067
37 King Street, Covent Garden, London WC2E 8JS
Tel: 020 7240 3718
Email: ..... info@royalscottishcorporation.org.uk
Object: B

KIRSTIN ROYLE TRUST
Founded: 1995 CR1048717
6/8 Valleyfield Street, Edinburgh EH3 9LS
Email: .... kirstinroyletrust@hotmail.com
Objects: W6,W3,W7,W5,W10,1A,A,1B,O,P,W8

KRASZNA-KRAUSZ FOUNDATION
CR326601
3 Downs Court Road, Purley, Surrey CR8 1BE
Tel: 020 7435 1831
Email: .... info@kraszna-krausz.org.uk
Objects: 1A,A,1B

L

LA PROVIDENCE
Founded: 1718 CR219318
The French Hospital, 41 La Providence, Rochester, Kent ME1 1NB
Tel: 01634 843107
Email: .... theclerk@lineone.net
Objects: 1A,W4,C

LAKELANDS DAY CARE HOSPICE, CORBY
CR1062120
Lakelands, Butland Road, Oakley Vale, Corby, Northamptonshire NN18 8LX
Tel: 01536 747755
Objects: F,E,W5,G,N,O,3,P

LAMBETH ELFRIDA RATHBONE SOCIETY (RATHBONE)
CR1096727
8 Chatsworth Way, West Norwood, London SE27 9HR
Tel: 020 8670 4039
Email: ...... a.preston@rathbonesociety.org.uk
Objects: W3,W5,Z

LANCEFIELD CENTRE, THE
Founded: 1990 CR803214
20a Lancefield Street, London W10 4PB
Tel: 020 8960 6006
Email: .... lancefieldcent@aol.com

THE LANDMARK TRUST
Founded: 1965 CR243312
Shottesbrooke, Maidenhead, Windsor & Maidenhead SL6 3SW
Tel: 01628 825920
Email: .... info@landmarktrust.org.uk
Objects: W2,V,3

LANDSCAPE DESIGN TRUST
CR288510
Bank Chambers, 1 London Road, Redhill, Surrey RH1 1LY
Tel: 01737 779257
Email: .... info@landscape.co.uk
Objects: W2,G,H,3

LANDSCAPE RESEARCH GROUP
CR287160
4 Gwyns Piece, Lambourn, Hungerford, West Berkshire RG17 8YZ
Email: .... admin@landscaperesearch.org

THE LANGFORD TRUST FOR ANIMAL HEALTH AND WELFARE
Founded: 1990 CR900380
School of Veterinary Science, Langford House, Langford, North Somerset BS40 5DU
Tel: 0117 928 9207
Email: .... langford-trust@bristol.ac.uk
Objects: W1,G

THE LANGLEY HOUSE TRUST
CR290059
PO Box 181, Witney, Oxfordshire OX28 6WD
Tel: 01993 774075
Email: .... info@langleyhousetrust.org
Objects: O,3,C

L'ARCHE
Founded: 1972 CR264166
10 Briggate, Silsden, Keighley, West Yorkshire BD20 9JT
Tel: 01535 656186
Email: .... info@larche.org.uk
Objects: F,W5,G,O,3,C,P,K

LAST CHANCE ANIMAL RESCUE
CR1002349
Head Office, Hartfield Road, Edenbridge, Kent TN8 5NH
Tel: 01227 722 929; 01732 865 530
Email: .. general@lastchanceanimalrescue.co.uk

LATIN LINK
CR1020826
87 London Street, Reading RG1 4QA
Tel: 0118 957 7100
Email: .... info@latinlink.org.uk
Objects: F,W3,W2,W7,W5,G,W10,W15,V,W16,R,W4,U,H,T,O,Y,C,P,Z,W8,L

LATTITUDE GLOBAL VOLUNTEERING (FORMERLY GAP ACTIVITY PROJECTS)
CR272761
44 Queen's Road, Reading RG1 4BB
Tel: 0118 959 4914
Email: .... volunteer@lattitude.org.uk

LAURA CRANE TRUST
CR1058464
PO Box 437, Huddersfield, West Yorkshire HD1 9QH
Tel: 01484 510013
Email: .... admin@lauracranetrust.org

THE LEADERS OF WORSHIP AND PREACHERS TRUST (LWPT)
Founded: 1849 CR1107967
Head Office, 89 High Street, Rickmansworth, Hertfordshire WD3 1EF
Tel: 01923 775856
Email: .... headoffice@lpma.co.uk
Objects: 1A,A,3,C

LEAGUE OF FRIENDS OF THE WHITCHURCH HOSPITAL (SHROPSHIRE)
Founded: 1991 CR1002033
The Bungalow, Yockings Gate Mews, Black Park, Whitchurch, Shropshire SY13 4JP
Tel: 01948 664828

LEAGUE OF JEWISH WOMEN
Founded: 1943 CR1104023
6 Bloomsbury Square, London WC1A 2LP
Tel: 020 7242 8300
Email: . . . . Jackie@theljw.org
Objects: F,S,E,W7,G,2,W4,3,P,W8

THE LEAGUE OF REMEMBRANCE
Founded: 1918 CR213364
55 Great Ormond Street, London WC1N 3HZ
Tel: 020 7829 7818
Email: . . . . info@leagueofremembrance.com
Objects: W9,1A,W4,3,P

LEAGUE OF THE HELPING HAND, THE
Founded: 1908 CR208792
PO Box 342, Burgess Hill, West Sussex
RH15 5AQ
Tel: 01444 236099
Email: . . . . secretary@ill.org.uk
Objects: W5,1A,A

LEAGUE OF WELLDOERS
Founded: 1893 CR224436
119-133 Limekiln Lane, Liverpool, Merseyside
L5 8SN
Tel: 0151 207 1984
Email: . . . . welldoers@btconnect.com
Objects: W3,E,W4,3,P

LEARNING THROUGH ACTION TRUST
CR1014350
Learning Through Action Centre, Fair Cross, Stratfield Saye, Reading RG7 2BT
Tel: 0870 770 7985
Email: . . . . ltacentreoffice@aol.com
Objects: F,W3,G,H,3,P,K

LEARNING THROUGH LANDSCAPES TRUST
Founded: 1990 CR803270
Third Floor, Southside Offices, The Law Courts, Winchester, Hampshire SO23 9DL
Tel: 01962 846258
Email: . . . . schoolgrounds-uk@ltl.org.uk
Objects: F,W6,W3,W2,W7,W5,G,W10,2,H,3

LEATHER AND HIDE TRADES BENEVOLENT INSTITUTION
Founded: 1860 CR206133
Treasurer: Mr Tim F Bigden
Secretary: Mrs Karen Harriman
143 Barkby Road, Leicester, Leicestershire
LE4 9LG
Tel: 0116 274 1500
Fax: 0116 274 1500
Email: . . . . karenharriman@btconnect.com
Web: . . . . http://www.lhtbi.org.uk
Objects: W11,1A,A
Financial assistance available to former workers in the leather and hide or skin trades and their widows who are in need. Also one-off grants for special needs.

LEE ABBEY FELLOWSHIP
CR1094097
Lee Abbey, Lynton, Devon EX35 6JJ
Tel: 01598 752621
Email: . . . . finance@leeabbey.org.uk

LEE HOUSE, WIMBLEDON
Founded: 1875 CR222043
Lee House, 2 Lancaster Avenue, Wimbledon, London SW19 5DE
Tel: 020 8946 0369
Objects: W4,3,C,W8

LEEDS CENTRE FOR DEAF AND BLIND PEOPLE
Founded: 1876 CR227169
Centenary House, North Street, Leeds, West Yorkshire LS2 8AY
Tel: 0113 243 8328
Email: . . . . info@centenaryhouse.fsnet.co.uk
Objects: W6,W7,P

LEEDS CHILDREN'S CHARITY
CR224649
6-8 Lower Ground, York Place, Leeds, West Yorkshire LS1 2DS
Tel: 0113 245 4281
Email: . . . . office@leedstosilverdale.com

LEEDS REC
Founded: 1990 CR1000406
Sheepscar House, Sheepscar Street South, Leeds, West Yorkshire LS7 1AD
Tel: 0113 243 8421
Email: . . . . leedsrec@btinternet.com
Objects: F,W10,3

LEEDS TRAINING TRUST
Founded: 1990 CR1000380
Mitchell House, 139 Richardshaw Lane, Pudsey, Leeds, West Yorkshire LS28 6AA
Tel: 0113 255 2417

LEGISLATION MONITORING SERVICE FOR CHARITIES
CR1057767
Church House, Great Smith Street, Westminster, London SW1P 3JZ
Tel: 020 7222 1265
Email: . . . . info@lmsconline.org.uk
Objects: F,H,3

LENNOX CHILDRENS CANCER FUND
Founded: 1992 CR1011325
57 Mawney Road, Romford, Essex RM7 7HL
Tel: 01708 734366

LEO TRUST, THE
Founded: 1993 CR1017367
Boldshaves Oast, Frogshole, Woodchurch, Ashford, Kent TN26 3RA
Tel: 01233 860060
Email: . . . . leotrust@btconnect.com
Objects: F,W5,3,P

LEONARD CHESHIRE DISABILITY
Founded: 1948 CR218186; SC005117
Legacy Department, 66 South Lambeth Road, London SW8 1RL
Tel: 020 3242 0418
Email: . . . . info@LCDisability.org
Objects: M,E,W5,G,V,D,N,U,O,3,P

LEONARD CHESHIRE DISABILITY SCOTLAND
CR218186; SC005117
Supporter Services, Murrayburgh House, 17 Corstorphine Road, Edinburgh EH12 6DD

Tel: 0131 346 9040
Email: . . . . scotland@lc-uk.org
Objects: W5,3

LEPRA
CR213251; SC039715
28 Middleborough, Colchester, Essex CO1 1TG
Tel: 01206 216700
Email: . . . . fundraising@lepra.org.uk
Objects: W6,M,W3,W5,G,1B,N,W4,U,O,3,W8

THE LEPROSY MISSION ENGLAND AND WALES
Founded: 1874 CR1050327
Goldhay Way, Orton Goldhay, Peterborough, Cambridgeshire PE2 5GZ
Tel: 01733 370505
Objects: F,W6,M,W3,W5,G,1A,1B,N,R,W4,U,H,O,3,C,P,W8,K

LES BOURGS HOSPICE, GUERNSEY
Andrew Mitchell House, Rue du Tertre, St Andrews, Guernsey GY6 8SF
Tel: 01481 251111
Email: . . . . info@lesbourgs.com

LET'S FACE IT SUPPORT NETWORK FOR THE FACIALLY DISFIGURED
CR1043461
72 Victoria Avenue, Westgate-on-Sea, Kent CT8 8BH
Tel: 01843 833724
Email: . . . . chrisletsfaceit@aol.com

LEUKAEMIA BUSTERS
CR1157147
Southampton General Hospital, Southampton, Hampshire SO16 6YD
Tel: 023 8077 5590
Email: . . . . contact@leukaemiabusters.org.uk
Object: W3

LEUKAEMIA CARE
Founded: 1967 CR259483; SC039207
One Birch Court, Blackpole East, Worcester, Worcestershire WR3 8SG
Tel: 01905 755977; 0800 169 6680 (CARE Line); 0845 521 3456 (Fundraising)
Email: . . . . legacies@leukaemiacare.org.uk
Objects: F,W3,1A,A,V,W4,H,3

LEWIS W. HAMMERSON MEMORIAL HOME
Founded: 1993 CR286002
50A The Bishops Avenue, London N2 0BE
Tel: 020 8458 4523
Objects: W7,W5,W4,3,C

LICENSED TRADE CHARITY
Founded: 2004 CR230011
Heatherley, London Road, Ascot, Windsor & Maidenhead SL5 8DR
Tel: 01344 884440
Email: . . . . info@licensedtradecharity.org.uk
Objects: F,W3,W5,G,W11,1A,A,2,W4,B,P

LIFE ACADEMY
Founded: 1964 CR801246
9 Chesham Road, Guildford, Surrey GU1 3LS

Tel: 01483 301170
Email: .... info@pra.uk.com
Objects: F,G,2,H,3

LIFELINE 4 KIDS / HANDICAPPED CHILDREN'S AID COMMITTEE

Founded: 1961 CR200050
Chairman: Mr Roger Adelman
215 West End Lane, West Hampstead, London NW6 1XJ
Tel: 020 7794 1661
Fax: 020 7794 1161
Email: .... mail@lifeline4kids.org
Web: www.lifeline4kids.org
Objects: M,W3,J,W5

Most people realise the degree of stress suffered when a child is born with, or acquire a disability, how many do something about it?
It is 55 years since a number of caring parents joined together to help children less fortunate than their own.
Appeals are investigated and means tested. If successful, funds are allocated and specialist items are purchased directly by us.
We never award cash grants. We are a voluntary charity without paid staff or office expenses so virtually every penny raised is used to alleviate distress. We are determined never to let a child's cry for help go unheard.

See advert on previous page

THE LIFETRAIN TRUST

Founded: 1990 CR803697
Felbury House, Holmbury St Mary, Dorking, Surrey RH5 6NL
Tel: 01306 730929
Email: .... info@lifetrain.org.uk
Objects: F,W3,W5,G,W10,V,3,P

LIGHT INFANTRY REGIMENTAL ASSOCIATION (SOMERSET)

CR800595
Light Infantry Office (Somerset), The Rifles, 14 Mount Street, Taunton, Somerset TA1 3QB
Tel: 01823 333434
Objects: W9,1A,2,P

LIGHTHOUSE PROJECT

Founded: 1968 CR519859
Sefton House, Bridle Road, Bootle, Merseyside L30 4UG
Tel: 0151 530 2566
Email: .... ho@lighthouseproject.co.uk
Objects: F,G,W4,3

THE LIND TRUST

Founded: 1990 CR803174
Drayton Hall, Hall Lane, Drayton, Norwich, Norfolk NR8 6DP

LINDSEY LODGE HOSPICE, SCUNTHORPE

Founded: 1990 CR702871
Burringham Road, Scunthorpe, North Lincolnshire DN17 2AA
Tel: 01724 270835
Email: . . fundraising@lindseylodgehospice.org.uk
Objects: W9,W6,W7,W5,W10,W11,N,W4,3,W8

LING TRUST LIMITED

Founded: 1991 CR1003366
13 East Stockwell Street, Colchester, Essex CO1 1SS
Tel: 01206 769246

LIONHEART (REGISTERED AS ROYAL INSTITUTION OF CHARTERED SURVEYORS' BENEVOLENT FUND LTD)

CR261245
Surveyor Court, Westwood Way, Coventry, West Midlands CV4 8BF
Tel: 024 7646 6696
Email: .... info@lionheart.org.uk
Objects: F,W6,W3,W7,W5,W11,1A,A,V,W4,O,W8

LISTENING BOOKS

Founded: 1972 CR264221
12 Lant Street, London SE1 1QH
Tel: 020 7407 9417
Email: .... info@listening-books.org.uk
Objects: W6,W3,S,W5,G,2,W4,Y,3

LISTER INSTITUTE OF PREVENTIVE MEDICINE, THE

CR206271
PO Box 1083, Bushey, Hertfordshire WD23 9AG
Tel: 01923 801886
Email: .... secretary@lister-institute.org.uk
Objects: W6,W3,W7,1A,W4,W8

LITTLE FOUNDATION

Founded: 1990 CR803551
c/o MacKeith Press, 30 Furnival Street, London EC4A 1JQ
Tel: 020 7831 4918
Objects: W3,1B

THE LITTLE SISTERS OF THE POOR

CR234434
Sr Caroline Lloyd
St Peter's Residence (CC), 2a Meadow Road, London SW8 1QH
Tel: 020 7735 0788
Fax: 020 7582 0973
Email: .... mp.lond@lsplondon.co.uk
Web: .... www.littlesistersofthepoor.co.uk
Object: W4

The Little Sisters of the Poor, an international congregation of Religious Sisters welcome into their homes elderly persons of modest means and of all nationalities and denominations. There are currently 15 homes in the UK, Jersey and Ireland.

LIVABILITY (BUILDING ON THE HERITAGE OF JOHN GROOMS AND THE SHAFTESBURY SOCIETY)

CR1116530
6 Mitre Passage, London SE10 0ER
Tel: 020 7452 2000
Email: .... info@livability.org.uk
Objects: M,W3,E,W5,G,V,N,U,O,3,C,K

LIVER CANCER SURGERY APPEAL

CR1061703
The Old Farm House, Epsom Road, Merrow, Guildford, Surrey GU4 7AB
Tel: 01483 546321
Email: . . livercancersurgeryappeal@yahoo.co.uk

LIVERPOOL MERCHANTS' GUILD

Founded: 1869 CR206454
110-114 Duke Street, Liverpool, Merseyside L1 5AG
Tel: 0151 703 1080
Objects: 1A,A,W4,B

LIVING PAINTINGS TRUST, THE
Founded: 1989 CR1049103
Queen Isabelle House, Unit 8, Kingsclere Park, Kingsclere, Newbury, West Berkshire RG20 4SW
Tel: 01635 299771
Objects: W6,S,G,H,3,P

LIVING SPACE
Founded: 1991 CR1002762
38 Marsh Hill, London E9 5PE
Tel: 020 8985 5575
Email: office@livingspace.org
Objects: D,C

LIVING STREETS
Founded: 1929 CR1108448; SC039808
88-94 Wentworth Street, London E1 7SA
Tel: 020 7377 4900
Email: info@livingstreets.org.uk
Objects: F,W6,W3,W2,W7,W5,2,W4,H

LLANGOLLEN INTERNATIONAL MUSICAL EISTEDDFOD
CR504620
Eisteddfod Office, Royal International Pavilion, Abbey Road, Llangollen, Denbighshire LL20 8SW
Tel: 01978 862007
Email: info@international-eisteddfod.co.uk

LLIW VALLEY WOMEN'S AID
Founded: 1991 CR1005646
PO Box 503, Portardawe, Swansea SA8 4WN
Tel: 01792 869480
Email: info@luma.org.uk
Objects: W3,D,3,C,W8

LLOYD FOUNDATION, THE
Founded: 1972 CR314203
Fairway, Round Oak View, Tillington, Hereford, Herefordshire HR4 8EQ
Tel: 01432 760409
Objects: W3,G,1A,A,1B

THE LODGING HOUSE MISSION
SC017283
35 East Campbell Street (CC), Glasgow G1 5DT
Tel: 0141 552 0285
Email: enquiries@lhm-glasgow.co.uk
Objects: F,W9,W3,E,W5,G,W11,W4,3,P,W8

LONDON BROOK ADVISORY CENTRE
Founded: 1992 CR1013037
421 Highgate Studios, 53-79 Highgate Road, London NW5 1TL
Tel: 020 7284 6040

LONDON CATALYST
Founded: 1872 CR1066739
45 Westminster Bridge Road, London SE1 7JB
Tel: 020 7021 4631
Email: london.catalyst@peabody.org.uk
Objects: F,W6,M,W3,E,W7,W5,A,1B,N,W4,O,C

LONDON CENTRE FOR PSYCHOTHERAPY
Founded: 1953 CR267244
32 Leighton Road, London NW5 2QE
Tel: 020 7482 2002; 020 7482 2282
Email: info@lcp-psychotherapy.org.uk
Objects: F,G,2,O,3

LONDON SCHOOL OF THEOLOGY
CR312778
Green Lane, Northwood, Middlesex HA6 2UW
Tel: 01923 456000
Email: enquiries@lst.ac.uk

LONDON SHIPOWNERS' & SHIPBROKERS' BENEVOLENT SOCIETY
Founded: 1852 CR213348
The Annexe, 20 St. Dunstan's Hill, London EC3R 8HL
Tel: 020 7283 6090
Objects: W11,1A,A

LONDON SPORTS FORUM FOR DISABLED PEOPLE
CR1055683
Unit 2B07, London South Bank University, Technopark, 90 London Road, London SE1 6LN
Tel: 020 7717 1699
Email: info@interactive.uk.net
Objects: F,W6,W3,J,W7,W5,G,H,3

LONDON WEST TRAINING SERVICES
Founded: 1991 CR1002148
207 Waterlow Road, London SE1 8XD
Tel: 020 7928 2439
Email: lwts@lwts.org.uk
Objects: F,G,3

LONDON YOUTH (FORMERLY THE FEDERATION OF LONDON YOUTH CLUBS)
Founded: 1887 CR303324
47 - 49 Pitfield Street, London N1 6DA
Tel: 020 7549 8800
Email: info@londonyouth.org.uk

LOOK: NATIONAL FEDERATION OF FAMILIES WITH VISUALLY IMPAIRED CHILDREN
Founded: 1991 CR1140471
c/o Deaf Cultural Centre, Ladywood Road, Birmingham, West Midlands B16 8SZ
Tel: 0121 428 5038; 0121 427 7111
Email: steve@look-uk.org
Objects: F,W6,W3,G,V,2,H,P

LORD WHISKY SANCTUARY FUND
CR283483
Park House, Stelling Minnis, Canterbury, Kent CT4 6AN
Tel: 01303 862622
Fax: 01303 863007
Email: lord.whisky@btinternet.com
Web: www.lordwhisky.co.uk
Objects: F,W1
The Lord Whisky Centre and Tea Rooms opened in November 1994, providing a veterinary clinic for those on low income, a behaviour clinic, and dog and owner training classes. The Tea Rooms are open everyday from 10am-4pm. The sanctuary is funded entirely by donations and legacies which are much appreciated by the founder, Margaret Todd MBE, Park House, Stelling Minnis, Nr Canterbury, Kent CT4 6AN.

LOROS: LEICESTERSHIRE AND RUTLAND ORGANISATION FOR THE RELIEF OF SUFFERING

CR506120
LOROS Fundraising Office, Groby Road, Leicester, Leicestershire LE3 9QE
Tel: 0116 231 8431
Email: . . . . fundraising@loros.co.uk
Objects: F,W9,W6,W7,W5,G,W10,W11,N,W4,O,3,W8

LUCY FAITHFULL FOUNDATION, THE

Founded: 1992 CR1013025
Bordesley Hall, The Holloway, Alvechurch, Birmingham, West Midlands B48 7QA
Tel: 01527 591922
Email: . . . . office@lucyfaithfull.org
Objects: F,W3,G,H,O,3

THE LULLABY TRUST (FORMERLY FSID)

Founded: 1971 CR262191
11 Belgrave Road, London SW1V 1RB
Tel: . . . 020 7802 3200; 020 7233 2090 (Helpline)
Email: . . . . office@lullabytrust.org.uk
Objects: F,W3,G,A,1B,H,3,W8

LYMPHOMA ASSOCIATION

CR1068395
PO Box 386, Aylesbury, Buckinghamshire HP20 2GA
Tel: . . 01296 619419 Fundraising; 01296 619400 Admin
Email: . . . . fundraising@lymphoma.org.uk
Objects: F,W3,2,W4,H,3

LYNEAL TRUST

CR516224
The Shirehall, Abbey Foregate, Shrewsbury, Shropshire SY2 6ND
Tel: 01743 252728
Email: . . . . . . pushkar.trivedi@shropshire.gov.uk
Objects: W5,V,3

LYTTELTON WELL LIMITED

Founded: 1990 CR1001139
Church Street, Malvern, Worcestershire WR14 2AY
Tel: 01684 573702
Email: . . . . manager@lytteltonwell.co.uk
Objects: F,W3,R,W4,3,W8

M

M.F.P.A. TRUST FUND FOR THE TRAINING OF HANDICAPPED CHILDREN IN THE ARTS

CR328151
88 London Road, Holybourne, Alton, Hampshire GU34 4EL
Tel: 01420 88755
Objects: W3,G,1A,A,1B

MACCLESFIELD ACCOMMODATION CARE AND CONCERN

Founded: 1990 CR1133376
1 Glegg Street, Macclesfield, Cheshire SK11 7AJ
Tel: 01625 502540
Objects: F,W3,D,3

MACINTYRE CARE

Founded: 1966 CR250840
602 South Seventh Street, Central Milton Keynes, Milton Keynes, Buckinghamshire MK9 2JA
Tel: 01908 230100
Email: . . . . fundraising@macintyre-care.org
Objects: F,M,E,W5,G,D,O,3,C,P,K

MACMILLAN CANCER SUPPORT

CR261017; SC039907, IoM 604
UK Office, 89 Albert Embankment, London SE1 7UQ
Tel: 0800 107 4448
Email: . . . . leavealegacy@macmillan.org.uk

MACULAR SOCIETY

Macular Society

Founded: 1987 CR1001198; SC042015, IoM 1123
Crown Chambers, South Street, Andover, Hampshire SP10 2BN
Tel: 01264 321988
Email: . . . . legacies@macularsociety.org
Web: . . . . www.macularsociety.org
Objects: F,W6,2,W4,H,Z,W

Macular disease causes irreversible sight loss in more than one in five people over 90. Many are unable to drive, read or recognise faces easily, seriously affecting quality of life. Where treatment is available, it does not restore lost sight. There is no cure. The Macular Society is the only UK charity dedicated to people with macular disease. We sponsor research to find a cure and offer information and advice through our helpline, counselling and local support groups. Legacies are vital in helping us support and reassure people coping with macular sight loss and bringing hope for future generations. Thank you for thinking of us.

MAIDSTONE & NORTHWEST CROSSROADS

Founded: 1992 CR1090904
The Lodge, Holborough Road, Snodland, Kent ME6 5PJ
Tel: 01634 249090
Objects: W6,M,W3,W7,W5,W10,N,W4,3,P,W8

MAKRO-AJY

Founded: 1927 CR305963
Balfour House, 741 High Road, London N12 0BQ
Tel: 020 8369 5000
Objects: F,W3,J,S,G,H

MALCOLM SARGENT FESTIVAL CHOIR

Founded: 1996 CR1055426
34 North End Road, London W14 0SH

Tel: 020 7602 6818; 020 7352 6805
Email: . . . . malcolm.sargent@virgin.net
Objects: W3,S,1B,2,W4,3

MANCHESTER & CHESHIRE DOGS' HOME

Founded: 1893 CR1001346
Crofters House, Moss Brook Road, Harpurhey, Manchester, Greater Manchester M9 5PG
Tel: 0844 504 1212
Fax: 0161 277 6949
Email: . . . . appeals@dogshome.net
Web: . . . . www.dogshome.net
Objects: W1,G,3

The Home, founded in 1893 to take in and care for lost and stray dogs in order to re-unite them with their owners or to find new and caring homes for them, continues over a hundred years later to care for thousands of dogs annually. The Home is a charity maintained by voluntary donations to carry out its work in conjunction with local authorities. We receive no Government Funding. Our greatest challenge is to maintain our care of thousands of dogs each year on two sites - Manchester and Cheshire.

See advert on this page

MANCHESTER DEVELOPMENT EDUCATION PROJECT LTD

Founded: 1990 CR1000590
c/o Manchester Metropolitan University, 799 Wilmslow Road, Manchester, Greater Manchester M20 2RR
Tel: 0161 921 8020
Email: . . . . info@dep.org.uk
Objects: F,W3,G,W10,H,3

MANCHESTER EDUCATION BUSINESS SOLUTIONS LTD

Founded: 1990 CR1093728
3rd Floor, Paragon House, 48 Seymour Grove, Old Trafford, Manchester, Greater Manchester M16 0LN
Tel: 0161 772 1000

THE MANOR PREPARATORY SCHOOL TRUST

Founded: 1990 CR900347
Faringdon Road, Shippon, Abingdon, Oxfordshire OX13 6LN
Tel: . . . . . 01235 554814 Bursary; 01235 858458 School Office
Email: . . . . bursar@manorprep.org
Objects: W3,G,3

MANOR TRAINING AND RESOURCE CENTRE LTD

Founded: 1990 CR1000516
306-308 Prince of Wales Road, Sheffield, South Yorkshire S2 1FF
Tel: 0114 264 2194
Email: . . . . kimg@matrec.org.uk
Objects: G,3

MARE AND FOAL SANCTUARY
CR1141831
Accounts Department, Honeysuckle Farm, Buckland Road, Newton Abbot, Devon TQ12 4SA
Tel: 01626 355969
Email: .... office@mareandfoal.org
Objects: W1,O

MARFAN ASSOCIATION UK
Founded: 1984 CR802727
Rochester House, 5 Aldershot Road, Fleet, Hampshire GU51 3NG
Tel: 01252 810472; 01252 617320 Answerphone
Email: .... contactus@marfan-association.org.uk
Objects: F,M,W3,J,G,N,2,U,H,O,P

MARIE CURIE
CR207994; SC038731
89 Albert Embankment, London SE1 7TP
Tel: 0800 716 146
Email: .... info@mariecurie.org.uk
Objects: M,E,G,N,H,O

MARIE STOPES INTERNATIONAL
CR265543
1 Conway Street, Fitzroy Square, London W1T 6LP
Tel: 020 7034 2343
Email: .... fundraising@mariestopes.org.uk

THE MARINE CONNECTION
CR1062222
Lime House, Regency Close, Uckfield, East Sussex TN22 1DS
Tel: 07931 366352
Email: .... info@marineconnection.org
Objects: W1,W3,W2,G,2,H,3

MARINE CONSERVATION SOCIETY (MCS)
Founded: 1991 CR1004005; SC037480
Overross House, Ross Park, Ross-on-Wye, Herefordshire HR9 7US
Tel: 01989 566017
Email: .... info@mcsuk.org
Objects: F,W1,J,W2,G,2,H

MARITIME VOLUNTEER SERVICE - MVS (THE MARITIME FOUNDATION)
CR1048454
202 Lambeth Road, London SE1 7JW
Tel: 020 7928 8100
Object: G

MARKET RESEARCH BENEVOLENT ASSOCIATION
Founded: 1977 CR274190
11 Tremayne Walk, Camberley, Surrey GU15 1AH
Tel: 01276 0684 826
Email: .... marketresearchba@yahoo.co.uk
Objects: F,1A,A,V,N,O

MARLBOROUGH BRANDT GROUP, THE
Founded: 1991 CR1001398
Upper Office, Dutch Park, Elmtree Park, Manton, Marlborough, Wiltshire SN8 1PS
Tel: 01672 861116
Email: .... info@mbg.org
Objects: G,U,H,3

MARLEBONE BANGLADESH SOCIETY
Founded: 1991 CR1001900
19 Stamford Street, London NW8 8ER
Tel: 020 7724 7427
Email: .... info@mbs-uk.org
Objects: F,W3,W5,G,W10,W4,B,3,P,W8

MARRIAGE CARE
Founded: 1946 CR218159
Clitherow House, 1 Blythe Mews, Blythe Road, London W14 0NW
Tel: 020 7371 1341
Email: .... info@marriagecare.org.uk
Objects: F,W9,W5,G,W10,2,W4,3,W8

MARTHA TRUST
Founded: 1983 CR1067885
Homemead Lane, Hacklinge, Deal, Kent CT14 0PG
Tel: 01304 615223
Email: .... contact@marthatrust.org.uk
Objects: E,W5,3

MARTINDALE (HILDA) EDUCATIONAL TRUST
Founded: 1952
c/o Registry, Royal Holloway, University of London, Egham, Surrey TW20 0EX
Tel: 01784 276158
Email: .... hildamartindaletrust@rhul.ac.uk
Objects: G,1A,A,3,W8

MARTINEAU COMMUNITY NURSERY
Founded: 1991 CR1012831
1 Elwood Street, London N5 1EB
Tel: 020 7359 9911
Email: .... martineau.community@virgin.net
Objects: W3,G,2,3

MARWELL WILDLIFE
CR275433
Colden Common (CC), Winchester, Hampshire SO21 1JH
Tel: 01962 777407; 01962 777913
Email: .... fundraising@marwell.org.uk
Objects: W1,W3,W2,S,W5,G,A,1B,2

MARY FEILDING GUILD
Founded: 1877 CR205563
103-107 North Hill, London N6 4DP
Tel: 020 8340 3915
Objects: D,W4,3,C

THE MARY HARE FOUNDATION
CR1002680
Arlington Manor, Snelsmore Common, Newbury, West Berkshire RG14 3BQ
Tel: 01635 244204
Email: .... foundation@maryhare.org.uk
Objects: W7,G,3

MARY WARD CENTRE, THE
Founded: 1891 CR223066
42 Queen Square, London WC1N 3AQ
Tel: 020 7269 6000
Email: .... info@marywardcentre.ac.uk
Object: G

MASONIC SAMARITAN FUND
Founded: 1990 CR1130424
60 Great Queen Street, London WC2 5BL
Tel: 020 7404 1550
Email: .... info@msfund.org.uk
Objects: 1A,A,N,2

MAST APPEAL
CR1000695
M A S T Appeal Office, Macclesfield District General Hospital, Prestbury Road, Macclesfield, Cheshire SK10 3BL
Tel: 01625 661988
Objects: N,3

MASTER TAILORS' BENEVOLENT ASSOCIATION
Founded: 1887 CR212136
35 Dewlands, Godstone, Surrey RH9 8BS
Tel: 01883 743469
Objects: W11,1A,A

THE MATHILDA & TERENCE KENNEDY INSTITUTE OF RHEUMATOLOGY TRUST
Founded: 1966 CR260059
1 Aspenlea Road, Hammersmith, London W6 8LH
Tel: 020 8383 4444
Email: . . . . c.boden@kirtrust.org
Object: 3

MATILWALA FAMILY CHARITABLE TRUST, THE
Founded: 1992 CR1012756
9 Brookview, Fulwood, Preston, Lancashire PR2 8FG
Tel: 01772 706501

MATTHEW TRUST - HELPING THE MENTALLY ILL IN THE COMMUNITY AND VICTIMS OF AGGRESSION
Founded: 1977 CR294966
PO Box 604, London SW6 3AG
Tel: 020 7736 5976
Email: . . . . matthewtrust@ukonline.co.uk
Objects: F,M,G,1A,A,V,N,B,O,3,P

THE MAYFIELD TRUST
Founded: 1991 CR1002398
Horley Green Road, Claremount, Halifax, West Yorkshire HX3 6AS
Tel: 01422 322552
Objects: F,W3,J,W5,G,1A,A,1B,V,D,2,R,3,C,P,K

ME (MYALGIC ENCEPHALOPATHY) ASSOCIATION
Founded: 1976 CR801279
7 Apollo Office Court, Radclive Road, Gawcott, Buckingham, Buckinghamshire MK18 4DF
Tel: 01280 818964
Email: . . . . . . meconnect@meassociation.org.uk
Objects: F,W5,G,2,H

THE MEATH EPILEPSY TRUST
CR200359
Westbrook Road, Godalming, Surrey GU7 2QH
Tel: 01483 415095
Email: . . . . info@meath.org.uk
Objects: E,N,O,3

MEDECINS SANS FRONTIERES MSF (DOCTORS WITHOUT BORDERS)
Founded: 1993 CR1026588
Lower Ground Floor, Chancery Exchange, 10 Furnival Street, London EC4A 1AB
Tel: 020 7404 6600
Email: . . . . office-ldn@london.msf.org
Object: U

MEDICAL COUNCIL ON ALCOHOL, THE
Founded: 1967 CR265242
5 St Andrew's Place, London NW1 4LB
Tel: 020 7487 4445
Email: . . . . info@m-c-a.org.uk
Objects: F,W9,W3,J,W7,W5,G,W10,W15,W16,N,2,W4,H,Z,W8,W

MEDICAL RESEARCH FOUNDATION
CR1138223
c/o Medical Research Council, One Kemble Street, London WC2B 4AN
Tel: 0207 395 2268
Email: . . . . enquiries@mrf.mrc.ac.uk
Web: . . . www.medicalresearchfoundation.org.uk
Objects: G,N,W

The Medical Research Foundation (MRF) is the Medical Research Council (MRC)'s registered charity. The MRC is the UK's major public funder of medical research. We support the country's very best scientists, doctors and nurses to investigate many of today's most pressing health problems. To date, 27 MRC-funded scientists have won Nobel Prizes for their achievements in biomedical research. To ensure that this standard of excellence continues, we place great importance on training and developing the next generation of researchers. You can support the MRC through a legacy in your will, or through a regular standing order or a one-off donation to the Medical Research Foundation.

See advert on previous page

THE MEDICALERT FOUNDATION BRITISH ISLES & IRELAND
CR233705
MedicAlert House, 327-329 Witan Court, Upper Fourth Street, Milton Keynes, Buckinghamshire MK9 1EH
Tel: 020 7833 3034; 0800 581 420
Email: . . . . info@medicalert.org.uk

MENCAP IN KIRKLEES
Founded: 1990 CR702494
The Stables, Buckden Mount, 8 Thornhill Road, Huddersfield, West Yorkshire HD3 3AU
Tel: 01484 340811
Email: . . . . info@mencapinkirklees.org.uk
Objects: F,W3,E,W5,W4,3,P

MENCAP (ROYAL MENCAP SOCIETY)
CR222377
Mencap National Centre, 123 Golden Lane, London EC1Y 0RT
Tel: 020 7696 5615
Email: . . . . legacies@mencap.org.uk
Objects: F,W3,E,W5,G,V,D,H,C,P

MENIERE'S SOCIETY - HELPING PEOPLE WITH VERTIGO, TINNITUS AND DEAFNESS
Founded: 1984 CR297246
The Rookery, Surrey Hills Business Park, Wotton, Dorking, Surrey RH5 6QT
Tel: 0845 120 2975
Email: . . . . info@menieres.org.uk
Objects: F,J,2,H

MENINGITIS NOW
CR803016; SC037790
Fern House, Bath Road, Stroud, Gloucestershire GL5 3TJ
Tel: 01453 768000
Email: . . . . info@meningitisnow.org
Objects: F,M,W3,W7,W5,G,W10,W15,1A,W4,H,O,W

MENTAL HEALTH FOUNDATION

Founded: 1949 CR801130; SC039714
Colechurch House, 1 London Bridge Walk, London SE1 2SX
Tel: 020 7803 1121
Email: mhf@mhf.org.uk
Objects: F,W3,J,E,W5,G,A,W4,H,O,C,P,K

MERCHANT NAVY WELFARE BOARD

CR212799
8 Cumberland Place, Southampton, Hampshire SO15 2BH
Tel: 023 8033 7799
Email: enquiries@mnwb.org.uk

MERCHANT SEAMEN'S WAR MEMORIAL SOCIETY

CR207500
Sachel Court, Springbok Farm Estate, Alfold, Cranleigh, Surrey GU6 8EX
Tel: 01403 752555
Email: t.goacher@mswmsociety.org.uk

MERCURY PHOENIX TRUST

Founded: 1992 CR1013768
The Mill, Mill Lane, Cookham, Windsor & Maidenhead SL6 9QT
Tel: 01628 527874

MERCY SHIPS

CR1053055; SC039743
Mercy Ships UK, The Lighthouse, 12 Meadway Court, Stevenage, Hertfordshire SG1 2EF
Tel: 01438 727800
Email: info@mercyships.org.uk

MERSEY KIDNEY RESEARCH

Founded: 1964 CR250895
Room 3,312A, School of Clinical Sciences, UCD Building, Royal Liverpool University Hospital, Liverpool, Merseyside L69 3GA
Tel: 0151 706 3598
Email: annmkr@liv.ac.uk

MERSEYSIDE BROOK ADVISORY CENTRE

Founded: 1990 CR703015
81 London Road, Liverpool, Merseyside L3 8JA
Tel: 0151 207 4000
Objects: F,W3,3,W8

MERSEYSIDE CHINESE COMMUNITY DEVELOPMENT ASSOCIATION

Founded: 1989 CR1001288
The Pagoda of Hundred Harmony, Chinese Community Centre, Henry Street, Liverpool, Merseyside L1 5BU
Tel: 0151 233 8833
Objects: F,W3,G,W10,W4,3

MERTON MUSIC FOUNDATION

Founded: 1991 CR1004122
MMF Office Chaucer Centre, Canterbury Road, Morden, Surrey SM4 6PX
Tel: 020 8640 5446
Email: admin@mmf.org.uk
Objects: W3,G,3

MERU

CR269804
Unit 2, Eclipse Estate, 30 West Hill, Epsom, Surrey KT19 8JD
Tel: 01372 725203
Email: info@meru.org.uk

THE METHODIST CHURCH

CR1132208
Methodist Church House, 25 Marylebone Road, London NW1 5JR
Tel: 020 7486 5502
Email: helpdesk@methodistchurch.org.uk
Objects: W3,G,W10,1A,A,1B,N,2,R,W4,U,B,Y,3,P, W8,L

METHODIST CHURCH FUNDS

25 Marylebone Road, London NW1 5JR
Tel: 020 7467 5266
Email: missionfunding@methodistchurch.org.uk
Objects: 1A,A,W4

METHODIST HOMES

Founded: 1943 CR1083995
Epworth House, Stuart Street, Derby, Derbyshire DE1 2EQ
Tel: 01332 296200
Email: enquiries@mha.org.uk
Objects: E,D,N,W4,H,3,C,P

METHODIST LONDON MISSION FUND

Founded: 1861
1 Central Buildings, Westminster, London SW1H 9NH
Tel: 020 7222 8010
Email: info@methodistlondon.org.uk
Objects: F,J,A,1B,R

METHODIST MINISTERS' HOUSING SOCIETY

Founded: 1948
Methodist Church House, 25 Marylebone Road, London NW1 5JR
Tel: 020 7467 5272
Email: admin@mmhs.org.uk
Object: D

METHODIST RELIEF AND DEVELOPMENT FUND

CR291691
Finance Accounts Payable, 25 Marylebone Road, London NW1 5JR
Tel: 020 7467 5132
Email: mrdf@methodistchurch.org.uk
Objects: W3,W2,W5,A,1B,W4,U,H,W8

METROPOLITAN POLICE BENEVOLENT FUND

Founded: 2008 CR1125409
Charities Support Officer: Mr William Tarrant
Treasurer: Mr Stephen Skirten
Charities Section, 9th Floor, Empress State Building, Lillie Road, London SW6 1TR
Tel: 020 7161 1667
Email: william.tarrant@met.police.uk
Objects: W11,1A,A,1B,2,W4,O,Y,I

Summary of Objects

The charity is predominantly funded via contributions from police officers, however donations from members of the public are greatly appreciated. The objects of the charity are to:

- Provide financial support by way of a grant or a loan to serving, former, ex and retired police officers and their Widows, Widowers and dependants who are sick or injured suffering financial hardship or distress.
- Provide grants to other charities who exist for the relief of serving, former, ex and retired police officers and their Widows, Widowers and dependants.
- Assist serving, former, ex and retired police officers and their Widows, Widowers and dependants in such

ways as the Trustees think fit, provided that these shall be exclusively charitable.
• Assist close family of deceased police officers who died in the line of duty to attend police memorial services.

MIDDLE EAST CHRISTIAN OUTREACH LTD

Founded: 1976 CR272327
22 Culverden Park Road, Tunbridge Wells, Kent TN4 9RA
Tel: 01892 521541
Email: .... info@twoffice.co.uk
Objects: R,H

MIDDLESEX ASSOCIATION FOR THE BLIND

CR207007
Head Office: The Sight Centre, Unit 3-4, Freetrade House, Lowtner Road, Stanmore, Middlesex HA7 1EP
Tel: 020 8423 5141
Email: .... info@aftb.org.uk

MIDLANDS AIR AMBULANCE CHARITY (FORMERLY COUNTY AIR AMBULANCE)

Founded: 1991 CR1143118
Chief Executive: Hanna Sebright
Air Operations Manager: Becky Steele
Head Office (CD), Hawthorn House, Dudley Road, Stourbridge, West Midlands DY9 8BQ
Tel: 0800 840 2040
Fax: 01384 486621
Email: .... info@midlandsairambulance.com
Web: .... www.midlandsairambulance.com
Objects: M,N,3

MIGRAINE ACTION ASSOCIATION

Founded: 1958 CR207783
27 East Street, Leicester, Leicestershire LE1 6NB
Email: .... info@migraine.org.uk
Objects: F,W3,J,W5,1A,A,1B,2,H,3,W8

THE MIGRAINE TRUST

Founded: 1965 CR1081300; SC042911
2nd Floor, 55-56 Russell Square, London WC1B 4HP
Tel: 020 7436 1336
Email: .... info@migrainetrust.org
Objects: F,W3,W5,G,A,W4,H,3,W8

MILITARY MINISTRIES INTERNATIONAL

CR284203
Havelock House, Barrack Road, Aldershot, Hampshire GU11 3NP
Tel: 01252 311222
Email: .... headoffice@m-m-i.org.uk
Objects: W9,R

MILL GROVE CHRISTIAN CHARITABLE TRUST

Founded: 1899 CR1078661
Crescent Road, South Woodford, London E18 1JB
Tel: 020 8504 2702
Email: .... millgrove@btinternet.com
Objects: W3,E,3

MILL HOUSE ANIMAL SANCTUARY - SAVE OUR OLD TIRED HORSES AND OTHER ANIMALS SANCTUARY

CR512905
Mayfields Road, Fullwood, Sheffield, South Yorkshire S10 4PR
Tel: 01226 762732; 0114 230 2907
Email: millhouseanimalsanctuary@btinternet.com

MIND

Founded: 1946 CR219830
Granta House, 15-19 Broadway, Stratford, London E15 4BQ
Tel: .. 020 8519 2122; 0845 766 0163 MIND Info Line
Email: .... contact@mind.org.uk
Objects: F,G,W10,1A,A,1B,2,W4,H,W8

MIND IN EXETER AND EAST DEVON LTD

CR1056071
4 Charlotte Mews, Pavilion Place, Exeter, Devon EX2 4HA
Tel: 01392 204499
Email: .... central@mindex.org.uk
Objects: F,E,W5,G,D,3,P,W8

THE MISCARRIAGE ASSOCIATION

CR1076829
17 Wentworth Terrace, Wakefield, West Yorkshire WF1 34W
Tel: 01924 200799 Helpline/Answerphone; 01924 200795 Admin
Email: ..... info@miscarriageassociation.org.uk
Objects: F,2,3,W8

MISSIO

CR1056651
23 Eccleston Square, London SW1V 1NU
Tel: 020 7821 9755
Email: .... legacy@missio.org.uk
Objects: R,U,H

MISSION CARE

Founded: 1912 CR284967
Graham House, 2 Pembroke Road, Bromley, Kent BR1 2RU
Tel: 020 8289 7925
Email: .... admin@missioncare.org.uk
Objects: M,G,D,C,P

THE MISSION TO SEAFARERS

Founded: 1856 CR1123613; SCO41938
St Michael Paternoster Royal, College Hill, London EC4R 2RL
Tel: 020 7248 5202
Email: .... general@missiontoseafarers.org
Objects: F,R

MOBILITY TRUST

Founded: 1972 CR1070975
17b Reading Road, Pangbourne, West Berkshire RG8 7LR
Tel: 0118 984 2588
Objects: M,W5,3

MODEL HOUSE LLANTRISANT LIMITED, THE

Founded: 1991
Model House Craft & Design Centre, Bull Ring, Llantrisant, Rhondda Cynon Taff CF72 9EB
Tel: 01443 237758
Objects: W3,W5,G,W4,3,W8

MONEY ADVICE TRUST

Founded: 1991 CR1099506
21 Garlick Hill, London EC4V 2AU
Tel: 020 7653 9721
Email: .... info@moneyadvicetrust.org
Objects: F,1B

MONOUX (SIR GEORGE) EXHIBITION FOUNDATION

CR310903

Life Long Learning Services, PO Box 416, Buildings 7 & 8, Uplands Business Park, Blackhorse Lane, Walthamstow, London E17 5QT

Tel: 020 8496 3509

Objects: 1A,A

MOON HALL SCHOOL

Founded: 1990 CR803481

Feldemore, Pasturewood Road, Holmbury St Mary, Dorking, Surrey RH5 6LQ

Tel: 01306 731464

Email: . . . . . . enquiries@moonhall.surrey.sch.uk

Objects: F,W3,W5,G,H,3

MOORCROFT RACEHORSE WELFARE CENTRE

CR1076278

Huntingrove Stud, Slinfold, Horsham, West Sussex RH13 0RB

Tel: 07929 666408

Email: . . . . info@mrwc.org.uk

Objects: W1,O

MOORFIELDS EYE HOSPITAL - SPECIAL TRUSTEES

CR228064

City Road, London EC1V 2PD

Tel: 020 7566 2643

MORDEN COLLEGE

Founded: 1695 CR215551

19 St Germans Place, Blackheath, London SE3 0PW

Tel: 020 8463 8330

Email: . . . . info@mordencollege.org

Objects: 1A,A,1B,W4,C

MORGAN (JUNIUS S) BENEVOLENT FUND

Founded: 1890 CR206126

Norfolk House, 31 St James's Square, London SW1Y 4JR

Tel: 020 7597 3166

Email: . . . . jane.minett@sghambros.com

Objects: 1A,A

MORRIS CERULLO WORLD EVANGELISM

Founded: 1990 CR1001361

PO Box 277, Hemel Hempstead, Hertfordshire HP2 7DH

Tel: 01442 232432

Objects: 2,R

MORTHYNG LIMITED

Founded: 1990 CR1000381

14-16 Ship Hill, Rotherham, South Yorkshire S60 2HG

Tel: 01709 372900

Email: . . . . morthyng@btinternet.com

Objects: W3,W2,W5,G,W10,W11,W4,3,W8,K

MORTIMER SOCIETY LIMITED, THE

Founded: 1983 CR287579

Frindsbury House, 42 Hollywood Lane, Frindsbury, Rochester, Kent ME3 8AL

Tel: 01634 719942

Objects: W5,3

MOTABILITY

Founded: 1977 CR299745

Warwick House, Roydon Road, Harlow, Essex CM19 5PX

Tel: 0845 166 8786

Email: . . . . fundraising@motability.co.uk

Objects: M,W5,1A,A,3

MOTHERS' UNION

Founded: 1876 CR240531

Mary Sumner House, 24 Tufton Street, London SW1P 3RB

Tel: 020 7222 5533

Email: . . . . mu@themothersunion.org

Objects: F,M,W3,V,2,R,U,H,3,P,W8

MOTIONHOUSE

Founded: 1990 CR328693

Spencer Yard, Leamington Spa, Warwickshire CV31 3SY

Tel: 01926 887052

Objects: W3,S,G,W10,W4,W8

MOTOR NEURONE DISEASE ASSOCIATION - ENGLAND, WALES AND NORTHERN IRELAND

CR294354

PO Box 246, Northampton, Northamptonshire NN1 2PR

Tel: 01604 250505; 08457 626262 MND Connect

Email: . . . . fundraising@mndassociation.org

Objects: F,M,W5,1A,2,H,3

MRS SMITH AND MOUNT TRUST, THE

Founded: 1992 CR1009718

White Horse Court, 25C North Street, Bishop's Stortford, Hertfordshire CM23 2LD

Tel: 01279 506421

Email: . . . . charities@pwwsolicitors.co.uk

Objects: F,W3,E,W5,G,W10,A,1B,D,W4,O,C,K

MRSA ACTION UK

CR1115672

6 Lunesdale Road (CC), Kirkham, Lancashire PR4 2HS

Tel: 07762 741114

Email: . . . . info@mrsaactionuk.net

MSSC (MARINE SOCIETY AND SEA CADETS)

MSSC

MARINE SOCIETY & SEA CADETS

CR313013; SC037808

202 Lambeth Road, London SE1 7JW

Tel: 020 7654 7000

Fax: 020 7401 2537

Email: . . . . vboyle@ms-sc.org / general email: legacy@ms-sc.org

Pass on your love of the sea to thousands of young people across the UK and seafarers worldwide by including MSSC (Marine Society & Sea Cadets) in your Will. Your vital gift will support thousands of young people to challenge themselves, gain qualifications and build life skills to further their education and careers, based on the customs and traditions of the Royal Navy for the very best head start in life. Leave a legacy with MSSC and you will also support seafarers access courses, qualifications and financial help to further their career at sea.

MULBERRY TRUST, THE
Founded: 1991 CR1005893
PO Box 147, Aylesbury, Buckinghamshire
HP18 0WD
Tel: 01844 290154

MULTIPLE SCLEROSIS SOCIETY
CR1139257; SC041990
MS National Centre, 372 Edgware Road, London
NW2 6ND
Tel: 020 8438 0700
Email: . . . . legacies@mssociety.org.uk
Objects: F,J,E,G,A,2,H,P

MULTIPLE SCLEROSIS SOCIETY SCOTLAND
CR1139257; SC041990
Office for Scotland, Ratho Park, 88 Glasgow Road, Ratho Station, Newbridge, Midlothian
EH28 8PP
Tel: 0131 335 4050
Email: . . . . legacies@mssociety.org.uk

MULTIPLE SCLEROSIS TRUST (MS TRUST)
Founded: 1993 CR1088353
Spirella Building, Bridge Road, Letchworth, Hertfordshire SG6 4ET
Tel: 01462 476700
Email: . . . . info@mstrust.org.uk
Objects: F,W3,W5,G,W4,H,3,W8,K

MUSCULAR DYSTROPHY UK
Founded: 1959 CR205395; SC039445
61A Great Suffolk Street, London SE1 0BU
Tel: . . . . 020 7803 4800; 0800 652635 (Helpline)
Email: . . . . info@muscular-dystrophy.org
Objects: F,M,W5,H

MUSEUM OF EAST ASIAN ART, THE
Founded: 1990 CR328725
12 Bennett Street, Bath, Bath & North East Somerset BA1 2QL
Tel: 01225 464640
Email: . museum@east-asian-art.freeserve.co.uk
Objects: W9,W6,W3,W2,S,W7,W5,G,W10,W11, W12,W4,H,3,W8

MUSIC IN HOSPITALS, ENGLAND, WALES AND NORTHERN IRELAND
CR1051659
Case House, 85-89 High Street, Walton-on-Thames, Surrey KT12 1DZ
Tel: 01932 260810
Email: . . . . info@musicinhospitals.org.uk
Objects: W9,W6,W3,S,E,W7,W5,W10,W4,O,3,P, W8,K

MUSIC LIBRARIES TRUST, THE
Founded: 1982 CR284334
Jerwood Library of the Performing Arts, Trinity Laban, King Charles Court, Old Royal Naval College, King William Walk, Greenwich, London
SE10 9JF
Tel: 020 8305 4425
Email: . . . . e.speller@trinitylaban.ac.uk
Objects: J,S,G,1A,A,1B,H

MY SIGHT NOTTINGHAMSHIRE
CR511288
Ortzen Street, Radford, Nottingham, Nottinghamshire NG7 4BN
Tel: 0115 970 6806
Email: . . . . info@nrsb.org.uk

MYELIN PROJECT
Founded: 1990 CR1000614
32 The Croft, Hadfield, Glossop, Derbyshire
SK13 1HN
Tel: 01457 865639
Email: . . . . info@myelinproject.co.uk

MYELOMA UK
SC026116
22 Logie Mill, Beaverbank Business Park, Edinburgh EH7 4HG
Tel: 0131 557 3332
Email: . . . . myelomauk@myeloma.org.uk

N

NABS
CR1070556
6th Floor, 388 Oxford Street, London W1C 1JT
Tel: 020 7290 7070
Email: . . . . nabs@nabs.org.uk
Objects: F,W11,A

NACRO - THE CRIME REDUCTION CHARITY
Founded: 1966 CR226171
Park Place, 10-12 Lawn Lane, London SW8 1UD
Tel: 020 7840 7200
Email: . . . . communications@nacro.org.uk
Objects: F,W3,J,G,1A,A,2,H,3,C,K

NAGRYS LTD
Founded: 1990 CR803104
45 Cheyne Walk, London NW4 3QH
Object: G

NARCOLEPSY ASSOCIATION (UK)
Founded: 1981 CR326361
PO Box 13842, Penicuik, Midlothian EH26 8WX
Tel: 0845 450 0394
Email: . . . . info@narcolepsy.org.uk
Objects: F,W3,W5,2,H,3,P

NASH CHARITY
Founded: 1922 CR229447
Peachey and Co, 95 Aldwych, London WC2B 4JF
Tel: 020 7316 5200
Objects: W9,1A,A,1B

NAT (NATIONAL AIDS TRUST)
Founded: 1987 CR297977
New City Cloisters, 196 Old Street, London
EC1V 9FR
Tel: 020 7814 6767
Email: . . . . info@nat.org.uk
Objects: W3,J,W5,G,W10,W15,D,W4,H,Y,Z,W8

NATIONAL ALLIANCE OF WOMEN'S ORGANISATIONS (NAWO)
Founded: 1989 CR803701
1-3 Berry Street, London EC1V 0AA
Tel: 020 7490 4100
Objects: F,J,G,H

NATIONAL ANIMAL WELFARE TRUST

National Animal Welfare Trust
Charity No 1090499

Founded: 1971 CR1090499
Chief Executive: Ms Clare Williams

Tylers Way, Watford, Hertfordshire WD25 8WT
Tel: . . . . 020 8950 0177 (option 1)
Fax: 020 8420 4454
Email: . . . . headoffice@nawt.org.uk
Web: . . . . www.nawt.org.uk

Objects: Q,W1,G,W4,H

The National Animal Welfare Trust was set up to find homes for unwanted dogs, cats and other domestic animals. Once in the Trust's care no healthy animal is put to sleep, however long its stay. The Trust has five Rescue Centres: the Hertfordshire centre based at the above address, the Somerset centre at Heaven's Gate Farm near Langport, the Berkshire Centre at Trindledown Farm, near Great Shefford, the Cornish Centre at Wheal Alfred Kennels, Hayle and the Essex Centre at Clacton-on-Sea.

See advert on this page

NATIONAL ANKYLOSING SPONDYLITIS SOCIETY (NASS)

Founded: 1976 CR272258; SC041347
4 Albion Court, Hammersmith, London W6 0QT
Tel: 020 8741 1515
Email: . . . . nass@nass.co.uk

Objects: F,J,G,2,H,O

NATIONAL ASSOCIATION FOR THE RELIEF OF PAGET'S DISEASE

Founded: 1973 CR266071
The Paget's Association, Suite 5, Moorfield House, Moorside Road, Swinton, Manchester, Greater Manchester M27 0EW
Tel: 0161 799 4646
Email: . . . . helpline@paget.org.uk

Objects: F,J,W5,G,A,1B,2,W4,H,3

NATIONAL ASSOCIATION FOR VOLUNTARY AND COMMUNITY ACTION (NAVCA)

Founded: 1991 CR1001635
The Tower, 2 Furnival Square, Sheffield, South Yorkshire S1 4QL
Tel: . . 0114 278 6636; 0114 278 7025 Textphone
Email: . . . . navca@navca.org.uk

Objects: F,J,G,2,H

NATIONAL ASSOCIATION OF CHILD CONTACT CENTRES - NACCC

CR1078636
1 Heritage Mews, High Pavement, Nottingham, Nottinghamshire NG1 1HN
Tel: 0845 450 0280
Email: . . . . contact@naccc.org.uk

Objects: W3,2,H,T,3

NATIONAL ASSOCIATION OF SWIMMING CLUBS FOR THE HANDICAPPED

Founded: 1966 CR247772
The Willows, Mayles Lane, Wickham, Hampshire PO17 5ND
Tel: 01329 833689
Objects: F,J,G,H,O,3,P

NATIONAL AUTISTIC SOCIETY

Founded: 1962 CR269425; SC039427
393 City Road, London EC1V 1NG
Tel: 020 7833 2299
Email: .... legacies@nas.org.uk
Objects: F,W3,W5,G,W15,2,W4,H,3,C,P,Z

THE NATIONAL BENEVOLENT CHARITY

Founded: 1812 CR212450
Peter Hervé House, Eccles Court, Tetbury, Gloucestershire GL8 8EH
Tel: 01666 505500
Email: .... ce@nbi.org.uk

NATIONAL BLIND CHILDREN'S SOCIETY

CR1051607; SC042089
Bradbury House, 33 Market Street, Highbridge, Somerset TA9 3BW
Tel: 01278 764764
Email: .... enquiries@nbcs.org.uk
Objects: W6,W3

THE NATIONAL BRAIN APPEAL

Founded: 1984 CR290173
Unit 5, Nunhold Farm Business Centre, Dark Lane, Hatton, Warwick, Warwickshire CV35 8XB
Tel: 01926 840011
Email: .... theresa.dauncey@uclh.nhs.uk
Objects: F,N,O

NATIONAL BURNS MEMORIAL HOMES, MAUCHLINE, AYRSHIRE

SC001850
c/o Mitchells Roberton Solicitors (CC), George House, 36 North Hanover Street, Glasgow G1 2AD
Tel: 0141 552 3422
Email: .... ajc@mitchells-roberton.co.uk
Objects: W4,3,C

NATIONAL CARAVAN COUNCIL LIMITED BENEVOLENT FUND

CR271625
Catherine House, Victoria Road, Aldershot, Hampshire GU11 1SS
Tel: 01252 318251
Email: .... info@nationalcaravan.co.uk
Objects: W6,W7,W5,W11,1A,A,W4,W8

NATIONAL CHILDBIRTH TRUST

Founded: 1956 CR801395
Alexandra House, Oldham Terrace, Acton, London W3 6NH
Tel: ..... 0870 770 3236 Admin; 0870 444 8707 Enquiries
Email: .... enquiries@nct.org.uk
Objects: F,M,W3,J,G,2,H,3,P,W8,K

NATIONAL CHILDREN'S BUREAU

Founded: 1963 CR258825
8 Wakley Street (CD), London EC1V 7QE
Tel: 020 7843 6000
Email: .... fundraising@ncb.org.uk
Objects: F,W3,J,G,2,H,3

NATIONAL CHILDREN'S ORCHESTRA OF GREAT BRITAIN

Founded: 1978 CR803026
57 Buckingham Road, Weston-super-Mare, North Somerset BS24 9BG
Tel: 01934 418855
Email: .... g.jones@nco.org.uk
Objects: W3,S,3

NATIONAL CHURCHES TRUST

Founded: 1952 CR207402
31 Newbury Street, London EC1A 7HU
Tel: 020 7600 6090
Objects: W2,A,1B,3

NATIONAL COASTWATCH INSTITUTION

CR1045645
1 Barras Street, Liskeard, Cornwall PL14 6AD
Tel: 0300 111 1202
Email: .... nci@springfresh.co.uk

NATIONAL COMMUNITIES RESOURCE CENTRE LTD

Founded: 1991 CR1005555
Trafford Hall, Ince Lane, Wimbolds Trafford, Cheshire CH2 4JP
Tel: 01244 300246
Objects: W3,W2,G,W10,D,H

NATIONAL COUNCIL FOR PALLIATIVE CARE

Founded: 1991 CR1005671
The Fitzpatrick Building, 188-194 York Way, London N7 9AS
Tel: 020 7697 1520
Email: .... enquiries@ncpc.org.uk
Objects: F,W3,J,W5,G,W10,W4,H

NATIONAL COUNCIL FOR VOLUNTARY ORGANISATIONS (NCVO)

CR225922
Regent's Wharf, 8 All Saints Street, London N1 9RL
Tel: .. 020 7713 6161; 0800 279 8798 Help Desk
Email: .... ncro@ncro-rol.org.uk
Objects: F,J,G,2,H,K

NATIONAL COUNCIL FOR VOLUNTARY YOUTH SERVICES

Founded: 1936 CR1093386
Second Floor, Solecast House, 13-27 Brunswick Place, London N1 6DX
Tel: 020 7253 1010
Email: .... mail@ncvys.org.uk
Objects: W3,J,G,2,H,P

NATIONAL COUNCIL OF WOMEN OF GREAT BRITAIN

Founded: 1895 CR1001015
Administrative Office, 72 Victoria Road, Darlington, Co. Durham DL1 5JG
Tel: 01325 367375
Email: .... info@ncwgb.org
Objects: G,2,H,P,W8

THE NATIONAL DEAF CHILDREN'S SOCIETY

Founded: 1944 CR1016532; SC040779
Castle House, Ground Floor South, 37-45 Paul Street, London EC2A 4LS
Tel: .. 020 7014 1102; 0808 800 8880 Freephone helpline (voice/text)
Email: .... fundraising@ndcs.org.uk
Objects: F,M,W3,J,W7,G,W10,A,2,B,H,3,P

NATIONAL ECZEMA SOCIETY

Founded: 1976 CR1009671
Hill House, Highgate Hill, London N19 5NA
Tel: 020 7281 3553
Email: mcox@eczema.org
Objects: F,W3,G,W10,2,W4,H,W8

NATIONAL EQUINE (AND SMALLER ANIMALS) DEFENCE LEAGUE

CR280700
The Animals' Refuge, Oak Tree Farm, Wetheral Shields, Carlisle, Cumbria CA4 8JA
Tel: 01228 560082
Email: admin@animalrefuge.co.uk
Objects: W1,W2

NATIONAL EXAMINATION BOARD IN OCCUPATIONAL SAFETY AND HEALTH, THE (NEBOSH)

Founded: 1979 CR1010444
Meridian Business Park, 3 Dominus Way, Leicester, Leicestershire LE19 1QW
Tel: 0116 263 4700
Email: info@nebosh.org.uk
Objects: G,3

NATIONAL EYE RESEARCH CENTRE

CR1156134
Bristol Eye Hospital, Lower Maudlin Street, Bristol BS1 2LX
Tel: 0117 9290024
Email: info@nerc.co.uk

NATIONAL FEDERATION OF WOMENS INSTITUTES

Founded: 1990 CR803793
104 New Kings Road, London SW6 4LY
Tel: 020 7371 9300
Email: hq@nfwl.org.uk
Objects: S,G,2,H,3,P,W8

NATIONAL FOUNDATION FOR EDUCATIONAL RESEARCH IN ENGLAND AND WALES - (NFER)

CR313392
The Mere, Upton Park, Slough SL1 2DQ
Tel: 01753 574123
Email: enquiries@nfer.ac.uk
Objects: G,2

NATIONAL FRUIT COLLECTION

Founded: 1990 CR328674
Crop Technology Centre, Brogdale Farm, Brogdale Road, Faversham, Kent ME13 8XZ
Tel: 01795 533225
Email: contact@nationalfruitcollection.org.uk
Objects: W2,G,2,W12

NATIONAL HEALTH SERVICE PENSIONERS' TRUST

Founded: 1991 CR1002061
PO Box 456, Esher, Surrey KT10 1DP
Tel: 01372 805760
Email: frankjackson1945@yahoo.com
Objects: W11,1A,A,1B,2

NATIONAL HEART FORUM

Founded: 1990 CR803286
Tavistock House South, Tavistock Square, London WC1H 9LG
Tel: 020 7383 7638
Email: nhf-post@heartforum.org.uk
Objects: J,G,2,H

NATIONAL INSTITUTE OF ADULT CONTINUING EDUCATION

Founded: 1991 CR1002775
21 De Montfort Street, Leicester, Leicestershire LE1 7GE
Tel: 0116 204 4200
Email: enquiries@niace.org.uk
Objects: F,J,G,2,H

NATIONAL MEMORIAL ARBORETUM

Founded: 1994 CR1043992
Croxall Road, Alrewas, Staffordshire DE13 7AR
Tel: 01283 792 333
Email: legacynma@thenma.org.uk
Objects: W9,W2,S,W12,3

NATIONAL OSTEOPOROSIS SOCIETY

CR1102712; SC039755
Legacy Manager: Ms Liz Parry
Chairman: Catherine Tompkins
Manor Farm, Skinners Hill, Camerton, Bath, Bath and North East Somerset BA2 0PJ
Tel: 01761 473261
Email: legacies@nos.org.uk
Web: www.nos.org.uk
Objects: F,W3,W5,G,1B,2,W4,H,3,W8

The National Osteoporosis Society is the only UK wide charity dedicated to improving the prevention, diagnosis and treatment of osteoporosis. We run national education campaigns to increase awareness of this disease and its prevention. We provide advice and information through a range of publications, run a specialist nurse-led national helpline and outreach vital support to through our network of local groups. We fund pioneering research into the causes, treatment and prevention of osteoporosis and we actively lobby the government as well as educate key health professionals to ensure people affected by osteoporosis can obtain the treatment and support they need.

NATIONAL POLICE FUND

CR207608
3 Mount Mews, High Street, Hampton, Middlesex TW12 2SH
Tel: 020 8941 7661
Email: office@nationalpolicefund.org.uk
Objects: W3,G,W11,A,1B,W4

NATIONAL SOCIETY (C OF E) FOR PROMOTING RELIGIOUS EDUCATION

Founded: 1811 CR313070
Church House, Great Smith Street, Westminster, London SW1P 3AZ
Tel: 020 7898 1789
Email: info@natsoc.c-of-e.org.uk
Objects: F,W3,J,G,2,W4,H,3

NATIONAL SOCIETY FOR THE PREVENTION OF CRUELTY TO CHILDREN (NSPCC)

NSPCC

***Founded:* 1884 CR216401; SC037717**
Weston House, 42 Curtain Road, London EC2A 3NH
Tel: 020 7825 2939
Email: .... legacyinfo@nspcc.org.uk
Web: ...... www.nspcc.org.uk/giftsinwills
Objects: F,W3,J,G,W15,X,H,O,3,P

At the NSPCC we're leading the fight against child abuse in the UK and Channel Islands. We help children who've been abused to rebuild their lives, we protect children at risk, and we find the best ways of preventing child abuse from ever happening. We help children and families directly through local services, and provide training and support to people who work with children. We also provide Childline, our 24/7 service for children, as well as a Helpline for adults who are worried about a child. Much of this work is only possible thanks to the generosity of those who support us through gifts in wills. Once your loved ones are taken care of, a small percentage of whatever is left could help give future generations the safe childhood they deserve.

NATIONAL STAR COLLEGE OF FURTHER EDUCATION
CR220239
Ullenwood, Cheltenham, Gloucestershire GL53 9QU
Tel: 01242 527631
Objects: W3,W5,G,O

NATIONAL TALKING EXPRESS
CR801993
c/o The Katherine Road Community Centre, 254 Katherine Road, London E7 8PN
Tel: 020 3609 7255
Email: .... nte.office@talktalk.net
Objects: W6,W5,2,H,3

NATIONAL TALKING NEWSPAPERS AND MAGAZINES (TNAUK)
CR293656
National Recording Centre, Heathfield, East Sussex TN21 8DB
Tel: 01435 866102
Email: .... legacyservices@rnib.org.uk
Objects: F,W6,M,W5,G,H,3

THE NATIONAL TRUST FOR SCOTLAND
Founded: 1931SC007410
Development Dept, Hermiston Quay, 5 Cultins Road, Edinburgh EH11 4DF
Tel: 0131 458 0407
Email: .... legacy@nts.org.uk
Objects: W2,S,2

NATIONAL TRUST, THE
Founded: 1895 CR205846
Heelis, Kemble Drive, Swindon, Wiltshire SN2 2NA
Tel: 0844 800 1895
Email: .... legacies@nationaltrust.org.uk
Objects: W1,W3,W2,S,W5,G,V,2,W4,H,P

NATIONAL YOUTH BALLET
Founded: 1990 CR1000932
The Old Dairy, Wintersell Farm, Dwelly Lane, Edenbridge, Kent TN8 6QD
Tel: 01732 864781

NATIONAL YOUTH THEATRE OF GREAT BRITAIN
CR306075
443-445 Holloway Road, London N7 6LW
Tel: 020 7281 3863
Email: .... info@nyt.org.uk
Objects: W3,J,G,P

NATURE IN ART TRUST
Founded: 1982 CR1000553
Wallsworth Hall, Twigworth, Gloucester, Gloucestershire GL2 9PA
Tel: 0845 450 0233
Email: .... enquiries@nature-in-art.org.uk
Objects: S,G,W12,3

NAUTICAL INSTITUTE
Founded: 1971 CR1002462
202 Lambeth Road, London SE1 7LQ
Tel: 020 7928 1351
Email: .... sec@nautinst.org
Objects: J,G,2,B,H,3

NAUTILUS WELFARE FUND
CR218742
NUMAST Welfare Funds, Nautilus House, Mariners' Park, Seabank Road, Wallasey, Merseyside CH45 7PH
Tel: 0151 639 8454
Email: .... welfare@nautilusint.org
Objects: F,M,W11,1A,A,D,N,W4,B,3,C

NBFA ASSISTING THE ELDERLY
Founded: 1957 CR1147446
32 Buckingham Palace Road, London SW1W 0RE
Tel: 020 7828 0200
Email: .... info@nbfa.org.uk
Objects: M,W5,V,W4,P

NEA (NATIONAL ENERGY ACTION)
Founded: 1985 CR290511
Level Six (Elswick) West One, Forty Banks, Newcastle upon Tyne, Tyne & Wear NE1 3PA
Tel: 0191 261 5677
Email: .... info@nea.org.uk
Objects: F,J,W7,W5,G,W15,W4,H,Y,Z

NETHERLANDS BENEVOLENT SOCIETY
Founded: 1874 CR213032
PO Box 36, Burwash, Etchingham, East Sussex TN19 7WR
Tel: 01932 355885
Email: .... info@koningwillemfonds.org.uk
Objects: F,1A,A,2,B,3

NETWORK 81
Founded: 1986 CR1061950
1-7 Woodfield Terrace, Stansted, Essex CM24 8AJ
Tel: 0870 770 3262
Email: .... network81@tesco.net
Objects: F,W3,G,H,3

NEURO-DISABILITY RESEARCH TRUST
CR267953
West Hill, Putney, London SW15 3SW
Tel: 020 8780 4568
Email: . . . . nrt@rhn.org.uk
Object: W5

NEUROSCIENCE SUPPORT GROUP AT THE QUEEN'S MEDICAL CENTRE
CR1001538
D Floor, School of Biomedical Sciences, University of Nottingham Medical School, Queen's Medical Centre, Nottingham, Nottinghamshire NG7 2UH
Tel: 0845 458 3208
Email: . . . . info@nsgqmc.org.uk

NEW BRIDGE
Founded: 1956
Head Office, 27A Medway Street, London SW1P 2BD
Tel: 020 7976 0779
Email: . . . . info@newbridgefoundation.org.uk
Objects: F,W3,J,G,3

NEW COVENANT CHURCH
Founded: 1991 CR1004343
506-510 Old Kent Road, London SE1 5BA
Tel: 020 7231 9817
Email: . . . . admin@newcovenant.org.uk
Objects: F,W3,W5,G,W10,2,R,W4,H,T,P,W8

NEW FOREST AGRICULTURAL SHOW SOCIETY, THE
Founded: 1992 CR1004255
The Showground, New Park, Brockenhurst, Hampshire SO42 7QH
Tel: 01590 622400
Email: . . . . info@newforestshow.co.uk
Objects: A,1B,3

NEW FRONTIERS INTERNATIONAL
Founded: 1991 CR1060001
17 Clarendon Villas, Hove, Brighton & Hove BN3 3RE
Tel: 01273 234555
Email: . . . . office@newfrontiers.xtn.org
Objects: G,R

NEW HOPE
Founded: 1991 CR1080784
Administration Office, Top Floor, 67 Queens Road, Watford, Hertfordshire WD17 2QN
Tel: 01923 210680
Email: . . . . info@wnht.org
Objects: F,E,W5,W10,W16,W4,3,C,W8

NEW HORIZONS (TEESSIDE)
CR1096895
Park Side C.M.H.R.C, Park Road North, Middlesbrough, North Yorkshire TS1 3LF
Tel: 01642 217847
Email: . . . . enquiries@newhorizonsteesside.com
Objects: F,E,W5,W10,D,3,C,Z

NEW LIFE CROYDON
Founded: 1991 CR1123257
5 Cairo New Road, Croydon, Surrey CR0 1XP
Tel: 020 8680 7671
Email: . . . . chris.parker@nlcc.croydon.org.uk
Objects: W3,G,R

NEWBURY AND DISTRICT AGRICULTURAL SOCIETY, THE
Founded: 1991 CR1003898
Newbury Showground, Priors Court Road, Hermitage, Thatcham, West Berkshire RG18 9QZ
Tel: 01635 247111
Email: . . . . . . office@newburyshowground.co.uk
Objects: W1,W3,W2,G,2,W4

NEWGROUND TOGETHER
Founded: 1990 CR702800
Bob Watts Building, Nova Scotia Wharf, Bolton Road, Blackburn, Lancashire BB2 3GE
Tel: 01254 265163
Objects: F,W1,W3,W2,W5,G,W10,W4,3,W8

NEWHAM ASIAN WOMEN'S PROJECT
CR1001834
661 Barking Road, Plaistow, London E13 9EX
Tel: 020 8472 0528
Email: . . . . info@nawp.org
Objects: F,W3,G,W10,D,C,W8

NEWHAM EDUCATION EMPLOYER PARTNERSHIP LIMITED
Founded: 1990 CR1000041
Unit 3, 51-57 High Street South, East Ham, London E6 6EJ
Tel: 020 8430 5252
Email: . . . . marion.faust@newham.gov.uk
Objects: W3,G,3

NEWLIFE FOUNDATION FOR DISABLED CHILDREN
Founded: 1991 CR1001817
Hemlock Way, Cannock, Staffordshire WS11 7GF
Tel: 01543 468888
Objects: F,G,A,1B,3

NEWMARTIN COMMUNITY YOUTH TRUST
CR298557
The Newmartin Youth Centre, 25 Claughton Road, London E13 9PN
Tel: 020 8471 1749
Email: . . . . lindar@ncytrust.org

NEWPORT (SHROPSHIRE) COTTAGE HOSPITAL TRUST LIMITED
Founded: 1990 CR1001348
Upper Bar, Newport, Shropshire TF10 7EH
Tel: 01952 820893
Object: E

NEWSTRAID BENEVOLENT FUND - OLDBEN
Founded: 1839FS20BEN
Barnetson Court, Braintree Road, Great Dunmow, Essex CM6 1HS
Tel: 01371 874198
Email: . . . . oldben@newstraid.co.uk
Objects: F,1A,A,D,2,H,C

NEWTEC
Founded: 1990 CR802868
22 Deanery Road, Stratford, London E15 4LP
Tel: 020 8519 5843
Email: . . . . enq@newtec.ac.uk
Objects: G,3,W8

NFSH CHARITABLE TRUST LTD (THE HEALING TRUST)
Founded: 1955 CR1094702
21 York Road, Northampton, Northamptonshire NN1 5QG

Tel: 01604 603247
Email: . . . . office@thehealingtrust.org.uk
Objects: F,W1,W9,W6,W3,J,E,W7,W5,G,W10, W11,W15,2,W4,U,H,P,W8,K

NIGEL MOORES FAMILY CHARITABLE FOUNDATION

Founded: 1991 CR1002366
Macfarlane and Co, 2nd Floor, Cunard Building, Water Street, Liverpool, Merseyside L3 1DS
Tel: 0151 236 6161

NIGHTINGALE HOUSE

Founded: 1840 CR207316
105 Nightingale Lane, London SW12 8NB
Tel: 020 8673 3495
Email: . . . . info@nightingale.org.uk
Objects: W6,E,W7,W5,W10,D,N,W4,3

NOISE ASSOCIATION

CR1102775
Broken Wharf House, 2 Broken Wharf, London EC4V 3DT
Tel: . . . . . . 020 7329 0774; 01634 316542 (Press enquiries)
Email: . . . . info@ukna.org.uk

NOMAD HOMELESS ADVICE AND SUPPORT UNIT

Founded: 1991 CR1078089
90 - 92 West Street, Sheffield, South Yorkshire S1 4EP
Tel: 0114 263 6624
Email: . . . . director@nomadsheffield.co.uk
Objects: F,D,3,C

NORDOFF-ROBBINS MUSIC THERAPY CENTRE

CR280960
2 Lissenden Gardens, London NW5 1PP
Tel: 020 7267 4496
Email: . . . . admin@nordoff-robbins.org.uk

NORFOLK AND NORWICH ASSOCIATION FOR THE BLIND

Founded: 1805 CR207060
106 Magpie Road, Norwich, Norfolk NR3 1JH
Tel: 01603 629558
Email: . . . . office@nnab.co.uk
Objects: F,W6,M,S,G,V,3,C,P

THE NORFOLK HOSPICE, TAPPING HOUSE

CR1062800
Common Road (West), Snettisham, King's Lynn, Norfolk PE31 7PF
Tel: 01485 542891
Email: . . . . enquiries@norfolkhospice.org.uk

NORFOLK WILDLIFE TRUST

CR208734
Bewick House, 22 Thorpe Road, Norwich, Norfolk NR1 1RY
Tel: 01603 625540
Email: . . . . info@norfolkwildlifetrust.org.uk
Objects: W2,2

NORTH DEVON HOSPICE

CR286554
Deer Park, Barnstaple, Devon EX32 0HU
Tel: 01271 344248
Email: . . . . info@northdevonhospice.org.uk
Objects: F,W3,E,W5,G,W15,N,W4

NORTH EAST ENGLAND GUIDE ASSOCIATION

CR1000858
Unit 7, Alpha Court, Monks Cross Drive, Huntington, York, North Yorkshire YO32 9WN
Tel: 01904 676076
Email: . . . . northeast@girlguiding.org.uk
Objects: W3,G,2

NORTH EAST SENSORY SERVICES

SC009537
21 John Street, Aberdeen AB25 1BT
Tel: 0845 271 2345
Email: . . . . info@grampianblind.org
Objects: F,W6,3

NORTH HUMBERSIDE MOTOR TRADES GROUP TRAINING ASSOCIATION

Founded: 1990 CR702894
The Riley Centre, Parkfield Drive, Anlaby Road, Kingston upon Hull, East Riding of Yorkshire HU3 6TB
Tel: 01482 353022
Email: . . . . edward@motortradesgta.org
Objects: G,2

NORTH OF ENGLAND REFUGEE SERVICE, THE

Founded: 1991 CR1091200
2 Jesmond Road West, Newcastle upon Tyne, Tyne & Wear NE2 4PQ
Tel: 0191 245 7311
Email: . . . . info@refugee.org.uk

NORTH STAFFS HEART COMMITTEE

CR1054889
Sneyd Cottage (CD), 5 Herm Close, Seabridge, Newcastle-under-Lyme, Staffordshire ST5 3LL
Tel: 01782 622463
Email: . . . . . . tony.berry@northstaffsheart.org.uk

NORTH WEST SURREY ASSOCIATION OF DISABLED PEOPLE

CR1058774
Provincial House, 26 Commercial Way, Woking, Surrey GU21 6EN
Tel: 01483 750973
Email: . . . . home@nwsadp.org.uk

NORTHAMPTONSHIRE ASSOCIATION OF YOUTH CLUBS (NAYC)

Founded: 1990 CR803431
Kings Park, Kings Park Road, Moulton Park, Northampton, Northamptonshire NN3 6LL
Tel: 01604 647580
Email: . . . . nayc@nayc.org

NORTHERN COUNTIES KIDNEY RESEARCH FUND

CR700037
The Freeman Hospital, High Heaton, Newcastle upon Tyne, Tyne & Wear NE7 7DN
Tel: 0191 213 7093
Fax: 0191 223 1233
Email: . . . . info@nckrf.org.uk
Web: . . . . www.nckrf.org.uk

Fundraising in the North for research in the North. This Newcastle-based Fund began in 1971, becoming independent in 1988. It relies on bequests, covenants and donations, having no professional fund-raisers. All income is dedicated to research into kidney failure and kidney transplantation. Achievements include funding six full-time research workers, and establishing a pathology laboratory and establishing a transplant laboratory studying kidney graft rejection - still the greatest cause of graft loss. Newcastle has one of the largest clinical and research programmes in kidney transplant and kidney disease. To maintain it's pre-eminence, it needs the support of those who wish the north of the country to flourish. Please help us!

See advert on this page

NORTHERN IRELAND COMMUNITY RELATIONS COUNCIL

Founded: 1990XR16701
Glendinning House, 6 Murray Street, Belfast BT1 6DN
Tel: 028 9022 7500
Email: info@nicrc.org.uk
Objects: 1B,H,T

NORTHERN IRELAND HOSPICE

XN45696
Head Office, 18 O'Neill Road, Newtownabbey, County Antrim, Belfast BT36 6WB
Tel: 028 9078 1836
Email: fundraising@nihospice.org

NORTHUMBRIA COALITION AGAINST CRIME LIMITED

Founded: 1990 CR702756
Block 33, Northumbria Police Headquarters, Newcastle upon Tyne, Tyne & Wear NE20 0BL
Tel: 01661 868424
Email: lesley@ncac.org.uk
Objects: W3,J,G,2,H,3

NORTON FOUNDATION, THE

Founded: 1990 CR702638
PO Box 10282, Redditch, Worcestershire B97 9ZA
Objects: W3,1A,A,1B,2

NORWOOD

CR1059050
Broadway House, 80-82 The Broadway, Stanmore, Middlesex HA7 4HB
Tel: 020 8954 4555
Email: norwood@norwood.org.uk
Objects: Q,F,W6,M,W3,E,W7,W5,G,W10,3,C,P,K

THE NOT FORGOTTEN ASSOCIATION (NFA)

Founded: 1920 CR1150541
Fourth Floor, 2 Grosvenor Gardens, London SW1W 0DH
Tel: 020 7730 2400; 020 7730 3600
Email: info@nfassociation.org
Objects: W9,W5,P

NOTTINGHAM AND NOTTINGHAMSHIRE REC

Founded: 2005 CR1104984
67 Lower Parliament Street, Nottingham, Nottinghamshire NG1 3BB
Tel: 0115 958 6515
Email: mail@nottsrec.com
Objects: F,G,D,3,K

NUFFIELD HEALTH
CR205533; SC041793
40 - 44 Coombe Road, New Malden, Surrey KT3 4QF
Email: .... donations@nuffieldheath.org.uk
Objects: N,2,3

NUFFIELD ORTHOPAEDIC CENTRE APPEAL
CR1006509
Nuffield Orthopaedic Centre, Headington, Oxfordshire OX3 7HE
Tel: 01865 227722

NUGENT CARE
Founded: 1881 CR222930
99 Edge Lane, Liverpool, Merseyside L7 2PE
Tel: 0151 261 2000
Email: .... info@nugentcare.org
Objects: Q,F,W3,E,W7,W5,G,1A,A,W16,D,W4,H, O,3,C,P

NVISION (BLACKPOOL, FYLDE & WYRE SOCIETY FOR THE BLIND)
CR1009955
Princess Alexandra Home, Bosworth Place, Blackpool FY4 1SH
Tel: 01253 362692
Email: .... kevin@nvision-nw.co.uk
Objects: F,W6,M,J,E,O,3,P

NZ - UK LINK FOUNDATION
Founded: 1990 CR802457
New Zealand House, Haymarket, London SW1Y 4TQ
Tel: .... 07776 147885 (mobile)
Email: .... link@linkuknz.demon.co.uk
Objects: S,G,1A

O

OAKWOOD SCHOOL FUND
Founded: 1990 CR1000982
Oakwood School, Balcombe Road, Horley, Surrey RH6 9AE
Tel: 01293 785363

OASIS CHARITABLE TRUST
CR1026487
1 Kennington Road, London SE1 7QP
Tel: 020 7921 4200
Email: .... enquiries@oasisuk.org

OCD ACTION
CR1035213
107-109 Aberdeen Centre, 22-24 Highbury Grove, London N5 2EA
Tel: 020 7226 4000
Email: .... info@ocdaction.org.uk
Objects: F,2,H,3

OCKENDEN INTERNATIONAL
Founded: 1951 CR1053720
PO Box 1275, Woking, Surrey GU22 2FT
Objects: W3,W10,U,3,W8

OFF THE RECORD (BRISTOL)
Founded: 1965 CR1085351
2 Horfield Road, St Michael's Hill, Bristol BS2 8EA
Tel: 0117 922 6747
Objects: F,W3

OFFICERS' ASSOCIATION
Founded: 1920 CR201321
1st Floor, Mountbarrow House, 6-20 Elizabeth Street, London SW1W 9RB
Tel: 0845 873 7153
Email: .... postmaster@oaed.org.uk
Objects: F,W9,1A,A,D,3

OFFICERS' ASSOCIATION SCOTLAND
SC010665
New Haig House, Logie Green Road, Edinburgh EH7 4HR
Tel: 0131 557 2782
Objects: F,W9,M,1A,A

OILY CART COMPANY, THE
Founded: 1990 CR1000799
Smallwood School Annexe, Smallwood Road, London SW17 0TW
Tel: 020 8672 6329
Email: .... oilies@oilycart.org.uk
Objects: W3,S,W5,G,3,P

OMF INTERNATIONAL (UK)
Founded: 1865 CR1123973; SC039645
UK Headquarters, Station Approach, Borough Green, Sevenoaks, Kent TN15 8BG
Tel: 01732 887299
Email: .... omf@omf.org.uk
Objects: 2,R,H

ONE PARENT FAMILIES SCOTLAND (FORMERLY SCOTTISH COUNCIL FOR SINGLE PARENTS)
SC006403
13 Gayfield Square, Edinburgh EH1 3NX
Tel: .... 0808 801 0323 (Free helpline)
Email: .... info@opfs.org.uk
Objects: F,W3,J,G,W11,V,D,2,H,W8

ONE TO ONE (JAC)
CR801096
Carradine House, 237 Regents Park Road, London N3 3LF
Tel: 020 8343 4234
Email: .... admin@one-to-one.org
Objects: F,M,W3,E,W5,G,W10,A,1B,N,U,O

ONEKIND
SC041299
50 Montrose Terrace, Edinburgh EH7 5DL
Tel: 0131 661 9734
Email: .... info@onekind.org
Objects: F,W1,H

OPEN AIR MISSION
CR215409
4 Harrier Court, Woodside Road, Slip End, Luton, Bedfordshire LU1 4DQ
Tel: 01582 841141
Email: .... oamission@btinternet.com
Object: R

OPEN LEARNING FOUNDATION, THE
Founded: 1990 CR1000055
3 Devonshire Street, London W1W 5BA
Tel: 020 7636 4186
Email: .... olf2@btconnect.com
Objects: G,2,H

OPEN SIGHT
CR1055498
County Office, 25 Church Road, Bishopstoke, Eastleigh, Hampshire SO50 6BL

Tel: 023 8064 1244
Email: . . . . info@opensight.org.uk

OPEN SPACES SOCIETY (FORMERLY COMMONS, OPEN SPACES & FOOTPATHS PRESERVATION SOCIETY)

Founded: 1865 CR214753
25A Bell Street, Henley-on-Thames, Oxfordshire RG9 2BA
Tel: 01491 573535
Email: . . . . hq@oss.org.uk
Objects: F,W2,S,1B,2,H,P

OPERATION MOBILISATION

Founded: 1992 CR1008196
The Quinta, Weston Rhyn, Oswestry, Shropshire SY10 7LT
Tel: 01691 773388
Email: . . . . info@uk.om.org

OPPORTUNITY INTERNATIONAL UK

Founded: 1992 CR1107713; SC039692
Angel Court, 81 St Clements, Oxford, Oxfordshire OX4 1AW
Tel: 01865 725304
Email: . . . . impact@opportunity.org.uk
Objects: U,3

OPUS DEI CHARITABLE TRUST

Founded: 1991 CR1005860
6 Orme Court, London W2 4RL
Tel: 020 7229 7574
Objects: G,3

ORBIS UK

Founded: 1986 CR1061352
Fourth Floor, Fergusson House, 124-128 City Road, London EC1V 2NJ
Tel: 020 7608 7260
Email: . . . . info@orbis.org.uk
Objects: W6,G,N,U,3

ORCHID CANCER APPEAL

ORCHID
FIGHTING MALE CANCER

CR1080540
Ms Rebecca Porta
231-233 North Gower Street, London NW1 2NR
Tel: 020 3465 5766
Email: . . . . info@orchid-cancer.org.uk

Orchid exists to save men's lives from testicular, prostate and penile cancers through pioneering research and promoting awareness. **Orchid** is the only UK registered charity to focus entirely on male specific cancers. Every year over 37,400 men will be diagnosed with testicular, prostate or penile cancer. Despite the huge number of men getting these cancers, there is still poor awareness amongst the general public. Early detection, diagnosis and treatment can make a huge difference, helping to increase survival rates and improve quality of life. Every year thousands of people use our services for information and support. We rely entirely on voluntary contributions. Please help us save men's lives.

ORDER OF ST JOHN

Founded: 1888 CR235979
Priory House, 25 St John's Lane, Clerkenwell, London EC1M 4PP
Tel: 020 7251 3292
Objects: W6,W3,J,W5,W10,N,2,W4,3,W8

ORFACT: ORPHANS RELIEF FUND AND CHARITABLE TRUST

CR803125
The Studio, Jubilee Close, Kingsbury, London NW9 8TR
Tel: 020 8205 8272; 020 8358 4483
Email: . . . . info@orfact.org

ORMSBY CHARITABLE TRUST, THE

Founded: 1990 CR1000599
Wasing Old Rectory, Shalford Hill, Aldermaston, Reading RG7 4NB
Tel: 0118 981 9663
Objects: W6,W3,W7,W5,A,1B,W4

ORPHEUS CENTRE

CR1105213
Orpheus Centre, North Park Lane, Godstone, Surrey RH9 8ND
Tel: 01883 744664
Email: . . . . marketing@orpheus.org.uk
Objects: W6,W3,S,W7,W5,G,D

ORTHOMOLECULAR ONCOLOGY

CR1078066
Flat 8, Fifth Floor, Northwood Hall, Hornsey Lane, London N6 5PL
Tel: 020 8374 4298
Email: . . . . canceraction@cwgsy.net

ORTHOPAEDIC INSTITUTE LIMITED

Founded: 1971 CR1044906
The Robert Jones and Agnes Hunt Orthopaedic Hospital NHS Foundation Trust, Oswestry, Shropshire SY10 7AG
Tel: 01691 404661
Email: . . . . . enquiries@orthopaedic-institute.org

ORTHOPAEDIC RESEARCH UK

Founded: 1988 CR1111657
Furlong House, 10a Chandos Street, London W1G 9DQ
Tel: 020 7436 1919
Email: . . . . info@oruk.org
Objects: G,A,1B,W4

OSCAR BIRMINGHAM

Founded: 1990 CR1109849
251-253 Rookery Road, Handsworth, Birmingham, West Midlands B21 9PU
Tel: 0121 551 6553
Email: . . . . admin@oscarbirmingham.org.uk

OSTEOPATHIC CENTRE FOR CHILDREN, LONDON

Founded: 1991 CR1003934
15a Woodbridge Street, London EC1R 0ND
Tel: 020 7490 5510
Objects: W3,G,N,H,3

OUR LADY OF FIDELITY CHARITABLE TRUST

Founded: 1991 CR1002216
15-17 Marten Road, Folkestone, Kent CT20 2JR
Tel: 0131 325 3713
Objects: W3,E,G,2

THE OUTWARD BOUND TRUST

CR1128090; SC039613
Hackthorpe Hall, Hackthorpe, Penrith, Cumbria CA10 2HX

Tel: 01931 740000
Email: . . . . enquiries@outwardbound.org.uk
Objects: W3,G,3,P

OVACOME: THE OVARIAN CANCER SUPPORT CHARITY

Founded: 1996 CR1058026
B5 New City Cloisters, 196 Old Street, London EC1V 9FR
Tel: 0845 371 0554 (Support line); 020 7299 6654 (Admin)
Email: . . . . ovacome@ovacome.org.uk

OVERSEAS BISHOPRICS' FUND

Founded: 1841 CR245334
Church House, Great Smith Street, London SW1P 3AZ
Tel: 020 7898 1677
Objects: 1A,A,1B,R,U,3

OXFAM

Founded: 1942 CR202918; SC039042
Oxfam House, John Smith Drive, Cowley, Oxford, Oxfordshire OX4 2JY
Tel: 0300 200 1331
Email: . . . . legacy@oxfam.org.uk

OXFORD COLLEGES INTERNATIONAL (FORMERLY NORTH LONDON SCHOOLS TRUST)

Founded: 1991 CR1002034
11 Golders Green Road, London NW11 8DY
Tel: 020 8905 5467
Email: . . . . ggcol@easynet.co.uk
Objects: G,3

OXFORD HOUSE IN BETHNAL GREEN

Founded: 1884 CR208582
Derbyshire Street, Bethnal Green, London E2 6HG
Tel: 020 7739 9001
Email: . . . . admin@oxfordhouse.org.uk
Objects: F,W3,J,S,G,W10,2,P

OXFORD MISSION

CR211618
PO Box 86, Romsey, Hampshire SO51 8YD
Tel: 01794 515004
Email: . . . . oxfordmission@aol.com
Objects: W3,W5,2,W4,U,W8

OXFORD PRESERVATION TRUST

CR203043
10 Turn Again Lane, Oxford, Oxfordshire OX1 1QL
Tel: 01865 242918
Fax: 01865 246706
Email: . . . info@oxfordpreservation.org.uk
Web: http://www.oxfordpreservation.org.uk
Objects: W2,1B,2
Protection of Oxford's setting and townscape through land ownership and representation. Conservation projects & education programme.

OXFORDSHIRE CHINESE COMMUNITY & ADVICE CENTRE

CR1006710
44b Princes Street, Oxford, Oxfordshire OX4 1DD
Tel: 01865 204188
Email: . . . . occac@dial.pipex.com

OXFORDSHIRE RURAL COMMUNITY COUNCIL

Founded: 1990 CR900560
Jericho Farm, Worton, Witney, Oxfordshire OX29 4SZ
Tel: 01865 883488
Email: . . . . orcc@oxonrcc.org.uk
Objects: F,J,1B,H,3

P

P3 (PEOPLE POTENTIAL POSSIBILITIES)

CR703163
Eagle House, Cotmanhay Road, Ilkeston, Derbyshire DE7 8HU
Tel: 0115 850 8190
Email: . . . . info@p3charity.org

PACE CENTRE LTD, THE

Founded: 1992 CR1011133
Philip Green House, Coventon Road, Aylesbury, Buckinghamshire HP19 9JL
Tel: 01296 392739
Objects: W3,G,O,3

PACT (PRISON ADVICE & CARE TRUST)

CR219278
29 Peckham Road, London SE5 8UA
Tel: 020 7735 9535
Email: . . . . info@prisonadvice.org.uk

PAGET GORMAN SOCIETY

CR1008041
2 Dowlands Bungalows, Dowlands Lane, Smallfield, Surrey RH6 9SD
Tel: 01342 842308
Email: . . . . pru.phillips@googlemail.com

PAPWORTH TRUST

Founded: 1917 CR211234
Bernard Sunley Centre, Papworth Everard, Cambridge, Cambridgeshire CB23 3RG
Tel: 01480 357200
Email: . . . . info@papworth.org.uk
Objects: F,W6,M,W3,W7,W5,G,D,W4,O,3,C,K

PAPYRUS PREVENTION OF YOUNG SUICIDE

CR1070896
47 Bewsey Street, Warrington, Cheshire WA2 7JQ
Tel: 01925 572444; 0800 068 4141 HOPELineUK
Email: . . . . admin@papyrus-uk.org

PARKINSON'S UK

CR258197; SC037554
215 Vauxhall Bridge Road, Legacy Department, London SW1V 1EJ
Tel: . . 020 7931 8080; 0808 800 0303 Freephone Helpline
Email: . . . . enquiries@parkinsons.org.uk
Objects: F,M,W3,J,W5,G,W10,V,N,2,W4,H,O,3,P,K

News from The Passage

The Passage is about long term, lasting solutions and seeks to address the root causes that led to a person becoming homeless in the first place so that their cycle of homelessness can be broken for good. Recent achievements include:

- 92% of all new rough sleepers in South Westminster were either supported to return to their home area or linked into support services and accommodation off the streets within 2 contacts by The Passage Street Outreach team during 2011/12.
- The Passage helped 117 entrenched rough sleepers off the streets of South Westminster during the same period.
- For the 3rd year running every client moving on from The Passage's supported accommodation scheme and into their own tenancy has sustained that tenancy.
- Over the last 10 years The Passage has helped nearly 600 homeless people into full time employment.

The Passage has ninety staff and a volunteer to staff ratio of over 3:1. It costs nearly £4 million per year to run The Passage, and half of that income is dependent on voluntary donations. For every £1 donated in voluntary income, over 90% goes straight to our frontline services.

PARTIALLY SIGHTED SOCIETY
Founded: 1973 CR254052
1 Bennetthorpe, Doncaster, South Yorkshire DN2 6AA
Tel: 01302 965195
Email: .... reception@partsight.org.uk
Objects: F,W6,M,J,G,H,3,P

PARTIS COLLEGE
Founded: 1824 CR200606
Violet Wills Wing, Newbridge Hill, Bath, Bath & North East Somerset BA1 3QD
Tel: 01225 421532
Email: .... partiscoll@aol.com
Objects: D,W4,3,W8

THE PASSAGE

THE PASSAGE
to ending homelessness

Founded: 1980 CR1079764
Business Director: Mr Andrew Hollingsworth
St Vincent's Centre, Carlisle Place, London SW1P 1NL
Tel: 020 7592 1856
Fax: 020 7592 1870
Email: .... info@passage.org.uk
Web: .... www.passage.org.uk
Objects: E,W16,C

The Passage's Mission is to provide resources that encourage, inspire, and challenge homeless people to transform their lives. It fulfils its mission by providing:

- **Resource Centre services offering basic care, Health including mental health, substance misuse and primary care, Housing and advice, education, training and employment**
- **Street outreach services to contact rough sleepers**
- **Hostel accommodation with support and advice**
- **Home for Good supporting those who have been resettled**

See advert on previous page

PATIENTS ASSOCIATION
Founded: 1963 CR1006733
PO Box 935, Harrow, Middlesex HA1 3YJ
Tel: .... 020 8423 9111; 0845 608 4455 Helpline
Objects: F,W6,W3,W7,W5,2,W4,H,3,W8

PAUL FOUNDATION
Founded: 1991 CR1003143
Haycroft, Sherborne, Cheltenham, Gloucestershire GL54 3NB
Tel: 01451 844500
Objects: W3,A,1B

PAUL STRICKLAND SCANNER CENTRE
CR298867
Mount Vernon Hospital, Northwood, Middlesex HA6 2RN
Tel: 01923 844290
Objects: N,3

PAWS AND CLAWS ANIMAL RESCUE SERVICE, MID-SUSSEX
CR281075
Coombe Down, London Road, Sayers Common, Hurstpierpoint, West Sussex BN6 9HZ
Tel: 01444 831286
Email: .... info@pawsandclaws-ars.org.uk

PDSA
Founded: 1917 CR208217; SC037585
Head Office, Whitechapel Way, Priorslee, Telford, Shropshire TF2 9PQ
Tel: 01952 290999
Email: .... legacies@pdsa.org.uk
Objects: F,W1,M,2,H,3

PEABODY TRUST
Founded: 1862 CR206061
45 Westminster Bridge Road, London SE1 7JB
Tel: 020 7021 4000
Email: .... company.secretary@peabody.org.uk
Objects: W6,W3,E,W7,W5,G,W10,D,W4,3,C,W8

PEACE HOSPICE CARE
Founded: 1991 CR1002878
Reynolds Porter Chamberlain, 278-282 High Holborn, London WC1V 7HA
Tel: 020 7242 2877
Email: .... fundraising@peacehospice.org.uk
Objects: F,E,W10,N,W4,3,W8

PELICAN TRUST LIMITED
CR703143
20-22 Crofton Road, Allenby Industrial Estate, Lincoln, Lincolnshire LN3 4NL
Tel: 01522 513533
Email: .... jayne@pelicantrust.org
Objects: S,W5,G,O,3,K

PEMBROKE HOUSE, HOME FOR AGED EX-NAVAL MEN, THEIR WIVES AND WIDOWS AND FORMER WRENS
CR206243
11 Oxford Road, Gillingham, Kent ME7 4BS
Tel: 01634 852431
Email: .... pembrokehouse@rnbt.org.uk
Objects: W9,1A,A,N

PENNY BROHN CANCER CARE
Founded: 1980 CR284881
Chapel Pill Lane, Pill, Bristol BS20 0HH
Tel: . 01275 370110 Switchboard; 08451 232310 Helpline
Email: .... info@pennybrohn.org
Objects: F,W3,J,W5,G,W10,W4,H,O,3,W8

PENTREATH LTD
Founded: 1991 CR1004477
1st Floor Offices, Formal Ind Est, Treswithian, Camborne, Cornwall TR14 0PY
Tel: 01209 719632
Email: .... penreath@penreath.co.uk
Objects: F,W5,G,O,3,K

PEOPLE'S TRUST FOR ENDANGERED SPECIES
Founded: 1977 CR274206
3 Cloisters House, 8 Battersea Park Road, London SW8 4BG
Tel: 020 7498 4533
Email: .... enquiries@ptes.org
Web: .... www.ptes.org
One in ten British species faces the risk of extinction. Globally, an estimated 10,000 to 100,000 species are

becoming extinct every year. Each loss creates a gap in the ecosystem on which we all depend for everything from medicine to water. This situation is devastating for us and for future generations, but there is nothing natural or inevitable about it. It is absolutely avoidable. That is why PTES exists. A legacy of any size will enable us to plan ahead and use our resources in the best way to ensure the survival of our wildlife. Thank you.

PERENNIAL - GARDENERS' ROYAL BENEVOLENT SOCIETY

SC040180
115/117 Kingston Road, Leatherhead, Surrey KT22 7SU
Tel: 0845 230 1839
Email: . . . . info@perennial.org.uk
Objects: W3,W5,1A,A,V,D,N,B,H,3,C

PERTH & KINROSS SOCIETY FOR THE BLIND

SC001152
St Paul's Centre, 14 New Row, Perth, Perth & Kinross PH1 5QA
Tel: 01738 626969
Email: . . . . pkbs.perth@virgin.net

PERTH ASSOCIATION FOR MENTAL HEALTH

SC002072
Caladh Centre, 6 Milne Street, Perth, Perth & Kinross PH1 5QL
Tel: 01738 639657
Email: . . . . admin@pamh.co.uk

PESTALOZZI INTERNATIONAL VILLAGE TRUST

CR1098422
Sedlescombe, Battle, East Sussex TN33 0UF
Tel: 01424 870444
Email: . . . . office@pestalozzi.org.uk

PET RESCUE WELFARE ASSOCIATION

Founded: 2001 CR1116170
Llewerllyd Farm, Long Acres Lane, Dyserth, Denbighshire LL18 6BP
Tel: 01745 571061
Web: . . . . www.pet-rescuecharity.co.uk
Object: W1

Small enough to care, large enough to make a difference.

See advert on this page

THE PETER TRUST

CR1080159
St Mary's Presbytery, 40 Park Lane, Rothwell, Leeds, West Yorkshire LS26 0ES
Tel: 0113 282 2320
Email: . . . . psmythe@stmarys.fslife.co.uk
Objects: 1A,1B,U,3

BRITISH SMALL ANIMAL VETERINARY ASSOCIATION - PETSAVERS

Founded: 1974 CR1024811
Woodrow House, 1 Telford Way, Waterwells Business Park, Quedgeley, Gloucestershire GL2 2AB
Tel: 01452 726723
Email: . . . . info@petsavers.org.uk
Objects: W1,G,1A,A,1B,2,3

PHAB
Founded: 1957 CR283931
Summit House, Wandle Road, Croydon, Surrey CR0 1DF
Tel: 020 8667 9443
Email: .... info@phab.org.uk
Objects: F,W3,J,S,W5,G,1A,1B,V,2,W4,H,3,P

PHARMACIST SUPPORT
Founded: 1841 CR1158974
5th Floor (CD), 196 Deansgate, Manchester, Greater Manchester M3 3WF
Tel: 0808 168 2233
Email: .... info@pharmacistsupport.org
Objects: F,W5,W11,W15,1A,W4,O,Y

PHILHARMONIA ORCHESTRA
CR250277
First Floor, 125 High Holborn, London WC1V 6QA
Tel: 020 7242 5001
Email: .... info@philharmonia.co.uk
Object: S

PHYLLIS TUCKWELL HOSPICE CARE
CR264501
The Fundraising Department, Waverley Lane, Farnham, Surrey GU9 8BL
Tel: 01252 729400
Email: fundraising@phyllistuckwellhospice.org.uk
Object: N

PIED PIPER TRUST, THE
Founded: 1992 CR1011611
Gloucestershire Royal Hospital, Great Western Road, Gloucester, Gloucestershire GL1 3NN
Tel: 01452 394119
Objects: W3,1B,N

PILGRIMS' FRIEND SOCIETY
Founded: 1807 CR1134979
175 Tower Bridge Road, London SE1 2AL
Tel: 0300 300 1400
Email: .... info@pilgrimsfriend.org.uk
Objects: D,W4,3,C

PILGRIMS HOSPICES IN EAST KENT
CR293968
56 London Road, Canterbury, Kent CT2 8JA
Tel: 01227 812601
Email: .... eastkent@pilgrimshospice.org

PIMLICO OPERA
Founded: 1991 CR1003836
The Coach House, 12 St Thomas Street, Winchester, Hampshire SO23 9HF
Tel: 01962 868600
Objects: S,G,3

PINE RIDGE DOG SANCTUARY
Founded: 1958 CR256728
Priory Road (CC), Ascot, Windsor & Maidenhead SL5 8RJ
Tel: 01344 882689
Fax: 01344 882689
Email: .... pineridgedogs@yahoo.co.uk
Objects: W1,W15,W4

Pine Ridge Dog Sanctuary has been saving stray and unwanted dogs since 1958. Established by the late Bernard Cuff. We spay and neuter all dogs, if old enough, prior to rehoming. We also help the elderly or needy families with veterinary costs. We can only do this through the generosity of animal lovers who support our work with regular donations. Please do not let the dogs down, they are relying on you. Please remember Pine Ridge in your Will. Legacies are of utmost importance to enable us to continue our work in giving the dogs the love and care they deserve.

THE PLAIN TRUTH
CR1098217
PO Box 4421, Worthing, West Sussex BN14 8WQ
Tel: 01638 741549
Email: .... ptruth@netcomuk.co.uk

PLANT HERITAGE (NCCPG)
Founded: 1991 CR1004009; SC041785
12 Home Farm, Loseley Park, Guildford, Surrey GU3 1HS
Tel: 01483 447540
Email: .... info@plantheritage.org.uk
Objects: W2,2

POD CHARITABLE TRUST
Founded: 1977 CR279743
Mount Hall, Llanfair Caereinion, Welshpool, Powys SY21 0BH
Tel: 01938 810374
Email: .... podcharity@btinternet.com
Objects: W3,O,3,P

POLDEN PUCKHAM CHARITABLE FOUNDATION
Founded: 1991 CR1003024
BM PPCF, London WC1N 3XX
Objects: W2,1B

POLESWORTH GROUP HOMES ASSOCIATION
Founded: 1991 CR1003230
Laurel End, Laurel Avenue, Tamworth, Staffordshire B78 1LT
Tel: 01827 896124
Objects: W5,3,C

THE POLICE DEPENDANTS' TRUST
Founded: 1966 CR251021
3 Mount Mews, High Street, Hampton, Middlesex SW12 2SH
Tel: 020 8941 6907
Email: .... office@pdtrust.org
Objects: M,W3,1A,A,V

POLICE MEMORIAL TRUST
CR289371
219 Kensington High Street, London W8 6BD
Tel: 020 7734 8385
Object: W12

POLICE REHABILITATION CENTRE
CR210310
Flint House, Reading Road, Goring-on-Thames, Reading RG8 0LL
Tel: 01491 874499
Email: .... enquiries@flinthouse.co.uk

THE POLICE TREATMENT CENTRES
CR1147449; SC043396
St Andrews, Harlow Moor Road, Harrogate, North Yorkshire HG2 0AD
Tel: 01423 504448
Email: . enquiries@thepolicetreatmentcentres.org

POLISH EX-COMBATANTS ASSOCIATION
Founded: 1946 CR249509
240 King's Street, London W6 0RF
Tel: 020 8741 1911; 020 8748 6136
Objects: F,H

PONTEFRACT FAMILY CENTRE

Founded: 1982 CR1100754
4 Harropwell Lane, Pontefract, West Yorkshire WF8 1QY
Tel: 01977 706932
Objects: E,W5,W4,3,P

PONTESBURY PROJECT FOR PEOPLE WITH SPECIAL NEEDS, THE

Founded: 1990 CR702609
Hill Farm, Pontesford, Shrewsbury, Shropshire SY5 0UH
Tel: 01743 791975

POPPYSCOTLAND (THE EARL HAIG FUND SCOTLAND)

SC014096
New Haig House, Logie Green Road, Edinburgh EH7 4HQ
Tel: 0131 550 1567
Email: .... supportercare@poppyscotland.org.uk
Objects: F,W9,M,J,1A,A,1B,2,H,3,K

PORCHLIGHT

CR267116
2nd Floor, Watling Chambers, 18-19 Watling Street, Canterbury, Kent CT1 2UA
Tel: 01227 760078
Email: .... getinvolved@porchlight.org.uk
Objects: F,W3,W16,D,W4,Y,3,C,Z,W8

POSITIVE EAST

Founded: 1990 CR1001582
159 Mile End Road, Stepney, London E1 4AQ
Tel: 020 7791 2855
Email: ...... patrick.barker@positiveeast.org.uk
Objects: F,W3,W10,3,W8

POSITIVE PLACE

Founded: 1992 CR1009957
52 Deptford Broadway, London SE8 4PH
Tel: 020 8694 9988
Email: .... info@thepositiveplace.org.uk
Objects: 2,3

POSITIVELY UK

Founded: 1987 CR1007685
345 City Road, London EC1V 1LR
Tel: .... 020 7713 0444 (admin) 9:30-5
Email: .... info@positivelyuk.org
Objects: F,W3,G,H,3,P,W8

POTENTIAL PLUS UK [FORMERLY NATIONAL ASSOCIATION FOR GIFTED CHILDREN (NAGC)]

Founded: 1966 CR313182
Suite 1.2, Challenge House, Sherwood Drive, Bletchley, Milton Keynes, Buckinghamshire MK3 6DP
Tel: 01908 646433
Email: .... amazingchildren@potentialplusuk.org
Objects: F,W3,J,G,2,H,3,P

POTTERY & GLASS TRADES' BENEVOLENT FUND

Founded: 1881 CR208227
Flat 57, Witley Court, Coram Street, London WC1N 1HD
Tel: 020 7837 2231
Objects: W11,1A,A,B

PRACTICAL ACTION (FORMERLY ITDG)

Founded: 1966 CR247257
The Schumacher Centre, Bourton on Dunsmore, Rugby, Warwickshire CV23 9QZ
Tel: 01926 634400
Fax: 01926 634401
Email: ..... legacy@practicalaction.org.uk
Web: .... www.practicalaction.org
Objects: W2,U,W8

Founded in 1966 by radical economist and author of Small is Beautiful, Dr E F Schumacher.
Together we can:
•directly help nearly one million families transform their lives
•protect poor people from preventable disease by providing them with access to safe drinking
•reduce the impact of natural disasters like earthquakes and flooding on the communities whose lives they threaten
•ensure sustainable access to energy sources that power schools, hospitals, villages and improve livelihoods
For further information on making or changing your will and thus changing lives, please contact our Legacy Officer, Liz Webb.

PRADER-WILLI SYNDROME ASSOCIATION (UK)

Founded: 1981 CR284583
Suite 4.4, Litchurch Plaza, Litchurch Lane, Derby, Derbyshire DE24 8AA
Tel: 01483 724784
Objects: F,W3,J,W5,G,W10,W15,2,H,P,W8,W

PRAXIS CARE

XN80842
27-31 Lisburn Road, Belfast BT9 7AA
Tel: 028 9024 8665
Email: .... info@praxiscare.co.uk
Objects: W3,E,W5,W4,C,P

PRE-SCHOOL LEARNING ALLIANCE

Founded: 1961 CR1096526
The Fitzpatrick Building, 188 York Way, London N7 9AD
Tel: 020 7697 2500
Email: .... info@pre-school.org.uk

PRESBYTERIAN CHURCH IN IRELAND

XN45376
Assembly Buildings, Fisherwick Place, Belfast BT1 6DW
Tel: 028 9032 2284
Email: .... clerk@presbyterianireland.org
Objects: F,W3,W7,G,W15,1A,1B,R,W4,U,H,3,C,Z,W8,L

PRESBYTERIAN CHURCH OF WALES

CR1132022
Tabernacle Chapel, 81 Merthyr Road, Whitchurch, Cardiff CF14 1DD
Tel: 029 2062 7465
Email: .... swyddfa.office@ebcpcw.org.uk

PRESTON AND WESTERN LANCASHIRE REC

Founded: 1990 CR1095261
Town Hall Annexe, Birley Street, Preston, Lancashire PR1 2RL
Tel: 01772 906422
Email: .... admin@prestonrec.org.uk
Objects: F,S,W10,2,3

PREVENT UNWANTED PETS (PUP)

CR702569

14 Friars Close, Tyldesley, Manchester, Greater Manchester M29 8QB

Tel: 07772 722709

Email: . . . . aguest@cat.com

PRIMARY IMMUNODEFICIENCY ASSOCIATION (PIA)

Founded: 1990 CR1107233

Alliance House, 12 Caxton Street, London SW1H 0QS

Tel: 020 7976 7640

Email: . . . . info@pia.org.uk

Objects: F,W3,W5,1B,2,H,3,P

THE PRINCE'S TRUST

CR1079675

Prince's Trust House (CC), 9 Eldon Street, London EC2M 7LS

Tel: 020 7543 1299

Email: . . . . getinvolved@princes-trust.org.uk

Objects: F,W3,W5,G,W10,1A,A,H,3

THE PRINCE'S FOUNDATION FOR THE BUILT ENVIRONMENT

CR1069969

19-22 Charlotte Road, London EC2A 3SG

Tel: 020 7613 8500

Email: . . . . enquiry@princes-foundation.org

Objects: F,W3,W2,G,2,3

PRINCESS ALICE HOSPICE

CR1010930

West End Lane, Esher, Surrey KT10 8NA

Tel: 01372 468811

Email: . . . . legacies@pah.org.uk

Objects: F,G,N,O,3

PRINTERS' CHARITABLE CORPORATION

Founded: 1827 CR208882

Suite B, Underwood House, 235 Three Bridges Road, Crawley, West Sussex RH10 1LS

Tel: 01293 542820

Email: . info@printerscharitablecorporation.co.uk

Objects: F,W11,1A,A,N,2,B,3,C

PRISON FELLOWSHIP ENGLAND AND WALES

CR1102254

PO Box 68226, London SW1P 9WR

Tel: 020 7799 2500

Email: . . . . info@prisonfellowship.org.uk

Objects: F,W3,R,W4,T,O,3,W8

PRISON REFORM TRUST

PRISON
REFORM
TRUST

Founded: 1981 CR1035525

Finance and Development Officer: Ms Charlotte Story

2nd Floor, The Old Trading House, 15 Northburgh Street, London EC1V 0JR

Tel: 020 7689 7731

Fax: 020 7251 5076

Email: . charlotte.story@prisonreformtrust.org.uk

Web: . . . . www.prisonreformtrust.org.uk

Objects: F,H

We aim to create a just, humane and effective penal system. We do this by inquiring into the workings of the system; informing prisoners, staff and the wider public; and by influencing parliament, government and officials towards reform.

PRISONERS ABROAD

Founded: 1978 CR1093710

89-93 Fonthill Road, London N4 3JH

Tel: 020 7561 6820

Email: . . . . info@prisonersabroad.org.uk

Objects: F,J,G,1A,A,U,H,3

PRISONERS' EDUCATION TRUST

CR1084718

The Foundry, 17 – 19 Oval Way, London SE11 5RR

Tel: 020 3752 5680

Email: . . . . info@prisonerseducation.org.uk

Objects: G,1A,A,O,3

PRISONERS' FAMILIES & FRIENDS SERVICE

CR251847

20 Trinity Street, London SE1 1DB

Tel: 020 7403 4091

Email: . . . . info@pffs.org.uk

Objects: F,W3,3,W8

PRISONERS OF CONSCIENCE APPEAL FUND

CR213766

PO Box 61044, London SE1 1UP

Tel: 020 7407 6644

Email: . . . . info@prisonersofconscience.org

Objects: G,A,O

PRO CORDA - NATIONAL SCHOOL FOR YOUNG CHAMBER MUSIC PLAYERS

CR1116213

Leiston Abbey House, Theberton Road, Leiston, Suffolk IP16 4TB

Tel: 01728 831354

Email: . . . . mail@procorda.com

Objects: W3,S,G,1A,3

PROFESSIONAL ASSOCIATION FOR CHILDCARE AND EARLY YEARS (PACEY)
CR295981
Royal Court, 81 Tweedy Road, Bromley, Kent BR1 1TG
Tel: 0300 003 0005
Email: . . . . info@pacey.org.uk
Objects: F,W3,J,G,2,W4,H

PROFESSIONALS AID COUNCIL
Founded: 1921 CR207292
10 St Christopher's Place, London W1U 1HZ
Tel: 020 7935 0641
Email: . . . . admin@paca.org.uk
Objects: W3,J,G,W11,1A,A,W4

PROGRESSIO
Founded: 1940 CR294329
Units 9-12, The Stableyard, Broomgrove Road, London SW9 9TL
Tel: 020 7733 1195
Email: . . . . ciir@ciir.org
Objects: W3,W2,W7,W5,G,W10,W4,U,H,3,W8

PROJECT ABILITY
SC005226
Trongate, 103, Glasgow, Glasgow G1 5HD
Tel: 0141 552 2822
Email: . . . . . . development@project-ability.co.uk
Objects: W3,S,W5,W10,3,K

PROSPECT EDUCATION (TECHNOLOGY) TRUST LTD
Founded: 1990 CR803497
100 West Hill, Wandsworth, London SW15 2UT
Tel: 020 8877 0357
Objects: W3,G,3

PROSPECTS FOR PEOPLE WITH LEARNING DISABILITIES
Founded: 1976 CR1060571
69 Honey End Lane, Reading RG30 4EL
Tel: 0118 950 8781
Email: . . . . info@prospects.org.uk
Objects: M,E,W5,R,3,C,P,K

PROSTATE ACTION
Founded: 1994 CR1135297
6 Crescent Stables, 139 Upper Richmond Road, London SW15 2TN
Tel: 020 8788 7720
Email: . . . . info@prostateaction.org.uk
Objects: F,1B,H,3

PROSTATE CANCER RESEARCH CENTRE
CR1156027
Britannia House, 7 Trinity Street, London SE1 1DB
Tel: 020 7848 7546
Email: . . . info@prostate-cancer-research.org.uk
Object: W

See advert on this page

PROSTATE CANCER UK

Founded: 1996 CR1005541; SC039332
Director of Fundraising: Mr James Beeby
Fourth Floor, The Counting House, 53 Tooley Street, London SE1 2QN
Tel: 0800 082 1616
Fax: 020 3310 7107
Email: . . . . legacies@prostatecanceruk.org
Web: . . . . prostatecanceruk.org
Objects: F,H,W

One man dies of prostate cancer every hour. Prostate Cancer UK fights to help more men survive prostate cancer and enjoy a better quality of life. We support men, find answers and lead change.

PROTESTANT TRUTH SOCIETY

CR248505
184 Fleet Street, London EC4A 2HJ
Tel: 020 7405 4960
Email: . . . . pts@protestant-truth.org

PROVIDENCE ROW

Founded: 1860 CR1140192
The Dellow Centre, 82 Wentworth Street, London E1 7SA
Tel: 020 7375 0020
Email: . . . . info@providencerow.org.uk
Objects: F,E,W4,3,C,W8

PROVISION TRADE BENEVOLENT INSTITUTION

Founded: 1835 CR209173
17 Clerkenwell Green, London EC1R 0DP
Tel: 020 7253 2114
Objects: W11,1A,A,2,B

PROWDE'S EDUCATIONAL FOUNDATION

Founded: 1722 CR310255
39 Stanley Street, Southsea, Hampshire PO5 2DS
Objects: W3,G,1A,A

PSORIASIS ASSOCIATION

Founded: 1968 CR257414; SC039886
Dick Coles House, 2 Queensbridge, Northampton, Northamptonshire NN4 7BF
Tel: . . 01604 251620; 08456 760076 Helpline No.
Email: helen.mcateer@psoriasis-association.org.uk
Objects: F,W6,W3,J,W7,W5,G,W10,1B,2,W4,H,W8,W

THE PSP ASSOCIATION

CR1037087
PSP House, 167 Watling Street West, Towcester, Northamptonshire NN12 6BX
Tel: 01327 322410
Email: . . . . psp@pspeur.org

PSYCHIATRY RESEARCH TRUST

Founded: 1982 CR284286
16 De Crespigny Park, Denmark Hill, London SE5 8AF
Tel: 020 7703 6217
Email: . . . . psychiatry_research_trust@kcl.ac.uk
Object: 1A

PUBLIC LAW PROJECT, THE

Founded: 1991 CR1003342
150 Caledonian Road, London N1 9RD
Tel: 020 7697 2190
Email: . . . . admin@publiclawproject.org.uk
Objects: W3,W5,G,W4,3

PURLEY PARK TRUST LTD

CR261726
Huckleberry Close, Purley-on-Thames, Reading RG8 8EH
Tel: 0118 942 7608
Objects: E,W5,3,Z

Q

QED UK

Founded: 1991 CR1004608
Quest House, 243 Manningham Lane, Bradford, West Yorkshire BD8 7ER
Tel: 01274 483267
Email: . . . . info@qed-uk.org
Objects: F,J,G,W10,3,P

QUAKERS (YEARLY MEETING OF THE RELIGIOUS SOCIETY OF FRIENDS IN BRITAIN)

Founded: 1652
Friends House, 173 Euston Road, London NW1 2BJ
Tel: 020 7663 1000
Email: . . . . rachelr@quaker.org.uk
Objects: F,J,W2,G,W10,D,2,R,U,H,T,3

QUAKERS: YOUNG FRIENDS' GENERAL MEETING OF THE RELIGIOUS SOCIETY OF FRIENDS

CR1064763
YFGM Office, Friends House, 173-177 Euston Road, London NW1 2BJ
Tel: 020 7663 1050
Email: . . . . yfgm@quaker.org.uk

QUARRIERS

SC001960
Fundraising, The Exchange, Quarrier's Village, Bridge of Weir, Renfrewshire PA11 3SX
Tel: 01505 616057
Email: . . . . fundraising@quarriers.org.uk

QUEEN ALEXANDRA HOSPITAL HOME

Founded: 1919 CR208721
Boundary Road, Worthing, West Sussex BN11 4LJ
Tel: 01903 213458
Email: . . . . ceo@qahh.org.uk
Objects: W9,W5,V,N

QUEEN ALEXANDRA'S ROYAL ARMY NURSING CORPS ASSOCIATION (QARANC)

CR270278
Regimental Headquarters QARANC, AMS HQ, Slim Road, Camberley, Surrey GU15 4NP
Tel: 01276 412754; 01276 412791
Email: . . . . regtsecqaranc@hotmail.com
Objects: W9,1A

QUEEN ELIZABETH'S FOUNDATION FOR DISABLED PEOPLE
CR251051
Leatherhead Court, Woodlands Road, Leatherhead, Surrey KT22 0BN
Tel: 01372 841127
Email: .... cynthia.robinson@qefd.org
Objects: F,M,E,W5,G,V,O,3

THE QUEEN'S NURSING INSTITUTE
Founded: 1887 CR213128
1A Henrietta Place, London W1G 0LZ
Tel: 020 7549 1400
Email: .... sheena.frempong@qni.org.uk
Objects: F,W6,J,W7,W5,G,W10,W11,1A,A,W4,B,H,W8

QUEEN VICTORIA SCHOOL, DUNBLANE
SC013381
Dunblane, Stirling FK15 0JY
Tel: 0131 310 2927; 01786 822288
Email: .... stephen.dougan@qvs.org.uk
Objects: W9,W3,G,W11

QUEEN VICTORIA SEAMEN'S REST - FOR UNEMPLOYED, RETIRED AND ACTIVE SEAFARERS
Founded: 1843 CR1106126
121-131 East India Dock Road, Poplar, London E14 6DF
Tel: 020 7987 5466
Email: .... personalassistant@qvsr.org.uk

R

RAEC AND ETS BRANCH ASSOCIATION
Founded: 1957 CR231250
RHQ AGC, Worthy Down, Winchester, Hampshire SO21 2RG
Tel: 01962 887970
Email: .... raecandets.assoc@milnet.uk.net
Objects: W9,A

RAF ASSOCIATION
Founded: 1943 CR226686; SC037673
Atlas House, 41 Wembley Road, Leicester, Leicestershire LE3 1UT
Tel: 0116 266 5224
Email: .... liz.fredericks@rafa.org.uk
Objects: F,W9,A,V,2,U,B,C,P

RAILWAY BENEFIT FUND
Founded: 1858 CR206312
Electra Way, Crewe Business Park, Crewe, Cheshire CW1 6HS
Tel: 01270 251316
Email: ...... director@railwaybenefitfund.org.uk
Objects: W6,W3,W7,W5,W10,W11,1A,A,W4,W8

RAINBOW KIDZ
CR1114717
55 Wordsworth Avenue, London E18 2HD
Tel: 020 8530 5111; 07788 100279
Email: .... info@rainbow-kidz.org.uk

RAINER
Founded: 1788 CR229132
Rectory Lodge, High Street, Brasted, Westerham, Kent TN16 1JF
Tel: 01959 578200
Email: .... mail@raineronline.org
Objects: W3,G,D,3,P,Z,I

RAINY DAY TRUST (INCORPORATING THE POTTERY & GLASS TRADES' BENEVOLENT FUND)
Founded: 1843 CR209170
Brooke House, 4 The Lakes, Northampton, Northamptonshire NN4 7YD
Tel: 01604 622023
Email: .... info@rainydaytrust.org.uk
Objects: W9,W6,J,W7,W5,W10,W11,1A,A,V,2,W4,W8

RAMBLERS' ASSOCIATION
Founded: 1935 CR1093577; SC039799
2nd Floor, Camelford House, 87-89 Albert Embankment, London SE1 7TW
Tel: 020 7339 8500
Email: .... rememberus@ramblers.org.uk
Objects: W2,S,G,2,P

RAPE & ABUSE LINE (HIGHLANDS & ISLANDS)
SC007515
PO Box 10, Dingwall, Highland IV15 9HA
Tel: ... 0808 800 0123 Freephone (Answered by females); 0808 800 0122 Freephone (Answered by males)
Object: F

RAPE CRISIS - SOUTH LONDON
CR1085104
PO Box 383, Croydon, Surrey CR9 2AW
Tel: 0845 122 1331 Helpline; 020 8683 3311; 020 8239 1124 Minicom
Email: .... info@rasasc.org.uk
Objects: F,W3,G,3,W8

RAVENSCOURT
Founded: 1990 CR1000296
15 Ellasdale Road, Bognor Regis, West Sussex PO21 2SG
Tel: 01243 862157
Objects: O,3

RAYNAUD'S & SCLERODERMA ASSOCIATION
CR326306
112 Crewe Road, Alsager, Cheshire ST7 2JA
Tel: 01270 872776
Email: .... info@raynauds.org.uk
Objects: F,W3,W5,1A,A,2,W4,H

RAYSTEDE CENTRE FOR ANIMAL WELFARE
Founded: 1952 CR237696
The Broyle, Ringmer, Lewes, East Sussex BN8 5AJ
Tel: 0844 875 1252
Email: .... info@raystede.org
Objects: W1,2

RCH CONVALESCENT CENTRES
Founded: 1899 CR207528
245 Victoria Avenue, Ockbrook, Derby, Derbyshire DE72 3RL
Tel: 01332 280552
Email: .... keithalldread@aol.com
Objects: W6,W7,W5,W11,V,N,W4,3

REACH CHARITY - HELPING CHILDREN WITH UPPER LIMB DIFFERENCES LIVE LIFE WITHOUT LIMITS
CR1134544
c/o TEH, Pearl Assurance House, Brook Street, Tavistock, Devon PL19 0BN
Tel: 0845 130 6225
Email: .... reach@reach.org.uk
Web: .... www.reach.org.uk
Objects: F,W3,W5,O,3
Reach is a family support organisation. It provides information and advice on treatment and living with an upper limb deficiency. We have branches throughout the UK. For further information contact: Jo Dixon at above address.

REACH VOLUNTEERING
Founded: 1979 CR278837
89 Albert Embankment, London SE1 7TP
Tel: 020 7582 6543
Email: .... mail@reachskills.org.uk
Objects: F,W9,W6,W3,J,W2,W7,W5,W11,2,W12, W4,3,W8,K

REACT - (RAPID EFFECTIVE ASSISTANCE FOR CHILDREN WITH POTENTIALLY TERMINAL ILLNESS)
Founded: 1990 CR802440; SCD38067
St Luke's House, 270 Sandycombe Road, Kew, Richmond, Surrey TW9 3NP
Tel: 020 8940 2575
Email: .... react@reactcharity.org
Objects: M,W3,1A,V,N

RED SHIFT THEATRE COMPANY LTD
Founded: 1981 CR1004213
TRG2 Trowbray House, 108 Weston Street, London SE1 3QB
Tel: 020 7378 9787
Email: .... mail@redshifttheatreco.co.uk
Objects: S,3

REDBRIDGE CVS
Founded: 1991 CR1005075
3rd Floor, Forest House, 16-20 Clements Road, Ilford, Essex IG1 1BA
Tel: 020 8553 1004
Email: .... info@redbridgecvs.net
Objects: F,W3,J,G,W10,2,H,3

REDBRIDGE, EPPING & HARROW CROSSROADS - CARING FOR CARERS
Founded: 1991 CR1005208
106 Charter Avenue, Newbury Park, Ilford, Essex IG2 7AD
Tel: 020 8518 4090; 020 8554 0790
Objects: M,W3,W5,W10,2,W4,3

REDCAR & CLEVELAND MIND
Founded: 1991 CR1142520
Dove House, 5 Turner Street, Redcar, Redcar & Cleveland TS10 1AY
Tel: 01642 296052
Email: .... main@randcmind.org
Objects: F,J,E,W5,2,H,O,3,P

REDDITCH CITIZENS ADVICE BUREAU
Founded: 1967 CR1003414
Suite E, Canon Newton House, Kingfisher Shopping Centre, Redditch, Worcestershire B97 4HA
Tel: 08444 152221
Email: .... manager@redditchcab.cabnet.org.uk
Objects: F,W9,W6,W3,W7,W5,G,W10,W11,D,W4, 3,W8

REDR UK
CR1079752
250a Kennington Lane, London SE11 5RD
Tel: 020 7840 6000
Email: .... info@redr.org
Objects: F,W3,G,W10,2,W4,U,H,3,W8,K

REDWINGS HORSE SANCTUARY
Founded: 1984 CR1068911
Hapton, Norwich, Norfolk NR15 1SP
Tel: 01508 481000
Fax: 0870 458 1947
Email: .... legacies@redwings.co.uk
Web: .... www.redwings.org.uk
Objects: Q,F,W1,G,N,H,O,3
Working to provide and promote the care and protection of horses, ponies, donkeys and mules.
See advert on previous page

REDWINGS HORSE SANCTUARY, ADA COLE
CR1068911
Broadlands, Epping Road, Roydon, Nazeing, Essex EN9 2DH
Tel: 01508 481000; 08700 400033
Email: .... info@redwings.co.uk

REFUGEE COUNCIL, THE
Founded: 1981 CR1014576
1-11 Broadway (CD), Gredley House, Stratford, London E15 4BQ
Tel: .. 020 7346 6700; 020 7582 3660 Donations
Email: .... info@refugeecouncil.org.uk
Objects: F,J,E,G,W10,H,3,K

REFUGEE LEGAL CENTRE
Founded: 1992 CR1012804
Nelson House, 153-157 Commercial Road, London E1 2DA
Tel: 020 7780 3200
Email: .... rlc@refugee-legal-centre.org.uk
Objects: F,W10,3

RELATE BRIGHTON, HOVE, EASTBOURNE, WORTHING AND DISTRICTS
CR1091414
58 Preston Road, Brighton, Brighton & Hove BN1 4QF
Tel: 01273 697997
Email: .... reception@brightonrelate.org.uk
Objects: F,3,P

RELATE, THE RELATIONSHIP PEOPLE
Founded: 1938 CR207314
Relate Premier House, Carolina Court, Lakeside, Doncaster, South Yorkshire DN4 5RA
Tel: 0845 456 1310
Email: .... enquiries@relate.org.uk
Objects: F,G,H,3

RELATIVES & RESIDENTS ASSOCIATION
Founded: 1993 CR1020194
1 The Ivories, 6-18 Northampton Street, London N1 2HY
Tel: 020 7359 8148
Email: .... info@relres.org
Objects: F,J,G,2,W4,H,P

RELEASE - THE NATIONAL DRUGS & LEGAL HELPLINE
Founded: 1967 CR801118
388 Old Street, London EC1V 9LT
Tel: 020 7729 9904
Email: . . . . ask@release.org.uk
Objects: F,G,H,3

RELIEF FUND FOR ROMANIA
Founded: 1989 CR1046737
PO Box 2122, London SE21 9AD
Email: . . . . mail@relieffundforromania.co.uk
Objects: U,3

REMEDI
Founded: 1973 CR1063359
Elysium House, 126-128 New Kings Road, London SW6 4LZ
Tel: 020 7384 2929
Email: . . . . info@remedi.org.uk
Objects: W3,W5,A,1B,N,W4,O

RESCARE - NATIONAL SOCIETY FOR CHILDREN AND ADULTS WITH LEARNING DISABILITIES AND THEIR FAMILIES
Founded: 1984 CR5631419
Steven Jackson House, 31 Buxton Road, Heaviley, Stockport, Greater Manchester SK2 6LS
Tel: 0161 474 7323
Email: . . . . office@rescare.org.uk
Objects: F,W5,1A,2,H,3

THE RESEARCH INSTITUTE FOR THE CARE OF OLDER PEOPLE
CR1042559
The RICE Centre, Royal United Hospital, Bath, Bath & North East Somerset BA1 3NG
Tel: 01225 476420
Objects: F,G,N,2,W4,3

RESTORE - BURN AND WOUND RESEARCH
CR1003899
Studio 214, Canalot Studios, 222 Kensal Road, London W10 5BN
Tel: 020 3735 6652
Email: . . . . clerk@restore-research.org.uk
Objects: W6,W3,W7,W5,W10,W15,N,W4,W8,W

RESTRICTED GROWTH ASSOCIATION
Founded: 1970 CR261647
PO Box 99, Lydney, Gloucester, Gloucestershire GL15 9AW
Tel: 0300 111 1970
Email: . . . . office@restrictedgrowth.co.uk
Objects: Q,F,W3,2,H,P

RETAIL TRUST
Founded: 1832 CR1090136; SC039684
Marshall Hall, Marshall Estate, Hammers Lane, Mill Hill, London NW7 4DQ
Tel: . 020 8358 7236; 0845 766 0113 Retail Trust Helpline
Email: . . . . helpline@retailtrust.org.uk
Objects: F,W9,M,W3,J,E,W5,G,W10,W11,1A,A,D, W4,H,3,C,W8

RETIRED GREYHOUND TRUST
Founded: 1975 CR269668
Park House, Park Terrace, Worcester Park, Surrey KT4 7JZ
Tel: 020 8335 3016
Fax: 020 8337 5426
Email: . . . greyhounds@retiredgreyhounds.co.uk

THE RETIRED NURSES NATIONAL HOME
Founded: 1934 CR1090202
Riverside Avenue, Bournemouth BH7 7EE
Tel: 01202 396418
Email: . . . . anything@rnnh.co.uk
Objects: M,N,3,C,P

RETRAINING OF RACEHORSES (ROR)
CR1084787
75 High Holborn, London WC1V 6LS
Tel: 020 7152 0178
Email: . . . . info@ror.org.uk

RETT UK
CR1137820
Langham House West, Mill Street, Luton, Bedfordshire LU1 2NA
Tel: 01582 798910
Email: . . . . info@rettsyndrome.org.uk
Objects: F,W5,3

REVITALISE RESPITE HOLIDAYS
Founded: 1963 CR295072
212 Business Design Centre, 52 Upper Street, London N1 0QH
Tel: 0303 303 0147
Email: . . . . info@vitalise.org.uk
Objects: W6,W3,W5,W10,V,N,H,3

RFEA LTD - FINDING JOBS FOR EX FORCES PERSONNEL
Founded: 1885 CR1061212
49 Pall Mall, London SW1Y 5JG
Tel: 020 7321 2011
Email: . . . . rfeaadminho@ctp.org.uk
Objects: F,W9,2,3,K

RICABILITY
Founded: 1991 CR1007726
30 Angel Gate, City Road, London EC1V 2PT
Tel: . . . . 020 7427 2460; 020 7427 2469 Minicom
Email: . . . . mail@ricability.org.uk
Objects: W6,W7,W5,W4,H,3

RICHARD LEWIS AWARD FUND, THE
Founded: 1992 CR1010272
Manor Barn, 8 Manor Way, Eastbourne, East Sussex BN20 9BN
Objects: W3,S,G,1B

RICHMOND FELLOWSHIP
Founded: 1959 CR200453
Richmond Fellowship, 80 Holloway Road, Islington, London N7 8JG
Tel: 020 7697 3300
Email: communications@richmondfellowship.org.uk
Objects: F,E,G,D,O,3,C,P,K

RIDING FOR THE DISABLED ASSOCIATION (NORTHERN IRELAND) INCORPORATING CARRIAGE DRIVING
Founded: 1969 CR244108
Lady Juliet Frazer, 72 Hillmount Road, Cullybackey, Ballymena, Co. Antrim BT42 1NZ
Email: . . . . rdaniregion@yahoo.co.uk
Objects: F,M,J,W5,G,V,2,H,O,3

THE RIGHT TO LIFE CHARITABLE TRUST
CR1099319
PO Box 354, Sevenoaks, Kent TN13 9GA
Tel: 01732 460911
Email: . . . . eleanor@righttolife.org.uk

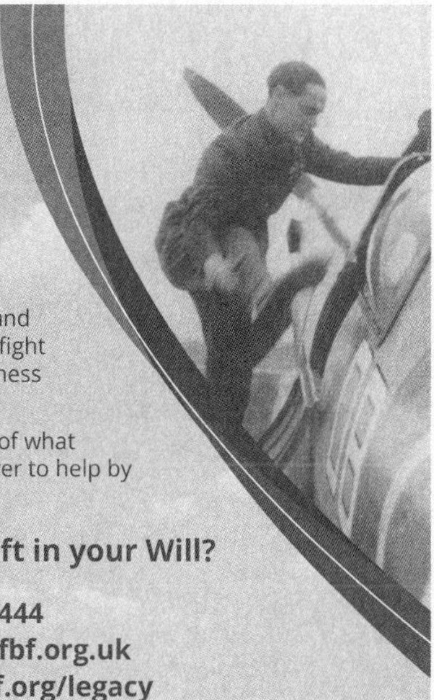

RIVER & ROWING MUSEUM FOUNDATION

Founded: 1990 CR1001051
Mill Meadows, Henley-on-Thames, Oxfordshire RG9 1BF
Tel: 01491 415600
Email: . . . . museum@rrm.co.uk
Objects: W3,W2,S,G,W12,H

RIVERSIDE VINEYARD CHURCH

Founded: 1992 CR1013545
The Vineyard Centre, 513 Browells Lane, Feltham, Middlesex TW13 7EQ
Tel: 020 8890 3535
Objects: W3,2,R

ROALD DAHL'S MARVELLOUS CHILDREN'S CHARITY

Founded: 1991 CR1137409
81A High Street, Great Missenden, Buckinghamshire HP16 0AL
Tel: 01494 890465
Objects: W3,1A,A,1B,N

ROBERT OWEN COMMUNITIES

Founded: 1986 CR517845
The Boatshed, Unit C, Dart Marine Park, Steamer Quay Road, Totnes, Devon TQ9 5AL
Tel: 01803 868550
Email: . . . . admin@roc-uk.org
Objects: E,W5,C

ROCK WORK OPPORTUNITY CENTRE LTD

Founded: 1992 CR1011392
230 Bristol Avenue, Blackpool FY2 0JF
Tel: 01253 593173
Email: . . . . dt@rockwork.freeserve.co.uk

ROKPA UK OVERSEAS PROJECTS

CR1059293; SC038628
ROKPA UK, Kagyu Samye Ling, Eskdalemuir, Langholm, Dumfries & Galloway DG13 0QL
Tel: . . . . 01387 373232 ext. 230
Email: . . . . charity@rokpauk.org

ROOM, THE NATIONAL COUNCIL FOR HOUSING AND PLANNING

Founded: 1900 CR252002
41 Botolph Lane, London EC3R 8DL
Tel: 020 7929 9494
Email: . . . . room@rtpi.org.uk
Objects: F,J,W2,S,G,D,2,H,3

ROTHERHAM CROSSROADS CARING FOR CARERS

Founded: 1990 CR1062664
Unit H, The Point, Broadmarsh, Rotherham, South Yorkshire S60 1BP
Tel: 01709 360272
Objects: W6,M,W7,W5,W4,3,P

ROTHERHAM HOSPICE, THE

CR700356
Broom Road (CC), Rotherham, South Yorkshire S60 2SW
Tel: . . 01709 308917 Fundraising/Administration; 01709 308918 Lottery
Email: . . . fundraising@rotherhamhospice.org.uk
Objects: E,W5,W15,N,W4,3

ROUND TABLE CHILDREN'S WISH
CR1060225
857 Wimborne Road, Bournemouth BH9 2BQ
Tel: 01202 514515
Email: .... info@rtcw.org
Objects: W3,3

THE ROWANS HOSPICE
CR299731
Purbrook Heath Road (CC), Purbrook, Waterlooville, Hampshire PO7 5RU
Tel: 023 9225 0001
Email: .... info@rowanshospice.co.uk
Objects: F,M,E,W5,W10,N,W4,3

ROXBURGHE HOUSE
CRExempt
Royal Victoria House, Jedburgh Road, Dundee DD2 1SP
Tel: 01382 423132

ROXBURGHE HOUSE (DUNDEE)
SC011042
Royal Victoria Hospital, Jedburgh Road, Dundee DD2 1SP
Tel: 01382 423132
Email: .... jenniffer.calder@nhs.net
Objects: W5,N,W4,3,W8

ROY CASTLE LUNG CANCER FOUNDATION
CR1046854; SC037596
4-6 Enterprise Way, Wavertree Technology Park, Wavertree, Liverpool, Merseyside L13 1FB
Tel: 033 3323 7200
Email: .... foundation@roycastle.org
Objects: F,W3,J,G,A,H

ROYAL ACADEMY OF ARTS
CR1125383
Burlington House, Piccadilly, London W1J 0BD
Tel: 020 7300 5677

ROYAL AGRICULTURAL BENEVOLENT INSTITUTION
Founded: 1860 CR208858
Shaw House, 27 West Way, Oxford, Oxfordshire OX2 0QH
Tel: . Switchboard: 01865 724931; Helpline: 0300 303 7373
Email: .... info@rabi.org.uk
Objects: M,W5,W11,W15,A,W4,B,Y,W14

ROYAL AIR FORCE BENEVOLENT FUND – RAFBF
Founded: 1919 CR1081009; SCO38109
Controller: Air Marshal David Murray
67 Portland Place, London W1B 1AR
Tel: 020 7307 3444
Fax: 020 7636 7005
Email: .... legacy@rafbf.org.uk
Web: .... www.rafbf.org
Object: W9

See advert on previous page

ROYAL ALEXANDRA AND ALBERT SCHOOL, THE

Founded: 1758 CR311945
Secretary: Mrs Diana Bromley
Gatton Park, Reigate, Surrey RH2 0TD
Tel: 01737 649000
Fax: 01737 649002
Email: . . . . bursar@gatton-park.org.uk
Web: . . . . http://www.raa-school.co.uk.
Objects: W3,G,1A,B,3

A voluntary-aided junior and secondary boarding and flexi boarding school for boys and girls aged from 7-18, catering especially for those without one or both parents or whose circumstances make boarding education advantageous.
Children of all abilities admitted. Superb facilities, bursaries available.
Management: Jointly by School Foundation and Surrey Education Authority through Governing Body.
See advert on previous page

ROYAL ALFRED SEAFARERS' SOCIETY

Founded: 1865 CR209776
Head Office, Weston Acres, Woodmansterne Lane, Banstead, Surrey SM7 3HA
Tel: 01737 353763
Email: . . . . enquiries@royalalfred.org.uk
Objects: W9,W5,W11,N,W4,3,C

ROYAL ARCHAEOLOGICAL INSTITUTE

CR254543
c/o Society of Antiquaries, Burlington House, Piccadilly, London W1J 0BE
Tel: 0116 243 3839
Email: . . . . admin@royalarchinst.org
Objects: W2,1A,A,1B,H

ROYAL ARMY MEDICAL CORPS BENEVOLENCE

CR1129091
RHQ RAMC, Slim Road, Camberley, Surrey GU15 4NP
Tel: 01276 412791
Objects: W9,1A,A

ROYAL ARMY PAY CORPS REGIMENTAL ASSOCIATION

Founded: 1928 CR270477
RHQ AGC, Worthy Down, Winchester, Hampshire SO21 2RG
Tel: 01962 887436
Email: . . . . regsec.rapc@virgin.net
Objects: W9,1A,A,V,2,P

ROYAL ARMY SERVICE CORPS AND ROYAL CORPS AND ROYAL CORPS OF TRANSPORT BENEVOLENT FUND

Founded: 1927 CR273525
Dettingen House, The Princess Royal Barracks, Deepcut, Camberley, Surrey GU16 6RW
Tel: 01252 833391
Objects: F,W9,W5,1A,A,1B,W12,W4,P

ROYAL ARTILLERY CHARITABLE FUND

Founded: 1839 CR210202
General Secretary: Lt Col I A Vere Nicoll MBE
Artillery House, Royal Artillery Barracks, Larkhill, Salisbury, Wiltshire SP4 8QT
Tel: 01980 845895
Email: . . . . Rarhq-racf-raa-gensec@mod.uk
Objects: F,W9,J,G,1A,A,1B,V,B,P

For relief and assistance of all past and present members of the Royal Regiment of Artillery, and their families and dependants, and the families and dependants of any deceased members, who are in need.

ROYAL ASSOCIATION FOR DEAF PEOPLE (RAD)

Founded: 1841 CR1081949
Century House South, Riverside Office Centre, North Station Road, Colchester, Essex CO1 1RE
Tel: . . . 0845 688 2525 - Minicom: 0845 688 2527
Email: . . . . info@royaldeaf.org.uk
Objects: F,J,S,W7,W5,H,T,3,P

ROYAL BLIND

Founded: 1793SC017167
Box No: 500, Gillespie Crescent, Edinburgh EH10 4HZ
Tel: 0131 229 1456
Email: . . . . enquiries@royablind.org
Objects: F,W6,M,W3,W5,G,N,W4,3

ROYAL BOTANIC GARDENS, KEW, FOUNDATION AND FRIENDS

Founded: 1990 CR803428
The Herbarium, Kew Green, Richmond, Surrey TW9 3AB
Tel: 020 8332 3249
Email: . . . . legacies@kew.org
Objects: W2,S,G,2,W12,3

ROYAL BRITISH LEGION

CR219279
Haig House, 199 Borough High Street, London SE1 1AA
Tel: 020 3207 2100
Email: . . . . info@britishlegion.org.uk
Objects: F,E,A,B,O,C,K

ROYAL BRITISH LEGION INDUSTRIES

Founded: 1925 CR0210053
Royal British Legion Village, Aylesford, Kent ME20 7NL
Tel: 01622 717202
Email: . . . . sales@rbli.co.uk
Objects: W9,W5,D,O,C,K

ROYAL BRITISH LEGION SCOTLAND (RBLS)

SC003323
New Haig House, Logie Green Road, Edinburgh EH7 4HR
Tel: 0131 557 2782
Email: . . . . admin@rblscotland.org
Objects: F,W9,J,S,2,B,H,P

ROYAL BRITISH LEGION WOMEN'S SECTION

CR219279
Haig House, 199 Borough High Street, London SE1 1AA
Tel: 020 3207 2188
Email: . . . . women@britishlegion.org.uk
Objects: F,W9,M,W3,W5,G,1A,A,V,D,2,W4,3,P, W8

ROYAL COLLEGE OF ANAESTHETISTS

Founded: 1992 CR1013887
Churchill House, 35 Red Lion Square, London WC1R 4SG
Tel: 020 7092 1500
Email: . . . . info@rcoa.ac.uk

ROYAL COLLEGE OF MIDWIVES TRUST

Founded: 1881 CR210064
15 Mansfield Street, London W1G 9NH

Tel: 020 7312 3535
Email: .... info@rcm.org.uk
Objects: F,W3,J,G,N,2,U,B,H,3,W8

ROYAL COLLEGE OF PSYCHIATRISTS
CR228636
21 Precot Street (CC), London E1 8BB
Tel: .... 020 7235 2351 ext. 127
Email: .... dhart@rcpsych.ac.uk

ROYAL COLLEGE OF SURGEONS OF EDINBURGH
SC005317
CC Health Awards & Grants, 18 Nicolson Street, Edinburgh EH8 9DW
Tel: 0131 527 1600
Email: .... c.mccartney@rcsed.ac.uk

ROYAL COMMONWEALTH EX-SERVICES LEAGUE
Founded: 1921 CR231322
199 Borough High Street, London SE1 1AA
Tel: 020 3207 2413
Email: .. mgordon-roe@commonwealthveterans.org.uk
Objects: F,W9,J,1A,A,1B,U,W8

ROYAL COMMONWEALTH SOCIETY
CR226748
25 Northumberland Avenue, London WC2N 5AP
Tel: 020 7766 9240
Email: .... fundraising@thercs.org
Objects: W3,S,G

ROYAL ELECTRICAL & MECHANICAL ENGINEERS BENEVOLENT FUND
CR246967
RHQ REME, Headquarters DEME (A), Isaac Newton Road, Arborfield, Reading RG2 9NJ
Tel: 0118 976 3219
Email: .... deme-welfare-RO2@mod.uk
Objects: F,W9,M,J,G,1A,A,V,D,R,U,B,T,O,C,K

ROYAL ENGINEERS ASSOCIATION
Founded: 1868 CR258322
Brompton Barracks, Chatham, Kent ME4 4UG
Tel: 01634 847005
Email: .... info@reaha.org.uk
Objects: F,W9,J,1A,A,1B,V,W4,P,W8

ROYAL ENGINEERS CENTRAL CHARITABLE TRUST
Founded: 1991 CR1003032
Regimental HQ, Ravelin Building, Brompton Barracks, Dock Road, Chatham, Kent ME4 4UG
Tel: 01634 822355
Email: .... info@reahq.org.uk
Objects: W9,1A,A,1B,2,W12

ROYAL FOUNDATION OF ST. KATHARINE
Founded: 1147 CR223849
2 Butcher Row, London E14 8DS
Tel: 020 7790 3540
Email: ...... michael@stkatherine.demon.co.uk
Objects: F,S,G,D,R,H,P

THE ROYAL HOMES
Founded: 1885 CR210760
Queen Alexandra's Court, St Mary's Road, Wimbledon, London SW19 7DE
Tel: 020 8946 5182
Email: .... rhowd_qac@ssafa.org.uk
Objects: 1A,D,3,W8

ROYAL HORTICULTURAL SOCIETY – THE UK'S LEADING GARDENING CHARITY
CR222879; SC038262
80 Vincent Square, London SW1P 2PE
Tel: 020 7821 3125
Email: .... developmentoffice@rhs.org.uk

THE ROYAL HOSPITAL FOR NEURO-DISABILITY
Founded: 1854 CR205907
West Hill (CC), Putney, London SW15 3SW
Tel: 020 8780 4563
Email: .... fundraising@rhn.org.uk
Objects: W5,N,O

ROYAL HUMANE SOCIETY
Founded: 1774 CR231469
Brettenham House, Lancaster Place, London WC2E 7EP
Tel: 020 7836 8155
Email: .... rhs@supanet.co.uk
Objects: W9,W6,W3,W7,W5,W10,1A,W4,P,W8

ROYAL LIFE SAVING SOCIETY UK
CR1046060; SC037912
River House, High Street, Broom, Warwickshire B50 4HN
Tel: 01789 773994
Email: .... lifesavers@rlss.org.uk
Objects: W3,G,W4,3

ROYAL LITERARY FUND
Founded: 1790 CR219952
3 Johnson's Court, off Fleet Street, London EC4A 3EA
Tel: 020 7353 7150
Email: .... egunnrlf@globalnet.co.uk
Objects: 1A,A,B

ROYAL LIVERPOOL PHILHARMONIC SOCIETY, THE
Founded: 1841 CR1002122
Philharmonic Hall, Hope Street, Liverpool, Merseyside L1 9BP
Tel: 0151 210 2895
Email: .... lisa.murray@liverpoolphil.com
Objects: S,G

ROYAL LONDON SOCIETY FOR BLIND PEOPLE
Founded: 1838 CR307892
Victoria Charity Centre, 11 Belgrave Road, London SW1V 1RB
Tel: 020 7808 6170
Email: .... ceosoffice@rlsb.org.uk
Objects: F,W6,M,W3,W5,G,W4,B,H,O,3,P,K

ROYAL MARINES ASSOCIATION
Founded: 1946 CR206003
Central Office, Building 32, Whale Island, Portsmouth, Hampshire PO2 8ER
Tel: 023 9265 1519
Email: .... chiefexec@rma.org.uk
Objects: F,W9,1B,2,P

ROYAL MARINES CHARITABLE TRUST FUND
CR1134205
Building 32, H M S Excellent, Whale Island, Portsmouth, Hampshire PO2 8ER
Tel: 023 9254 7201
Email: .... fundraising@rmctf.org.uk
Objects: W9,1A,A

THE ROYAL MARSDEN CANCER CHARITY

Founded: 1851 CR1095197
203 Fulham Road, London SW3 6JJ
Tel: 020 7808 2274
Email: .... charity@royalmarsden.org

ROYAL MASONIC BENEVOLENT INSTITUTION

Founded: 1842 CR207360
60 Great Queen Street, London WC2B 5AZ
Tel: 020 7596 2400
Email: .... enquiries@rmbi.org.uk
Objects: F,1A,V,W4,B,3,C

ROYAL MASONIC TRUST FOR GIRLS AND BOYS

Founded: 1982 CR285836
60 Great Queen Street, London WC2B 5AZ
Tel: 020 7405 2644
Email: .... info@rmtgb.org
Objects: W3,G,1A,1B

ROYAL MEDICAL BENEVOLENT FUND

Founded: 1836 CR207275
24 King's Road, Wimbledon, London SW19 8QN
Tel: 020 8540 9194
Email: .... info@rmbf.org
Objects: W11,1A,A

THE ROYAL MEDICAL FOUNDATION

Founded: 1855 CR312046
Epsom College, College Road, Epsom, Surrey KT17 4JQ
Tel: 01372 821010
Email: . caseworker@royalmedicalfoundation.org
Objects: W3,W5,G,1A,A,W4,B

ROYAL MERCHANT NAVY SCHOOL FOUNDATION

Founded: 1827 CR309047
Bear Wood, Wokingham RG41 5BG
Tel: 0118 978 1865
Email: .... admin@merchantnavy.org.uk
Objects: W3,G,1A,A

ROYAL MILITARY POLICE ASSOCIATION

CR261630
Regimental Headquarters, Royal Military Police, Roussillon Barracks, Chichester, West Sussex PO19 6BL
Tel: 01243 534237
Email: .... rmpa@rhqrmp.freeserve.co.uk
Objects: W9,J,1A,1B,V,2,P

ROYAL MILITARY POLICE CENTRAL BENEVOLENT FUND (1946)

Founded: 1944 CR248713
Defence College of Policing & Guarding, PP38, Southwick Park, Fareham, Hampshire PO17 6EJ
Tel: 023 9228 4206
Email: .... regsec_rhqrmp@btconnect.com
Objects: F,W9,J,1A,A,1B,V,P

ROYAL NATIONAL COLLEGE FOR THE BLIND (RNC)

Founded: 1872 CR1000388
Venns Lane, Hereford, Herefordshire HR1 1DT

Tel: 01432 376371
Email: . . . . fundraising@rnc.ac.uk
Objects: W6,W5,G,O,3

ROYAL NATIONAL INSTITUTE OF BLIND PEOPLE (RNIB)

Founded: 1868 CR226227
105 Judd Street, London WC1H 9NE
Tel: . . . . 020 7388 1266; 0845 766 9999 Helpline
Email: . . . . helpline@rnib.org.uk
Objects: F,W6,M,W3,J,S,W5,G,A,V,D,W4,H,O,C,P

ROYAL NATIONAL LIFEBOAT INSTITUTION (RNLI)

Founded: 1824 CR209603; SC037736
West Quay Road, Poole, Dorset BH15 1HZ
Tel: 0300 3000 124
Objects: F,W9,W6,M,W3,J,W7,W5,G,W10,W11,W4,U,H,3,W8

ROYAL NAVAL & ROYAL MARINE CHILDREN'S FUND

Founded: 1903 CR1075015
311 Twyford Avenue, Portsmouth, Hampshire PO1 8RN
Tel: 023 9263 9534
Email: . . . . mab52@btconnect.com
Objects: F,W9,M,W3,G,1A,B,C

ROYAL NAVAL ASSOCIATION - ONCE NAVY, ALWAYS NAVY

Founded: 1950 CR266982
Room 209, Semaphore Tower, PP70, HM Naval Base, Portsmouth, Hampshire PO1 3LT
Tel: 02392 723823
Email: . . . . paddy@royalnavalassoc.com
Objects: F,W9,J,G,1A,A,1B,2,B,H,P

THE ROYAL NAVAL BENEVOLENT TRUST (GRAND FLEET & KINDRED FUNDS)

Founded: 1922 CR206243
Events and Publicity Officer: Ms Corinne Day
Chief Executive: Commander Stephen Farrington QGM RN
Castaway House (CD), 311 Twyford Avenue, Portsmouth, Hampshire PO2 8RN
Tel: . . . 023 9269 0112 Administration; 023 9266 0296 Welfare
Fax: 023 9266 0852
Email: . . . . rnbt@rnbt.org.uk
Web: . . . . www.rnbt.org.uk
Objects: F,W9,1A,A

The RNBT was established in 1922 to give help, in cases of need, to those who are serving or have served as ratings in the Royal Navy or as other ranks in the Royal Marines, and their dependants.

See advert on previous page

ROYAL NAVY SUBMARINE MUSEUM

Founded: 1996 CR1142123
Haslar Jetty Road, Gosport, Hampshire PO12 2AS
Tel: 023 9251 0354
Email: rnsubs@submarine.museum.demon.co.uk
Objects: W2,G,W12

ROYAL NORTHERN COLLEGE OF MUSIC

CR504948
124 Oxford Road, Manchester, Greater Manchester M13 9RD
Tel: 0161 907 5200
Email: . . . . info@rncm.ac.uk
Objects: W3,S,G,3

ROYAL PARKS FOUNDATION

CR1097545
The Old Police House, Hyde Park, London W2 2UH
Tel: 020 7036 8043
Email: . . . . . . support@royalparksfoundation.org

ROYAL PINNER SCHOOL FOUNDATION

Founded: 1845 CR1128414
110 Old Brompton Road, London SW7 3RB
Tel: 020 7373 6168
Objects: W3,G,1A,A,2,3

THE ROYAL SCHOOL FOR DEAF CHILDREN MARGATE AND WESTGATE COLLEGE

CR1127209
Victoria Rd, Margate, Kent CT9 1NB
Tel: 01843 227561
Email: . . . . enquiries@rsdcm.org.uk
Objects: W3,W7,G

ROYAL SCHOOL FOR THE BLIND, LIVERPOOL

Founded: 1791 CR526090
Church Road, North Wavertree, Liverpool, Merseyside L15 6TQ
Tel: 0151 733 1012
Email: . . . . rsblind@globalnet.co.uk
Objects: W6,W3,W5,G

ROYAL SCHOOL FOR THE DEAF DERBY

CR1062507
Ashbourne Road, Derby, Derbyshire DE22 3BH
Tel: 01332 362512
Email: . . . . principal@rsdd.org.uk

ROYAL SCHOOL OF NEEDLEWORK

Founded: 1872 CR312774
Apartment 12A, Hampton Court Palace, East Molesey, Surrey KT8 9AU
Tel: 020 8943 1432
Email: . . . . . . enquiries@royal-needlework.co.uk
Objects: W2,S,G,H

ROYAL SIGNALS ASSOCIATION

CR284923
Regimental HQ Royal Signals, Blandford Camp, Dorset DT11 8RH
Tel: 01258 482089; 01258 482082
Email: . . . welfare@royalsignalsassociation.co.uk
Objects: W9,A

THE ROYAL SOCIETY FOR THE PREVENTION OF ACCIDENTS

Founded: 1916 CR207823
Edgbaston Park, 353 Bristol Road, Birmingham, West Midlands B5 7ST
Tel: 0121 248 2000
Email: . . . . info-ni@rospa.com
Objects: F,W3,J,G,2,W4,H,3

THE ROYAL SOCIETY FOR THE PROMOTION OF HEALTH

Founded: 1876 CR215520
38A St George's Drive, London SW1V 4BH
Tel: 020 7630 0121
Email: . . . . rsph@rsph.org
Objects: W6,W3,W2,W7,W5,G,2,W4,H,3,W8

THE ROYAL SOCIETY OF CHEMISTRY
Founded: 1920 CR207890
Thomas Graham House, 290 Cambridge Science Park, Milton Road, Cambridge, Cambridgeshire CB4 0WF
Tel: 01223 432683
Email: .... development@rsc.org
Objects: F,J,W11,1A,2,B,Y,3

ROYAL SOCIETY OF MUSICIANS OF GREAT BRITAIN
Founded: 1738 CR208879
26 Fitzroy Square, London W1T 6BT
Tel: 020 7629 6137
Email: .. enquiries@royalsocietyofmusucians.org
Objects: 1A,A

THE ROYAL SOCIETY OF ST GEORGE CHARITABLE TRUST
Founded: 1971 CR263076
127 Sandgate Road, Folkestone, Kent CT20 2BL
Tel: 01303 241795
Email: .... info@rssg.u-net.com
Objects: W3,G,1A,A,1B,2

ROYAL SOCIETY, THE
Founded: 1660 CR207043
The Royal Society, 6-9 Carlton House Terrace, London SW1Y 5AG
Tel: 020 7451 2500
Email: .... claire.glen@royalsoc.ac.uk
Objects: W2,1A,A,1B,2,3

THE ROYAL STAR & GARTER HOMES
Founded: 1916 CR210119
15 Castle Mews, Hampton, Middlesex TW12 2NP
Tel: 020 8481 7676
Email: ..... generalenquiries@starandgarter.org
Objects: W9,W5,N,W4,O,3

ROYAL TANK REGIMENT BENEVOLENT FUND
Founded: 1919 CR248487
Stanley Barracks, Bovington, Wareham, Dorset BH20 6JB
Tel: 01929 403331
Objects: F,W9,1A,A,1B

ROYAL THEATRICAL FUND
Founded: 1839 CR222080
11 Garrick Street, London WC2E 9AR
Tel: 020 7836 3322
Email: .... admin@trtf.com
Objects: W6,M,W5,1A,A,N,W4,O

ROYAL ULSTER CONSTABULARY GEORGE CROSS - POLICE SERVICE NORTHERN IRELAND BENEVOLENT FUND
XN48380
77-79 Garnerville Road, Belfast BT4 2NX
Tel: 028 9076 4200; 028 9076 4215
Email: .... benfund.pfni@btconnect.com
Objects: W9,W6,W3,J,W7,W5,W15,1A,1B,2,W4, O,Y,3,P,W8

ROYAL VARIETY CHARITY
Founded: 1908 CR206451
Brinsworth House (CD), 72 Staines Road, Twickenham, Middlesex TW2 5AL
Tel: 020 8898 8164
Email: .... admin@eabf.org.uk
Objects: M,J,1A,A,V,N,B

ROYAL WOLVERHAMPTON SCHOOL
CR1092221
Penn Road, Wolverhampton, West Midlands WV3 0EG
Tel: 01902 341230
Email: .... kp@royal.wolverhampton.sch.uk

RP FIGHTING BLINDNESS
Founded: 1975 CR271729
PO Box 350, Buckingham, Buckinghamshire MK18 1GZ
Tel: . 01280 821334; RP Helpline: 08451 232354
Email: .... info@rpfightingblindness.org.uk
Objects: F,A,1B,2,H

RSABI
SC009828
The Rural Centre, West Mains of Ingliston, Newbridge, Midlothian EH28 8LT
Tel: 0300 111 4166
Email: .... rsabi@rsabi.org.uk
Objects: F,W6,W3,W7,W5,W11,1A,A,W4,W8

RSPB (THE ROYAL SOCIETY FOR THE PROTECTION OF BIRDS)
CR207076; SC037654
The Lodge, Sandy, Bedfordshire SG19 2DL
Tel: 01767 693276
Email: .... legacy.team@rspb.org.uk

RSPCA
CR219099
Wilberforce Way, Southwater, Horsham, West Sussex RH13 9RS
Tel: 0300 123 0125
Email: .... ncowles@rspca.org.uk
Objects: F,W1,M,G,N,2,H,O

RUDOLF STEINER PRESS
Founded: 1992 CR1013276
Hillside House, The Square, Forest Row, East Sussex RH18 5ES
Tel: 01342 824433
Email: .... office@rudolfsteinerpress.com
Objects: H,3

RUTHERFORD HOUSE
SC015111
1 Hill Street, Edinburgh EH2 3JP
Tel: 0131 220 1735
Email: .... info@rutherfordhouse.org.uk
Objects: G,R

RWE NPOWER BENEVOLENT SOCIETY
Founded: 1991 CR1000443
INNOGY, Trigonos, Windmill Hill Business Park, Whitehill Way, Swindon, Wiltshire SN5 6PB
Tel: 01793 877777
Objects: F,M,W3,J,E,G,N,H,O,C,P,K

S

SADACCA LIMITED
Founded: 1990 CR702393
48 Wicker Street, Sheffield, South Yorkshire S3 8JB
Tel: 0114 275 3915
Email: .... sadacca@yahoo.co.uk
Objects: F,W3,S,E,W5,G,W10,2,W4,3,P

SAILORS' FAMILIES' SOCIETY
Founded: 1821 CR224505
Francis ReckittHouse, Newland, Kingston upon Hull, East Riding of Yorkshire HU6 7RJ
Tel: 01482 342331
Email: . . . . info@sailors-families.org.uk
Objects: F,W3,G,1A,A,V,3,C

SAILORS' SOCIETY
Founded: 1818 CR237778
350 Shirley Road (CC), Southampton, Hampshire SO15 3HY
Tel: 023 8051 5950
Email: . . . . admin@biss.org.uk
Objects: F,M,J,W11,1A,A,B,3

SAINT JOHN OF GOD HOSPITALLER SERVICES
Founded: 2005 CR1108428
Saint Bede's House, Morton Park Way, Darlington, Co. Durham DL1 4XZ
Tel: 01325 373700
Email: . . . . enquiries@hospitaller.org.uk

SAINT MICHAEL'S HOSPICE (HARROGATE)
CR518905
Crimple House, Hornbeam Park Avenue, Harrogate, North Yorkshire HG2 8QL
Tel: . . . . . 01423 879687; 01423 872658 Nursing
Email: . . . . info@saintmichaelshospice.org

SALFORD FOUNDATION LIMITED
Founded: 1991 CR1002482
1st Floor Charles House, Albert Street, Eccles, Manchester, Greater Manchester M30 0PD
Tel: 0161 787 8500

SALISBURY CATHEDRAL TRUST
CR291252
The Manor (CC), Manningford Abbots, Pewsey, Wiltshire SN9 6HZ
Tel: 01672 564809
Email: . . . . robingamble@salisburycathedraltrust.fsnet.co.uk

SALTER'S HILL CHARITY LTD
CR288379
Keepers Cottage, Falcon Lane, Ledbury, Herefordshire HR8 2JN
Tel: 01531 671080
Email: . . . . rob.woolf@saltershill.org.uk
Objects: E,W5

THE SALVATION ARMY - UNITED KINGDOM WITH THE REPUBLIC OF IRELAND
CR214779; SC009359
Territorial Headquarters, 101 Newington Causeway, London SE1 6BN
Tel: 020 7367 4800
Email: . . . . legacy.enquiry@salvationarmy.org.uk
Objects: F,W9,M,W3,S,E,W5,G,V,D,N,2,R,W4,U,H,T,O,3,C,P,W8,K

SAMARITAN'S PURSE
Samaritan's Purse
INTERNATIONAL RELIEF

Founded: 1990 CR1001349
Victoria House, Victoria Road, Buckhurst Hill, Essex IG9 5EX
Tel: 020 8559 1180
Fax: 020 8502 9062
Email: . . . . . info@samaritans-purse.org.uk
Web: www.samaritans-purse.org.uk; www.operationchristmaschild.org.uk
Samaritan's Purse International Relief. Helping in Jesus' name. Samaritan's Purse is committed to providing long term support for the victims of war, poverty, famine, disease and natural disaster whilst sharing the Good News of Jesus Christ.
See advert on previous page

SAMARITANS
Founded: 1953 CR219432; SC040604
The Upper Mill, Kingston Road, Ewell, Surrey KT17 2AF
Tel: 08709 000032
Email: . . . . admin@samaritans.org
Objects: F,W9,W6,W3,W7,W5,W10,W11,2,R,W4,3,W8

SANDES SOLDIERS' & AIRMEN'S CENTRES
CR250718
Unit 7, 30 Island Street, Belfast BT4 1DH
Tel: 028 9050 0250
Email: . . . . info@sandes.org.uk
Objects: F,W9,R,3,P

SANDS - STILLBIRTH AND NEONATAL DEATH SOCIETY
Founded: 1978 CR299679
28 Portland Place, London W1B 1LY
Tel: . . . . 020 7436 5881 Helpline; 020 7436 7940 Administration
Email: . . . . support@uk-sands.org
Objects: F,J,G,1A,2,H,3,P,W8,K

SANE
Founded: 1986 CR296572
1st Floor Cityside House, 40 Adler Street, London E1 1EE
Tel: 020 7375 1002; 0845 767 8000 Saneline (Local call)
Email: . . . . info@sane.org.uk
Objects: F,G,A,R,H

SAT-7 TRUST
CR1060612
The Coach House, 43 New Road, Chippenham, Wiltshire SN15 1HL
Tel: 01249 765865
Email: . . . . respond@sat7trust.org
Objects: W3,W15,1B,R,W4,W8

SAVE OUR SEALS FUND (SOSF)
SC025489
c/o Animal Concern, PO Box 5178, Dumbarton, West Dunbartonshire G82 5YJ
Tel: 01389 841639
Email: . . . . seals@jfrobins.force9.co.uk
Objects: W1,W2

SAVE THE CHILDREN

Founded: 1919 CR213890; SC039570
Chair: Peter Bennett-Jones CBE
Chief Executive: Tanya Steele
Honorary Treasurer: Gareth Davies
Patron: HM Queen Elizabeth II
President: HRH The Princess Royal
Legacy and In Memory (CD), 1 St John's Lane, London EC1M 4AR
Tel: 020 7012 6400
Email: . . . . . leavelife@savethechildren.org.uk
Web: . . . www.savethechildren.org.uk/leavelife
Objects: F,W3,J,G,U,H,3

Save the Children believes every child deserves a future. In the UK and around the world, we give children a healthy start in life, the opportunity to learn, and protection from harm.

Leaving a gift in your will can make a lasting difference to the world the next generation grows up in. After you've provided for your loved ones, your will can give vital support to children who might not otherwise survive. For more information, please e-mail leavelife@savethechildren.org.uk

SBA THE SOLICITORS' CHARITY

Founded: 1858 CR1124512
1 Jaggard Way, Wandsworth Common, London SW12 8SG
Tel: 020 8675 6440
Email: . . . . sec@sba.org.uk
Objects: F,W11,1A,A,V,B

SCHOOL-HOME SUPPORT SERVICE (UK)

CR1084696
Unit 6, Bow Exchange, 5 Yeo Street, London E3 3QP
Tel: 020 7538 3479
Email: . . . . mail@schoolhomesupport.org.uk
Objects: F,W3,J,G,3

SCHOOLMISTRESSES & GOVERNESSES BENEVOLENT INSTITUTION

Founded: 1843 CR205366
Unit 2, Bybow Farm, Orchard Way, Wilmington, Dartford, Kent DA2 7ER
Tel: 01322 293822
Email: . . . . sarah.brydon@sgbi.net / gillian.mumford@sgbi.net
Objects: W11,1A,A,V,W4,U,B,W14,3,W8

SCOLIOSIS ASSOCIATION UK

Founded: 1981 CR285290
4 Ivebury Court, 323-327 Latimer Road, London W10 6RA
Tel: . . . . 020 8964 5343; 020 8964 1166 Helpline
Email: . . . . sauk@sauk.org.uk
Objects: F,J,2,H,3,P

SCOPE

Founded: 1952 CR208231
Legacy Manager: Mr Thomas Dixon
6 Market Road (CD14), London N7 9PW
Tel: 020 7619 7293
Email: . . . . giftsinwills@scope.org.uk
Web: . . . . . http://www.scope.org.uk/giftsinwills

By leaving a gift in your Will to Scope, you will be supporting disabled people and their families for generations to come.

SCOTS GUARDS CHARITABLE FUND

CR249900
Scots Guards Office, The Castle, Edinburgh EH1 2YT
Tel: 0131 310 5042
Email: . . . . finance@rhqscotsguards.co.uk
Objects: W9,1A,A,1B,2

SCOTSCARE

Founded: 1611 CR207326
22 City Road, London EC1Y 2AJ
Tel: . . . . 020 7240 3718; 0800 652 2989 Helpline
Email: . . . . info@scotscare.com
Objects: F,1A,A,V,D,B,C

SCOTTISH CATHOLIC INTERNATIONAL AID FUND (SCIAF)

SC012302
19 Park Circus, Glasgow G3 6BE
Tel: 0141 354 5555
Email: . . . . sciaf@sciaf.org.uk

SCOTTISH CENTRE FOR CHILDREN WITH MOTOR IMPAIRMENTS

SC008428
The Craighalbert Centre, 1 Craighalbert Way, Cumbernauld, North Lanarkshire G68 0LS
Tel: 01236 456100
Email: . . . . kirstenbruce@craighalbert.org.uk
Objects: W3,W5,G

SCOTTISH LANGUAGE DICTIONARIES LTD

SC032910
25 Buccleuch Place, Edinburgh EH8 9LN
Tel: 0131 650 4149
Email: . . chris.robinson@scotsdictionaires.org.uk
Objects: W3,G,2,W4,3

SCOTTISH NATIONAL FEDERATION FOR THE WELFARE OF THE BLIND

SC002185
Redroofs, Balgavies, Forfar, Angus DD8 2TH
Tel: 01307 830265
Email: . . . . secyj@snfwb.wanadoo.co.uk
Objects: F,W6,G,2

SCOTTISH OUT OF SCHOOL CARE NETWORK

SC020520
Floor 2, 100 Wellington Street, Glasgow G2 6DH
Tel: 0141 564 1284
Email: . . . . info@soscn.org
Objects: F,W3,W5,W15,2,H

SCOTTISH SOCIETY FOR THE PREVENTION OF CRUELTY TO ANIMALS (SCOTTISH SPCA)

SC006467
Braehead Mains, 603 Queensferry Road, Edinburgh EH4 6EA
Tel: 03000 999999
Email: . . . . enquiries@scottishspca.org
Objects: W1,2,3

SCOTTISH TERRIER EMERGENCY CARE SCHEME

CR275666
8 Cornwall Close, Westwood, Nottingham, Nottinghamshire NG16 5JS
Tel: 01773 783794
Email: . . . . karen.elkin@ntlworld.com

SCOTTISH VETERANS' RESIDENCES

SC015260
53 Canongate, Edinburgh EH8 8BS
Tel: 0131 556 0091
Email: . . . . info@svronline.org
Objects: W9,W16,D,3,C

SCOTTISH WAR BLINDED

Founded: 1915SC002652
PO Box 500, Gillespie Crescent, Edinburgh EH10 4HZ
Tel: 0131 229 1456
Objects: F,W9,W6,E,G,1A,A,1B,D,3,K

THE SCOUT ASSOCIATION

Founded: 1907 CR306101; SC038437
Gilwell Park, Chingford, London E4 7QW
Tel: 020 8433 7212
Email: . . . . info@scout.org.uk
Objects: W3,G,2,P

SCOUTS SCOTLAND (THE SCOTTISH COUNCIL THE SCOUT ASSOCIATION)

SC017511
Scottish Headquarters, Fordell Firs, Hillend, Dunfermline, Fife KY11 7HQ
Tel: 01383 419073
Email: . . . . shq@scouts.scot
Objects: W3,G,2

SCRIPTURE UNION ENGLAND AND WALES

Scripture union

Founded: 1867 CR213422
National Director: Rev Tim Hastie-Smith
207-209 Queensway, Bletchley, Buckinghamshire MK2 2EB
Tel: 01908 856000
Fax: 01908 856111
Email: . . . . info@scriptureunion.org.uk
Web: . . . . www.scriptureunion.org.uk
Objects: W3,W15,V,R,H

We are a Christian charity with a mission to share the good news with the next generation. Alongside direct mission we support churches, schools and local communities to bring the good news about Jesus Christ to children and young people. Through a network of volunteers, staff and Mission Partners we run Christian holidays, church based events and school Christian groups. Alongside this we produce a wide range of Christian printed and digital publications and support those who use our resources through training programmes. Please see our website for more information: www.scriptureunion.org.uk

See advert on previous page

SEA RANGER ASSOCIATION

Founded: 1973 CR269659
4 Grand Drive, Raynes Park, London SW20 0JT
Tel: 020 8540 3694
Email: . . . . info@searangers.org.uk
Objects: W3,G,3,P

SEAGULL PRINT LIMITED

Founded: 1991 CR1003168
667-669 Garratt Lane, London SW17 0PB
Tel: 020 8944 7366
Email: . . . . lynnr@seagullprint.co.uk
Objects: F,W5,G,O,3,K

SEAL AND BIRD RESCUE TRUST

CR1000313
The Barns, Mill Common Road, Ridlington, North Walsham, Norfolk NR28 9TY
Tel: 01692 650338
Email: . . . . sbrt@talktalk.net

SEASHELL TRUST (FORMERLY ROYAL SCHOOLS FOR THE DEAF MANCHESTER)

Founded: 1823 CR1092655
Stanley Road, Cheadle Hulme, Chester, Cheshire SK8 6RQ
Tel: 0161 610 0100
Email: . . . . info@seashelltrust.org.uk
Objects: W3,G,O,3,P

SECOND CHANCE: A CHARITY FOR CHILDREN WHO NEED SPECIAL HELP

CR1001462
Second Chance House (CC), Somers Road Bridge, Portsmouth, Hampshire PO5 4NS
Tel: 023 9287 2790
Email: . . . . second.chance@ukonline.co.uk
Objects: W3,G

SEEABILITY (THE ROYAL SCHOOL FOR THE BLIND)

Founded: 1799 CR255913
Newplan House, 41 East Street, Epsom, Surrey KT17 1BL
Tel: 01372 755042
Email: . . . . enquiries@seeability.org
Objects: F,W6,W3,E,W5,G,2,W4,O,3,C,K

SELF HELP AFRICA

CR298830
Westgate House, Dickens Court, Hills Lane, Shrewsbury, Shropshire SY1 2HT
Tel: 01743 277170
Email: . . . . infouk@selfhelpafrica.org

SELF UNLIMITED

CR250058
14 Nursery Court, Kibworth Business Park, Harborough Road, Kibworth, Leicester, Leicestershire LE8 0EX
Tel: 0116 279 6225
Email: . . . . info@selfunlimited.co.uk
Objects: E,W5,G,D,3,C,K

SEMTA

Founded: 1990 CR1000328
14 Upton Road, Watford, Hertfordshire WD18 0JT
Tel: 01923 238441
Objects: G,3

SENSE (THE NATIONAL DEAFBLIND & RUBELLA ASSOCIATION)

Founded: 1956 CR289868
101 Pentonville Road, London N1 9LG
Tel: 0300 330 9257
Email: . . . . legacy@sense.org.uk
Objects: F,W6,W3,J,E,W7,W5,G,V,D,2,W4,U,H, O,3,C,P,K

SEQUAL TRUST (SPECIAL EQUIPMENT & AIDS FOR LIVING)

the sequal trust .org.uk

Founded: 1969 CR260119
3 Ploughmans Corner, Wharf Road, Ellesmere, Shropshire SY12 0EJ
Tel: 01691 624222
Fax: 01691 624222
Email: . . . . info@thesequaltrust.org.uk
Web: . . . . http://www.thesequaltrust.org.uk
Object: W5

The Sequal Trust, founded in 1969, is a national charity which fund raises to provide communication aids to British Citizens of all ages with speech, movement or severe learning difficulties. Applicants are accepted who do not have the funds to buy such vital equipment themselves and whose local authorities have no budget for such devices. Liaison is conducted with the person's health care professional, in order to ensure that the recommended speech aid fully meets the needs of the individual, to allow them to lead more independent lives and so 'Set lively minds free'.

SERVICE TO THE AGED

Founded: 1991 CR1001916
c/o Cohen Arnold & Co, New Burlington House, 1075 Finchley Road, London NW11 0PU
Tel: 020 8731 0777
Objects: N,W4,C

SESAME INSTITUTE UK

Founded: 1964 CR263155
Christchurch, 27 Blackfriars Road, London SE1 8NY
Tel: 020 7633 9690
Email: . . . . info@sesame-institute.org
Objects: F,W6,W3,W7,W5,G,2,R,W4,O,3,P,W8,K

SEVENOAKS DAY NURSERY TRUST

Founded: 1988 CR299319
Rear of Community Centre, Otford Road, Sevenoaks, Kent TN14 5DN
Tel: 01732 460384
Objects: W3,G,W15,3,W8

SEVENTH-DAY ADVENTIST CHURCH

Founded: 1901 CR1044071
British Isles HQ, SDA Church, Stanborough Park, Watford, Hertfordshire WD25 9JZ
Tel: 01923 672251
Email: . . . . sda@adventist.org.uk
Objects: F,M,G,1A,1B,N,R,U,H,3

SEVERN GORGE COUNTRYSIDE TRUST

Founded: 1991 CR1004508
Wesley Rooms Annexe, Jockey Bank, Ironbridge, Telford, Shropshire TF8 7PD
Tel: 01952 433880
Objects: W2,3

SGM LIFEWORDS

CR219055
1A The Chandlery, 50 Westminster Bridge Road, London SE1 7QY
Tel: 020 7730 2155
Email: . . . . uk@sgmlifewords.com

SHAFTESBURY YOUNG PEOPLE (FORMERLY SHAFTESBURY HOMES & ARETHUSA)

CR311697
The Chapel, Royal Victoria Patriotic Building, John Archer Way, Trinity Road, London SW18 3SX
Tel: 020 8875 1555
Email: . . . . info@shaftesbury.org.uk
Objects: Q,W3,3

SHALOM EMPLOYMENT ACTION CENTRE

Founded: 1990 CR802730
395 High Street North, London E12 6PG
Tel: 020 8472 3571

SHAPE

Founded: 1976 CR279184
Deane House Studios, 27 Greenwood Place, London NW5 1LB
Tel: . . . . . 0845 521 3457; 020 7424 7333 Shape Tickets; 020 7424 7330 Minicom
Email: . . . . info@shapearts.org.uk
Objects: W6,W3,S,W7,W5,G,2,W4,H,3,K

SHARE COMMUNITY LTD
Founded: 1970 CR264894
64 Altenburg Gardens, London SW11 1JL
Tel: 020 7924 2949
Email: . . . . info@sharecommunity.org.uk
Objects: W6,W7,W5,G,O,3,P,K

SHARED CARE NETWORK
Founded: 1990 CR1104216
63-66 Easton Business Centre, Felix Road, Bristol BS5 0HE
Tel: . . . . 0117 941 5361; 0117 941 5364 Minicom
Email: . . . . shared-care@bristol.ac.uk
Objects: Q,W6,W3,W7,W5,2,P

SHAW TRUST
CR287785; SC039856
Fox Talbot House, Greenways Business Park, Bellinger Close, Chippenham, Wiltshire SN15 1BN
Tel: 01225 716350
Email: . . . . fundraising@shaw-trust.org.uk

SHEFFIELD MEDIA AND EXHIBITION CENTRE LIMITED, THE
Founded: 1991 CR1002020
The Showroom, 7 Paternoster Row, Sheffield, South Yorkshire S1 2BX
Tel: 0114 279 6511
Objects: S,G,H,3,P,K

SHELTER CYMRU - HELPING HOMELESS AND BADLY HOUSED PEOPLE IN WALES
CR515902
25 Walter Road, Swansea SA1 5NN
Tel: 01792 469400
Email: . . . . fundraising@sheltercymru.org.uk
Objects: F,D

SHELTER - NATIONAL CAMPAIGN FOR HOMELESS PEOPLE

Founded: 1966 CR263710; SC002327
88 Old Street, London EC1V 9HU
Tel: 0344 515 2062
Email: . . . . joel_dunster@shelter.org.uk
Web: . . . . http://www.shelter.org.uk/legacy
Objects: F,W9,W6,W3,W7,W5,W10,W11,W15, W16,W4,H,3,Z,W8
Shelter helps millions of people every year struggling with bad housing or homelessness.
Remembering Shelter in your will is one of the most important and lasting ways that you can help people to keep a roof over their heads.

SHENLEY PARK TRUST
Founded: 1990 CR803520
The Bothy, Shenley Park, Radlett Lane, Shenley, Hertfordshire WD7 9DW
Tel: 01923 852629
Objects: W2,3

THE SHEPPARD TRUST - HOUSING FOR ELDERLY LADIES

The Sheppard Trust

Sheltered housing for elderly ladies of limited means

Founded: 1855 CR1133356
12 Lansdowne Walk, London W11 3LN
Tel: 020 7727 5500
Fax: 020 7727 7730
Email: ... clarescottbooth@sheppardtrust.org
To provide low cost, self-contained, unfurnished, sheltered flats for elderly ladies of limited means. Applicants must be at least 65 years old and able to care for themselves. They should be of a Christian faith.

SHINGLES SUPPORT SOCIETY
Founded: 1996 CR291657
41 North Road, London N7 9DP
Tel: 020 7607 9661
Objects: F,W9,W6,W3,W7,W5,W10,W11,N,W4,H,3,W8

SHIPSTON HOME NURSING
CR1061405
Old Schoolroom, Behind 32 Church Street, Shipston-on-Stour, Warwickshire CV36 4AP
Tel: 01608 661379
Objects: N,W4,3

SHIPWRECKED MARINERS' SOCIETY
Founded: 1839 CR212034
Chief Executive: Commodore M.S. Williams CBE, RN
1 North Pallant, Chichester, West Sussex PO19 1TL
Tel: 01243 789329; 01243 787761
Fax: 01243 530853
Email: .... general@shipwreckedmariners.org.uk
Web: .... www.shipwreckedmariners.org.uk
Objects: W11,1A,W4
Founded in 1839 to provide practical and financial assistance to survivors of shipwreck, the Society's main function today is to make grants to ex-merchant seafarers, fishermen and their dependants. Annual grant expenditure is currently £1.4 million in over 2,200 cases of need.

See advert on previous page

SHIPWRECKED MARINERS' SOCIETY
Founded: 1839 CR212034
Chief Executive: Commodore M.S. Williams CBE, RN
1 North Pallant, Chichester, West Sussex PO19 1TL
Tel: 01243 789329; 01243 787761
Fax: 01243 530853
Email: .... general@shipwreckedmariners.org.uk
Web: .... www.shipwreckedmariners.org.uk
Objects: W11,1A,W4
Founded in 1839 to provide practical and financial assistance to survivors of shipwreck, the Society's main function today is to make grants to ex-merchant seafarers, fishermen and their dependants. Annual grant expenditure is currently £1.4 million in over 2,200 cases of need.

SHIRE HORSE SOCIETY
CR210619
East of England Showground, Oundle Road, Peterborough, Cambridgeshire PE2 6XE
Tel: 01733 234451
Email: .... info@eastofengland.org.uk

SHUMEI EIKO LIMITED
Founded: 1991 CR1002647
Chaucer College Canterbury, University Road, Canterbury, Kent CT2 7LJ
Tel: 01227 787800
Object: G

SHUTTLEWOOD CLARKE FOUNDATION, THE
Founded: 1990 CR803525
Ulverscroft Grange, Ulverscroft, Leicester, Leicestershire LE67 9QB
Tel: 01530 244914
Objects: E,W5,W4,3

THE SICK CHILDREN'S TRUST (THE SCT)
Founded: 1982 CR284416
88 Leadenhall Street, Lower Ground Floor, London EC3A 3BP
Tel: 020 7931 8695
Email: .... info@sickchildrenstrust.org
Objects: W3,E,3,C,P

SICKLE CELL SOCIETY
Founded: 1979 CR1046631
54 Station Road, Harlesden, London NW10 4UA
Tel: 020 8961 7795; 020 8961 4006
Email: .... sicklecellsoc@btinternet.com
Objects: F,M,J,G,1A,A,V,H,3,P

SIGHT CONCERN BEDFORDSHIRE
CR1117209
Kings House, 245 Ampthill Road, Bedford, Bedfordshire MK42 9AZ
Tel: 01234 311555
Email: .... simoncarter@sightconcern.org.uk

SIGHTSAVERS
Founded: 1950 CR207544; SC038110
Grosvenor Hall, Bolnore Road, Haywards Heath, West Sussex RH16 4BX
Tel: 01444 446600
Email: .... info@sightsavers.org
Objects: W6,M,G,1B,N,2,U,H,O

THE SIGNALONG GROUP
CR1039788
Stratford House, Waterside Court, Neptune Close, Rochester, Kent ME2 4NZ
Tel: 0845 450 8422
Email: .... mkennard@signalong.org.uk
Objects: F,W3,W5,W15,1B,H

'SIGNALS' MEDIA ARTS CENTRE LIMITED
Founded: 1999 CR802376
Victoria Chambers, St Runwald Street, Colchester, Essex CO1 1HF
Tel: 01206 560255
Email: .... info@signals.org.uk
Objects: W3,W2,S,W7,W5,G,W10,W4,3,W8,K

SIGNHEALTH - THE HEALTHCARE CHARITY FOR DEAF PEOPLE
CR1011056
5 Baring Road, Beaconsfield, Buckinghamshire HP9 2NB

Tel: 01494 687600
Email: .... info@signhealth.org.uk

SILCOATES SCHOOL

Founded: 1820 CR529281
Wrenthorpe, Wakefield, West Yorkshire WF2 0PD
Tel: 01924 291614
Objects: W3,G,1A

SILOAM CHRISTIAN MINISTRIES - EDUCATION, MEDICAL AID, SOCIAL AND OTHER RELIEF AS AN EXPRESSION OF GOD'S LOVE WORLDWIDE

CR327396
4 Chapel Court, Holly Walk, Leamington Spa, Warwickshire CV32 4YS
Tel: 01926 335037; 0800 027 7917
Email: .... info@siloam.org.uk
Objects: W6,W3,W7,W5,W10,1A,1B,R,W4,U,W8

THE SILVANUS TRUST

CR285768
Unit 4, Winstone Beacon, Trematon, Saltash, Cornwall PL12 4RU
Tel: 01752 846400
Email: .... info@silvanus.org.uk
Objects: W2,G,1A,A,1B,3

SIMON COMMUNITY, THE

Founded: 1963 CR283938
129 Malden Road, London NW5 4HS
Tel: 020 7485 6639
Email: .... info@simoncommunity.org.uk

SIOBHAN DAVIES DANCE/ SIOBHAN DAVIES STUDIOS

Founded: 1992 CR1010786
Siobhan Davies Studios, 85 St George's Road, London SE1 6ER
Tel: 020 7091 9650
Email: .... info@siobhandavies.com
Objects: S,G,2,3

SIR ALISTER HARDY FOUNDATION FOR OCEAN SCIENCE

Founded: 1990 CR1001233
The Laboratory, Citadel Hill, Plymouth, Devon PL1 2PB
Tel: 01752 633288
Email: .... sahfos@wpo.nerc.ac.uk
Objects: W2,G

SIR JAMES KNOTT TRUST, THE

CR1001363
16-18 Hood Street, Newcastle upon Tyne, Tyne & Wear NE1 6JQ
Tel: 0191 230 4016
Objects: F,W9,W6,M,W3,W2,S,E,W7,W5,G,A,1B, D,W4,O,C,P

SIR JOSIAH MASON TRUST

CR209283
Mason Court, Hillborough Road, Birmingham, West Midlands B27 6PF
Tel: 0121 245 1002
Email: .... leslie.robinson@sjmt.org.uk
Objects: G,D,W4,3,C

SIR RICHARD STAPLEY EDUCATIONAL TRUST

Founded: 1919 CR313812
Administrator
Chairman: Dr Mary Wheater
Stapley Trust, Richmond, Surrey TW9 3AL
Email: .... admin@stapleytrust.org
Web: .... www.stapleytrust.org
Objects: G,1A,A

The maximum amount of support is £1,200. Grants are awarded to students on an approved course at a university in the UK leading to a post graduate degree (Masters MPhil or PhD) and to students on courses leading to a second degree in medicine, dentistry or veterinary studies. Students must be over 24 on the 1st October of the proposed academic year, with a 1st or good 2i degree (65% or higher), and residing in the UK when making their application. Applicants must not be in receipt of full awards (tuition and maintenance) from other bodies. Grants are awarded for one academic year. All enquiries should be made to admin@stapleytrust.org. Application forms are available in early January. The closing date for applications is the 31st March or the first 300 applications received.

THE SISTERS OF THE SACRED HEARTS OF JESUS AND MARY

Founded: 1903 CR1004590
Chigwell Convent, 803 Chigwell Road, Woodford Green, Essex IG8 8AU
Tel: 020 8504 1624
Objects: W3,G,N,R,W4,U,T,3

SKILLSHARE INTERNATIONAL

Founded: 1990 CR802576
Imperial House, St Nicholas Circle, Leicester, Leicestershire LE1 4LF
Tel: 0116 254 1862
Email: .... info@skillshare.org
Objects: W3,W2,W5,G,W10,W4,U,3,W8

SKINNER'S COMPANY, THE

Founded: 1327 CR307846
Skinners' Hall, 8 Dowgate Hill, London EC4R 2SP
Tel: 020 7213 0562
Objects: W3,W2,W5,G,1A,A,1B,D,W4,B,C,W8

SOBELL HOUSE HOSPICE CHARITY LIMITED

CR1118646
Churchill Hospital, Headington, Oxford, Oxfordshire OX3 7LJ
Tel: 01865 857007
Email: .... mail@sobellhospice.org
Object: N

SOCIAL MARKET FOUNDATION

Founded: 1990 CR1000971
11 Tufton Street, London SW1P 3QB
Tel: 020 7222 7060
Objects: G,H,3

SOCIETY FOR MUCOPOLYSACCHARIDE DISEASES

Founded: 1982 CR1143472
MPS House, Repton Place, White Lion Road, Amersham, Buckinghamshire HP7 9LP
Tel: 0845 389 9901
Email: .... mps@mpssociety.co.uk
Objects: F,W3,W5,A,V,N,2,H,P

SOCIETY FOR PROMOTING THE TRAINING OF WOMEN

Founded: 1859 CR313700
168 Sandyhurst Lane, Ashford, Kent TN25 4NX
Tel: 01233 624031
Objects: G,1A,3,W8

SOCIETY FOR THE ASSISTANCE OF LADIES IN REDUCED CIRCUMSTANCES
Founded: 1886 CR205798
Lancaster House, 25 Hornyold Road, Malvern, Worcestershire WR14 1QQ
Tel: 0300 365 1886
Email: .... info@salrc.org.uk
Objects: 1A,A,1B,Y,W8

SOCIETY FOR THE PROTECTION OF ANCIENT BUILDINGS
Founded: 1877 CR1113753; SC039244
37 Spital Square, London E1 6DY
Tel: 020 7377 1644
Email: .... development@spab.org.uk
Objects: F,W2,S,G,2,H,3

SOCIETY FOR THE PROTECTION OF ANIMALS ABROAD (SPANA)
Founded: 1923 CR209015
14 John Street, London WC1N 2EB
Tel: 020 7831 3999
Email: .... legacies@spana.org
Objects: W1,W2,G,A,1B,2,U

SOCIETY FOR THE STUDY OF ADDICTION TO ALCOHOL AND OTHER DRUGS
Founded: 1992 CR1009826
SSA, Leeds Addiction Unit, 19 Springfield Mount, Leeds, West Yorkshire LS2 9NG
Tel: 0113 295 1338
Objects: 1A,1B,2,H

SOCIETY OF FRIENDS OF FOREIGNERS IN DISTRESS
Founded: 1803 CR212593
68 Burhill Road, Hersham, Walton-on-Thames, Surrey KT12 4JF
Tel: 01932 244916
Objects: W10,1A,A,3

SOCIETY OF JESUS CHARITABLE TRUST, THE
Founded: 1990 CR803659
114 Mount Street, London W1K 3AH
Tel: 020 7499 0285
Objects: R,3

SOCIETY OF ST VINCENT DE PAUL
XN45800
Northern Ireland Regional Office, 196-200 Antrim Road, Belfast BT15 2AJ
Tel: 028 9035 1561
Email: .... info@svpni.co.uk

SOCIETY OF THE PRECIOUS BLOOD
Founded: 1990 CR900512
Burnham Abbey, Taplow, Maidenhead, Windsor & Maidenhead SL6 OPW
Tel: 01628 604080
Objects: 2,R

SOFA (FURNITURE REUSE CHARITY)
Founded: 1984 CR1002980
Towles Building, Nottingham Road, Loughborough, Leicestershire LE11 1DY
Tel: 01509 262557
Email: .... office@sofareuse.org
Objects: F,M,W2,G,W15,Y,3

SOIL ASSOCIATION
CR206862
South Plaza, Marlborough Street, Bristol BS1 3NX
Tel: 0117 314 5000
Email: .... info@soilassociation.org
Object: 2

THE SOLDIERS' & AIRMEN'S SCRIPTURE READERS ASSOCIATION (SASRA)
Founded: 1838 CR235708; SC039130
Havelock House, Barrack Road, Aldershot, Hampshire GU11 3NP
Tel: 01252 310033
Email: .... admin@sasra.org.uk
Objects: W9,2,R,3

SOMERSET COURT AUTISTIC TRUST
CR291850
20 Willifield Way, London NW11 7XT
Tel: 020 8455 0880
Email: .... dig12@btinternet.com
Objects: M,V,C

SOMERSET WILDLIFE TRUST
CR238372
Tonedale Mill, Wellington, Taunton, Somerset TA21 OAW
Email: .... enquiries@somersetwildlife.org
Objects: F,W3,J,G,2

SONS OF DIVINE PROVIDENCE
Founded: 1952 CR1088675
13 Lower Teddington Road, Hampton Wick, Kingston-upon-Thames, Surrey KT1 4EU
Tel: 020 8977 5130
Email: .... mail@sodp.fsnet.co.uk
Objects: E,W5,G,D,R,W4,U,3,C

SOS CHILDREN
Founded: 1968 CR1069204
Terrington House, 13-15 Hills Road, Cambridge, Cambridgeshire CB2 1NL
Tel: 01223 365589
Email: .... info@soschildren.org
Objects: W3,U

SOS, THE
Founded: 1955 CR208231
3 Nelson Court, Woodards View, Shoreham-by-Sea, West Sussex BN43 5LR
Tel: 01273 462727
Email: .... georgehammond@btinternet.com
Objects: F,W3,J,W5,G,1A,A,1B,2

SOUND SEEKERS
Founded: 1992 CR1013870
UCL Ear Institute, 332-336 Gray's Inn Road, London WC1X 8EE
Tel: 020 7833 0035
Email: .... admin@sound-seekers.org.uk
Objects: W3,W7,G,2,U,3

SOUTH AMERICAN MISSION SOCIETY
CR221328
Allen Gardiner Cottage, Pembury Road, Tunbridge Wells, Kent TN2 3QU
Tel: 01892 538647
Email: .... finsec@samsgb.org
Objects: F,W6,W3,W7,W5,G,W10,R,W4,U,H,T,3, W8

SOUTH ASIAN CONCERN CHARITABLE TRUST
Founded: 1991 CR1002270
PO Box 43, Sutton, Surrey SM2 5WL

Tel: 020 8770 9717
Email: .... info@southasianconcern.org
Objects: G,W10,R,H,3

SOUTH LONDON MISSION
Headquarters, Central Hall, 256 Bermondsey Street, London SE1 3UJ
Tel: 020 7407 2014
Objects: F,M,W3,E,G,W10,R,W4,H,3,C,P

SOUTH LONDON YMCA
CR1099051
The Old House, 2 Wellesley Court Road, Croydon, Surrey CR0 1LE
Tel: 020 8667 9249
Email: .... admin@croydonymca.org
Objects: F,W3,G,3,C,P

SOUTH WEST EQUINE PROTECTION
CR1087579
Unit B5, Yelverton Business Park, Crapstone, Devon PL20 7PE
Tel: 01822 854823
Email: .... mail@swep.org.uk

SOUTH YORKSHIRE COMMUNITY FOUNDATION
Founded: 1986 CR1140947
Unit 3, G1 Building, 6 Leeds Road, Sheffield, South Yorkshire S9 3TY
Tel: ..... 0114 242 4857/0114 242 4294 (grants)
Email: .. admin@sycf.org.uk/grants@sycf.org.uk

SOUTH YORKSHIRE HOUSING ASSOCIATION, CARE & SUPPORTED HOUSING
Founded: 1997 CR501639
43-47 Wellington Street, Sheffield, South Yorkshire S1 4HF
Tel: 0114 290 0250
Email: .... care@syha.co.uk
Objects: D,3,C

SOUTHERN AREA HOSPICE SERVICES
XN47329/2
St John's House (CC), Courtenay Hill, Newry, Co. Down BT34 2EB
Tel: 028 3025 1333
Email: ... info@southernareahospiceservices.org
Objects: M,N

SOUTHERN HOUSING FOUNDATION
27412
Southern Housing Group, Fleet House, 59-61 Clerkenwell Road, London EC1M 5LA
Tel: 020 7251 6091
Email: .... foundation@shgroup.co.uk
Objects: W3,G,1A,1B,D,P,K

SOUTHWARK CHILDREN'S FOUNDATION
Founded: 1991 CR1002774
Eveline Lowe Primary School, Marlborough Grove, London SE1 5JT
Tel: 020 7237 3207
Objects: W3,J,S,G,V,2,H,3

SOUTHWARK DIOCESAN WELCARE
Founded: 1894 CR1107859
St John's Community Centre, 19 Frederick Crescent, London SW9 6XN
Tel: 020 7820 7910
Email: .... centraloffice@welcare.org
Objects: F,W3,J,G,W15,2,Y,3,P,Z,W8

SOVA
CR1073877
1st Floor, Chichester House, 37 Brixton Road, London SW9 6DZ
Tel: 020 7793 0404
Email: .... mail@sova.org.uk
Objects: F,W3,J,G,W10,O,3,P,W8,K

SPADEWORK LIMITED
Founded: 1985 CR291198
Teston Road, Offham, West Malling, Kent ME19 5NA
Tel: 01732 870002
Objects: W5,G,3,K

SPANISH GOSPEL MISSION
CR1017224
70 Butts Road, Barton-upon-Humber, North Lincolnshire DN18 5JH
Tel: 01652 661340
Email: ... office@spanish-gospel-mission.org.uk
Object: R

SPARKS - THE CHILDREN'S MEDICAL RESEARCH CHARITY
Founded: 1991 CR1003825; SC039482
Heron House, 10 Dean Farrar Street, London SW1H 0DX
Tel: 020 7799 2111
Email: .... info@sparks.org.uk
Objects: W3,A,1B

SPEAKABILITY (ACTION FOR DYSPHASIC ADULTS)
Founded: 1980 CR295094
1 Royal Street, London SE1 7LL
Tel: 020 7261 9572
Email: .... speakability@speakability.org.uk
Objects: F,W5,G,2,W4,H,3,P

SPEEDWELL TRUST
Parkanaur Forest Park, Dungannon, Co. Tyrone BT70 3AA
Tel: 028 8776 7392
Email: .... speedwell.trust@btinternet.com
Objects: W3,W2,G,T,3

SPINAL INJURIES ASSOCIATION
CR1054097
SIA House, 2 Trueman Place, Oldbrook, Milton Keynes MK6 2HH
Tel: 0845 678 6633 Switchboard; 0800 980 0501 Freephone Helpline
Email: .... siahouse@spinal.co.uk
Objects: F,W5,2,H,3

SPINAL MUSCULAR ATROPHY SUPPORT UK
Founded: 1985 CR1106815
40 Cygnet Court, Timothys Bridge Road, Stratford-upon-Avon, Warwickshire CV37 9NW
Tel: 08707 743651; 08707 743652
Email: .... M.D@smasupportuk.org.uk
Objects: F,W5,1A,3

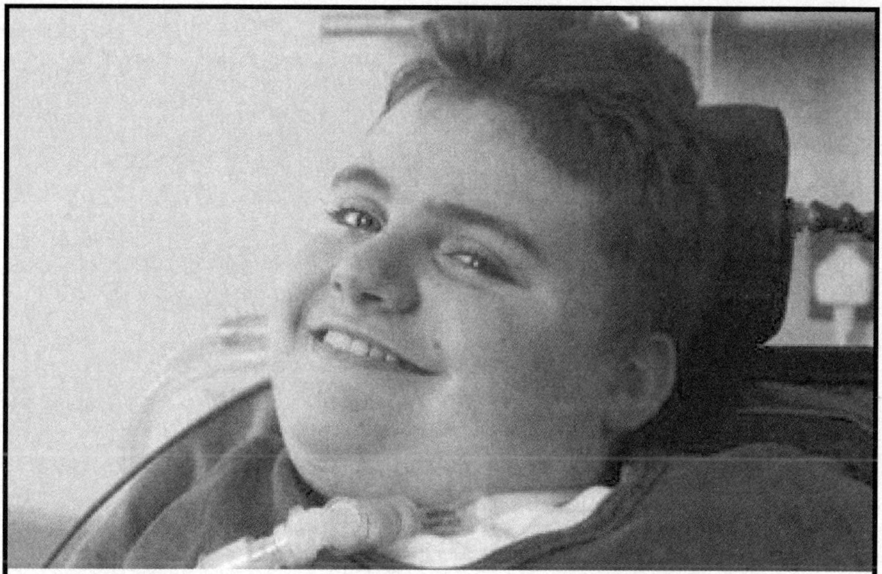

See advert on previous page

SPITALFIELDS CRYPT TRUST, LONDON

Founded: 1965 CR1075947
Acorn House, 116-118 Shoreditch High Street, London E1 6JN
Tel: 020 7613 5677
Email: .... info@sct.org.uk
Objects: E,G,O,3,C,P

SPITALFIELDS MARKET COMMUNITY TRUST

Founded: 1991 CR1004003
Spitalfields City Farm, Weaver Street, London E1 5HJ
Tel: 020 7247 8762

SPORTS COUNCIL TRUST COMPANY, THE

Founded: 1990 CR803779
3rd Floor, Victoria House, Southampton Row, London WC1B 4SE
Tel: 020 7273 1648
Objects: W6,W3,W7,W5,W10,A,1B,W4

SPRING HARVEST

Founded: 1992 CR1014540
14 Horsted Square, Uckfield, East Sussex TN22 1QG
Tel: 01825 769111
Objects: G,V,3

SPRING PROJECT, THE

CR1067992
PO BOX 20, Morpeth, Northumberland NE61 3YP
Tel: 01670 510725
Email: .... info@springproject.org.uk
Objects: R,3

SPRINGHILL HOSPICE (ROCHDALE)

CR701798
Broad Lane, Rochdale, Greater Manchester OL16 4PZ
Tel: 01706 649920
Email: ...... enquiries@springhillhospice.org.uk

SPURGEON'S CHILD CARE

CR1081182
74 Wellingborough Road, Rushden, Northamptonshire NN10 9TY
Tel: 01933 412412
Email: .... scc@spurgeons.org
Objects: F,W3,E,R,U,H,3,P,W8

SSAFA, THE ARMED FORCES CHARITY

CR210760; SC038056
Queen Elizabeth House (CC), 4 St Dunstan's Hill, London EC3R 8AD
Tel: 020 7463 9257
Email: .... legacy@ssafa.org.uk
Objects: F,W9,W6,W3,J,W7,W5,1A,A,V,D,2,W4, H,O,3,C,W8,K

ST ANDREW'S CHILDREN'S SOCIETY

SC005754
7 John's Place (CD), Leith, Edinburgh EH6 7EL
Tel: 0131 454 3370
Email: .... info@standrews-children.org.uk
Objects: Q,F,W3,3

ST ANDREW'S (ECUMENICAL) TRUST

Founded: 1991 CR1004126
Lambeth Palace, London SE1 7JU
Tel: 020 7898 1221
Objects: G,1A,R,B

ST ANDREW'S SOCIETY FOR LADIES IN NEED

Founded: 1874 CR208541
20 Denmark Gardens, Holbrook, Ipswich, Suffolk IP9 2BG
Tel: 01473 327408
Email: .... mpope1@btinternet.com
Objects: 1A,A,V,W4,W8

ST ANDREWS SCOTTISH SOLDIERS CLUB FUND

Founded: 1974 CR233297
37 King Street, Covent Garden, London WC2E 8JS
Email: .... info@scotscare.com
Object: A

ST ANNE'S COMMUNITY SERVICES

Founded: 1971 CR502224
6 St Mark's Avenue, Leeds, West Yorkshire LS2 9BN
Tel: 0113 243 5151
Email: .... info@st.annes.org.uk
Objects: F,E,W5,G,D,3,C,P

ST ANN'S HOSPICE

CR258085
St Ann's Road North, Heald Green, Cheadle, Greater Manchester SK8 3SZ

Tel: 0161 498 3631
Email: .... enquiries@sah.org.uk

ST ANTHONY'S HOSPITAL, NORTH CHEAM

CR1068661
801 London Road, North Cheam, Surrey SM3 9DW
Tel: 020 8337 6691
Email: .... info@stanthonys.org.uk
Objects: N,3

ST AUGUSTINE'S FOUNDATION

Founded: 1979 CR307961
c/o Cathedral House, The Precincts, Canterbury, Kent CT1 2EH
Tel: 01227 762862
Objects: 1B,R

ST AUSTELL CHINA CLAY MUSEUM LIMITED

Founded: 1991 CR1001838
Wheal Martyn, Carthew, St Austell, Cornwall PL26 8XG
Tel: 01726 850362
Email: .... info@chinaclaycountry.co.uk
Objects: W2,S,G,W12,3

ST BARNABAS

Founded: 1897 CR206792
73 High Street, Southwold, Ipswich, Suffolk IP18 6DS
Tel: 01502 723308
Objects: V,W4,3,C

ST BARNABAS HOSPICE TRUST

CR1053814
Fundraising Office, 12 Cardinal Close, Lincoln, Lincolnshire LN2 4SY
Tel: 01522 540300
Email: ... fundraising@stbarnabashospice.co.uk
Objects: F,E,N,W4,3,W8

ST BARNABAS SOCIETY, THE

Founded: 1992 CR1009910
4 First Turn, Wolvercote, Oxford, Oxfordshire OX2 8AH
Tel: 01865 513377
Email: ..... secretary@stbarnabassociety.org.uk
Objects: 1A,A

ST BENEDICT'S HOSPICE, SUNDERLAND

CR1019410
St Benedict's Way, Ryhope, Sunderland, Tyne & Wear SR2 0NY
Tel: 0191 512 8436
Email: .... anne.oliver@sotw.nhs.uk

ST BRIGID'S SCHOOL LIMITED

Founded: 1991 CR1003157
Plas Yn Green, Mold Road, Denbigh, Denbighshire LL16 4BH
Tel: 01745 815228
Email: .... bursarst.brigids@denbighshire.gov.uk
Objects: G,3

ST CATHERINE'S HOSPICE

Founded: 1983 CR281362
Malthouse Road, Crawley, West Sussex RH10 6BH
Tel: 01293 447333
Email: .... info@stch.org.uk
Objects: F,E,G,N,O,3

ST CHRISTOPHER'S FELLOWSHIP

CR207782
1 Putney High Street, London SW15 1SZ
Tel: 020 8780 7800
Email: .... info@stchris.org.uk

ST CHRISTOPHER'S HOSPICE

CR210667
51-59 Lawrie Park Road, London SE26 6DZ
Tel: 020 8768 4500
Email: .... enquiries@stchris.ftech.couk
Objects: F,E,G,N,H,3

ST CLARE WEST ESSEX HOSPICE CARE TRUST

Founded: 1990 CR1063631
St Clare Hospice Centre, Hastingwood Road, Harlow, Essex CM17 9JX
Tel: 01279 413590
Email: .... fund@stclare-hospice.co.uk
Objects: F,M,E,N,3

ST COLUMBA'S HOSPICE (EDINBURGH)

SC003634
Challenger Lodge, Boswall Road, Edinburgh EH5 3RW
Tel: 0131 551 1381
Email: .... fund@stcolumbashospice.org.uk

ST CUTHBERT'S CENTRE

Founded: 1990 CR803638
The Philbeach Hall,, 51 Philbeach Gardens, Earls Court, London SW5 9EB
Tel: 020 7835 1389
Email: .... dropin@stcuthbertscentre.org.uk
Objects: F,E,G,3

ST DAVID'S FOUNDATION HOSPICE CARE

Founded: 1992 CR1010576
Cambrian House, St Johns Road, Newport NP19 8GR
Tel: 01633 271364
Email: ..... enquiries@stdavidsfoundation.co.uk
Objects: N,3

ST DAVID'S HOSPICE

CR1038543
Abbey Road, Llandudno, Conwy LL30 2EN
Tel: 01492 879058
Email: ...... enquiries@stdavidshospice.org.uk
Objects: N,3

ST ELIZABETH'S - POSITIVE LIVING & LEARNING FOR PEOPLE WITH EPILEPSY & OTHER COMPLEX NEEDS

Founded: 1901 CR1068661
Perry Green (CC), Much Hadham, Hertfordshire SG10 6EW
Tel: 01279 843451
Email: .... enquiries@stelizabeths.org.uk

ST FRANCIS' CHILDREN'S SOCIETY

CR211670
Collis House, 48 Newport Road, Woolstone, Milton Keynes, Buckinghamshire MK15 0AA
Tel: 01908 572700
Email: .... enquiries@sfcs.org.uk
Objects: Q,3

ST FRANCIS LEPROSY GUILD

Founded: 1895 CR208741
73 St Charles Square, London W10 6EJ

Tel: 020 8969 1345
Email: . . . . enquiries@stfrancisleprosy.org
Objects: W6,W3,W7,W5,G,A,1B,D,N,2,R,W4,O,C,W8,K

ST GEORGE'S COMMUNITY CHILDREN'S PROJECT LIMITED

Founded: 1989 CR802017
St George's Centre, 7 Chilston Road, Tunbridge Wells, Kent TN4 9LP
Tel: 01892 543982
Email: . . . . info@stgeorgesproject.org
Objects: W3,G,3

ST GEORGE'S CRYPT (LEEDS)

Founded: 1930 CR250016
St George's Crypt, Great George Street, Leeds, West Yorkshire LS1 3BR
Tel: 0113 245 9061
Email: . . . . admin@stgeorgescrypt.org.uk
Objects: F,M,W3,E,D,N,R,3,C,P

ST GEORGE'S HOSPITAL CHARITY

CR241527
St George's Hospital, Blackshaw Road, London SW17 0QT
Tel: 020 8725 4522
Email: . . . . giving@stgeorges.nhs.uk
Objects: W6,W3,W7,W5,W15,1A,A,1B,W16,N,W4,O,W8,W

ST GILES HOSPICE

CR509014
Fisherwick Road, Whittington, Lichfield, Staffordshire WS14 9LH
Tel: 01543 432538
Email: . . . . mail@st-giles-hospice.org.uk
Objects: E,G,N,3

ST JOHN AMBULANCE

CR1077265
27 St. John's Lane, London EC1M 4BU
Tel: 020 7324 4000
Objects: M,W3,J,E,G,N,2,U,H,3,C,P,K

ST JOHN CYMRU WALES

CR250523
Priory House, Beignon Close, Ocean Way, Cardiff CF24 5PB
Tel: 029 2044 9629
Email: . . . . fundraising@stjohnwales.org.uk

ST JOSEPH'S HOSPICE

Founded: 1905 CR1113125
Mare Street, Hackney, London E8 4SA
Tel: 020 8525 6000
Email: . . . . info@stjh.org.uk
Objects: W5,W10,N,W4,3

ST JOSEPH'S HOSPICE ASSOCIATION (JOSPICE INTERNATIONAL)

Founded: 1966 CR1090151
Ince Road, Thornton, Liverpool, Merseyside L23 4UE
Tel: 0151 924 3812
Email: . . . . enquiries@jospice.org.uk
Objects: N,R,U

ST JOSEPH'S SOCIETY (FORMERLY THE AGED POOR SOCIETY)

Founded: 1708 CR1010058
St Joseph's Almshouse, 42 Brook Green, London W6 7BW
Tel: 020 7603 9817

ST KATHARINE & SHADWELL TRUST

Founded: 1990 CR1001047
Unit 1.4, 11-29 Fashion Street, London E1 6PX
Tel: 020 7422 7523
Objects: G,A,1B,H

ST LOYE'S FOUNDATION

CR235434
Beaufort House, 51 New North Road, Exeter, Devon EX4 4EP
Tel: 01392 255428
Email: . . . . helpingus@stloyes.co.uk
Objects: F,W9,W6,M,J,W7,W5,G,W11,W4,H,O,3,W8

ST LUKE'S HEALTHCARE FOR THE CLERGY

Founded: 1892 CR1123195
14 Fitzroy Square, London W1T 6AH
Tel: 020 7388 4954
Email: . . . . admin@stlukeshealthcare.org.uk
Objects: F,N,3

ST LUKE'S HOSPICE, HARROW & BRENT

CR298555
Kenton Grange, Kenton Road, Harrow, Middlesex HA3 0YG
Tel: 020 8382 8000
Email: . . . . info@stlukes-hospice.org

ST MARGARET'S SOMERSET HOSPICE

CR279473
Head Office, Heron Drive, Bishops Hull, Taunton, Somerset TA1 5HA
Tel: . . . . 01823 259394 (Fundraising)
Email: . . . . admin@st-marg-hospice.org.uk
Objects: F,E,G,N,O,3

ST MARK'S HOSPITAL FOUNDATION

Founded: 1835 CR1140930
Northwick Park, Watford Road, Harrow, Middlesex HA1 3UJ
Tel: 020 8235 4092
Email: . . . . foundation@nhs.net

(COMMUNITY OF) ST MARY AT THE CROSS

Founded: 1866 CR209261
The Mother Abbess: Dame Mary Therese
Edgware Abbey, 94A Priory Field Drive, Edgware, Middlesex HA8 9PU
Tel: 020 8958 7868
Fax: 020 8958 1920
Email: . . . . info@edgwareabbey.org.uk
Web: . . . . http://www.edgwareabbey.org.uk
Objects: W5,W4,3

Edgware Abbey is a place of peace, offering Benedictine Hospitality for those seeking rest and spiritual renewal. Henry Nihill House provides high quality care for frail elderly people and those with physical disability.

ST MARY'S CONVENT & NURSING HOME, LONDON

CR1080751
Burlington Lane, Chiswick, London W4 2QE
Tel: 020 8994 4641
Objects: W7,W5,W11,N,W4,W8

ST MICHAEL'S FELLOWSHIP

CR1035820
136 Streatham High Road, London SW16 1BW
Tel: 020 8835 9570
Email: . . . . . admin@stmichaelsfellowship.org.uk

ST MICHAEL'S HOSPICE (NORTH HAMPSHIRE)
Founded: 1991 CR1002856
Basil De Ferranti House, Aldermaston Road, Basingstoke, Hampshire RG24 9NB
Tel: 01256 844744
Email: .... info@stmichaelshospice.org.uk
Objects: F,W9,W6,M,W3,J,E,W7,W5,G,W10, W11,N,W4,O,3,P,W8

ST MONICA TRUST
Founded: 1925 CR202151
Cote Lane, Westbury-on-Trym, Bristol BS9 3UN
Tel: 0117 949 4044
Email: .... info@stmonicatrust.org.uk
Objects: M,W5,G,1A,A,1B,D,N,2,W4,O,3,C,P

ST PATRICKS MISSIONARY SOCIETY (KILTEGAN FATHERS)
CR269640
20 Beauchamp Road, East Molesey, Surrey KT8 0PA
Tel: 020 8979 1890
Email: .... spsuk@aol.com
Objects: F,W3,W2,W10,2,R,W4,U,T,W8

ST PETER'S HOME AND SISTERHOOD
Founded: 1861 CR240675
St Peter's Convent, St Columbus House, Maybury Hill, Woking, Surrey GU22 8AB
Tel: 01483 750739
Objects: F,G,3

ST PETERS TRUST FOR KIDNEY, BLADDER & PROSTATE RESEARCH
CR1060924
Royal Free Charity, (Fund 543), Royal Free Hospital, Pond Street, London NW3 2QG
Tel: 020 7472 6677
Email: .... rfh.stpeterstrust@nhs.net
Objects: W3,1B,2,W4,H

ST RAPHAEL'S HOSPICE
CR1068661
London Road, North Cheam, Sutton, Surrey SM3 9DX
Tel: 020 8099 7777
Email: .... fundraising@straphaels.org.uk
Objects: F,E,G,N,W4,3

ST RICHARD'S HOSPICE, WORCESTER
Founded: 1984 CR515668
Wildwood Drive, Worcester, Worcestershire WR5 2QT
Tel: 01905 763963
Email: .... enquiries@strichards.org.uk
Objects: F,G,N,3

ST SAVIOUR'S PRIORY
Founded: 1866 CR231926
18 Queensbridge Road, London E2 8NS
Tel: 020 7739 6775
Objects: W3,E,R,W4,3

ST THOMAS'S COMMUNITY NETWORK
Founded: 1990 CR1093430
Blue Coat Base, Beechwood Road, Dudley, West Midlands DY2 7QA
Tel: 01384 818990
Email: .... stcn@bcnet.org.uk
Objects: F,J,S,G,2,3

ST URSULA'S HIGH SCHOOL TRUST
Founded: 1990 CR900498
Brecon Road, Westbury on Trym, Bristol BS9 4DT
Tel: 0117 962 2616
Objects: W3,G,3

ST VINCENT DE PAUL SOCIETY (ENGLAND & WALES)
CR1053992
9 Larcom Street, Walworth, London SE17 1RX
Tel: 020 7703 3030
Email: .... info@svp.org.uk
Objects: F,W3,E,W7,W5,V,2,W4,U,C,P

STAFFORDSHIRE WILDLIFE TRUST
Founded: 1969 CR259558
The Wolseley Centre, Wolseley Bridge, Stafford, Staffordshire ST17 0WT
Tel: 01889 880100
Email: .... info@staffs-wildlife.org.uk
Objects: W2,G,2,3

STAPLES TRUST
Founded: 1992 CR1010656
Allington House, 150 Victoria Street, London SW1E 5AE
Tel: 020 7410 0330

STARS FOUNDATION FOR CEREBRAL PALSY
CR1103090
3 Nelson Court, Woodards View, Shoreham-by-Sea, West Sussex BN43 5LR
Tel: 01273 462727
Email: .... enquiry@starsorg.co.uk

STEEPHILL SCHOOL
Founded: 1990 CR803152
off Castle Hill, Fawkham, Longfield, Kent DA3 7BG
Tel: 01474 702107
Email: .... steephillprep@hotmail.com
Objects: W3,G

STEP BY STEP PARTNERSHIP LTD
Founded: 1990 CR900308
36 Crimea Road, Aldershot, Hampshire GU11 1UD
Tel: 01252 346105
Email: .... generalmanager@emmaus.co.uk
Objects: F,W3,E,G,D,3,C,P

STEP FORWARD (TOWER HAMLETS)
Founded: 1990 CR802597
234 Bethnal Green Road, London E2 0AA
Tel: 020 7739 3082
Objects: F,W3,G,3

STEPPING STONE PROJECT (ROCHDALE) LTD
Founded: 1991 CR1004375
Central Office, PO Box 153, Rochdale, Greater Manchester OL16 1FR
Tel: 01706 353000

STEPS CHARITY WORLDWIDE
CR1094343
Warrington Lane (CD), Lymm, Cheshire WA13 0SA
Tel: 0871 717 0044
Email: .... info@steps-charity.org.uk

STOCKFIELD COMMUNITY ASSOCIATION
Founded: 1991 CR1003108
St Philip's Gate, 5 Waterloo Street, Birmingham, West Midlands B2 5PG
Tel: 0121 200 3242
Email: .... acs@acollins-sol.co.uk

STOKE ON TRENT CITIZENS ADVICE BUREAU
Founded: 1990 CR1001204
Advice House, Cheapside, Hanley, Stoke-on-Trent, Staffordshire ST1 1HL
Tel: 01782 408600
Objects: F,W9,W6,W3,W7,W5,W10,W4,3,W8

STOLL (FORMERLY SIR OSWALD STOLL FOUNDATION)
Founded: 1916 CR207939
446 Fulham Road, London SW6 1DT
Tel: 020 7385 2110
Email: .... fundraising@stoll.org.uk
Objects: F,W9,W5,D,W4,3,C

STONHAM
CR22981R
Octavia House, 50 Banner Street, London EC1Y 8TX
Tel: 020 7549 0000
Email: ...... takki.sulaiman@homegroup.org.uk
Objects: F,W3,W5,W10,D,3,C,P,W8

STRODE PARK FOUNDATION FOR PEOPLE WITH DISABILITIES
Founded: 1946 CR227794
Strode Park House, Herne, Herne Bay, Kent CT6 7NE
Tel: 01227 373292
Email: .... info@strodepark.org.uk
Objects: F,M,W3,E,W5,G,N,O,3,C

THE STROKE ASSOCIATION
CR211015; SC037789
Stroke Association House, 240 City Road, London EC1V 2PR
Tel: 020 7566 1505
Email: .... legacy@stroke.org.uk

STUDENT CHRISTIAN MOVEMENT
Founded: 1889 CR1125640
308F, The Big Peg, 120 Vyse Street, The Jewellery Quarter, Birmingham, West Midlands B18 6ND
Tel: 0121 200 3355
Email: .... scm@movement.org.uk
Objects: W3,G,2,H,3,P

SUFFOLK MIND
CR1003061
Hyntle Barn (CD), Hill Farm, Silver Hill, Hintlesham, Ipswich, Suffolk IP8 3NJ
Tel: 0300 111 6000
Email: .... info@suffolkmind.org.uk
Objects: F,W3,E,W5,G,W10,W15,W16,D,W4,O,W14,3,C,P,W8,K

SUFFOLK REGIMENT OLD COMRADES ASSOCIATION
Founded: 1881 CR427780
The Keep, Gibraltar Barracks, Bury St Edmunds, Suffolk IP33 3PN
Tel: 01603 400290
Objects: W9,1A,A,2,B,C

SUMATRAN ORANGUTAN SOCIETY
CR1085600
The Old Music Hall, 106-108 Cowley Road, Oxford, Oxfordshire OX4 1JE
Tel: 01865 403 341
Email: .... helen@orangutans-sos.org

SUMNER'S (SIR JOHN) TRUST
Founded: 1927 CR218620
No. 1, Colmore Square, Birmingham, West Midlands B4 6AA
Objects: W9,W6,W3,W2,W7,W5,W10,W11,1A,A,1B,W4,W8

SUNSET HOME ALMSHOUSES
Founded: 1913 CR1070355
21 Rodney Road, Cheltenham, Gloucestershire GL50 1HX
Tel: 01242 522180
Objects: W4,3,C

SUPPORT AND HOUSING ASSISTANCE FOR PEOPLE WITH DISABILITIES (WANDSWORTH), ALSO KNOWN AS: SHAD WANDSWORTH
Founded: 1990 CR1001264
5 Bedford Hill, Balham, London SW12 9ET
Tel: 020 8675 6095
Email: .... info@shad.org.uk
Objects: J,W5,D,2,3

SUPPORT IN MIND SCOTLAND (PREVIOUSLY THE NATIONAL SCHIZOPHRENIA FELLOWSHIP)
SC013649
Unit 6, Newington Business, Dalkeith Road Mews, Edinburgh EH16 5GA
Tel: 0131 662 4359
Email: ...... info@supportinmindscotland.org.uk

SUPPORT NETWORK - BENEVOLENT FUND OF THE INSTITUTION OF MECHANICAL ENGINEERS
Founded: 1913 CR209465
Support Network, 3 Birdcage Walk, London SW1H 9JJ
Tel: 020 7304 6812; 020 7304 6816
Email: .... info@supportnetwork.org.uk
Objects: F,M,S,W7,W5,G,W10,W11,W15,1A,V,W4,U,H,Y,P,Z,W8

SURREY WILDLIFE TRUST
CR208123
School Lane, Pirbright, Woking, Surrey GU24 0JN
Tel: 01483 795444
Email: .... grace.moran@surreywt.org.uk

SUSSEX DEAF ASSOCIATION
Founded: 1912 CR1166507
Manager: Ms Chrissie Jenner
Chairman: Mr P Cornish
Valley Social Centre, Whitehawk Way, Brighton, Brighton & Hove BN2 5HE
Tel: 01273 671899
Fax: 01273 625283
Email: .... info@sussexdeaf.com
Web: .... http://www.sussexdeaf.com
Objects: F,W6,W3,J,E,W7,W5,G,W10,W15,1A,2,W4,H,3,P,K

SUSSEX HORSE RESCUE TRUST

CR297576
Hempstead Farm, Hempstead Lane, Uckfield, East Sussex TN22 3DL
Tel: 01825 762010
Email: .... sussexhorsetrust@yahoo.com
Objects: W1,O

SUSSEX WILDLIFE TRUST

CR207005
Woods Mill, Henfield, West Sussex BN5 9SD
Tel: 01273 492630
Email: .... enquiries@sussexwt.org.uk
Objects: W1,W2,G,2,H

SUTTON ASSOCIATION FOR THE BLIND

CR1092429
1st Floor, 3 Robin Hood Lane, Sutton, Surrey SM1 2SW
Tel: 020 8409 7166/7
Email: .... info@suttonvision.org.uk
Objects: F,W6,W4,O,3

SWALE CITIZENS ADVICE BUREAU

Founded: 1972 CR1103010
17 Station Street, Sittingbourne, Kent ME10 3DU
Tel: 0870 121 2105
Objects: F,3

SWAN LIFELINE

Founded: 1986 CR1156995
Chairman: Ms Kay Webb
PO Box 364, Sunbury-on-Thames, Middlesex TW16 9BH
Tel: 01753 859397
Email: .... kaywebbsll@btinternet.com
Web: .... www.swanlifeline.org.uk
Objects: W1,W2,3

Voluntary 24 hour Swan rescue and treatment centre for Thames Valley and home counties with the aim of releasing back to the wild whenever possible. Funded by public donations. Become a Friend of Swan Lifeline.

See advert on this page

THE SWAN SANCTUARY

the Swan sanctuary

Founded: 1990 CR1002582
Trustee: Ms Dorothy Beeson BEM
Trustee: Mr Stephen Knight
Felix Lane, Shepperton, Middlesex TW17 8NN
Tel: 01932 240790
Email: .... info@theswansanctuary.org.uk
Web: .... www.theswansanctuary.org.uk
Objects: W1,W2

The Swan Sanctuary is a charity dedicated to the care and treatment of swans and waterfowl with an established reputation, not only within the British Isles but worldwide

See advert on next page

SWANSEA & DISTRICT FRIENDS OF THE BLIND
Founded: 1960 CR211343
3 De La Beche Street, Swansea SA1 3EY
Tel: 01792 655424
Email: . . . . john_allan_10@hotmail.com
Objects: W6,P

SWEET CHARITY
Founded: 1918 CR1109578; SC038665
76-78 Red Lion Street, London WC1R 4NA
Tel: 020 7404 5222
Email: . . . . info@sweetcharity.net
Objects: F,W6,W7,W5,W11,1A,A,V,W4,3,W8

SWINBROOK NURSERY CENTRE
Founded: 1991 CR1001843
39-41 Acklam Road, London W10 5YU
Tel: 020 8968 5833
Email: . . . . swinbrooknursery@hotmail.com
Objects: W3,W10,3

SWINDON AND CRICKLADE RAILWAY
CR1067447
47 Corby Avenue, Swindon, Wiltshire SN3 1PS
Tel: 01793 536570
Objects: W2,W12,3

SWINDON & DISTRICT CITIZENS ADVICE BUREAU
Founded: 1939 CR1115564
Faringdon House, 1 Faringdon Road, Swindon, Wiltshire SN1 5AR
Tel: 01793 618781
Email: . . . . . bureau.swindoncab@cabnet.org.uk
Objects: F,W9,W6,W3,W7,W5,G,W10,W11,2,W4,3,W8

SWINDON COUNSELLING SERVICE
Founded: 1990 CR1066502
23 Bath Road, Swindon, Wiltshire SN1 4AS
Tel: 01793 514550
Objects: F,3

SWINDON REC
Founded: 1990 CR900449
Faringdon House, 1 Faringdon Road, Swindon, Wiltshire SN1 5AR
Tel: 01793 528545
Objects: F,J,G,W10,3

SWINFEN CHARITABLE TRUST
CR1077879
Dene House, Dene Farm Lane, Wingham, Canterbury, Kent CT3 1NU
Tel: 01227 721024
Email: . . . swinfencharitabletrust@btinternet.com

SWISS BENEVOLENT SOCIETY
Founded: 1870 CR1111348
79 Endell Street, London WC2H 9DY
Email: . . . . info@swissbenevolent.org.uk
Objects: F,1A,A,2,B

SYNERGY ADDICTION
Founded: 1990 CR1001149
The Victoria Centre, Pettits Lane, Romford, Essex RM1 4HP

Tel: 01708 740072
Email: .... admin@synergyaddiction.com
Objects: F,O,3

T

TACT (THE ADOLESCENT AND CHILDREN'S TRUST)

Founded: 1965 CR1018963
303 Hither Green Lane, Hither Green, London SE13 6TJ
Tel: 020 8695 8142
Email: .... enquiries@tactcare.org.uk
Objects: Q,F,W3,G,H,3

TAILORS' BENEVOLENT INSTITUTE

Founded: 1837 CR212954
68 Nightingale Road, Petts Wood, Orpington, Kent BR5 1BQ
Tel: 01689 824405
Objects: W11,A

TALIESIN TRUST LTD, THE

Founded: 1991 CR1004108
Ty Newydd, Llanystumdwy, Criccieth, Gwynedd LL52 0LW
Tel: 01766 522811
Email: .... post@tynewydd.org
Objects: W6,W3,S,W7,W5,G,W10,W4,3,W8

TAMARISK TRUST

CR208812
Unit 1A, First Floor, The Old Print Works, 25 Tapster Street, Barnet, Hertfordshire EN5 5TH
Tel: 020 8447 0541
Email: .... info@tamarisktrust.org.uk
Objects: M,W5,3

TATE FOUNDATION

CR1085314
Tate Foundation, Millbank, London SW1P 4RG
Tel: 020 7887 8637
Email: .... legacy.enquiries@tate.org.uk
Objects: S,G,W12

TAVISTOCK CENTRE FOR COUPLE RELATIONSHIPS

Founded: 1948 CR209706
Tavistock Centre, Belsize Lane, London NW3 5BA
Tel: . 020 7435 7111; 020 7447 3723 Information
Email: .... tccr@tccr.org.uk
Objects: F,G,H,3

TEACHER SUPPORT NETWORK

Founded: 1877 CR1072583
Drayton Park, 40A Drayton Park, London N5 1EW
Tel: 020 7697 2750
Email: .... enquiries@teachersupport.info
Objects: F,G,W11,1A,A,2,3

TEDWORTH CHARITABLE TRUST, THE

Founded: 1990 CR328524
Allington House, 150 Victoria Street, London SW1E 5AE
Tel: 020 7410 0330

TEESSIDE HOSPICE CARE FOUNDATION, MIDDLESBROUGH

Founded: 1982 CR512875
1 Northgate Road, Linthorpe, Middlesbrough, North Yorkshire TS5 5NW
Tel: 01642 816777
Email: .... teessidehospice@hotmail.com
Objects: F,M,W3,E,W5,G,N,W4,O,3,P

TEESSIDE POSITIVE ACTION

Founded: 1990 CR1121302
15 Baker Street, Middlesbrough, North Yorkshire TS1 2LF
Tel: 01642 254598
Objects: F,W3,W5,G,H,3,W8

TEIKYO FOUNDATION (UK)

Founded: 1990 CR1001232
Framewood Road, Wexham, Buckinghamshire SL2 4QS
Tel: 01753 663756

TEIKYO UNIVERSITY OF JAPAN IN DURHAM

Founded: 1990 CR1000091
c/o Teikyo Foundation, Framewood Road, Wexham, Buckinghamshire SL2 4QS
Tel: 01753 663756

TELEPHONES FOR THE BLIND FUND

Founded: 1967 CR255155
7 Huntersfield Close, Reigate, Surrey RH2 0DX
Tel: 01737 248032
Objects: W6,1A,A,3

TENOVUS SCOTLAND

SC009675
Royal College of Physicians and Surgeons, 234 St. Vincent Street, Glasgow G2 5RJ
Tel: 0845 521 0783; 01292 311276
Email: .... gen.sec@talk21.com

TENOVUS - THE CANCER CHARITY

CR1054015
43 The Parade, Cardiff CF24 3AB
Tel: 029 2048 2000
Email: .... post@tenovus.com
Objects: F,M,W3,J,W5,G,W10,1A,A,1B,2,W4,H,3, W8

TERRENCE HIGGINS TRUST

Founded: 1983 CR288527
314-320 Gray's Inn Road, London WC1X 8DP
Tel: . . 020 7812 1600; 0845 122 1200 THT Direct Helpline
Email: .... info@tht.org.uk
Objects: F,M,J,W5,G,W10,D,2,H,3,P,K

THE FASHION & TEXTILE CHILDREN'S TRUST

Founded: 1968 CR257136
Lynnhaven House, 9 Columbine Way, Gislingham, Eye, Suffolk IP23 8HL
Tel: ...... 01379 788644; 07976 152807 Mobile
Email: .... info@ftct.org.uk
Objects: W3,G,1A,A,1B

THAMES VALLEY CHARITABLE TRUST, THE

Founded: 1990 CR802595
28-30 Beaumont Road, Windsor, Windsor & Maidenhead SL4 1JP
Tel: 01753 861115

THANET EARLY YEARS PROJECT & PALS

Founded: 1991 CR1100011
The Curran Building, Newlands Primary School, Dumpton Lane, Ramsgate, Kent CT11 7AJ

Tel: 01843 591200
Email: .... maria@thanetearlyyears.org
Objects: W3,G,W10,3,W8

THEATRES TRUST CHARITABLE FUND
Founded: 1976 CR274697
22 Charing Cross Road, London WC2H 0QL
Tel: 020 7836 8591
Email: .... info@theatrestrust.org.uk
Objects: F,W2,S,H

THE THEATRICAL GUILD
Founded: 1892 CR206669
PO Box 22712, London N22 5WQ
Tel: 020 8889 7570
Email: .... admin@ttg.org.uk
Objects: F,W11,1A,A

THEM WIFIES LIMITED
Founded: 1990 CR702946
Floor 2, British India House, Carliol Square, Newcastle upon Tyne, Tyne & Wear NE1 6UF
Tel: 0191 261 4090
Objects: W3,G,K

THE THIRD AGE TRUST / THE UNIVERSITIES OF THE THIRD AGE / U3A NATIONAL OFFICE
CR288007
Old Municipal Buildings, 19 East Steet, Bromley, Kent BR1 1QE
Tel: 020 8466 6139
Email: .... national.office@u3a.org.uk
Objects: G,2,W4

THOMAS CORAM FOUNDATION FOR CHILDREN
CR312278
49 Mecklenburgh Square, London WC1N 2QA
Tel: 020 7520 0300
Objects: Q,W3,3

THOMAS HOWELL'S TRUST
Founded: 1991 CR1004185
c/o The Drapers Company, Drapers Hall, Throgmorton Avenue, London EC2N 2DQ
Tel: 020 7588 5001
Objects: W3,A,1B

THOMAS MORE PROJECT, THE
Founded: 1992 CR1009917
33 Fallodon Way, Henleaze, Bristol BS9 4HZ
Tel: 0117 962 0887; 0117 962 9899
Objects: W5,D

THOMAS WALL TRUST
Founded: 1920 CR206121
PO Box 52781, London EC2P 2UT
Tel: 020 7638 1753
Objects: W3,G,1A,A,1B,W4,3

THOROUGHBRED REHABILITATION CENTRE
Founded: 1993 CR1089564
Whinney Hill, Aughton Road, Halton, Lancaster, Lancashire LA2 6PQ
Tel: 01524 812649
Email: .... fundraising@thetrc.co.uk

THRIVE

Founded: 1978 CR277570
The Geoffrey Udall Centre, Trunkwell Park, Beech Hill, Reading RG7 2AT
Tel: 0118 988 5688
Email: . . . . info@thrive.org.uk
Objects: F,W6,M,W2,W5,G,2,W4,H,O,3,P,K

THROMBOSIS RESEARCH INSTITUTE

TRI Thrombosis Research Institute

Founded: 1987 CR800365
Director: Professor The Lord Kakkar
Institute Secretary: Mr James To
Emmanuel Kaye Building, Manresa Road, Chelsea, London SW3 6LR
Tel: 020 7351 8300
Fax: 020 7351 8324
Email: . . . . instsec@tri-london.ac.uk
Web: . . . . www.tri-london.ac.uk
Object: W

See advert on previous page

THYROID UK

Founded: 2001 CR1125270
32 Darcy Road, St Osyth, Clacton-on-Sea, Essex CO16 8QF
Tel: 01255 820407
Email: . . . . enquiries@thyroiduk.org
Objects: F,G,H

TIGGYWINKLES, THE WILDLIFE HOSPITAL TRUST

Tiggywinkles.

Founded: 1978 CR286447
Aston Road, Haddenham, Aylesbury, Buckinghamshire HP17 8AF
Tel: 01844 292292
Email: . . . . mail@tiggywinkles.org
Web: . . . . www.tiggywinkles.com
Object: W1

Specialising in hedgehogs, Tiggywinkles, the Wildlife Hospital Trust, has been working for over 30 years rescuing, treating and rehabilitating ALL sick, injured and orphaned British wildlife. Without large reserves and no Government or Lottery funding, Tiggywinkles is dependent upon the compassion of the general public and corporate sponsorship to continue its life-saving work. The hospital has a committed team of hardworking veterinary staff and volunteers dedicated to caring for their patients. For the vital work of Tiggywinkles to continue help is desperately needed and always so greatly appreciated. Please HELP US HELP THEM.

See advert on this page

TIMBER TRADES' BENEVOLENT SOCIETY

Founded: 1897 CR207734
Masons Croft, 19 Church Lane, Oulton, Stone, Staffordshire ST15 8UL
Tel: 08448 922205
Email: .... info@ttbs.org.uk
Objects: W11,1A,A,B

TOBACCO PIPE MAKERS & TOBACCO TRADE BENEVOLENT FUND

Founded: 2010 CR1135646
Forum Court, 83 Copers Cope Road, Beckenham, Kent BR3 1NR
Tel: 020 8663 3050
Objects: W11,1A,A,W4

TOGETHER FOR MENTAL WELLBEING FORMERLY TOGETHER, WORKING FOR WELLBEING

Founded: 1879 CR211091
12 Old Street, London EC1V 9BE
Tel: 020 7780 7300
Email: .... contact-us@together-uk.org
Objects: F,M,S,E,W5,G,W10,2,W4,B,H,O,3,C,P,K

TOMMY'S, THE BABY CHARITY

CR1060508
Tommy's Head Office, Nicholas House, 3 Laurence Pountney Hill, London EC4R 0BB
Tel: ... 0870 770 7070; 0870 777 7676 Donation
Email: .... mailbox@tommys.org
Objects: F,A,H,3,W8

TOMORROW'S PEOPLE TRUST LTD

CR1102759
1st Floor Minster House, York Road, Eastbourne, East Sussex BN21 4ST
Tel: 020 7036 6990
Email: .... headoffice@tomorrows-people.co.uk

TORRIDGE TRAINING SERVICES LTD

Founded: 1990 CR900128
Woodville, Heywood Road, Bideford, Devon EX39 3PG
Tel: 01237 479491
Email: .... admin@ttser.demon.co.uk
Objects: G,3

TOURISM FOR ALL UK

Founded: 1981 CR279169
c/o Vitalise, Shap Road Industrial Estate, Shap Road, Kendal, Cumbria LA9 6NZ
Tel: .... 0845 124 9971 Info
Email: .... info@tourismforall.org.uk
Objects: F,W6,J,W7,W5,V,2,W4,H,3

TOWER HAMLETS AND CANARY WHARF FURTHER EDUCATIONAL TRUST, THE

Founded: 1991 CR1002772
c/o London Borough of Tower Hamlets, 3rd Floor, Mulberry Place, 5 Clove Crescent, London E14 2BG
Tel: 0207 364 4888
Object: G

TOWER HAMLETS MISSION

Founded: 1870 CR259535
31 Mile End Road, London E1 4TP
Tel: 020 7790 3040; 020 7790 6278
Email: .... enquiry@thmission.force9.co.uk
Objects: O,3,C

TOWN & COUNTRY PLANNING ASSOCIATION

Founded: 1899 CR214348
17 Carlton House Terrace, London SW1Y 5AS
Tel: 020 7930 8903
Email: .... tcpa@tcpa.org.uk
Objects: W2,G,D,2,H

TOWNROW (ARTHUR) PENSIONS FUND

Founded: 1966 CR252256
PO Box 48, Chesterfield, Derbyshire S40 1XT
Tel: 01246 238086
Objects: 1A,3,W8

TOY TRUST, THE

Founded: 1991 CR1001634
British Toy and Hobby Assn Limited, 80 Camberwell Road, London SE5 0EG
Tel: 020 7701 7271
Email: .... admin@btha.co.uk
Objects: F,M,W3,E,1A,A,1B,V,N,U,H,O,P

TOYNBEE HALL

Founded: 1884 CR211850
28 Commercial Street, Tower Hamlets, London E1 6LS
Tel: 020 7247 6943
Email: .... info@toynbeehall.org.uk
Objects: F,M,W3,S,E,G,W10,V,D,W4,H,3,C,P,W8

TREBAH GARDEN TRUST

Founded: 1990 CR1000067
Mawnan Smith, Falmouth, Cornwall TR11 5JZ
Tel: 01326 250448
Email: .... mail@trebah-garden.co.uk
Objects: W2,G,2

TREE AID

CR1135156
Brunswick Court, Brunswick Square, Bristol BS2 8PE
Tel: 0117 909 6363
Email: .... info@treeaid.org.uk
Objects: W2,U,W8

TREE COUNCIL, THE

CR279000
4 Dock Offices, Surrey Quays Road, London SE16 2XU
Tel: 020 7407 9992
Email: .... info@treecouncil.org.uk
Web: .... www.treecouncil.org.uk
Object: W2

Founded in 1974, The Tree Council promotes the improvement of the environment by the planting and conservation of trees and woods in town and country throughout the UK. It is responsible for an annual programme that includes Seed Gathering Season, National Tree Week, and Walk in the Woods month, supporting the groups organising local events. It also co-ordinates the national volunteer Tree Warden scheme and operates a fund giving tree-planting grants to schools and communities.

TREE OF HOPE
CR1149254; SC042611
43a Little Mount Sion, Tunbridge Wells, Kent TN1 1YP
Tel: 01892 535525
Email: . . . . info@treeofhope.org.uk

TRELOAR TRUST - WORKING FOR STUDENTS WITH DISABILITY
Founded: 1908 CR1092857
London Road, Holybourne, Alton, Hampshire GU34 4GL
Tel: 01420 526567
Email: . . . . fundraising@treloar.org.uk

THE TRICYCLE THEATRE
Founded: 1980 CR276892
269 Kilburn High Road, London NW6 7JR
Tel: . . . . 020 7372 6611; 020 7625 5105 Minicom
Email: . . . . development@tricycle.co.uk

TRINITARIAN BIBLE SOCIETY
Founded: 1831 CR233082; SC038379
Tyndale House, 200 Dorset Road, London SW19 3NN
Tel: 020 8543 7857
Email: . . . . info@tbsbibles.org
Objects: W3,W7,W5,W10,1A,1B,2,R,W4,H,W8

TRINITY HOSPICE
Founded: 1891 CR1013945
30 Clapham Common North Side, London SW4 0RN
Tel: 020 7787 1000
Email: . . . . enquiries@trinityhospice.org.uk
Objects: F,W6,M,W3,W7,W5,W10,N,W4,O,3,W8

TRINITY HOUSE
Founded: 1514 CR211869
Corporate Department, Trinity House, Tower Hill, London EC3N 4DH
Tel: 020 7481 6900
Objects: W9,W3,W5,G,W11,W15,A,1B,W4,B,Y,C, W8

TRINITY HOUSING RESOURCE CENTRE
Founded: 1991 CR1003826
Villa Road, Handsworth, Birmingham, West Midlands B19 1BL
Tel: 0121 554 8745; 0121 554 8746

TROLLOPE SOCIETY, THE
Founded: 1990 CR803130
Maritime House, Clapham Old Town, London SW4 0JW
Tel: 020 7720 6789
Objects: S,2,H

TROOP AID
CR1123888
Unit 21, Radway Road, Shirley, Solihull, West Midlands B90 4NR
Tel: 0121 711 7215
Email: . . . . info@troopaid.co.uk

THE TRUST FOR EDUCATION
Founded: 1990 CR1000408
c/o Wrigleys, 19 Cookridge Street, Leeds, West Yorkshire LS2 3AG
Tel: 0113 244 6100
Objects: W3,G,1B

TRUST FOR LONDON
Founded: 1891 CR205629
6 Middle Street, London EC1A 7PH
Tel: 020 7606 6145
Email: . . . . info@trustforlondon.org.uk
Objects: A,1B

TTE MANAGEMENT & TECHNICAL TRAINING
Founded: 1991 CR1001390
Edison House, Middlesbrough Road East, South Bank, Middlesbrough, North Yorkshire TS6 6TZ
Tel: 01642 462266
Email: . . . . info@tte.co.uk
Objects: W3,G,W4,3

TUBEROUS SCLEROSIS ASSOCIATION
Founded: 1977 CR1039549; SC042780
PO Box 4923, Sheffield, South Yorkshire S2 9EU
Tel: 0114 270 1723
Email: . emma.damian-grint@tuberous-sclerosis.org

TURN2US (FORMERLY KNOWN AS THE DISTRESSED GENTLEFOLK'S AID ASSOCIATION)
Founded: 1897 CR207812; SCO40987
Hythe House, 200 Shepherds Bush Road, London W6 7NL
Tel: 020 7396 6700; 0800 413 220
Email: . . . . info@turn2us.org.uk
Objects: F,W9,J,W5,W11,1A,A,W4

TURNERS COURT YOUTH TRUST
Founded: 1991 CR309562
9 Red Cross Road, Goring, Reading RG8 9HG
Tel: 01491 874234
Email: . . . . turnerscourt@turnerscourt.org.uk
Objects: F,W3,G,3

TURNING POINT
Founded: 1999 CR234887
Standon House, 21 Mansell Street, London E1 8AA
Tel: 020 7481 7600
Email: . . . . info@turning-point.co.uk

TWINS & MULTIPLE BIRTHS ASSOCIATION
Founded: 1978 CR1076478
2 The Willows, Gardner Road, Guildford, Surrey GU1 4PG
Tel: 0870 770 3305
Email: . . . . enquiries@tamba.org.uk
Objects: F,W3,G,2,H,P

TYDFIL TRAINING CONSORTIUM LIMITED
Founded: 1990 CR702622
William Smith Building, High Street, Merthyr Tydfil CF47 8AP
Tel: 01685 371747
Email: . . . . training@tydfil.com
Objects: F,W6,W3,W7,W5,G,W11,W4,3,W8

U

UCCF: THE CHRISTIAN UNIONS
Founded: 1928 CR306137
Blue Boar House, 5 Blue Boar Street, Oxford, Oxfordshire OX1 4EE
Tel: 01865 253650
Email: . . . . rmc@uccf.org.uk
Objects: W3,G,R,H,3

UCL CANCER INSTITUTE RESEARCH TRUST
CR299617
Paul O'Gorman Building, University College London, 72 Huntley Street, London WC1E 6BT
Tel: 020 7679 6697
Email: . . . . royalfreecrt@ucl.ac.uk
Object: N

UCL HOSPITALS CHARITABLE FOUNDATION
CR1077638
2nd Floor West, 250 Euston Road, London NW1 2PQ
Tel: 020 7380 9558
Email: . . . . helen.sandwell@uclh.nhs.uk

UK SKILLS
Founded: 1991 CR1001586
5 Portland Place, London W1B 1PW
Tel: 020 7580 1011
Email: . . . . ukskills@ukskills.org.uk
Objects: W3,J,G,H,3

THE UK STEM CELL FOUNDATION
CR1110009
Abbey House, 83 Princes Street, Edinburgh EH2 2ER
Tel: 020 7670 5370
Email: . . . . info@ukscf.org

THE ULSTER DEFENCE REGIMENT BENEVOLENT FUND
XN48435
Building 44, Anderson House, Holywood, Co. Down BT18 9QA
Tel: 028 9042 0137
Email: . . . . udrbenfund@aftercareservice.org
Object: W9

UMBRELLA - WORKING FOR POSITIVE MENTAL HEALTH
Founded: 1991 CR1006778
354 Goswell Road, London EC1V 7LQ
Tel: 020 7278 3709
Email: . . . . info@umbrellacare.org.uk
Objects: G,D,3,C

UNICEF UK
CR1072612; SC043677
30A Great Sutton Street, London EC1V 0DU
Tel: 0300 330 5580
Email: . . . . helpdesk@unicef.org.uk

UNISON WELFARE
Founded: 1910 CR1023552
1 Mabledon Place, London WC1H 9AJ
Tel: 020 7551 1620
Email: . . . . welfare@unison.co.uk
Objects: F,1A,A,2

UNITARIAN & FREE CHRISTIAN CHURCHES, GENERAL ASSEMBLY OF
Founded: 1825 CR250788
Essex Hall, 1-6 Essex Street, London WC2R 3HY
Tel: 020 7240 2384
Email: . . . . info@unitarian.org.uk
Objects: F,W3,J,G,2,R,H,3

UNITED LAW CLERKS' SOCIETY
Founded: 1832 CR277276
J A Dungay, Innellan House, 109 Nutfield Road, Merstham, Surrey RH1 3HD
Tel: 01737 643261
Objects: A,B

UNITED RESPONSE
Founded: 1973 CR265249
Vantage House, 1 Weir Road, Wimbledon Park, London SW19 8UX
Tel: 020 8246 5200
Email: . . . . info@unitedresponse.org.uk
Objects: E,W5,W10,D,O,3,C,P,K

UNIVERSAL BENEFICENT SOCIETY, THE (UBS)
Founded: 1857 CR220978
6 Avonmore Road, London W14 8RL
Tel: 020 7605 4200
Email: . . . . ubs@independentage.org.uk
Objects: F,1A,A,W4,B

UNIVERSITIES FEDERATION FOR ANIMAL WELFARE (UFAW)
Founded: 1926 CR207996
The Old School, Brewhouse Hill, Wheathampstead, Hertfordshire AL4 8AN
Tel: 01582 831818
Email: . . . . ufaw@ufaw.org.uk
Objects: F,W1,G,1A,A,1B,2,B,H,3

UNIVERSITIES UK
Founded: 1990 CR1001127
Woburn House, 20 Tavistock Square, London WC1H 9HQ
Tel: 020 7419 4111
Email: . . . . info@universitiesuk.ac.uk
Objects: G,2,H

UNIVERSITY OF ABERDEEN DEVELOPMENT TRUST
SC002938
King's College, Aberdeen AB24 3FX
Tel: 01224 272281
Email: . . . . giving@abdn.ac.uk
Objects: W3,W2,G,1A,N,W12,B,W

UNIVERSITY OF CAMBRIDGE VETERINARY SCHOOL TRUST (CAMVET)
XO 979/86
Department of Veterinary Medicine, Madingley Road, Cambridge, Cambridgeshire CB3 0ES
Tel: . . . . 01223 337630 / 764475
Email: . . . . trust.office@vet.cam.ac.uk
Objects: W1,2

UNIVERSITY OF CAPE TOWN TRUST
Founded: 1990 CR803042
83a Esher High Street, Esher, Surrey KT10 9QA
Tel: 01372 477116
Email: . . . . uct-trust@tecres.net
Objects: W3,G,1B,U

URBAN SAINTS
Founded: 1906 CR223798
Kestin House, 45 Crescent Road, Luton, Bedfordshire LU2 0AH
Tel: 01582 589850
Email: . . . . email@urbansaints.org
Objects: W3,J,G,V,2,R,U,H

URBAN THEOLOGY UNIT
Founded: 1971 CR1115390
210 Abbeyfield Road, Sheffield, South Yorkshire S4 7AZ
Tel: 0114 243 5342
Email: . . . . office@utusheffield.org.uk
Objects: G,2,H

THE URE ELDER FUND
SC003775
1 George Square, Glasgow G2 1AL
Tel: 0141 248 5011
Objects: 1A,A,B,W8

UROSTOMY ASSOCIATION
Founded: 1971 CR1131072
Central Office, 18 Foxglove Avenue, Uttoxeter, Staffordshire ST14 8UN
Email: . . . secretary@urostomyassociation.org.uk
Objects: F,W3,J,W5,2,W4,H,O,P,W8

US (UNITED SOCIETY, FORMERLY USPG)
Founded: 1701 CR234518
Harling House, 47-51 Great Suffolk Street, London SE1 0BS
Tel: 020 7921 2200
Email: . . . . info@weareUs.org.uk
Objects: W6,M,W3,W7,W5,G,W10,1A,A,1B,N,2, R,W4,U,H,T,O,W8

UXBRIDGE UNITED WELFARE TRUSTS
Founded: 1991 CR217066
Trustees Room, Woodbridge House, New Windsor Street, Uxbridge, Middlesex UB8 2TY
Tel: 01895 232976
Objects: A,1B

V

VALE WILDLIFE HOSPITAL
CR702888
Station Road, Beckford, Tewkesbury, Gloucestershire GL20 7AN
Tel: 01386 882288
Email: . . . . info@valewildlife.org.uk
Objects: W1,W2,G,3

VALERIE TAYLOR TRUST
CR1122245
115 Penn Place, Northway, Rickmansworth, Hertfordshire WD3 1QQ
Tel: 07967 711235
Email: . . . . admin@valerietaylortrust.org

THE VEGAN SOCIETY
CR279228
Donald Watson House, 21 Hylton Street, Hockley, Birmingham, West Midlands B18 6HJ
Tel: 0845 458 8244
Email: . . . . info@vegansociety.com

VEGETARIAN SOCIETY OF THE UK LTD, THE

Founded: 1968 CR259358
Parkdale, Dunham Road, Altrincham, Greater Manchester WA14 4QG
Tel: 0161 925 2000
Email: . . . . support@vegsoc.org
Objects: F,W1,W3,W2,G,2,R,H,P

VEGFAM (FEEDS THE HUNGRY WITHOUT EXPLOITING ANIMALS)

Founded: 1963 CR232208
Honorary Secretary / Trustee: Ms Sandra Ozolins
c/o Cwm Cottage (CD), Cwmynys, Cilycwm, Llandovery, Carmarthenshire SA20 0EU
Tel: 01550 721197
Fax: . . . . Please Telephone First
Web: . . . . . www.vegfamcharity.org.uk/home.html
Inland Revenue Ref: XN8555. **Self Assessment Gift Aid Ref:** XAD67AG

Online Donations: https://www.charitychoice.co.uk/vegfam

ABOUT VEGFAM
Vegfam "Feeds The Hungry Without Exploiting Animals" by funding sustainable, self-supporting projects: seeds and tools for vegetable growing, fruit/nut tree planting, irrigation and water wells. Also emergency relief in times of crisis and disaster. Vegfam helps people to help themselves.

WHY DONATIONS ARE NEEDED
Vegfam projects provide food security for children and adults worldwide - alleviating hunger, malnutrition, starvation and thirst. As little as £5 enables a family in India to be self-sufficient in fruit/nuts/vegetables or a family in Africa to have access to a safe water supply.

WHERE DONATIONS ARE SPENT
Beneficiaries: flood/earthquake survivors, HIV/AIDS sufferers, homeless people, marginalised communities, orphanages, refugees, schools/colleges, trafficked women and children, villagers and tribal people. In addition, the people who benefit from Vegfam funded projects are often suffering from disease and disabilities. For many, Vegfam is their only hope of help.

From 2008 to 2011, Vegfam funded 37 projects in 22 countries, helping over 950,000 people.

All donations and legacies are gratefully received and make a real difference to people's lives.

Please support our life saving work. Thank you.
See advert on previous page

VETLIFE

Founded: 1978 CR224776
7 Mansfield Street, London W1G 9NQ
Tel: 020 7908 6385
Email: . . . . info@vbf.org.uk
Objects: W11,1A,A,D,2,3

VICTIM SUPPORT

CR298028
Octavia House, 50 Banner House, London EC1Y 8ST
Tel: 020 7336 1730
Email: . . . . info@victimsupport.org.uk

VICTIM SUPPORT SCOTLAND

SC002138
15-23 Hardwell Close, Edinburgh EH8 9RX
Tel: . . . 0131 662 5420; 0845 603 9213 (Helpline)
Email: . . . . info@victimsupportsco.org.uk
Objects: F,3

VICTORIA AND ALBERT MUSEUM

South Kensington, London SW7 2RL
Tel: 020 7942 2716
Email: . . . . legacy@vam.ac.uk
Objects: S,G,W12

VICTORIA CONVALESCENT TRUST

Founded: 1897 CR1064585
62 Wilson Street, London EC2A 2BU
Objects: W9,W6,W3,W7,W5,W10,W11,1A,A,2, W4,W8

VIETNAMESE MENTAL HEALTH SERVICES

Founded: 1991 CR1001991
Thomas Calton Centre, Alpha Street, Peckham, London SE15 4NX
Tel: 020 7639 2288
Email: . . . . vietnamesemhs@aol.com
Objects: F,E,W5,W10,O,3,C

VILLAGE AID

Founded: 1990 CR1067322
Unit 1B, Riverside Business Park, Buxton Road, Bakewell, Derbyshire DE45 1GS
Tel: 01629 814434
Email: . . . . jo@villageaid.org
Objects: 2,U,3

VISION AID OVERSEAS

CR1081695
12 The Bell Centre, Newton Road, Crawley, West Sussex RH10 9FZ
Tel: 01293 535016
Email: . . . . info@visionaidoverseas.org
Objects: W6,W3,W5,G,W10,N,2,R,W4,U,3,W8

VISION SUPPORT

CR1068565
Units 1 and 2, The Ropeworks, Whipcord Lane, Chester, Cheshire CH1 4DZ
Tel: 01244 381515
Email: . . . . information@visionsupport.org.uk
Objects: F,W6,M,W3,W7,W5,W4,O,3,P,W8,K

VITILIGO SOCIETY

CR1069607
125 Kennington Road, London SE11 6SF
Tel: 020 7840 0844
Objects: F,2,H

VOICE OF THE LISTENER (& VIEWER) TRUST

CR296207
101 King's Drive, Gravesend, Kent DA12 5BQ
Tel: 01474 352835
Email: . . . . info@vlv.org.uk
Objects: W3,S,G

VOLUNTARY ACTION CAMDEN

CR802186
293-299 Kentish Town Road, London NW5 2TJ
Tel: 020 7284 6550
Email: . . . . vac@vac.org.uk

VOLUNTARY ACTION CARDIFF

Founded: 1991 CR1068623
3rd Floor, Brunel House, 2 Fitzalan Place, Cardiff CF24 0BE
Tel: 029 2048 5722; 029 2046 4196
Email: . . . . enquiries@vacardiff.org.uk
Objects: F,W3,J,W5,G,W10,A,2,W4,H,3,W8

VOLUNTARY ACTION KIRKLEES
Founded: 1991 CR1086938
15 Lord Street, Kirklees, Huddersfield, West Yorkshire HD1 1QB
Tel: 01484 518457
Email: ...... info@voluntaryactionkirklees.co.uk
Objects: F,J,3

VOLUNTARY ACTION NORTH EAST LINCOLNSHIRE
Founded: 1991 CR1002624
14 Town Hall Street, Grimsby, North East Lincolnshire DN31 1HN
Tel: 01472 231123
Email: .... peter@vanel.org.uk
Objects: F,J,G,2

VOLUNTEER CENTRE WOLVERHAMPTON
Founded: 1984 CR1079891
Volunteer Centre, 5 Cleveland Street, Wolverhampton, West Midlands WV1 3HL
Tel: 01902 572323
Email: .... info@wolvesvb.org.uk
Objects: F,W1,W9,W6,W3,J,W2,W7,W5,W10, W12,W4,H,3,W8

VOLUNTEER READING HELP
Founded: 1973 CR296454
Charity House, 14-15 Perseverance Works, 38 Kingsland Road, London E2 8DD
Tel: 0870 774 4300
Email: .... info@vrh.org.uk
Objects: W3,G,3

VRANCH HOUSE SCHOOL AND CENTRE
Founded: 1991 CR1002700
Vranch House, Pinhoe Road, Exeter, Devon EX4 8AD
Tel: 01392 468333

VSA (FORMERLY VOLUNTARY SERVICE ABERDEEN)
SC 012950
38 Castle Street, Aberdeen AB11 5YU
Tel: 01224 212021
Email: .... fundraising@vsa.org.uk

VSO
CR313757; SCO39117
100 London Road, Kingston upon Thames, Surrey KT2 6QJ
Tel: 020 8780 7500
Email: .... enquiry@vso.org.uk
Objects: W6,W3,J,W2,W7,W5,G,W10,W4,U,H,P, W8

W

WAKEFIELD HOSPICE
CR518392
Aberford Road, Wakefield, West Yorkshire WF1 4TS
Tel: 01924 213900
Email: .... legacies@wakefieldhospice.co.uk
Objects: N,3

WALDENSIAN CHURCH MISSIONS
CR277255
85 St Andrew's Road, Cambridge, Cambridgeshire CB4 1DH
Tel: 01223 315753
Email: .... erica.newbury@gmail.com
Object: R

WAR ON WANT
Founded: 1952 CR208724
Fenner Brockway House, 37-39 Great Guildford Street, London SE1 0ES
Tel: 020 7620 1111
Email: .... kthompson@waronwant.org
Objects: F,W3,G,A,U,H,W8

WASTE MANAGEMENT INDUSTRY TRAINING AND ADVISORY BOARD, THE
Founded: 1991 CR1006826
Peterbridge House, 3 The Lakes, Northampton, Northamptonshire NN4 7HE
Tel: 01604 231950
Email: .... info.admin@wamitab.org.uk
Objects: G,W11,3

WATERAID

WaterAid

CR288701; SC039479
47-49 Durham Street, London SE11 5JD
Tel: 020 7793 4594
Fax: 020 7793 4545
Email: ...... supportercare@wateraid.org
Web: .... www.wateraid.org
Object: U

Water and sanitation underpin health, education and livelihoods, yet hundreds of millions of people live without these basic human rights. WaterAid works with local partners to deliver taps and toilets to some of the world's poorest and most marginalised communities. We campaign and influence decision makers to invest in water and sanitation, where it's needed the most.

WaterAid believes in a future where everyone, everywhere has clean water to drink and somewhere safe to use the toilet. With your help we can build this future; one where people are free from water related diseases, where children can go to school and communities can thrive. A future where people live with dignity and hope.

Leave a gift in your will to WaterAid and you'll transform lives for generations. Leave the world with water. Find out more at www.wateraid.org/uk/will

WATERSIDE CENTRE, THE
Founded: 1990 CR1001330
63 Waterside, Kings Langley, Hertfordshire WD4 8HE
Tel: 01923 260092
Objects: E,W5,3

WATFORD MENCAP
CR1004431
Langwood House, Suites 1 & 2, 63-81 High Street, Rickmansworth, Hertfordshire WD3 1EQ
Tel: 01923 713620
Email: .... admin@watfordmencap.org.uk

WATSON'S (ANN) TRUST

Founded: 1721 CR226675
Flat 4, 14 College Street, Sutton-on-Hull, Hull, Kingston upon Hull HU7 4UP
Tel: 01482 709626
Objects: W3,G,1A,A,D,W4,B,W8

WDC, WHALE AND DOLPHIN CONSERVATION

Founded: 1987 CR1014705; SC040231
Brookfield House (CD15), 38 St Paul Street, Chippenham, Wiltshire SN15 1LJ
Tel: 01249 449500
Fax: 01249 449501
Email: . . . . legacies@whales.org
Web: . . . . whales.org
Objects: W1,W2,G,1A,A,1B,2,H

WDC, Whale and Dolphin Conservation is the leading global charity dedicated to the conservation and protection of whales and dolphins. We know that whales and dolphins are amazing, and we have the scientific evidence to back this up. They pass on knowledge from one generation to the next, they play games just for fun, and we even know that some of them are smart enough to use tools. But, sadly they face many threats and they need our help to protect them against hunting, captivity, horrific injury and death in fishing nets, pollution, the dangers of increased boat traffic and more.

Our vision is a world where every whale and dolphin is safe and free. With a gift to WDC in your Will, you can help us achieve this.

WEARSIDE WOMEN IN NEED

Founded: 1990 CR1000934
1st Floor, The Elms, Concord, Washington, Tyne & Wear NE37 2BA
Tel: 0191 416 3550
Email: . . . . wwinelms@aol.com
Objects: F,W3,D,C,W8

WELDMAR HOSPICECARE TRUST

Founded: 1990 CR1000414
Hammick House, Bridport Road, Poundbury, Dorchester, Dorset DT1 3SD
Tel: 01305 269898
Email: . . . . reception@weld-hospice.org.uk
Objects: E,N,3

WELLCHILD

Founded: 1977 CR289600
16 Royal Crescent, Cheltenham, Gloucestershire GL50 3DA
Tel: 01242 530007
Email: . . . . info@wellchild.org.uk
Objects: W3,1B

WELLDON ACTIVITY GROUP

Founded: 2002 CR1091034
Welldon Centre, Welldon Crescent, Harrow, Middlesex HA1 1JZ
Tel: 020 8861 0764
Objects: E,W5,W10,W4,3

WELSH KITE TRUST / YMDDIRIEDOLAETH BARCUDIAID CYMRU

CR1058210
"Samaria", Nantmel, Llandrindod Wells, Powys LD1 6EN
Tel: 01597 825981
Email: . . . . info@welshkitetrust.org

WELSH UNLIMITED (POPETH CYMRAEG)

Founded: 1990 CR1074898
Pwll y Grawys, Denbigh, Denbighshire LL16 3LF
Tel: 01745 812287
Email: . . . . gwybod@popethcymraeg.com
Objects: F,S,G,W4

WELSH WATER ELAN TRUST, THE

Founded: 1990 CR1001347
Stayley, Pentrosfa, Llandrindod Wells, Powys LD1 5AL
Tel: 01597 822838
Email: . . . . merolt@yahoo.com
Objects: W2,3

WELSHPOOL AND LLANFAIR LIGHT RAILWAY PRESERVATION CO LIMITED

Founded: 1990 CR1000378
15 Valley Avenue, London N12 9PG
Tel: 020 8445 5581
Email: . . . . regdavies@btinternet.com
Objects: W2,S,G,2,3,K

WESC FOUNDATION

CR1058937
Countess Wear, Exeter, Devon EX2 6HA
Tel: 01392 454336
Email: . . . . fundraising@westengland.org.uk
Objects: F,W6,M,W3,G,N,O,P

AUTISM WESSEX

Founded: 1990 CR1000792
22 Bargates, Christchurch, Dorset BH23 1QL
Tel: 01202 483360
Email: . . . . enquiries@autismwessex.org.uk
Objects: F,W3,W5,G,2,3,C,P

WESSEX FOUNDATION, THE

Founded: 1991 CR1002373
The Magdalen Project, Magdalen Farm, Winsham, Chard, Somerset TA20 4PA
Tel: 01460 30144
Email: . . . . . . admin@themagdalenproject.org.uk
Objects: W6,W3,W2,S,W7,W5,G,W10,V,W4,O,3,P,W8,K

WEST HAMPSTEAD COMMUNITY CENTRE

Founded: 1990 CR1135778
17 Dornfell Street, London NW6 1QN
Tel: . . . . info@westhampsteadcc.org.uk
Objects: F,W3,S,W7,W5,G,W10,V,W4,P,W8,K

WEST KENT MIND

Founded: 1995 CR1044977
34 St John's Road, Sevenoaks, Kent TN13 3LW
Tel: 01732 744950
Email: . . . . . . admin@sevenoaksareamind.org.uk
Objects: F,J,E,W5,G,2,3,C,P

WEST KENT YMCA - HELPING YOUNG PEOPLE BUILD THEIR FUTURE

Founded: 1990 CR803529
Ryder House, 1-23 Belgrave Road, Tunbridge Wells, Kent TN1 2BP

Tel: 01892 542209
Email: .... info@westkentymca.org.uk
Objects: F,W3,S,E,W5,G,D,3,C,K

WEST LONDON DAY CENTRE
Founded: 1887 CR1133739
19 Thayer Street, London W1U 2QJ
Tel: 020 7935 6179
Email: .... office@wlm.org.uk
Objects: F,W9,J,E,G,N,R,W4,O,3,C,W8

WEST SCOTLAND DEAF CHILDREN'S SOCIETY, A REGISTERED ASSOCIATION OF THE NATIONAL DEAF CHILDREN'S SOCIETY
SC012285
281a Central Chambers, 93 Hope Street, Glasgow G2 6LD
Tel: 0141 243 2958
Email: .... wsdcs@btconnect.com

WESTMINSTER AMALGAMATED CHARITY
Founded: 1961 CR207964
School House, Drury Lane, London WC2B 5SU
Tel: 020 7395 9460
Objects: W6,W3,W7,W5,W10,1A,A,1B,W4,W8

WESTMINSTER FRENCH PROTESTANT SCHOOL FOUNDATION
Founded: 1747 CR1094943
34 Rowan Walk, Bromley, Kent BR2 8QN
Objects: W3,G,1A

THE WESTMINSTER SOCIETY FOR PEOPLE WITH LEARNING DISABILITIES
CR801081
16a Croxley Road, London W9 3HL
Tel: 020 8968 7376
Email: .... westminstersociety@wspld.org

WESTON HOSPICECARE
Founded: 1990 CR900328
Jackson-Barstow House, 28 Thornbury Road, Uphill, Weston-super-Mare, North Somerset BS23 4YQ
Tel: 01934 423900
Email: .... info@westonhospicecare.org.uk
Objects: M,3

WHEELPOWER - BRITISH WHEELCHAIR SPORT
Founded: 1972 CR265498
Head of Fundraising: Mr Paul Rushton
Stoke Mandeville Stadium, Guttmann Road, Stoke Mandeville, Buckinghamshire HP21 9PP
Tel: 01296 395995
Fax: 01296 424171
Email: .... info@wheelpower.org.uk
Web: .... www.wheelpower.org.uk
Objects: F,J,W5,G,2,H,O,P

Each year, thousands of men, women and children become disabled due to an accident or illness or are born with a disability.
WheelPower help disabled people to play sport and lead healthy active lives.

WHEN YOU WISH UPON A STAR
CR1060963
2nd Floor, Futurist House, Valley Road, Basford, Nottinghamshire NG5 1JE
Tel: 0115 979 1210

WHITCHESTER CHRISTIAN CENTRE, HAWICK
SC011436
Borthaugh, Hawick, Scottish Borders TD9 7LN
Tel: ...... 01450 377477; 01450 370809 Admin
Email: .... enquiries@whitchester.org.uk

WHITE HORSE CARE TRUST, THE
Founded: 1990 CR900633
Washbourne House, 77A High Street, Wroughton, Wiltshire SN4 9JU
Tel: 01793 846000
Email: .... staff@whct.co.uk
Objects: W5,D,N,O,3

WHITEHALL AND INDUSTRY GROUP, THE
Founded: 1991 CR1061584
22 Queens Annes Gate, London SW1H 9AA
Tel: 020 7222 1166
Email: .... info@wig.co.uk
Objects: J,G,2

WHITELANDS SPRINGFIELD AND TYNING COMMUNITY ASSOCIATION
Founded: 1990 CR900420
39 Walnut Buildings, Radstock, Bath, Bath & North East Somerset BA3 3LJ
Tel: 01761 435101

WHO CARES? TRUST - WORKING WITH CHILDREN AND YOUNG PEOPLE IN CARE
CR1010518
Kemp House, 152-160 City Road, London EC1V 2NP
Tel: 020 7251 3117
Email: .... mailbox@thewhocarestrust.org.uk
Objects: Q,F,W3,J,H,3

THE WILBERFORCE TRUST
CR1087065
Wilberforce House, 49 North Moor Road, Huntington, York, North Yorkshire YO32 9QN
Tel: 01904 760037
Email: .... enquiry@wilberforcetrust.org.uk
Objects: W6,W5,3,C

WILD FUTURES (THE MONKEY SANCTUARY)
CR1102532
Murrayton House (CC), St Martins, Looe, Cornwall PL13 1NZ
Tel: 01503 262532
Email: .... info@wildfutures.org
Objects: W1,W2

THE WILDERNESS FOUNDATION UK
CR1118493
Trinity House, 2 Whitbread's Business Centre, Whitbread's Farm Lane, Chatham Green Essex CM3 3FE
Tel: 0300 123 3073
Email: .... info@wildernessfoundation.org.uk
Objects: W1,W3,W2,S,W5,G,W15,V,U,T,O,3,P, W8

WILDFOWL & WETLANDS TRUST

WWT

Founded: 1946 CR1030884; SC039410
Chief Executive: Mr Martin Spray CBE
Slimbridge, Gloucestershire GL2 7BT
Tel: 01453 891900
Fax: 01453 890827
Email: . . . . enquiries@wwt.org.uk
Web: . . . . www.wwt.org.uk
Objects: W1,W2,G,2

Founded by the late Sir Peter Scott, WWT works to save wetlands for wildlife and people at nine UK centres and internationally.

THE WILDLIFE AID FOUNDATION

Founded: 1987 CR1138944
Managing Trustee: Mr Simon Cowell
Randalls Farmhouse (CD), Randalls Road, Leatherhead, Surrey KT22 0AL
Tel: . 09061 800 132 - 24Hr Helpline calls 50p per minute
Fax: 01372 375183
Email: . . . . office@wildlifeaid.org.uk
Web: . . . . www.wildlifeaid.org.uk
Objects: W1,G,3

See advert on this page

WILDLIFE TRUSTS, THE

Founded: 1912 CR207238
The Kiln, Mather Road, Newark-on-Trent, Newark, Nottinghamshire NG24 1WT
Tel: 01636 677711
Email: . . . . pdorans@wildlifetrusts.org
Objects: W3,J,W2,G,H

WILLIAM SUTTON TRUST

Founded: 1900 CR205847
12 Elstree Way, Borehamwood, Hertfordshire WD6 1JE
Tel: 020 8235 7000
Email: . . . . south@williamsutton.org.uk
Objects: W9,W6,W3,W7,W5,W10,D,W4,3,C,W8

WILLOW FOUNDATION

CR1106746
Willow House, 18 Salisbury Square, Hatfield, Hertfordshire AL9 5BE
Tel: 01707 259777
Email: . . . . info@willowfoundation.org.uk

WILTONS MUSIC HALL

Founded: 1991 CR1003041
Wilton's Music Hall, Graces Alley, Wellclose Square, London E1 8JB
Tel: 01622 690691
Objects: S,G

WILTSHIRE WILDLIFE TRUST

Founded: 1962 CR266202
Wiltshire Wildlife Trust Head Office, Elm Tree Court, Long Street, Devizes, Wiltshire SN10 1NJ

Tel: 01380 725670
Email: .... info@wiltshirewildlife.org
Objects: F,W1,J,W2,G,2,H,3

THE WIMBLEDON GUILD
CR200424
Guild House, 30-32 Worple Road, Wimbledon, London SW19 4EF
Tel: 020 8946 0735
Objects: F,W9,M,W5,A,D,N,W4,P

WINCANTON RECREATIONAL TRUST
Founded: 1991 CR1003992
Homestead Farm, Barrow Lane, Charlton Musgrove, Wincanton, Somerset BA9 8HW
Tel: 01963 34017

WINNICOTT FOUNDATION - IMPROVING CARE FOR PREMATURE AND SICK BABIES - SUPPORTING IMPERIAL'S NEONATAL UNITS AT ST MARY'S HOSPITAL AND QUEEN CHARLOTTE'S HOSPITALS
CR292668
Sam Segal Unit, Clarence Wing, St Mary's Hospital, Imperial College Healthcare NHS Trust, Praed Street, London W2 1NY
Tel: 020 3312 6773
Email: .... info@winnicott.org.uk

WIRRAL COUNCIL FOR VOLUNTARY SERVICE
CR1003070
46 Hamilton Square, Birkenhead, Merseyside CH41 5AR
Tel: 0151 647 5432
Email: .... admin@wirralcvs.org.uk
Objects: F,J,G,H

WISDOM HOSPICE (ROCHESTER), FRIENDS OF
CR284894
High Bank, Rochester, Kent ME1 2NU
Tel: 01634 831163
Email: .... info@fowh.org.uk

WOKING AND SAM BEARE HOSPICES
Founded: 1991 CR1082798, 1115439
Woking & Sam Beare Hospices, Hill View Road, Woking, Surrey GU22 7HW
Tel: 01483 881750
Email: .... mail@woking-hospice.freeserve.co.uk
Objects: N,3

WOKING HOMES - A RESIDENTIAL RETIREMENT HOME (A RAILWAY CHARITY)
CR1120447
Oriental Road, Woking, Surrey GU22 7BE
Tel: 01483 763558
Email: .... administration@woking-homes.co.uk

WOLVERHAMPTON MULTI-HANDICAP CARE AND RELIEF SERVICE
Founded: 1990 CR703005
Easterling House, Hilton Street, Springfields, Wolverhampton, West Midlands WV10 0LF
Objects: W3,W5,3

WOMANKIND WORLDWIDE
Founded: 1989 CR328206
Marketing Officer: Ms Rosey Ellum
Head of Fundraising and Marketing: Ms Disha Sughand
2nd Floor, Development House, 56-64 Leonard Street, London EC2A 4LT
Tel: 020 7549 0360
Fax: 020 7549 0361
Email: .... info@womankind.org.uk
Web: .... www.womankind.org.uk
Objects: U,Y,W8

Womankind Worldwide is an international women's human rights charity working to help women transform their lives around the world. We partner with women's rights organisations and movements who are changing the world. We work to end violence against women, increase women's civil and political participation and to increase women's control over their own livelihoods. For 27 years Womankind Worldwide has been helping courageous individuals transform their lives.

WOMEN IN PRISON
Founded: 1992 CR1118727
Unit 10, The Ivories, 6 Northampton Street, London N1 2HY
Tel: 020 7359 6674
Email: .... salma@womeninprison.org.uk
Objects: F,W3,G,W10,1A,A,W4,O,3,W8

WOMEN IN SUPPORTED HOUSING
Founded: 1991 CR1040476
Vernon House, 80 Edna Street, Hyde, Cheshire SK14 1DR
Tel: 0161 366 1355
Email: .... wishtameside@btconnect.com
Objects: F,D,3,C,W8

WOMEN'S ENVIRONMENTAL NETWORK
Founded: 1992 CR1010397
PO Box 30626, London E1 1TZ
Tel: 020 7481 9004
Email: .... info@wen.org.uk
Objects: F,W2,W10,2,H,W8

WOMEN'S ROYAL NAVAL SERVICE BENEVOLENT TRUST
Founded: 1941 CR206529
311 Twyford Avenue, Portsmouth, Hampshire PO2 8RN
Tel: 023 9265 5301
Email: .... generalsecretary@wrnsbt.org.uk
Objects: Q,F,W9,1A,A,2,Y,W8

WOMEN'S TECHNOLOGY / BLACKBURNE HOUSE
Founded: 1992 CR1010546
Blackburne House, Hope Street, Liverpool, Merseyside L8 7PE
Tel: 0151 709 4356
Objects: G,3,W8

WOOD GREEN, THE ANIMALS CHARITY
CR298348
The Legacy Department, Kings Bush Farm, London Road, Godmanchester, Cambridgeshire PE29 2NH
Tel: 01480 830014
Email: .... info@woodgreen.org.uk

THE WOODLAND TRUST
Founded: 1972 CR294344; SC038885
Autumn Park, Dysart Road, Grantham, Lincolnshire NG31 6LL

Tel: 01476 581111
Email: .... legacies@woodland-trust.org.uk
Objects: F,W1,W6,W3,J,W2,W7,W5,G,W10,W11,A,1B,2,W4,H,P,W8

WOODLANDS HOSPICE CHARITABLE TRUST, LIVERPOOL
CR1048934
University Hospital Aintree Campus, Longmoor Lane, Liverpool, Merseyside L9 7LA
Tel: 0151 529 2299
Email: .... carole.riley@aintree.nhs.uk

WOODROFFE BENTON FOUNDATION
Founded: 1988 CR1075272
16 Fernleigh Court, Harrow, Middlesex HA2 6NA
Tel: 020 8421 4120
Objects: M,W2,W5,G,A,1B,N,W4,C,P

WOODSIDE ANIMAL WELFARE TRUST
CR1143122
Elfordleigh, Plympton, Plymouth, Devon PL7 5ED
Tel: 01752 347503
Email: generalenquiries@woodsidesanctuary.org.uk

WORDSLEY HOUSING SOCIETY
Founded: 1990 CR1001178
30 Brook Street, Wordsley, Stourbridge, West Midlands DY8 5YW
Tel: 01384 480770
Objects: F,V,O,3,C,P

WORKERS' EDUCATIONAL ASSOCIATION
Founded: 1903 CR1112775
4 Luke Street, London EC2 4XW
Tel: 020 7426 3450
Email: .... national@wea.org.uk
Objects: S,G,2,3

WORKING MEN'S COLLEGE FOR MEN AND WOMEN
Founded: 1854 CR312803
44 Crowndale Road, Camden, London NW1 1TR
Tel: 020 7255 4700
Email: .... info@wmcollege.ac.uk
Objects: W6,W5,G,W10,W4,3,W8

WORKS TRUST, THE
Founded: 1990 CR1000463
Prospect House, 19-21 Bucknall Old Road, Hanley, Stoke-on-Trent, Staffordshire ST1 2AF
Tel: 01782 263919
Email: ... heritage@the-works-trust.demon.co.uk
Objects: W2,W12,3

WORLD CANCER RESEARCH FUND
Founded: 1990 CR1000739
19 Harley Street, London W1G 9QJ
Tel: 020 7343 4200
Email: .... giftsinwills@wcrf.org
Objects: 1A,2,H,3

WORLD CHRISTIAN MINISTRIES
Founded: 1991 CR1001691
6 Belfield Close, Marldon, Paignton, Devon TQ3 1NZ
Tel: 01803 663681
Objects: M,E,G,R,U

WORLD HORSE WELFARE
Founded: 1927 CR206658; SC038384
UK Head Office, Anne Colvin House, Snetterton, Norfolk NR16 2LR
Tel: 0870 870 1927
Email: .... hq@ilph.org
Objects: Q,F,W1,G,A,1B,2,U,B,H,O

WORLD LAND TRUST
Founded: 1990 CR1001291
Blyth House, Bridge Street, Halesworth, Suffolk IP19 8AB
Tel: 01986 874422
Email: .... info@worldlandtrust.org
Object: W2

WORLD MEDICAL FUND
CR1063756
St Helens, Low Road, Saddlebow, Norfolk PE34 3FN
Tel: 0800 783 3822
Email: .... info@ukwmf.org

WORLD OWL TRUST
CR1107529
World Owl Centre, Muncaster Castle, Ravenglass, Cumbria CA18 1RQ
Tel: 01229 717393
Email: .... barbara@owls.org

WORLD PARROT TRUST
Founded: 1989 CR800944
Glanmor House, Hayle, Cornwall TR27 4HB
Tel: 01736 751026
Email: .... uk@parrots.org
Objects: W1,W2,2,H

WORLDWIDE CANCER RESEARCH
SC022918
Madras House, St Andrews, Fife KY16 9EH
Tel: 01334 477910
Email: . enquiries@worldwidecancerresearch.org
Object: A

WORLDWIDE HARVEST MINISTRIES TRUST
Founded: 1991 CR1005119
41 Marlow Road, Maidenhead, Windsor & Maidenhead SL6 7AQ
Tel: 01628 621727
Objects: 1A,N,2,R,U

WRITERS & SCHOLARS EDUCATIONAL TRUST
Founded: 1971 CR325003
6-8 Amwell Street, London EC1R 1UQ
Tel: 020 7278 2313
Email: .... hugo@indexoncensorship.org
Objects: F,J,S,W5,G,W10,W4,H,3,W8

WWF-UK
Founded: 1961 CR1081247; SC039593
The Living Planet Centre, Rufford House, Brewery Road, Woking, Surrey GU21 4LL
Tel: 01483 426333
Email: .... legacy@wwf.org.uk
Objects: W1,W2,G,A,1B,2,U,H

WYTHAM HALL LIMITED
Founded: 1983 CR289328
117 Sutherland Avenue, London W9 2QJ
Tel: 020 7289 1978
Email: .... enquiries@wythamhall.co.uk
Objects: F,G,D,N,O,C,P

Y

YATELEY INDUSTRIES FOR THE DISABLED LTD

Founded: 1935 CR229571
Mill Lane (CD119), Yateley, Hampshire GU46 7TF
Tel: 01252 872337
Email: .... sandram@yateleyindustries.net
Objects: E,W5,G,V,D,O,3,C,P,K

YELDALL CHRISTIAN CENTRES

Founded: 1990 CR1000038
Yeldall Manor, Blakes Lane, Hare Hatch, Reading RG10 9XR
Tel: 0118 940 1093
Email: .... info@yeldall.org.uk
Objects: F,O,3

YHA (ENGLAND AND WALES)

Founded: 1930 CR306122
Trevelyan House, Dimple Road, Matlock, Derbyshire DE4 3YH
Tel: 01629 592600
Email: .... fundraising@yha.org.uk
Objects: W3,W2,S,G,V,2,P

YMCA CAMBRIDGESHIRE & PETERBOROUGH

Founded: 1990 CR1069810
The Cresset, Rightwell, Bretton, Peterborough, Cambridgeshire PE3 8DX
Tel: 01733 269621
Email: ...... peterboroughymca@btinternet.com
Objects: F,W3,G,D,T,3,C

YMCA ENGLAND

Founded: 1844 CR212810
640 Forest Road, London E17 3DZ
Tel: 020 8520 5599
Email: .... Roomsponsor@ymca.org.uk
Objects: F,M,W3,S,E,G,U,H,C,P

YMCA - SLOUGH

Founded: 1991 CR1002442
30 Ladbrooke Road, Chalvey, Slough SL1 2SR
Tel: 01753 810684
Objects: G,D,C

YORKSHIRE CANCER RESEARCH

CR516898
Jacob Smith House (CC), 7 Grove Park Court, Harrogate, North Yorkshire HG1 4DP
Tel: 01423 501269
Email: .... hq@ycr.org.uk

YORKSHIRE COUNTY CRICKET CLUB CHARITABLE YOUTH TRUST, THE

Founded: 1991 CR1001497
9 St Winifreds Road, Harrogate, North Yorkshire HG2 8LN
Tel: 01423 887978

YORKSHIRE SCULPTURE PARK

CR1067908
West Bretton, Wakefield, West Yorkshire WF4 4LG
Tel: . 01924 830579 Office; 01924 832631 Visitor Information
Email: .... info@ysp.co.uk
Objects: S,G

YORKSHIRE WILDLIFE TRUST

CR210807
1 St George's Place, York, North Yorkshire YO24 1GN
Tel: 01904 659570
Email: .... info@ywt.org.uk
Objects: W1,W2,G,2,3

YOUNG CLASSICAL ARTISTS TRUST

CR326490
West Wing, Somerset House, Strand, London WC2R 1LA
Tel: 020 7379 8477
Email: .... info@ycat.co.uk

YOUTH ALIYAH - CHILD RESCUE

Founded: 1944 CR1077913
126 Albert Street, London NW1 7NE
Tel: 020 7485 8375
Email: .... info@youthaliyah.org.uk
Objects: Q,W3,G,1B,N,U

YOUTH FOR CHRIST

CR263446
PO Box 5254, Little Cornbow, Halesowen, West Midlands B63 3DG
Tel: 0121 550 8055
Email: .... yfc@yfc.co.uk

YOUTH MUSIC

CR1075032
1 America Street, London SE1 0NE
Tel: 020 7902 1060
Email: .... info@youthmusic.org.uk
Objects: W3,G,A,1B

YOUTH SPORT TRUST

Founded: 1994 CR1086915
3rd Floor, The Podium, One Eversholt Street, London NW1 2DN
Tel: 020 7842 8932
Email: .... fundraising@youthsporttrust.org
Objects: W3,G,3

YOUTH WITH A MISSION

CR264078
Highfield Oval, Ambrose Lane, Harpenden, Hertfordshire AL5 4BX
Tel: 01582 463216
Email: .... enquiries@oval.com
Objects: R,T,3

Z

ZOOLOGICAL SOCIETY OF GLASGOW & WEST SCOTLAND

Founded: 1936SC002651
Morrisbank, Deans Road, Bathgate, West Lothian EH48 1JU
Objects: W1,J,W2,G,2,H

ZOOLOGICAL SOCIETY OF LONDON, THE

CR208728
Regent's Park, London NW1 4RY
Tel: 020 7449 6443
Email: .... remember@zsl.org
Objects: W1,W2

ADOPTION SERVICES

The names of the Societies are listed under the areas in which their administrative headquarters are situated, though their activities are not necessarily confined to those areas. Local Authority Social Services Departments are also recognised Adoption Agencies. Societies based in England, Scotland and Wales were contacted individually to verify current details.

ENGLAND

Bristol

CCS ADOPTION (CLIFTON CHILDREN'S SOCIETY)
162 Pennywell Road, Easton, Bristol BS5 0TX
Tel: 0845 122 0077
Email: . . . . info@ccsadoption.org

Cambridgeshire

CORAM CAMBRIDGESHIRE ADOPTION
Coram Cambridgeshire Adoption, Lincoln House, The Paddocks Business Centre, 2nd Floor, Cherry Hinton Road, Cambridge, Cambridgeshire CB1 8DH
Tel: 0300 123 1093
Email: enquiries@coramcambridgeshireadoption.org.uk

Co. Durham

DFW ADOPTION
Agriculture House, Stonebridge, Durham, Co. Durham DH1 3RY
Tel: 0191 386 3719
Email: . . . . office@dfw.org.uk

Devon

FAMILIES FOR CHILDREN DEVON
Southgate Court, Buckfast, Buckfastleigh, Devon TQ11 0EE
Tel: 01364 645480
Email: . . . . mail@familiesforchildren.org.uk

Greater Manchester

CARITAS DIOCESE OF SALFORD
Cathedral Centre, 3 Ford Street, Salford, Greater Manchester M3 6DP
Tel: 0161 817 2250

Hertfordshire

ACTION FOR CHILDREN, THE CHILDREN'S CHARITY
3 Boulevard, Ascot Road, Watford, Hertfordshire WD18 8AJ
Tel: 01923 361 500

Lancashire

CARITAS CARE LIMITED
218 Tulketh Road, Preston, Lancashire PR2 1ES
Tel: 01772 732313
Email: . . . . info@caritascare.org.uk

London

BRITISH ASSOCIATION FOR ADOPTION AND FOSTERING
Saffron House, 6-10 Kirby Street, London EC1N 8TS
Tel: 020 7421 2600
Email: . . . . mail@baaf.org.uk

SSAFA
19 Queen Elizabeth Street, London SE1 2LP
Tel: 0845 1300 975
Email: . . . . info@ssafa.org.uk

TACT (THE ADOLESCENT AND CHILDREN'S TRUST)
TACT Adoption Services, 303 Hither Green Lane, Hither Green, London SE13 6TJ
Tel: 0800 232 1157
Email: . . . . enquiries@tactcare.org.uk

Middlesex

NORWOOD JEWISH ADOPTION SOCIETY
Broadway House, 80-82 The Broadway, Stanmore, Middlesex HA7 4HB
Tel: 020 8809 8809
Email: . . . . info@norwood.org.uk

Milton Keynes

ST FRANCIS CHILDREN'S SOCIETY
Collis House, 48 Newport Road, Woolstone, Milton Keynes MK15 OAA
Tel: 01908 572700
Email: . . . . enquiries@sfcs.org.uk

Nottinghamshire

FAITH IN FAMILIES
7 Colwick Road, West Bridgford, Nottingham, Nottinghamshire NG2 5FR
Tel: 0115 955 8811
Email: . . . . enquiries@ccfnotts.co.uk

FAMILY CARE
28 Magdala Road, Nottingham, Nottinghamshire NG3 5DF
Tel: 0115 960 3010
Email: . . . . . . info@familycare-nottingham.org.uk

Reading

FOSTERING ADOPTION TEAM - RBC (READING BOROUGH COUNCIL)
Placement Choice & Stability, PO Box 2943, Reading RG1 9NT
Tel: 0118 955 3740
Email: . . . . adoption@reading.gov.uk

PARENTS AND CHILDREN TOGETHER
7 Southern Court, South Street, Reading RG1 4QS
Tel: 0300 456 4800
Email: . . . . info@pactcharity.org

South Yorkshire

ADOPTION AND FAMILY WELFARE SOCIETY
Jubilee House, 1 Jubilee Road, Wheatley, Doncaster, South Yorkshire DN1 2UE
Tel: 01302 349909
Email: . . . . info@yorkshireadoptionagency.org.uk

Staffordshire

SACCS FLYING COLOURS FOSTERING CARE
The Dairy House, Brockton Hall, Brockton, Eccleshall, Stafford, Staffordshire ST21 6LY
Tel: 01785 857100
Email: . . . . . . info@flyingcoloursfostercare.co.uk

Surrey

CABRINI CHILDREN'S SOCIETY
49 Russell Hill Road, Purley, Surrey CR8 2XB
Tel: 020 8668 2181
Email: . . . . info@cabrini.org.uk

CHRISTIAN FAMILY CONCERN
Wallis House, 42 South Park Hill Road, South Croydon, Surrey CR2 7YB
Tel: 020 8688 0251
Email: . . . . . . info@christianfamilyconcern.org.uk

Tyne & Wear

ST CUTHBERT'S CARE
St Cuthberts House, West Road, Newcastle upon Tyne, Tyne & Wear NE15 7PY
Tel: 0191 228 0111
Email: . . . . enquiries@stcuthbertscare.org.uk

NORTHERN IRELAND

Belfast

ADOPTION ROUTES
18 Heron Road, Belfast BT3 9LE
Tel: 028 9073 6080

FAMILY CARE SOCIETY (BELFAST)
97 Malone Avenue, County Antrim, Belfast BT9 6EQ
Tel: 028 9069 1133
Email: . . . . email@family-care-society.org

Co. Londonderry

FAMILY CARE SOCIETY (LONDONDERRY)
1a Millar Street, Londonderry, Co. Londonderry BT48 6SU
Tel: 028 7136 8592

SCOTLAND

Edinburgh

BARNARDO'S SCOTLAND - GIVING CHILDREN BACK THEIR FUTURE
235 Corstorphine Road, Edinburgh EH12 7AR
Tel: 0131 334 9893
Email: . . . . martin.crewe@barnardos.org.uk

SCOTTISH ADOPTION
161 Constitution Street, Edinburgh EH6 7AD
Tel: 0131 553 5060
Email: . . . . info@scottishadoption.org

ST ANDREWS CHILDREN'S SOCIETY LTD
7 John's Place, Edinburgh EH6 7EL
Tel: 0131 454 3370
Email: . . . . info@standrews-children.org.uk

Glasgow

ST MARGARET'S CHILDREN AND FAMILY CARE SOCIETY
26 Newton Place, Glasgow G3 7PY
Tel: 0141 332 8371
Email: . . . . info@stmargaretsadoption.org.uk

WALES

Cardiff

ST. DAVID'S CHILDREN'S SOCIETY (WALES)
28 Park Place, Cardiff CF10 3BA
Tel: 029 2066 7007
Email: . . . . info@stdavidscs.org

ALMSHOUSES

For those seeking almshouse accommodation, lists of local almshouse charities and their contact names and addresses should be obtainable from local authority Housing Departments or Social Services Departments and from Citizens' Advice Bureaux. Alternatively, the Almshouse Association can provide a list of the almshouse trusts in a locality.

The Almshouse Association
Billingbear Lodge, Maidenhead Road, Wokingham RG40 5RU
Tel: 01344 452922 Fax: 01344 862062
E-mail: naa@almshouses.org Web: www.almshouses.org

For the last thousand years, almshouses have provided accommodation for older people and they continue to give this service today.

Early almshouses were called Hospitals, in the sense that they provided hospitality and shelter for those in need. Part of our national heritage, almshouses show the most complete examples of vernacular domestic architecture from the 12th century to the present day. There are more than 2,600 groups of almshouses in the United Kingdom, providing over 35,000 homes for people. New almshouses continue to be built today, some as extensions of existing trusts and others as new foundations.

The Almshouse Association is itself a charity which aims to assist and advise trustees of almshouses on their many problems. There are approximately 1,700 almshouse charities in membership of the Association throughout the United Kingdom. One of the main tasks is helping trustees to improve the accommodation in their almshouses up to modern housing standards. This often involves arranging or assisting with funding towards the cost of the work. A Common Investment Fund and Comprehensive Insurance Policy have been established for almshouse charities to help trustees further with the financial running of their trusts.

The Association publishes an Annual Report and quarterly Gazette to keep members up to date with legislation and other information and a series of regional meetings and training days are arranged annually. An Associate membership is available to individuals and bodies who are interested in supporting the work of the Association.

CITIZENS ADVICE BUREAUX

Citizens Advice Bureaux help people with legal, financial and other advice throughout the UK. They are all registered charities and rely on volunteers and donations to keep them going. The following pages list selected CAB offices throughout England, Scotland, Wales and Northern Ireland and are organised according to county/unitary authority/region.

For more information, contact the local CAB office, or visit www.citizensadvice.org.uk

CHANNEL ISLANDS

Guernsey

Guernsey
Bridge Avenue, The Bridge, St Sampsons, Guernsey GY2 4QS
Tel: 01481 242266

Jersey

St Helier
The Annexe, St Paul's Gate, New Street, St Helier, Jersey JE2 3WP
Tel: 01534 724942
Email: . . . . advice@cab.org.je

ENGLAND

Bath & North East Somerset

Bath
2 Edgar Buildings, George Street, Bath, Bath & North East Somerset BA1 2EE
Tel: 0344 848 7919

Bedfordshire

Ampthill
The Court House, Woburn Street, Ampthill, Bedfordshire MK45 2HX
Tel: 0844 477 1600

Bedford
7a St Paul's Square, Bedford, Bedfordshire MK40 1SQ
Tel: 01234 354384

Dunstable
Grove House, 76 High Street North, Dunstable, Bedfordshire LU6 1NF
Tel: . . . . 01582 661384; 01582 670003 Appts

Leighton Buzzard
Bossard House, West Street, Leighton Buzzard, Bedfordshire LU7 1DA
Tel: 01525 373878

Luton
24-26 King Street, Luton, Bedfordshire LU1 2DP
Tel: 01582 731616

Blackpool

Blackpool
6-10 Whitegate Drive, Devonshire Square, Blackpool FY3 9AQ
Tel: 01253 308400
Email: . . . . advice@blackpoolcab.org.uk

Bournemouth

Bournemouth
The West Wing, Town Hall, Bourne Avenue, Bournemouth BH2 6DX
Tel: 01202 290967

Bracknell Forest

Bracknell
42 The Broadway, Bracknell, Bracknell Forest RG12 1AG
Tel: 0844 499 4107

Bristol

Bristol
12 Broad Street, Bristol BS1 2HL
Tel: 03444 111444

Buckinghamshire

Amersham
Barn Hall Annexe, Chiltern Avenue, Amersham, Buckinghamshire HP6 5AH
Tel: 0845 092 0137

Aylesbury
2 Pebble Lane, Aylesbury, Buckinghamshire HP20 2JH
Tel: 0844 4994714

Buckingham
Wheeldon House, Market Hill, Buckingham, Buckinghamshire MK18 1JX
Tel: 01280 816707

High Wycombe
8 Easton Street, High Wycombe, Buckinghamshire HP11 1NJ
Tel: 0844 499 4108

Milton Keynes
Acorn House, 361 Midsummer Boulevard, Milton Keynes, Buckinghamshire MK9 3HP
Tel: 01908 604475

Cambridgeshire

Cambridge
66 Devonshire Road, Cambridge, Cambridgeshire CB1 2BL
Tel: 0344 848 7979
Email: . . . . advice@cambridgecab.org.uk

Ely
70 Market Street, Ely, Cambridgeshire CB7 4LS
Tel: 0344 878 7979

Huntingdon
Town Hall, Market Hill, Huntingdon, Cambridgeshire PE29 3LE
Tel: 01480 388900

March
March Library, City Road, March, Cambridgeshire PE15 9LT
Tel: 0344 245 1292

Peterborough
16-17 St Marks Street, Peterborough, Cambridgeshire PE1 2TU
Tel: 0844 499 4120; 01733 558383
Email: . . . . info@peterboroughcab.org.uk

St Neots
CAB Portacabin, Cambridgeshire, St Neots, Cambridgeshire PE19 1AJ
Tel: 0344 245 1292

Wisbech
9 Church Mews, Wisbech, Cambridgeshire PE13 1HL
Tel: 0344 245 1292

Cheshire

Birchwood
46 Benson Road, Birchwood, Warrington, Cheshire WA3 7PQ
Tel: 01925 824952

Chester
Folliot House, 53 Northgate Street, Chester, Cheshire CH1 2HQ
Tel: 0844 576 6111

Crewe
50 Victoria Street, Crewe, Cheshire CW1 2JE
Tel: 01270 303003

Crewe and Nantwich
The Gables, Beam Street, Nantwich, Cheshire CW5 5NF
Tel: 01270 303004

Ellesmere Port
1 Whitby Road, Ellesmere Port, Cheshire CH65 8AA
Tel: 0151 355 3428

Lymm
Lymm Library, Davies Way, Lymm, Cheshire WA13 0QW
Tel: 01925 753247

Macclesfield
Sunderland House, Sunderland Street, Macclesfield, Cheshire SK11 6JF
Tel: . . . 01625 426303 Client Line; 01625 432847
Email: . . . . advice@cecab-north.org.uk

Runcorn
Runcorn Office, Ground Floor, Grosvenor House, Runcorn, Cheshire WA7 2HF
Tel: 0845 130 4055

Widnes
Unit 6, Lugsdale Road, Widnes, Cheshire WA8 6DJ
Tel: 0845 130 4055
Email: . . . . advice@haltoncab.org.uk

Winsford
The Brunner Guildhall, High Street, Winsford, Cheshire CW7 2AU
Tel: 0844 576 6111

Co. Durham

Barnard Castle
21 Galgate, Barnard Castle, Co. Durham DL12 8EQ
Tel: 01833 631486
Email: . . . . teesdalecab@hotmail.com

Chester-le-Street
1a Front Street, Chester-le-Street, Co. Durham DH3 3BQ
Tel: 0191 389 3000

Darlington
Bennet House, 14 Horsemarket, Darlington, Co. Durham DL1 5PT
Tel: . . . . 01325 256999 Advice Line
Email: . . . . bureau@darlingtoncab.cabnet.org.uk

Durham
39 Claypath, Durham, Co. Durham DH1 1RH
Tel: . . . . 0191 384 2638; 0191 383 2885 - appointment line

Hartlepool
87 Park Road, Hartlepool, Co. Durham TS26 9HP
Tel: 01429 273223

Peterlee
17-19 The Upper Chare, Castledene Shopping Centre, Peterlee, Co. Durham SR8 1BW
Tel: 0191 586 2639

Wear Valley
Four Clocks, 154a Newgate Street, Bishop Auckland, Co. Durham DL14 7EH
Tel: 01388 606661
Email: . . . . enquiries@wearvalleycab.org.uk

Cornwall

Bodmin
Shire Hall, Mount Folly Square, Bodmin, Cornwall PL31 2DQ
Tel: 01208 74835

Bude
Neetside, Bude, Cornwall EX23 8LB
Tel: 01288 354531

Falmouth
Mulberry Passage, Market Strand, Falmouth, Cornwall TR11 3DB
Tel: 0844 499 4188

Liskeard
Duchy House, 21 Dean Street, Liskeard, Cornwall PL14 4AB
Tel: 0844 499 4188

Newquay
The Public Library, Marcus Hill, Newquay, Cornwall TR7 1BD
Tel: 0844 499 4188

Penzance
The Guildhall, St John's Road, Penzance, Cornwall TR18 2QR
Tel: 0844 499 4188

Truro
The Library, Union Place, Truro, Cornwall TR1 1EP
Tel: 0844 499 4188

Cumbria

Barrow-in-Furness
Ramsden Hall, Abbey Road, Barrow-in-Furness, Cumbria LA14 5QW
Tel: 0844 4994132

Carlisle
5-6 Old Post Office Court, Carlisle, Cumbria CA3 8LE
Tel: 01228 633900

Copeland
Tangier Buildings, Gregg's Lane, (off Tangier Street), Whitehaven, Cumbria CA28 7UH
Tel: 01946 693321

Eden
2 Sandgate, Penrith, Cumbria CA11 7TP
Tel: 01768 863564

Ulverston
Town Hall Annexe, Theatre Street, Ulverston, Cumbria LA12 7AQ
Tel: 01229 585585

Windermere
The Library, Ellerthwaite Road, Windermere, Cumbria LA23 2AJ
Tel: 01539 446464

Workington
Vulcans Lane, Workington, Cumbria CA14 2BT
Tel: 01900 604735

Derbyshire

Clay Cross
126 High Street, Clay Cross, Chesterfield, Derbyshire S45 9EE
Tel: 0844 848 9800
Email: . . . . mail@nedcab.org.uk

Glossop
1st Floor, Bradbury Community House, Market Street, Glossop, Derbyshire SK13 8AR
Tel: 01298 214550

Staveley
6 - 8 Broad Pavement, Chesterfield, Derbyshire S40 1RP
Tel: 01246 209164

Devon

Barnstaple
Ground Floor, Belle Meadow Court, Albert Lane, Barnstaple, Devon EX32 8RJ
Tel: 01271 377077

Bideford
28a Bridgeland Street, Bideford, Devon EX39 2PZ
Tel: 01237 473161

Exeter
Wat Tyler House, 3 King William Street, Exeter, Devon EX4 6PD
Tel: 0844 4994101

Exmouth
The Town Hall, St Andrew's Road, Exmouth, Devon EX8 1AW
Tel: 01395 264645

Honiton
Honiton Library and Information Centre, 48-50 New Street, Honiton, Devon EX14 IBS
Tel: 01404 44213

North Devon
Ilfracombe Outreach, c/o The Ilfracombe Centre, 44 High Street, Ilfracombe, Devon EX34 8AL
Tel: 01271 377181

Okehampton
The Ockment Centre, North Street, Okehampton, Devon EX20 1AR
Tel: 01837 52574

Paignton
29 Palace Avenue, Paignton, Devon TQ3 3EQ
Tel: 01803 521726

Tavistock
Kingdon House, North Street, Tavistock, Devon PL19 0AN
Tel: 01822 612359

Teignbridge
Bank House Centre, 5b Bank Street, Newton Abbot, Devon TQ12 2JL
Tel: 01626 203141

Teignmouth
Teignmouth Library, Fore Street, Teignmouth, Devon TQ14 8DY
Tel: 01626 776770
Email: . . . . enquiries@teignbridgecab.org.uk

Tiverton (Mid-Devon)
Mid Devon District CAB, The Town Hall, St Andrew Street, Tiverton, Devon EX16 6PG
Tel: 01884 234926

Torquay
Debt Advice Unit, 11 Castle Road, Torquay, Devon TQ1 3BB
Tel: 01803 297803

Totnes
The Cottage, Follaton House, Plymouth Road, Totnes, Devon TQ9 5NE
Tel: 01803 862392

Dorset

Bridport
45 South Street, Bridport, Dorset DT6 3NY
Tel: 01308 456594
Email: . . . . advice@bridport-cab.org.uk

Christchurch
2 Sopers Lane, Christchurch, Dorset BH23 1JG
Tel: . 01202 482023 Advice; 01202 488442 Appts Only

Dorchester
1 Acland Road, Dorchester, Dorset DT1 1JW
Tel: 0845 231 0400

Gillingham
The Courtyard, Newbury Court, Gillingham, Dorset SP8 4QX
Tel: 01747 822117

Sherborne
Manor House, Newland, Sherborne, Dorset DT9 3JL
Tel: 0844 848 7939

Wareham
Mill Lane, Wareham, Dorset BH20 4RA
Tel: 01929 551257
Email: . . . . . . bureau@purbeckcab.cabnet.org.uk

Weymouth
2 Mulberry Terrace, Great George Street, Weymouth, Dorset DT4 8NQ
Tel: 01305 782798

Wimborne
Hanham Road, Wimborne, Dorset BH21 1AS
Tel: 01202 884738

East Riding of Yorkshire

Boothferry
80 Pasture Road, Boothferry, Goole, East Riding of Yorkshire DN14 6HE
Tel: . 01405 762054 Advice; 01405 720866 Appts Only
Email: .... bureau@boothferrycab.cabnet.org.uk

Bridlington
5a Prospect Arcade, Bridlington, East Riding of Yorkshire YO15 2AL
Tel: .... 01482 393180; 01262 605644 Appts

East Sussex

Crowborough
Croham Lodge, Croham Road, Crowborough, East Sussex TN6 2RH
Tel: 03444111444

Eastbourne
Unit 6, Highlight House, 8 St Leonards Road, Eastbourne, East Sussex BN21 3UH
Tel: 03444 111 444

Hailsham
Southview, Western Road, Hailsham, East Sussex BN27 3DN
Tel: 03444111444

Lewes
The Barn, 3 North Court, Lewes, East Sussex BN7 2AR
Tel: 03444 111444

Seaford
37 Church Street, Seaford, East Sussex BN25 1HG
Tel: 03444 111444

Essex

Barking
55 Ripple Road, Barking, Essex IG11 7NT
Tel: 020 8594 6715/ 0208 507 5969

Billericay
Burghstead Lodge, 143 High Street, Billericay, Essex CM12 9AB
Tel: 03444 770808/ 0300 546 2595

Braintree, Halstead & Witham
Collingwood Road, Witham, Essex CM8 2DY
Tel: 0844 499 4719

Brentwood
8 - 12 Crown Street, Brentwood, Essex CM14 4BA
Tel: 0344 477 0808

Chelmsford
Burgess Well House, Coval Lane, Chelmsford, Essex CM1 1FW
Tel: 01245 257144; 01245 354720

Colchester
Blackburn House, Ground Floor, 32 Crouch Street, Colchester, Essex CO3 3HH
Tel: 03444 770808

Epping
TheReUSe Centre, Bower Hill Industrial Estate, Bower Hill, Epping, Essex CM16 7BN
Tel: 03444 770808

Grays
Voluntary & Community Resource Centre, High Street, Thurrock, Grays, Essex RM17 6XP
Tel: 03444 770808

Loughton
St Mary's Parish Centre, High Road, Loughton, Essex IG10 1BB
Tel: 03444 770808

Maldon
St Cedds House, Princes Road, Maldon, Essex CM9 5NY
Tel: 01621 841195
Email: ...... bureau@maldoncab.cabnet.org.uk

Rochford
Rochford Day Centre, Back Lane, Rochford, Essex SS4 1AY
Tel: 0344 477 0808

Saffron Walden
Barnard's Yard, Saffron Walden, Essex CB11 4EB
Tel: 01799 618 840

Southend-on-Sea

CITIZENS ADVICE BUREAU (CAB)
1 Church Road, Southend-on-Sea, Essex SS1 2AL
Tel: 01702 610610

Tendring
18 Carnarvon Road, Clacton-on-Sea, Essex CO15 6QF
Tel: 0844 477 0808

Waltham Abbey
Side Entrance, Town Hall, Highbridge Street, Waltham Abbey, Essex EN9 1DE
Tel: 03444 770808

Wickford
Gibraltar Walk, High Street, Wickford, Essex SS12 9AX
Tel: 0300 456 2595/ 03444 77 0808

Gloucestershire

Cirencester
2-3 The Mews, Cricklade Street, Cirencester, Gloucestershire GL7 1HY
Tel: 01285 652908

Gloucester
75-81 Eastgate Street, Gloucester, Gloucestershire GL1 1PN
Tel: . 01452 528017 Advice; 01452 527202 Appts

Stroud
Unit 8, 1st Floor Brunel Mall, London Road, Stroud, Gloucestershire GL5 2BP
Tel: 01453 762084

Greater Manchester

Altrincham
20 Stamford New Road, Altrincham, Greater Manchester WA14 1EJ
Tel: 0844 499 4103

Ashton-under-Lyne
9 George Street, Ashton-under-Lyne, Greater Manchester OL6 6AQ
Tel: 0161 330 2156

Bolton
26-28 Mawdsley Street, Bolton, Greater Manchester BL1 1LF
Tel: 0808 801 0011/ 03444889622

Bury
1-3 Blackburn Street, Radcliffe, Greater Manchester M26 1NN
Tel: 0845 120 3757

Irlam & Cadishead
126 Liverpool Road, Irlam, Manchester, Greater Manchester M44 5BE
Tel: 0844 826 9695/ 0300 456 2554
Email: . . . . email@salford.cabnet.org.uk

Longsight
384 Dickenson Road, Longsight, Manchester, Greater Manchester M13 0WQ
Tel: 0845 122 1112

Manchester
Swan Buildings, 20 Swan Street, Manchester, Greater Manchester M4 5JW
Tel: 0161 834 9057

Oldham
1 & 2 Ashcroft Court, Peter Street, Oldham, Greater Manchester OL1 1HP
Tel: 0344 488 9622

Prestwich
7 Fairfax Road, Prestwich, Greater Manchester M25 1AS
Tel: 0845 120 3757

Radcliffe
1-3 Blackburn Street, Radcliffe, Manchester, Greater Manchester M26 1NN
Tel: 0844 826 9320

Sale
73 Chapel Road, Sale, Greater Manchester M33 7EG
Tel: 0844 499 4103

Salford
25a Hankinson Way, Salford Precinct, Salford, Greater Manchester M6 5JA
Tel: 0844 826 9695/ 0300 456 2554

Salford - Mental Health Services
Prestwich Psychiatric Hospital, Bury New Road, Prestwich, Greater Manchester M25 3BL
Tel: 0161 772 3506
Email: . . . . main.bureau@smhscab.org.uk

Stretford
Stretford Library, 55 Bennett Street, Stretford, Greater Manchester M32 8SG
Tel: 0844 499 4103

Withington
Withington Methodist Church, 439 Wimslow Road, Withington, Manchester, Greater Manchester M20 4AN
Tel: 08444 111 444

Hampshire

Aldershot
39 High Street, Aldershot, Hampshire GU11 1BJ
Tel: 03444111444/ 01252 333 618
Email: . . . . advice@aldershotcab.org.uk

Alton
7 Cross And Pillory Lane, Alton, Hampshire GU34 1HL
Tel: 01420 544 807/ 03444 111 306
Email: . . . . . altonoutreach@easthantscab.org.uk

Andover
35 London Street, Hampshire, Andover, Hampshire SP10 2NU
Tel: 01264 365534

Ash
Ash Hill Road, Ash, Aldershot, Hampshire GU12 5DP
Tel: 01252 315569
Email: . . . . ashcan@cabnet.org.uk

Basingstoke
19-20 Westminster House, The Library, Potters Walk, Basingstoke, Hampshire RG21 7LS
Tel: 01256 322814

Bishop's Waltham
Well House, 2 Brook Street, Bishop's Waltham, Hampshire SO32 1AX
Tel: 03444 111 306/ 01489 890 940
Email: . administration@winchesterdistrictcab.org.uk

Fareham
1st Floor, Country Library Building, Osborn Road, Fareham, Hampshire PO16 7EN
Tel: 03444 111 306

Farnborough
Elles Hall Community Centre, Meudon Avenue, Farnborough, Hampshire GU14 7LE
Tel: 03444 111306/ 01252 513 051

Fleet
Civic Offices, Harlington Way, Fleet, Hampshire GU51 4AE
Tel: 01252 617922

Fordingbridge
The Rainbow Centre, 39 Salisbury Street, Fordingbridge, Hampshire SP6 1AB
Tel: 01425 652643
Email: . . . . advice@newforest.cabnet.org

Hythe
The Grove, 25 St Johns Street, Hythe, Southampton, Hampshire SO45 6BZ
Tel: 03444 111 306
Email: . . . . advice@newforest.cabnet.org.uk

Leigh Park
Leigh Park Community Centre, Dunsbury Way, Leigh Park, Havant, Hampshire PO9 5BG
Tel: 023 9271 7707

Lymington
Court Mews, 28a New Street, Lymington, Hampshire SO41 9AP
Tel: 03444 111306
Email: . . . . advice@newforest.cabnet.org

New Milton
Shop 5, Parklands Place, 39-41 Old New Milton Road, New Milton, Hampshire BH25 6AS
Tel: 03444 111 306
Email: . . . . advice@newforest.cabnet.org.uk

Petersfield
The Old Surgery, 18 Heath Road, Petersfield, Hampshire GU31 4DY
Tel: 03444 111 306/01730 710 281

Portsmouth
1-3a London Road, Dugald Drummond Street, Portsmouth, Hampshire PO2 0BQ
Tel: 023 9265 6300

Ringwood
5 Fridays Court, High Street, Ringwood, Hampshire BH24 1AB
Tel: 01425 473330

Romsey
5 Abbey Walk, Church Street, Romsey, Hampshire SO51 8JQ
Tel: 01794 516378

Southampton
3 Kings Park Road, Southampton, Hampshire SO15 2AT
Tel: 023 8022 1406; 023 8033 3868

Whitehill and Bordon
Forest Community Centre, Pinehill Road, Bordon, Hampshire GU35 0BS
Tel: 03444 111 306/ 01420 477 005

Winchester
The Winchester Centre, 68 St Georges Street, Winchester, Hampshire SO23 8AH
Tel: 01962 848000
Email: . . . . advice@winchestercab.org,uk

Yateley
Royal Oak Close, Yateley, Hampshire GU46 7UD
Tel: 01252 878410

Herefordshire

Hereford
8 St Owen Street, Hereford, Herefordshire HR1 2PJ
Tel: 0844 826 9685
Email: . . . . info@herefordshirecab.org.uk

Leominster
11 Corn Square, Leominster, Herefordshire HR6 8LR
Tel: 0844 826 9685

Hertfordshire

Abbots Langley
The Old Stables, St Lawrence's Vicarage, High Street, Abbots Langley, Hertfordshire WD5 0AS
Tel: 03444 111 444/ 0344 245 1296

Barnet
30 Station Road, Barnet, Hertfordshire EN5 1PL
Tel: 0300 456 8365

Bishop's Stortford
74 South Street, Bishop's Stortford, Hertfordshire CM23 3AZ
Tel: 03444 111 444

Borehamwood
Community Centre, Vanstone Suite, 2 Allum Lane, Elstree, Borehamwood, Hertfordshire WD6 3PJ
Tel: . . . . 0870 121 2025 Phone advice; 0208 953 9961 Appointments

Buntingford
The Manor House, 21 High Street, Buntingford, Hertfordshire SG9 9AB

Bushey
8 Rudolph Road, Bushey, Hertfordshire WD23 3DU
Tel: 03444 111 444

Cheshunt
Old Bishop's College, Churchgate, Cheshunt, Hertfordshire EN8 9XP
Tel: 03444 111 444

Hatfield
1st Floor, Queensway House, Queensway, Hatfield, Hertfordshire AL10 0LW
Tel: 01707 280 413 (Advice Line)/ 03444 111 444

Hemel Hempstead
Dacre House, 19 Hillfield Road, Hemel Hempstead, Hertfordshire HP2 4AA
Tel: 03444 111 444

Hertford
No 4, Yeoman's Court, Ware Road, Hertford, Hertfordshire SG13 7HJ
Tel: 0344 411 1444

Hitchin
Thomas Bellamy House, Bedford Road, Hitchin, Hertfordshire SG5 1HL
Tel: 0845 688 9897
Email: . . . . info@nhsdistrictcab.org.uk

Letchworth
66-68 Leys Avenue, Letchworth, Hertfordshire SG6 3EG
Tel: 03444 111 444
Email: . . . . infor@nhdistrictcab.cabnet.org.uk

Potters Bar
Wyllyotts Centre, 1 Wyllyotts Place, Darkes Lane, Potters Bar, Hertfordshire EN6 2HN
Tel: 03444 111 444

Rickmansworth
Northway House, High Street, Rickmansworth, Hertfordshire WD3 1EH
Tel: 03444 111 444/0344 245 1296

Royston
Town Hall, Royston, Hertfordshire SG8 7BZ
Tel: 03444 111 444
Email: . . . . infor@nhdistrictcab.cabnet.org.uk

South Oxhey
4 Bridlington Road, South Oxhey, Watford, Hertfordshire WD19 7AF
Tel: 03444111444/ 0344 245 1296

St Albans
Civic Centre, St Albans, Hertfordshire AL1 3JE
Tel: 01727 811118/03444 111 444

Stevenage
Swingate House, Danestrete, Stevenage, Hertfordshire SG1 1AF
Tel: 0845 120 3789; 01438 759300 Answerphone

Ware and District
Meade House, 85 High Street, Ware, Hertfordshire SG12 9AD
Tel: 0844 848 9700

Watford
St Mary's Churchyard, High Street, Watford, Hertfordshire WD17 2BE
Tel: 03444 111 444

Isle of Wight

Newport
Advice Hub, 7 High Street, Newport, Isle of Wight PO30 1SS
Tel: 03444 111 444

Kent

Bexleyheath
2 Townley Road, Bexleyheath, Kent DA7 7HL
Tel: 020 8303 5100/ 01322 517 150

Bromley
Community House, South Street, Bromley, Kent BR1 1RH
Tel: 020 8315 1940

Dartford
Trinity Resource Centre, High Street, Dartford, Kent DA1 1DE
Tel: 01322 472 979

Deal
26 Victoria Road, Deal, Kent CT14 7BJ
Tel: 0344 848 7978

Dover, Deal & District
Maison Dieu Gardens, Maison Dieu Road, Dover, Kent CT16 1RW
Tel: 0844 848 7978

Edenbridge
The Eden Centre, Four Elms Road, Edenbridge, Kent TN8 6BY
Tel: 0300 422 888

Erith
42 Pier Road, Erith, Kent DA8 1TA
Tel: 01322 571 150

Faversham
43 Stone Street, Faversham, Kent ME13 8PH
Tel: 0844 499 4125

Folkestone
Folkstone Library, 2 Grace Hill, Folkestone, Kent CT20 1HD
Tel: 0844 499 4118

Gillingham
Kingsley House, 37-39 Balmoral Road, Gillingham, Kent ME7 4PF
Tel: 01634 383 760
Email: .... info@cabmedwayadvice.org.uk

Herne Bay
185-187 High Street, Herne Bay, Kent CT6 5AF
Tel: 01227 740647 (To make appointments only); 0844 499 4128 (Adviceline)

Maidstone
2 Bower Terrace, Tonbridge Road, Maidstone, Kent ME16 8RY
Tel: 01622 752420; 01622 757882
Email: .... advice@maidstonecab.org.uk

Margate
2nd Floor, Mill Lane House, Mill Lane, Margate, Kent CT9 1LB
Tel: . 01843 225973 Advice; 01843 232666 Appts
Email: .... enquiries@thanetcitizensadvice.co.uk

Sevenoaks
Buckhurst Lane (next to the library), Sevenoaks, Kent TN13 1HW
Tel: 01732 440 488
Email: .... info@sevenoakscab.org.uk

Sittingbourne
17 Station Street, Sittingbourne, Kent ME10 3DU
Tel: 0844 499 4124

Swanley and District
16 High Street, Swanley, Kent BR8 8BG
Tel: 01322 664949

Tonbridge
3-4 River Walk, Tonbridge, Kent TN9 1DT
Tel: 01732 361 709

Tunbridge Wells
5th Floor, Vale House, Clarence Road, Tunbridge Wells, Kent TN1 1LS
Tel: 08701 264856 Advice; 01892 617256 Admin Answerphone Only
Email: .... advice@twcab.cabnet.org.uk

Kingston upon Hull

Hull
1st Floor, The Wilson Centre, Alfred Gelder Street, Hull, Kingston upon Hull HU1 2AG
Tel: .... 01482 224608 General Line

Lancashire

Bacup
Ground Floor, Stubbylee Hall, Stubbylee Lane, Bacup, Lancashire OL13 0DE
Tel: 0300 456 2552/ 0844 499 4121

Barnoldswick
10 Rainall Road, Barnoldswick, Lancashire BB18 5AF
Tel: 01282 814814
Email: .... pris@cabnet.org.uk

Blackburn
Central Library, Town Hall Street, Blackburn, Lancashire BB1 1AG
Tel: 03444 889 622
Email: .... info@blackburncab.org.uk

Chorley
35-39 Market Street, Chorley, Lancashire PR7 2SW
Tel: 0344 245 1294/ 0300 330 0650

Clitheroe
19-21 Wesleyan Row, Parson Lane, Clitheroe, Lancashire BB7 2JY
Tel: 01200 428966

Colne
Town Hall, Albert Road, Colne, Nelson, Lancashire BB8 0AQ
Tel: 01282 867188

Hyndburn
New Era Centre, Paradise Street, Accrington, Lancashire BB5 1PB
Tel: 01254 304114; 01254 394210

Kirkham
Council Offices, Moor Street, Kirkham, Preston, Lancashire PR4 2AU
Tel: 01772 682588
Email: .... kirkhamcab@cabnet.org.uk

Lancaster
87 King Street, Lancaster, Lancashire LA1 1RH
Tel: 03444 889 622
Email: .... enquiries@northlancashire.org.uk

Morecambe and Heysham
Oban House, 87-89 Queen Street, Morecambe, Lancashire LA4 5EN
Tel: .... 0844 499 4197 (Advice); 01524 400405 Appts
Email: .... enquiries@northlancashire.org.uk

Nelson
61-63 Every Street, Nelson, Lancashire BB9 7LT
Tel: 01282 616750

Preston
Town Hall Annexe, Birley Street, Preston, Lancashire PR1 2QE
Tel: . 01772 822416 Advice; 01772 906434 Appts

Leicestershire

Coalville
Council Offices, Whitwick Road, Coalville, Leicestershire LE67 3FJ
Tel: . . 0300 330 1025/ 0300 456 8400 (Macmillan helpline)
Email: .... advice@swlcab.org.uk

Harborough
District Council, The Symington Building, Adam & Eve Street, Market Harborough, Leicestershire LE16 7AF
Tel: . . 0300 330 1025/ 0300 456 8400 (Macmillan helpline)
Email: .... advice@leicscab.org.uk

Loughborough
Woodgate Chambers, 70 Woodgate, Loughborough, Leicestershire LE11 2TZ
Tel: 0300 330 1025

Melton Mowbray
Melton Borough Council Offices, Parkside, Stattion Approach, Burton Street, Melton Mowbray, Leicestershire LE13 1AE
Tel: 0300 330 1025

Lincolnshire

Boston
The Len Medlock, Voluntary Centre, St Georges Road, Boston, Lincolnshire PE21 8YB
Tel: 0844 499 4199

East Lindsey
20 Algitha Road, Skegness, Lincolnshire PE25 2AG
Tel: 0844 491 4199

Gainsborough
26 North Street, Gainsborough, Lincolnshire DN21 2HU
Tel: 0844 499 4199

Lincoln & District
Beaumont Lodge, Beaumont Fee, Lincoln, Lincolnshire LN1 1UL
Tel: 0844 499 4199

Sleaford
The Advice Centre, Moneys Yard, Carre Street, Sleaford, Lincolnshire NG34 7TW
Tel: 0844 499 4199

Stamford
39 High Street, Stamford, Lincolnshire PE9 2BB
Tel: 0844 499 4199

London

Barnet
40-44 Church End, Barnet, London NW4 4JT
Tel: 0300 456 8365

Beckenham and Penge
20 Snowdown Close, Avenue Road, Penge, London SE20 7RU
Tel: . . . . 020 8778 0921; 020 8776 9209 Minicom

Bermondsey
8 Market Place, Southwark Park Road, Bermondsey, London SE16 3UQ
Tel: 0344 499 4134

Brent
270-272 High Road, Willesden, London NW10 2EY
Tel: 0845 050 5250
Email: . . . . brent.cab@brentcab.co.uk

Chelsea
Old Town Hall, Kings Road, Chelsea, London SW3 5EE
Tel: 08448269708

Fulham
Avonmore Library & Neighbourhood Centre, 7 North End Crescent, Fulham, London W14 8TG
Tel: 020 7385 1322
Email: . . . . advice@hfcab.org.uk

Hackney
300 Mare Street, Hackney, London E8 1HE
Tel: 020 8525 6350

Holborn
3rd Floor, Holborn Library, 32-38 Theobalds Road, Holborn, London WC1X 8PA
Tel: 0300 330 0646

Kensington
140 Ladbroke Grove, Kensington, London W10 5ND
Tel: 0844 826 9708

Kentish Town
242 Kentish Town Road, Kentish Town, London NW5 2AB
Tel: 0300 330 0646

Morden
7 Crown Parade, Crown Lane, Morden, London SM4 5DA
Tel: 0344 243 8430
Email: . . . . advice@mertoncab.org.uk

Palmers Green
Town Hall, Green Lanes, Palmers Green, London N13 4XD
Tel: 0870 126 4664

Peckham
97 Peckham High Street, Peckham, London SE15 5RS
Tel: 0344 499 4134

Putney & Roehampton
Roehampton CAB, 166 Roehampton Lane, Roehampton, London SW15 4HR
Tel: 020 7042 0333

Sheen
Sheen Lane Centre, Sheen Lane, Sheen, London SW14 8LP
Tel: 0208 712 7800

Strand
Royal Courts of Justice, Strand, London WC2A 2LL
Tel: . . . 08458563534; 020 7947 6880 - voicemail

Streatham Hill
Ilex House, 1 Barrhill Road, Streatham Hill, London SW2 4RJ
Tel: 0344 245 1298

Walthamstow
Church Hill Business Centre, 6 Church Hill, Walthamstow, London E17 3AG
Tel: 0208 521 5125

Wandsworth
14 York Road, Battersea, London SW11 3QA
Tel: 020 7042 0333

Whitechapel
32, Greatorex Street, Whitechapel, London E1 5NP
Tel: 0844 826 9699
Email: . . . . . . towerhamlets@eastendcab.org.uk

Woolwich
Old Town Hall, Polytechnic Street, Woolwich, London SE18 6PN
Tel: 020 8853 9499
Email: . . . . greenwichcab@btopenworld.com

Merseyside

Anfield
36-38 Breckfield Road North, Anfield, Liverpool, Merseyside L5 4NH
Tel: 0344 848 7700

Bootle
Goddard Hall, 297 Knowsley Road, Bootle, Merseyside L20 5DF
Tel: 0151 288 5683

Crosby
Prince Street, Crosby, Liverpool, Merseyside L22 5PB
Tel: 0151 282 5666

Formby
11a Duke Street, Formby, Liverpool, Merseyside L37 4AN
Tel: 01704 875078; 01704 873009

Garston
Garston Community House, Garston Village, 2 Speke Road, Liverpool, Merseyside L19 2PA
Tel: 0344 848 7700/ 0151 427 3980
Email: .... info@southliverpoolcab.org.uk

Halewood
The Halewood Centre, Roseheath Drive, Halewood, Merseyside L26 9UH
Tel: 0845 122 1300
Email: .... advice@knowsleycab.org.uk

Heswall
Hillcroft, Rocky Lane, Heswall, Wirral, Merseyside CH60 0BY
Tel: 0844 477 2121

Kirkby
1st Floor, 2 Newton Gardens, Kirkby, Knowsley, Merseyside L32 8RR
Tel: 0845 122 1300
Email: .... advice@knowsleycab.org.uk

Liverpool
2nd Floor, 1 Union Court, Cook Street, Liverpool, Merseyside L2 4SJ
Tel: 0151 285 8534; 0844 848 7700
Email: .... bureau@liverpoolcab.org

Netherley
Belle Vale Business Centre, Childwall Valley Road, Netherley, Liverpool, Merseyside L25 2RJ
Tel: 0844 848 7700

Prescot
10a Church Street, Prescot, Merseyside L34 3LA
Tel: 0845 122 1300; 0151 477 6012
Email: .... advice@knowsleycab.org.uk

Southport
24 Wright Street, Southport, Merseyside PR9 0TL
Tel: 01704 385627

St Helens
Millenium Centre, Corporation Centre, St Helens, Merseyside WA10 1HJ
Tel: . 08448 269694 Advice; 01744 737866 Appts

Wallasey
237-243 Liscard Road, Wallasey, Merseyside CH44 5TH
Tel: 0844 477 2121
Email: .... advice@wirralcab.org.uk

Wirral
57 New Chester Road, New Ferry, Bebington, Wirral, Merseyside CH62 1AB
Tel: 0344 477 2121
Email: .... advice@wirralcab.org.uk
1- 3 Acacia Grove, West Kirby, Wirral, Merseyside CH48 4DD
Tel: 0844 477 2121

Middlesex

Enfield
Unit 3, Vincent House, 2E Nags Head Road, Ponders End, Enfield, Middlesex EN3 7FN
Tel: 020 8375 4170

Harrow
Harrow Civic Centre, Civic 9, Station Road, Harrow, Middlesex HA1 2XH
Tel: 0208 427 9477

Sunbury-on-Thames
Sunbury Library, The Parade, Staines Road West, Sunbury-on-Thames, Middlesex TW16 7AB
Tel: 01932 827 187

Twickenham
5th Floor, Regal House, 70 London Road, Twickenham, Middlesex TW1 3QS
Tel: ....
0208 712 7800/ 0844 826 9700

0844 826 9700

Uxbridge
The Colonnade, Civic Centre, High Street, Uxbridge, Middlesex UB8 1UW
Tel: 0344 848 7903

Norfolk

Dereham
Assembly Rooms, Ruthen Place, Dereham, Norfolk NR19 2TX
Tel: 03444 111 444

Diss & Thetford
Shelfanger Road, Diss, Norfolk IP22 4EH
Tel: . 01379 651333 Diss; 01842 752777 Thetford
Email: .... advice@disscab.cabnet.org.uk

Great Yarmouth
2 Stonecutters Way, Great Yarmouth, Norfolk NR30 1HF
Tel: 01493 856665
Email: .... advice@yarevalleycab.org.uk

Holt
Kerridge Way, Holt, Norfolk NR25 6DN
Tel: 03444 111 444
Email: .... advice@midnorfolkcab.org.uk

North Walsham & District
The CAB Offices, New Road, North Walsham, Norfolk NR28 9DE
Tel: 01692 402570

Thetford
Level 3, Breckland House, Thetford, Norfolk IP24 1BT
Tel: 01842 752777
Email: ...... advice@thetfordcab.cabnet.org.uk

Watton
The Cabin, Harvey Street, Watton, Norfolk IP25 6EB
Tel: 03444 111 444

West Norfolk
Whites House, 26 St Nichols Street, King's Lynn, Norfolk PE30 1LY
Tel: 03444 111 444

North East Lincolnshire

Grimsby
4 Town Hall Street, Grimsby, North East Lincolnshire DN31 1HN
Tel: 01472 252500

North Lincolnshire

Scunthorpe
12 Oswald Road, Scunthorpe, North Lincolnshire DN15 7PT
Tel: 0870 126 4854 Advice; 01724 870941 Appts

North Somerset

Weston-super-Mare
The Badger Centre, 3-6 Wadham Street, Weston-super-Mare, North Somerset BS23 1JY
Tel: 0870 121 2017

North Yorkshire

Hambleton
277 High Street, Northallerton, North Yorkshire DL7 8DW
Tel: 0845 122 8689 Advice; 01609 776551 Appts
Email: . . . . advice@hambletoncab.cabnet.org.uk

Harrogate
Audrey Burton House, Queensway, Harrogate, North Yorkshire HG1 5IX
Tel: 01423 503576
Email: . . advice@cravenandharrogatecab.org.uk

Middlesbrough
3 Bolckow Street, Middlesbrough, North Yorkshire TS1 1TH
Tel: 0344 499 4110

Richmond
23 Newbiggin, Richmond, North Yorkshire DL10 4DX
Tel: 01748 826 532/ 03444 111 444
Email: . . . . . enquiries@richmondshirecab.org.uk

Ryedale
Stanley Harrison House, Norton Road, Norton, Malton, Malton, North Yorkshire YO17 9RD
Tel: 03444 111 444
Email: . . . . . . bureau@ryedalecab.cabnet.org.uk

Selby
Rear of 4 Park Street, Selby, North Yorkshire YO8 4PW
Tel: 01757 701 320/ 03444 111 444

Skipton
St Andrew's Church Hall, Newmarket Street, Skipton, North Yorkshire BD23 2JE
Tel: 01756 701 371
Email: . . . . advice@skiptoncab.cabnet.org.uk

Whitby
Church House, Flowergate, Whitby, North Yorkshire YO21 3BA
Tel: 0845 120 2930 Advice; 01723 368710 Appts

York
West Offices, Station Rise, York, North Yorkshire YO1 6GA
Tel: . . . . 03444 111 444 Advice Line
Email: . . . . admin@yorkcab.org.uk

Northamptonshire

Daventry
The Abbey, Market Square, Daventry, Northamptonshire NN11 4XG
Tel: . . . . 0844 855 2122; 01327 701693 Minicom

Kettering
5 Horsemarket, Kettering, Northamptonshire NN16 0DG
Tel: 0844 855 2122

Northampton
Town Centre House, 7/8 Mercers Row, Northampton, Northamptonshire NN1 2QL
Tel: 0844 855 2122

Wellingborough
2b High Street, Wellingborough, Northamptonshire NN8 4HR
Tel: 0870 126 4865
Email: . . . . . . advice@wellingboroughcab.org.uk

Northumberland

Amble
The Fourways, Bridge Street, Amble, Northumberland NE65 0DR
Tel: 01665 604135

Ashington
39-91 Station Road, Ashington, Northumberland NE63 8RS
Tel: 01670 818360
Email: . . . . cab@wansbeck80.fsnet.co.uk

Berwick-upon-Tweed
Berwick, 5 Tweed Street, Berwick-upon-Tweed, Northumberland TD15 1NG
Tel: 01289 330222

Blyth Valley
Eric Tolhurst Centre, 3-13 Quay Street, Blyth, Northumberland NE24 2AS
Tel: 01670 367779
Email: . emailenquiries@blythvalley.cabnet.org.uk

Castle Morpeth
Tower Buildings, 9 Oldgate, Morpeth, Northumberland NE61 1PY
Tel: 01670 518814

Hexham
The Community Centre, Gilesgate, Hexham, Northumberland NE46 3NP
Tel: 01434 605254
Email: . . westnorthumberlandcab@cabnet.org.uk

Nottinghamshire

Bassetlaw
Central Avenue, Worksop, Nottinghamshire S80 1EJ
Tel: 08448563411

Beeston
Ground Floor, Council Offices, Foster Avenue, Beeston, Nottinghamshire NG9 1AB
Tel: 0844 499 1193
Email: . . . . bureau@eastwood.cabnet.org.uk

Eastwood
Library and Information Centre, Wellington Place, Eastwood, Nottingham, Nottinghamshire NG16 3GB
Tel: 0844 499 4194

Sutton-in-Ashfield
22 Market Street, Sutton-in-Ashfield, Nottinghamshire NG17 1AG
Tel: 0870 126 4873

Oxfordshire

Didcot
Dales,, 9-15 High Street, Didcot, Oxfordshire OX11 8EQ
Tel: 03444 111 444

Oxford
95 St Aldates, Oxford, Oxfordshire OX1 1DA
Tel: 03444 111 444

Poole

Poole
54 Lagland Street, Poole BH15 1QG
Tel: .... 01202 680838 Advice line
Email: .... advice@poolecab.co.uk

Reading

Reading
Minster Street, Reading RG1 2JB
Tel: .... 0845 071 6379 Advice; 01189 583 5313 Training Services line

Woodley
Headley Road (Next to Library), Woodley, Reading RG5 4JA
Tel: 08444 994 126
Email: .... public@wokingham-cab.org.uk

Redcar & Cleveland

Redcar & Cleveland
88 Westgate, Guisborough, Redcar & Cleveland TS14 6AP
Tel: 01642 469880

Rutland

Oakham
56 High Street, Oakham, Rutland LE15 6AL
Tel: 0845 120 3705
Email: .... advice@rutlandcab.org.uk

Shropshire

Bridgnorth and District
Westgate, Bridgnorth, Shropshire WV16 5AA
Tel: 0844 499 1100

Ludlow
Stone House, Corve Street, Ludlow, Shropshire SY8 1DG
Tel: 0844 499 1100

Oswestry
34 Arthur Street, Oswestry, Shropshire SY11 1JN
Tel: 0844 499 1100

Slough

Slough
Hasland, 27 Church Street, Slough SL1 1PL
Tel: 0845 120 3712

Somerset

Frome
5 King Street, Frome, Somerset BA11 1BH
Tel: 01373 465496

Shepton Mallet
9/9a Market Place, Shepton Mallet, Somerset BA4 5AZ
Tel: 01749 343010
Email: .... advice@mendipcab.org.uk

Yeovil
40 - 42 Hendford, Yeovil, Somerset BA20 1UW
Tel: 01935 421167
Email: .... cab@southsomcab.org.uk

South Gloucestershire

Yate
Kennedy Way, Yate, South Gloucestershire BS37 4DQ
Tel: 0870 121 2019

South Yorkshire

Mexborough
Behind New Surgery, Adwick Road, Mexborough, South Yorkshire S64 0DB
Tel: 01709 572400/01709 572404

Rotherham
Wellgate Old Hall, 120-126 Wellgate, Rotherham, South Yorkshire S60 2LN
Tel: 01709 515680

Sheffield
Mental Health Unit CAB, Michael Carlisle Centre, Nether Edge Hospital, Osborne Road, Sheffield, South Yorkshire S11 9BF
Tel: 0114 271 8025
Sheffield Debt Support Unit, Unit 9b The Old Dairy, Broadfield Road, Sheffield, South Yorkshire S8 0XQ

Staffordshire

Cheadle
Rear of Lulworth House, 51 High Street, Cheadle, Staffordshire ST10 1JY
Tel: 03444111444

East Staffordshire
Suite 8, Anson Court, Horninglow Street, Burton-on-Trent, Staffordshire DE14 1NG
Tel: 01283 566722/ 0344 245 1280
Email: .... info@eaststaffordshirecab.co.uk

Lichfield
29 Levetts Fields, Lichfield, Staffordshire WS13 6HY
Tel: 03444111444

Newcastle-under-Lyme
25-27 Well Street, Newcastle-under-Lyme, Staffordshire ST5 1BP
Tel: 03444111444(advice) 01782201234 (admin)

Rugeley
7 Brook Square, Rugeley, Staffordshire WS15 2DU
Tel: 03444111444

Stafford
Stafford District, Vol Services Centre, 131-141 North Walls, Stafford, Staffordshire ST16 3AD
Tel: 01785 258673; 01785 242524

Stafford & Stone (Stone)
Stone Town Council Offices, 15 Station Road, Stone, Staffordshire ST15 8JP
Tel: 03444111444

Stoke-on-Trent District
Advice House, Cheapside, Hanley, Stoke-on-Trent, Staffordshire ST1 1HL
Tel: 01782 408600
Email: .... advice@stoke-cab.org.uk

Suffolk

Beccles
12 New Market, Beccles, Suffolk NR34 9HB
Tel: 01502 717715

Brandon
11 High Street, Brandon, Suffolk IP27 0AQ
Tel: 01842 811511
Email: .... advice@brandoncab.co.uk

Bungay
8 Chaucer Street, Bungay, Suffolk NR35 1DT
Tel: 01986 895827

Bury St Edmunds
The Risbygate Centre, 90 Risbygate Street, Bury St Edmunds, Suffolk IP33 3AA
Tel: 01284 753675

Felixstowe & District
2-6 Orwell Road, Felixstowe, Suffolk IP11 7HD

Haverhill - Centre for Voluntary Agencies
Lower Downslade, Haverhill, Suffolk CB9 9HB
Tel: 01440 704012

Ipswich
19 Tower Street, Ipswich, Suffolk IP1 3BE
Tel: 01473 219777

Leiston
14 Colonial House, Station Road, Leiston, Suffolk IP16 4JD
Tel: 01728 832193

Mildenhall
Willow House, 40 St Andrews Street, Mildenhall, Bury St Edmunds, Suffolk IP28 7HB
Tel: 01638 712094
Email: . . . . mildenhall@brandoncab.co.uk

Newmarket
Foley Gate, Wellington Street, Newmarket, Suffolk CB8 0HY
Tel: 01638 665999
Email: . . . adviser@newmarketcab.cabnet.org.uk

North East Suffolk (Lowestoft)
The Advice Centre, 36 Gordon Road, Lowestoft, Suffolk NR32 1NL
Tel: 01502 518510

Stowmarket
5 Milton Road South, Stowmarket, Suffolk IP14 1EZ
Tel: 01449 676060; 01449 676280

Sudbury
Belle Vue, Newton Road, Sudbury, Suffolk CO10 2RG
Tel: 01787 374671
Email: . . . . . . bureau@sudburycab.cabnet.org.uk

Surrey

Addlestone
The Old Library, Church Road, Addlestone, Surrey KT15 1RW
Tel: 01932 842666

Camberley
Rear of Library, Knoll Road, Camberley, Surrey GU15 3SY
Tel: 01276 684342/ 01276 417 900

Caterham
Soper Hall, Harestone Valley Road, Caterham, Surrey CR3 6YN
Tel: 01883 344777

Cranleigh
Village Way, Cranleigh, Surrey GU6 8AF
Tel: 0344 848 7969

Croydon
1 Overbury Crescent, New Addington, Croydon, Surrey CR0 0LR
Tel: 01689 846890

Epsom
The Old Town Hall, The Parade, Epsom, Surrey KT18 5AG
Tel: 01372 237 000

Esher
Harry Fletcher House, High Street, Esher, Surrey KT10 9RN
Tel: 01372 464770

Farnham
Montrose House, South Street, Farnham, Surrey GU9 7RN
Tel: 0844 848 7969

Frimley
Beech House, Church Road, Frimley, Camberley, Surrey GU16 7AD
Tel: 01276 21711
Email: . . . bureau@heathlandscab.cabnet.org.uk

Guildford
15-21 Haydon Place, Guildford, Surrey GU1 4LL
Tel: 01483 576699
Email: . . . . guildford@cabnet.org.uk

Haselmere
Well Lane House, Well Lane, High Street, Haslemere, Surrey GU27 2LB
Tel: 0844 848 7969

Horley
c/o Horley Help Shop, 4 Victoria Square, Consort Way, Horley, Surrey RH6 7AF
Tel: 0844 477 9394
Email: . . . . info@redhillcab.cabnet.org.uk

Leatherhead
The Georgian House, Swan Mews, High Street, Leatherhead, Surrey KT22 8AE
Tel: . 01372 375522 Advice; 01372 361160 Appts

Leatherhead & Dorking
Lyons Court, Dorking, Surrey RH4 1AB
Tel: 01306 876805

Mitcham
Kellaway House, 326 London Road, Mitcham, Surrey CR4 3ND
Tel: 0344 243 8430

North Cheam
The Central Library, St Nicholas Way, Sutton, Surrey SM1 1EA
Tel: 020 8405 3552

North Surrey Domestic Abuse Outreach Service
Elm Grove, Hersham Road, Walton-on-Thames, Surrey KT12 1LH
Tel: 01932 248660

Oxted
1st Floor Library Building, 14 Gresham Road, Oxted, Surrey RH8 0BQ
Tel: 01883 730 259/ 03444 111 444

Richmond
ASCA, 233 Lower Mortlake Road, Richmond, Surrey TW9 2LL
Tel: 0844 826 9700

Staines
Community Link, Knowle Green, Staines, Surrey TW18 1XA
Tel: . . 01784 444220 (advice line); 01784 444215 (appointment line only)

Sutton
The Central Library, St Nicholas Way, Sutton, Surrey SM1 1EA
Tel: 020 8405 3552

Thornton Heath
Strand House, Zion Road, Thornton Heath, Surrey CR7 8RG
Tel: 020 8684 2236

Wallington
Carshalton & Wallington CAB, 68 Parkgate Road, Wallington, Surrey SM6 0AH
Tel: 020 8405 3552

Waverley
10 Queen Street, Godalming, Surrey GU7 1BD
Tel: 0844 848 7969

Woking
Provencial House, 26 Commercial Way, Woking, Surrey GU21 6EN
Tel: 0844 375 2975

Tyne & Wear

Gateshead
Davidson Building, Swan Street, Gateshead, Tyne & Wear NE8 1BG
Tel: . . . . . 0191 478 5100 (admin) 0344 245 1288

Washington
The Elms, 19 Front Street, Washington, Tyne & Wear NE37 2SW
Tel: 0191 416 6848

Warwickshire

Bedworth
25 Congreve Walk, Bedworth, Warwickshire CV12 8LX
Tel: 0844 855 2322
Email: . . . . info@brancab.org.uk

Rugby
1st Floor, Chestnut House, 32 North Street, Rugby, Warwickshire CV21 2AG
Tel: 08448552322
Email: . . . . adviser@brancab.org.uk

Stratford-upon-Avon
25 Meer Street, Stratford-upon-Avon, Warwickshire CV37 6QB
Tel: . 01789 293299 Advice; 01789 261966 Appts
Email: . . . . . enquiries@stratforduponavon.org.uk

Warwick District
10 Hamilton Terrace, Leamington Spa, Warwickshire CV32 4LY
Tel: 0844 855 2322

West Berkshire

Newbury
16 Bartholomew Street, Newbury, West Berkshire RG14 5LL
Tel: 08444 779980

West Midlands

Bilston
William Leigh House, 15 Walsall Street, Bilston, Wolverhampton, West Midlands WV14 0AT
Tel: 01902 572006

Birmingham
Ground Floor, Gazette Buildings, 168 Corporation Street, Birmingham, West Midlands B4 6TF
Tel: . . . . 0344 477 1010/ 0121 683 6900 (admin)

Brierley Hill
Brierley Hill Library, 122 High Street, Brierley Hill, West Midlands DY5 3ET
Tel: 01384 816222
Email: . . . . dudleybureau@dudleycabx.org

Coventry
Kirby House, Little Park Street, Coventry, West Midlands CV1 2JZ
Tel: 024 76223284

Cradley Heath
Cradley Heath Community Centre, Reddal Hill Road, Cradley Heath, West Midlands B64 5JG
Tel: 0121 500 2703

Dudley District (Halesowen)
Level 5 Halesowen Library, Queensway Mall, The Cornbow, Halesowen, West Midlands B63 4AZ
Tel: . . . . 03444 111 444/ 03444111445 (text)
Email: . . . . dudleybureau@dudleycabx.org

Dudley District (Stourbridge)
69 Market Street, Stourbridge, West Midlands DY8 1AQ
Tel: . . . . . . 03444 111 444/ 03444 111 445 (text)
Email: . . . . dudleybureau@dudleycabx.org

Handsworth
171 Churchill Parade, Birchfield Road, Handsworth, Birmingham, West Midlands B19 1LL
Tel: . . . . . . 08444 771010; 0121 687 5323 Admin

Kingstanding
Perry Common Library, College Road, Birmingham, West Midlands B44 0HH
Tel: . 08444 771010 (Info line) 10:00am - 3:00pm; 0121 244 1090 (Admin Office)

Low Hill
Ground Floor, Housing Office, Showell Circus, Wolverhampton, West Midlands WV10 9JL
Tel: 01902 572006

Northfield
Northfield Library, 77 Church Road, Northfield, Birmingham, West Midlands 31 2LB
Tel: . . 08444 771010 (Info 10am-3pm); 0121 687 5767 (Admin Office)

Oldbury
Municipal Buildings, Halesowen Street, Oldbury, Warley, West Midlands B69 2AB
Tel: 03444 111 444

Sandell (Smethwick)
370-372 High Street, Smethwick, Warley, West Midlands B66 3PJ
Tel: 0121 558 8500

Tipton
St Paul's Community Centre, Brick Kiln Street, Tipton, West Midlands DY4 9BP
Tel: 03444 111 444

Walsall
139-144 Lichfield Street, (opposite the Town Hall), Walsall, West Midlands WS1 1SE
Tel: . . . . 01922 700600 Advice Line
Email: . . advice@cab.walsall.org.uk/office@cab.walsall.org.uk

West Bromwich
22 Lombard Street, West Bromwich, West Midlands B70 8RT
Tel: 03444 111 444

Wolverhampton
26 Snow Hill, Wolverhampton, West Midlands WV2 4AD
Tel: 01902 572006

Yardley
Tyseley CAB, 744-746 Warwick Road, Tyseley, Birmingham, West Midlands B11 2HG
Tel: 03444 77 1010

West Sussex

Bognor Regis
Town Hall, Clarence Road, Bognor Regis, West Sussex PO21 1LD
Tel: 0844 477 1171
Email: ...... bureau@bognorcab.cabnet.org.uk

Burgess Hill
Delmon House, 38 Church Road, Burgess Hill, West Sussex RH15 9AE
Tel: 0844 477 1171

Chichester
Bell House, 6 Theatre Lane, Chichester, West Sussex PO19 1SR
Tel: 0844 477 1171

Crawley
The Orchard, 1-2 Gleneagles Court, Brighton Road, Southgate, Crawley, West Sussex RH10 6AD
Tel: 0844 477 1171

East Grinstead
Cantelupe House, Cantelupe Road, East Grinstead, West Sussex RH19 3BZ
Tel: 0844 477 1171

Haywards Heath
Oaklands, Paddockhall Road, Haywards Heath, West Sussex RH16 1HG
Tel: 0844 477 1171

Horsham
Lower Tanbridge Way, Horsham, West Sussex RH12 1PJ
Tel: 0844 477 1171
Email: .... advice@horshamcab.org.uk

Lancing and Sompting
Parish Hall, South Street, Lancing, West Sussex BN15 8AJ
Tel: 01903 755585; 01903 754194
Email: ...... bureau@lancingcab.cabnet.org.uk

Littlehampton
14-16 Anchor Springs, Littlehampton, West Sussex BN17 6BP
Tel: 0844 477 1171
Email: ..... enquiries@littlehampton-cab.org.uk

Shoreham-by-Sea
Pond Road, Shoreham-by-Sea, West Sussex BN43 5WU
Tel: 01273 453756

Worthing
11 North Street, Worthing, West Sussex BN11 1DU
Tel: 08448 487912
Email: .... contact@worthingcab.org

West Yorkshire

Batley
Town Hall Annexe, Brunswick Street, Batley, West Yorkshire WF17 5DT
Tel: 08448 487970

Chapeltown
Willow House, New Roscoe Buildings, Cross Francis Street, Chapeltown, Leeds, West Yorkshire LS7 4BZ
Tel: 0113 262 9479

Dewsbury
Units 5-6 Empire House, Wakefield Old Road, Dewsbury, West Yorkshire WF12 8DJ
Tel: 0844 848 7970

Elland
65/67 Southgate, Elland, West Yorkshire HX5 0DQ
Tel: 01422 842848

Halifax
37 Harrison Road, Halifax, West Yorkshire HX1 2AF
Tel: 01422 842848

Hebden Bridge
New Oxford House, Albert Street, Hebden Bridge, West Yorkshire HX7 8AH
Tel: 01422 842848

Huddersfield
2nd Floor, Standard House, Half Moon Street, Huddersfield, West Yorkshire HD1 2JF
Tel: .... 0844 848 7970 Advice
Email: .... bureau@skcab.org.uk

Keighley
The Library Annexe, Spencer Street, Keighley, West Yorkshire BD21 2BN
Tel: 0845 120 2909

Leeds
Central Office, 31 New York Street, Leeds, West Yorkshire LS2 7DT
Tel: 0844 477 4788

Otley
The Courthouse, Courthouse Street, Otley, West Yorkshire LS21 1BG
Tel: 0844 477 4788

Shipley
6 - 8 Windsor Road, Shipley, West Yorkshire BD18 3EQ
Tel: 0845 120 2909

Spen Valley
The Town Hall, Church Street, Cleckheaton, West Yorkshire BD19 3RH
Tel: 0844 848 7970

Todmorden
Tormorden Community College, Burnley Road, Todmorden, West Yorkshire OL14 7BX
Tel: ...... 01422 842848 Telephone Advice Line

Wiltshire

Chippenham
3 Avon Reach, Monkton Hill, Chippenham, Wiltshire SN15 1EE
Tel: 0845 120 3707

Kennet
New Park Street, Devizes, Wiltshire SN10 1DY
Tel: 0844 375 2775
Email: .... bureau.kennetcab@cabnet.org.uk

Salisbury and District
18 College Street, Salisbury, Wiltshire SP1 3AL
Tel: 0844 375 2775
Email: .... advice@cabsalisbury.org.uk

Swindon
Faringdon House, 1 Faringdon Road, Swindon, Wiltshire SN1 5AR
Tel: 0844 499 4114
Email: .... advice@swindon.cabnet.org.uk

Tidworth
The Community Centre, Wyle Road, Tidworth, Wiltshire SP9 7QQ
Tel: 01980 843377

Trowbridge
1 Mill Street, Trowbridge, Wiltshire BA14 8BE
Tel: 0844 375 2775

Wokingham

Wokingham
First Floor, 26-28 Market Place, Wokingham RG40 1AP
Tel: 0844 499 4126
Email: public@wokingham-cab.org.uk

Worcestershire

Bromsgrove and District
50-52 Birmingham Road, Bromsgrove, Worcestershire B61 0DD
Tel: 01527 831480; 01527 557397 (Housing advice only)

Evesham
116 High Street, Evesham, Worcestershire WR11 4EJ
Tel: 01386 443737
Email: enquiries@wychavoncab.cabnet.org.uk

Malvern Hills
The Grange, Grange Road, Malvern, Worcestershire WR14 3HA
Tel: 01684 563611
Email: bureau@malvernhills-cab.org.uk

Redditch
Suite E Cannon Newton House, Kingfisher Shopping Centre, Redditch, Worcestershire B97 4HA
Tel: 0844 415 2221

Worcester
The Hopmarket, The Foregate, Worcester, Worcestershire WR1 1DL
Tel: 01905 611371
Email: advice@worcestercab.cabnet.org.uk

Wyre Forest
21-23 New Road, Kidderminster, Worcestershire DY10 1AF
Tel: 01562 823953

NORTHERN IRELAND

Belfast

Falls
8 Springfield Road, Belfast BT12 7AG
Tel: 028 9050 3000
Email: fallscab@citizensadvice.co.uk

Co. Antrim

Antrim
10D High Street, Antrim, Co. Antrim BT41 1AN
Tel: 028 9442 8176
Email: antrimdistrictcab@citizensadvice.co.uk

Ballymena
28 Mount Street, Ballymena, Co. Antrim BT43 6BW
Tel: 028 2564 4398
Email: ballymenacab@citizensadvice.co.uk

Carrickfergus
65 North Street, Carrickfergus, Co. Antrim BT38 7AE
Tel: 028 9335 1808

Larne
Park Lodge, 49 Victoria Road, Riverdale, Larne, Co. Antrim BT40 1RT
Tel: 028 2826 0379

Lisburn
Bridge Community Centre, 50 Railway Street, Lisburn, Co. Antrim BT28 1XG
Tel: 028 9266 2251
Email: lisburncab@citizensadvice.co.uk

Rathcoole
Dunanney Centre, Rathmullan Drive, Rathcoole, Co. Antrim BT37 9DQ
Tel: 028 9085 2271; 028 9085 2400
Email: enewtownabbey@citizensadvice.co.uk

Co. Armagh

Armagh
9 McCrums Court, Armagh, Co. Armagh BT61 7RS
Tel: 028 3752 4041
Email: armaghcab@citizensadvice.co.uk

Craigavon District (Lurgan)
The Town Hall, 6 Union Street, Lurgan, Co. Armagh BT66 8DY
Tel: 028 3835 3260
Email: criagavondistrictcab@citizensadvice.co.uk

Co. Down

Ards
75 West Street, Newtownards, Co. Down BT23 4EN
Tel: 028 9182 3966
Email: ardscab@citizensadvice.co.uk

Banbridge
77 Bridge Street, Banbridge, Co. Down BT32 3JL
Tel: 028 4062 2201
Email: banbridgecab@citizensadvice.co.uk

Bangor
Hamilton House, 1a Springfield Avenue, Bangor, Co. Down BT20 5BY
Tel: 028 9127 0009

Down District
Maghinnis House, 8-10 Irish Street, Downpatrick, Co. Down BT30 6BP
Tel: 028 4461 4110; 028 4461 7907 Minicom
Email: downpatrickcab@citizensadvice.co.uk

Newry and Mourne District
Ballybot House, 28 Cornmarket, Newry, Co. Down BT35 8BG
Tel: 028 3026 2934
Email: newrycab@citizensadvice.co.uk

North Down (Holywood)
Queens Hall, Sullivan Place, Holywood, Co. Down BT18 9JF
Tel: 028 9042 8288
Email: northdowncab@citizensadvice.co.uk

Co. Londonderry

Causeway
24 Lodge Road, Coleraine, Co. Londonderry BT52 1NB
Tel: 028 7034 4817
Email: causewaycab@citizensadvice.co.uk

Londonderry
Embassy Court, 3 Strand Road, Londonderry, Co. Londonderry BT48 7BJ
Tel: 028 7136 2444
Email: lmanderrycab@citizensadvice.co.uk

Co. Tyrone

Dungannon
5-6 Feeneys Lane, Dungannon, Co. Tyrone BT70 1TX
Tel: 028 8772 5299
Email: . . . . dungannoncab@citizensadvice.co.uk

Strabane
17 Dock Street, Strabane, Co. Tyrone BT82 8EE
Tel: 028 7138 2665
Email: . . . . . . strabanecab@citizensadvice.co.uk

SCOTLAND

Aberdeen

Aberdeen
41 Union Street, Aberdeen AB11 5BN
Tel: 01224 586255
Email: . . bureau@aberdeencab.casonline.org.uk

Aberdeenshire

Banff and Buchan
Townhouse, Broad Street, Peterhead, Aberdeenshire AB42 1BY
Tel: 01779 471515
Email: . . . . bureau@banffcab.cabnet.org.uk

Angus

Arbroath
11 Millgate, Arbroath, Angus DD11 1NN
Tel: 01241 870661
Email: . . bureauarbroath@arbroathcab.casonline.org.uk

Forfar
19 Queen Street, Forfar, Angus DD8 3AJ
Tel: 01307 467096
Email: . . . . . . bureau@forfarcab.casonline.org.uk

Montrose
32 Castle Street, Montrose, Angus DD10 8AG
Tel: 01674 673263

Clackmannanshire

Alloa
47 Drysdale Street, Alloa, Clackmannanshire FK10 1JA
Tel: 01259 723880
Email: . . . . . . bureau@alloacab.casonline.org.uk

Dumfries & Galloway

Annan
19a Bank Street, Annan, Dumfries & Galloway DG12 6AA
Tel: 01461 201012
Email: . . . . . bureau@annancab.casonline.org.uk

Castle Douglas
3 St Andrew Street, Castle Douglas, Dumfries & Galloway DG7 1DE
Tel: 01556 502190
Email: . . . bureau@cdouglascab.casonline.org.uk

Dumfries
81-85 Irish Street, Dumfries, Dumfries & Galloway DG1 2PQ
Tel: 01387 252456
Email: . . . bureau@dumfriescab.casonline.org.uk

Stranraer
23 Lewis Street, Stranraer, Dumfries & Galloway DG9 7AB
Tel: 01776 706355
Email: . . . bureau@stranraercab.casonline.org.uk

Dundee

Dundee
Dundee Central Library, Level 4, Wellgate Centre, Dundee DD1 2DB
Tel: 01382 307494
Email: . . . . bureau@dundeecab.casonline.org.uk

East Ayrshire

Kilbirnie
43 Main Street, Kilbirnie, East Ayrshire KA25 7BX
Tel: 01505 682830
Email: . . . . bureau@kilbirniecab.casonline.org.uk

Kilmarnock
3 John Dickie Street, Kilmarnock, East Ayrshire KA1 1HW
Tel: 01563 544744

East Lothian

Haddington
46 Court Street, Haddington, East Lothian EH41 3NP
Tel: 01620 824471
Email: . . . . cab@haddingtoncab.casonline.org.uk

Musselburgh
141 High Street, Musselburgh, East Lothian EH21 7DD
Tel: 0131 653 2748; 0131 653 2544
Email: bureau@musselburghcab.casonline.org.uk

Edinburgh

Edinburgh
58 Dundas Street, Edinburgh EH3 6QZ
Tel: . . . . 0131 558 3681/ 0131 558 1500 (advice)

Gorgie / Dalry
Fountainbridge Library, 137 Dundee Street, Edinburgh EH11 1BG
Tel: . . . . . 0131 474 8080 Advice; 0131 558 3681 Appointments
Email: . gorgiedalry@citizensadviceedinburgh.co.uk

Leith
12 Bernard Street, Leith, Edinburgh EH6 6PP
Tel: 0131 554 8144
Email: . . . . . leith@citizensadviceedinburgh.co.uk

Pilton
661 Ferry Road, Pilton, Edinburgh EH4 2TX
Tel: 0131 202 1153
Email: . . . . pilton@citizensadviceedinburgh.co.uk

Falkirk

Denny
24 Duke Street, Denny, Falkirk FK6 6DD
Tel: 01324 823118; 01324 825333

Grangemouth and Bo'ness
1 Kerse Road, Grangemouth, Falkirk FK3 8HW
Tel: 01324 483467
Email: . bureau@grangemouthcab.casonline.org.uk

Glasgow

Bridgeton
35 Main Street, Glasgow G40 1QB
Tel: 0141 554 0336

Castlemilk
27 Dougrie Drive, Castlemilk, Glasgow G45 9AD
Tel: 0141 634 0338
Email: . . . . . . bureau@cmilkcab.casonline.org.uk

Drumchapel
195c Drumry Road East, Drumchapel, Glasgow G15 8NS
Tel: . . . . . 0141 944 0205 Advice; 0141 944 2612
Email: . bureau@drumchapelcab.casonline.org.uk

East Renfrewshire
216 Main Street, Barrhead, Glasgow G78 1SN
Tel: 0141 881 2032
Email: . . bureau@eastrenfrewshirecab.casonline.org.uk

Easterhouse
46 Shandwick Square, Easterhouse, Glasgow G34 9DT
Tel: . . . . . 0141 771 2328 Advice; 0141 773 1349
Email: . . adminuser@easterhousecab.casonline.org.uk

Maryhill
25 Avenuepark Street, Glasgow G20 8TS
Tel: 0141 946 6373
Email: . . . . bureau@maryhillcab.casonline.org.uk

Parkhead
1361-1363 Gallowgate, Parkhead, Glasgow G31 4DN
Tel: 0141 554 0004
Email: . . . . info@parkheadcab.org.uk

Highland

Inverness
103 Academy Street, Inverness, Highland IV1 1LX
Tel: 01463 237664

Lochaber
Dudley Road, Fort William, Highland PH33 6JB
Tel: 01397 705311

Nairn
6 High Street, Nairn, Highland IV12 4BJ
Tel: 01667 456677
Email: . . . . . . bureau@nairncab.casonline.org.uk

Ross and Cromarty
'Balallan', 4 Novar Road, Ross-shire, Alness, Highland IV17 0QG
Tel: 01349 883333
Email: . . . . adviser@alnesscab.casonline.org.uk

Thurso
7a Brabster Street, Thurso, Caithness, Highland KW14 7AP
Tel: 01847 894243; 01847 896796
Email: . . . . bureau@cnesscab.cabnet.org.uk

Midlothian

Dalkeith
8 Buccleuch Street, Dalkeith, Midlothian EH22 1HA
Tel: 0131 663 3688
Email: . . . . bureau@dalkeithcab.casonline.org.uk

Penicuik
14a John Street, Penicuik, Midlothian EH26 8AB
Tel: 01968 675259

Moray

Elgin
30-32 Batchen Street, Elgin, Moray IV30 1BH
Tel: 01343 550088
Email: . . . . . bureau@moraycab.casonline.org.uk

North Ayrshire

Arran
Park Terrace, Lamlash, Isle of Arran, North Ayrshire KA27 8NB
Tel: 01770 600210
Email: . . . . . . bureau@arrancab.casonline.org.uk

Largs
36 Boyd Street, Largs, North Ayrshire KA30 8LE
Tel: 01475 673586
Email: . . . . . . bureau@largscab.casonline.org.uk

North Ayrshire
The Three Towns Centre for Enterprise, Moffat House, 12-14 Nineyard Street, Saltcoats, North Ayrshire KA21 5HS
Tel: 01294 467848
Email: . . . bureau@saltcoatscab.casonline.org.uk

Saltcoats
18-20 Countess Street, Saltcoats, North Ayrshire KA21 5HW
Tel: 01294 602328

North Lanarkshire

Airdrie
Resource Centre, 14 Anderson Street, Airdrie, North Lanarkshire ML6 0AA
Tel: 01236 754109
Email: . . . . . advice@airdriecab.casonline.org.uk

Bellshill
6 Hamilton Road, Bellshill, North Lanarkshire ML4 1AQ
Tel: 01698 748615
Email: . . . manager@bellshillcab.casonline.org.uk

Coatbridge
Unit 10, Fountain Business Centre, Ellis Street, Coatbridge, North Lanarkshire ML5 3AA
Tel: 01236 421447; 01236 421448
Email: . adviser@coatbridgecab.casonline.org.uk

Cumbernauld
2 Annan House, 3rd Floor, Town Centre, Cumbernauld, North Lanarkshire G67 1DP
Tel: 01236 723201
Email: bureau@cumbernauldcab.casonline.org.uk

Motherwell and Wishaw
32 Civic Square, Motherwell, North Lanarkshire ML1 1TP
Tel: 01698 259389; 01698 251981
Email: bureau2@motherwellcab.casonline.org.uk

Orkney Islands

Orkney
Anchor Buildings, 6 Bridge Street, Kirkwall, Orkney Islands KW15 1HR
Tel: 01856 875266

Perth & Kinross

Perth
4-12 New Row, Perth, Perth & Kinross PH1 5QB
Tel: . 01738 624301 Advice; 01738 564304 Appts
Email: karencampbell@perthcab.casonline.org.uk

Renfrewshire

Paisley
45 George Street, Paisley, Renfrewshire PA1 2JY
Tel: 0141 889 2121
Email: . . . . bureau@paisleycab.casonline.org.uk

Scottish Borders

Galashiels
111 High Street, Galashiels, Scottish Borders TD1 1RZ
Tel: 01896 753889
Email: bureau@centralborderscab.casonline.org.uk

Hawick
1 Towerdykesside, Hawick, Scottish Borders TD9 9EA
Tel: 01450 374266
Email: . enquiries@roxburghcab.casonline.org.uk

Peebles
42 Old Town, Peebles, Scottish Borders EH45 8JF
Tel: 01721 721722
Email: . . manager@peeblescab.casonline.org.uk

Shetland Islands

Lerwick
Market House, 14 Market Street, Lerwick, Shetland Islands ZE1 0JP
Tel: 01595 694696
Email: . . . . sicab@zetnet.co.uk

South Lanarkshire

Clydesdale
10-12 Wide Close, Lanark, South Lanarkshire ML11 7LX
Tel: 01555 664301
Email: . . advice@clydesdalecab.casonline.org.uk

East Kilbride
9 Olympia Way, Town Centre, East Kilbride, South Lanarkshire G74 1JT
Tel: 01355 263698
Email: . . . . . bureau@ekilbridecab.cabnet.org,uk

Hamilton
Almada Tower, 67 Almada Street, Hamilton, South Lanarkshire ML3 0HQ
Tel: 01698 283477

Stirling

Stirling
The Norman MacEwan Centre, Cameronian Street, Stirling FK8 2DX
Tel: 01786 470239
Email: sessionsupervisor@sterlingcab.casonline.org.uk

West Dunbartonshire

Dumbarton
Bridgend House, 179 High Street, Dumbarton, West Dunbartonshire G82 1NW
Tel: 01389 744690
Email: . . . . info@dumbartoncab.co.uk

West Lothian

West Lothian
Suite 7, Shiel House, Craigshill, Livingston, West Lothian EH54 5EH
Tel: . . . . 01506 432977 Advice Lines
Email: . . . . enquiries@cabwestlothian.org.uk

Western Isles

Barra
Castlebay, Isle of Barra, Western Isles HS9 5XD
Tel: 01871 810608
Email: . . . . . . bureau@barracab.casonline.org.uk

Harris
Pier Road, Tarbert, Isle of Harris, Western Isles HS3 3BG
Tel: 01859 502431
Email: . . . . bureau@harriscab.cabnet.org.uk

Lewis
41-43 Westview Terrace, Stornoway, Isle of Lewis, Western Isles HS1 2HP
Tel: 01851 705727
Email: . . . . . . bureau@lewiscab.casonline.org.uk

Uist
45 Winfield Way, Balivanich, Isle of Benbecula, Western Isles HS7 5LH
Tel: 01870 602421
Email: . . . . bureau@uistcab.casonline.org.uk

WALES

Anglesey

Canolfan Cynghori Ynys Mon
6 Victoria Terrace, Holyhead, Anglesey LL65 1UT
Tel: 0844 477 2020

Blaenau Gwent

Blaina
High Street, Blaina, Blaenau Gwent NP13 3AN
Tel: 01495 292659

Bridgend

Bridgend
Ground Floor, 26 Dunraven Place, Bridgend CF31 1JD
Tel: 0844 477 2020

Maesteg
Council Offices, Talbot Street, Maesteg, Bridgend CF34 9BY
Tel: 0844 477 2020

Caerphilly

Bargoed
41b Hanbury Road, Bargoed, Caerphilly CF81 8QU
Tel: 0844 477 2020

Caerphilly
2B De Clare House, 5 Alfred Owen Way, Pontygwindy Industrial Estate, Caerphilly CF83 2WB
Tel: 0844 477 2020

Carmarthenshire

Ammanford
14 Iscennen Road, Ammanford, Carmarthenshire SA18 3BG
Tel: 01269 590721

Carmarthen
113 Lammas Street, Carmarthen, Carmarthenshire SA31 3AP
Tel: 01267 234488

Llanelli
4a Cowell Street, Llanelli, Carmarthenshire SA15 1UU
Tel: 0844 477 2020

Ceredigion

Aberystwyth
12 Cambrian Place, Aberystwyth, Ceredigion SY23 1NT
Tel: 01970 612817

Cardigan
Napier Street, Cardigan, Ceredigion SA43 1ED
Tel: 01239 613707
Email: ... enquiries@cardigancab.cabnet.org.uk

Conwy

Clych Conwy District
7 South Parade, Llandudno, Conwy LL30 2LN
Tel: 0844 477 2020

Denbighshire

Denbigh
23 High Street, Denbigh, Denbighshire LL16 3HY
Tel: 01745 814336

Llangollen
37 Hall Street, Llangollen, Denbighshire LL20 8EP
Tel: 01978 860983

Rhyl
11 Water Street, Rhyl, Denbighshire LL18 1SP
Tel: 01745 334568

Ruthin
The Old Fire Station, Market Street, Ruthin, Denbighshire LL15 1BE
Tel: 01824 703483

Flintshire

Holywell
The Old Library, Post Office Lane, Holywell, Flintshire CH8 7LH
Tel: 01352 711262

Mold
The Annexe Terrig House, Chester Street, Mold, Flintshire CH7 1EG
Tel: 01352 753520

Merthyr Tydfil

Merthyr Tydfil
Tramroadside North, Merthyr Tydfil CF47 0AP
Tel: 01685 379997; 01685 382188

Monmouthshire

Abergavenny
26a Monk Street, Abergavenny, Monmouthshire NP7 5NP
Tel: .. 08444 772020; 01873 735867 Admin Line
Email: .... abergavennycab@yahoo.co.uk

Chepstow
The Gate House, High Street, Chepstow, Monmouthshire NP16 5LH
Tel: 0844 477 2020

Monmouth
23a Whitecross Street, Monmouth, Monmouthshire NP25 3BY
Tel: 0844 477 2020

Neath Port Talbot

Neath
44 Alfred Street, Neath, Neath Port Talbot SA11 1EH
Tel: 0844 477 2020

Port Talbot
36 Forge Road, Port Talbot, Neath Port Talbot SA13 1NU
Tel: 0844 477 2020

Newport

Newport
8 Corn Street, Newport NP20 1DJ
Tel: 0844 477 2020

Risca
Park Road, Risca, Newport NP11 6BJ
Tel: 0844 477 2020

Pembrokeshire

Haverfordwest
43 Cartlett, Haverfordwest, Pembrokeshire SA61 2LH
Tel: 0844 477 2020
Email: .... hwestcab@yahoo.com

Powys

Brecon
11 Glamorgan Street, Brecon, Powys LD3 7DW
Tel: 0845 601 8421

Newtown
Ladywell House, Frolic Street Entrance, Park Street, Newtown, Powys SY16 1QS
Tel: 01686 624390
Email: .... montycab@powys.org.uk

Ystradgynlais
Welfare Hall, Brecon Road, Ystradgynlais, Powys SA9 1JJ
Tel: 0845 601 8421

Rhondda Cynon Taff

Cynon Valley
Old Library, Duffryn Road, Mountain Ash, Rhondda Cynon Taff CF45 4DA
Tel: ...... 08444772020; 08444 772020 Advice
Email: .... cynonvalleycab@talk21.com

Rhondda Taff
5 Gelliwastad Road, Pontypridd, Rhondda Cynon Taff CF37 2BP
Tel: 0844 477 2020

Swansea

SWANSEA CITIZENS ADVICE BUREAU
Llys Glas, Pleasant Street, Swansea SA1 5DS
Tel: 01792 474882
Email: .... enquiries@swanseacab.org.uk

Torfaen

Cwmbran
21 Caradoc Road, Cwmbran, Torfaen NP44 1PP
Tel: 01633 482464

Vale of Glamorgan

Barry
119 Broad Street, Barry, Vale of Glamorgan CF62 7TZ
Tel: 0844 477 2020

Wrexham

Wrexham
35 Grosvenor Road, Wrexham LL11 1BT
Tel: 01978 364639

HOSPICE SERVICES

This section comprises selected hospices/palliative care in-patient services in the UK. Hospice or palliative care may also be provided at home (with support from specially trained staff), in a hospital or at a hospice day centre. A full list, together with other useful information, is published in the Hospice and Palliative Care Directory available from Hospice UK, who can be reached at:
Hospice House, 34 – 44 Britannia Street, London WC1X 9JG
Tel: 020 7520 8200
Email: info@hospiceuk.org
Web: www.hospiceuk.org

THAMES HOSPICE
Pine Lodge, Hatch Lane, Windsor, Berkshire SL4 3RW
Tel: 01753 842121
Email: .... contact@thameshospice.org.uk

CHANNEL ISLANDS

Guernsey

LES BOURGS HOSPICE
Andrew Mitchell House, Rue de Tertre, St Andrew's, Guernsey GY6 8SF
Tel: 01481 251111
Email: .... info@lesbourgs.com

Jersey

JERSEY HOSPICE CARE
Clarkson House, Mont Cochon, St Helier, Jersey JE2 3JB
Tel: 01534 876555
Email: .. administration@jerseyhospicecare.com

ENGLAND

Bedfordshire

KEECH HOSPICE CARE
Great Bramingham Lane, Streatley, Luton, Bedfordshire LU3 3NT
Tel: 01582 492339
Email: .... info@keech.org.uk

SUE RYDER - ST JOHN'S HOSPICE
St John's, Moggerhanger, Bedford, Bedfordshire MK44 3RJ
Tel: 01767 640622

Blackpool

TRINITY - THE HOSPICE IN THE FYLDE
Low Moor Road, Bispham, Blackpool FY2 0BG
Tel: 01253 358881
Email: ..... trinity.enquiries@trinityhospice.co.uk

Brighton & Hove

MARTLETS HOSPICE
Wayfield Avenue, Hove, Brighton & Hove BN3 7LW
Tel: 01273 273400

THE SUSSEX BEACON
Bevendean Road, Brighton, Brighton & Hove BN2 4DE
Tel: 01273 694222

Bristol

BRISTOL HAEMATOLOGY & ONCOLOGY CENTRE
Horfield Road, Bristol BS2 8ED
Tel: 0117 342 2416

Buckinghamshire

WILLEN HOSPICE
Willen Village, Milton Road, Milton Keynes, Buckinghamshire MK15 9AB
Tel: 01908 663636

Cambridgeshire

EAST ANGLIA'S CHILDREN'S HOSPICES
42 High Street, Milton, Cambridge, Cambridgeshire CB24 6DF
Tel: 01223 205180

Cheshire

EAST CHESHIRE HOSPICE
Millbank Drive, Macclesfield, Cheshire SK10 3DR
Tel: 01625 610364
Email: .... admin@echospice.org.uk

HALTON HAVEN HOSPICE
Barnfield Avenue, Murdishaw, Runcorn, Cheshire WA7 6EP
Tel: 01928 712728

HOSPICE OF THE GOOD SHEPHERD
Gordon Lane, Backford, Chester, Cheshire CH2 4DG
Tel: . 01244 851091; 01244 851811 (Fundraising)

ST LUKE'S (CHESHIRE) HOSPICE
Grosvenor House, Queensway, Winsford, Cheshire CW7 4AW
Tel: 01606 551246
Email: .... enquiries@stlukes-hospice.co.uk

ST ROCCO'S HOSPICE
Lockton Lane, Bewsey, Warrington, Cheshire WA5 0BW
Tel: 01925 575780
Email: .... enquiries@stroccos.org.uk

Co. Durham

WILLOW BURN HOSPICE
Maidenlaw Hospital, Lanchester, Co. Durham DH7 0QS
Tel: 01207 529224
Email: .... enquiries@willowburn.co.uk

Cornwall

MOUNT EDGCUMBE HOSPICE
Porthpean Road, St Austell, Cornwall PL26 6AB
Tel: 01726 65711

Cumbria

EDEN VALLEY HOSPICE
Durdar Road, Carlisle, Cumbria CA2 4SD
Tel: 01228 810801

ENNERDALE PALLIATIVE CARE UNIT
Dalegarth Ward, West Cumberland Hospital, Whitehaven, Cumbria CA28 8JG
Tel: .... 01946 693181 ext. 4058

HOSPICE AT HOME WEST CUMBRIA
Workington Community Hospital, Park Lane, Workington, Cumbria CA14 2RW
Tel: 01900 705200
Email: . info@hospiceathomewestcumbria.org.uk

Derbyshire

ASHGATE HOSPICE
Ashgate Road, Old Brampton, Chesterfield, Derbyshire S42 7JE
Tel: 01246 568801
Email: .... info@ashgatehospice.nhs.uk

Devon

HOSPISCARE
Dryden Road, Exeter, Devon EX2 5JJ
Tel: 01392 688000

ROWCROFT HOSPICE
Rowcroft House, Avenue Road, Torquay, Devon TQ2 5LS
Tel: 01803 210800
Email: .. rachael.bryett@rowcroft-hospice.org.uk

Dorset

JOSEPH WELD HOSPICE
Herringston Road, Dorchester, Dorset DT1 2SL
Tel: 01305 215300

East Sussex

ST MICHAEL'S HOSPICE
25 Upper Maze Hill, St Leonards-on-Sea, East Sussex TN38 0LB
Tel: 01424 445177
Email: .... info@stmichaelshospice.co.uk

ST PETER & ST JAMES HOSPICE AND CONTINUING CARE CENTRE
North Chailey, North Common Road, North Chailey, Lewes, East Sussex BN8 4ED
Tel: 01444 471598
Email: .... enquiries@stpeter-stjames.org.uk

ST WILFRID'S HOSPICE
2-4 Mill Gap Road, Eastbourne, East Sussex BN21 2HJ
Tel: 01323 644500
Email: .... hospice@stwhospice.org

Essex

FAIR HAVENS HOSPICE
124-126 Chalkwell Avenue, Westcliff-on-Sea, Essex SS0 8HN
Tel: 01702 220350
Email: .... cwood@havenhospices.org.uk

FARLEIGH HOSPICE
Farleigh Hospice, North Court Road, Chelmsford, Essex CM1 7FH
Tel: 01245 457300
Email: .... info@farleighhospice.org

HAVENS HOSPICES, INCORPORATES FAIR HAVENS HOSPICE AND LITTLE HAVENS HOSPICE
47 Second Avenue, Westcliff-on-Sea, Essex SS0 8HX
Tel: 01702 220350
Email: .... sseiffert@havenshospices.org.uk

ST FRANCIS HOSPICE
The Hall, Havering-Atte-Bower, Romford, Essex RM4 1QH
Tel: 01708 753319
Email: .... fundraising@sfh.org.uk

ST HELENA HOSPICE
Barncroft Close, Highwoods, Colchester, Essex CO4 9JU
Tel: 01206 845566
Email: ...... enquiries@sthelenahospice.org.uk

ST LUKE'S HOSPICE (BASILDON AND DISTRICT) LIMITED
Fobbing Farm, Nethermayne, Basildon, Essex SS16 5NJ
Tel: 01268 524973
Email: ..... careservices@stlukeshospice.co.uk

Gloucestershire

SUE RYDER - LECKHAMPTON COURT HOSPICE
Leckhampton Court, Church Road, Leckhampton, Cheltenham, Gloucestershire GL53 0QJ
Tel: 01242 230199

Greater Manchester

BEECHWOOD CANCER CARE CENTRE
Chelford Grove, Stockport, Greater Manchester SK3 8LS
Tel: 0161 476 0384
Email: . enquiries@beechwoodcancercarecentre.co.uk

BOLTON HOSPICE
Queens Park Street, Bolton, Greater Manchester BL1 4QT
Tel: 01204 663066
Email: .... admin@boltonhospice.org

BURY HOSPICE
Dumers Lane, Radcliffe, Manchester, Greater Manchester M26 2QD
Tel: 0161 725 9800

DR KERSHAW'S HOSPICE
Turf Lane, Royton, Oldham, Greater Manchester OL2 6EU
Tel: 0161 624 2727
Email: ..... appeals@drkershawshospice.org.uk

FRANCIS HOUSE CHILDREN'S HOSPICE
390 Parrswood Road, East Didsbury, Manchester, Greater Manchester M20 5NA
Tel: 0161 434 4118

SPRINGHILL HOSPICE
Broad Lane, Rochdale, Greater Manchester OL16 4PZ
Tel: 01706 649920
Email: .... info@springhill.org.uk

ST ANN'S HOSPICE, HEALD GREEN
St Ann's Road North, Heald Green, Cheadle, Greater Manchester SK8 3SZ
Tel: 0161 437 8136

WIGAN & LEIGH HOSPICE
Kildare Street, Hindley, Wigan, Greater Manchester WN2 3HZ
Tel: 01942 525566
Email: .... enquiries@wlh.org.uk

Hampshire

COUNTESS OF BRECKNOCK HOUSE, WAR MEMORIAL HOSPITAL
Charlton Road, Andover, Hampshire SP10 3LB
Tel: 01264 835288
Email: . info@countessofbrecknockhospice.co.uk

OAKHAVEN HOSPICE TRUST
Oakhaven Hospice (CD), Lower Pennington Lane, Lymington, Hampshire SO41 8ZZ
Tel: 01590 670346
Email: .... mike@oakhavenhospice.co.uk

THE ROWANS HOSPICE
Purbrook Heath Road, Purbrook, Waterlooville, Hampshire PO7 5RU
Tel: 023 9225 0001
Email: .... info@rowanshospice.co.uk

ST MICHAEL'S HOSPICE (NORTH HAMPSHIRE)
Basil de Ferranti House, Aldermaston Road, Basingstoke, Hampshire RG24 9NB
Tel: 01256 844744
Email: .... info@stmichaelshospice.org.uk

Hartlepool

HARTLEPOOL AND DISTRICT HOSPICE
Alice House, Wells Avenue, Hartlepool TS24 9DA
Tel: 01429 855555

Herefordshire

ST MICHAEL'S HOSPICE (INCORPORATING THE FREDA PEARCE FOUNDATION)
Bartestree, Hereford, Herefordshire HR1 4HA
Tel: 01432 851000
Email: . rshackelford@st-michaels-hospice.org.uk

Hertfordshire

HOSPICE OF ST FRANCIS
Spring Garden Lane, Off Shooters way, Northchurch, Berkhamsted, Hertfordshire HP4 3GW
Tel: 01442 869550; 01442 869555
Email: .... admin@stfrancis.org.uk

Isle of Wight

EARL MOUNTBATTEN HOSPICE
Halberry Lane, Newport, Isle of Wight PO30 2ER
Tel: 01983 528989

Kent

ELLENORLIONS HOSPICES, NORTHFLEET
Coldharbour Road, Northfleet, Gravesend, Kent DA11 7HQ
Tel: 01474 320007

PILGRIMS HOSPICE IN CANTERBURY
56 London Road, Canterbury, Kent CT2 8JA
Tel: 01227 459700

PILGRIMS HOSPICE IN THANET
Ramsgate Road, Margate, Kent CT9 4AD
Tel: 01843 233920

WISDOM HOSPICE
High Bank, Rochester, Kent ME1 2NU
Tel: 01634 830456

Lancashire

DERIAN HOUSE CHILDREN'S HOSPICE
Chancery Road, Astley Village, Chorley, Lancashire PR7 1DH
Tel: 01257 271271
Email: .... info@derianhouse.co.uk

ST CATHERINE'S HOSPICE (PRESTON)
Lostock Hall, Lostock Lane, Preston, Lancashire PR5 5XU
Tel: 01772 629171
Email: .... admin@stcatherines.co.uk

ST JOHN'S HOSPICE
Slyne Road, Lancaster, Lancashire LA2 6ST
Tel: 01524 382538
Email: .... ask@sjhospice.org.uk

Leicestershire

LOROS (LEICESTERSHIRE & RUTLAND HOSPICE)
Groby Road, Leicester, Leicestershire LE3 9QE
Tel: 0116 231 3771
Email: .... administration@loros.co.uk

RAINBOWS CHILDREN'S HOSPICE
Lark Rise, Loughborough, Leicestershire LE11 2HS
Tel: 01509 638000
Email: .... administration@rainbows.co.uk

Lincolnshire

ST BARNABAS HOSPICE
36 Nettleham Road, Lincoln, Lincolnshire LN2 1RE
Tel: 01522 511566

London

GREENWICH & BEXLEY COMMUNITY HOSPICE
185 Bostall Hill, Abbey Wood, London SE2 0GB
Tel: 020 8312 2244
Email: .... kateheaps@gbch.org.uk

LONDON LIGHTHOUSE
111-117 Lancaster Road, Ladbroke Grove, London W11 1QT
Tel: 020 7313 2900
Email: info.ladbrokegrove@tht.org.uk

MARIE CURIE HOSPICE, HAMPSTEAD
11 Lyndhurst Gardens, Hampstead, London NW3 5NS
Tel: 020 7853 3400
Email: info@mariecurie.org.uk

MILDMAY HOSPITAL UK
Spencer House, Austin Street, London E2 7NB
Tel: 020 7613 6300
Email: comms@mildmay.org

NORTH LONDON HOSPICE
47 Woodside Avenue, North Finchley, London N12 8TF
Tel: 020 8343 8841
Email: nlh@northlondonhospice.co.uk

RICHARD HOUSE CHILDREN'S HOSPICE
Richard House Drive, Beckton, London E16 3RG
Tel: 020 7540 0200
Email: info@richardhouse.org.uk

ST CHRISTOPHER'S HOSPICE
51-59 Lawrie Park Road, Sydenham, London SE26 6DZ
Tel: 020 8768 4500
Email: info@stchristophers.org.uk

ST JOHN'S HOSPICE
Hospital of St John & St Elizabeth, 60 Grove End Road, St John's Wood, London NW8 9NH
Tel: 020 7806 4040

ST JOSEPH'S HOSPICE
Mare Street, Hackney, London E8 4SA
Tel: 020 8525 6000
Email: info@stjh.org.uk

TRINITY HOSPICE
30 Clapham Common North Side, Clapham, London SW4 0RN
Tel: 020 7787 1000
Email: enquiries@trinityhospice.org.uk

Merseyside

MARIE CURIE HOSPICE, LIVERPOOL
Speke Road, Woolton, Liverpool, Merseyside L25 8QA
Tel: 0151 801 1400
Email: info@mariecurie.org.uk

QUEENSCOURT HOSPICE
Town Lane, Southport, Merseyside PR8 6RE
Tel: 01704 544645
Fax: 01704 549622
Email: fundraising@queenscourt.org.uk
Queenscourt Hospice provides care for the people of Southport, Formby and West Lancashire. We care for patients with serious illnesses, enabling them to achieve the best possible quality of life at each new stage in the Hospice and at Home through our In-Patient unit, Queenscourt Connect and Queenscourt at Home services.

ST JOHN'S HOSPICE IN WIRRAL
Mount Road, Bebington, Merseyside CH63 6JE
Tel: 0151 334 2778
Email: info@wirralhospice.org

ST JOSEPH'S HOSPICE ASSOCIATION (JOSPICE INTERNATIONAL)
Ince Road, Thornton, Liverpool, Merseyside L23 4UE
Tel: 0151 924 3812
Email: enquiries@jospice.org.uk

Norfolk

EAST ANGLIA'S CHILDREN'S HOSPICES
Quidenham, Norwich, Norfolk NR16 2PH
Tel: 01953 888603/4

North East Lincolnshire

ST ANDREW'S HOSPICE
Peaks Lane, Grimsby, North East Lincolnshire DN32 9RP
Tel: 01472 350908

North Yorkshire

SAINT MICHAEL'S HOSPICE
Crimple House, Hornbeam Park Avenue, Harrogate, North Yorkshire HG2 8QL
Tel: 01423 879687

ST CATHERINE'S HOSPICE
Throxenby Lane, Scarborough, North Yorkshire YO12 5RE
Tel: 01723 351421
Email: general@st-catherineshospice.org.uk

ST LEONARD'S HOSPICE
185 Tadcaster Road, York, North Yorkshire YO24 1GL
Tel: 01904 708553
Email: enquiries@stleonardshospice.org.uk

TEESSIDE HOSPICE CARE FOUNDATION
1a Northgate Road, Linthorpe, Middlesbrough, North Yorkshire TS5 5NW
Tel: 01642 811060
Email: marketing@teessidehospice.co.uk

Nottinghamshire

BEAUMOND HOUSE COMMUNITY HOSPICE
32 London Road, Newark, Nottinghamshire NG24 1TW
Tel: 01636 610556
Email: info@beaumondhouse.co.uk

JOHN EASTWOOD HOSPICE
Mansfield Road, Sutton-in-Ashfield, Nottinghamshire NG17 4HJ
Tel: 01623 622626

Oxfordshire

HELEN & DOUGLAS HOUSE

Helen & Douglas House
HOSPICE CARE FOR CHILDREN AND YOUNG ADULTS

14a Magdalen Road, Oxford, Oxfordshire OX4 1RW
Tel: 01865 799150
Fax: 01865 202702
Email: . . . admin@helenanddouglas.org.uk
Web: . . . . . . www.helenanddouglas.org.uk
Our mission is to enable young people with life shortening conditions to live as well and fully as possible. We provide specialist level palliative care through medical and nursing expertise, emotional and practical support.
We have to raise 88% of the funds we need; so whether your gift is large or small, it will make a difference and help to ensure that we can be here for families both now and in the future.

KATHARINE HOUSE HOSPICE
East End, Adderbury, Banbury, Oxfordshire OX17 3NL
Tel: 01295 811866
Email: . . . . general@khh.org.uk

SUE RYDER - NETTLEBED HOSPICE
Nettlebed, Henley-on-Thames, Oxfordshire RG9 5DF
Tel: 01491 641384

Shropshire

SEVERN HOSPICE
Bicton Heath, Shrewsbury, Shropshire SY3 8HS
Tel: 01743 236565
Email: . . . . admin@severnhospice.org.uk

South Yorkshire

ST JOHN'S HOSPICE
Weston Road, Balby, Doncaster, South Yorkshire DN4 8JS
Tel: 01302 796666

ST LUKES HOSPICE
Little Common Lane, off Abbey Lane, Sheffield, South Yorkshire S11 9NE
Tel: 0114 236 9911

Staffordshire

ST GILES HOSPICE
Fisherwick Road, Whittington, Lichfield, Staffordshire WS14 9LH
Tel: 01543 432031
Email: . . . . enquiries@st-giles-hospice.org.uk

Stockton-on-Tees

BUTTERWICK HOSPICE CARE
Middlefield Road, Stockton-on-Tees TS19 8XN
Tel: 01642 607742

Suffolk

ST ELIZABETH HOSPICE
565 Foxhall Road, Ipswich, Suffolk IP3 8LX
Tel: 01473 727776
Email: . . . . enquiries@stelizabethhospice.org.uk

ST NICHOLAS HOSPICE CARE
Hardwick Lane, Bury St Edmunds, Suffolk IP33 2QY
Tel: 01284 766133
Email: . . . . enquiries@stnh.org.uk

Surrey

PRINCESS ALICE HOSPICE
West End Lane, Esher, Surrey KT10 8NA
Tel: 01372 468811
Email: . . . . enquiries@pah.org.uk

ST RAPHAEL'S HOSPICE
London Road, North Cheam, Surrey SM3 9DX
Tel: 020 8335 4575
Email: . . . . enquiries@straphaels.org.uk

Tyne & Wear

MARIE CURIE HOSPICE, NEWCASTLE
Marie Curie Drive, Newcastle upon Tyne, Tyne & Wear NE4 6SS
Tel: 0191 219 1000
Email: . . . . info@mariecurie.org

ST BENEDICT'S HOSPICE
Monkwearmouth Hospital, Newcastle Road, Sunderland, Tyne & Wear SR5 1NB
Tel: 0191 569 9192

ST CLARE'S HOSPICE (JARROW)
Primrose Terrace, Jarrow, Tyne & Wear NE32 5HA
Tel: 0191 529 7100
Email: . . . . . . fundraising@stclareshospice.co.uk

ST OSWALD'S HOSPICE
Regent Avenue, Gosforth, Newcastle upon Tyne, Tyne & Wear NE3 1EE
Tel: 0191 285 0063

Warwickshire

THE MYTON HOSPICES
Myton Lane, Myton Road, Warwick, Warwickshire CV34 6PX
Tel: 01926 492518
Email: . . . . enquiry@mytonhospice.org

West Midlands

ACORNS CHILDREN'S HOSPICE TRUST
103 Oak Tree Lane, Selly Oak, Birmingham, West Midlands B29 6HZ
Tel: 0121 248 4850

ACORNS WALSALL
Walstead Road, Walsall, Birmingham, West Midlands WS5 4LZ
Tel: 01922 422500

COMPTON HOSPICE
39 Compton West Street, Wolverhampton, West Midlands WV3 9DW
Tel: 0845 225 5497
Email: . . . . admin@comptonhospice.org.uk

JOHN TAYLOR HOSPICE
76 Grange Road, Erdington, Birmingham, West Midlands B24 0DF
Tel: 0121 465 2000
Email: . . . . . . enquiries@jhntaylorhospice.org.uk

MARIE CURIE HOSPICE, SOLIHULL
911-913 Warwick Road, Solihull, West Midlands B91 3ER
Tel: 0121 254 7800
Email: . . . . info@mariecurie.org.uk

ST MARY'S HOSPICE
176 Raddlebarn Road, Selly Park, Birmingham, West Midlands B29 7DA
Tel: 0121 472 1191
Email: . . . . info@bsmh.org.uk

West Sussex

CHESTNUT TREE HOUSE CHILDREN'S HOSPICE
Dover Lane, Poling, Arundel, West Sussex BN18 9PX
Tel: . 01903 871800/01903 871 820 (fundraising)
Email: . . . enquiries@chestnut-tree-house.org.uk
Web: . . . . www.chestnut-tree-house.org.uk
Beds: 10 HC/DC/BS/MND/V/HSN

MACMILLAN SPECIALIST PALLIATIVE SERVICE
Midhurst Community Hospital, Dodsley Lane, Midhurst, West Sussex GU29 9AW
Tel: 01730 811121

ST CATHERINE'S HOSPICE
Malthouse Road, Crawley, West Sussex RH10 6BH
Tel: 01293 447333
Email: . . . . info@stch.org.uk

ST WILFRID'S HOSPICE
Grosvenor Road, Donnington, Chichester, West Sussex PO19 8FP
Tel: 01243 775302
Email: . . . . general@stwh.co.uk

West Yorkshire

KIRKWOOD HOSPICE
21 Albany Road, Dalton, Huddersfield, West Yorkshire HD5 9UY
Tel: 01484 557900

MARIE CURIE HOSPICE, BRADFORD
Maudsley Street, Bradford, West Yorkshire BD3 9LE
Tel: 01274 337000
Email: . . . . . bradfordhospice@mariecurie.org.uk

MARTIN HOUSE - HOSPICE CARE FOR CHILDREN AND YOUNG PEOPLE
Martin House
hospice care for children and young people

Grove Road, Boston Spa, Wetherby, West Yorkshire LS23 6TX
Tel: 01937 844569
Fax: 01937 541363
Web: . . . . www.martinhouse.org.uk

THE PRINCE OF WALES HOSPICE
Halfpenny Lane, Pontefract, West Yorkshire WF8 4BG
Tel: 01977 708868
Email: .... reception@pwh.org.uk

ST GEMMA'S HOSPICE
329 Harrogate Road, Moortown, Leeds, West Yorkshire LS17 6QD
Tel: 0113 218 5506
Email: .... fundraising@st-gemma.co.uk

SUE RYDER
Manorlands Hospice, Hebden Road, Oxenhope, Keighley, West Yorkshire BD22 9HJ
Tel: 01535 642308

SUE RYDER - WHEATFIELDS HOSPICE
Grove Road, Headingley, Leeds, West Yorkshire LS6 2AE
Tel: 0113 278 7249

WAKEFIELD HOSPICE
Aberford Road, Wakefield, West Yorkshire WF1 4TS
Tel: 01924 213900
Email: .. barbara.baker@wakefieldhospice.co.uk

Wiltshire

DOROTHY HOUSE HOSPICE CARE
Winsley, Bradford-on-Avon, Wiltshire BA15 2LE
Tel: 01225 722988
Email: ...... info@dorothyhouse-hospice.org.uk

PROSPECT HOSPICE
Moormead Road, Swindon, Wiltshire SN4 9BY
Tel: 01793 813355
Email: .... info@prospect-hospice.net

NORTHERN IRELAND

Belfast

MARIE CURIE HOSPICE, BELFAST
Kensington Road, Belfast BT5 6NF
Tel: 028 9088 2000
Email: .... belfasthospice@mariecurie.org.uk

NORTHERN IRELAND HOSPICE
Somerton House, 74 Somerton Road, Belfast BT15 3LH
Tel: 028 9078 1836
Email: .... information@nihospicecare.com

Co. Down

SOUTHERN AREA HOSPICE SERVICES
St Johns House, Courtenay Hill, Newry, Co. Down BT34 2EB
Tel: 028 3026 7711
Email: ... info@southernareahospiceservices.org

Co. Londonderry

FOYLE HOSPICE
61 Culmore Road, Londonderry, Co. Londonderry BT48 8JE
Tel: 028 7135 1010
Email: ... care@foylehospice.com/fundraising@foylehospice.com

SCOTLAND

Aberdeen

ROXBURGHE HOUSE
Dept of Palliative Medicine, Ashgrove Road, Cornhill Site, Aberdeen AB25 2ZH
Tel: 0845 456 6000

Edinburgh

ST COLUMBA'S HOSPICE
15 Boswall Road, Edinburgh EH5 3RW
Tel: 0131 551 1381
Email: .... info@stcolumbashospice.org.uk

WAVERLEY CARE MILESTONE
113 Oxgangs Road North, Edinburgh EH14 1EB
Tel: 0131 441 6989
Email: .... milestone@waverleycare.org

Fife

HOSPICE WARD (WARD 16)
Queen Margaret Hospital, Whitefield Road, Dunfermline, Fife KY12 0SU
Tel: 01383 627016

Glasgow

MARIE CURIE HOSPICE, HUNTERS HILL
1 Belmont Road, Hunters Hill, Glasgow G21 3AY
Tel: 0141 531 1300
Email: .... info@mariecurie.org.uk

THE PRINCE & PRINCESS OF WALES HOSPICE
71 Carlton Place, Glasgow G5 9TD
Tel: 0141 429 5599
Email: .... info@ppwh.org.uk

Highland

HIGHLAND HOSPICE, NESS HOUSE
1 Bishop's Road, Inverness, Highland IV3 5SB
Tel: 01463 243132

North Lanarkshire

ST ANDREW'S HOSPICE
Henderson Street, Airdrie, North Lanarkshire ML6 6DJ
Tel: 01236 766951

Orkney Islands

ORKNEY MACMILLAN HOUSE
Balfour Hospital, New Scapa Road, Kirkwall, Orkney Islands KW15 1BH
Tel: 01856 888000

Perth & Kinross

CHILDREN'S HOSPICE ASSOCIATION SCOTLAND - RACHEL HOUSE
Avenue Road, Kinross, Perth & Kinross KY13 8FX
Tel: 01577 865777

Renfrewshire

ARDGOWAN HOSPICE
12 Nelson Street, Greenock, Renfrewshire PA15 1TS
Tel: 01475 726830

ST VINCENT'S HOSPICE
Old Howwood Road, Howwood, Johnstone, Renfrewshire PA9 1AF
Tel: 01505 705635

Stirling

STRATHCARRON HOSPICE
Randolph Hill, Fankerton by Denny, Stirling FK6 5HJ
Tel: 01324 826222
Email: ...... enquiries@strathcarronhospice.org

WALES

Denbighshire

MACMILLAN UNIT
Denbigh Infirmary, Ruthin Road, Denbigh, Denbighshire LL16 3ES
Tel: 01745 818100

Newport

ST ANNE'S HOSPICE
Harding Avenue, Malpas, Newport NP20 6ZE
Tel: 01633 820282

Rhondda Cynon Taff

Y BWTHYN
Pontypridd and District Hospital, The Common, Pontypridd, Rhondda Cynon Taff CF37 4AL
Tel: 01443 486144

Swansea

TY OLWEN PALLIATIVE CARE SERVICE
Morriston Hospital, ABM University NHS Trust, Swansea SA6 6NL
Tel: 01792 703412

Vale of Glamorgan

MARIE CURIE HOSPICE, HOLME TOWER
Bridgeman Road, Penarth, Vale of Glamorgan CF64 3YR
Tel: 029 2042 6000
Email: .... info@mariecurie.org.uk

Wrexham

NIGHTINGALE HOUSE HOSPICE, WREXHAM / TY'R EOS
Nightingale House, Chester Road, Wrexham LL11 2SJ
Tel: 01978 316800
Email: . . caroline.siddall@nightingalehouse.co.uk

FREE LEGAL ADVICE

If in doubt as to how to find legal advice services, consult the Citizens Advice Bureau (CAB) in the area concerned (see directory listing for the local office). The following organisations provide specialist services or information.

ENGLAND

Greater Manchester

EQUALITY AND HUMAN RIGHTS COMMISSION
Arndale House, Arndale Centre, Manchester, Greater Manchester M4 3AQ
Tel: 0161 829 8100
Email: . . . . info@equalityhumanrights.com

London

ADVISORY SERVICE FOR SQUATTERS
Angel Alley, 84b Whitechapel High Street, London E1 7QX
Tel: 020 3216 0099
Email: . . . . advice@squatter.org.uk

AT EASE ADVICE, INFORMATION AND COUNSELLING SERVICE
Bunhill Fields Meeting House, Quaker Court, Banner Street, London EC1Y 8QQ
Tel: 020 7490 5223
Email: . . . . nfo@atease.org.uk

EQUALITY AND HUMAN RIGHTS COMMISSION
Fleetbank House, 2-6 Salisbury Square, London EC4Y 8JX
Tel: 020 7832 7800
Email: . . . . info@equalityhumanrights.com

FAMILY RIGHTS GROUP
The Print House, 18 Ashwin Street, London E8 3DL
Tel: 0808 801 0366 Freephone Advice; 020 7923 2628 Admin
Email: . . . . office@frg.org.uk

FREE REPRESENTATION UNIT
Ground Floor, 60 Gray's Inn Road, London WC1X 8LU
Tel: 020 7611 9555
Email: . . . . admin@freerepresentationunit.org.uk

IMMIGRATION ADVICE SERVICE
70 Borough High St, London SE1 1XF
Tel: 0844 974 4000
Email: . . . . info@iasservices.org.uk

JOINT COUNCIL FOR THE WELFARE OF IMMIGRANTS
115 Old Street, London EC1V 9RT
Tel: 020 7251 8708

MARY WARD LEGAL CENTRE
10 Great Turnstile, London WC1V 7JU
Tel: 020 7831 7079
Email: . . . . enquiries@marywardlegal.org.uk

MIND
Granta House, 15-19 Broadway, Stratford, London E15 4BQ
Tel: 020 8519 2122
Email: . . . . willsandtrust@mind.org.uk

ONE PARENT FAMILIES - GINGERBREAD
520 Highgate Studios,, 53-79 Highgate Road,, London NW5 1TL.
Tel: 020 7428 5400

RELEASE
124-128 City Road, London EC1V 2NJ
Tel: 020 7324 2989
Email: . . . . ask@release.org.uk

UK COUNCIL FOR INTERNATIONAL STUDENT AFFAIRS (UKCISA)
9-17 St Albans Place, Islington, London N1 0NX
Tel: 020 7288 4330

VICTIM SUPPORT
Hallam House, 56-60 Hallam Street, London W1W 6JL
Tel: 020 7268 0200
Email: . . . . legacies@victimsupport.org.uk

SCOTLAND

Glasgow

EQUALITY AND HUMAN RIGHTS COMMISSION
151 West George Street, Glasgow G2 2JJ
Tel: 0141 228 5910
Email: . . . . . scotland@equalityhumanrights.com

WALES

Cardiff

EQUALITY AND HUMAN RIGHTS COMMISSION
Ground Floor, 1 Caspian Point, Caspian Way, Cardiff Bay, Cardiff CF10 4DQ
Tel: 02920 447710
Email: . . . . wales@equalityhumanrights.com

LAW CENTRES

The following selected Law Centres provide free legal advice and representation in areas of social welfare law only. They are listed according to alphabetical order of county / unitary authority / region in England, Scotland, Wales and Northern Ireland and by numbered postal districts in Greater London. For further information contact the Law Centres Network: Floor 1, Tavis House, 1-6 Tavistock Square, London WC1H 9NA. E-mail: info@lawcentres.org.uk Web: www.lawcentres.org.uk

ENGLAND

Bedfordshire

LUTON LAW CENTRE
6th Floor, Cresta House, Alma Street, Luton, Bedfordshire LU1 2PL
Tel: 01582 481000; 01582 482000
Email: .... admin@lutonlawcentre.co.uk

Bristol

AVON & BRISTOL LAW CENTRE
2 Moon Street, Bristol BS2 8QE
Tel: 0117 924 8662
Email: .... mail@ablc.org.uk

Cumbria

CUMBRIA LAW CENTRE
8 Spencer Street, Carlisle, Cumbria CA1 1BG
Tel: 01228 515129
Email: .... reception@comlaw.co.uk

Derbyshire

DERBYSHIRE LAW CENTRE
1 Rose Hill East, Chesterfield, Derbyshire S40 1NU
Tel: 01246 550 674
Email: .... clc@chesterfieldlawcentre.org.uk

DERBY CITIZENS ADVICE AND LAW CENTRE
Stuart House, Green Lane, Derby, Derbyshire DE1 1RS
Tel: 01332 228 700
Email: .. advice@citizensadviceandlawcentre.org

Gloucestershire

GLOUCESTER LAW CENTRE
3rd Floor, 75-81 Eastgate Street, Gloucester, Gloucestershire GL1 1PN
Tel: 01452 423492
Email: ..... contact@gloucesterlawcentre.co.uk

Greater Manchester

BURY LAW CENTRE
Unit 1, Bury Business Centre, Kay Street, Bury, Bury, Greater Manchester BL9 6BU
Tel: 0161 272 0666
Email: .... info@burylawcentre.co.uk

ROCHDALE LAW CENTRE
15 Drake Street, Rochdale, Greater Manchester OL16 1RE
Tel: 01706 657766
Email: .... info@rochdalelawcentre.org.uk

SOUTH MANCHESTER LAW CENTRE
584 Stockport Road, Longsight, Manchester, Greater Manchester M13 0RQ
Tel: 0161 225 5111
Email: .... admin@smlc.org.uk

Isle of Wight

ISLE OF WIGHT LAW CENTRE
Exchange House, St Cross Lane, Newport, Isle of Wight PO30 5BZ
Tel: 01983 524715
Email: .... iowlc@iowlc.org.uk

London

BATTERSEA LAW CENTRE (SWLLC)
125 Bolingbroke Grove, London SW11 1DA
Tel: 020 7585 0716
Email: . solicitors@battersealawcentre.fsnet.co.uk

BRENT COMMUNITY LAW CENTRE
389 Willesden High Road, London NW10 2JR
Tel: 020 8451 1122
Email: .... brentlaw@brentlaw.org.uk

CAMBRIDGE HOUSE LAW CENTRE
1 Addington Square, London SE5 0HF
Tel: 020 7358 7025
Email: .... info@ch1889.org

CAMDEN COMMUNITY LAW CENTRE
2 Prince of Wales Road, London NW5 3LQ
Tel: 020 7284 6510
Email: .... admin@cclc.org.uk

CENTRAL LONDON LAW CENTRE
14 Irving Street, London WC2H 7AF
Tel: 020 7839 2998
Email: .... renata@londonlawcentre.org.uk

GREENWICH COMMUNITY LAW CENTRE
187 Trafalgar Road, Greenwich, London SE10 9EQ
Tel: 020 8305 3350
Email: .... info@gclc.co.uk

HACKNEY COMMUNITY LAW CENTRE
8 Lower Clapton Road, London E5 0PD
Tel: . 020 8985 8364; 020 8985 5236 Emergency
Email: .... info@hclc.org.uk

HAMMERSMITH AND FULHAM COMMUNITY LAW CENTRE LIMITED
363 North End Road, Fulham, London SW6 1NW
Tel: 020 3080 0330
Email: . . . . hflaw@hflaw.org.uk

HARINGEY LAW CENTRE
754-758 High Rd, London N17 0AL
Tel: 020 8808 5354
Email: . . . . tottenhamlawcentre@tiscali.co.uk

ISLINGTON LAW CENTRE
38 Devonia Road, London N1 8JH
Tel: 020 7288 7630
Email: . . . . info@islingtonlaw.org.uk

LAMBETH LAW CENTRE
Unit 4, The Co-op Centre, 11 Mowll Street, London SW9 6BG
Tel: 020 7840 2000
Email: . . . . admin@lambethlawcentre.org

NORTH KENSINGTON LAW CENTRE
Unit 15, Baseline Studios, Whitchurch Road, London W11 4AT
Tel: 020 8969 7473
Email: . . . . info@nklc.co.uk

PADDINGTON LAW CENTRE
439 Harrow Road, London W10 4RE
Tel: 020 8960 3155
Email: . . . . paddingtonlaw@btconnect.com

PLUMSTEAD COMMUNITY LAW CENTRE
105 Plumstead High Street, London SE18 1SB
Tel: 020 8855 9817

SOUTHWARK LAW CENTRE
Hanover Park House, 14-16 Hanover Park, London SE15 5HG
Tel: 020 7732 2008

SPRINGFIELD ADVICE AND LAW CENTRE LIMITED
Admissions Buildings, Springfield University Hospital, 61 Glenburnie Road, London SW17 7DJ
Tel: 020 8767 6884
Email: . . . . info@springfieldlawcentre.org.uk

TOWER HAMLETS LAW CENTRE
789 Commercial Road, Limehouse, London E14 7HG
Tel: 020 7538 4909
Email: . . . . info@thlc.co.uk

Merseyside

VAUXHALL LAW & INFORMATION CENTRE
VNC Millennium Resource Centre, Blenheim Street, Liverpool, Merseyside L5 8UX
Tel: 0151 482 254
Email: . . . . advice@lawcentre.vnc.org.uk

Middlesex

HILLINGDON LAW CENTRE
12 Harold Avenue, Hayes, Middlesex UB3 4QW
Tel: 020 8561 9400
Email: . . . . info@hillingdonlawcentre.co.uk

Surrey

KINGSTON & RICHMOND LAW CENTRE (SWLLC)
Siddeley House, 50 Canbury Park Road, Kingston on Thames, Surrey KT2 6LX
Tel: 020 8767 2777
Email: . . . . kingston@swllc.org

SURREY LAW CENTRE
34-36 Chertsey Street, Guildford, Surrey GU1 4HD
Tel: 01483 215000
Email: . . . . info@surreylawcentre.org

WANDSWORTH & MERTON LAW CENTRE (SWLLC)
112 London Road, Morden, Surrey SM4 5AX
Tel: 020 8543 4069

Tyne & Wear

NEWCASTLE LAW CENTRE LIMITED
Mea House, Ellison Place, Newcastle upon Tyne, Tyne & Wear NE1 8XS
Tel: 0191 2304777
Email: . . . . info@newcastlelawcentre.co.uk

West Midlands

BIRMINGHAM COMMUNITY LAW CENTRE
The Bangladesh Centre, 97 Walford Road, Sparkbrook, Birmingham, West Midlands B11 1NP
Tel: 0121 772 623
Email: . . . . . admin@birminghamlawcentre.org.uk

COVENTRY LAW CENTRE
Oakwood House, St Patricks Road Entrance, Coventry, West Midlands CV1 2HL
Tel: 024 7622 3053
Email: . . . . enquiries@covlaw.org.uk

West Yorkshire

BRADFORD LAW CENTRE
31 Manor Row, Bradford, West Yorkshire BD1 4PS
Tel: 01274 306617
Email: . . . . info@bradfordlawcentre.co.uk

KIRKLEES LAW CENTRE
Units 11/12, Empire House, Wakefield Old Road, Dewsbury, West Yorkshire WF12 8DJ
Tel: 01924 439829
Email: . . . . manager@kirkleeslc.org.uk

Wiltshire

WILTSHIRE LAW CENTRE
Swindon Advice and Support Centre, Sanford Street, Swindon, Wiltshire SN1 1QH
Tel: 01793 486926
Email: . . . . info@wiltslawcentre.co.uk

NORTHERN IRELAND

Belfast

LAW CENTRE (NORTHERN IRELAND)
124 Donegall Street, Belfast BT1 2GY
Tel: 028 9024 4401
Email: . . . . admin.belfast@lawcentreni.org

Co. Londonderry

LAW CENTRE (NORTHERN IRELAND) WESTERN AREA OFFICE
Western Area Office, 9 Clarendon Street, Londonderry, Co. Londonderry BT48 7EP
Tel: 028 7126 2433
Email: .... admin.derry@lawcentreniwest.org

SCOTLAND

Glasgow

CASTLEMILK LAW AND MONEY ADVICE CENTRE
155 Castlemilk Drive, Castlemilk, Glasgow G45 9UG
Tel: 0141 634 0313
Email: .... mail@castlemilklawcentre.co.uk

ETHNIC MINORITIES LAW CENTRE
41 St Vincent Place, Glasgow G1 2ER
Tel: 0141 204 2888
Email: .... admin@emlc.org.uk

WALES

Cardiff

CARDIFF LAW CENTRE
41-42 Clifton Street, Cardiff CF24 1LS
Tel: 029 2049 8117
Email: .... cardiff.lawcentre@dial.pipex.com

LOCAL ASSOCIATIONS OF AND FOR DISABLED PEOPLE

Information on local associations of and for disabled people was originally supplied by the Royal Association for Disability and Rehabilitation (RADAR). RADAR merged with Disability Alliance and the National Centre for Independent Living to form Disability Rights UK. Disability Rights UK can be contacted at: Ground floor, CAN Mezzanine, 49-51 East Road, London N1 6AH. Tel: 020 7250 8181.

Information from DIAL UK is also listed. DIAL UK is now managed by Scope. For more information, please visit www.scope.org.uk/dial or call 0808 800 3333.

ENGLAND

Cambridgeshire

FRIENDS WITH DISABILITIES
5 Grieve Court, Cambridge, Cambridgeshire CB4 1FR
Tel: 01223 425595
Email: . . . gerri@disability-cambridgeshire.org.uk

Cornwall

DISABILITY CORNWALL
Units 1G & H Guildford Road Industrial Estate, Guildford Road, Hayle, Cornwall TR27 4QZ
Tel: . . . . . . 01736 756655; 01736 759500 (DIAL)
Email: . . . . info@disabilitycornwall.org.uk

Dorset

CMT UNITED KINGDOM
3 Groveley Road, Christchurch, Dorset BH23 3HB
Tel: 0800 6526316
Email: . . . . enquiries@cmt.org.uk

North Yorkshire

NORTH YORKSHIRE CENTRE FOR INDEPENDENT LIVING
Unit 26 Cayley Court, Hopper Hill Road, Eastfield, Scarborough, North Yorkshire YO11 1YJ
Tel: 01723588002
Email: . . . . admin@nycil.org.uk

Wiltshire

INDEPENDENT LIVING CENTRE (WILTSHIRE & BATH)
St George's Road, Semington, Trowbridge, Wiltshire BA14 6JQ
Tel: 01380 871007
Email: . welcome.ilc.semington@googlemail.com

ENGLAND - NON RADAR MEMBERS

Buckinghamshire

CENTRE FOR INTEGRATED LIVING
330 Saxon Gate West, Milton Keynes, Buckinghamshire MK9 2ES
Tel: 01908 231344
Email: . . . . info@mkcil.org.uk

DISABILITY INFORMATION NETWORK
6 The Courtyard, Gatehouse Close, Aylesbury, Buckinghamshire HP19 8DP
Tel: 01298 487924
Email: . . . . bucksdin@hotmail.com

Cheshire

HALTON DISABILITY INFORMATION SERVICES
Collier Street, Runcorn, Cheshire WA7 1HB
Tel: . . . 01928 717445; 01928 718999 (Minicom)

Isle of Wight

DIAL ISLE OF WIGHT
The Riverside Centre, The Quay, Newport, Isle of Wight PO30 2QR
Tel: 01983 522823
Email: . . . . dial.iw@hotmail.co.uk

Lancashire

WEST LANCS DISABILITY HELPLINE
Whelmar House, 2nd Floor, Southway, Skelmersdale, Lancashire WN8 6NN
Tel: . . . 01695 51819; 0800 220676 (Advice line)
Email: . . . . enquiries@wldh.org.uk

Leicestershire

MOSAIC : SHAPING DISABILITY SERVICES
2 Oak Spinney Park, Ratby Lane, Leicester, Leicestershire LE3 3AW
Tel: 0116 231 8720
Email: . . . . enquiries@mosaic1898.co.uk

London

DISABILITY ACTION IN ISLINGTON
90-92 Upper Street, London N1 0NP
Tel: . . . . 020 7226 0137; 020 7359 1891 Minicom

REAL
. . . . Jack Dash House, 2 Lawn House Cl, London E14 9YQ
Tel: 0207 001 2177
Email: . . . . hello@real.org.uk

North Lincolnshire

CARERS' SUPPORT CENTRE
Jessie Wilcox House, 11 Redcombe Lane, Brigg, North Lincolnshire DN20 8AU
Tel: 01652 650585
Email: . . . . info@carerssupportcentre.com

North Somerset

DIAL
Room 5, Roselawn, 28 Walliscote Road, Weston-super-Mare, North Somerset BS23 1UJ
Tel: 01934 419426
Email: . . . . mail@westondial.co.uk

North Yorkshire

SELBY AND DISTRICT DIAL
12 Park Street, Selby, North Yorkshire YO8 4PW
Tel: 01757 210495
Email: . . . . selbydial@tiscali.co.uk

Northamptonshire

ADVICE DAVENTRY
The Abbey, off Market Square, Daventry, Northamptonshire NN11 4XG
Tel: 01327 701646

South Yorkshire

DISABILITY INFORMATION SERVICE
c/o Central Library, Walker Place, Rotherham, South Yorkshire S65 1JH
Tel: 01709 373658

West Yorkshire

CALDERDALE DART
Suite 5, Rimani House, 14-16 Hall Street, Halifax, West Yorkshire HX1 5BD
Tel: 01422 346040
Email: . . . . calderdaledart@hotmail.co.uk

DISABILITY ADVICE BRADFORD
103 Dockfield Road, Shipley, West Yorkshire BD17 7AR
Tel: 01274 594173
Email: . . . . enquiry@disabilityadvice.org.uk

ONE VOICE - FEDERATION OF DISABLED PEOPLE
17-18 Queensgate Market Arcade, Huddersfield, West Yorkshire HD1 2RA

ENGLAND - RADAR MEMBERS

Birmingham

CARES
The Carers Hub, 76-78 Boldmere Road, Sutton Coldfield, Birmingham B73 5TJ
Tel: 0333 006 9711
Email: . . . . . . info@birminghamcarershub.org.uk

Brighton & Hove

BLUEBIRD SOCIETY FOR THE DISABLED
176 Portland Road, Hove, Brighton & Hove BN3 5QN
Tel: 01273 207664
Email: . . . . bluebirdsociety@waitrose.com

BRIGHTON & HOVE FEDERATION OF DISABLED PEOPLE
Montague House, Somerset Street Entrance, Montague Place, Brighton, Brighton & Hove BN2 1JE
Tel: 01273 203016
Email: . . . . disabilityadvice@bhfederation.org.uk

Bristol

THE WEST OF ENGLAND CENTRE FOR INCLUSIVE LIVING
Link House, Britton Gardens, Kingswood, Bristol BS15 1TF
Tel: 0117 947 9911
Email: . . . . hello@wecil.co.uk

Cambridgeshire

DIAL PETERBOROUGH
John Mansfield Centre, Eastern Avenue, Dogsthorpe, Peterborough, Cambridgeshire PE3 8DX
Tel: 01733 265551
Email: . . . . dialpeterborough@btconnect.com

Cheshire

DIAL HOUSE CHESTER
DIAL House, Hamilton Place, Chester, Cheshire CH1 2BH
Tel: 01244 345655
Email: . . . . . contactus@dialhousechester.org.uk

DISABILITY INFORMATION BUREAU
Pierce Street, Macclesfield, Cheshire SK11 6ER
Tel: 01625 501759
Email: . . . . info@dibservices.org.uk

VALE ROYAL DISABILITY SERVICES
VRDS Head Office, 4 Hartford Business Centre, Chester Road, Hartford, Northwich, Cheshire CW8 2AB
Tel: 01606 888400
Email: . . . . office@vrds.org.uk

Co. Durham

EVOLUTION (DARLINGTON CVS)
Church Row, Darlington, Co. Durham DL1 5QD
Tel: 01325 266888
Email: . . . . . . enquiries@evolutiondarlington.com

Cornwall

CORNWALL DISABLED ASSOCIATION
1 Riverside House, Heron Way, Newham, Truro, Cornwall TR1 2XN
Tel: 01872 273518
Email: . . . . info@cornwalldisabled.co.uk

Cumbria

ALLERDALE DISABILITY ASSOCIATION
Curwen Centre, Curwen Park, Workington, Cumbria CA14 4YB
Tel: 0845 129 9954
Email: . . . . access@adanet.org.uk

BARROW AND DISTRICT DISABILITY ASSOCIATION
71-77 School Street, Barrow-in-Furness, Cumbria LA14 1EJ
Tel: 01229 432599
Email: . . . . info@bdda.org.uk

Derbyshire

DISABILITY DIRECT
227 Normanton Road, Normanton, Derby, Derbyshire DE23 6UT
Tel: . . . 01332 299449; 01332 368585 (Minicom)
Email: . . . . info@disabilitydirectderby.co.uk

Devon

PLYMOUTH AND DISTRICT DISABLED FELLOWSHIP
Astor Hall, 157 Devonport Road, Stoke, Plymouth, Devon PL1 5RB
Tel: 01752 562729

Dorset

DISABILITY ACTION
Christchurch Hospital, Fairmile Road, Christchurch, Dorset BH23 2JX
Tel: 01202 705496

Essex

DIAL BASILDON & SOUTH ESSEX
75 Southernhay, Basildon, Essex SS14 1EU
Tel: 01265 286676
Email: . . . . enquiries@dialbasildon.co.uk

Gloucestershire

NEWENT ASSOCIATION FOR THE DISABLED
Sheppard House, Onslow Road, Newent, Gloucestershire GL18 1TL
Tel: 01531 821227

Greater Manchester

BURY & DISTRICT DISABLED ADVISORY COUNCIL
Seedfield Resource Centre, Parkinson Street, Bury, Greater Manchester BL9 6NY
Tel: 0161 253 6888
Email: . . . . info@baddac.org.uk

DISABILITY STOCKPORT
16 Meyer Street, Cale Green, Stockport, Greater Manchester SK3 8JE
Tel: . . 0161 480 7248; 0161 480 7248 (Minicom)
Email: . . . . email@disabilitystockport.org.uk

Hertfordshire

DISABILITY INFORMATION SERVICE FOR HERTFORDSHIRE (D.I.S.H.)
PO Box 979, St Albans, Hertfordshire AL1 9JF
Tel: . . . . 0800 181 067 (Helpline)
Email: . . . . info@dish.uk.net

HERTFORDSHIRE ACTION ON DISABILITY
The Woodside Centre, The Commons, Welwyn Garden City, Hertfordshire AL7 4DD
Tel: 01707 324581
Email: . . . . info@hadnet.org.uk

Isle of Man

MANX FOUNDATION FOR THE PHYSICALLY DISABLED
Masham Court, Victoria Avenue, Douglas, Isle of Man IM2 4AW
Tel: 01624 628926

Kent

DIAL
9a Gorrell Road, Whitstable, Kent CT5 1RN
Tel: 01227 771155; 01227 771645

DIAL NORTH WEST KENT
7 The Hives, Northfleet, Kent DA11 9DE
Tel: 01474 356962
Email: . . . . info@dialnwk.org.uk

Kingston upon Hull

COUNCIL OF DISABLED PEOPLE
35 Ferensway, Hull, Kingston upon Hull HU2 8NA
Tel: 01482 326140

Lancashire

DIAL WEST LANCASHIRE
49 Westgate, Sandy Lane, Skelmersdale, Lancashire WN8 8LP
Tel: 0800 220 676

Lincolnshire

CLUB 87 FOR THE YOUNGER DISABLED
The Old Orchard, Davy's Lane, Bracebridge Heath, Lincoln, Lincolnshire LN4 2NB
Tel: 01522 527583

DISABILITY LINCS
Ancaster Day Centre, Boundary Street, Lincoln, Lincolnshire LN5 8NJ
Tel: 01522 870602
Email: . . . . enquiries@disabilitylincs.org.uk

London

ACTION DISABILITY KENSINGTON & CHELSEA
ADKC Centre, Whitstable House, Silchester Road, London W10 6SB
Tel: . . . . 020 8960 8888; 020 8964 8066 Minicom
Email: . . . . adkc@adkc.org.uk

FITZGIBBON ASSOCIATES
Omnibus Business Centre, 39-41 North Road, London N7 9DP
Tel: 0845 111 6543

HAMMERSMITH & FULHAM ACTION ON DISABILITY (HAFAD)
Greswell Centre, Greswell Street, London SW6 6PX
Tel: 020 7471 8510
Email: info@hafad.org.uk

HARINGEY CONSORTIUM OF DISABLED PEOPLE AND CARERS
551B High Road Tottenham, London N17 6SB
Tel: 020 8801 5757; 020 8801 9576
Email: director.hcdc@btconnect.com

SOUTHWARK DISABLEMENT ASSOCIATION
Aylesbury Day Centre, Room 48, 2 Bradenham Close, London SE17 2QB
Tel: 020 7701 1391
Email: sda@dircon.co.uk

Merseyside

WIRED - WIRRAL INFORMATION RESOURCE FOR EQUALITY & DISABILITY
Wirral Business Centre, Arrowbrook Road, Wirral, Merseyside SH 49 1SX
Tel: 0151 670 0777 or 0151 222 7990
Email: contact@wired.me.uk

Middlesex

LONDON BOROUGH OF HARROW SOCIAL SERVICES DEPARTMENT
Civic Centre, Station Road, Harrow, Middlesex HA1 2XF
Tel: 020 8863 5611

Norfolk

CENTRE 81
Tarworks Road, Great Yarmouth, Norfolk NR30 1QR
Tel: 01493 852573
Email: admin@centre81.com

HAND
38a Bull Close, Magdalen Street, Norwich, Norfolk NR3 1SX

North Yorkshire

DIAC YORK
Room 2, Nursery Block, Priory Street Centre, 17 Priory Street, York, North Yorkshire Y01 6ET
Tel: 01904 638467

DISABILITY ACTION YORKSHIRE
Unit i4A, Hornbeam Park Oval, Harrogate, North Yorkshire HG2 8RB
Tel: 01423 855410
Email: fundraising@da-y.org.uk

SCARBOROUGH AND DISTRICT DISABLEMENT ACTION GROUP
Allatt House, 5 West Parade Road, Scarborough, North Yorkshire YO12 5ED
Tel: 01723 379397; 01723 379397 (Minicom)
Email: scardag@onyxnet.co.uk

Northumberland

BERWICK BOROUGH DISABILITY FORUM
Voluntary Centre, 5 Tweed Street, Berwick-upon-Tweed, Northumberland TD15 1NG
Tel: 01289 308888

BLYTH VALLEY DISABLED FORUM
20 Stanley Street, Blyth, Northumberland NE24 2BU
Tel: 01670 360927

DISABILITY ASSOCIATION
Austin House, 11 Sandersons Arcade, Morpeth, Northumberland NE61 1NS
Tel: 01670 504488

NORTHUMBRIAN CALVERT TRUST
Kielder Water, Hexham, Northumberland NE48 1BS
Tel: 01434 250232

Nottinghamshire

DISABILITY NOTTINGHAMSHIRE
1 Byron Street, Mansfield, Nottinghamshire NG18 5NX
Tel: 01623 625891; 01623 656556 (Minicom)
Email: advice@disabilitynottinghamshire.org.uk

DISABLED PEOPLE'S ADVOCACY: NOTTINGHAMSHIRE
Voluntary Action Centre, 7 Mansfield Road, Nottingham, Nottinghamshire NG1 3FB
Tel: 0115 934 9504

South Gloucestershire

COUNCIL FOR THE DISABLED
c/o Kingswood Borough Council, Civic Centre, High Street, Kingswood, Thornbury, South Gloucestershire BS15 2TR

South Yorkshire

DIAL
9 Doncaster Road, Barnsley, South Yorkshire S70 1TH
Tel: 01226 240273
Email: dialbarnsley2@hotmail.com

DIAL (DONCASTER)
Shaw Wood Business Park, Shaw Wood Way, Doncaster, South Yorkshire DN2 5TB
Tel: 01302 327800; 01302 768297 (Minicom)
Email: advice@dialdoncaster.co.uk

FEDERATION FOR THE DISABLED SELF-HELP GROUPS
Five Arches Community Centre, Penrith Road, Shirecliffe, Sheffield, South Yorkshire S5 8UA

Suffolk

AVENUES EAST
Acorn Business Centre, Papermill Lane, Bramford, Ipswich, Suffolk IP8 4BZ
Tel: 01473 836777; 01473 836779 (Textphone)
Email: enquiries@optua.org.uk

DIAL
Waveney Centre for Independent Living, 161 Rotterdam Road, Lowestoft, Suffolk NR32 2EZ
Tel: 01502 511333
Email: info@dialnet.f2s.com

DISABLED ADVICE BUREAU
Room 11, 19 Tower Street, Ipswich, Suffolk IP1 3BE
Tel: 01473 217313
Email: dab.ipswich@btopenworld.com

Surrey

ACCESS GROUP GUILDFORD (FORMERLY GUILDFORD ACCESS FOR THE DISABLED)
c/o Guildford Borough Council, Millmead House, Millmead, Guildford, Surrey GU2 4BB
Tel: 01483 444056

DISABILITY INITIATIVE SERVICES LTD
Resource Centre, Knoll Road, Camberley, Surrey GU15 3SY
Tel: 01276 676302
Email: . . . . info@disabilityinitiative.org.uk

DISABILITYCROYDON
Room 2.07, Strand House, Zion Road, Thornton Heath, Surrey CR7 8RG
Tel: 020 8684 5538
Email: . . . . info@disabilitycroydon.org.uk

Tyne & Wear

CITY OF SUNDERLAND COUNCIL FOR THE DISABLED
100 Norfolk Street, Sunderland, Tyne & Wear SR1 1EA
Tel: 0191 514 3346

NORTH TYNESIDE DISTRICT DISABILITY FORUM
The Shiremoor Centre, Earsdon Road, Shiremoor, North Shields, Tyne & Wear NE27 9HJ
Tel: 0191 200 8570
Email: . . . . info@ntdf.co.uk

Warwickshire

DIAL
New Ramsden Centre, School Walk, Attleborough, Nuneaton, Warwickshire CV11 4PJ
Tel: 024 7634 9954
Email: . . . . enquiries@nbdial.com

West Midlands

COUNCIL OF DISABLED PEOPLE (WARWICKSHIRE & COVENTRY)
Room 6, Koco Building, Unit 15, The Arches Industrial Estate, Spon End, Coventry, West Midlands CV1 3JQ
Tel: 01926 889349; 01926 889349
Email: . . . . info@cdp.org.uk

DISABLED ASSOCIATION
7 Albion Street, Brierley Hill, West Midlands DY5 3EE

FELLOWSHIP OF THE DISABLED
9 Wingate Road, Bentley, Walsall, West Midlands WS2 0AS

FELLOWSHIP OF THE PHYSICALLY HANDICAPPED
3 Avon House, Peak Drive, Gornal, Dudley, West Midlands DY3 2BY

VOLUNTARY ASSOCIATION FOR THE PHYSICALLY HANDICAPPED
1 Barns Lane, Rushall, West Midlands WS4 1HQ

WEST MIDLANDS FAMILY PLACEMENT SERVICES
Trinity House, Trinity Road, Dudley, West Midlands DY1 1JB
Tel: 01384 458585
Email: . . . . wmfp@barnardos.org.uk

West Sussex

VOICE FOR DISABILITY
7 St. John's Parade, Allinora Crescent, Goring, West Sussex BN12 4HJ
Tel: 01903 2444457
Email: . . . . info@wsad.org.uk

West Yorkshire

DIAL (LEEDS)
The Mary Thornton Suite, Armley Grange Drive, Leeds, West Yorkshire LS12 3QH
Tel: . 0113 214 3630; 0113 214 3627 (Textphone)
Email: . . . . dial.leeds@btconnect.com

DIAL (WAKEFIELD)
Highfield House Resource Centre, Love Lane, Castleford, Wakefield, West Yorkshire WF10 5RT
Tel: 01977 723933/4; 01977 724 081 (Textphone)
Email: . . . . advice@dialwakefield.co.uk

KEIGALEY DISABLED PEOPLE'S CENTRE
Temple Row Centre, 23 Temple Row, Keighley, West Yorkshire BD21 2AH
Tel: 01535 606700

Wiltshire

WESSEX REHABILITATION ASSOCIATION
Glanville Centre, Salisbury District Hospital, Salisbury, Wiltshire SP2 8BJ
Tel: . . . . 01722 336262 ext. 4057

NORTHERN IRELAND

Belfast

PHABLINE
24-26 North Street Arcade, Belfast BT1 1PB

SCOTLAND - NON RADAR MEMBERS

East Dunbartonshire

CONTACT POINT IN EAST DUNBARTONSHIRE
The Park Centre, 45 Kerr Street, Kirkintilloch, East Dunbartonshire G66 1LF
Tel: . . 0141 578 0183; 0141 578 0183 (Minicom)
Email: . . . . contactp@yahoo.com

Edinburgh

GRAPEVINE LOTHIAN DISABILITY INFORMATION SERVICE
Norton Park Centre, 57 Albion Road, Edinburgh EH7 5QY
Tel: . . 0131 475 2370; 0131 475 2370 (Minicom)
Email: . . . . grapevine@lothiancil.org.uk

Falkirk

DUNDAS DISABILITY INFORMATION SERVICE
Falkirk Council, Oxgangs Road, Grangemouth, Falkirk FK3 9EF

Glasgow

CAREPARTNERS
154-156 Raeberry Street, Maryhill, Glasgow G20 6EA

Renfrewshire

DISABILITY RESOURCE CENTRE (PAISLEY)
74 Love Street, Paisley, Renfrewshire PA3 2EA
Tel: 0141 848 1123

Scottish Borders

THE BRIDGE
6a Roxburgh Street, Galashiels, Scottish Borders TD1 1PF
Tel: 01896 755370

WALES - NON RADAR MEMBERS

Rhondda Cynon Taff

LLANTRISANT AND DISTRICT DIAL
Ambulance Hall, Pontyclun, Llan Harry, Rhondda Cynon Taff CF7 8HY
Tel: 01443 237937

RACIAL EQUALITY COUNCILS

Racial Equality Councils (RECs), formerly known as Community Relations Councils, are autonomous, voluntary organisations. RECs work to eliminate racial discrimination and to promote equality of opportunity between different racial and ethnic groups.

Members of RECs are drawn from statutory and voluntary bodies, ethnic minority organisations and individuals who support their aims. RECs can advise individual complainants of their rights under the Race Relations Act 1976 and provide information and assistance to organisations on developing and implementing equal opportunity policies.

For more information go to www.bforec.co.uk

ENGLAND

Bournemouth

DORSET RACE EQUALITY COUNCIL
The Link, 3-5 Palmerston Road, Dorset, Bournemouth BH1 4HN
Tel: 01202 392954
Email: . . . . enquiries@dorsetrec.org.uk

Buckinghamshire

AYLESBURY VALE EQUALITY & HUMAN RIGHTS COUNCIL
The Gateway, Gatehouse Road, Aylesbury, Buckinghamshire HP19 8FF
Tel: 01296 425332
Email: . . . . office@avrec.org.uk

Cambridgeshire

CAMBRIDGE ETHNIC COMMUNITY FORUM (CECF)
21B Sturton Street, Cambridge, Cambridgeshire CB1 2SN
Tel: 01223 655 241
Email: . . . . reception@cecf.co.uk

Cheshire

CHESHIRE HALTON & WARRINGTON REC
The Unity Centre, 17 Cuppin Street, Chester, Cheshire CH1 2BN
Tel: 01244 400730
Email: . . . . office@chawrec.org.uk

Essex

BARKING & DAGENHAM REC
Unit 2, 30 Thames Road, Barking, Essex IG11 0HZ
Tel: 020 8594 2773
Email: . . . . bardag-rec@yahoo.co.uk

Gloucestershire

RACE EQUALITY COUNCIL FOR GLOUCESTERSHIRE ("GLOSREC")
15 Brunswick Road, Gloucester, Gloucestershire GL1 1HG
Tel: 01452 301290
Email: . . . . enquiries@glosrec.org.uk

Lancashire

PRESTON & WESTERN LANCASHIRE REC
Town Hall Annexe, Birley Street, Preston, Lancashire PR1 2RL
Tel: 01772 906422
Email: . . . . admin@prestonrec.org.uk

Leicestershire

HUMAN RIGHTS & EQUALITIES CHARNWOOD
66 Nottingham Road, Loughborough, Leicestershire LE11 1EU
Tel: 01509 261651
Email: . . . . info@rg

THE RACE EQUALITY CENTRE
2nd Floor, Phoenix Yard, 5-9 Upper Brown Street, Leicester, Leicestershire LE1 5TE
Tel: 0116 2042790
Email: . administrator@theraceequalitycentre.org.uk

London

EALING EQUALITY COUNCIL
The Lido Centre, 63 Mattock Lane, Ealing, London W13 9LA
Tel: 020 8579 3861
Email: . . . . info@ealingrec.org.uk

ENFIELD RACIAL EQUALITY COUNCIL
Community House, 311 Fore Street, Edmonton, London N9 0PZ
Tel: 020 8373 6271
Email: . . . . info@enfieldrec.org.uk

HARINGEY RACE AND EQUALITY COUNCIL
14 Turnpike Lane, London N8 0PT
Tel: 020 8889 6871
Email: . . . . info@

WALTHAM FOREST RACE EQUALITY COUNCIL
Community Place, 806 High Road, Leyton, London E10 6AE
Tel: 020 8279 2425
Email: . . . . info@

Middlesex

HOUNSLOW RACIAL EQUALITY COUNCIL
49-53 Derby Road, Hounslow, Middlesex
TW3 3UQ
Tel: 020 8572 5532
Email: . . . . info@hounslowrec.co.uk

Northamptonshire

NORTHAMPTONSHIRE RIGHTS AND EQUALITY COUNCIL
Northampton College, R Building, Booth Lane, Northampton, Northamptonshire NN3 3RF
Tel: 01604 400808
Email: . . . . info@northamptonshirerec.org.uk

Suffolk

IPSWICH AND SUFFOLK COUNCIL FOR RACIAL EQUALITY
46A St Matthew's Street, Ipswich, Suffolk IP1 3EP
Tel: 01473 408111; 01473 400082
Email: . . . . office@iscre.org.uk

Surrey

KINGSTON RACE AND EQUALITIES COUNCIL
Neville House, 55 Eden Street, Kingston upon Thames, Surrey KT1 1BW
Tel: 020 8547 2332
Email: . . . . enquiries@kingstonrec.org

Warwickshire

WARWICKSHIRE RACE EQUALITY PARTNERSHIP
Room 127, Morgan Conference Suite, Warwickshire College, Rugby Centre, Technology Drive, Rugby, Warwickshire CV21 1AR
Tel: 01788 863117
Email: . . . . info@wrep.org.uk

West Midlands

CENTRE FOR EQUALITY & DIVERSITY
16A Stone Street, Dudley, West Midlands
DY1 1NS
Tel: 01384 456166
Email: . . . . admin@cfed.org.uk

Wiltshire

WILTSHIRE RACIAL EQUALITY COUNCIL
Bridge House, Stallard Street, Trowbridge, Wiltshire BA14 9AE
Tel: 01225 766439
Email: . . . . wiltsrec@gmail.com

SCOTLAND

Aberdeen

GRAMPIAN REGIONAL EQUALITY COUNCIL LTD
41 Union Street, Aberdeen AB11 5BN
Tel: 01224 595505
Email: . . . . info@grec.co.uk

Edinburgh

EDINBURGH AND LOTHIANS REGIONAL EQUALITY COUNCIL LIMITED
14 Forth Street, Edinburgh EH1 3LH
Tel: 0131 556 0441
Email: . . . . admin@lrec.org.uk

Glasgow

WEST OF SCOTLAND REGIONAL EQUALITY COUNCIL
Napiershall Street Centre, 39 Napiershall Street, Glasgow G20 6EZ
Tel: 0141 337 6626
Email: . . . . admin@wsrec.co.uk

WALES

Newport

SEWREC
137 Commercial Street, Newport NP20 1LN
Tel: 01633 250006
Email: . . . . info@sewrec.org.uk

Swansea

SWANSEA BAY REGIONAL EQUALITY COUNCIL
Third Floor, Grove House, Grove Place, Swansea SA1 5DF
Tel: 01792 457035
Email: . . . . info@sbrec.org.uk

UK COMMUNITY FOUNDATIONS

Community Foundation Network represents the community foundation movement in the UK. Our aim is to help clients create lasting value from their local giving through the network of community foundations.

Community foundations are charities located throughout the UK dedicated to strengthening local communities, creating opportunities and tackling issues of disadvantage and exclusion. Community foundations target grants that make a genuine difference to the lives of local people. They manage funds donated by individuals and organisations, building endowment and acting as the vital link between donors and local needs, connecting people with causes, and enabling clients to achieve far more than they could ever by themselves.

There are three categories of community foundations: Members are established community foundations; Associates are aspiring foundations; and Affiliates are foundations outside the UK, partner organisations in the UK or other grant-makers that are committed to improving local communities.

Further information can be obtained from UK Community Foundations, 12 Angel Gate, 320-326 City Road, London EC1V 2PT Tel: 020 7713 9326 E-mail: network@ukcommunityfoundations.org
Web: www.communityfoundations.org.uk

ENGLAND

Bedfordshire

BEDFORDSHIRE AND LUTON COMMUNITY FOUNDATION
The Old School, Southill Road, Cardington, Bedfordshire MK44 3SX
Tel: 01234 834930

Bournemouth

DORSET COMMUNITY FOUNDATION
Abchurch Chambers, 24 St Peters Road, Bournemouth BH1 2LN
Tel: 01202 292255
Email: . . . . philanthropy@dorsetcf.org

Bristol

QUARTET COMMUNITY FOUNDATION
Royal Oak House, Royal Oak Avenue, Bristol BS1 4GB
Tel: 0117 989 7700
Email: . . . . info@quartetcf.org.uk

Buckinghamshire

BUCKINGHAMSHIRE COMMUNITY FOUNDATION (A)
Foundation House, 119a Bicester Road, Aylesbury, Buckinghamshire HP19 9BA
Tel: 01296 330134
Email: . . . . info@buckscf.org.uk

MILTON KEYNES COMMUNITY FOUNDATION
Acorn House, 381 Midsummer Boulevard, Milton Keynes, Buckinghamshire MK9 3HP
Tel: 01908 690276
Email: . . . . . info@mkcommunityfoundation.co.uk

Cambridgeshire

CAMBRIDGESHIRE COMMUNITY FOUNDATION
The Quorum, Barnwell Road, Cambridge, Cambridgeshire CB5 8RE
Tel: 01223 410535
Email: . . . . info@cambscf.org.uk

Cheshire

CHESHIRE COMMUNITY FOUNDATION
Warren House, Rudheath Way, Northwich, Cheshire CW9 7LT
Tel: 01606 330607
Email: office@cheshirecommunityfoundation.org.uk

Co. Durham

COUNTY DURHAM COMMUNITY FOUNDATION
Whitfield Court, St John's Road, Durham, Co. Durham DH7 8XL
Tel: 0191 378 6340
Email: . . . . info@cdcf.org.uk

Cornwall

CORNWALL COMMUNITY FOUNDATION
Suite 1, Sheers Barton, Lawhitton, Launceston, Cornwall PL15 9NJ
Tel: 01566 779333/01566 779865
Email: . . . . office@cornwallfoundation.com

Cumbria

CUMBRIA COMMUNITY FOUNDATION (A)
Dovenby Hall, Dovenby, Cockermouth, Cumbria CA13 0PN
Tel: 01900 825760
Email: . . . . enquiries@cumbriafoundation.org

Derbyshire

DERBYSHIRE COMMUNITY FOUNDATION
Foundation House, Unicorn Business Park, Wellington Street, Ripley, Derbyshire DE5 3EH
Tel: 01773 514850
Email: . info@derbyshirecommunityfoundation.co.uk

Devon

DEVON COMMUNITY FOUNDATION (A)
The Factory, Leat Street, Tiverton, Devon EX16 5LL
Tel: 01884 235887
Email: .... admin@devoncf.com

East Sussex

SUSSEX COMMUNITY FOUNDATION
15 Western Road, Lewes, East Sussex BN7 1RL
Tel: 01273 409440
Email: .... info@sussexgiving.org.uk

Essex

EAST LONDON COMMUNITY FOUNDATION (A)
Office 7, Chadwell Heath Industrial Park, Kemp Road , Dagenham, Essex RM8 1SL
Tel: 0300 303 1203
Email: .... enquiries@elcf.org.uk

ESSEX COMMUNITY FOUNDATION
121 New London Road, Chelmsford, Essex CM2 0QT
Tel: 01245 355947
Email: .... general@essexcf.org.uk

Gloucestershire

GLOUCESTERSHIRE COMMUNITY FOUNDATION
Barnett Way, Barnwood, Gloucester, Gloucestershire GL4 3RS
Tel: 01452 656385

Greater Manchester

COMMUNITY FOUNDATION FOR GREATER MANCHESTER
Speakers House, 39 Deansgate, Manchester, Greater Manchester M3 2BA
Tel: 0161 214 0940
Email: .... info@forevermanchester.com

Hampshire

HAMPSHIRE AND THE ISLE OF WIGHT COMMUNITY FOUNDATION
Dame Mary Fagan House, Chineham Court, Lutyens Close, Basingstoke, Hampshire RG24 8AG
Tel: 01256 776101
Email: .... hiwcfadmin@hantscf.org.uk

Herefordshire

HEREFORDSHIRE COMMUNITY FOUNDATION
The Fred Bulmer Centre, Wall Street, Hereford, Herefordshire HR4 9HP
Tel: 01432 272550
Email: .... info@herefordshirefoundation.org

Hertfordshire

HERTFORDSHIRE COMMUNITY FOUNDATION
Foundation House, 2-4 Forum Place, Hatfield, Hertfordshire AL10 0RN
Tel: 01707 251351
Email: .... office@hertscf.org.uk

Kent

KENT COMMUNITY FOUNDATION
Office 23, Evegate Park Barn, Evegate, Smeeth, Ashford, Kent TN25 6SX
Tel: 01303 814500
Email: .... admin@kentcf.org.uk

Lancashire

COMMUNITY FOUNDATION FOR LANCASHIRE
Suite 22, The Globe Centre, St James Square, Accrington, Lancashire BB5 0RE
Tel: 0151 232 2444
Email: .... info@lancsfoundation.org.uk

Leicestershire

LEICESTERSHIRE, LEICESTER AND RUTLAND COMMUNITY FOUNDATION
3 Wycliffe Street, Leicester, Leicestershire LE1 5LR
Tel: 0116 262 4916
Email: ... grants@llrcommunityfoundation.org.uk

Lincolnshire

LINCOLNSHIRE COMMUNITY FOUNDATION
4 Mill House, Moneys Yard, Sleaford, Lincolnshire NG34 7TW
Tel: 01529 305825

London

LONDON COMMUNITY FOUNDATION
Unit 7 Piano House, 9 Brighton Terrace, Lambeth, London SW9 8DJ
Tel: 020 7582 5117
Email: .... info@londoncf.org.uk

ST KATHARINE & SHADWELL TRUST
One Bishops Square, London E1 6AD

Merseyside

COMMUNITY FOUNDATION FOR MERSEYSIDE (A)
3rd Floor, Stanley Buildings, 43 Hanover Street, Liverpool, Merseyside L1 3DN
Tel: 0151 232 2444
Email: .... info@cfmerseyside.org.uk

Milton Keynes

MILTON KEYNES COMMUNITY FOUNDATION
Acorn House, 381 Midsummer Boulevard, Central Milton Keynes, Milton Keynes MK9 3HP
Tel: 01908 690276
Email: ..... info@mkcommunityfoundation.co.uk

Norfolk

NORFOLK COMMUNITY FOUNDATION
St James Mill, Whitefriars, Norwich, Norfolk NR3 1SH
Tel: 01603 623958
Email: . . . . grahamtuttle@norfolkfoundation.com

North Yorkshire

TWO RIDINGS COMMUNITY FOUNDATION
Suite 134, The Innovation Centre, York Science Park, York, North Yorkshire YO10 5DG
Tel: 01759 377400
Email: . . . . office@trcf.org.uk

Northamptonshire

NORTHAMPTONSHIRE COMMUNITY FOUNDATION
18 Albion Place, Northampton, Northamptonshire NN1 1UD
Tel: 01604 230033
Email: . . . . enquiries@ncf.uk.com

Nottinghamshire

NOTTINGHAMSHIRE COMMUNITY FOUNDATION
Pine House B, Ransom Wood Business Park, Southwell Road West, Mansfield, Nottinghamshire NG21 0HJ
Tel: 01623 620002
Email: . . . . enquiries@nottscf.org.uk

Oxfordshire

OXFORDSHIRE COMMUNITY FOUNDATION
3 Woodins Way, Oxford, Oxfordshire OX1 1HD
Tel: 01865 798666
Email: . . . . ocf@oxfordshire.org

Reading

BERKSHIRE COMMUNITY FOUNDATION
Arlington Business Park, Theale, Reading RG7 4SA
Tel: 0118 930 3021

Shropshire

COMMUNITY FOUNDATION FOR SHROPSHIRE AND TELFORD (A)
Meeting Point House, Southwater Square, Telford, Shropshire TF3 4HS
Tel: 01952 201858
Email: . . . contact@cfshropshireandtelford.org.uk

Somerset

SOMERSET COMMUNITY FOUNDATION
Yeoman House, Royal Bath and West Showground, Shepton Mallet, Somerset BA4 6QN
Tel: 01749 344949
Email: . . . . info@somersetcf.org.uk

South Yorkshire

SOUTH YORKSHIRE COMMUNITY FOUNDATION
G1 Building, Unit 3, 6 Leeds Road, Sheffield, South Yorkshire SN 3TY
Tel: 0114 242 4857
Email: . . . . admin@sycf.org.uk

Staffordshire

STAFFORDSHIRE COMMUNITY FOUNDATION
Communications House, University Court, Stoke-on-Trent, Staffordshire ST18 0ES
Tel: 01785 339540
Email: . . . . office@staffsfoundation.org.uk

Stockton-on-Tees

TEES VALLEY COMMUNITY FOUNDATION
Wallace House, Falcon Court, Stockton-on-Tees TS18 3TXB
Tel: 01642 260860
Email: . . . . info@teesvalleyfoundation.org

Suffolk

SUFFOLK COMMUNITY FOUNDATION
The Old Barns, Peninsula Business Centre, Ipswich, Suffolk IP9 2BB
Tel: 01473 602602
Email: . . . . info@suffolkfoundation.org.uk

Surrey

COMMUNITY FOUNDATION FOR SURREY
1 Bishops Wharf, Walnut Tree Close, Guildford, Surrey GU1 4RA
Tel: 01483 409230
Email: . . . . info@cfsurrey.org.uk

Tyne & Wear

COMMUNITY FOUNDATION TYNE & WEAR AND NORTHUMBERLAND
Cale Cross, 156 Pilgrim Street, Newcastle upon Tyne, Tyne & Wear NE1 6SU
Tel: 0191 222 0945
Email: . . . general@communityfoundation.org.uk

West Midlands

BIRMINGHAM AND BLACK COUNTRY COMMUNITY FOUNDATION
Nechells Baths, Nechells Park Road, Nechells, Birmingham, West Midlands B7 5PD
Tel: 0121 322 5560
Email: . . . . team@bbccf.org.uk

HEART OF ENGLAND COMMUNITY FOUNDATION (ALSO COVERS COVENTRY AND WARWICKSHIRE) (A)
c/o PSA Peugeot Citroen, Torrington Avenue, Tile Hill, Coventry, West Midlands CV4 9AP
Tel: 024 76883297
Email: . . . . info@heartofenglandcf.co.uk

West Yorkshire

COMMUNITY FOUNDATION FOR CALDERDALE
1855 Building, 1st Floor, Discovery Road, Halifax, West Yorkshire HX1 2NG
Tel: 01422 349700
Email: . . . . enquiries@cffc.co.uk

LEEDS COMMUNITY FOUNDATION
Ground Floor, 51a St Paul Street, Leeds, West Yorkshire LS1 2TE
Tel: 0113 242 2426
Email: . . info@leedscommunityfoundation.org.uk

ONE COMMUNITY FOUNDATION
c/o Chadwick Lawrence Solicitors, 13 Railway Street, Huddersfield, West Yorkshire HD1 1JS
Tel: 01484 468397

WAKEFIELD DISTRICT COMMUNITY FOUNDATION
Vincent House, 136 Westgate, Wakefield, West Yorkshire WF2 9SR
Tel: 01924 239181

Wiltshire

THE COMMUNITY FOUNDATION FOR WILTSHIRE & SWINDON
Sandcliffe House, 21 Northgate Street, Devizes, Wiltshire SN10 1JX
Tel: 01380 729284
Email: .... info@wscf.org.uk

Worcestershire

WORCESTERSHIRE COMMUNITY FOUNDATION
Community House, Stourport Road, Kidderminster, Worcestershire DY11 7QE
Tel: 01562 733133
Email: .... vikki@worcscf.org.uk

NORTHERN IRELAND

Belfast

COMMUNITY FOUNDATION FOR NORTHERN IRELAND
Community House, Citylink Business Park, Albert Street, Belfast BT12 4HQ
Tel: 028 9024 5927
Email: .... info@communityfoundationni.org

Co. Fermanagh

FERMANAGH TRUST
Fermanagh House, Broadmeadow Place, Enniskillen, Co. Fermanagh BT74 7HR
Tel: 028 6632 0210
Email: .... info@fermanaghtrust.org

SCOTLAND

Edinburgh

SCOTTISH COMMUNITY FOUNDATION
2nd Floor, Calton House, 22 Calton Road, Edinburgh EH8 8DP
Tel: 0131 524 0300
Email: ...... grants@foundationscotland.org.uk

WALES

Cardiff

COMMUNITY FOUNDATION IN WALES
St Andrews House, 24 St Andrews Crescent, Cardiff CF10 3DD
Tel: 029 20379580
Email: .... info@cfiw.org.uk

VOLUNTARY ORGANISATIONS FOR BLIND & PARTIALLY SIGHTED PEOPLE

Nearly half of the UK's local societies for blind and partially sighted people have resource centres holding classes in braille, typing and cooking. All provide advice and information. Local societies have their own organisations, Visionary - linking local sight loss charities (Tel: 020 8417 0942), and the RNIB supports local activities through centres for blind and partially sighted people in the UK.

Registration and welfare of blind people is undertaken by local authorities. See also organisations listed in the object index under Blind people.

ENGLAND

Bath & North East Somerset

DEAF PLUS VISION PLUS
2 Queens Parade, Bath, Bath & North East Somerset BA1 2NJ
Tel: 01225 446555
Email: .... bath.office@deaf.org

Bedfordshire

SIGHT CONCERN (BEDFORDSHIRE)
Kings House, 245 Ampthill Road, Bedford, Bedfordshire MK42 9AZ
Tel: 01234 311555
Email: .... office@sightconcern.org.uk

Blackpool

BLACKPOOL, FYLDE & WYRE SOCIETY FOR THE BLIND
Resource Centre, Bosworth Place, Blackpool FY4 1SH
Tel: 01253 362692
Email: .... info@vnision-nw.co.uk

Bournemouth

BOURNEMOUTH SOCIETY FOR THE VISUALLY IMPAIRED
5 Victoria Park Road, Bournemouth BH9 2RB
Tel: 01202 546644
Email: .... enquiries@bsvi.org.uk

Brighton & Hove

SUSSEX LANTERN (FORMERLY BRIGHTON SOCIETY FOR THE BLIND)
William Moon Lodge, The Linkway, Brighton, Brighton & Hove BN1 7EJ
Tel: 01273 507251
Email: .... info@bsblind.co.uk

Bristol

ACTION FOR BLIND PEOPLE SOUTHWEST
10 Stillhouse Lane, Bedminster, Bristol BS3 4EB
Tel: 0117 953 7750
Email: ...... bristol@actionforblindpeople.org.uk

Buckinghamshire

BUCKSVISION
Resource and Training Centre, 143 Meadowcroft, Aylesbury, Buckinghamshire HP19 9HH
Tel: 01296 487556
Email: .... reception@bucksvision.co.uk

Cambridgeshire

CAMSIGHT
167 Green End Road, Cambridge, Cambridgeshire CB4 1RW
Tel: 01223 420033
Email: .... info@camsight.org.uk

HUNTINGDONSHIRE SOCIETY FOR THE BLIND
8 St Mary's Street, Huntingdon, Cambridgeshire PE29 3PE
Tel: 01480 453438
Email: .... info@huntsblind.co.uk

PETERBOROUGH ASSOCIATION FOR THE BLIND
The Former Pharmacy, c/o The Medical Centre, Saltersgate, Peterborough, Cambridgeshire PE1 4YL
Tel: 01733 703570

RNIB PETERBOROUGH
Bakewell Road, Orton Southgate, Peterborough, Cambridgeshire PE2 6XU
Tel: 01733 375000

RNIB TALKING BOOK SERVICE
PO Box 173, Peterborough, Cambridgeshire PE2 6WS
Tel: 0303 123 9999

Cheshire

IRIS VISION RESOURCE CENTRE
14 Chapel Street, Crewe, Cheshire CW2 7DQ
Tel: 01270 250316
Email: .... info@iriscentre.org.uk

MACCLESFIELD EYE SOCIETY
15 Queen Victoria Street, Macclesfield, Cheshire SK11 6LP
Tel: 01625 422602

WARRINGTON, WIDNES AND DISTRICT SOCIETY FOR THE BLIND
Fairfield & Howley Centre, Fairfield, Warrington, Cheshire WA1 3AJ
Tel: 01925 632700
Email: . . . . info@warringtonvip.co.uk

Co. Durham

COUNTY DURHAM SOCIETY FOR THE BLIND & PARTIALLY SIGHTED
4 Red Hill Villas, Durham, Co. Durham DH1 4BA
Tel: 0191 386 8175
Email: . . . . info@cdslops.co.uk

Cornwall

CORNWALL COMMUNITY VOLUNTEER SERVICE
Community Centre, South Terrace, Camborne, Cornwall TR14 8SU
Tel: 01209 718844

ISIGHT CORNWALL
The Sight Centre, Newham Road, Truro, Cornwall TR1 2DP
Tel: 01872 261110
Email: . . . . info@isightcornwall.org.uk

Cumbria

BARROW AND DISTRICTS SOCIETY FOR THE BLIND
67-69 Cavendish Street, Barrow-in-Furness, Cumbria LA14 1QD
Tel: 01229 820698
Email: . . . . info@barrowblindsociety.org.uk

CARLISLE SOCIETY FOR THE BLIND
9 Brunswick Street, Carlisle, Cumbria CA1 1PB
Tel: 01228 593104

EDEN VOLUNTARY SOCIETY FOR THE BLIND & PARTIALLY SIGHTED
1 Mostyn Hall, Friargate, Penrith, Cumbria CA11 7XR
Tel: . . . . . . 01768 891724 (answerphone service)

SOUTH LAKES SOCIETY FOR THE BLIND
Stricklandgate House, 92 Stricklandgate, Kendal, Cumbria LA9 4PU
Tel: 01539 742633

WEST CUMBRIA SOCIETY FOR THE BLIND
22 Lowther Street, Whitehaven, Cumbria CA28 7DG
Tel: 01946 592474
Email: . . . . sightloss.lifeline@hotmail.com

Derbyshire

DERBYSHIRE ASSOCIATION FOR THE BLIND
65-69 Nottingham Road, Derby, Derbyshire DE1 3QS
Tel: 01332 292262

Devon

DEVON INSIGHT
Station House, Holman Way, Topsham, Exeter, Devon EX3 0EN
Tel: 01392 876666
Email: . . . . devon-blind@btconnect.com

HEARING & SIGHT CENTRE
Guild House, 156 Manormead Road, Plymouth, Devon PL3 5QL
Tel: . . 01752 201766; 01752 241087 (Textphone)
Email: . . . . guild@plymouthguild.otg.uk

NEWTON ABBOT CARE OF THE BLIND SOCIETY
37B Knowles Hill Road, Newton Abbot, Devon TQ12 2PP
Tel: 01626 366001

East Sussex

EAST SUSSEX ASSOCIATION OF BLIND AND PARTIALLY SIGHTED PEOPLE (ESAB)
Prospect House, 7-9 George Street, Hailsham, East Sussex BN27 1AD
Tel: 01323 832252
Email: . . . . info@eastsussexblind.org

EASTBOURNE BLIND SOCIETY
124-142 Longstone Road, Eastbourne, East Sussex BN22 8DA
Tel: 01323 729511

HASTINGS & ROTHER VOLUNTARY ASSOCIATION FOR THE BLIND
3 Upper Maze Hill, St Leonards-on-Sea, East Sussex TN38 OLQ
Tel: 01424 436359
Email: . . . . hrvab@freeuk.com

Essex

COLCHESTER SOCIETY FOR THE BLIND
29 Lucy Lane South, Stanway, Colchester, Essex CO3 0HE
Tel: 01206 533711

ESSEX BLIND CHARITY
Read House, 23 The Esplanade, Frinton-on-Sea, Essex CO13 9AU
Tel: 01255 673654
Email: . . . . info@essexblind.co.uk

Gloucestershire

INSIGHT GLOUCESTERSHIRE
81 Albion Street, Cheltenham, Gloucestershire GL52 2RZ
Tel: 01242 221170
Email: . . . . enquiries@insight-glos.org.uk

Greater Manchester

BURY SOCIETY FOR THE BLIND & PARTIALLY SIGHTED PEOPLE
Wolstenholme House, 4 Tenterten Street, Bury, Greater Manchester BL9 0EG
Tel: 0161 763 7014

HEYWOOD BLIND WELFARE SOCIETY
Social Centre for the Blind, 1 Starkey Street, Heywood, Greater Manchester OL10 4JS
Tel: 01706 369382

OLDHAM METROPOLITAN SOCIETY FOR THE BLIND
8 Montgomery House, Hawthorn Road, Hollinwood, Oldham, Greater Manchester OL8 3QG
Tel: 0161 682 8019

WHITEFIELD BLIND AID SOCIETY
23 Frankton Road, Whitefield, Manchester, Greater Manchester M45 7FB
Tel: 0161 766 7915

WIGAN, LEIGH AND DISTRICT SOCIETY FOR THE BLIND
Room 8, 28 Upper Dicconson Street, Wigan, Greater Manchester WN1 2AG
Tel: 01942 242891
Email: .... wiganleighblind@btinternet.com

Hampshire

PORTSMOUTH ASSOCIATION FOR THE BLIND
48 Stubbington Avenue, North End, Portsmouth, Hampshire PO2 0HY
Tel: 023 9266 1717
Email: .... portsmouthblind@btconnect.com

SOUTHAMPTON SIGHT
3 Bassett Avenue, Bassett, Southampton, Hampshire SO16 7DP
Tel: 023 8076 9882

Hertfordshire

HERTFORDSHIRE SOCIETY FOR THE BLIND
The Woodside Centre, The Commons, Welwyn Garden City, Hertfordshire AL7 4SE
Tel: 01707 324680
Email: .... office@hertsblind.com

Isle of Man

MANX BLIND WELFARE SOCIETY
Corrin Court, Heywood Avenue, Onchan, Douglas, Isle of Man IM3 3AP
Tel: 01624 674727
Email: .... enquiries@mbws.org.im

Isle of Wight

ISLE OF WIGHT SOCIETY FOR THE BLIND
137 Carisbrooke Road, Newport, Isle of Wight PO30 1DD
Tel: 01983 522205
Email: .... enquiries@iwsb.org.uk

Kent

KENT ASSOCIATION FOR THE BLIND
72 College Road, Maidstone, Kent ME15 6SJ
Tel: 01622 691357
Email: ..... amanda.croft-pearman@kab.org.uk

ROYAL LONDON SOCIETY FOR THE BLIND
Dorton Campus, Wildernesse Avenue, Seal, Sevenoaks, Kent TN15 0EB
Tel: 01732 592500
Email: .... web-master@rlsb.org.uk

Kingston upon Hull

HULL AND EAST RIDING INSTITUTE FOR THE BLIND
Beech Holme, Beverley Road, Hull, Kingston upon Hull HU5 1NF
Tel: 01482 342297

Lancashire

ACCRINGTON AND DISTRICT BLIND SOCIETY
32 Bank Street, Accrington, Lancashire BB5 1HP
Tel: 01254 233332

BLACKBURN AND DISTRICT BLIND SOCIETY
1-2 Thwaites House, Railway Road, Blackburn, Lancashire BB1 5AX
Tel: 01254 54143; 01254 65535

BURNLEY AND DISTRICT SOCIETY FOR THE BLIND
3 Bedford Avenue, Burnley, Lancashire BB12 6AE
Tel: 01282 438507

GALLOWAY'S SOCIETY FOR THE BLIND
Howick House, Howick Park Avenue, Penwortham, Preston, Lancashire PR1 0LS
Tel: 01772 744148
Email: .... peter.taylor@galloways.org.uk

Leicestershire

VISTA
1a Sailsbury Road, Leicester, Leicestershire LE1 7QR
Tel: 0116 249 0909
Email: .... info@vistablind.org.uk

Lincolnshire

LINCOLN & LINDSEY BLIND SOCIETY
Bradbury House, Ramsgate, Louth, Lincolnshire LN11 0NB
Tel: 01507 605604
Email: .... info@llbs.co.uk

London

ACTION FOR BLIND PEOPLE - PART OF RNIB GROUP
105 Judd Street, London WC1H 9NE
Tel: 0303 123 9999
Email: .... supportercare@afbp.org.uk

BLINDAID

BlindAid

Lantern House, 102 Bermondsey Street, London SE1 3UB
Tel: 020 7403 6184
Fax: 020 7234 0708
Email: .... enquiries@blindaid.org.uk
Web: .... www.blindaid.org.uk
BlindAid has over 180 years of experience. Working in the 12 Inner London Boroughs, we provide vital home visits to over 600 isolated blind and visually impaired people offering friendship, company and conversation.

BRENT VISUALLY HANDICAPPED GROUP
Cameron House, 80 Pound Lane, Willesden, London NW10 2HT
Tel: .... 020 8451 4354 Answerphone

THE HARINGEY PHOENIX GROUP
Winkfield Resource Centre, 33 Winkfield Road, Wood Green, London N22 5RP
Tel: 020 8889 7070
Email: ..... haringeyphoenixgroup@yahoo.co.uk

IN TOUCH ISLINGTON
99 Shepperton Road, London N1 3DF
Tel: 020 7359 6827

JEWISH CARE
Amelie House, Maurice & Vivienne Wohl Campus, 221 Golders Green Road, London NW11 9DQ
Tel: 020 8922 2000
Email: .... info@jcare.org

MERTONVISION
c/o The Guardian Centre, 67 Clarendon Road, Colliers Wood, London SW19 2DX
Tel: 020 8540 5446
Email: .... info@mertonvision.org.uk

NEWHAM VOLUNTARY ASSOCIATION FOR THE BLIND
Jordan Hall, Curwen Centre, 2 London Road, Plaistow, London E13 0DE
Tel: 020 8548 1977

RNIB HEADQUARTERS
105 Judd Street, London WC1H 9NE
Tel: 020 7388 1266
Email: .... helpline@rnib.org.uk

ROYAL NATIONAL INSTITUTE OF BLIND PEOPLE (RNIB)
105 Judd Street, London WC1H 9NE
Tel: 0845 600 0313
Email: .... legacyservices@rnib.org.uk

Merseyside

BRADBURY FIELDS
The Bradbury Centre, Youens Way, Liverpool, Merseyside L14 2EP
Tel: 0151 221 0888
Email: .... info@bradburyfields.org.uk

CATHOLIC BLIND INSTITUTE
Yew Tree Lane, Liverpool, Merseyside L12 9HN
Tel: 0151 220 2525

GALLOWAY'S SOCIETY FOR THE BLIND
Paton House, 22 Wright Street, Southport, Merseyside PR9 0TL
Tel: 01704 534555
Email: .... southeast@galloways.org.uk

WIRRAL SOCIETY OF THE BLIND AND PARTIALLY SIGHTED
Ashville Lodge, Ashville Road, Birkenhead, Merseyside CH41 8AU
Tel: 0151 652 8877

Middlesex

MIDDLESEX ASSOCIATION FOR THE BLIND
Suite 18 - Freetrade House, Lowther Road, Stanmore, Middlesex HA7 1EP
Tel: 020 8423 5141; 0845 838 0480
Email: .... info@aftb.org.uk

Norfolk

NORFOLK AND NORWICH ASSOCIATION FOR THE BLIND
106 Magpie Road, Norwich, Norfolk NR3 1JH
Tel: 01603 629558
Email: .... office@nnab.org.uk

North Somerset

VISION NORTH SOMERSET
3 Neva Road, Weston-super-Mare, North Somerset BS23 1YD
Tel: 01934 419393
Email: .... celia.henshall@visionns.org.uk

North Yorkshire

HARROGATE & DISTRICT SOCIETY FOR THE BLIND (INC. RIPON)
Russell Sergeant House, 23 East Parade, Harrogate, North Yorkshire HG1 5LF
Tel: 01423 565915
Email: .... enquiries@hdsb.org.uk

SCARBOROUGH BLIND AND PARTIALLY SIGHTED SOCIETY (INCLUDING WHITBY & RYEDALE)
183 Dean Road, Scarborough, North Yorkshire YO12 7JH
Tel: 01723 354417

SELBY DISTRICT VISION
Unit 12, The Prospect Centre, Prospect Way, Selby, North Yorkshire YO8 8BD
Tel: 01757 709800
Email: .... info@selbydistrictvision.co.uk

TEESSIDE AND DISTRICT SOCIETY FOR THE BLIND
Stockton Road, Newport, Middlesbrough, North Yorkshire TS5 4AH
Tel: 01642 247518

Northamptonshire

NORTHAMPTONSHIRE ASSOCIATION FOR THE BLIND
37 Harbour Road, Kingsthorpe, Northampton, Northamptonshire NN2 8AG
Tel: 01604 719193
Email: .... helpline@nab.org.uk

Northumberland

NORTHUMBERLAND COUNTY BLIND ASSOCIATION
Reiver House, Stathers Lane, Morpeth, Northumberland NE61 1TD
Tel: 01670 574316
Email: .... enquiries@ncba.org.uk

Oxfordshire

BANBURY SOCIETY FOR THE VISUALLY IMPAIRED
7 Willoughby Road, Banbury, Oxfordshire OX16 9DZ
Tel: 01865 725595

OXFORDSHIRE ASSOCIATION FOR THE BLIND
Bradbury Lodge, Gordon Woodward Way, Abingdon Road, Oxford, Oxfordshire OX1 4XL
Tel: 01865 725595
Email: .... director@oxeyes.org.uk

Poole

DORSET BLIND ASSOCIATION
17 Bournemouth Road, Lower Parkstone, Poole BH14 0EF
Tel: 01202 712869
Email: .... info@dorsetblind.org.uk

Reading

BERKSHIRE COUNTY BLIND SOCIETY
Midleton House, 5 Erleigh Road, Reading RG1 5LR
Tel: 0118 987 2803
Email: .... office@bcbs.org.uk

READING ASSOCIATION FOR THE BLIND
Walford Hall, Carey Street, Reading RG1 7JS
Tel: 0118 957 2960
Email: .... readingblind@yahoo.co.uk

Shropshire

SHROPSHIRE VOLUNTARY ASSOCIATION FOR THE BLIND
SVAB Office, The Lantern, Meadow Farm Drive, Shrewsbury, Shropshire SY1 4NG
Tel: 01743 210508

South Yorkshire

BARNSLEY BLIND AND PARTIALLY SIGHTED ASSOCIATION
The Resource Centre, 22 Regent Street South, Barnsley, South Yorkshire S70 2HT
Tel: 01226 200618

SHEFFIELD ROYAL SOCIETY FOR THE BLIND (SRSB)
5 Mappin Street, Sheffield S1 4DT
Tel: 0114 272 2757
Fax: 0870 706 5171
Email: .... steve@srsb.org.uk
Web: .... www.srsb.org.uk
SRSB provides opportunity, support, friendship and services to blind and partially sighted people in Sheffield, helping them to achieve whatever they wish to do and whatever they aspire to be.

SHEFFIELD VOLUNTARY TRUST FOR THE WELFARE OF THE BLIND AND PARTIALLY SIGHTED
Sheffield City Council, Sheffield, South Yorkshire S1 2JQ
Tel: 0114 273 4973

Suffolk

EAST SUFFOLK ASSOCIATION FOR THE BLIND
Mallard House Business Centre, The Old Station, Little Bealings, Woodbridge, Suffolk IP13 6LT
Tel: 01473 611011

IPSWICH BLIND SOCIETY LTD
19 Tower Street, Ipswich, Suffolk IP1 3BE
Tel: .... 01473 219712 24hr Answerphone
Email: .... ipswichblindsociety@tiscali.co.uk

WEST SUFFOLK VOLUNTARY ASSOCIATION FOR THE BLIND
4 Bunting Road, Moreton Hall Estate, Bury St Edmunds, Suffolk IP32 7BX
Tel: 01284 748800
Email: .... info@wsvab.org

Surrey

CROYDON VOLUNTARY ASSOCIATION FOR THE BLIND
Bedford Hall, 72-74 Wellesley Road, Croydon, Surrey CR0 2AR
Tel: 020 8688 2486

KINGSTON-UPON-THAMES ASSOCIATION FOR THE BLIND
Adams House, Vicarage Lane, New Malden, Surrey KT3 3FF
Tel: 020 8605 0060

SUTTON VISION
1st Floor, 3 Robin Hood Lane, Sutton, Surrey SM1 2SW
Tel: 020 8409 7166/7
Email: .... info@suttonvision.org.uk

Tyne & Wear

BLIND SOCIETY FOR NORTH TYNESIDE
Parkside House, Elton Street, Wallsend, Tyne & Wear NE28 8QU
Tel: 0191 262 0869

COMMUNITY FOUNDATION (FORMERLY TYNE & WEAR FOUNDATION)
9th Floor, Cale Cross, 156 Pilgrim Street, Newcastle upon Tyne, Tyne & Wear NE1 6SU
Tel: 0191 222 0945
Email: ... general@communityfoundation.org.uk

GATESHEAD & SOUTH TYNESIDE SIGHT SERVICE (FORMERLY NORTHUMBRIA SIGHT SERVICE)
Badbury Centre, Bensham Hospital, Saltwell Road, Gateshead, Tyne & Wear NE8 4YL
Tel: 0191 478 5959

LONGBENTON VOLUNTARY COMMITTEE FOR THE BLIND
Beech House, 12 The Spinney, Killingworth Village, Newcastle upon Tyne, Tyne & Wear NE12 6BG
Tel: 0191 268 1569

NEWCASTLE SOCIETY FOR BLIND PEOPLE
3rd Floor, MEA House, Ellison Place, Newcastle upon Tyne, Tyne & Wear NE1 8XS
Tel: 0191 232 7292
Email: .... enquiries@nsbp.co.uk

SUNDERLAND AND NORTH DURHAM ROYAL SOCIETY FOR THE BLIND
8 Foyle Street, Sunderland, Tyne & Wear SR1 1LB
Tel: 0191 567 3939
Email: .... office@sundrsb.org.uk

TYNEMOUTH BLIND WELFARE SOCIETY
Pearey House, Preston Park, North Shields, Tyne & Wear NE29 9JR
Tel: 0191 257 4388

West Midlands

BEACON CENTRE FOR THE BLIND
Wolverhampton Road East, Wolverhampton, West Midlands WV4 6AZ
Tel: 01902 880111
Email: .... enquiries@beacon4blind.co.uk

COVENTRY RESOURCE CENTRE FOR THE BLIND
33 Earlsdon Avenue South, Coventry, West Midlands CV5 6TH
Tel: 024 7671 7522

FOCUS BIRMINGHAM
48-62 Woodville Road, Harborne, Birmingham, West Midlands B17 9AT
Tel: . . . . 0121 478 5200 (Switchboard); 0121 478 5222 (Helpline)

RNIB BIRMINGHAM
58-72 John Bright Street, Birmingham, West Midlands B1 1BN
Tel: 0121 665 4200

WALSALL SOCIETY FOR THE BLIND
Hawley House, 11 Hatherton Road, Walsall, West Midlands WS1 1XS
Tel: 01922 627683

West Sussex

4SIGHT (FORMERLY WEST SUSSEX ASSOCIATION FOR THE BLIND)
Bradbury Centre, 36 Victoria Drive, Bognor Regis, West Sussex PO21 2TE
Tel: 01243 828555
Email: . . . . enquiries@4sightsussex.co.uk

WORTHING SOCIETY FOR THE BLIND
75 Richmond Road, Worthing, West Sussex BN11 4AQ
Tel: 01903 235782
Email: . . . . info@wsftb.org.uk

West Yorkshire

HALIFAX SOCIETY FOR THE BLIND
34 Clare Road, Halifax, West Yorkshire HX1 2HX
Tel: 01422 352383

KEIGHLEY AND DISTRICT ASSOCIATION FOR THE BLIND
1 Albert Street, Keighley, West Yorkshire BD21 2AT
Tel: 01535 602354
Email: . . . . enquiries@keighleyblind.org

LEEDS JEWISH BLIND SOCIETY
The Margery & Arnold Ziff Community Centre, 311 Stonegate Road, Leeds, West Yorkshire LS17 6AZ
Tel: 0113 268 4211

THE LEEDS SOCIETY FOR DEAF & BLIND PEOPLE
Centenary House, North Street, Leeds, West Yorkshire LS2 8AY
Tel: 0113 243 8328

PUDSEY VOLUNTARY COMMITTEE FOR THE WELFARE OF THE BLIND
8 Monson Avenue, Calverley, Pudsey, West Yorkshire LS28 5NP
Tel: 0113 229 5257

SHIPLEY AND BAILDON BLIND WELFARE ASSOCIATION
8 Hill End Grove, Bradford, West Yorkshire BD7 4RP
Tel: 01274 571074

SOCIETY FOR THE BLIND OF DEWSBURY, BATLEY AND DISTRICT
The Whitfield Centre, 180 Soothill Lane, Batley, West Yorkshire WF17 6HP
Tel: 01924 445222

WAKEFIELD SOCIETY FOR THE BLIND
c/o Bardon, Runtlings, Ossett, West Yorkshire WF5 8JJ
Tel: 01924 262643

WEST RIDING BLIND ASSOCIATION
Parkside Centre, Leeds Road, Outwood, Wakefield, West Yorkshire WF1 2PN
Tel: 01924 215555

Worcestershire

SIGHT CONCERN WORCESTERSHIRE
The Bradbury Centre, 2 Sansome Walk, Worcester, Worcestershire WR1 1LH
Tel: 01905 723245
Email: . . . . info@sightconcern.co.uk

NORTHERN IRELAND

Co. Armagh

LURGAN BLIND WELFARE COMMITTEE
15 Market Street, Lurgan, Co. Armagh BT66 8AR

SCOTLAND

Dumfries & Galloway

DUMFRIES & GALLOWAY ASSOCIATION FOR THE BLIND
Mount St Michael, Craigs Road, Dumfries, Dumfries & Galloway DG1 4UT
Tel: 01387 248784

Dundee

DUNDEE BLIND & PARTIALLY SIGHTED SOCIETY
Thomas Herd House, 10-12 Ward Road, Dundee DD1 1LX
Tel: 01382 227101
Email: . . . . sandra.gollan@dbpss.org.uk

Edinburgh

RNIB SCOTLAND
12-14 Hillside Crescent, Edinburgh EH7 5EA
Tel: 0131 652 3140
Email: . . . . rnibscotland@rnib.org.uk

Fife

FIFE SOCIETY FOR THE BLIND
Fife Sensory Impairment Centre, Wilson Avenue, Kirkcaldy, Fife KY2 5EF
Tel: 01592 644979
Email: . . . . info@fsbinsight.co.uk

Glasgow

JEWISH BLIND SOCIETY (SCOTLAND)
Walton Community Centre, May Terrace, Giffnock, Glasgow G46 6LD
Tel: 0141 620 1800

VISIBILITY (FORMERLY GLASGOW AND WEST OF SCOTLAND SOCIETY FOR THE BLIND)
2 Queens Crescent, Glasgow G4 9BW
Tel: 0141 332 4632
Email: .... info@visibility.org.uk

Highland

HIGHLAND SOCIETY FOR BLIND PEOPLE
38 Ardconnel Street, Inverness, Highland IV2 3EX
Tel: 01463 233663
Email: .... denise@highlandblindcraft.co.uk

WALES

Cardiff

CARDIFF INSTITUTE FOR THE BLIND
Shand House, 20 Newport Road, Cardiff CF24 0YB
Tel: 029 2048 5414
Email: .... postmaster@cibi.co.uk

Gwynedd

NORTH WALES SOCIETY FOR THE BLIND
325 High Street, Bangor, Gwynedd LL57 1YB
Tel: 01248 353604

Merthyr Tydfil

MERTHYR TYDFIL INSTITUTE FOR THE BLIND
Unit 4, Triangle Business Park, Pentrebach, Merthyr Tydfil CF48 4TQ
Tel: 01685 370072
Email: .... info@mtib.co.uk

Swansea

SWANSEA AND DISTRICT FRIENDS OF THE BLIND
3 De La Beche Street, Swansea SA1 3EY
Tel: 01792 655424
Email: .... john_allen_10@hotmail.com

VISION IMPAIRED WEST GLAMORGAN
2 Gonhill, West Cross, Swansea SA3 5PL
Tel: 01792 776360
Email: .... judith@cibi.co.uk

Torfaen

GWENT ASSOCIATION FOR THE BLIND
Badbury House, Park Buildings, Park Road, Pontypool, Torfaen NP4 6JH
Tel: 01495 764650

VOLUNTARY ORGANISATIONS & RESIDENTIAL HOMES FOR DEAF PEOPLE

This information was originally supplied by the Royal National Institute for Deaf People (RNID) who are now known as Action on Hearing Loss. The charity has detailed lists of local organisations and clubs for deaf people. Telephone numbers below are for voice only unless otherwise specified. Action on Hearing Loss should be contacted at the following address:
19-23 Featherstone Street, London EC1Y 8SL Tel: 0808 808 0123 Textphone: 0808 808 9000
Email: informationline@hearingloss.org.uk Web: www.actiononhearingloss.org.uk

ENGLAND

Bath & North East Somerset

ACTION ON HEARING LOSS BATH SUPPORTED HOUSING
112 Freeview Road, Twerton, Bath, Bath & North East Somerset BA2 1DZ
Tel: 01225 342930

ACTION ON HEARING LOSS NEWBRIDGE HILL
51 Newbridge Hill, Lower Weston, Bath, Bath & North East Somerset BA1 3PR
Tel: . . . 01225 443019; 01225 443019 Textphone
Email: . . . . . . ursula.forbush@hearingloss.org.uk

ACTION ON HEARING LOSS POOLEMEAD
Poolemead House, Watery Lane, Twerton-on-Avon, Bath, Bath & North East Somerset BA2 1RN
Tel: . . . . 01225 332818 Voice/Textphone; 01225 332818

Blackpool

BLACKPOOL, FYLDE AND WYRE SOCIETY FOR THE DEAF
Wynfield House, 115 Newton Drive, Blackpool FY3 8LZ
Tel: 01253 300728

Brighton & Hove

ACTION ON HEARING LOSS WILBURY GARDENS
13 Wilbury Gardens, Hove, Brighton & Hove BN3 6HQ
Tel: . . . . 01273 205044 Voice/Minicom
Email: . . . . scrinne.maer@hearingloss.org.uk

Cambridgeshire

CAMSIGHT
167 Green End Road, Cambridge, Cambridgeshire CB4 1RW
Tel: 01223 246237 Voice; 01223 411801 Minicom
Email: . . . . office@cambsdeaf.org

Cheshire

DEAFNESS SUPPORT NETWORK
144 London Road, Northwich, Cheshire CW9 5HH
Tel: 01606 47831
Email: . . . . dsn@dsnonline.co.uk

Cornwall

ACTION ON HEARING LOSS PENDEAN COURT
16 Pendean Court, Barras Cross, Liskeard, Cornwall PL14 6DZ
Tel: . . . 01579 340201; 01579 340450 Textphone

Devon

ACTION ON HEARING LOSS PIPPIN HOUSE
8 Keyberry Park, Newton Abbot, Devon TQ12 1BZ
Tel: . . . 01626 354521; 01626 337251 Textphone

East Sussex

HEARING CONCERN LINK
27-28 The Waterfront, Eastbourne, East Sussex BN23 5UZ

Essex

FOLEY HOUSE
115 High Garrett, Braintree, Essex CM7 5NU
Tel: . . . . 01376 326652 Voice
Email: . . . . enquiries@foleyhouse.org.uk

ROYAL ASSOCIATION FOR DEAF PEOPLE
Century House South, Riverside Office Centre, North Station Road, Colchester, Essex CO1 1RE
Tel: . . 0845 688 2525; 0845 688 2527 (Minicom)
Email: . . . . info@royaldeaf.org.uk

Greater Manchester

MANCHESTER DEAF CENTRE
Crawford House, Booth Street East, Manchester, Greater Manchester M13 9GH
Tel: . . . . . . 0161 273 3415 Voice; 0161 273 3415 Minicom

Hampshire

SONUS
Spitfire House, 28-29 High Street, Southampton, Hampshire SO14 2DF
Tel: 023 8051 6516
Email: . . . . enquiries@sonus.org.uk

Isle of Wight

EASTHILL HOME FOR DEAF PEOPLE
7 Pitt Street, Ryde, Isle of Wight PO33 3EB
Tel: . . . . 01983 564068 Voice/Minicom

Kent

ACTION ON HEARING LOSS CLIFFE AVENUE
15 Cliffe Avenue, Westbrook, Margate, Kent CT9 5DU
Tel: ..... 01843 232122; 01843 232624 Minicom

ACTION ON HEARING LOSS ROPER HOUSE
St Dunstans Street, Canterbury, Kent CT2 8BZ
Tel: ...... 01227 462155; 01227 781915 Voice/Textphone

Lancashire

EAST LANCASHIRE DEAF SOCIETY
6-8 Heaton Street, Blackburn, Lancashire BB2 2EF
Tel: ... 01254 844550; 01254 262460 (Minicom)
Email: .... burnley@elds.org.uk

Leicestershire

ACTION DEAFNESS
Orchardson Avenue, Leicester, Leicestershire LE4 6DP
Tel: .. 0116 257 4800 Voice; 0116 257 4850 Text
Email: .... enquiries@actiondeafness.org.uk

London

ACTION ON HEARING LOSS BRONDESBURY ROAD
113 Brondesbury Road, Queens Park, London NW6 6RY
Tel: ...... 020 7328 8540 Voice; 020 7328 8544 Minicom

JEWISH DEAF ASSOCIATION
Julius Newman House, Woodside Park Road, Off High Road, North Finchley, London N12 8RP
Tel: ..... 020 8446 0502 (Voice); 020 8446 4037 (Textphone)
Email: .... mail@jda.dircon.co.uk

Merseyside

MERSEYSIDE SOCIETY FOR DEAF PEOPLE
Queens Drive, West Derby, Liverpool, Merseyside L13 0DJ
Tel: .... 0151 228 0888 Voice/Minicom

SOUTHPORT CENTRE FOR THE DEAF
19A Stanley Street, Southport, Merseyside PR9 0BY
Tel: .... 01704 537001 Voice/Minicom

North Yorkshire

DEAF SOCIETY YORK & DISTRICT
Centre for the Deaf, Bootham House, 61 Bootham, York, North Yorkshire YO3 7BT
Tel: .... 01904 623459 Voice/Minicom

Nottinghamshire

NOTTINGHAMSHIRE DEAF SOCIETY
22 Forest Road West, Nottingham, Nottinghamshire NG7 4EQ
Tel: .... 0115 970 0516 Voice/Minicom
Email: .... nds@nottsdeaf.org.uk

Reading

READING DEAF CENTRE
131 Cardiff Road, Reading RG1 8JF
Tel: .... 0118 959 4969 Voice/Minicom

South Yorkshire

SHEFFIELD CENTRAL DEAF CLUB
Victoria Hall Methodist Church, Norfolk Street, Chapel Walk, Sheffield, South Yorkshire S1 2PD
Tel: .... 0114 275 5307 Voice; 0114 275 5307 Minicom
Email: .... andrew.brown26@btconnect.com

Surrey

ACTION ON HEARING LOSS GIBRALTAR CRESCENT
36a Gibraltar Crescent, Epsom, Surrey KT19 9BT
Tel: ...... 020 8393 0865 Voice; 020 8393 7623 Minicom

West Midlands

ACTION ON HEARING LOSS MULBERRY HOUSE
70 Lichfield Street, Walsall, West Midlands WS4 2BY
Tel: 01922 615218 Voice; 01922 722658 Mincom

ACTION ON HEARING LOSS OLIVE LANE
60 Olive Lane, Halesowen, West Midlands B62 8LZ
Tel: . 0121 559 0031; 0121 559 0280 (Textphone)
Email: .... rosie.foster@rnid.org.uk

BID SERVICES
Ladywood Road, Birmingham, West Midlands B16 8SZ
Tel: 0121 246 6100
Email: .... info@bid.org.uk

COVENTRY DEAF SOCIAL CLUB
Henry Fry Centre, Hertford Place, Coventry, West Midlands CV1 3JZ
Tel: .... 024 7622 2321 Voice/Minicom
Email: .... henryfry@dsl.pipex.com

NORTHERN IRELAND

Co. Londonderry

ACTION ON HEARING LOSS HARKNESS GARDENS
1-2 Harkness Gardens, Brigade Road, Londonderry, Co. Londonderry BT47 6GG
Tel: ...... 028 7134 1005 Voice; 028 7134 2262 Minicom

SCOTLAND

Aberdeen

ABERDEEN AND NE SOCIETY FOR THE DEAF
13 Smithfield Road, Aberdeen AB24 4NR
Tel: ... 01224 494566; 01224 495675 (Minicom)
Email: .... info@aneds.org.uk

Dundee

DEAF ACTION
36 Roseangle, Dundee DD1 4LY
Tel: ...... 01382 221124; 01382 224052; 01382 227052 Voice/Minicom
Email: .... tynesideadmin@deafaction.org

Edinburgh

DEAF ACTION
49 Albany Street, Edinburgh EH1 3QY
Tel: ...... 0131 556 3128; 0131 557 0419 (Text)
Email: .... admin@deafaction.org

Glasgow

DEAF CONNECTIONS
Glasgow Centre for the Deaf, 100 Norfolk Street, Glasgow G5 9EJ
Tel: .... 0141 420 1759 Voice/Text
Email: .... enquiries@deafconnections.co.uk

VOLUNTEER CENTRES & COUNCILS FOR VOLUNTARY SERVICES

Volunteer Centres are local agencies whose main purpose is to match up would-be volunteers with suitable opportunities and promote good practice in volunteering. They provide training and support as required and help develop new opportunities for volunteering in their communities. Volunteer Centres are unique in that their primary concern is with the well-being of volunteers, rather than the organisations they assist.

Councils for Voluntary Services provide a range of specialist expertise and information with the aim of helping local people run successful community organisations. Advice ranges from help finding funding and making effective use of resources to holding forums. CVS also aim to encourage more people to volunteer and get involved in voluntary and community action.

For more information go to http://www.navca.org.uk/

Other useful volunteering resources:
NCVO, Regent's Wharf, 8 All Saints Street, London N1 9RL Tel: 020 7713 6161
Email: ncvo@ncvo.org.uk Web: www.volunteering.org.uk;
Volunteer Scotland, Jubilee House, Forthside Way, Stirling FK8 1QZ
Tel: 01786 479593 Fax: 01786 479593 Web: www.volunteerscotland.net; or
Volunteer Now, 34 Shaftesbury Square, Belfast, Co. Antrim BT2 7DB Tel: 028 9023 2020
Email: info@volunteernow.co.uk Web: www.volunteernow.co.uk

ENGLAND

Bedfordshire

VOLUNTEER CENTRE BEDFORD
43 Bromham Road, Bedford, Bedfordshire MK40 2AA
Tel: 01234 213100

Bracknell Forest

BRACKNELL FOREST VOLUNTARY ACTION
BFVA, Ground Floor, Amber House, Market Street, Bracknell, Bracknell Forest RG12 1JB
Tel: 01344 304404

Brighton & Hove

VOLUNTEER CENTRE BRIGHTON AND HOVE
113 Queens Road, Second Floor, Community Base, Hove, Brighton & Hove BN1 3XG
Tel: 01273 737 888

Bristol

VOLUNTEER BRISTOL
Royal Oak House, Royal Oak Avenue, Bristol BS1 4GB
Tel: 0117 989 7733

Buckinghamshire

COMMUNITY IMPACT BUCKS
Unit B The Firs, Bierton, Aylesbury, Buckinghamshire HP22 5DX
Tel: 0845 3890389

Cambridgeshire

CAMBRIDGE VOLUNTEER CENTRE
Llandaff Chambers, 2 Regent Street, Cambridge, Cambridgeshire CB2 1AX
Tel: 01223 356549

FENLAND VOLUNTEER BUREAU
69 Queens Road, Wisbech, Cambridgeshire PE13 2PE
Tel: 01945 582192

PETERBOROUGH COUNCIL FOR VOLUNTARY SERVICE
3 Lincoln Court, Lincoln Road, Peterborough, Cambridgeshire PE1 2RP
Tel: 01733 311016; 01733 342683

Cheshire

CHESTER VOLUNTARY ACTION
Folliott House, 53 Northgate Street, Chester, Cheshire CH1 2HQ
Tel: 01244 316587

CONGLETON VOLUNTEER BUREAU
54 Lawton Street, Congleton, Cheshire CW12 1RS
Tel: 01260 299022

(CREWE & NANTWICH VB) NANTWICH BRANCH
Nantwich Office, Beam Street, Nantwich, Cheshire CW5 5DE
Tel: . . . . All Enquiries to the Main Office

CREWE & NANTWICH VOLUNTARY ACTION
Ashton House, 1a Gatefield Street, Crewe, Cheshire CW1 2JP
Tel: 01270 211545
Email: .... enquiries@cvce.org.uk

CVS CHESHIRE EAST
81 Park Lane, Macclesfield, Cheshire SK11 6TX

HALTON & ST HELEN'S VOLUNTARY & COMMUNITY ACTION
Sefton House, Public Hall Street, Runcorn, Cheshire WA7 1NG
Tel: 01928 592405
Email: .... info@haltonsthelensvca.org.uk

HALTON YOUNG VOLUNTEERS BUREAU
Information Shop for Young People, 2 Frederick Street, Widnes, Cheshire WA8 6PG
Tel: 0151 420 7888

(MACCLESFIELD CVS VB) KNUTSFORD BRANCH
St John's Wood Millenium Community Centre, Longridge, Knutsford, Cheshire WA16 8PA
Tel: 01565 652538

VOLUNTEER CENTRE WARRINGTON
9 Suez Street, Warrington, Cheshire WA1 1EF
Tel: 01925 637609

Co. Durham

2D (SUPPORT FOR THE VOLUNTARY AND COMMUNITY SECTOR OF TEESDALE & WEAR VALLEY)
Unit 9, Crook Business Centre, New Road, Crook, Co. Durham DL15 8QX
Tel: 01388 762220

DERWENTSIDE CVS & VOLUNTEER BUREAU
The Tommy Amstrong Centre, Clifford Road, Stanley, Co. Durham DH9 0XG
Tel: 01207 218855

DURHAM ASSOCIATION OF YOUTH AND COMMUNITY ORGANISATIONS (D.A.Y.C.O.)
Thornley Community Association, Hartlepool Street North, Hartlepool, Co. Durham DH6 3AB
Tel: 01429 821311

EASINGTON & DISTRICT VOLUNTEER BUREAU
13 Upper Yoden Way, Peterlee, Co. Durham SR8 1AX
Tel: 0191 586 5427

EVOLUTION DARLINGTON
Church Row, Darlington, Co. Durham DL1 5QD
Tel: 01325 266888

HARTLEPOOL VOLUNTARY DEVELOPMENT AGENCY
Rockhaven, 36 Victoria Road, Hartlepool, Co. Durham TS26 8DD
Tel: 01429 262641
Email: .... info@hvda.co.uk

Cornwall

(CORNWALL CFV) BUDE BRANCH
Neetside, The Crescent, Bude, Cornwall EX23 8LB
Tel: 01288 352700

(CORNWALL CFV) NORTH CORNWALL BRANCH
1 Hamley Court, Dennison Road, Bodmin, Cornwall PL31 2LL
Tel: 01208 79565

(CORNWALL CFV) VOLUNTEER CENTRE CARADON
Shop B, 6 Church Street, Liskeard, Cornwall PL14 3AG
Tel: 01579 344818

(PENWITH VB) HAYLE BRANCH
Unit 4 Foundry House, Foundry Square, Hayle, Cornwall TR27 4HH
Tel: 01736 757364

PENWITH VOLUNTEER BUREAU
Parade Street, Penzance, Cornwall TR18 4BU
Tel: 01736 330988

RESTORMEL VOLUNTEER CENTRE CORNWALL REST FOR VOLUNTEERS
17 Duke Street, St Austell, Cornwall PL25 5PQ
Tel: 01726 71087

VOLUNTEER CORNWALL
Acorn House, Heron Way, Newham, Truro, Cornwall TR1 2XN
Tel: 01872 265305

Cumbria

WEST CUMBRIA VOLUNTEER CENTRE
12a Selby Terrace, Maryport, Cumbria CA15 6NF
Tel: 01900 819191

Derbyshire

AMBER VALLEY CVS VOLUNTEER BUREAU
Market Place, Ripley, Derbyshire DE5 3HA
Tel: 01773 512076

CHESTERFIELD & NE DERBYSHIRE VOLUNTEER CENTRE
35 Rose Hill, Chesterfield, Derbyshire S40 1TT
Tel: 01246 276777
Email: .... info@chesterfieldvc.org.uk

EREWASH CVS VOLUNTEER CENTRE
Springfield House, 4/5 Granby Street, Ilkeston, Derbyshire DE7 8HN
Tel: 0115 850 8860
Email: .... enquiries@erewashcvs.org.uk

GLOSSOP & DISTRICT VOLUNTEER BUREAU
Howard Town House, High Street East, Glossop, Derbyshire SK13 8DA
Tel: 01457 865722
Email: .... info@gvb.org.uk

NEW MILLS AND DISTRICT VOLUNTEER CENTRE
33-35 Union Road, High Peak, New Mills, Derbyshire SK22 3EL
Tel: 01663 744196

VOLUNTEER CENTRE BUXTON & DISTRICT
16 Eagle Parade, Buxton, Derbyshire SK17 6EQ
Tel: 01298 23970

VOLUNTEER CENTRE DERBYSHIRE DALES
Ashbourne Business Centre, Dig Street, Ashbourne, Derbyshire DE6 1GF
Tel: 01335 348602

Devon

CREDITON & DISTRICT VOLUNTEER CENTRE
The Old Surgery, 55 The High Street, Crediton, Devon EX17 3JX
Tel: 01363 777711

DAWLISH & EAST TEIGNBRIDGE VOLUNTEER BUREAU
The Manor, Old Town Street, Dawlish, Devon EX7 9AW
Tel: 01626 888321

INVOLVE - VOLUNTARY ACTION IN MID DEVON
Raymond Penny House, Phoenix Lane, Tiverton, Devon EX16 6LU
Tel: 01884 255734

NORTH DEVON VOLUNTEERING DEVELOPMENT AGENCY
149 High Street, Ilfracombe, Devon EX34 9EZ
Tel: 01271 866300

TEIGNBRIDGE VOLUNTEER CENTRE
Forde House, Brunel Road, Newton Abbot, Devon TQ12 4XX
Tel: 01626 215902
Email: .... funding@teigncvs.org.uk

(TORRIDGE VB) HOLSWORTHY BRANCH
Holsworth Volunteer Centre, Unit 1, Manor Court, Victoria Square, Holsworthy, Devon EX22 6AA
Tel: 01409 254484

(TORRIDGE VB) TORRINGTON BRANCH
1st Floor, Castle Hill, South Street, Torrington, Devon EX38 8AA
Tel: 01805 626123

WEST DEVON COMMUNITY AND VOLUNTARY SERVICES
The Carlton Centre, St James Street, Okehampton, Devon EX20 1DW
Tel: 01837 53392

WEST DEVON CVS & VOLUNTEER CENTRE
5 King Street, Tavistock, Devon PL19 0DS
Tel: 01822 618230

Dorset

DORCHESTER VOLUNTEER BUREAU
1 Colliton Walk, Dorchester, Dorset DT1 1TZ
Tel: 01305 269214

HANDS ROCHESTER VOLUNTEER CENTRE
Kingsley House, 37 - 39 Balmoral Road, Gillingham, Dorset ME7 4PF
Tel: 01634 380030
Email: .... enquiries@ handsrochestervolunteercentre.org

ISLAND VOLUNTEERS FOR YOU (IVY)
19 Easton Street, Portland, Dorset DT5 1BS
Tel: 01305 823789
Email: .... island.volunteers@virgin.net

VOLUNTEER CENTRE DORSET
1 Colliton Walk, Dorchester, Dorset DT1 1TZ
Tel: 01305 269214

East Riding of Yorkshire

EAST RIDING (CENTRAL) CVS VOLUNTEER BUREAU
Morley's House, Morley's Yard, Walkergate, Beverley, East Riding of Yorkshire HU17 9BY
Tel: 01482 871077
Email: .... office@ervas.org.uk

East Sussex

EASTBOURNE ASSOCIATION OF VOLUNTARY SERVICES (EAVS)
8 Saffrons Road, Eastbourne, East Sussex BN21 1DG
Tel: 01323 639373
Email: .... eastbourneinfo@3va.org.uk

HASTINGS VOLUNTARY ACTION
Jackson Hall, Portland Place, Hastings, East Sussex TN34 1QN
Tel: 01424 446060
Email: .. infoworker@hastingsvoluntaryaction.org

PEACEHAVEN & TELSCOMBE VOLUNTEER BUREAU
43 Longridge Avenue, Saltdean, East Sussex BN2 8LG
Tel: 01273 390408

SUSSEX DOWNS CVS VOLUNTEER CENTRE
66 High Street, Lewes, East Sussex BN7 1XG
Tel: 01273 470108
Email: .... lewesinfo@3va.org.uk

UCKFIELD VOLUNTEER & INFORMATION CENTRE
Unit 3, 79 High Street, Uckfield, East Sussex TN22 1AS
Tel: 01825 760019
Email: .... uvic@btconnect.com

Essex

BARKING & DAGENHAM VOLUNTEER CENTRE
Starting Point, 16 Pickering Road, Barking, Essex IG11 8PG
Tel: 020 3288 2168
Email: .... bardagvb@hotmail.co.uk

BASILDON, BILLERICAY AND WICKFORD CVS VOLUNTEER BUREAU
The George Hurd Centre, Audley Way, Basildon, Essex SS14 2FL
Tel: 01268 294124
Email: .... admin@bbwcvs.org.uk

CASTLE POINT VOLUNTEER CENTRE
The Tyrells Centre, 39 Seamore Avenue, Thundersley, Benfleet, Essex SS7 4EX
Tel: .... 0800 840 4714 / 01268 638416

CHELMSFORD VOLUNTEER CENTRE
Burgess Well House, Coval Lane, Chelmsford, Essex CM1 1FW
Tel: 01245 250731

CLACTON & DISTRICT VOLUNTEER BUREAU
26 High Street, Clacton-on-Sea, Essex CO15 1UQ
Tel: 01255 427888

COLCHESTER CVS & VOLUNTEER CENTRE
Winsley's House, High Street, Colchester, Essex CO1 1UG
Tel: 01206 505250

MALDON CVS & VOLUNTEER CENTRE
The Square, Holloway Road, Heybridge, Maldon, Essex CM9 4ER
Tel: 01621 851891

SOUTHEND SAVS CENTRE
29-31 Alexandra Street, Southend-on-Sea, Essex SS1 1BW
Tel: 01702 356000

VOLUNTARY ACTION EPPING FOREST
Homefield House, Civic Offices Site, High Street, Epping, Essex CM16 4BZ
Tel: 01992 564178
Email: .... admin@vaef.org.uk

VOLUNTEER CENTRE UTTLESFORD
London Road, Saffron Walden, Essex CB11 4ER
Tel: 01799 510525

Gloucestershire

CHELTENHAM VOLUNTEER CENTRE
Sandford Park Offices, College Road, Cheltenham, Gloucestershire GL53 7HX
Tel: 01242 257727
Email: enquiries@volunteeringcheltenham.org.uk

COTSWOLD COUNCIL FOR VOLUNTARY SERVICE
The Volunteer Centre, 23 Sheep Street, Cirencester, Gloucestershire GL7 1QW
Tel: 01285 658802

COTSWOLD COUNCIL FOR VOLUNTARY SERVICE
23 Sheep Street, Cirencester, Gloucestershire GL7 1QW
Tel: 01285 658802

COTSWOLD COUNCIL FOR VOLUNTARY SERVICE (FAIRFORD CENTRE)
3 London Street, Fairford, Gloucestershire GL7 4AH
Tel: 01285 713852

FOREST VOLUNTARY ACTION FORUM
Rheola House, Belle Vue Centre, Cinderford, Gloucestershire GL14 2AB
Tel: 01594 822073
Email: .... info@svas.org.uk

GLOUCESTER ASSOCIATION FOR VOLUNTARY AND COMMUNITY ACTION
75-81 Eastgate Street, Gloucester, Gloucestershire GL1 1PN
Tel: 01452 332424
Email: .... volunteering@gavca.org.uk

(VCA) DURSLEY VOLUNTEER CENTRE
Community Shop, 24 Parsonage Street, Dursley, Gloucestershire GL11 4AA
Tel: 01453 548801

VOLUNTEER & COMMUNITY ACTION
The Old Town Hall, The Shambles, High Street, Stroud, Gloucestershire GL5 1AP
Tel: 01453 759005

Greater Manchester

BOLTON CVS & VOLUNTEER CENTRE
The Bolton Hub, Bold Street, Bolton, Greater Manchester BL1 1LS
Tel: 01204 546010

ROCHDALE CVS
Sparrow Hill, Rochdale, Greater Manchester OL16 1QT
Tel: 01706 631291

VOLUNTEER CENTRE SALFORD
The Old Town Hall, off Irwell Place, Eccles, Salford, Greater Manchester M30 0EJ
Tel: 0161 707 7067

VOLUNTEER CENTRE TAMESIDE
95-97 Penny Meadow, Ashton-under-Lyne, Greater Manchester OL6 6EP
Tel: 0161 339 2345

WIGAN & LEIGH CVS
93 Church Street, Leigh, Greater Manchester WN7 1AZ
Tel: 01942 514234
Email: .... info@cvswl.org

Hampshire

BASINGSTOKE CCS VOLUNTEER BUREAU
The Orchard, White Hart Lane, Basingstoke, Hampshire RG21 4AF
Tel: 01256 423850
Email: .. sarah.robinson@voluntaryservices.com

COMMUNITY FIRST NEW FOREST (FORMERLY NEW FOREST VOLUNTARY SERVICE COUNCIL)
Public Offices, 65 Christchurch Road, Ringwood, Hampshire BH24 1DH
Tel: 01425 482773
Email: .... admin@cfnf.org.uk

EAST HAMPSHIRE VOLUNTEER BUREAU (BORDON BRANCH)
St. Mark's Church, Forest Centre, Bordon, Hampshire GU35 0TN
Tel: 01420 475 536

GOSPORT VOLUNTEER CENTRE
Martin Snape House, 96 Pavilion Way, Gosport, Hampshire PO12 1FG
Tel: 023 9258 8347

HART VOLUNTEER BUREAU
Civic Offices, Harlington Way, Fleet, Hampshire GU51 4AE
Tel: 01252 815652
Email: ... voluntarybureau@hartvolaction.org.uk

HAVANT VOLUNTEER CENTRE
Havant Council or Community Service, 47 Market Parade, Havant, Hampshire PO9 1PY
Tel: 023 9248 1845
Email: . . . . volunteering@havantccs.org.uk

VOLUNTEER CENTRE EASTLEIGH
One Community, 16 Romsey Road, Eastleigh, Hampshire SO50 9AL
Tel: 023 8090 2457
Email: . . . . volunteer@1community.org.uk

VOLUNTEER CENTRE TEST VALLEY (ANDOVER BRANCH)
2nd Floor, East Wing, Wessex Chambers, South Street, Andover, Hampshire SP10 2BN
Tel: 01264 362600
Email: . . . . volunteers@tvcs.org.uk

VOLUNTEER CENTRE WINCHESTER
The Winchester Centre, 68 St Georges's Street, Winchester, Hampshire SO23 8AH
Tel: 01962 848030

Herefordshire

HAY & DISTRICT COMMUNITY SUPPORT
Oxford Road, Hay on Wye, Hereford, Herefordshire HR3 5AL
Tel: 01497 821031

HEREFORDSHIRE VOLUNTARY ACTION
Berrows Business Centre, Bath Street, Hereford, Herefordshire HR1 2HE
Tel: 01432 343932

LEDBURY & DISTRICT VOLUNTEER BUREAU
Salters Yard, Bye Street, Ledbury, Herefordshire HR8 2AA
Tel: 01531 635339

Hertfordshire

(DACORUM VB) BERKHAMSTED BRANCH
Berkhamsted Civic Centre, 161-166 High Street, Berkhamsted, Hertfordshire HP4 3HB
Tel: 01442 228933

ROYSTON & DISTRICT VOLUNTEER CENTRE
Royston Hospital, London Road, Royston, Hertfordshire SG8 9EN
Tel: 01763 243020
Email: . . . . info@roystonvolunteer.org.uk

ST ALBANS VOLUNTEER CENTRE
31 Catherine Street, St Albans, Hertfordshire AL3 5BJ
Tel: 01727 852657; 01727 852656
Email: . . . . enquiries@cvsstalbans.org.uk

VOLUNTEER CENTRE BROXBOURNE & EAST HERTS
Silverline House, 1-3 Albury Grove Road, Cheshunt, Hertfordshire EN8 8NS
Tel: 01992 638633

VOLUNTEER CENTRE DACORUM
The Roundhouse, Marlowes, Hemel Hempstead, Hertfordshire HP1 1BT
Tel: 01442 247209; 01442 214734

THE VOLUNTEER CENTRE HERTSMERE
Allum Lane Community Centre, Allum Lane, Elstree, Hertfordshire WD6 3PJ
Tel: 020 8207 4504

VOLUNTEER CENTRE THREE RIVERS
Basing House, 46 High Street, Rickmansworth, Hertfordshire WD3 1HP
Tel: 01923 711174

VOLUNTEER CENTRE WATFORD
149 The Parade, Watford, Hertfordshire WD17 1RH
Tel: 01923 248304
Email: . . . . volunteering@watfordcvs.net

WELWYN HATFIELD CVS VOLUNTEER BUREAU
40 Town Centre, Hatfield, Hertfordshire AL10 0JJ
Tel: 01707 274861

Isle of Wight

ISLAND VOLUNTEERS
39 Quay Street, Newport, Isle of Wight PO30 5BA

Kent

CANTERBURY & HERNE BAY VOLUNTEER CENTRE
Tower Works, Simmonds Road, Canterbury, Kent CT1 3RA
Tel: 01227 452278

COMMUNITY LINKS BROMLEY
Community House, South Street, Bromley, Kent BR1 1RH
Tel: 020 8315 1900
Email: . . . admin@communitylinksbromley.org.uk

COMMUNITY LINKS BROMLEY
Community House, South Street, Bromley, Kent BR1 1RH
Tel: 020 8315 1905

DOVER DISTRICT VOLUNTEERING CENTRE
26 Victoria Road, Deal, Kent CT14 7BJ
Tel: 01304 367898

DOVER DISTRICT VOLUNTEERING CENTRE
26 Victoria Road, Deal, Kent CT14 7BJ
Tel: 01304 367898

HANDS AND GILLINGHAM VOLUNTEER BUREAU
62 Watling Street, Gillingham, Kent ME7 2YN
Tel: 01634 577984

MALLING AREA VOLUNTEER CENTRE
18 Twisden Road, East Malling, Maidstone, Kent ME19 6SA
Tel: 01732 843346
Email: . . . . mallingvb@mallingvb.org

NEW ASH GREEN VOLUNTEER CENTRE
Youth Centre, Ash Road, New Ash Green, Kent DA3 8JY
Tel: 01474 879168

SHEPWAY VOLUNTEER CENTRE
URC Community Centre, Castle Hill Avenue, Folkestone, Kent CT20 2QL
Tel: 01303259007

SWALE CVS
Central House, Central Avenue, Sittingbourne, Kent ME10 4NU
Tel: 01795 473828

THANET VOLUNTEER BUREAU
Forresters Hall, Meeting Street, Ramsgate, Kent CT11 9RT
Tel: 01843 590935; 01843 597115

TONBRIDGE VOLUNTEER BUREAU
3 St Mary's Road, Tonbridge, Kent TN9 2LD
Tel: 01732 357978

TUNBRIDGE WELLS & DISTRICT VOLUNTEER BUREAU
Wood House, Wood Street, Tunbridge Wells, Kent TN1 2QS
Tel: 01892 540131

VOLUNTARY ACTION MAIDSTONE
39-48 Marsham Street, Maidstone, Kent ME14 1HH
Tel: 01622 677337

NORTH WEST VOLUNTARY CENTRE
33 Essex Road, Dartford, Kent DA1 2AU
Tel: 01322 272476

NORTH WEST VOLUNTARY CENTRE
45 Windmill Street, Gravesham, Gravesend, Kent DA12 1BA
Tel: 01474 322729

VOLUNTEER CENTRE BEXLEY
Crayford Manor House, Mayplace Road East, Crayford, Dartford, Kent DA1 4HB
Tel: 01322 524682
Email: information@bvsc.co.uk

VOLUNTEER CENTRE SEVENOAKS
Bradbourne School, Bradbourne Vale Road, Sevenoaks, Kent TN13 3LE
Tel: 01732 454785
Email: volunteeringsevenoaks@vawk.org.uk

VOLUNTEER CENTRE SWANLEY & DISTRICT
Library and Information Centre, London Road, Swanley, Kent BR8 7AE
Tel: 01322 669292; 0845 2412180

WHISTABLE VOLUNTEER CENTRE
St Mary's Hall, Oxford Street, Whitstable, Kent CT5 1DD
Tel: 01227 772248
Email: manager@whitstablevc.org.uk

Kingston upon Hull

HULL CVS: VOLUNTEER CENTRE HULL
The Strand, 75 Beverley Road, Hull, Kingston upon Hull HU3 1KL
Tel: 01482 324474
Email: enquires@hull-cvs.co.uk

Lancashire

BLACKPOOL VOLUNTEERING CENTRE
South Lodge, Stanley Park, West Park Drive, Blackpool, Lancashire FY3 9EQ
Tel: 01253301004
Email: blackpoolvc3@yahoo.co.uk

(COALVILLE & DISTRICT CVS VB) ASHBY BRANCH
The Cornerstone, Sulyard St, Lancaster, Lancashire LA1 1PX
Tel: 01524555900

HYNDEBURN & RIBBLE VALLEY CVS
1 Swan Mews, Off Castle Street, Clitheroe, Lancashire BB7 2BX
Tel: 01200 422721
Email: dorothyshears@hyndeburnandribblevalleycvs.org

WEST LANCASHIRE CVS VOLUNTEER BUREAU
Certacs House, 10-12 Westgate, Skelmersdale, Lancashire WN8 8AZ
Tel: 01695 733737

Leicestershire

(COALVILLE AND DISTRICT CVS VB) ASHBY, MEASHAM, AND MOIRA BRANCHES
17 Ashby Road, Moira, Leicestershire DE12 6DJ
Tel: 01283 551261

(COSBY, BLABY & DISTRICT) NARBOROUGH BRANCH
Council Offices, Deford Road, Narborough, Leicestershire LE19 3EP
Tel: 01162750555

LUTTERWORTH & BROUGHTON ASTLEY VC (BROUGHTON ASTLEY BRANCH)
The Community Cabin, 38a Main Street, Broughton Astley, Leicestershire LE9 6RD

NORTH WEST LEICESTERSHIRE VOLUNTEER CENTRE
9 Newarke Street, Leicester, Leicestershire LE1 5SN
Tel: 01162575050

VOLUNTARY ACTION FOR OADBY & WIGSTON
132a Station Road, Wigston, Leicestershire LE18 2DL
Tel: 0116 2887828

VOLUNTARY ACTION HINCKLEY & BOSWORTH
50, Gwendoline Avenue, Hinckley, Leicestershire LE10 0EZ
Tel: 01455610115

VOLUNTARY ACTION LEICESTER
9 Newarke Street, Leicester, Leicestershire LE1 5SN
Tel: 0116 258 0666
Email: info@valonline.org.uk

VOLUNTARY ACTION SOUTH LEICESTERSHIRE
The Settling Rooms, St Mary's Place, Springfield Street, Market Harborough, Leicestershire LE16 7DR
Tel: 01858433232

VOLUNTEER CENTRE - BLABY DISTRICT
Parker House, 254 Braunstone Lane, Braunstone, Leicestershire LE3 3AS
Tel: 0116 223 8338
Email: info@volunteerblabydistrict.org.uk

VOLUNTEER CENTRE LUTTERWORTH
One Stop Shop, Wycliffe House, Gilmorton Road, Lutterworth, Leicestershire LE17 4DY
Tel: 01455 555570
Email: . . . . info.luttvc@onestopshop.org.uk

VOLUNTEER CENTRE SHEPSHED
9a Charnwood Road, Shepshed, Leicestershire LE12 9QE
Tel: 01509 508040

Lincolnshire

BOSTON & DISTRICT VOLUNTEER CENTRE
The Len Medlock Voluntary Centre, St George's Road, Boston, Lincolnshire PE21 8YB
Tel: 01205510888

KESTEVEN VOLUNTARY ACTION
26-27 St Catherine's Road, Grantham, Lincolnshire NG31 6TT

LOUTH AREA VOLUNTARY CENTRE (MABLETHORPE)
The Interagency Building, Stanley Avenue, Mablethorpe, Lincolnshire LN12 2AP
Tel: 01507 479632

NORTH KESTEVEN CVS LTD
The Old Mart, Church Lane, Sleaford, Lincolnshire NG34 7DF
Tel: 01529 308450
Email: . northkesteven@voluntarycentreservices.org.uk

SOUTH LINK CVS
The Len Medlock Voluntary Centre, St Georges Road, Boston, Lincolnshire PE21 8YB
Tel: 01205 365580

VOLUNTARY CENTRE SERVICES WEST LINDSEY
Unit 9, The Lindsey Centre, Gainsborough, Lincolnshire DN21 2BT
Tel: 01427 613470
Email: . info@voluntarysupportwestlindsey.org.uk

VOLUNTEER CENTRE LINCOLN
The Voluntary Sector Hub, Beaumont Fee, Lincoln, Lincolnshire LN1 1UW
Tel: 01522 551683
Email: . . . . info@info@vcslincoln.org.uk

VOLUNTEER CENTRE NORTH KESTEVEN
26 Carre Street, Sleaford, Lincolnshire NG34 7TR
Tel: 01529 308450
Email: . . . . info@volunteercentrenk.org.uk

London

ENFIELD VOLUNTARY ACTION
Community House, 311 Fore Street, London N9 0PZ
Tel: 020 8373 6348
Email: . . . . admin@enfieldva.org.uk

HACKNEY VOLUNTARY ACTION
Unit 13, Springfield House, 5 Tyssen Street, London E8 2LY
Tel: 020 7241 4443

HAMMERSMITH & FULHAM VOLUNTEER CENTRE
148 King Street, Hammersmith, London W6 0QU
Tel: 020 8741 9876

ISLINGTON VOLUNTEER CENTRE
200a Pentonville Road, Islington, London N1 9JP
Tel: 020 7686 6800; 020 7833 9691

VOLUNTEER CENTRE CAMDEN
2 Grafton Yard, Camden, London NW5 2ND
Tel: 020 7424 9990
Email: volunteercentrecamden@camdenvb.org.uk

VOLUNTEER CENTRE GREENWICH
2nd Floor, 10 Woolwich New Road, Woolwich, London SE18 6AB
Tel: 020 8317 3817
Email: . . . . info@vcgreenwich.org.uk

VOLUNTEER CENTRE KENSINGTON & CHELSEA
Canalside House, 383 Ladbroke Grove, London W10 5AA
Tel: 020 8960 3722

VOLUNTEER CENTRE TOWER HAMLETS
Norvin House, 1st Floor, 45-55 Commercial Street, Tower Hamlets, London E1 6BD
Tel: 020 7377 0956
Email: . . . . info@towerhamlets.org.uk

VOLUNTEER CENTRE WANDSWORTH
170 Garratt Lane, Wandsworth, London SW18 4DA
Tel: 020 8870 4319

VOLUNTEER CENTRE WESTMINSTER
37 Chapel Street, London NW1 5DP
Tel: 020 7723 1216
Email: . . . . info@onewestminster.org.uk

THE VOLUNTEER NETWORK CENTRE
Emmanuel Parish Church, Romford Road, London E7 8BD
Tel: 020 8536 1937
Email: . . . . volunteers@vncnewham.co.uk

Merseyside

VOLUNTEER CENTRE LIVERPOOL
151 Dale Street, Liverpool, Merseyside L2 2AH
Tel: 0151 237 3975
Email: enquiries@volunteercentreliverpool.org.uk

VOLUNTEER CENTRE SEFTON
3rd Floor, Merseyside 3TC Centre, 16 Crosby Road North, Waterloo, Liverpool, Merseyside L22 0NY
Tel: 0151 920 0726

VOLUNTEER CENTRE SEFTON
Top Floor, Shakespeare Centre, Shakespeare Street, Southport, Merseyside PR8 5AB
Tel: 01704 501024

WIRRAL CVS VOLUNTEER CENTRE
Unit 30, Woodside Business Park, Shore Rd, Birkenhead, Merseyside CH41 1EL
Tel: 0151 647 5432
Email: . . . . karen@wirralcvs.org.uk

Middlesex

BINGHAM VB (WEST BRIDGEFORD & DISTRICT VB BRANCH)
Harlequin House, 7 High Street, Teddington, Middlesex TW11 8EL

HOUNSLOW VOLUNTEER BUREAU
45 Treaty Centre, High Street, Hounslow, Middlesex TW3 1ES
Tel: 020 8570 5083

Milton Keynes

VOLUNTEER CENTRE MILTON KEYNES
Acorn House, 383 Midsummer Boulevard, Central Milton Keynes, Milton Keynes MK9 3HP
Tel: 01908 662744

Norfolk

FAKENHAM COMMUNITY SERVICES
Community Health Services, Fakenham Medical Practice, Greenaway Lane, Fakenham, Norfolk NR21 8ET
Tel: 01328 862751

VOLUNTARY NORFOLK
83-87 Pottergate, Norwich, Norfolk NR2 1DZ
Tel: 01603 614474
Email: admin@voluntarynorfolk.org.uk

VOLUNTARY NORFOLK
The Market Surgery, 26 Norwich Road, Aylsham, Norfolk NR11 6BW
Tel: 01263 731478
Email: aylshamvsc@voluntarynorfolk.org.uk

VOLUNTARY NORFOLK (ATTLEBOROUGH BRANCH)
Attleborough Health Centre, Station Road, Attleborough, Norfolk NR17 2AS
Tel: 01603 614474

VOLUNTARY NORFOLK (BOWTHORPE BRANCH)
Bowthorpe Health Centre, Wendene, Norwich, Norfolk NR5 9HA

VOLUNTARY NORFOLK (BRUNDALL BRANCH)
Brundall Health Centre, The Dales, The Street, Brundall, Norwich, Norfolk NR13 5RP
Tel: 01603 712255

VOLUNTARY NORFOLK (CROMER BRANCH)
Benjamin Court, Intensive Service Centre, Roughton Road, Cromer, Norfolk NR27 0EU
Tel: 01263 517989
Email: cromervsc@voluntarynorfolk.org.uk

VOLUNTARY NORFOLK (DISS BRANCH)
The Health Centre, Mount Street, Diss, Norfolk IP22 4WG
Tel: 01379 644513
Email: dissvsc@voluntarynorfolk.org.uk

VOLUNTARY NORFOLK (EAST DEREHAM BRANCH)
Dereham Hospital, Northgate, Dereham, Norfolk NR19 2EX
Tel: 01362 692391
Email: eastderehamvsc@voluntarynorfolk.org.uk

VOLUNTARY NORFOLK (LAWSON ROAD BRANCH)
Lawsom Road Health Centre, Lawson Road, Norwich, Norfolk NR3 4LE
Tel: 01603 428104

VOLUNTARY NORFOLK LONG STRATTON BRANCH
Long Stratton Health Centre, Flowerpot Lane, Long Stratton, Norfolk NR15 2TS
Tel: 01508 531175
Email: longstrattonvsc@voluntarynorfolk.org.uk

VOLUNTARY NORFOLK (NORTH WALSHAM BRANCH)
North Walsham Hospital, Yarmouth Road, North Walsham, Norfolk NR28 9AP
Tel: 01692 408314

VOLUNTARY NORFOLK (THETFORD BRANCH)
Riversdale, Tanner Street, Thetford, Norfolk IP24 2BQ
Tel: 01842 761377

VOLUNTARY NORFOLK (THORPE ST ANDREW)
The Health Centre, Williams Loke, St Williams Way, Norwich, Norfolk NR7 0AJ
Tel: 01603 430205

VOLUNTARY NORFOLK (WYMONDHAM BRANCH)
Wymondham Health Centre, 18 Bridewell Street, Wymondham, Norfolk NR18 0AR
Tel: 01953 606201
Email: wymondhamvsc@voluntarynorfolk.org.uk

WEST NORFOLK VOLUNTARY & COMMUNITY ACTION
16 Tuesday Market Place, King's Lynn, Norfolk PE30 1JN
Tel: 01553 760568
Email: info@westnorfolkvca.org

North East Lincolnshire

NORTH EAST LINCOLNSHIRE VOLUNTEER CENTRE
14 Town Hall Street, Grimsby, North East Lincolnshire DN31 1HN
Tel: 01472 231123
Email: volunteer@vanel.org.uk

North Somerset

VOLUNTARY ACTION NORTH SOMERSET
The Badger Centre, 3-6 Wadham Street, Weston-super-Mare, North Somerset BS23 1JY
Tel: 01934 410192
Email: enquiries@vansweb.org.uk

North Yorkshire

BEDALE VOLUNTARY CENTRE
Bedale Hall, Bedale, North Yorkshire DL8 1AA
Tel: 01677 425329

HARROGATE & AREA VOLUNTEER CENTRE
Community House, 46-50 East Parade, Harrogate, North Yorkshire HG1 5RR
Tel: 01423 509004
Email: volunteer@harrogate.org

MIDDLESBOROUGH COUNCIL FOR VOLUNTARY DEVELOPMENT
St Mary's Centre, 82-90 Corporation Road, Middlesbrough, North Yorkshire TS1 2RW
Tel: 01642 249 300

RICHMONDSHIRE VOLUNTEER CENTRE
6 Flints Terrace, Richmond, North Yorkshire DL10 7AH
Tel: 01748 822335

RIPON CVS VOLUNTEER CENTRE
Sharow View, Allhallowgate, Ripon, North Yorkshire HG4 1LE
Tel: 01423504074

RYEDALE CVA VOLUNTEER ACTION
Ryedale Community House, Wentworth Street, Malton, North Yorkshire YO17 7BN
Tel: 01653 600120

STOKESLEY AND DISTRICT CCA VOLUNTEER CENTRE
The Community Care Association, Town Close, North Road, Stokesley, North Yorkshire TS9 5DH
Tel: 01642 710085

THIRSK VOLUNTEER CENTRE
14a Market Place, Thirsk, North Yorkshire YO7 1LB
Tel: 01845 523115

VOLUNTEER BUREAU OF CRAVEN
26 Otley St, Skipton, North Yorkshire BD23 1EW
Tel: 01756 701648
Email: .... info@cravenva.org.uk

VOLUNTEERING HAMBLETON
Community House, 10 South Parade, Northallerton, North Yorkshire DL7 8SE
Tel: 01609 780458

YORK CVS VOLUNTEER CENTRE
15 Priory Street, York, North Yorkshire YO1 6ET
Tel: 01904 621133

Northamptonshire

CORBY VOLUNTEER BUREAU
The TA Building, Elizabeth Street, Corby, Northamptonshire NN17 1PN
Tel: 01536 267873

DAVENTRY VOLUNTEER CENTRE
DDWF Building, 13 New Street, Daventry, Northamptonshire NN114BT
Tel: 01327 300614
Email: .... info@daventryvolunteers.org.uk

NORTHAMPTON VOLUNTEER CENTRE
15 St Giles Street, Northampton, Northamptonshire NN1 1JA
Tel: 01604 637522

OUNDLE VOLUNTEER ACTION
The Old Market Hall, Market Place, Oundle, Northamptonshire PE8 4BA
Tel: 01832 275433

SOUTH NORTHANTS VOLUNTEER BUREAU
The Volunteer Centre, Whittons Lane, Towcester, Northamptonshire NN12 6YZ
Tel: 01327 358264

VOLUNTEER CENTRE WELLINGBOROUGH
1-3 Orient Way, Wellingborough, Northamptonshire NN8 1AF
Tel: 01933 276933
Email: ... info@wellingborough-volunteers.org.uk

Northumberland

NORTH NORTHUMBERLAND VOLUNTARY ACTION
107 - 109 Station Road, Ashington, Northumberland NE63 8RS
Tel: 01670858688
Email: ..... enquire@northumberlandcva.org.uk

TYNEDALE VOLUNTARY ACTION
Hexham Community Centre, Gilesgate, Hexham, Northumberland NE46 3NP
Tel: 01434 601201

WANSBECK CENTRE FOR VOLUNTARY SERVICE
107 & 109 Station Road, Ashington, Northumberland NE63 8RS
Tel: 01670 858688

Nottinghamshire

(BASSETLAW BCVS INVOLVE PROJECT) RETFORD BRANCH
Community Shop, 18 West Street, Retford, Nottinghamshire DN22 6ES
Tel: 01777 709650

BASSETLAW COMMUNITY & VOLUNTEER SERVICE
The Old Abbey School, Priorswell Road, Worksop, Nottinghamshire S80 2BU
Tel: 01909 476118

EASTWOOD VOLUNTEER BUREAU
Wellington Place, Eastwood, Nottingham, Nottinghamshire NG16 3GB
Tel: 01773 535255

MANSFIELD VOLUNTEER CENTRE
Community House, 36 Wood Street, Mansfield, Nottinghamshire NG18 1QA
Tel: 01623 651177
Email: .... volunteer@mansfieldcvs.org

(NEWARK & SHERWOOD VB) FARNSFIELD BRANCH
Farnsfield Village Centre, Lower Hall, New Hill, Newark, Nottinghamshire NG22 8JM

(NEWARK & SHERWOOD VB) WESTERN DISTRICT BRANCH
Bedehouse Chapel, Bedehouse Lane, Barnbygate, Newark, Nottinghamshire NG24 1PU
Tel: 01636 707418

OUR CENTRE
6 Pond Street, Kirkby-in-Ashfield, Nottinghamshire NG17 7AH
Tel: 01623 753192

RUSHCLIFFE VOLUNTEER CENTRE
Level 3a Bridgford House, Pavilion Road, West Bridgford, Nottinghamshire NG2 5GJ
Tel: 0115 969 9060

STAPLEFORD CARE CENTRE
Church Street, Stapleford, Nottinghamshire NG9 8DB
Tel: 01158835000
Email: .... margaretsb@hotmail.co.uk

SUTTON IN ASHFIELD VOLUNTEER BUREAU
Sutton Centre, High Pavement, Sutton-in-Ashfield, Nottinghamshire NG17 1EE
Tel: 01623 515614
Email: .... ashfieldvolunteering@btconnect.com

VOLUNTEER CENTRE BROXTOWE
8 Chilwell Road, Beeston, Nottinghamshire NG9 1EJ
Tel: 0115 917 8080
Email: .... Lindab@vabroxtowe.org.uk

WEST BRIDGFORD & DISTRICT VOLUNTEER BUREAU
Park Lodge, Bridgford Road, West Bridgford, Nottinghamshire NG2 6AT
Tel: 0115 969 9060

Oxfordshire

WEST OXFORDSHIRE VOLUNTEER LINK-UP
Methodist Church, 10 Wesley Walk, Witney, Oxfordshire OX28 6ZJ
Tel: 01993 776277

Redcar & Cleveland

REDCAR & CLEVELAND VOLUNTARY DEVELOPMENT AGENCY
Westfield Farm, The Green, Dormanstown, Redcar, Redcar & Cleveland TS10 5NA
Tel: 01642 440571
Email: .... enquiries@rcvda.org.uk

Rutland

VOLUNTEER ACTION RUTLAND
Land's End Way, Oakham, Rutland LE15 6RB
Tel: 01572 722622

Shropshire

OSWESTRY COMMUNITY ACTION
QUBE, Oswald Road, Oswestry, Shropshire SY11 1RB
Tel: 01691 656882

SHREWSBURY VOLUNTARY ACTION
Abbots House Courtyard, 13 Butcher Row, Shrewsbury, Shropshire SY1 1UP
Tel: 01743 341700

SOUTH SHROPSHIRE VOLUNTEER EXCHANGE
2a Palmers House, 7 Corve Street, Ludlow, Shropshire SY8 1DB
Tel: 01584 877756

TELFORD VOLUNTEER DESK
Telford and Wrekin CVS, Meeting Point House, Southwater Square, Town Centre, Telford, Shropshire TF3 4HS
Tel: 01952 291350

Slough

SLOUGH VOLUNTEER BUREAU
1st Floor, Kingsway URC, Slough SL1 1SZ
Tel: 01753 528632

Somerset

BRIDGWATER VOLUNTEER BUREAU
The Lions, West Quay, Bridgwater, Somerset TA6 3HW
Tel: 01278 457685

TAUNTON DEANE VOLUNTEER BUREAU
Flook House, Belvedere Road, Taunton, Somerset TA1 1BT
Tel: 01823 284470
Email: .... enquiries@tauntoncvs.org.uk

South Gloucestershire

THORNBURY & DISTRICT VOLUNTEER CENTRE
The Town Hall, 35 High Street, Thornbury, South Gloucestershire BS35 2AR
Tel: 01454 413392

VOLUNTEER CENTRE YATE
Yate Library, 44 West Walk, Yate, South Gloucestershire BS37 4AX
Tel: 01454 324102

South Yorkshire

BARNSLEY VOLUNTARY ADVISORY SERVICE
33 Queens Road, Barnsley, South Yorkshire S71 1AN
Tel: 01226 295905

DONCASTER CVS VOLUNTEER BUREAU
Units 5 & 6 Trafford Court, Doncaster, South Yorkshire DN1 1PN
Tel: 01302 343300

VOLUNTARY ACTION SHEFFIELD (INCLUDING VOLUNTEER CENTRE SHEFFIELD)
The Circle, 33 Rockingham Lane, Sheffield, South Yorkshire S1 4FW
Tel: 0114 253 6600

Staffordshire

ADSIS
Alan Dean Centre, 23 Carter Street, Uttoxeter, Staffordshire ST14 8EY
Tel: 01889 560550

LICHFIELD & DISTRICT COMMUNITY AND VOLUNTARY SECTOR SUPPORT
Mansell House, 22 Bore Street, Lichfield, Staffordshire WS13 6LL
Tel: 01543 303030
Email: .... rosevakis@ldcvs.org.uk

STAFFORD VOLUNTEER CENTRE
Stafford District Voluntary Services, 131-141 North Walls, Stafford, Staffordshire ST16 3AD
Tel: 01785 279934

STAFFORDSHIRE MOORLANDS VOLUNTEER BUREAU
Bank House, 20 St Edward Street, Leek, Staffordshire ST13 5DS
Tel: 01538 398240

Suffolk

ALDEBURGH, LEISTON & SAXMUNDHAM VOLUNTEER CENTRE
Council Offices, 13 Main Street, Leiston, Suffolk IP16 4ER
Tel: 01728 832829

THE BECCLES VOLUNTEER CENTRE
4-4a The Score, Northgate, Beccles, Suffolk N34 7AR
Tel: 01502 710777

BURY ST EDMUNDS VOLUNTEER CENTRE LTD
86 Whiting Street, Bury St Edmunds, Suffolk IP33 1NX
Tel: 01284 766126

EYE & DISTRICT VOLUNTEER CENTRE
20 Broad Street, Eye, Suffolk IP23 7AF
Tel: 01379 871200

FELIXSTOWE VOLUNTEER CENTRE
108 Queens Road, Felixstowe, Suffolk IP11 7PG
Tel: 01394 284770

FRAMLINGHAM & DISTRICT VOLUNTEER CENTRE
10a Riverside, Framlingham, Suffolk IP13 9AG
Tel: 01728 621210

HAVERHILL & DISTRICT VOLUNTEER CENTRE
Haverhill Centre for Voluntary Agencies, Lower Downs Slade, Haverhill, Suffolk CB9 9HB
Tel: 01440 708444
Email: . . . . info@hvc.org.uk

IPSWICH & DISTRICT VOLUNTEER BUREAU
Room 32, 19 Tower Street, Ipswich, Suffolk IP1 3BE

STOWMARKET & DISTRICT VOLUNTEER CENTRE
Ipswich Road, Stowmarket, Suffolk IP14 1BE
Tel: 01449 612486

SUDBURY & DISTRICT VOLUNTEER CENTRE
The Christopher Centre, 10 Gainsborough Street, Sudbury, Suffolk CO10 2EU
Tel: 01787 880711

VOLUNTEER CENTRE LOWESTOFT
15 Milton Road East, Lowestoft, Suffolk NR32 1NT
Tel: 01502 562299

Surrey

CATERHAM VOLUNTEER CENTRE
Soper Hall, Harestone Valley Road, Caterham, Surrey CR3 6YN
Tel: 01883 344444

CROYDON VOLUNTEER CENTRE
2a Garnet Road, Thornton Heath, Surrey CR7 8RD
Tel: 020 8684 2727

FARNHAM VOLUNTEER CENTRE
Vernon House, 28 West Street, Farnham, Surrey GU9 7DR
Tel: 01252 725961

GUILDFORD VOLUNTEERS' BUREAU
39 Castle Street, Guildford, Surrey GU1 3UQ
Tel: 01483 565456

KINGSTON ON THAMES VOLUNTEER BUREAU
Siddeley House, 50 Canbury Park Road, Kingston on Thames, Surrey KT2 6LX
Tel: 020 8225 8685

(LINGFIELD & DORMANSLAND VB) OXTED BRANCH
Community Hub, 1st Floor, Oxted Library, 14 Gresham Road, Oxted, Surrey RH8 0BQ
Tel: 01883 722593

LINGFIELD & DORMANSLAND VOLUNTEER CENTRE
Lingfield Community Centre, High Street, Lingfield, Surrey RH7 6AB
Tel: 01342 836774
Email: . . . . lingfieldvc@btinternet.com

REIGATE & BANSTEAD CVS VOLUNTEER BUREAU
76 Station Road, Redhill, Surrey RH1 1PL
Tel: 01737762115
Email: . . . . volunteer@rbcus.org.uk

REIGATE AND BANSTEAD VOLUNTEER BUREAU
The Help Shop, Victoria Square, Consort Way, Horley, Surrey RH6 7AF
Tel: 01293 822677

RUNNYMEDE VOLUNTEER CENTRE
Unit 12-13, Sainsbury's Centre, Chertsey, Surrey KT16 9AG
Tel: 01932 571122

VOLUNTEER CENTRE CROYDON
2A Garnet Road, Thornton Heath, Surrey CR7 8RD
Tel: 020 8684 2727

VOLUNTEER CENTRE MERTON
The Vestry Hall, London Road, Mitcham, Surrey CR4 3UD
Tel: 020 8640 7355
Email: . . . . . . info@volunteercentremerton.org.uk

WOKING VOLUNTEER BUREAU
Provincial House, 26 Commercial Way, Woking, Surrey GU21 6EN
Tel: 01483 751456

Tyne & Wear

GATESHEAD VOLUNTEER BUREAU
John Haswell House, 8-9 Gladstone Terrace, Gateshead, Tyne & Wear NE8 4DY
Tel: 0191 478 4103

NORTH TYNESIDE VOLUNTARY ORGANISATIONS DEVELOPMENT AGENCY
The Shiremoor Centre, Earsdon Road, Shiremoor, Newcastle upon Tyne, Tyne & Wear NE27 0HJ
Tel: 01916432626
Email: . . . . admin@voda.org.uk

SOUTH TYNESIDE VOLUNTARY CENTRE
John Hunt House, 27 Beach Road, South Shields, Tyne & Wear NE33 2QA
Tel: 0191 456 9551

Warwickshire

(NORTH WARWICKSHIRE VB) KINGSBURY BRANCH
Kingsbury Library, Bromage Avenue, Kingsbury, Warwickshire B78 2HN
Tel: .... All Enquiries to the Main Office

STRATFORD-ON-AVON VOLUNTEER CENTRE
Suite 3, Arden Court, Arden Street, Stratford-on-Avon, Warwickshire CV37 6NT
Tel: 01789 262886

STRATFORD-ON-AVON VOLUNTEER CENTRE, ALCESTER BRANCH
Globe House, Priory Road, Alcester, Warwickshire B49 5DZ
Tel: 01789 763117

STRATFORD-ON-AVON VOLUNTEER CENTRE, SHIPSTON BRANCH
Medical Centre, Badgers Crescent, Shipston-on-Stour, Warwickshire CV36 4BQ
Tel: 01608 663122

STRATFORD ON AVON VOLUNTEER CENTRE, SOUTHAM BRANCH
The Grange, Coventry Road, Southam, Warwickshire CV33 0LY
Tel: 01926 817525

VOLUNTEER CENTRE NORTH WARWICKSHIRE
White Hart House, Long Street, Atherstone, Warwickshire CV9 1AX
Tel: 01827 717073
Email: .... info@vcnw.org.uk

VOLUNTEER CENTRE NUNEATON & BEDWORTH
4 School Road, Bulkington, Bedworth, Warwickshire CV12 9JB
Tel: 024 7631 5151

VOLUNTEER CENTRE RUGBY
60 Regent Street, Rugby, Warwickshire CV21 2PS
Tel: 01788 561293

WARWICKSHIRE COMMUNITY & VOLUNTARY ACTION - WARWICK DISTRICT
4-6 Clemens Street, Leamington Spa, Leamington Spa, Warwickshire CV31 2DL
Tel: 01926477512
Email: .... warwickinfo@wcava.org.uk

West Berkshire

WEST BERKSHIRE VOLUNTEER CENTRE
1 Bolton Place, Northbrook Street, Newbury, West Berkshire RG14 1AJ
Tel: 01635 49004

West Midlands

BIRMINGHAM VOLUNTEER CENTRE
138 Digbeth, Birmingham, West Midlands B5 6DR
Tel: 01216434343

DUDLEY CVS VOLUNTEER CENTRE
7 Albion Street, Brierley Hill, West Midlands DY5 3EE
Tel: 01384 573381

VOLUNTEER CENTRE COVENTRY
29 Warwick Road, Coventry, West Midlands CV1 1ES
Tel: 024 7622 0381
Email: .... info@volunteering-cov.org.uk

VOLUNTEER CENTRE SANDWELL
Municipal Buildings, Freeth Street, Oldbury, Warley, West Midlands B69 2AB
Tel: 0121 544 8326

West Sussex

ADUR VOLUNTEER CENTRE
Chesham House, 124 South Street, Lancing, West Sussex BN15 8AJ
Tel: 01903 854980
Email: .... info@adurva.org

CRAWLEY VOLUNTEER CENTRE
The Orchard, 1-2 Gleneagles Court, Brighton Road, Crawley, West Sussex RH10 6AD
Tel: 01293657000
Email: .... volbur@crawleycvs.org

EAST ARUN CVS VOLUNTEER BUREAU
The Dairy, 3-5 Church Street, Littlehampton, West Sussex BN17 5EL
Tel: 01903 731223

EAST GRINSTEAD CVS
Old Court House, College Land, East Grinstead, West Sussex RH19 3LS
Tel: 01342 328080

HORSHAM VOLUNTEER CENTRE
The Octagon, St Marks Court, Chart Way, Horsham, West Sussex RH12 1XL
Tel: 01403 232100

VOLUNTEER INFORMATION POINT, BURGESS HILL
38 Church Road, Burgess Hill, West Sussex RH15 9AE
Tel: 01444 870711

VOLUNTARY ACTION WORTHING
Worthing Town Hall, Chapel Road, Worthing, West Sussex BN11 1HA
Tel: 01903 528620
Email: .... volunteering@vaworthing.org.uk

West Yorkshire

KEIGHLEY VOLUNTEER CENTRE
8-10 North Street, Keighley, West Yorkshire BD21 3SE
Tel: 01535 609506

SHIPLEY & BINGLEY VOLUNTARY SERVICES
Cardigan House, Ferncliffe Road, Bingley, West Yorkshire BD16 2TA
Tel: 01274 781222
Email: .... admin@sbvs.org.uk

VOLUNTARY ACTION KIRKLEES
12 New Street, Huddersfield, West Yorkshire HD1 2AR
Tel: 01484 519053
Email: .... info@vkirklees.org.uk

VOLUNTARY ACTION LEEDS
Stringer House, 34 Lupton Street, Hunslet, Leeds, West Yorkshire LS10 2QW
Tel: 0113 395 0405
Email: . . . . volunteering@val.org.uk

VOLUNTEERING BRADFORD
19-25 Sunbridge Street, Bradford, West Yorkshire BD1 2AY
Tel: 01274 725434

VOLUNTEERING BRADFORD
19-25 Sunbridge Road, Bradford, West Yorkshire BD1 2AY
Tel: 01274 725434
Email: . . . . info@volunteeringbradford.org

Wiltshire

VOLUNTEER CENTRE SALISBURY
Greencroft House, 42-46 Salt Lane, Salisbury, Wiltshire SP1 1EG
Tel: 01722 421747
Email: . . . . info@wessexcommunityaction.org.uk

VOLUNTEER CENTRE SWINDON
1 John Street, Swindon, Wiltshire SN1 1RT
Tel: 01793 420557

Windsor & Maidenhead

MAIDENHEAD VOLUNTEER BUREAU
Highview, 6 North Road, Maidenhead, Windsor & Maidenhead SL6 1PL
Tel: 01628 673937

Wokingham

WOKINGHAM VOLUNTEER CENTRE
The Ritz Plaza, 10 Denton Road, Wokingham RG40 2DX
Tel: 0118 977 0749
Email: . . . . volunteer@wok-vol.org.uk

Worcestershire

BROMSGROVE & DISTRICT VOLUNTEER BUREAU
Britannic House, 13-15 Church Street, Bromsgrove, Worcestershire B61 8DD
Tel: 01527 577857

COMMUNITY ACTION WYRE FOREST
Suite B, 3rd floor, 26 Church Street, Kidderminster, Worcestershire DY10 2AR
Tel: 01562 751412
Email: . . . . cvs@communityactionwf.org.uk

DROITWICH SPA CVS
The Old Library Centre, 65 Ombersley Street East, Droitwich, Worcestershire WR9 8QS
Tel: 01905 779115
Email: . . . . admin@droitwichcvs.org.uk

COMMUNITY ACTION MALVERN & DISTRICT
3rd Floor, 29-30 Belle Vue Terrace, Malvern, Worcestershire WR14 4PZ
Tel: 01684 892381
Email: . . . . info@communityaction.org.uk

PERSHORE VOLUNTEER CENTRE
Pershore Volunteer Centre, 1 Billing House, Pershore, Worcestershire WR10 1EY
Tel: 01386 554299
Email: . . . . admin@pershorevolunteers.org

WORCESTER VOLUNTEER CENTRE
33 The Tything, Worcester, Worcestershire WR1 1JL
Tel: 01905 24741

NORTHERN IRELAND

Co. Antrim

VOLUNTARY SERVICE LISBURN
52a Bachelor's Walk, Lisburn, Co. Antrim BT28 1XN
Tel: 028 9260 2479

Co. Down

NEWRY CONFEDERATION OF COMMUNITY GROUPS
Ballybot House, 28 Cornmarket, Newry, Co. Down BT35 8BG
Tel: 028 302 61022
Email: . . . . info@ccgnewrycommunity.org

Co. Londonderry

LONDONDERRY CHURCHES VOLUNTARY WORK BUREAU
22 Bishop Street, Londonderry, Co. Londonderry BT48 6PP
Tel: 028 7127 1017

SCOTLAND

VOLUNTEER CENTRE - EAST DUNBARTONSHIRE
Unit 4/5, 18 - 20 Townhead, Kirkintilloch, Glasgow G66 1NL
Tel: 0141 578 6680
Email: . . . . admin@vced.org.uk

Aberdeen

VOLUNTARY SERVICE ABERDEEN (VSA)
38 Castle Street, Aberdeen AB11 5YU
Tel: 01224 212021
Email: . . . . info@vsa.org.uk

Aberdeenshire

VOLUNTEER CENTRE ABERDEENSHIRE
72a High Street, Banchory, Aberdeenshire AB31 5SS
Tel: 01330825027
Email: . . . . mail@avashire.org.uk

Angus

VOLUNTEER CENTRE ANGUS
32-34 Guthrie Port, Arbroath, Angus DD11 1RN
Tel: 01241 875525

Dumfries & Galloway

THIRD SECTOR, DUMFRIES AND GALLOWAY
Third Sector, Dumfries and Galloway, 16 Queensberry Street, Dumfries, Dumfries & Galloway DG1 1EX
Tel: 0300 303 8558
Email: . . . . info@thirdsectordumgal.org.uk

VOLUNTEER ACTION DUMFRIES & GALLOWAY (ANNANDALE & ESKDALE BRANCH)
16 High Street, Annan, Lochmaben, Dumfries & Galloway DG11 1NH
Tel: 01387 811571

Dundee

VOLUNTEER CENTRE DUNDEE
Number 10, 10 Constitution Road, Dundee DD1 1LL
Tel: 01382 305705
Email: .... info@volunteerdundee.org.uk

East Ayrshire

VOLUNTEER CENTRE EAST AYRSHIRE
28 Grange Street, Kilmarnock, East Ayrshire KA1 2DD
Tel: 01563 544765

Edinburgh

STRIVE
98 North High Street, Musselburgh, Edinburgh EH21 6AS
Tel: 0131 665 3300
Email: .... info@strive.me.uk

VOLUNTEER CENTRE EDINBURGH
222 Leith Walk, Edinburgh EH6 5EQ
Tel: 0131 225 0630
Email: ...... admin@volunteeredinburgh.org.uk

Falkirk

CVS FALKIRK & DISTRICT
Unit 6, The Courtyard, Callendar Business Park, Callendar Road, Falkirk FK1 1XR
Tel: 01324 692000
Email: .... info@cvsfalkirk.org.uk

Fife

FIFE VOLUNTARY ACTION
29a Canmore Street, Dunfermline, Fife KY12 7NU
Tel: 01383 732136
Email: .... info@fifevoluntaryaction.org.uk

FIFE VOLUNTARY ACTION
New Volunteer House, 16 East Fergus Place, Kirkcaldy, Fife KY1 1XT
Tel: 01592 645300
Email: .... info@fifevoluntaryaction.org.uk

FIFE VOLUNTARY ACTION
The Greig Institute, Forth Street, Leven, Fife KY8 4PF
Tel: 0800 389 6046
Email: .... info@fifevoluntaryaction.org.uk

FIFE VOLUNTARY ACTION
Volunteer House, 69-73 Crossgate, Cupar, Fife KY15 5AS
Tel: 01334 654080
Email: .... info@fifevoluntaryaction.org.uk

Glasgow

VOLUNTEER GLASGOW
Abbey House, 1st Floor, East, 10 Bothwell Street, Glasgow G2 6LU
Tel: 0141 226 3431
Email: .... info@volunteerglasgow.org

Highland

ROSS-SHIRE VOLUNTARY ACTION
Thorfin House, Bridgend Business Park, 1 Bridgend Road, Dingwall, Highland IV15 9SL
Tel: 01349 862 431
Email: .... rva@rossvolact.org.uk

VOLUNTEERING HIGHLAND
The Gateway, 1a Milburn Road, Inverness, Highland IV2 3PX
Tel: 01463 711393
Email: ..... enquiries@volunteeringhighland.org

Midlothian

VOLUNTEER CENTRE MIDLOTHIAN
32/6 Hardengreen Industrial Estate, Dalkeith, Midlothian EH22 3NX
Tel: 0131 660 1216
Email: .... info@volunteermidlothian.org.uk

Orkney Islands

VOLUNTARY ACTION ORKNEY/ VOLUNTEER CENTRE ORKNEY
Anchor Buildings, 6 Bridge Street, Kirkwall, Orkney Islands KW15 1HR
Tel: 01856 872897
Email: .... enquiries@vaorkney.org.uk

Perth & Kinross

VOLUNTEER CENTRE PERTH & KINROSS
The Gateway, North Methven Street, Perth, Perth & Kinross PH1 5PP
Tel: 01738 567076

Renfrewshire

ENGAGE RENFREWSHIRE
10 Falcon Crescent, Paisley, Renfrewshire PA3 1NS
Tel: 0141 887 7707
Email: .... info@engagerenfrewshire.com

VOLUNTEER CENTRE INVERCLYDE
175 Dalrymple Street, Greenock, Renfrewshire PA15 1JZ
Tel: 01475 787414
Email: . diane.mcallister@volunteerinverclyde.org.uk

Scottish Borders

BERWICKSHIRE ASSOCIATION FOR VOLUNTARY SERVICE
Platform 1, Station Road, Duns, Scottish Borders TD11 3HS
Tel: 01361 883137
Email: .... dughall.laing@bavs.org.uk

THE BRIDGE - ROXBURGH
1 Veitch's Close, Jedburgh, Scottish Borders TD8 6AY
Tel: 01835 863554
Email: .... roxburgh@the-bridge.uk.net

THE BRIDGE - TWEEDALE
Volunteer Resource Centre, School Brae, High Street, Brae, Peebles, Scottish Borders EH45 8AL
Tel: 01721 723123
Email: .... tweeddale@the-bridge.uk.net

South Ayrshire

VOLUNTARY ACTION SOUTH AYRSHIRE
27-29 Crown Street, Ayr, South Ayrshire KA8 8AG
Tel: 01292 432 661
Email: . enquiries@voluntaryactionsouthayrshire.org.uk

South Lanarkshire

SOLVE - VOLUNTEER CENTRE
14 Townhead Street, Hamilton, South Lanarkshire ML3 7BE
Tel: 01698 286902
Email: . . . . info@solve.uk.com

Stirling

VOLUNTEER CENTRE STIRLING
15 Friars Street, Stirling FK8 1HA
Tel: 01786 446071
Email: . . . . info@volunteeringstirling.org.uk

West Lothian

VOLUNTEER CENTRE WEST LOTHIAN
36 - 40 North Bridge Street, Bathgate, West Lothian EH48 4PP
Tel: 01506 650111
Email: . . . . volunteer@vcwl.co.uk

Western Isles

VOLUNTEER CENTRE WESTERN ISLES
95 Cromwell Street, Stornoway, Western Isles H51 2DG
Tel: 01851 700366
Email: . . bellann@volunteeringwesternisles.co.uk

WALES

Cardiff

CARDIFF VOLUNTARY COMMUNITY SERVICE
Brunel House, 2 Fitzalan Road, Cardiff CF24 0HA
Tel: 029 2022 7625

Denbighshire

DENBIGHSHIRE VOLUNTARY SERVICES COUNCIL
Naylor Leyland Centre, Well Street, Ruthin, Denbighshire LL15 1AF
Tel: 01824 702441

Gwynedd

CAERNARFON VOLUNTEER BUREAU
Santes Helen Road, Caernarfon, Gwynedd LL55 2YD
Tel: 01286 677337

Powys

LLANDRIDNOD WELLS VOLUNTEER BUREAU
c/o PAVO, Marlow, South Crescent, Llandrindod Wells, Powys LD1 5DH
Tel: 0845 0093288

RHAYADER AND DISTRICT COMMUNITY SUPPORT
The Arches, West Street, Rhayader, Powys LD6 5AB
Tel: 01597 810921
Email: . . . . carolyn@rdcs.org.uk

YSTRADGYNLAIS VOLUNTEER CENTRE
16 Station Road, Ystradgynlais, Powys SA9 1NT
Tel: 01639 849192

Wrexham

WREXHAM VOLUNTEER CENTRE
21 Egerton Street, Wrexham LL11 1ND
Tel: 01978 312556
Email: . . . . vb@avow.org

OBJECT INDEX

The following Object Index is based on the Object Codes listed at the start of the Digest (on page xxvi). Here we have further split these codes to reflect a charity's main areas of expertise (see below) and who the charity benefits.

The Charities' Main Areas of Expertise

ADOPTION, FOSTERING

ADVICE, COUNSELLING, INFORMATION

CARE EQUIPMENT, PRACTICAL SERVICES

CO-ORDINATION, LIAISON

CULTURAL PURSUITS

DAY CENTRES

EDUCATION, TRAINING

GRANTS TO INDIVIDUALS

GRANTS TO ORGANISATIONS

GRANTS TO ORGANISATIONS/CHARITIES

HOLIDAYS

HOUSING

MEDICAL TREATMENT, NURSING

MEMBER ORGANISATION

MISSIONARY & OUTREACH WORK AT HOME OR ABROAD

OVERSEAS AID OR SERVICE

PENSIONS, BENEFITS OR SCHOLARSHIPS

PUBLICATIONS AND/OR FREE LITERATURE

RECONCILIATION

REHABILITATION, THERAPY

SERVICES PROVIDER

SHELTERED ACCOMMODATION & HOSTELS

SOCIAL ACTIVITIES & RELATIONSHIPS

WORKSHOPS & OTHER EMPLOYMENT

The Charity Benefits

ANIMALS AND/OR BIRDS

ARMED SERVICES & EX-SERVICES

BLIND PEOPLE

CHILDREN, YOUNG PEOPLE

CONSERVATION & ENVIRONMENT

DEAF PEOPLE

DISABLED PEOPLE

ETHNIC MINORITIES

EX PROFESSIONAL OR TRADE WORKERS

RELIEF OF POVERTY

SOCIAL WELFARE & CASEWORK

WOMEN

ADVERTISER INDEX